American Language Hub

LEVEL 2
Teacher's Book

CHARLOTTE RANCE

macmillan education

Macmillan Education Limited
4 Crinan Street
London N1 9XW

Companies and representatives throughout the world

American Language Hub Level 2 Teacher's Book
ISBN 978-0-230-49703-0

American Language Hub Level 2 Teacher's Book with Teacher's App Pack
ISBN 978-0-230-49704-7

Written by Charlotte Rance

First published 2020

Teacher's Book credits:
Original design by emc design ltd
Page make-up by SPi Global
Illustrated by Andy Keylock
Cover design based on original design by Restless
Cover image by Getty Images/Linghe Zhao/Taxi

Author's acknowledgements
Charlotte Rance would like to thank the whole team for their hard work and invaluable support. Also, a special thank you to Stacey Hughes for all her advice and guidance. Finally, to her partner Matt Conway for his constant support.

The authors and publishers would like to thank the following for permission to reproduce their photographs:

4FR Photography/Nils Kahle W18; **Bananastock** W28, W29(bl); BananaStock/Punchstock W69(tl), W69(tr), W69(ml), W69(mr), W69(b); **Brand X** W15, W29(br), W58; **Corbis**/Fuse W30(t); **E+**/Andresr W10, E+/gradyreese W55; **Getty Images** Andresr W19, W33(b), Getty Images/PeopleImages, Yuri Arcurs W4, W13, Getty Images/Altrendo Images W3, Getty Images/Bananastock W68, Getty Images/iStockphoto/Thinkstock Images/BetaplusZ W17(tr), Getty Images/iStockphoto/barsik, Galina Barskaya W33(t), Getty Images/Marta Bieronska/EyeEm W1(tl), Getty Images/Blue Jean Images W41, Getty Images/iStockphoto/claudiaveja W67, Getty Images/Matteo Colombo W35(tl), Getty Images/Cultura W14, Getty Images/EyeEm W8, Getty Images/iStockphoto/DMEPhotography W9, Getty Images/Cultura RF/Frank and Helena W17(tl), Getty Images/iStockphoto/FlairImages W64(tl), Getty Images/Fuse W26(tr), W43(b), W64(mr), Getty Images/Tetra Images/Daniel Grill W7(tl), Getty Images/Tetra Images RF/Jamie Grill Photography W32(tr), Getty Images/Geber86 W26(tl), Getty Images/izusek, Izabela Habur W11, Getty Images/Hero Images W6, Getty Images/iStockphoto W53, Getty Images/Jupiterimages W46, Getty Images/Steve Kelley W71, Getty Images/KidStock/Blend Images W40, Getty Images/iStockphoto/MachineHeadz W70, Getty Images/Monkey Business W51, Getty Images/Morsa Images W38, Getty Images/Naufal MQ W39, Getty Images/Photodisc W1(tr), Getty Images/Blend Images/Jose Luis Pelaez Inc W20(tr), W32(tl), Getty Images/EyeEm/Deanna Pritzker W5, tty Images/EyeEm/Thanatham Piriyakarnjanakul W7(tl), Getty Images/Aurora Open/Olivier Renck W29(tr), Getty Images/Michael Roberts W23, Getty Images/Mint Images/Tim Robbins W24(tl), Getty Images/Cultura/Aleksander Rubtsov W45, Getty Images/Chris Ryan W52, Getty Images/iStockphoto/shironosov W29(mr), Getty Images/SolStock W29(tl), Getty Images/iStockphoto/Terraxplorer W7(tm), Getty Images/Thinkstock Images/Jupiterimages W20(tl), Getty Images/iStockphoto/Michael Utech W61, Getty Images/AJ Watt W43(tr), Getty Images/Wavebreak Media/Thinkstock W32(ml), Getty Images/filadendron, Todor Tsvetjov W2, Getty Images/Kalo Vicent W24(b), Getty Images/Dougal Waters W62, Getty Images/Westend61, W24(tr), W35(tr), Getty Images/Blend Images/Granger Wootz W64(bl); **Hero Images**/W34; **Image Source**/Image Source/Allen and Kleantho, W30(t), W64(br), Image Source/Alberto Guglielmi W66; **iStockphoto**/scanrail W49, iStockphoto/alexsl W54, Stockphoto/Peopleimages W59; **Jupiterimages** W64(ml); **Macmillan Education Limited**/Macmillan Australia W29(ml), W36, W63; **Photodisc** W33(m), W60, W64(tr); **Wavebreakmedia** Ltd/W37.

The author and publishers are grateful for permission to reprint the following copyright material:

Extracts from: '700 Classroom Activities New Edition' © David Seymour and Maria Popova 2005, published by Macmillan Education Limited. Used by permission. All Rights Reserved.

Extracts from: 'Learning Teaching 3rd Edition Student's Book' © Jim Scrivener 2011, published by Macmillan Education Limited. Used by permission. All Rights Reserved.

Extracts from: 'Teaching English Grammar' © Jim Scrivener 2010, published by Macmillan Education Limited. Used by permission. All Rights Reserved.

Student's Book credits:

Written by Daniel Brayshaw and Jon Hird

With thanks to Edward Price and Carol Goodwright for additional authoring and to Signature Manuscripts for the Grammar Hub pages.

Designed by emc design ltd
Illustrated by Peter Lubach, Rasmus Juul, Rose Frith represented by Lemonade Illustration
Picture research by Emily Taylor and Victoria Gaunt
Café Hub videos produced by Creative Listening
Café Hub video scripts written by James and Luke Vyner

Full acknowledgements for illustrations and photographs in the facsimile pages can be found in the Student's Book ISBN 978-1-380-01695-9 and in the Workbook ISBN 978-1-380-01697-3.

The authors and publishers are grateful for permission to reprint the following copyright material:

p36 Helliwell, J., Layard, R., & Sachs, J. (2016). World Happiness Report 2016. New York: Sustainable Development Solutions Network.

p42 Extract from 'One in five children just want to be rich when they grow up' by Keith Perry. Originally published in The Telegraph, 5 August 2014. © Telegraph Media Group Limited 2014. Reprinted with permission of The Telegraph.

p106 Eriksen M, Lebreton LCM, Carson HS, Thiel M, Moore CJ, Borerro JC, et al. (2014) Plastic Pollution in the World's Oceans: More than 5 Trillion Plastic Pieces Weighing over 250,000 Tons Afloat at Sea. PLoS ONE 9(12): e111913. https://doi.org/10.1371/journal.pone.0111913

p106 Extract from '38 million pieces of plastic waste found on uninhabited South Pacific island' by Elle Hunt. Originally published in The Guardian, 15 May 2017. © Copyright Guardian News & Media Ltd 2018. Reprinted with permission of The Guardian.

p107 Extract from 'Marine Conservation Society' © Marine Conservation Society (MCS) 2017. Reprinted with permission of Marine Conservation Society.

p106 Significant anthropogenic debris on remote island, Jennifer L. Lavers, Alexander L. Bond. Proceedings of the National Academy of Sciences Jun 2017, 114 (23) 6052-6055; DOI: 10.1073/pnas.1619818114 p112 Extract from 'Here is Facebook's guide to fake news' by Aatif Sulleyman. Originally published in The Independent, 9 May 2017. © Independent Digital News and Media Ltd 2017. Reprinted with permission of The Independent.

p114 Extract from 'How binge-watching has changed TV forever' by Sarah Rainey. Originally published in The Telegraph, 22 January 2015. © Telegraph Media Group Limited 2015. Reprinted with permission of The Telegraph. p164 Helliwell, J., Layard, R., & Sachs, J. (2017). World Happiness Report 2017, New York: Sustainable Development Solutions Network.

Printed and bound in Brazil.

2025
27

Contents

American Language Hub for Teachers

Student's Book Introduction

American Language Hub is a new six-level general English course for adult learners, which takes the complexity out of teaching English. It is designed to promote effective communication and helps to build learners' confidence with regular opportunities for meaningful practice. With its firm pedagogic foundation and syllabus aligned to the revised CEFR, American Language Hub has clear learning outcomes which make it easy to use in a variety of teaching situations.

1 RELATIONSHIPS

My best friend is the one who brings out the best in me.
Henry Ford

Iñupiat friends play in the first of the winter snow, Nome, Alaska.

OBJECTIVES

- find out about someone new
- talk about different types of people
- describe someone's personality
- greet people and give personal information, make introductions
- write information about yourself

Work with a partner. Discuss the questions.

1 Who's your best friend?
2 Look at the picture. Who was your best friend when you were a child?
3 What qualities do you look for in a friend?

RELATIONSHIPS 1

The engaging photograph and famous quotation help teachers to focus students and familiarize themselves with the ideas in the unit. Teachers can also encourage students to label the picture.

There is a quick warm up speaking activity. Teachers can use this time to prepare the class for their lesson and delay the main start for five minutes until all the students arrive.

Student's Book unit opener

The first page of every American Language Hub unit is the unit opener. It is an exciting visual opportunity for students to engage with the theme of the unit and see at a glance the CEFR learning objectives for each lesson.

Student's Book lessons 1 and 2

Reading and Listening

Reading and listening sections allow students to practice their receptive skills. All sections have tasks that move from global to detailed understanding so students can achieve a good overall comprehension. The key skills focus is clearly marked in the activity titles. The texts and scripts also present target vocabulary, grammar or pronunciation.

Grammar

The American Language Hub approach to grammar is inductive. Students are exposed to new language in context. Each grammar section prompts the student to notice the feature in context and to discover its form and use. Students then have further opportunities for controlled practice before using their new language in more authentic spoken or written output.

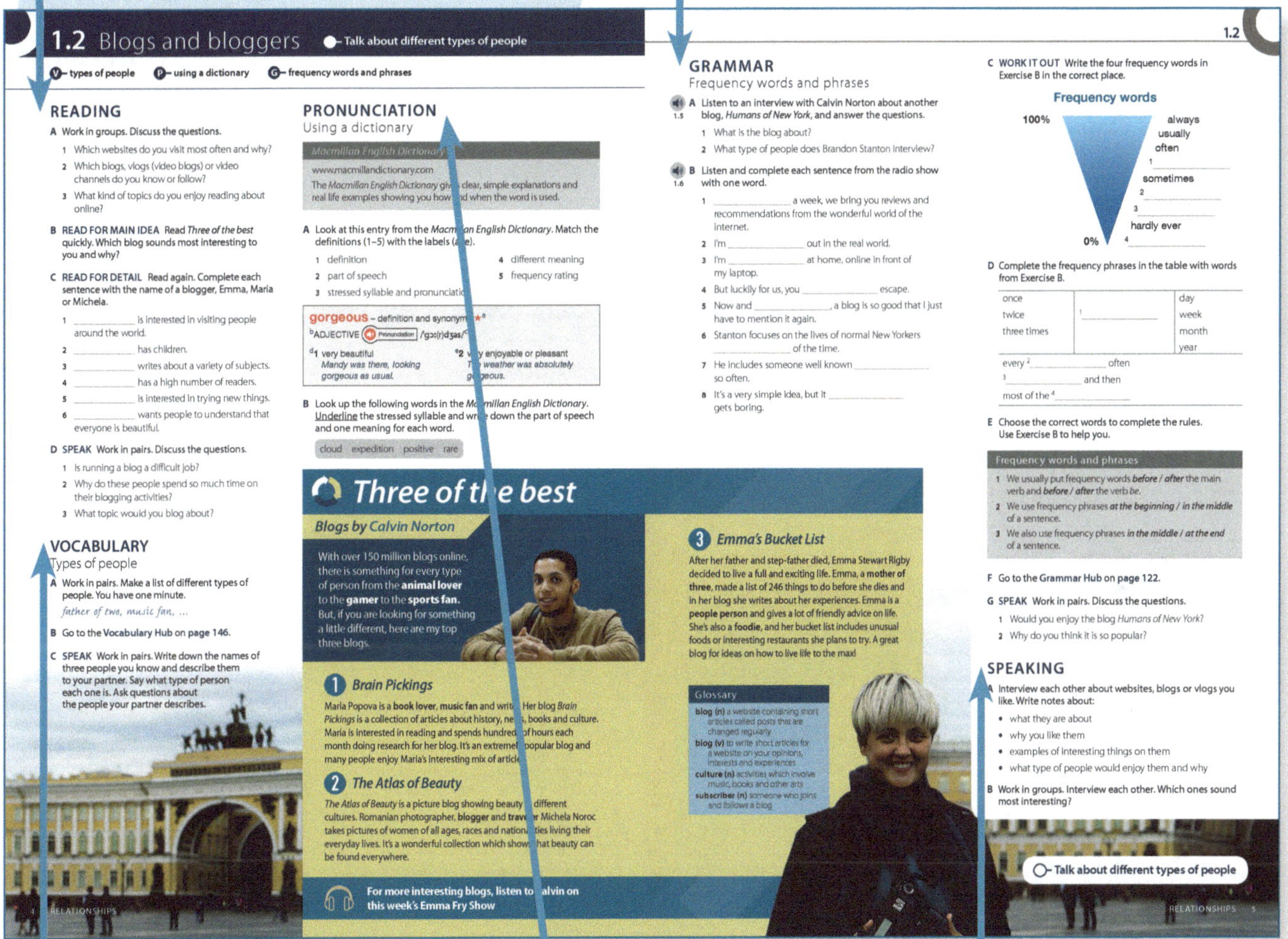

1.2 Blogs and bloggers — Talk about different types of people

V – types of people P – using a dictionary G – frequency words and phrases

READING

A Work in groups. Discuss the questions.
1 Which websites do you visit most often and why?
2 Which blogs, vlogs (video blogs) or video channels do you know or follow?
3 What kind of topics do you enjoy reading about online?

B READ FOR MAIN IDEA Read *Three of the best* quickly. Which blog sounds most interesting to you and why?

C READ FOR DETAIL Read again. Complete each sentence with the name of a blogger, Emma, Maria or Michela.
1 ________ is interested in visiting people around the world.
2 ________ has children.
3 ________ writes about a variety of subjects.
4 ________ has a high number of readers.
5 ________ is interested in trying new things.
6 ________ wants people to understand that everyone is beautiful.

D SPEAK Work in pairs. Discuss the questions.
1 Is running a blog a difficult job?
2 Why do these people spend so much time on their blogging activities?
3 What topic would you blog about?

VOCABULARY
Types of people

A Work in pairs. Make a list of different types of people. You have one minute.
father of two, music fan, ...

B Go to the Vocabulary Hub on page 146.

C SPEAK Work in pairs. Write down the names of three people you know and describe them to your partner. Say what type of person each one is. Ask questions about the people your partner describes.

PRONUNCIATION
Using a dictionary

Macmillan English Dictionary
www.macmillandictionary.com
The *Macmillan English Dictionary* gives clear, simple explanations and real life examples showing you how and when the word is used.

A Look at this entry from the *Macmillan English Dictionary*. Match the definitions (1–5) with the labels (a–e).
1 definition
2 part of speech
3 stressed syllable and pronunciation
4 different meaning
5 frequency rating

gorgeous – definition and synonyms
ADJECTIVE /ˈgɔː(r)dʒəs/
1 very beautiful *Mandy was there, looking gorgeous as usual.*
2 very enjoyable or pleasant *The weather was absolutely gorgeous.*

B Look up the following words in the *Macmillan English Dictionary*. Underline the stressed syllable and write down the part of speech and one meaning for each word.
cloud expedition positive rare

Three of the best
Blogs by Calvin Norton

With over 150 million blogs online, there is something for every type of person from the **animal lover** to the **gamer** to the **sports fan.** But, if you are looking for something a little different, here are my top three blogs.

1 *Brain Pickings*
Maria Popova is a **book lover, music fan** and writer. Her blog *Brain Pickings* is a collection of articles about history, news, books and culture. Maria is interested in reading and spends hundreds of hours each month doing research for her blog. It's an extremely popular blog and many people enjoy Maria's interesting mix of articles.

2 *The Atlas of Beauty*
The Atlas of Beauty is a picture blog showing beauty in different cultures. Romanian photographer, **blogger** and **traveler** Michela Noroc takes pictures of women of all ages, races and nationalities living their everyday lives. It's a wonderful collection which shows that beauty can be found everywhere.

3 *Emma's Bucket List*
After her father and step-father died, Emma Stewart Rigby decided to live a full and exciting life. Emma, a **mother of three**, made a list of 246 things to do before she dies and in her blog she writes about her experiences. Emma is a **people person** and gives a lot of friendly advice on life. She's also a **foodie**, and her bucket list includes unusual foods or interesting restaurants she plans to try. A great blog for ideas on how to live life to the max!

Glossary
blog (n) a website containing short articles called posts that are changed regularly
blog (v) to write short articles for a website on your opinions, interests and experiences
culture (n) activities which involve music, books and other arts
subscriber (n) someone who joins and follows a blog

For more interesting blogs, listen to Calvin on this week's Emma Fry Show

GRAMMAR
Frequency words and phrases

A 1.5 Listen to an interview with Calvin Norton about another blog, *Humans of New York*, and answer the questions.
1 What is the blog about?
2 What type of people does Brandon Stanton interview?

B 1.6 Listen and complete each sentence from the radio show with one word.
1 ________ a week, we bring you reviews and recommendations from the wonderful world of the internet.
2 I'm ________ out in the real world.
3 I'm ________ at home, online in front of my laptop.
4 But luckily for us, you ________ escape.
5 Now and ________, a blog is so good that I just have to mention it again.
6 Stanton focuses on the lives of normal New Yorkers ________ of the time.
7 He includes someone well known ________ so often.
8 It's a very simple idea, but it ________ gets boring.

C WORK IT OUT Write the four frequency words in Exercise B in the correct place.

Frequency words
100% always, usually, often, 1 ________, sometimes, 2 ________, 3 ________, hardly ever, 4 ________ 0%

D Complete the frequency phrases in the table with words from Exercise B.

once / twice / three times	1 ________	day / week / month / year
every 2 ________	often	
3 ________ and then		
most of the 4 ________		

E Choose the correct words to complete the rules. Use Exercise B to help you.

Frequency words and phrases
1 We usually put frequency words *before / after* the main verb and *before / after* the verb *be*.
2 We use frequency phrases *at the beginning / in the middle* of a sentence.
3 We also use frequency phrases *in the middle / at the end* of a sentence.

F Go to the Grammar Hub on page 122.

G SPEAK Work in pairs. Discuss the questions.
1 Would you enjoy the blog *Humans of New York*?
2 Why do you think it is so popular?

SPEAKING

A Interview each other about websites, blogs or vlogs you like. Write notes about:
- what they are about
- why you like them
- examples of interesting things on them
- what type of people would enjoy them and why

B Work in groups. Interview each other. Which ones sound most interesting?

Talk about different types of people

4 RELATIONSHIPS — RELATIONSHIPS 5

Vocabulary

American Language Hub teaches vocabulary in topic-related sets to help students categorize the new words they learn. Key vocabulary sets are built on and reviewed in the back of the book.

Pronunciation

In American Language Hub, lessons focus on both word level and sentence level pronunciation. This not only allows students to improve their accuracy, but also their fluency through sentence level intonation, which helps students understand how to add meaning through pronunciation.

Speaking

Each lesson starts with a CEFR unit objective which the lesson is designed to address. Students will usually use the grammar, vocabulary and pronunciation from the lesson to complete a speaking activity linked to the unit objective. American Language Hub allows students to safely practice speaking in pairs after most sections. This ensures that they feel confident to take an active role in the final speaking task.

Student's Book lesson 3

Reading and Listening Skill

Every unit includes a task designed to practice a key reading or listening skill. This ensures students are given the tools they need to effectively process a wide variety of texts and scripts. By the end of each book, students will have been exposed to 12 different key skills for reading or listening.

Skill labels

By focusing students' attention on the skills labels next to each exercise number, teachers can highlight which skills are being practiced and recycled.

1.3 Personality

Describe someone's personality

G – indefinite pronouns V – personality adjectives, adjective + preposition
P – word stress in multisyllable adjectives S – previewing a text

READING

A SPEAK Work in pairs. Discuss the questions.

1 Which do you do more often: write by hand or use a keyboard?
2 Which do you find easier? Why?
3 What kind of things do you write by hand (e.g. shopping lists)?

B Preview the text, and then answer the questions. Use the information in the box to help you.

Previewing a text

Before you read a text, look quickly at the title and any headings, pictures or diagrams. Use this information to decide what kind of text it is, what it's about and why someone might want to read it. This will make the text easier to understand.

1 What is the text about?
2 Is it from a science paper or a popular magazine? How do you know?
3 What do you think you will learn from the text?
4 Can you trust the information in the article?

C READ FOR MAIN IDEA Read *What does your handwriting say about you?* Was your preview correct?

D READ FOR SPECIFIC INFORMATION Read again and answer the questions.

1 What is graphology a study of?
2 How do graphologists help in court cases?
3 Do all graphologists agree that there is a link between handwriting and personality?

E SPEAK Work in pairs. Discuss the questions.

1 Do you believe there is a connection between handwriting and personality? Why/Why not?
2 Is it important for children to learn to write by hand these days? Why/Why not?

What does your *handwriting* say about you?

Everybody has their own style of handwriting, but can someone's handwriting tell you what they are like? The study of handwriting is called graphology. Graphologists are usually involved in legal cases. They are responsible for matching criminals to their handwriting or deciding if signatures are real. Some graphologists think handwriting can show anything: what kind of job you will be good at, how healthy you are and even what kind of partner you might be happy with. If you are interested in what your handwriting says about you, check out our information.

Letter size Small: Medium: Large:

You're probably a **hard-working** person. People with small handwriting are rarely **lazy**.

The research says you're **sensible**: you think carefully about the decisions you make.

Big writing – big personality! People with large writing are usually interested in parties and social events and are rarely shy.

Letter shape

Rounded letters: Rounded letters suggest you are a **creative** person. Are you good at art or music?

Pointed letters: You are **curious**. Your favorite question is 'Why?'!

Dotting your i

Dot high over the i: The research says you have a good imagination.

Dot low over the i: You are a **well-organized** person. Are your desk and room neat?

Spacing between words

Wide spacing: You're an **independent** type and you are happy on your own.

Narrow spacing: You're very **sociable** and you need other people in your life.

Your signature

Difficult to read: You are a private person. Like your signature, you can be difficult to read.

Easy to read: **Confident** people usually have signatures that are easy to read. You know what you are good at and you don't mind telling other people about it.

Does your handwriting match your personality? Don't be disappointed with the results if not. Not every graphologist believes there is a connection.

Glossary
legal (adj) relating to the law or lawyers
spacing (n) the amount of space between things

6 RELATIONSHIPS

1.3

GRAMMAR
Indefinite pronouns

A WORK IT OUT Look at the extract from the article and choose the correct words to complete the rules.

Everybody has their own style of handwriting, but can someone's handwriting tell you what they are like?

Indefinite pronouns

1 We use indefinite pronouns to talk about people or things *so we can say / without saying* who or what they are.
2 We use indefinite pronouns with *-body* and *-one* to talk about *people / things*.
3 After indefinite pronouns, we use *singular / plural* verbs.
4 We use *'s* with indefinite pronouns for *possessives / plural nouns*.

B PRACTICE Find and underline another example of an indefinite pronoun in the article.

C Go to the Grammar Hub on page 122.

VOCABULARY
Personality adjectives, adjective + preposition

A Match the personality adjectives in **bold** in *What does your handwriting say about you?* with the speakers below.

1 'I believe I can do anything if I try. I don't usually worry about things.' *confident*
2 'I love my job. I work a lot, but that's OK.'
3 'I can paint pictures, write stories and make music.'
4 'I plan my time carefully and I always know where to find my things.'
5 'I don't like work. I like doing nothing! My perfect day? Staying in bed with a pizza.'
6 'I like to think about things carefully before I do them.'
7 'I have a lot of friends and we meet and go out all the time.'
8 'I like learning new things and I ask a lot of questions.'
9 'I like to do things myself.'

B Look at the underlined phrases in the article. Complete the questions with the correct preposition.

1 Are you involved *in* any clubs, groups or teams? Which ones?
2 What are you good ___?
3 Who is responsible ___ doing the cooking in your home?
4 Are you happy ___ your cell phone? Why/Why not?
5 What websites, magazines or TV shows are you interested ___?
6 Are you interested ___ books and reading?

C SPEAK Work in pairs. Ask and answer the questions in Exercise B.

PRONUNCIATION
Word stress in multisyllable adjectives

1.7 A Listen and complete the table with the words in the box.

hard-working independent lazy sensible

1 Oo	2 Ooo	3 oOo	4 ooOo
		hard-working	

1.7 B Listen again and repeat the words.

1.8 C Look again at the article. Find the other personality adjectives in **bold** and write them in the correct place in Exercise A. Listen and check and repeat.

D SPEAK Work in pairs. Practice saying the words. Listen and check your partner's pronunciation.

SPEAKING HUB

A Work in pairs. You are going to study your classmates' handwriting. Follow the instructions.

1 Sign your name and write this sentence on a piece of paper.
The quick brown fox jumps over the lazy dog.
2 Swap papers and use the information in *What does your handwriting say about you?* to write five things about your partner's personality.

B DISCUSS Using your notes, tell your partner what their writing says about them.

Describe someone's personality

RELATIONSHIPS 7

Topics

American Language Hub topics contextualize the language input for the lesson. They have been selected to allow opportunities for personalization.

Speaking Hub

At the end of Lesson 3, students perform a longer speaking turn which is staged to allow planning and idea creation. Students should apply their learning from the whole unit in the performance of their long speaking turn.

Student's Book lesson 4

Functional Language

Each video provides a model for functional language so that students are able to access an ever-expanding bank of phrases. This language helps students to communicate effectively in a range of real-world situations.

Café Hub

The final lesson in each unit has a focus on video. Café Hub is an amusing situation comedy series. Meet Milly, Sam, Neena, Zac and Gaby as they take you through their adventures in London. Find out how they start their journey as complete strangers but become the best of friends.

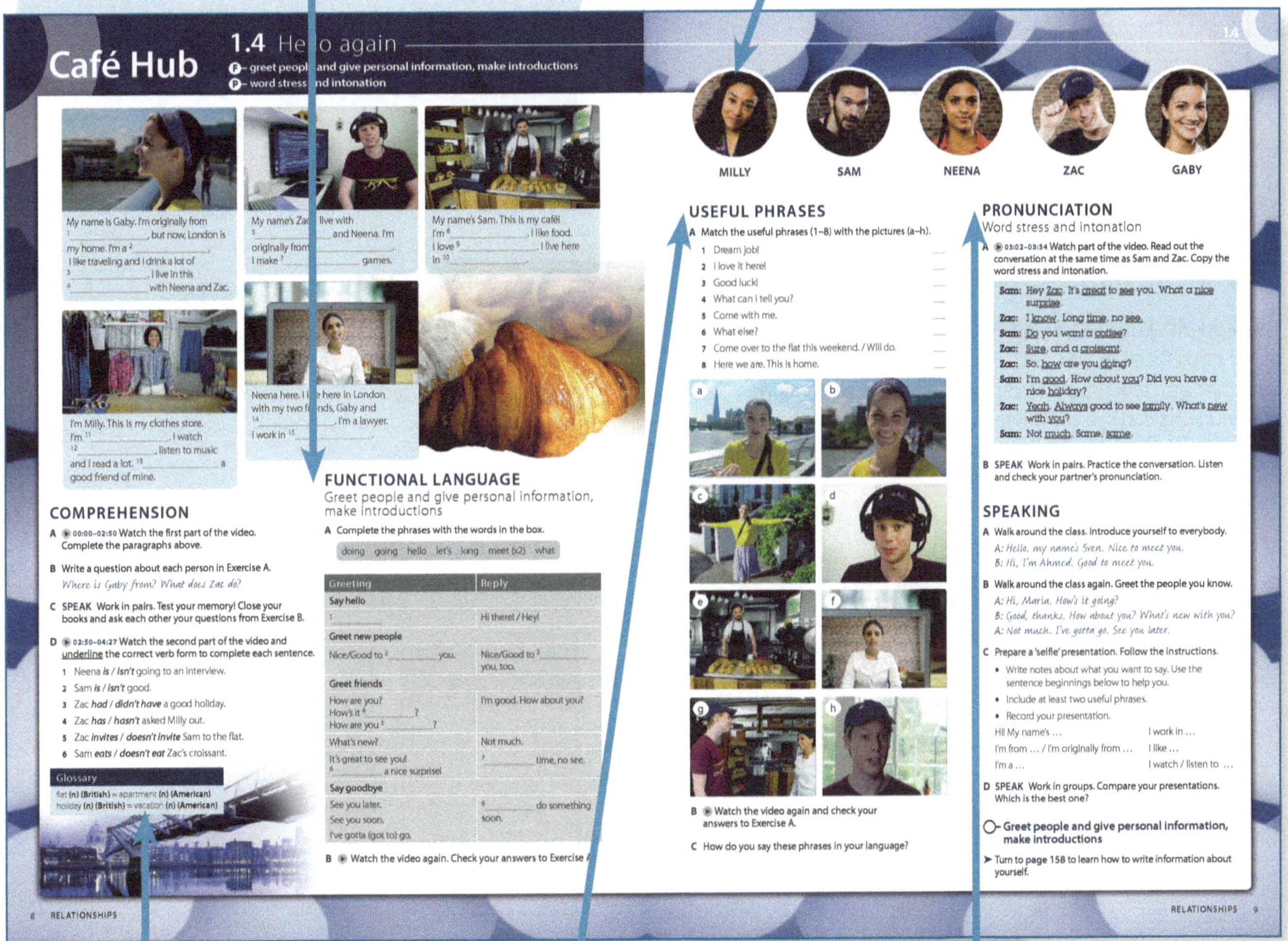

Café Hub

1.4 Hello again

F – greet people and give personal information, make introductions

P – word stress and intonation

My name is Gaby. I'm originally from [1] ________, but now, London is my home. I'm a [2] ________. I like traveling and I drink a lot of [3] ________. I live in this [4] ________ with Neena and Zac.

My name's Zac. I live with [5] ________ and Neena. I'm originally from [6] ________. I make [7] ________ games.

My name's Sam. This is my café! I'm [8] ________. I like food. I love [9] ________. I live here in [10] ________.

I'm Milly. This is my clothes store. I'm [11] ________. I watch [12] ________, listen to music and I read a lot. [13] ________ a good friend of mine.

Neena here. I live here in London with my two friends, Gaby and [14] ________. I'm a lawyer. I work in [15] ________.

COMPREHENSION

A 00:00–02:50 Watch the first part of the video. Complete the paragraphs above.

B Write a question about each person in Exercise A.
Where is Gaby from? What does Zac do?

C SPEAK Work in pairs. Test your memory! Close your books and ask each other your questions from Exercise B.

D 02:50–04:27 Watch the second part of the video and underline the correct verb form to complete each sentence.

1. Neena *is / isn't* going to an interview.
2. Sam *is / isn't* good.
3. Zac *had / didn't have* a good holiday.
4. Zac *has / hasn't* asked Milly out.
5. Zac *invites / doesn't invite* Sam to the flat.
6. Sam *eats / doesn't eat* Zac's croissant.

Glossary

flat (n) (British) = apartment (n) (American)
holiday (n) (British) = vacation (n) (American)

FUNCTIONAL LANGUAGE

Greet people and give personal information, make introductions

A Complete the phrases with the words in the box.

doing going hello let's long meet (x2) what

Greeting	Reply
Say hello	
[1] ________	Hi there! / Hey!
Greet new people	
Nice/Good to [2] ________ you.	Nice/Good to [3] ________ you, too.
Greet friends	
How are you? How's it [4] ________? How are you [5] ________?	I'm good. How about you?
What's new?	Not much.
It's great to see you! [6] ________ a nice surprise!	[7] ________ time, no see.
Say goodbye	
See you later. See you soon. I've gotta (got to) go.	[8] ________ do something soon.

B Watch the video again. Check your answers to Exercise A.

8 RELATIONSHIPS

MILLY SAM NEENA ZAC GABY

USEFUL PHRASES

A Match the useful phrases (1–8) with the pictures (a–h).

1. Dream job!
2. I love it here!
3. Good luck!
4. What can I tell you?
5. Come with me.
6. What else?
7. Come over to the flat this weekend. / Will do.
8. Here we are. This is home.

B Watch the video again and check your answers to Exercise A.

C How do you say these phrases in your language?

PRONUNCIATION

Word stress and intonation

A 03:02–03:34 Watch part of the video. Read out the conversation at the same time as Sam and Zac. Copy the word stress and intonation.

Sam: Hey Zac. It's great to see you. What a nice surprise.
Zac: I know. Long time, no see.
Sam: Do you want a coffee?
Zac: Sure, and a croissant.
Zac: So, how are you doing?
Sam: I'm good. How about you? Did you have a nice holiday?
Zac: Yeah. Always good to see family. What's new with you?
Sam: Not much. Same, same.

B SPEAK Work in pairs. Practice the conversation. Listen and check your partner's pronunciation.

SPEAKING

A Walk around the class. Introduce yourself to everybody.
A: Hello, my name's Sven. Nice to meet you.
B: Hi, I'm Ahmed. Good to meet you.

B Walk around the class again. Greet the people you know.
A: Hi, Maria. How's it going?
B: Good, thanks. How about you? What's new with you?
A: Not much. I've gotta go. See you later.

C Prepare a 'selfie' presentation. Follow the instructions.

- Write notes about what you want to say. Use the sentence beginnings below to help you.
- Include at least two useful phrases.
- Record your presentation.

Hi! My name's …
I'm from … / I'm originally from …
I'm a …
I work in …
I like …
I watch / listen to …

D SPEAK Work in groups. Compare your presentations. Which is the best one?

Greet people and give personal information, make introductions

Turn to page 158 to learn how to write information about yourself.

RELATIONSHIPS 9

Variety of English

The glossary boxes on these pages point out differences between American English and British English.

Useful Phrases

The video also provides an opportunity to learn a variety of useful phrases that students can use to bring authenticity to their language output.

Pronunciation

Lesson 4 has a focus on stress and intonation. Students notice the stress and rhythm of British and American English pronunciation in the video before preparing to speak themselves.

American Language Hub for Teachers

Student's Book Hubs

Writing Hub

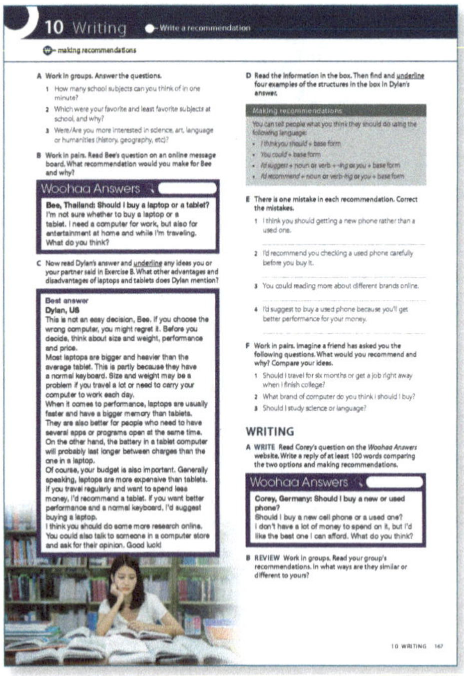

The Student's Book has an individual writing page at the back of the book for each unit. Each writing lesson is aligned to the unit topic and teaches a different writing genre and writing skill. Students can see completed writing models to analyze before they begin to write their own work.

Grammar Hub

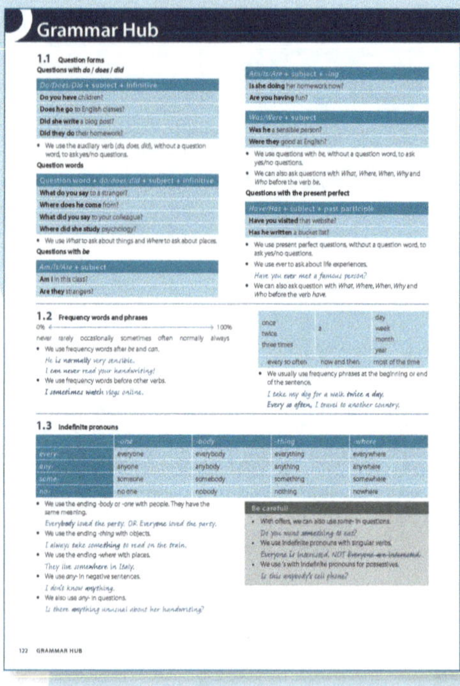

Clear explanations and further practice activities for each grammar point in the syllabus are provided at the back of the book. These can be used in class or set for homework to free up classroom time for communication.

Vocabulary Hub

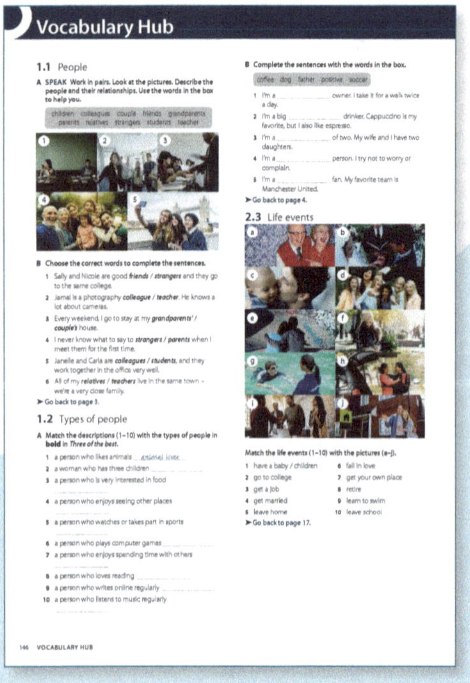

The Vocabulary Hub provides extra practice of key vocabulary presented in each unit. As with the Grammar Hub sections, these can either consolidate work done in class or be used for further self-study.

Communication Hub

The Communication Hub is used to set up longer communicative activities, such as information exchanges, quizzes and role plays.

Workbook

A Workbook is sold separately for American Language Hub. This includes 360 print activities practicing the language from the Student's Book. For each lesson there are corresponding practice exercises of grammar, vocabulary and pronunciation. There is further practice of the reading and listening skills from Lesson 3 and extension practice of the functional language from Lesson 4. There is also a page dedicated to the unit's writing genre and skill. All of these pages develop learning from the main lessons of the Student's Book.

Vocabulary and Grammar

The Workbook practices vocabulary and grammar that students have attended to in the Student's Book. By reminding themselves of the words and skills they have recently seen, students are better able to imbed learning and have it ready for recall during speaking practice.

Listening and Reading

The Workbook provides additional listening and reading texts that explore the topics in the Student's Book. These give students the opportunity to develop the key receptive skills from the unit.

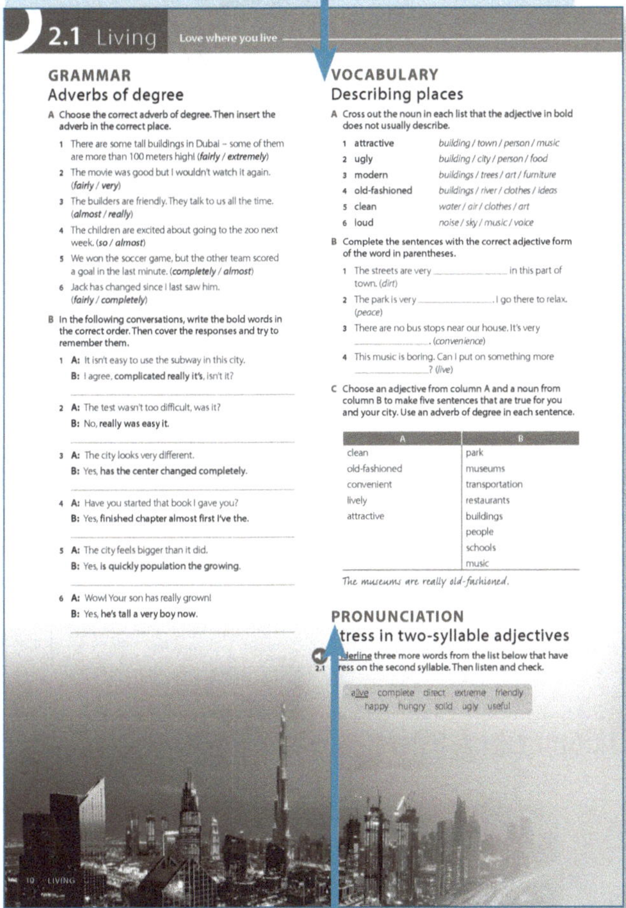

2.1 Living — Love where you live

GRAMMAR

Adverbs of degree

A Choose the correct adverb of degree. Then insert the adverb in the correct place.

1 There are some tall buildings in Dubai – some of them are more than 100 meters high! (*fairly / extremely*)
2 The movie was good but I wouldn't watch it again. (*fairly / very*)
3 The builders are friendly. They talk to us all the time. (*almost / really*)
4 The children are excited about going to the zoo next week. (*so / almost*)
5 We won the soccer game, but the other team scored a goal in the last minute. (*completely / almost*)
6 Jack has changed since I last saw him. (*fairly / completely*)

B In the following conversations, write the bold words in the correct order. Then cover the responses and try to remember them.

1 A: It isn't easy to use the subway in this city.
B: I agree, **complicated really it's**, isn't it?

2 A: The test wasn't too difficult, was it?
B: No, **really was easy it**.

3 A: The city looks very different.
B: Yes, **has the center changed completely**.

4 A: Have you started that book I gave you?
B: Yes, **finished chapter almost first I've the**.

5 A: The city feels bigger than it did.
B: Yes, **is quickly population the growing**.

6 A: Wow! Your son has really grown!
B: Yes, **he's tall a very boy now**.

VOCABULARY

Describing places

A Cross out the noun in each list that the adjective in bold does not usually describe.

1 **attractive** *building / town / person / music*
2 **ugly** *building / city / person / food*
3 **modern** *buildings / trees / art / furniture*
4 **old-fashioned** *buildings / river / clothes / ideas*
5 **clean** *water / air / clothes / art*
6 **loud** *noise / sky / music / voice*

B Complete the sentences with the correct adjective form of the word in parentheses.

1 The streets are very ________ in this part of town. (*dirt*)
2 The park is very ________. I go there to relax. (*peace*)
3 There are no bus stops near our house. It's very ________. (*convenience*)
4 This music is boring. Can I put on something more ________? (*live*)

C Choose an adjective from column A and a noun from column B to make five sentences that are true for you and your city. Use an adverb of degree in each sentence.

A	B
clean	park
old-fashioned	museums
convenient	transportation
lively	restaurants
attractive	buildings
	people
	schools
	music

The museums are really old-fashioned.

PRONUNCIATION

[S]tress in two-syllable adjectives

2.1 [Un]derline three more words from the list below that have [st]ress on the second syllable. Then listen and check.

alive complete direct extreme friendly happy hungry solid ugly useful

10 LIVING

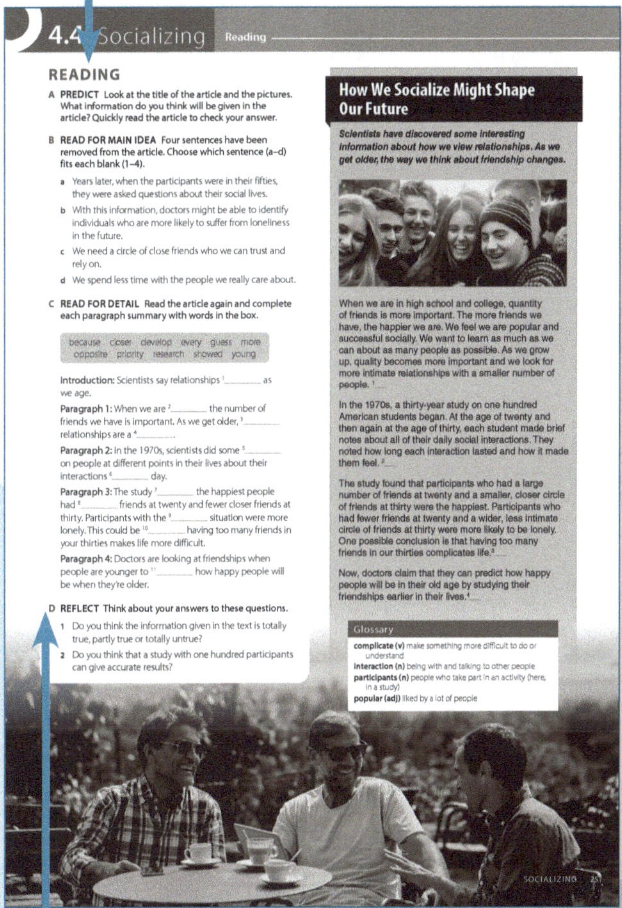

4.4 Socializing — Reading

READING

A **PREDICT** Look at the title of the article and the pictures. What information do you think will be given in the article? Quickly read the article to check your answer.

B **READ FOR MAIN IDEA** Four sentences have been removed from the article. Choose which sentence (a–d) fits each blank (1–4).

a Years later, when the participants were in their fifties, they were asked questions about their social lives.
b With this information, doctors might be able to identify individuals who are more likely to suffer from loneliness in the future.
c We need a circle of close friends who we can trust and rely on.
d We spend less time with the people we really care about.

C **READ FOR DETAIL** Read the article again and complete each paragraph summary with words in the box.

because closer develop every guess more opposite priority research showed young

Introduction: Scientists say relationships [1] ________ as we age.

Paragraph 1: When we are [2] ________ the number of friends we have is important. As we get older, [3] ________ relationships are a [4] ________.

Paragraph 2: In the 1970s, scientists did some [5] ________ on people at different points in their lives about their interactions [6] ________ day.

Paragraph 3: The study [7] ________ the happiest people had [8] ________ friends at twenty and fewer closer friends at thirty. Participants with the [9] ________ situation were more lonely. This could be [10] ________ having too many friends in your thirties makes life more difficult.

Paragraph 4: Doctors are looking at friendships when people are younger to [11] ________ how happy people will be when they're older.

D **REFLECT** Think about your answers to these questions.

1 Do you think the information given in the text is totally true, partly true or totally untrue?
2 Do you think that a study with one hundred participants can give accurate results?

How We Socialize Might Shape Our Future

Scientists have discovered some interesting information about how we view relationships. As we get older, the way we think about friendship changes.

When we are in high school and college, quantity of friends is more important. The more friends we have, the happier we are. We feel we are popular and successful socially. We want to learn as much as we can about as many people as possible. As we grow up, quality becomes more important and we look for more intimate relationships with a smaller number of people. [1] ___

In the 1970s, a thirty-year study on one hundred American students began. At the age of twenty and then again at the age of thirty, each student made brief notes about all of their daily social interactions. They noted how long each interaction lasted and how it made them feel. [2] ___

The study found that participants who had a large number of friends at twenty and a smaller, closer circle of friends at thirty were the happiest. Participants who had fewer friends at twenty and a wider, less intimate circle of friends at thirty were more likely to be lonely. One possible conclusion is that having too many friends in our thirties complicates life. [3] ___

Now, doctors claim that they can predict how happy people will be in their old age by studying their friendships earlier in their lives. [4] ___

Glossary

complicate (v) make something more difficult to do or understand
interaction (n) being with and talking to other people
participants (n) people who take part in an activity (here, in a study)
popular (adj) liked by a lot of people

SOCIALIZING 25

Pronunciation

The Workbook also consolidates the pronunciation topics from the Student's Book through further controlled practice.

Reflect

Each reading and listening page has a Reflect section so that students can use their Workbooks in class if they wish to reflect on their learning with their peers.

American Language Hub for Teachers

Teacher's Book

Procedural notes

The lessons include procedural notes for teachers. These offer support to teachers on how to deliver the lesson rather than telling them how to teach. The notes are designed to be brief and easy to read.

Worksheets

The bank of communicative worksheets at the back of the Teacher's Book provides additional controlled and freer practice of every vocabulary and grammar section.

Interleaved pages

Every level of American Language Hub has a Teacher's Book interleaved with pages of the Student's Book. The answers to all of the Student's Book activities are annotated on the page so there is no need for teachers to flip backward and forward to find information.

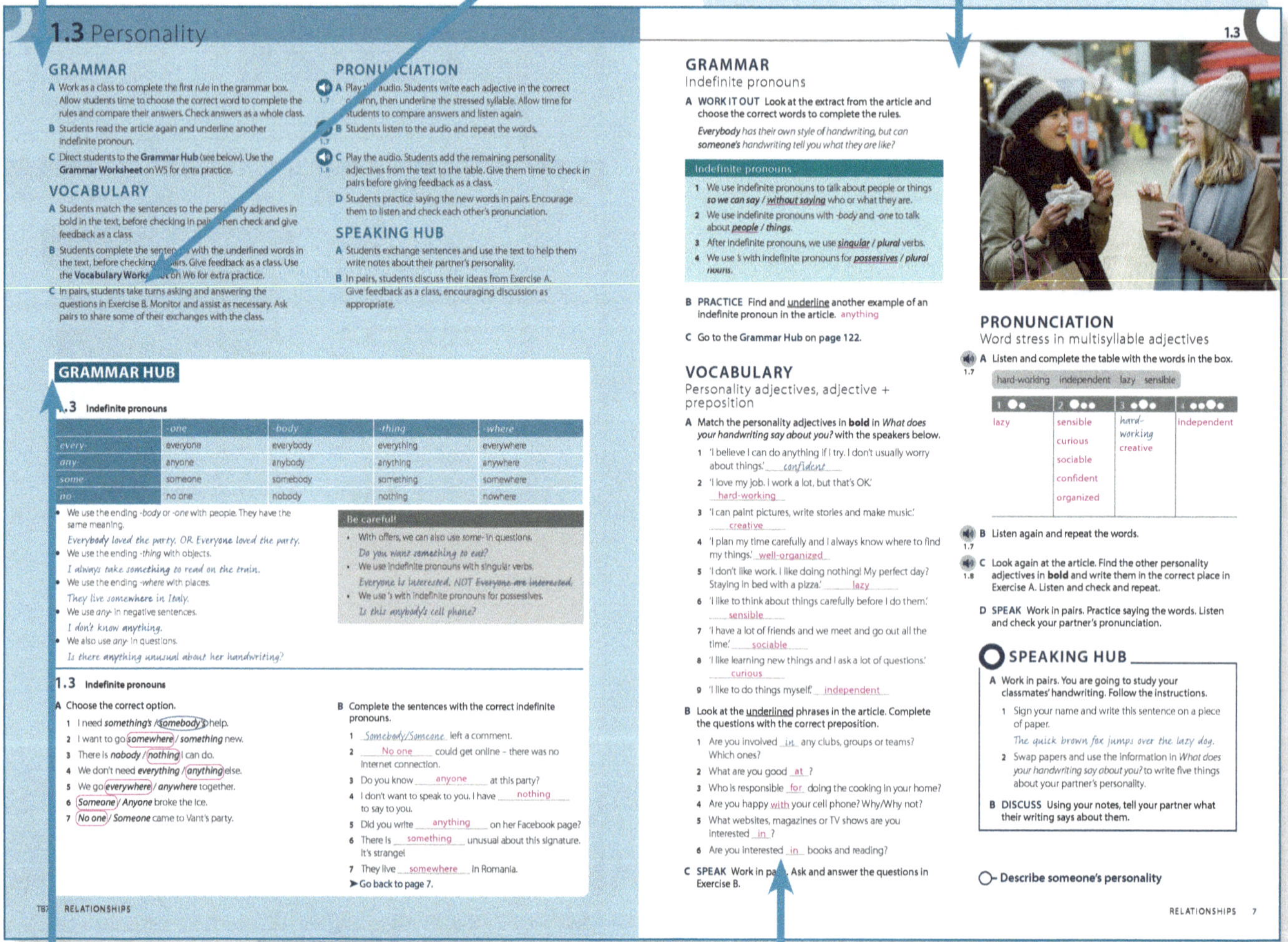

1.3 Personality

GRAMMAR

A Work as a class to complete the first rule in the grammar box. Allow students time to choose the correct word to complete the rules and compare their answers. Check answers as a whole class.

B Students read the article again and underline another indefinite pronoun.

C Direct students to the **Grammar Hub** (see below). Use the **Grammar Worksheet** on W5 for extra practice.

VOCABULARY

A Students match the sentences to the pers[illegible]ity adjectives in bold in the text, before checking in pai[illegible]hen check and give feedback as a class.

B Students complete the senten[illegible] with the underlined words in the text, before checking [illegible]airs. Give feedback as a class. Use the **Vocabulary Works[illegible]** on W6 for extra practice.

C In pairs, students take turns asking and answering the questions in Exercise B. Monitor and assist as necessary. Ask pairs to share some of their exchanges with the class.

PRONU[illegible]CIATION

1.7 A Play [illegible] audio. Students write each adjective in the correct [illegible]mn, then underline the stressed syllable. Allow time for students to compare answers and listen again.

1.7 B Students listen to the audio and repeat the words.

1.8 C Play the audio. Students add the remaining personality adjectives from the text to the table. Give them time to check in pairs before giving feedback as a class.

D Students practice saying the new words in pairs. Encourage them to listen and check each other's pronunciation.

SPEAKING HUB

A Students exchange sentences and use the text to help them write notes about their partner's personality.

B In pairs, students discuss their ideas from Exercise A. Give feedback as a class, encouraging discussion as appropriate.

GRAMMAR HUB

[illegible].3 Indefinite pronouns

	-one	-body	-thing	-where
every-	everyone	everybody	everything	everywhere
any-	anyone	anybody	anything	anywhere
some-	someone	somebody	something	somewhere
no-	no one	nobody	nothing	nowhere

- We use the ending -*body* or -*one* with people. They have the same meaning.
  Everybody loved the party. OR Everyone loved the party.
- We use the ending -*thing* with objects.
  I always take something to read on the train.
- We use the ending -*where* with places.
  They live somewhere in Italy.
- We use *any-* in negative sentences.
  I don't know anything.
- We also use *any-* in questions.
  Is there anything unusual about her handwriting?

Be careful!

- With offers, we can also use *some-* in questions.
  Do you want something to eat?
- We use indefinite pronouns with singular verbs.
  Everyone is interested. NOT ~~Everyone are interested.~~
- We use 's with indefinite pronouns for possessives.
  Is this anybody's cell phone?

1.3 Indefinite pronouns

A Choose the correct option.

1 I need *something's* / *somebody's* help.
2 I want to go *somewhere* / *something* new.
3 There is *nobody* / *nothing* I can do.
4 We don't need *everything* / *anything* else.
5 We go *everywhere* / *anywhere* together.
6 *Someone* / *Anyone* broke the ice.
7 *No one* / *Someone* came to Vant's party.

B Complete the sentences with the correct indefinite pronouns.

1 Somebody/Someone left a comment.
2 No one could get online – there was no Internet connection.
3 Do you know anyone at this party?
4 I don't want to speak to you. I have nothing to say to you.
5 Did you write anything on her Facebook page?
6 There is something unusual about this signature. It's strange!
7 They live somewhere in Romania.

➤ Go back to page 7.

TB7 RELATIONSHIPS

1.3

GRAMMAR

Indefinite pronouns

A WORK IT OUT Look at the extract from the article and choose the correct words to complete the rules.

***Everybody** has their own style of handwriting, but can **someone's** handwriting tell you what they are like?*

Indefinite pronouns

1 We use indefinite pronouns to talk about people or things *so we can say* / *without saying* who or what they are.
2 We use indefinite pronouns with *-body* and *-one* to talk about *people* / *things*.
3 After indefinite pronouns, we use *singular* / *plural* verbs.
4 We use 's with indefinite pronouns for *possessives* / *plural nouns*.

B PRACTICE Find and underline another example of an indefinite pronoun in the article. anything

C Go to the Grammar Hub on page 122.

VOCABULARY

Personality adjectives, adjective + preposition

A Match the personality adjectives in **bold** in *What does your handwriting say about you?* with the speakers below.

1 'I believe I can do anything if I try. I don't usually worry about things.' confident
2 'I love my job. I work a lot, but that's OK.' hard-working
3 'I can paint pictures, write stories and make music.' creative
4 'I plan my time carefully and I always know where to find my things.' well-organized
5 'I don't like work. I like doing nothing! My perfect day? Staying in bed with a pizza.' lazy
6 'I like to think about things carefully before I do them.' sensible
7 'I have a lot of friends and we meet and go out all the time.' sociable
8 'I like learning new things and I ask a lot of questions.' curious
9 'I like to do things myself.' independent

B Look at the underlined phrases in the article. Complete the questions with the correct preposition.

1 Are you involved in any clubs, groups or teams? Which ones?
2 What are you good at?
3 Who is responsible for doing the cooking in your home?
4 Are you happy with your cell phone? Why/Why not?
5 What websites, magazines or TV shows are you interested in?
6 Are you interested in books and reading?

C SPEAK Work in pa[illegible]. Ask and answer the questions in Exercise B.

PRONUNCIATION

Word stress in multisyllable adjectives

1.7 A Listen and complete the table with the words in the box.

hard-working independent lazy sensible

1 ●•	2 ●••	3 •●•	4 ••●•
lazy	sensible curious sociable confident organized	hard-working creative	independent

1.7 B Listen again and repeat the words.

1.8 C Look again at the article. Find the other personality adjectives in **bold** and write them in the correct place in Exercise A. Listen and check and repeat.

D SPEAK Work in pairs. Practice saying the words. Listen and check your partner's pronunciation.

SPEAKING HUB

A Work in pairs. You are going to study your classmates' handwriting. Follow the instructions.

1 Sign your name and write this sentence on a piece of paper.
The quick brown fox jumps over the lazy dog.
2 Swap papers and use the information in *What does your handwriting say about you?* to write five things about your partner's personality.

B DISCUSS Using your notes, tell your partner what their writing says about them.

Describe someone's personality

RELATIONSHIPS 7

Grammar explanations

Where the Student's Book asks the students to look at the Grammar Hub, the teacher can find this already annotated on the Teacher's Book page. For ease of use, the Grammar Hub reference activities at the end of the Student's Book have been added to the Teacher's Book pages at the location they will be used in the course. This makes it easier for teachers to mark homework in class or refer to succinct grammar explanations.

Annotated answers

The answers are annotated on the interleaved pages of the Student's Book. These provide a quick reference tool for teachers.

Teacher's Book: Macmillan Books for Teachers

Lead-in

Suggested lead-ins can be used to activate prior knowledge, generate interest in the lesson topic or focus on useful lexis.

Extra activities

Extra activity boxes help teachers extend the content of the lesson, both in and out of the classroom.

4.2 The future of free time

Present reasons to support or argue against predictions

G – making predictions P – *will* and *won't* V – suffixes

READING

A Work in pairs. Do you agree with the following sentences? Why/Why not?

In the next ten years …

we will do less work and spend more time socializing.

we will do a lot of our socializing in virtual worlds.

we will socialize with artificial intelligence.

B READ FOR MAIN IDEA Work in groups. Student A go to page 156, Student B go to page 153 and Student C go to page 152. Read your article and discuss the questions below.

1 What does the article say about our social lives?
2 What role will technology play?
3 Which expert or business leader is mentioned, and why?
4 What possible benefits of the development does the article mention?

C SPEAK Work in groups. Discuss your article and the following questions.

1 Which predictions do you think will happen?
2 Do you think these will be positive or negative developments for our social lives? Why?

34 SOCIALIZING

GRAMMAR

Making predictions

A WORK IT OUT Look at the sentences from the articles about the future of our social lives. Underline the modal verbs used to make predictions.

1 The good news is some people think it might not be long until every weekend is a long weekend.
2 However, experts agree that the way we use social media will change in the future.
3 Some experts even believe that one day it may be possible for robots to feel love.

B Find and underline four more examples of modal verbs in one of the articles you read in Reading Exercise B. Then work in pairs and compare your answers.

C Complete the rules with *will* or *might/may*.

Making predictions

1 We use ___will___ (*not*) + the base form of a verb when we are certain about our prediction.
2 We use ___might/may___ (*not*) + the base form of a verb when we are less certain about our prediction.

D Look at the sentences from *Robot relationships*. Then choose the correct words to complete the rules.

… humans will probably develop close relationships with robots.

… it definitely won't be long until robots look, sound and move like humans.

1 We use *probably* to make predictions with *will* and *won't* **less** / **more** certain.
2 We use *definitely* to make predictions with *will* and *won't* **less** / **more** certain.
3 We use *probably* and *definitely* **before** / **after** *will*.
4 We use *probably* and *definitely* **before** / **after** *won't*.

4.2 The future of free time

LEAD-IN

Students write anonymous predictions about what their classmates will do or become in the next five years. Collect all the predictions and read each one aloud. The class has to guess who the prediction is about and who wrote it.

READING

A Have a class discussion on whether they agree or not and why.

B Put students into groups of three. Direct students to the **Communication Hub**. Each student reads their corresponding article and answers the questions.

Article A: Work-life balance

1 *Shorter working weeks, longer weekends / more free time / soon every weekend might be a long weekend.*
2 *Better technology will do more of our work for us.*
3 *Carlos Slim – some of his employees work shorter weeks.*
4 *A better work-life balance / offices will use less energy and there will be fewer car trips.*

Article B: Social media

1 *The way we use social media will change in the future.*
2 *Virtual reality will make it possible to meet friends in 3D worlds.*
3 *Mark Zuckerberg – developing VR social media.*
4 *You will be able to meet friends 'inside' pictures and videos and in VR clubs and museums, etc.*

Article C: Robot relationships

1 *Humans will develop close relationships with robots.*
2 *Technology will make robots look, sound and move like humans. Scientists might be able to build robots that really understand human feelings.*
3 *Professor Hiroshi Ishiguro – he is mentioned because he has built a robot called Erica that can show basic feelings on her face.*
4 *Robots could take care of people.*

C Students take turns summarizing their article and discussing the questions as a group.

GRAMMAR

A Highlight the title of the section *(Making predictions)*. Ask students to read the three sentences and underline the modal verbs used to express prediction. Allow students to check their answers with a partner before checking with the whole class.

B Direct students back to the **Communication Hub** articles they read, and ask them to underline four examples of modal verbs. Give feedback as a class.

A: Work-life balance

... technology **will** *do more of ...*
This **will** *allow us to have ...*
... work-life balance **won't** *be the ...*
Office **will** *use less energy ...*
... there **will** *be fewer car trips ...*

B: Social media

... your friends **will** *soon put on ...*
... it **will** *be possible to meet ...*
... that you **will** *be able to ...*
It **will** *also be possible ...*
... you **might** *have to wait ...*

C: Robot relationships ...

humans **will** *probably develop ...*
... it definitely **won't** *be long ...*
... technology **might** *help scientists ...*
... your robot **might** *be able to ...*

C Focus students on the rules in the *Making predictions* box. Students work on their own to complete the rules. Remind them to use the sentences in Exercise A to help them. Check answers as a class.

D Read the sentences with the whole class. Students work on their own, completing Rules 1–4. They compare their answers in pairs before checking with the whole class.

METHODOLOGY HUB by Jim Scrivener

Getting feedback on teaching

Feedback from colleagues

Ask other teachers to come in and observe some of your lessons, and do an exchange observation with them, not to judge each other or score points but to learn from each other. The growth in trust and respect that comes from sharing ideas and skills in this way can really help all involved move forward, as well as having a markedly positive effect on the whole atmosphere of a school.

Even if a colleague cannot come in and observe a lesson, you could still set aside some uninterrupted time (perhaps 15 minutes or so) when they will sit and listen to you talk through your thoughts about the lesson. Your colleague could make a 'contract' with you that he or she will not offer suggestions or advice or help or opinions, but will simply listen and support you. This kind of helping is very simple to describe, but extremely powerful in action. It can be surprisingly beneficial to talk through one's own experience with another person who is really listening.

TEACHING IDEA by David Seymour and Maria Popova

One day

Explain that you are going to dictate one prediction about the future to each person. Invite students to mingle and collect (write down) the other students' opinions on their prediction. (Dictate each sentence quickly, but go through them two or three times so that students get another chance to write down their prediction. After the survey, elicit the results and write them on the board.)

Computers will take over the world.
Time travel will be possible.
We will find life in other solar systems.
Unintelligent clones will do all the hard work.
Disease will be eliminated.
People will live on Mars.
Everyone will live to be 200.
The environment will be destroyed.

SOCIALIZING TB34

Methodology Hub

Ideas for professional development from Jim Scrivener's *Learning Teaching, Third Edition* are presented in every unit to help new teachers pick up helpful tips to add to their repertoire or just reflect on a new way to use American Language Hub with their class.

Teaching Idea

Tips and ideas from the *Macmillan Books for Teachers* series are included in the teacher's notes to give some new ideas for instant communicative activities in the lesson. These can usually be used without paper preparation as warm-ups to get the class moving or as a flexible stage where there is time to fill.

American Language Hub for Teachers

Teacher's App

The American Language Hub Teacher's Book comes with a Teacher's App, which gives access to the Resource Center, Test Generator and Classroom Presentation Kit.

The Classroom Presentation Kit is designed to be displayed on an interactive whiteboard (IWB) or using a projector, it enables teachers to play video and audio or show interactive activities in class. It is not only user-friendly for the teacher but also for the student, with activities being clearly visible for the whole class. Answer-by-answer reveal enables teachers to elicit student responses and check answers one by one.

Tools

Embedded tools make it possible to highlight and annotate texts to prompt noticing or self-correction. Teachers have the option to turn on an audio script, which is timed to sync with the dialogue, when listening to audio.

Teachers can zoom into each activity with one click. Then they can either move smoothly through the activities or zoom out to see the whole page. They can also create a whiteboard area for additional notes.

Video

Teachers can also access the video and audio for the course, including the authentic video from *The Guardian*.

Homework

The app allows teachers to assign homework directly to their students' devices and alert them when they have activities to complete.

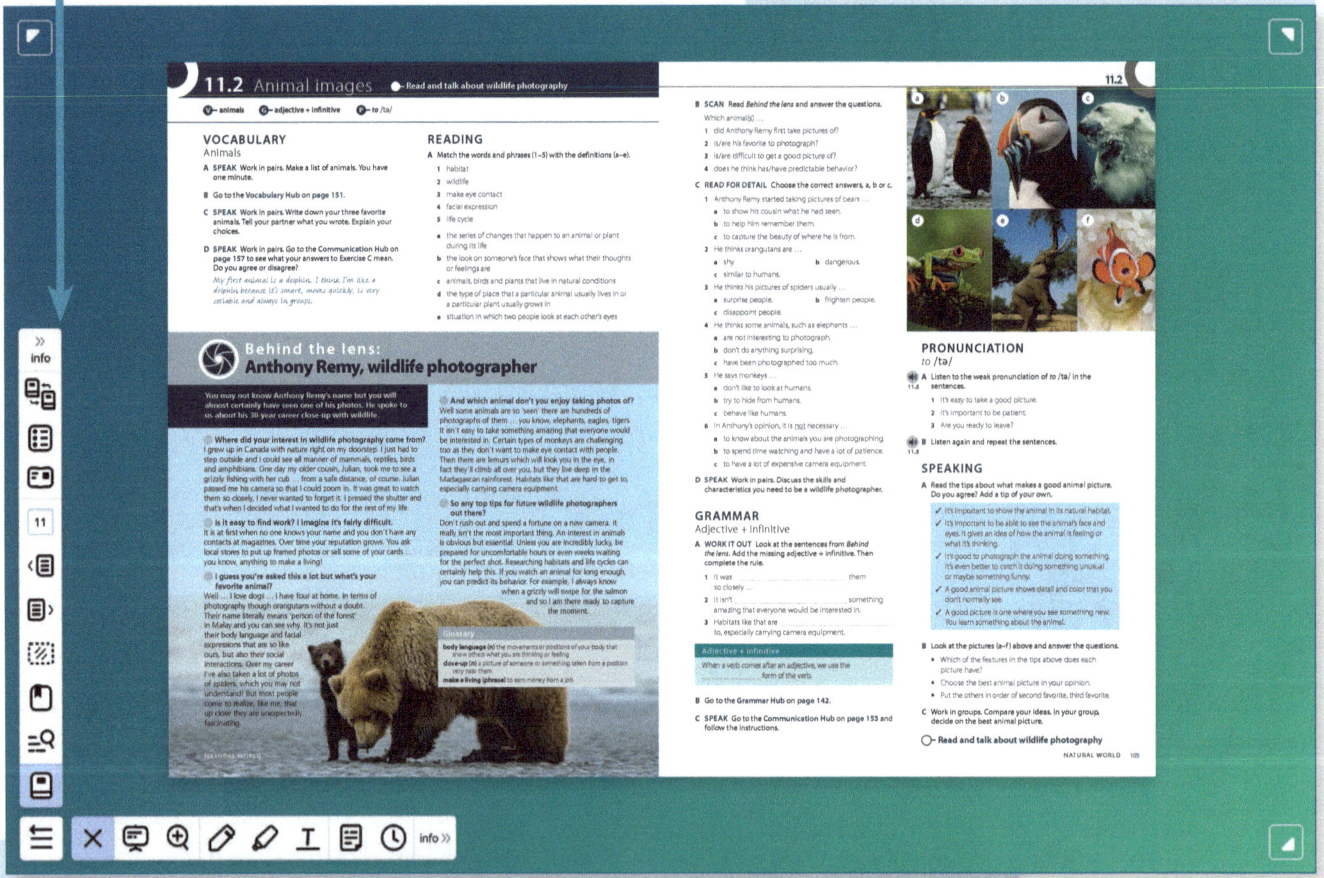

Preparation and Practice

Teachers can also configure student preparation and practice using the Teacher's App. Using the practice activities available, teachers can select and publish content to their students which they will receive through a push notification when they access their app. This enables teachers to personalize the amount and type of practice students do every week and to track their progress. Students can practice the grammar or vocabulary for the week before they go to class, allowing more time in the class for communication.

Test Generator

The Teacher's App also gives access to the Test Generator. In the Test Generator, teachers can create tests or use the pre-built tests for each level of the course and print these to assign to students. There are unit tests, mid- and end-of-course tests for each level, testing vocabulary, grammar and the four skills.

Student's App

Each Student's Book includes a code for the Student's App, to engage and encourage your students to practice their English on the move. Students can access grammar, vocabulary and pronunciation activities to prepare them for the lesson. Students are able to complete activities with varying levels of challenge and earn medals.

Preparation
Allows more time for communicative activities in the class by providing pre-lesson exposure to the language covered in the Student's Book.

Practice
Provides additional practice to consolidate, review and extend areas covered in the Student's Book.

Rewards
A reward system helps to maintain student motivation.

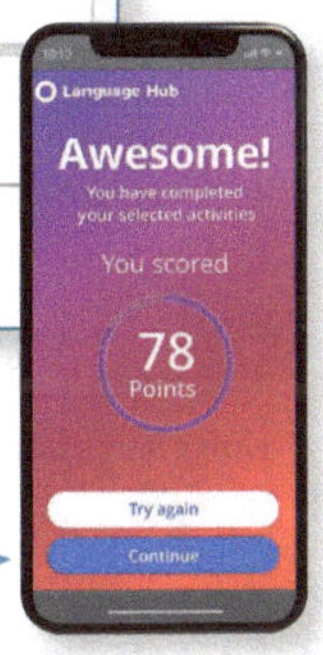

Video

Two types of video are available with the course. Café Hub is a situation comedy which models functional language. Video Hub uses content from *The Guardian* as a resource for authentic English. All the videos from the course relate to the unit topics, and offer listening practice and scaffolding for speaking output.

Video Hub

Café Hub

Contents

Welcome

USEFUL PHRASES

Classroom

0.1 **A** Write the words in the correct order to make useful questions for the classroom. Listen and check.

1. repeat / please / that, / Can / you / ? — Can you repeat that, please?
2. say / do / How / you / English / *trabajar* / in / ? — How do you say *trabajar* in English?
3. slowly, / Could / speak / more / please / you / ? — Could you speak more slowly, please?
4. do / pronounce / How / you / that / ? — How do you pronounce that?
5. spell / do / that / you / How / ? — How do you spell that?
6. *excellent* / What / mean / does / ? — What does *excellent* mean?

Dates

B SPEAK Work in pairs. Answer the questions.

1. Which months have exactly 30 days? — April, June, September, November
2. What are the days of the week? — Monday, Tuesday, Wednesday, Thursday, Friday, Saturday, Sunday
3. How do you say the ordinal numbers 1–20? — first, second, third, fourth, fifth, sixth, seventh, eighth, ninth, tenth, eleventh, twelfth, thirteenth, fourteenth, fifteenth, sixteenth, seventeenth, eighteenth, nineteenth, twentieth
4. What date is it today?

PRONUNCIATION

Word stress

0.2 **A** Listen and underline the stressed syllables. Then listen again and repeat the words.

happy po**lite** a**maz**ing **beau**tiful

The /ə/ sound

0.3 **B** Listen and underline the schwa /ə/ sound. Then listen again and repeat the words.

tel**e**vision m**a**gazine s**u**pport camp**u**s

Third person -s endings and simple past regular endings

0.4 **C** How do you pronounce the underlined sounds? Listen and repeat. Choose the correct option.

1	work**s**	**/s/** /z/ /ɪz/	4	play**ed**	**/d/** /t/ /ɪd/
2	ha**s**	/s/ **/z/** /ɪz/	5	watch**ed**	/d/ **/t/** /ɪd/
3	finish**es**	/s/ /z/ **/ɪz/**	6	want**ed**	/d/ /t/ **/ɪd/**

GRAMMAR

Tenses, structures and auxiliary verbs

A Choose the correct words to complete the questions.

1. What **do** / *does* / *are* you do?
2. *Are* / *Is* / **Can** you cook?
3. *Were* / *Will* / **Are** you reading a good book right now?
4. What *is* / *am* / **are** your parents' names?
5. Where *do* / **does** / *is* your best friend live?
6. Can you *swimming* / **swim** / *to swim*?

B SPEAK Work in pairs. Ask and answer the questions in Exercise A.

VOCABULARY

Word sets

A Look at the word sets. Cross out the odd one out. Check your answers with a partner and explain your choices.

1. serious ~~old~~ friendly happy
2. at five o'clock ~~next to me~~ in the afternoon on Tuesday — all others about time
3. across from the bank ~~four years ago~~ near the school behind the library — all others about places
4. ~~egg~~ bottle bag can — all others about containers
5. two years ago ~~in a month~~ last Friday yesterday evening — all others about past
6. banana apple ~~bread~~ orange — all others about fruit

Parts of speech

B Match the parts of speech in the box with the words in **bold**.

~~adjective~~ adverb article auxiliary noun preposition verb

1. My **favorite** subject is English. — *adjective*
2. I **read** emails in English at work. — verb
3. There are 12 students **in** our class. — preposition
4. **Do** you speak any other languages? — auxiliary
5. We have **a** test today. — article
6. This is my new English **book**. — noun
7. Please listen **carefully**. — adverb

Question words

C Complete the questions with the words in the box.

How many How much ~~What~~ When Where Who Why

1. *What* 's your name?
2. Where are you from?
3. When is your birthday?
4. How many brothers and sisters do you have?
5. Who do you know in this class?
6. Why are you studying English? Do you need it for work?
7. How much time do you spend studying English each week?

D SPEAK Work in pairs. Ask and answer the questions in Exercise C.

1 RELATIONSHIPS

> Relationship (n) the way in which two or more people or things are connected with or involve each other.
> Synonyms: connection (n), association (n).

My best friend is the one who brings out the best in me.

Henry Ford

> Ford is suggesting that your best friends in life are the people who help you to be a better person and reach your potential.

> Henry Ford (30 July 1863–7 April 1947) was an American businessperson, who founded the Ford Motor Company. He developed and manufactured the first automobile that many middle-class Americans could afford.

Inupiat friends play in the first of the winter snow, Nome, Alaska.

OBJECTIVES

- find out about someone new
- talk about different types of people
- describe someone's personality
- greet people and give personal information, make introductions
- write information about yourself

Work with a partner. Discuss the questions.

1 Who's your best friend?
2 Look at the picture. Who was your best friend when you were a child?
3 What qualities do you look for in a friend?

OBJECTIVES

Read the unit objectives to the class.

UNIT OPENER QUESTIONS

Ask students to read the quote and take one or two suggestions from the class about what they think it means.

Tell students to look at the picture on the page and ask prompt questions such as 'How do these children know each other?' If students share any good ideas or useful language, write these on the board.

Call on a student to read aloud the first question. Answer with a short description of your own best friend. Then ask students to discuss the questions with a partner or in a small group.

Monitor and help with grammar and vocabulary when necessary. When students have finished the activity, ask one or two pairs or groups to share their ideas with the class. Encourage the students to listen to one another and respond with their own ideas and opinions.

WORKSHEETS

Lesson 1.1 Breaking the ice

Grammar: Question forms (W1)

Vocabulary: People (W2)

Lesson 1.2 Blogs and bloggers

Grammar: Frequency words and phrases (W3)

Vocabulary: Types of people (W4)

Lesson 1.3 Personality

Grammar: Indefinite pronouns (W5)

Vocabulary: Personality adjectives, adjective + preposition (W6)

1.1 Breaking the ice

Find out about someone new

G question forms V people P the alphabet

LISTENING

A Complete the definitions with the words in the box.

conversation relationship successful tip topic

1 A private and informal talk between two people is a conversation.
2 A useful suggestion is a tip.
3 When you achieve the result you want, you are successful.
4 A subject that you write or speak about is a topic.
5 When two or more people or things are connected in some way, they have a relationship.

B SPEAK Work in groups. Discuss the questions.

1 What is happening in the photo at the top of the page?
2 Where do people usually meet for the first time?
3 How do you usually start a conversation with someone you have just met?

1.1 **C LISTEN FOR KEY WORDS** Listen to an interview with psychologist Isabelle Ackerman.

1 What topic does she talk about? meeting new people
2 What should you start a conversation with? a smile
3 What are two safe topics of conversation to 'break the ice'? interests and studies

Glossary

break the ice (phrase) to do or say something that makes people feel less shy or nervous in a social situation
politics (n) the activities of governments which control a country or area
psychology (n) the study of the mind and how it affects behavior
religion (n) the belief in the existence of a god or gods
social life (n) the time you spend enjoying yourself with friends

1.1 **D LISTEN FOR DETAIL** Listen again and complete each tip with the correct verb.

ask discuss feel give know say

1 Say something positive about the place or situation you are in, and then ask a question.
2 Ask about other people.
3 Don't be negative about other people because you don't know who they know.
4 Ask lots of questions and give lots of answers.
5 When you feel more relaxed, ask some personal questions.
6 Don't discuss topics like religion or politics with someone you don't know.

E SPEAK Work in groups. Discuss the questions.

1 What did you think of the tips in the podcast?
2 What other topics are easy to talk about with new people?

GRAMMAR

Question forms

1.2 **A WORK IT OUT** Complete the questions with the words in the box. Listen again and check your answers.

are did (x2) do (x2) have is (x2) were

1 What do you say to a stranger at a party or a new colleague at the office? simple present
2 Is it OK to talk about some topics, but not others? simple present
3 Have you ever met someone new and had no idea what to talk about? present perfect
4 Are you having fun? present progressive
5 What is your favorite band? simple present
6 Did you enjoy the ceremony? simple past
7 Were you at school together? simple past
8 Where did you study? simple past
9 Do you have children? simple present

1.1 Breaking the ice

LEAD-IN

Write something on the board that is important for you, e.g. a date, a name, a number, a place. Ask the class to guess what the numbers and words could mean by asking questions (e.g. *Are you 32 years old?*). Once they have guessed everything correctly, put students into small groups to do the activity themselves. Give feedback as a class, asking students to share what they found out.

LISTENING

A Ask the class to complete the definitions before checking their answers with a partner.

B Focus students on the picture. Ask where the people are and whether they know each other. Then tell the class to discuss Questions 2 and 3 in a small group. Monitor and correct any errors on the spot. Give feedback as a class.

1.1 **C** Give students time to read the questions and glossary box. Explain that it includes key words which might be useful to understand the audio. Play the audio. Give students time to answer the questions and compare their ideas in pairs, before checking answers as a class.

1.1 **D** Play the audio again, allowing time for students to complete the sentences. With a stronger class, you may ask students to complete the sentences and play the audio afterwards for them to check. If necessary, play the audio again before checking answers as a whole class.

E Encourage students to use information from the conversation to support their ideas when discussing the questions. Monitor and assist as necessary, before giving feedback as a class.

GRAMMAR

1.2 **A** Ask students to fill in the blanks with the words in the box. Play the audio for students to check their answers.

B Students read questions in Exercise A again and decide in which tense they are. Check answers as a whole class.

C Focus students on the grammar box. Read the rules as a class. Students circle the correct words to complete the rules. Remind students to use the sentences from Exercise A to help them.

D Direct students to the **Grammar Hub** (see TB3). Use the **Grammar Worksheet** on W1 for extra practice.

E Read the task with the whole class. Students work individually rewriting the questions. Check answers as a whole class.

F In pairs, students take turns asking and answering the questions in Exercise E for themselves. Monitor students and encourage them to ask further questions to get more information (e.g. *What's your brother's name?*). Ask different pairs to share their exchanges with the class.

AUDIO SCRIPT

1.1

Listening, Exercise C
P = Paul I = Isabelle

P: Hello, and welcome to *Everyday Psychology*. I'm Paul Ross, and with me today is psychologist and expert on relationships, Isabelle Ackerman.

I: Hello, Paul. Hello, listeners.

Ex C Q1 **P:** Isabelle, today's topic is meeting new people. Now, we regularly meet new people at work or in our social lives, but it can be difficult to talk to someone we don't know. I mean, what do you say to a stranger at a party or a new colleague at the office? Is it OK to talk about some topics, but not others? Have you ever met someone new and had no idea what to talk about? Today, you have some advice to help us 'break the ice' and start conversations with new people.

Ex C Q2 **I:** Yes, I do. Let's begin with a very simple tip. When you meet someone new, start with a smile. A smile can help us feel more relaxed, but that's easy to forget when you feel nervous.

P: And of course a friendly face is easier to talk to.

Ex D Q1 **I:** Yes. A nice way to continue a conversation is to say something positive. You could talk about the place or situation you are in and then ask a question. For example, at a party, try 'Are you having fun?' or 'I love this music! What is your favorite band?' To a new person at work, you can say 'Oh, I'm glad it's lunchtime. How's your first day going?'

P: So no complaining about the boss!

Ex D Q2 **I:** Not at first, no. But it is good to ask about other people. For example, in a new group of students, ask 'Do you know our teacher?' or, at a wedding ceremony, 'Did you enjoy the ceremony?' or 'How do you know the happy couple? Were you at school
Ex D Q3 together?' Don't be negative about other people because you don't know who they know.

P: Yes, that could be dangerous.

Ex C Q3 **I:** Interests and studies are always good, safe topics to talk about. Questions like 'What kind of music do you like?' or 'Where did you study?' are usually easy
Ex D Q4 to answer. Remember, ask lots of questions and give lots of answers. A successful conversation is like a game of tennis!

P: It takes hours and makes you tired?

Ex D Q5 **I:** Very funny. When you feel more relaxed, ask some personal questions. 'Where are you from?', 'Are you married?' and 'Do you have children?' are good
Ex D Q6 examples. But be careful. Don't discuss topics like religion or politics with someone you don't know.

P: Some great tips, Isabelle, thank you very much. That's all for this week. Remember, many great friends meet after a smile and a simple 'hello'. Good luck breaking the ice and meeting new people. Please join us for the next episode of *Everyday Psychology* – we'll be discussing the hot topic …

1.1 Breaking the ice

VOCABULARY

A Direct students to the **Vocabulary Hub** (see TB121) and have them complete the exercises. Allow time for students to compare answers in pairs before checking with the whole class. Use the **Vocabulary Worksheet** on W2 for extra practice.

B Monitor and take note of any language errors to go over at the end of the lesson. Ask one or two pairs to demonstrate their exchanges and encourage the whole class to respond to their ideas.

PRONUNCIATION

1.3 **A** Play the audio. Students listen to the alphabet and repeat.

1.3 **B** In pairs, students match the letters to the vowel sound they contain. Play the audio for students to check their answers.

C In pairs, students take turns to spell the words.

SPEAKING

A Model one or two questions. Then monitor and assist as necessary.

B Give students one minute to find a partner they don't know very well. Then, give students ten minutes to walk around the classroom asking and answering the questions they wrote in Exercise A.

GRAMMAR HUB

1.1 Question forms

Questions with *do* / *does* / *did*

Do/Does/Did + subject + infinitive
Do you have children?
Does he go to English classes?
Did she write a blog post?
Did they do their homework?

- We use the auxiliary verb (*do, does, did*), without a question word, to ask yes/no questions.

Question words

Question word + *do/does/did* + subject + infinitive
What do you say to a stranger?
Where does he come from?
What did you say to your colleague?
Where did she study psychology?

- We use *What* to ask about things and *Where* to ask about places.

Questions with *be*

Am/Is/Are + subject
Am I in this class?
Are they strangers?

Am/Is/Are + subject + *-ing*
Is she doing her homework now?
Are you having fun?

Was/Were + subject
Was he a sensible person?
Were they good at English?

- We use questions with *be*, without a question word, to ask yes/no questions.
- We can also ask questions with *What, Where, When, Why* and *Who* before the verb *be*.

Questions with the present perfect

Have/Has + subject + past participle
Have you visited that website?
Has he written a bucket list?

- We use present perfect questions, without a question word, to ask yes/no questions.
- We use *ever* to ask about life experiences.

  Have you ever met a famous person?
- We can also ask question with *What, Where, When, Why* and *Who* before the verb *have*.

1.1 Question forms

A Put the words in order to make questions.

1. you / do / go / skiing / want / to
   Do you want to go skiing?
2. does / what / do / he / weekends / on
   What does he do on weekends?
3. did / you / meet / where / for coffee
   Where did you meet for coffee?
4. you / tea / are / coffee / or / drinking
   Are you drinking tea or coffee?
5. your / new colleagues / were / at the office
   Were your new colleagues at the office?
6. you / been / have / ever / Mexico / to
   Have you ever been to Mexico?
7. tried / that / she / has / new restaurant
   Has she tried that new restaurant?

B Correct the mistakes in each sentence.

1. Why ~~you did~~ *did you* choose that topic?
2. Have you ever ~~meet~~ met a graphologist?
3. What ~~you are~~ are you talking about?
4. Did they ~~went~~ go to the movie theater last night?
5. Where ~~you did~~ did you put the new keyboard?
6. What ^is your best friend's name ~~is~~?
7. Did you ^do anything nice last weekend?

➤ Go back to page 3.

B Look at the questions in Exercise A. What tense are they? Write *simple present, simple past, present progressive* or *present perfect* next to each one.

C Choose the correct words to complete the rules. Use Exercise B to help you.

Question forms

1. We use the auxiliary verb (*do, does, did*) **before** / *after* the subject.
2. We use *be* (*am, is, are, was, were*) **before** / *after* the subject.
3. We use present perfect *have* **before** / *after* the subject.

D Go to the **Grammar Hub** on **page 122**.

E Rewrite the questions with the verb in parentheses in the correct place.

1. why you studying English? (*are*)
   Why are you studying English?
2. you have any brothers or sisters? (*do*)
   Do you have any brothers or sisters?
3. you ever met a famous person? (*have*)
   Have you ever met a famous person?
4. you do anything nice last weekend? (*did*)
   Did you do anything nice last weekend?
5. you like tea or coffee? (*do*)
   Do you like tea or coffee?
6. you a late-night or early-morning person? (*are*)
   Are you a late-night or early-morning person?
7. who your funniest friend? (*is*)
   Who is your funniest friend?
8. who the first person you talked to this morning? (*was*)
   Who was the first person you talked to this morning?
9. you ever been to a wedding? (*have*)
   Have you ever been to a wedding?
10. what the last good movie you saw? (*was*)
    What was the last good movie you saw?

F **SPEAK** Work in pairs. Ask and answer the questions in Exercise E.

VOCABULARY
People

A Go to the **Vocabulary Hub** on **page 146**.

B **SPEAK** Work in pairs. Answer the questions.

1. How many relatives do you have? How often do you see them all?
2. How many of your colleagues or other students in your class are also your friends?
3. Do you find it easy to talk to strangers? Why/Why not?

PRONUNCIATION
The alphabet

1.3 **A** Listen and repeat.

a b c d e f g h i j k l m n o p q r s t u v w x y z

A B C D E F G H I J K L M N O P Q R S T U V W X Y Z

1.4 **B** Work in pairs. Write the letters of the alphabet in the correct place. Listen and check.

/e/	/uː/	/ɑː/	/iː/	/aɪ/	/oʊ/	/eɪ/
f	u	r	e	i	o	a
l	q		b	y		h
m	w		c			j
n			d			k
s			g			
x			p			
			t			
			v			
			z			

C **SPEAK** Work in pairs. Look again at Vocabulary Exercise A on **page 146**. Take turns spelling the words.

SPEAKING

A Find out some information about your classmates. Write six questions using the ideas below to help you. Then write two more questions using your own ideas.

- ice breakers
  Hi, my name's ______. It's nice to meet you. So, …
- personal questions
- family and friends
  Do you come from a large family?
- interests and hobbies
- childhood and school
- work and study
- favorite things/places
- last weekend/vacation
  Where did you go for your last vacation?

B Work in pairs. Work with someone you do not know well and follow the instructions.

1. Stand up and meet the other people in the class. Take turns asking and answering the questions you wrote in Exercise A.
2. When you have broken the ice, sit down with your partner and tell him/her about the people you met. Was it easy to break the ice or do you need some more help?

Find out about someone new

1.2 Blogs and bloggers

Talk about different types of people

V types of people | P using a dictionary | G frequency words and phrases

READING

A Work in groups. Discuss the questions.

1 Which websites do you visit most often and why?
2 Which blogs, vlogs (video blogs) or video channels do you know or follow?
3 What kind of topics do you enjoy reading about online?

B READ FOR MAIN IDEA Read *Three of the best* quickly. Which blog sounds most interesting to you and why?

C READ FOR DETAIL Read again. Complete each sentence with the name of a blogger, Emma, Maria or Michela.

1 ___Michela___ is interested in visiting people around the world.
2 ___Emma___ has children.
3 ___Maria___ writes about a variety of subjects.
4 ___Maria___ has a high number of readers.
5 ___Emma___ is interested in trying new things.
6 ___Michela___ wants people to understand that everyone is beautiful.

D SPEAK Work in pairs. Discuss the questions.

1 Is running a blog a difficult job?
2 Why do these people spend so much time on their blogging activities?
3 What topic would you blog about?

VOCABULARY
Types of people

A Work in pairs. Make a list of different types of people. You have one minute.

father of two, music fan, …

B Go to the **Vocabulary Hub** on **page 146**.

C SPEAK Work in pairs. Write down the names of three people you know and describe them to your partner. Say what type of person each one is. Ask questions about the people your partner describes.

PRONUNCIATION
Using a dictionary

Macmillan English Dictionary

www.macmillandictionary.com

The *Macmillan English Dictionary* gives clear, simple explanations and real life examples showing you how and when the word is used.

A Look at this entry from the *Macmillan English Dictionary*. Match the definitions (1–5) with the labels (a–e).

1 definition d
2 part of speech b
3 stressed syllable and pronunciation c
4 different meaning e
5 frequency rating a

gorgeous – definition and synonyms ★[a]
[b]ADJECTIVE Pronunciation /ˈgɔː(r)dʒəs/[c]
[d]**1** very beautiful
Mandy was there, looking gorgeous as usual.
[e]**2** very enjoyable or pleasant
The weather was absolutely gorgeous.

B Look up the following words in the *Macmillan English Dictionary*. Underline the stressed syllable and write down the part of speech and one meaning for each word.

cloud expedition positive rare

cloud (noun)
expedition (noun)
positive (adjective) (noun)
rare (adjective)

Three of the best

Blogs by Calvin Norton

With over 150 million blogs online, there is something for every type of person from the **animal lover** to the **gamer** to the **sports fan.** But, if you are looking for something a little different, here are my top three blogs.

1 Brain Pickings

Maria Popova is a **book lover**, **music fan** and writer. Her blog *Brain Pickings* is a collection of articles about history, news, books and culture. (Ex C Q3) Maria is interested in reading and spends hundreds of hours each month doing research for her blog. It's an extremely popular blog and many people enjoy Maria's interesting mix of articles. (Ex C Q4)

2 The Atlas of Beauty

The Atlas of Beauty is a picture blog showing beauty in different cultures. Romanian photographer, **blogger** and **traveler** Michela Noroc takes pictures of women of all ages, races and nationalities living their everyday lives. (Ex C Q1) It's a wonderful collection which shows that beauty can be found everywhere. (Ex C Q6)

For more interesting blogs, listen to Calvin on this week's Emma Fry Show

1.2 Blogs and bloggers

LEAD-IN

Provide students with a copy of the following paragraph:

Although the history of coffeepots is relatively short, they have become an essential part of our culture. Practically everyone reads coffeepots, whether they're 'official' news coffeepots associated with news media, topic-based coffeepots related to one's work or hobbies or coffeepots purely for entertainment. The first coffeepot was created by Justin Hall in 1994. In 2004, Merriam-Webster declared 'coffeepot' the word of the year.

Tell them that the word 'coffeepot' stands for another word. Students have to guess the meaning of *coffeepot* through yes-no questions (e.g. *Is coffeepot a noun / verb / an object / a place?*). Remind them to use *coffeepot* in their questions.

READING

A Give students time to read the questions and glossary. Set them to work in small groups. Monitor their discussion and assist with grammar and vocabulary. Take feedback from one or two groups and encourage students to comment on one another's ideas.

B Tell students they have one minute to read the text and find out what it is about. Explain that it is not necessary to read the whole text in detail, just to understand the main idea. Students read and decide which blog might interest them and why. Take feedback from one or two students and encourage them to respond to one another's ideas.

C Ask students to look at the pictures. Ask questions to check understanding (e.g. *Do the photos correspond to any of the bloggers? How do you know? Who's standing on the plane?*). Students read the text again in detail and complete the sentences.

D In pairs, students discuss the questions. Encourage students to use information from the text to support their answers. Monitor and assist as necessary. Take feedback from one or two pairs and encourage students to respond to one another's ideas.

VOCABULARY

A Read the example phrases with the class. Give students a time limit of two minutes to work in pairs making a list of different types of people. Take feedback from one or two pairs and encourage students to respond to one another's ideas.

B Students turn to the **Vocabulary Hub** and complete the exercises. Use the **Vocabulary Worksheet** on W4 for extra practice.

C Model the activity. In pairs, students take turns describing the people they know to their partner and asking questions about the people their partner describes. Encourage students to use the words from the **Vocabulary Hub**.

PRONUNCIATION

A Ask students to read the entry for *gorgeous* from the Macmillan English Dictionary. Ask *What information did you get about the word?* Discuss with the class. Ask students to match definitions to the labels on the dictionary entry. Check answers with the class as a whole.

B Read the task with students. Ask them to check their answers individually before checking with the whole class.

cloud (noun) Students choose from two definitions; (countable and uncountable); one definition (un/countable); students choose from three definitions (countable).

expedition (noun) (countable) Students choose from three definitions.

positive (adjective) Students choose from five definitions; positive (noun) (countable) students choose from three definitions.

rare (adjective) Students choose from two definitions.

AUDIO SCRIPT

1.5

E = Emma C = Calvin

E: Hi. This is Emma Fry on chatfm.nett. Once a week, we bring you reviews and recommendations from the wonderful world of the internet. And today, we are talking blogs with journalist and blogger Calvin Norton from website *Three of the best*. Calvin, it's nice to see you.

C: You too Emma – it's a pleasure to be here. As you know, I'm rarely out in the real world. I'm normally at home, online, in front of my laptop …

E: But luckily for us, you occasionally escape! And today you have some blog recommendations for us.

C: Yes. Now, some of your listeners will know this first one already, I think, but, well, sorry! Now and then, a blog is so good that I just have to mention it again, and again! Run by a guy named Brandon Stanton, this is Humans of New York, a fantastic collection of pictures and extracts from interviews with people on the streets of New York.

E: Humans of New York? I think I've heard of it, actually.

C: You probably have. It has millions of followers on Facebook and Instagram.

E: Wow. And what's it about? I mean, who are the Humans of New York?

C: Well, Stanton focuses on the lives of normal New Yorkers most of the time. He includes someone well-known every so often. But I think it's actually the ordinary people that are the most interesting. New York is such a multi-cultural place and everyone on the blog has a different story to tell. It's a very simple idea, but it never gets boring.

E: And what kinds of things do Stanton and his 'humans' talk about?

C: Ha, well, this is why it's so interesting. He asks all sorts of personal questions and people really open up to him. Some people's stories are very funny and others are extremely sad. Some people even received help or became famous after their stories appeared on the blog.

E: Do all the people on the blog live in New York?

C: No, in fact, Stanton has traveled to countries including Iraq, Ukraine and Mexico. The stories from around the world are often about people who help others or who need help themselves. And there are now many similar blogs telling the stories of people from other cities around the world.

E: It sounds very interesting, Calvin. I'm going to check it out while we play a song. We'll be back with more recommendations from Calvin soon.

1.2 Blogs and bloggers

GRAMMAR

1.5 **A** Ask students if they have ever heard of *Humans of New York*. What do they think it is about? Explain the task and then play the audio. Give students some time to think about the questions after listening. Discuss their answers with the whole class.

1.5 **B** Go through the task. Play the audio again for students to complete the sentences as they hear the words. Stronger groups may enjoy completing the sentences before listening to the recording a second time to check.

C Focus students on the frequency scale and ask them to complete it with the frequency words from Sentences 1–4 in Exercise B. Students check answers in pairs before checking with the whole class.

D Explain that to talk about frequency, we can use words and phrases. Focus students on the table and ask them to complete the phrases using Exercise B if they need help.

E Focus students on the grammar box. Students circle the correct words to complete the rules. Remind them to look at the sentences from Exercise B to assist them. Ask stronger students to give the answer and elicit peer correction as appropriate.

F Direct students to the **Grammar Hub** (see below). Use the **Grammar Worksheet** on W3 for extra practice.

G Students discuss questions in pairs. Monitor and assist students as necessary. Take feedback from one or two pairs and encourage students to respond to one another's ideas.

SPEAKING

A Ask students to think about a website, blog or vlog that they enjoy. Elicit some comments and suggestions following the prompts. Tell students to write notes about the item of their choice using the five prompts.

B In groups, students interview one another about the website, blog or vlog they have chosen. Monitor and assist as necessary.

Extra activity
If you have time, put students into groups and ask them to research five useful websites, blogs/vlogs or apps for studying English. Give feedback as a class, adding any other sites, apps, etc that you would recommend.

GRAMMAR HUB

1.2 Frequency words and phrases

0% ⟵⟶ 100%

never rarely occasionally sometimes often normally always

- We use frequency words after *be* and *can*.

  He is normally very sensible.
  I can never read your handwriting!

- We use frequency words before other verbs.

  I sometimes watch vlogs online.

once twice three times	a	day week month year
every so often	now and then	most of the time

- We usually use frequency phrases at the beginning or end of the sentence.

  I take my dog for a walk twice a day.
  Every so often, I travel to another country.

1.2 Frequency words and phrases

A Write the missing letters.

1 I n<u>e v e</u> r get bored writing my blog.
2 She's s<u>o m e t i m e</u> s late for work.
3 They a<u>l w a y s</u> watch vlogs in their free time.
4 We're n<u>o r m a l l</u> y home before 11.
5 He o<u>c c a s i o n a l l</u> y checks his social media accounts at work.
6 I r<u>a r e l y</u> go online before starting work.
7 He r<u>e g u l a r l y</u> visits his relatives in Italy.

B Put the words and phrases of frequency in the correct place in each sentence. Sometimes more than one answer is possible.

1 We go on vacation. (*once a year*)
We go on vacation once a year.
2 They comment on online articles. (*now and then*)
Now and then, they comment on online articles.
3 I read online tips. (*every so often*)
I read online tips every so often.
4 She writes for popular magazines. (*most of the time*)
She writes for popular magazines most of the time.
5 He takes his dog to the park. (*three times a week*)
He takes his dog to the park three times a week.
6 We play computer games on Saturdays. (*always*)
We always play computer games on Saturdays.
7 We meet up for coffee on Sunday. (*usually*)
We usually meet up for coffee on Sunday.

➤ Go back to page 5.

GRAMMAR

Frequency words and phrases

1.5 **A** Listen to an interview with Calvin Norton about another blog, *Humans of New York*, and answer the questions.

1. What is the blog about? Interviews on the streets of New York.
2. What type of people does Brandon Stanton interview? Usually normal people, sometimes celebrities.

1.6 **B** Listen and complete each sentence from the radio show with one word.

1. ___Once___ a week, we bring you reviews and recommendations from the wonderful world of the internet.
2. I'm ___rarely___ out in the real world.
3. I'm ___normally___ at home, online in front of my laptop.
4. But luckily for us, you ___occasionally___ escape.
5. Now and ___then___, a blog is so good that I just have to mention it again.
6. Stanton focuses on the lives of normal New Yorkers ___most___ of the time.
7. He includes someone well known ___every___ so often.
8. It's a very simple idea, but it ___never___ gets boring.

C **WORK IT OUT** Write the four frequency words in Exercise B in the correct place.

Frequency words

100%
- always
- usually
- often
- 1 ___normally___
- sometimes
- 2 ___occasionally___
- 3 ___rarely___
- hardly ever
- 4 ___never___

0%

D Complete the frequency phrases in the table with words from Exercise B.

once twice three times	1 ___a___	day week month year
every 2 ___so___ often		
3 ___now___ and then		
most of the 4 ___time___		

E Choose the correct words to complete the rules. Use Exercise B to help you.

Frequency words and phrases

1. We usually put frequency words *before / after* the main verb and *before / after* the verb *be*.
2. We use frequency phrases *at the beginning / in the middle* of a sentence.
3. We also use frequency phrases *in the middle / at the end* of a sentence.

F Go to the **Grammar Hub** on **page 122**.

G **SPEAK** Work in pairs. Discuss the questions.

1. Would you enjoy the blog *Humans of New York*?
2. Why do you think it is so popular?

SPEAKING

A Interview each other about websites, blogs or vlogs you like. Write notes about:

- what they are about
- why you like them
- examples of interesting things on them
- what type of people would enjoy them and why

B Work in groups. Interview each other. Which ones sound most interesting?

3 *Emma's Bucket List*

After her father and step-father died, Emma Stewart Rigby decided to live a full and exciting life. Emma, a **mother of three**, made a list of 246 things to do before she dies and in her blog she writes about her experiences. Emma is a **people person** and gives a lot of friendly advice on life. She's also a **foodie**, and her bucket list includes unusual foods or interesting restaurants she plans to try. A great blog for ideas on how to live life to the max! Ex C Q2 Ex C Q5

Glossary

blog (n) a website containing short articles called posts that are changed regularly

blog (v) to write short articles for a website on your opinions, interests and experiences

culture (n) activities which involve music, books and other arts

subscriber (n) someone who joins and follows a blog

Talk about different types of people

1.3 Personality

Describe someone's personality

G indefinite pronouns **V** personality adjectives, adjective + preposition
P word stress in multisyllable adjectives **S** previewing a text

READING

A SPEAK Work in pairs. Discuss the questions.

1. Which do you do more often: write by hand or use a keyboard?
2. Which do you find easier? Why?
3. What kind of things do you write by hand (e.g. shopping lists)?

B Preview the text, and then answer the questions. Use the information in the box to help you.

Previewing a text

Before you read a text, look quickly at the title and any headings, pictures or diagrams. Use this information to decide what kind of text it is, what it's about and why someone might want to read it. This will make the text easier to understand.

1. What is the text about?
2. Is it from a science paper or a popular magazine? How do you know?
3. What do you think you will learn from the text?
4. Can you trust the information in the article?

C READ FOR MAIN IDEA Read *What does your handwriting say about you?* Was your preview correct?

D READ FOR SPECIFIC INFORMATION Read again and answer the questions.

1. What is graphology a study of?
   The study of handwriting.
2. How do graphologists help in court cases?
   match criminals to their handwriting
3. Do all graphologists agree that there is a link between handwriting and personality? No

E SPEAK Work in pairs. Discuss the questions.

1. Do you believe there is a connection between handwriting and personality? Why/Why not?
2. Is it important for children to learn to write by hand these days? Why/Why not?

What does your *handwriting* say about you?

Everybody has their own style of handwriting, but can someone's handwriting tell you what they are like?
Ex D Q1 The study of handwriting is called graphology. Graphologists are usually involved in legal cases. They are responsible for matching criminals to their handwriting or deciding if signatures are real. Ex D Q2 Some graphologists think handwriting can show anything: what kind of job you will be good at, how healthy you are and even what kind of partner you might be happy with.
If you are interested in what your handwriting says about you, check out our information.

Letter size

Small: Medium: Large:

You're probably a **hard-working** person. People with small handwriting are rarely **lazy**.

The research says you're **sensible**; you think carefully about the decisions you make.

Big writing – big personality! People with large writing are usually interested in parties and social events and are rarely shy.

Letter shape

Q Rounded letters: Rounded letters suggest you are a **creative** person. Are you good at art or music?

A Pointed letters: You are **curious**. Your favorite question is 'Why?'!

Dotting your i

Dot high over the i: The research says you have a good imagination.

Dot low over the i: You are a **well-organized** person. Are your desk and room neat?

Spacing between words

Wide spacing:

You're an **independent** type and you are happy on your own.

Narrow spacing:

You're very **sociable** and you need other people in your life.

Your signature

Difficult to read: You are a private person. Like your signature, you can be difficult to read.

Easy to read: **Confident** people usually have signatures that are easy to read. You know what you are good at and you don't mind telling other people about it.

Does your handwriting match your personality? Don't be disappointed with the results if not.
Ex D Q3 Not every graphologist believes there is a connection.

Glossary

legal (adj) relating to the law or lawyers
spacing (n) the amount of space between things

1.3 Personality

LEAD-IN

Ask students to write a short sentence on a piece of paper, e.g. *Today, it's sunny*, and fold it. Collect all the papers and put them on your desk. Open the papers one by one, show them to the class and ask who they think wrote it. Teach *handwriting*. Ask *Can you recognize your friend's handwriting? Is it easy or difficult? Why? What do you think your handwriting reflects?* Teach *personality*.

READING

A Focus students on the questions. Students discuss them in pairs. Monitor and assist as required. Take feedback from one or two pairs and encourage students to respond to one another's ideas.

B Pre-teach *graphology / graphologist*. Focus students on the skills box and make sure they understand the process. Give students a time limit of one minute to look at the headings, pictures and diagrams in the text before answering questions. Students share answers with the whole class.

1 *Handwriting and personality*
2 *A (popular) magazine (there are no citations, the language looks informal and there are pictures)*
3 *What your handwriting says about you. / To see if your handwriting matches your personality.*
4 *As it is not a scientific journal or paper, and there are no citations, you cannot fully trust the ideas.*

C Students read the text again and check their previews. Ask for a show of hands to see how many got the correct preview.

D Focus students on the glossary. Ask *Are the glossary words useful to understand the text?* Students read the text again to find the answers to questions. Tell students that identifying the key words in the questions (*graphology, graphologists, court cases*) may help them find the answer in the text. Allow time for students to compare and work on answers with a partner. Then check answers as a whole class.

E Remind students of the activity they did at the beginning of the class. Students discuss the questions in pairs. Encourage them to use the information from the text to support their answers. Monitor and assist as necessary. Take feedback from one or two pairs and have a class discussion.

Extra activity

Have a debate on one of the two questions: *Who thinks handwriting and personality are linked? Who thinks it is important for children to learn to write by hand?* Divide the class into two groups, in one those in favor and in the other those against the proposition. Eventually, after the discussion, you may want to hold a class vote on the propositions.

TEACHING IDEA by David Seymour and Maria Popova

Vocabulary: Tell the truth

Use this activity to practice vocabulary.

Write these topics on the board as prompts: *hobbies, job, house / apartment, home town, family / friends, personality.* In groups of three, students ask one another questions about them using the prompts. Some of the answers to the questions should be true and some should be false. Students listen to the other members of the group and write down anything they think is a lie.

When all the members of the group have asked and answered one another's questions, students challenge one another about the things they think are lies. The winner is the person who detected the most lies.

TEACHING IDEA by David Seymour and Maria Popova

Vocabulary: Nice people, nasty people

Use this activity to practice personality adjectives.

Write this conversation on the board:

A: *I like my cousin Roger.*

B: *Why?*

A: *Because he always sends cards and gives me lots of presents.*

B: *So you like him because he's generous.*

A: *That's right.*

Write the adjectives from this lesson on the board. Arrange students in pairs and ask them to take turns describing someone they know, without using the adjectives from the lesson. Their partner should choose the adjective that matches the description.

METHODOLOGY HUB by Jim Scrivener

Difficulties when reading a foreign language

Many learners approach reading texts expecting to read them thoroughly and to stop only when they have understood every word. Clearly, there is value in this as a way of improving their vocabulary and their understanding of grammar, but, as with listening, this kind of approach does not necessarily make them into better readers, because this plodding, word-by-word approach is not the way that we usually read in real life. In order to make students better readers, we need first of all to raise their awareness that it's not always essential to understand every word and that practicing some different reading techniques in English may be very useful to them. And if their basic strategy is to read slowly and ponderously, then a good first strategy could be to help them to read fast; not worrying about understanding every word; not, perhaps, even understanding most words, but still achieving a specific goal.

1.3 Personality

GRAMMAR

A Work as a class to complete the first rule in the grammar box. Allow students time to choose the correct word to complete the rules and compare their answers. Check answers as a whole class.

B Students read the article again and underline another indefinite pronoun.

C Direct students to the **Grammar Hub** (see below). Use the **Grammar Worksheet** on W5 for extra practice.

VOCABULARY

A Students match the sentences to the personality adjectives in bold in the text, before checking in pairs. Then check and give feedback as a class.

B Students complete the sentences with the underlined words in the text, before checking in pairs. Give feedback as a class. Use the **Vocabulary Worksheet** on W6 for extra practice.

C In pairs, students take turns asking and answering the questions in Exercise B. Monitor and assist as necessary. Ask pairs to share some of their exchanges with the class.

PRONUNCIATION

1.7 **A** Play the audio. Students write each adjective in the correct column, then underline the stressed syllable. Allow time for students to compare answers and listen again.

1.7 **B** Students listen to the audio and repeat the words.

1.8 **C** Play the audio. Students add the remaining personality adjectives from the text to the table. Give them time to check in pairs before giving feedback as a class.

D Students practice saying the new words in pairs. Encourage them to listen and check each other's pronunciation.

SPEAKING HUB

A Students exchange sentences and use the text to help them write notes about their partner's personality.

B In pairs, students discuss their ideas from Exercise A. Give feedback as a class, encouraging discussion as appropriate.

GRAMMAR HUB

1.3 Indefinite pronouns

	-one	*-body*	*-thing*	*-where*
every-	everyone	everybody	everything	everywhere
any-	anyone	anybody	anything	anywhere
some-	someone	somebody	something	somewhere
no-	no one	nobody	nothing	nowhere

- We use the ending *-body* or *-one* with people. They have the same meaning.
  *Every**body** loved the party. OR Every**one** loved the party.*
- We use the ending *-thing* with objects.
  *I always take some**thing** to read on the train.*
- We use the ending *-where* with places.
  *They live some**where** in Italy.*
- We use *any-* in negative sentences.
  *I don't know **any**thing.*
- We also use *any-* in questions.
  *Is there **any**thing unusual about her handwriting?*

Be careful!

- With offers, we can also use *some-* in questions.
  *Do you want **something** to eat?*
- We use indefinite pronouns with singular verbs.
  *Everyone **is** interested. NOT ~~Everyone are interested.~~*
- We use *'s* with indefinite pronouns for possessives.
  Is this anybody's cell phone?

1.3 Indefinite pronouns

A Choose the correct option.

1 I need *something's* / *somebody's* help. [circled: somebody's]
2 I want to go *somewhere* / *something* new. [circled: somewhere]
3 There is *nobody* / *nothing* I can do. [circled: nothing]
4 We don't need *everything* / *anything* else. [circled: anything]
5 We go *everywhere* / *anywhere* together. [circled: everywhere]
6 *Someone* / *Anyone* broke the ice. [circled: Someone]
7 *No one* / *Someone* came to Vant's party. [circled: No one]

B Complete the sentences with the correct indefinite pronouns.

1 *Somebody/Someone* left a comment.
2 No one could get online – there was no internet connection.
3 Do you know anyone at this party?
4 I don't want to speak to you. I have nothing to say to you.
5 Did you write anything on her Facebook page?
6 There is something unusual about this signature. It's strange!
7 They live somewhere in Romania.

➤ Go back to page 7.

GRAMMAR
Indefinite pronouns

A WORK IT OUT Look at the extract from the article and choose the correct words to complete the rules.

Everybody has their own style of handwriting, but can someone's handwriting tell you what they are like?

Indefinite pronouns

1 We use indefinite pronouns to talk about people or things *so we can say* / *without saying* who or what they are.
2 We use indefinite pronouns with *-body* and *-one* to talk about *people* / *things*.
3 After indefinite pronouns, we use *singular* / *plural* verbs.
4 We use *'s* with indefinite pronouns for *possessives* / *plural nouns*.

B PRACTICE Find and underline another example of an indefinite pronoun in the article. anything

C Go to the **Grammar Hub** on **page 122**.

VOCABULARY
Personality adjectives, adjective + preposition

A Match the personality adjectives in **bold** in *What does your handwriting say about you?* with the speakers below.

1 'I believe I can do anything if I try. I don't usually worry about things.' confident
2 'I love my job. I work a lot, but that's OK.' hard-working
3 'I can paint pictures, write stories and make music.' creative
4 'I plan my time carefully and I always know where to find my things.' well-organized
5 'I don't like work. I like doing nothing! My perfect day? Staying in bed with a pizza.' lazy
6 'I like to think about things carefully before I do them.' sensible
7 'I have a lot of friends and we meet and go out all the time.' sociable
8 'I like learning new things and I ask a lot of questions.' curious
9 'I like to do things myself.' independent

B Look at the underlined phrases in the article. Complete the questions with the correct preposition.

1 Are you involved in any clubs, groups or teams? Which ones?
2 What are you good at?
3 Who is responsible for doing the cooking in your home?
4 Are you happy with your cell phone? Why/Why not?
5 What websites, magazines or TV shows are you interested in?
6 Are you interested in books and reading?

C SPEAK Work in pairs. Ask and answer the questions in Exercise B.

PRONUNCIATION
Word stress in multisyllable adjectives

1.7 **A** Listen and complete the table with the words in the box.

hard-working independent lazy sensible

1 ●•	2 ●••	3 •●•	4 ••●•
lazy	sensible	hard-working	independent
	curious	creative	
	sociable		
	confident		
	organized		

1.7 **B** Listen again and repeat the words.

1.8 **C** Look again at the article. Find the other personality adjectives in **bold** and write them in the correct place in Exercise A. Listen and check and repeat.

D SPEAK Work in pairs. Practice saying the words. Listen and check your partner's pronunciation.

SPEAKING HUB

A Work in pairs. You are going to study your classmates' handwriting. Follow the instructions.

1 Sign your name and write this sentence on a piece of paper.
The quick brown fox jumps over the lazy dog.
2 Swap papers and use the information in *What does your handwriting say about you?* to write five things about your partner's personality.

B DISCUSS Using your notes, tell your partner what their writing says about them.

Describe someone's personality

Café Hub

1.4 Hello again

F – greet people and give personal information, make introductions
P – word stress and intonation

My name is Gaby. I'm originally from 1 Spain, but now, London is my home. I'm a 2 photographer, I like traveling and I drink a lot of 3 coffee. I live in this 4 flat/apartment with Neena and Zac.

My name's Zac. I live with 5 Gaby and Neena. I'm originally from 6 Seattle. I make 7 video games.

My name's Sam. This is my café! I'm 8 34. I like food. I love 9 croissants. I live here in 10 London.

I'm Milly. This is my clothes store. I'm 11 American. I watch 12 old movies, listen to music and I read a lot. 13 Neena's a good friend of mine.

Neena here. I live here in London with my two friends, Gaby and 14 Zac. I'm a lawyer. I work in 15 Central London.

COMPREHENSION

A ▶ **00:00–02:50** Watch the first part of the video. Complete the paragraphs above.

B Write a question about each person in Exercise A.

Where is Gaby from? What does Zac do?

C **SPEAK** Work in pairs. Test your memory! Close your books and ask each other your questions from Exercise B.

D ▶ **02:50–04:27** Watch the second part of the video and underline the correct verb form to complete each sentence.

1. Neena *is* / *isn't* going to an interview.
2. Sam *is* / *isn't* good.
3. Zac *had* / *didn't have* a good holiday.
4. Zac *has* / *hasn't* asked Milly out.
5. Zac *invites* / *doesn't invite* Sam to the flat.
6. Sam *eats* / *doesn't eat* Zac's croissant.

Glossary

flat **(n)** **(British)** = apartment **(n)** **(American)**
holiday **(n)** **(British)** = vacation **(n)** **(American)**

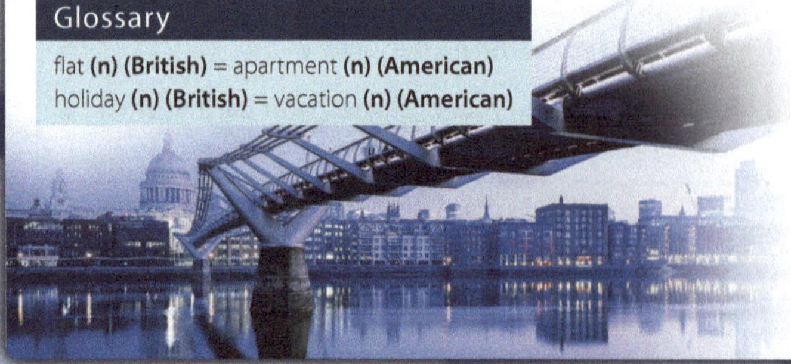

FUNCTIONAL LANGUAGE

Greet people and give personal information, make introductions

A Complete the phrases with the words in the box.

doing   going   hello   let's   long   meet (x2)   what

Greeting	Reply
Say hello	
1 Hello	Hi there! / Hey!
Greet new people	
Nice/Good to 2 meet you.	Nice/Good to 3 meet you, too.
Greet friends	
How are you? How's it 4 going? How are you 5 doing?	I'm good. How about you?
What's new?	Not much.
It's great to see you! 6 What a nice surprise!	7 Long time, no see.
Say goodbye	
See you later. See you soon. I've gotta (got to) go.	8 Let's do something soon.

B ▶ Watch the video again. Check your answers to Exercise A.

MILLY

SAM

NEENA

ZAC

GABY

USEFUL PHRASES

A Match the useful phrases (1–8) with the pictures (a–h).

1 Dream job! d
2 I love it here! b
3 Good luck! g
4 What can I tell you? e
5 Come with me. a
6 What else? f
7 Come over to the flat this weekend. / Will do. h
8 Here we are. This is home. c

a

b

c

d

e

f

g

h

B Watch the video again and check your answers to Exercise A.

C How do you say these phrases in your language?

PRONUNCIATION

Word stress and intonation

A 03:02–03:34 Watch part of the video. Read out the conversation at the same time as Sam and Zac. Copy the word stress and intonation.

Sam: Hey Zac. It's great to see you. What a nice surprise.
Zac: I know. Long time, no see.
Sam: Do you want a coffee?
Zac: Sure, and a croissant.
Zac: So, how are you doing?
Sam: I'm good. How about you? Did you have a nice holiday?
Zac: Yeah. Always good to see family. What's new with you?
Sam: Not much. Same, same.

B SPEAK Work in pairs. Practice the conversation. Listen and check your partner's pronunciation.

SPEAKING

A Walk around the class. Introduce yourself to everybody.

A: Hello, my name's Sven. Nice to meet you.
B: Hi, I'm Ahmed. Good to meet you.

B Walk around the class again. Greet the people you know.

A: Hi, Maria. How's it going?
B: Good, thanks. How about you? What's new with you?
A: Not much. I've gotta go. See you later.

C Prepare a 'selfie' presentation. Follow the instructions.

- Write notes about what you want to say. Use the sentence beginnings below to help you.
- Include at least two useful phrases.
- Record your presentation.

Hi! My name's …
I'm from … / I'm originally from …
I'm a …
I work in …
I like …
I watch / listen to …

D SPEAK Work in groups. Compare your presentations. Which is the best one?

Greet people and give personal information, make introductions

➤ Turn to **page 158** to learn how to write information about yourself.

1.4 Hello again

COMPREHENSION

A ▶ 00:00–02:50 Read through the text and look at the photos. Ask students to predict some of the missing words. Play the video and allow time afterwards for students to compare answers. Give feedback as a class.

B Look at the example question with students. Ask students to read the entries again. They work alone to write one question about each person in Exercise A. Monitor students and assist as necessary.

C In pairs, students take turns asking and answering the questions they wrote in Exercise B. When finished, students open their books to check each other's answers.

D ▶ 02:50–04:27 Play the second part of the video and ask students to underline the correct verb in each sentence. Students compare their answers in pairs. Give feedback as a class.

FUNCTIONAL LANGUAGE

A Students work alone to complete phrases in the grid with the words from the box. Allow time for students to compare answers in small groups.

B ▶ Play the video through in full for students to check their answers to Exercise A.

USEFUL PHRASES

A Encourage students to try and remember what was happening in each picture to complete the exercise.

B ▶ Play the video again for students to check their answers to Exercise A.

C Students look again at the phrases from Exercise A and translate them into their own language. In a multilingual class, you may want to pair students from different countries. Give feedback as a class and encourage discussion.

PRONUNCIATION

A ▶ 03:02–03:34 Elicit why some of the words in the conversation are underlined (*they're stressed*). Highlight that intonation is how our voices move up and down as we speak. Then play the clip again and have students copy the stress and intonation. Pause the clip if necessary.

B Students work in pairs practicing the conversation. Monitor and encourage natural correct stress and intonation.

SPEAKING

A Before beginning the exercise, model the conversation for students. Then, set a time limit for students to mingle and introduce themselves to their classmates.

B Again, model the conversation first before giving students time to mingle.

C Students work individually to write notes on what to say in their self-presentations. Encourage them to use the sentence beginnings in the exercise and to include at least two of the useful phrases from the lesson. Monitor and assist as required. Encourage students to practice their presentations before recording. Monitor and give feedback, before asking students to make their final recordings.

D In groups, students watch and compare their recordings before choosing the best.

▶ VIDEO SCRIPT

Café Hub 1.4 Hello Again
G = Gaby Z = Zac S = Sam M = Milly N = Neena

G: Hi, my name is Gaby. Nice to meet you. Come with me! I'm originally from Spain but now London is my home. I'm a photographer, I like to travel and I drink a lot of coffee. I love it here! Here we are. This is home. I live in this flat with two of my really good friends, Neena and …

Z: Zac. Ah! My name's Zac. Hey, how's it going? I live with Gaby and Neena. I'm originally from Seattle. I make video games. And … I have to test them! Dream job. OK, I'm gonna get some breakfast at Sam's cafe. See you later.

S: Hi there, my name's Sam. Nice to meet you! This is my cafe. What can I tell you? I'm 34. Erm … I like food! I love croissants and … I live here in London! See you later.

M: Hello! I'm Milly, this is my clothes store. I'm American … What else can I tell you? I watch old movies, listen to music and read a lot. Have you met Neena yet, she's a good friend of mine …

N: Hello, Neena here. Good to meet you! OK, I have to be quick, so … I live here in London with my friends Gaby and Zac. What else? Erm, I'm a lawyer and I work in Central London, but I'm looking for a new job and that is why I have to be quick! Because I've got a job interview right now!

Z: Neena! How's it going?
N: Interview!
Z: Of course! Good luck! See you later!
N: Bye!
S: Hey Zac! It's great to see you - what a nice surprise!
Z: I know! Long time, no see!
S: Do you want a coffee?
Z: Sure, and a croissant. So, how are you doing?
S: I'm good. How about you? Did you have a nice holiday?
Z: Yeah, it was great. Always good to see the family. What's new with you?
S: Not much. Same, same. Hey … Have you asked Milly out yet?
Z: No. Not yet …
S: Is that her?
Z: Unfortunately not. It's Gaby - oh no, I'm late! I've gotta go!
S: OK. Let's do something soon?
Z: Yeah, sure. Come over to the flat this weekend?
S: Will do. See you soon Zac. Hey, wait! You forgot …

NOTE: The Glossary boxes on these pages point out differences between American English and British English, which is used in the video clips.

1 Writing

Write information about yourself

W – checking your writing

Use it or lose it

Welcome. This is a blog for language learners written by … a language learner! My favorite tip for people interested in learning languages is 'use it or lose it'. It means 'practice the language and you won't forget it'. I started this blog to practice my English. Would you like to practice your English? Send me a message in English and I'll reply. Twice a week, I'll post the most interesting messages on the blog.

About me

I'm Karolina. Tea drinker, [1]~~bloger~~ and hard-working [2]~~langage~~ learner. [3]~~I've 20 years old~~ and I'm Polish. I study law in college, and English in my free time. I go to English classes [4]~~three times week~~ and I practice for half an hour every day. I have to be [5]~~wel organized~~ to get everything done! Of course, I'm [6]~~serious with~~ learning, but I also really enjoy it.

My blog [7]~~aren't~~ my only hobby. I'm a book lover and I'm also [8]~~interest in~~ old black and white movies. I read and watch in Polish and English.

I'm a curious, sociable person and [9]~~I like talk to people~~ who ask questions. I'm interested in creative types and I love meeting new people – especially other language learners (in the real world and online). I think that makes me a [10]~~person people~~. I hope you enjoy the blog. Remember … use it or lose it!

Refer students to this card as a model for the writing task.

A Read the home page of Karolina's blog and answer the questions.

1 What is her blog about and who is it for? Learning languages. People who want to practice English.
2 How can you help Karolina? Send her a message in English.

B Work in pairs. Read the *About me* section of Karolina's blog. Then cover the blog and discuss what you remember about:

1 her work or studies
2 her likes and dislikes
3 the type of person she is

C Work in pairs. In Karolina's *About me* section there are ten mistakes with grammar, vocabulary and spelling. Correct them. Use the information in the box to help you.

Checking your writing

Follow these tips to help make your writing better.

- Always read your writing slowly and carefully before you finish.
- Try and find and correct any mistakes.
- Check your grammar.
- Check the vocabulary and spelling and be careful with any new language.

D Which colors are the different types of mistakes in Karolina's writing?

1 grammar mistakes ___green___
2 vocabulary mistakes ___blue___
3 spelling mistakes ___red___

E Find and correct one mistake in each sentence. Then decide what type of mistake it is. Write grammar (*G*), vocabulary (*V*) or spelling (*S*).

1 I love to travell and I study tourism. ___travel___ ___S___
2 Why you did start this blog? ___did you___ ___G___
3 I try to learn a new word ever day. ___every___ ___V___
4 I usually am online during the evenings. ___am usually___ ___G___
5 I guess I'm an independant type. ___independent___ ___S___
6 I'm responsible with updating the website. ___responsible for___ ___V___
7 Are you want to know more about our group? ___Do you want___ ___G___
8 I've never write a blog before. ___written___ ___G___

WRITING

A PLAN You are going to write an *About me* section for your own blog, website or social media page. Take notes about your work or studies, your likes and dislikes and the type of person you are.

B WRITE Use your notes and Writing Exercise A to help you write your blog. Then check your writing using the list below and the strategies in the Writing skills box.

- [ ] I have mentioned my work or studies.
- [ ] I have mentioned some of my likes and dislikes.
- [ ] I have described my personality and the type of person I am.
- [ ] I have checked my work for mistakes with grammar, vocabulary and spelling.

C REVIEW Work in groups. Read the group's profiles. Can you recommend any blogs, websites, magazines, books, TV shows or movies the people in your group might be interested in?

Encourage students to look up relevant recommendations in English in their own time.

Answers

1 blogger
2 language
3 I'm 20 years old
4 three times a week
5 well organized
6 serious about
7 isn't
8 interested in
9 I like talking to people / I like to talk to people
10 people person

158 1 WRITING

WRITING

In this writing lesson, students will learn how to write an *About me* section for their own blog, website or social media page, using the strategies in the Writing skills box.

A Students read *Use it or lose it* and Karolina's blog, and answer the questions. Give them time to check their answers in pairs before giving feedback as a class.

B In pairs, students read the *About me* section of Karolina's blog, then close their books and discuss what they can remember about her studies, likes or dislikes and personality traits. Monitor and assist students as necessary.

Possible answers:

1 She studies law in college and English in her free time.
2 blogging, old black and white movies
3 hard-working, curious, sociable

C Focus students on the information in the box. In pairs, students correct the ten mistakes. Encourage them to use the Writing skills box to support them.

D Students match the types of mistakes with the colors used in Karolina's writing. Ask them to check their answers in pairs before checking with the whole class.

E Students correct the sentences and decide what type of mistake has been made in each. Ask students to check in pairs, before giving feedback as a class.

WRITING TASK

A Focus students on the task. Ask them to write notes about their work or studies, likes and dislikes and the type of person they think they are. Encourage them to use the words and phrases from the unit.

B Using their notes from Exercise A, students now write their *About me* sections. Encourage students to use the writing checklist to edit their work.

C In groups, students read their writing and make recommendations about blogs, websites, magazines, books, etc.

Unit 1 Review

VOCABULARY

A Complete the words for types of people.

1 someone who likes animals
a_nimal_ l_over_

2 someone who likes spending time with others
p_eople_ p_erson_

3 someone who plays video games
g_amer_

4 someone who is very interested in food
f_oodie_

5 a man who has two children
f_ather_ o_f_ t_wo_

6 someone who listens to music regularly
m_usic_ f_an_

B Complete the *About me* section of Emma's social media page with the personality adjectives in the box. There is one adjective you do not need.

creative curious ~~hard-working~~ independent sensible sociable well-organized

Hi, I'm Emma and I'm a student nurse. I study and work a lot [1](_hard-working_) and I make lists so I know what I am doing and when [2](_well-organized_). I always think carefully before I make decisions [3](_sensible_). I feel it is important to ask a lot of questions [4](_curious_) in my social life and at work. I have a good imagination and in my free time I like to write songs [5](_creative_). I also have a great group of friends and I love spending time with them [6](_sociable_).

C Choose the correct prepositions to complete the sentences.

1 In my family, we are all responsible *for* / *on* / *with* doing the housework.

2 I'm not interested *in* / *about* / *to* people who talk about themselves all the time.

3 As a child, I was involved *in* / *with* / *at* a lot of after-school clubs and activities.

4 I'm happy *at* / *with* / *on* my job.

GRAMMAR

A Complete the questions with the correct form of *do*, *be* or *have*.

1 Do you _have_ a pet?

2 _Are_ you from a large family?

3 _Did_ you have a party for your last birthday?

4 _Have_ you ever been to your country's capital city?

5 What _was_ your favorite book or toy when you were a child?

B Complete the article with the missing words.

Student Life Online
Your college, your site

This week, we asked students what blogs they read. This is what they said.

Erica: Most [1]_of_ the time, I read blogs about soccer.

Jake: [2]_Every_ so often, I read a cooking blog.

Ammar: I [3]_hardly_ ever read blogs. I don't have time.

Mark: Once a [4]_week_, on Sunday mornings, I sit down and read my favorite travel blog.

Tina: [5]_Now_ and then, I read news blogs.

Nazreen: I don't read blogs, but I do use Twitter. I check it at least ten [6]_times_ a day.

What are your favorite blogs? Leave your comments below.

C Choose the word which is *not* possible in each sentence.

1 *Everybody* / *Somebody* / *Anybody* can have nice handwriting.

2 I don't agree with *everything* / *anything* / *nothing* that the graphologists say.

3 Everyone *use* / *uses* / *has* a keyboard these days.

4 Do you know *anybody* / *anyone* / *anything* that is sociable?

FUNCTIONAL LANGUAGE

Reorder the words in the boxes to complete the conversations.

name's / Hi, / my / Erwin
myself / me / Let / introduce
meet / Nice / to / you

Erwin: [1]_Hi, my name's Erwin._

Laura: Oh, hi, Erwin.[2]_Let me introduce myself_. I'm Laura, the office manager.

Erwin: [3]_Nice to meet you_. I think you're going to be my boss!

nice / What / surprise / a
days / are / doing / What / you / these

Alan: Dan?

Dan: Alan! [4]_What a nice surprise_! How are you?

Alan: Oh, fine, thanks. [5]_What are you doing these days_?

Dan: I'm still teaching.

2 LIVING

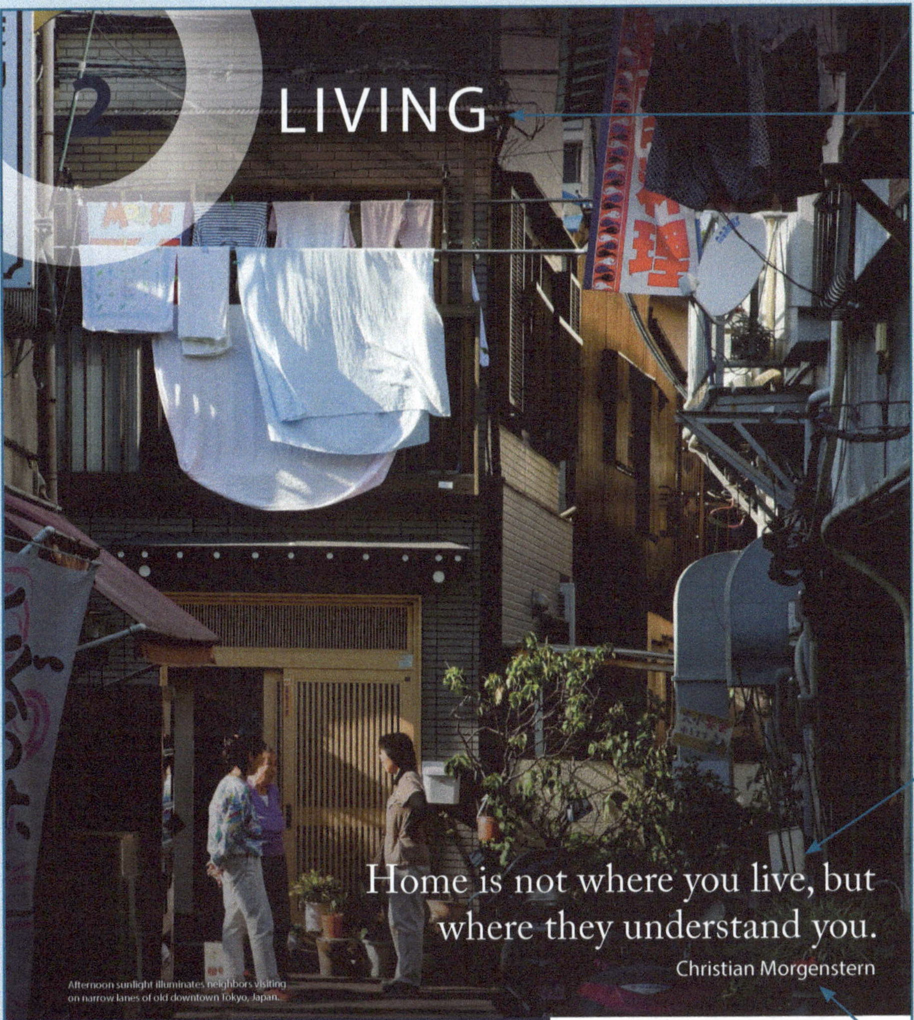

Afternoon sunlight illuminates neighbors visiting on narrow lanes of old downtown Tokyo, Japan.

Home is not where you live, but where they understand you.

Christian Morgenstern

Living (n) a particular type of life. Synonyms: life (n), lifestyle (n), existence (n).

Morgenstern is suggesting that your home is the place where people think and feel the way you do, not where you were actually born or live.

Christian Morgenstern (May 6, 1871–March 31, 1914) was a German poet from Munich. Morgenstern's poetry was inspired by English 'nonsense poetry' and is still very popular today.

OBJECTIVES

- talk about your neighborhood
- talk about your life and routine
- talk about life events
- ask for and give advice
- write an email of complaint

Work with a partner. Discuss the questions.

1 Read the quote. Where is 'home' for you?
2 Look at the picture. What do you think the people are talking about?
3 Do you know your neighbors?

LIVING 11

OBJECTIVES

Read the unit objectives to the class.

UNIT OPENER QUESTIONS

Encourage students to look at the quote and take one or two suggestions from the class about what they think it means.

Ask students to look at the picture on the page and encourage them to share their ideas. Ask prompt questions such as 'Where do you think this place is? Why?' If students share any good ideas or useful language, write these on the board.

Ask students to look at the questions at the bottom of the page. Answer with your explanation as to where your 'home' is. Students discuss the questions in pairs or in a small group.

Monitor and assist as necessary. When students have finished the activity, ask one or two pairs to share their ideas with the class. Encourage students to listen to one another and respond with their own ideas and opinions.

WORKSHEETS

Lesson 2.1 Love where you live

Grammar: Adverbs of degree (W7)

Vocabulary: Describing places (W8)

Lesson 2.2 The boomerang generation

Grammar: Simple present and present progressive (W9)

Vocabulary: Verb + preposition (W10)

Lesson 2.3 Time flies

Grammar: Simple past – regular and irregular verbs (W11)

Vocabulary: Life events (W12)

2.1 Love where you live

● Talk about your neighborhood

G adverbs of degree **V** describing places **P** stress in two-syllable adjectives

READING

A Work in pairs. Discuss the questions.

1 Do you love where you live? Why/Why not?
2 Look at the pictures. What can you see?
3 Look at the glossary. How can a building be environmentally friendly?

B SCAN Read *The forest in the sky* quickly and complete the sentences with the correct word or number from the text.

1 Bosco Verticale is an Italian name that means 'vertical ___forest___.'
2 The apartment buildings are in the city of ___Milan___ in Italy.
3 There are almost ___900___ trees on the balconies of the buildings.
4 The plants help make the noise from the ___traffic___ and people in the street quieter.
5 The apartment buildings are close to the city's services and ___transportation___.
6 The architects plan to build another forest city in ___China and the Netherlands___ in the future.

C READ FOR DETAIL Read again and answer the questions.

1 What are the four problems of life in central Milan that the writer mentions? noisy, polluted, hot, crowded
2 How do the Bosco Verticale buildings solve these problems?
3 What is the main problem with buildings like Bosco Verticale? They are expensive to build.
4 Does the writer think forest cities are a good idea? Yes, the writer believes they are worth the cost.

D SPEAK Work in pairs. Answer the questions.

1 Do you want to see forest cities in your country? Why/Why not?
Forest cities are a good idea because …
2 Should we pay more to live in clean cities? Why/Why not?
I don't think we should pay more to live in clean cities because …

THE FOREST IN THE SKY

Where in the world can you live on the top floor of a 111-meter high-rise building, near the center of a **lively** city, but still have breakfast under a tree on your balcony? Sounds almost impossible! Well, not if you live in the Bosco Verticale (vertical forest) buildings in Milan, Italy. Architect Stefano Boeri has created a completely new approach to designing buildings.

Like many big cities, Milan is **noisy** and **polluted**. It's hot in the summer and in the city center the green spaces are usually fairly **crowded**. But Boeri's team have found a very green answer to these problems.

Almost 900 trees grow high above Milan on the balconies of **modern** buildings. The trees keep the apartments cool in summer and warm in winter. They also produce oxygen, which keeps the air **clean**. The buildings are so **quiet** because the trees and plants stop the noise from the people and traffic in the streets below. Ex C Q2

Bosco Verticale is really **convenient** for the city's stores, services and transportation, it's **attractive**, and it's environmentally friendly. So, will there be more buildings like this in the future? Well, possibly. The architects want to build a new forest city in China and the Netherlands, but there is one more problem to solve. Buildings like this are extremely expensive. At 65 million euros, Bosco Verticale cost 5 percent more to build than a normal high-rise building. But if we want to live in cool, quiet cities with clean air, it will be worth the cost.

Glossary

architect (n) someone whose job is to design buildings
environmentally friendly (adj) something designed not to harm the natural environment
vertical (adj) standing, pointing or moving straight up

2.1 Love where you live

LEAD-IN

Draw three columns on the board with headings: *Things you like about your neighborhood, Things you don't like, Things that make no difference.* Say what you think about your neighborhood and teach *neighborhood, transportation, traffic, recycled (adj).* Students write two things about their neighborhood in each column. Ask students to share their ideas with the class. Write them in the corresponding columns. Do they coincide? Do they differ? Do they like living in their neighborhoods? Why? Why not?

READING

A Ask students to look at the photo. Does anyone recognize the building? (*Bosco Verticale in Milan, Italy*) How does it compare to their own homes? Are there any similar places in their cities / countries? Focus students on the glossary. Explain it contains key words they might need for their answers. Students discuss the questions in pairs. Monitor and assist as required. Take feedback from one or two pairs.

B Remind students that the purpose of scanning a text is to read it quickly looking for specific information. Tell them to underline the words they think will help them find the answers. Give them one minute to find the answers in the text.

C Students read the text again in detail, and answer the questions individually. Allow time for students to compare their answers with a partner. Then check answers as a whole class. Students can share personal experiences of seeing other buildings which are environmentally friendly in their city, or country or while traveling in other countries.

D Focus students on the questions. Model a possible ending for the first sentence and ask them to suggest other endings. Students discuss the two questions in pairs, using phrases from the article. Monitor and assist as necessary. Take feedback from one or two pairs and encourage students to comment on one another's ideas.

Extra activity

Put students into groups to design the ideal home. Ask them to write notes about furniture, design, number of rooms and location. Monitor and assist as necessary. Ask groups to present their houses to the class.

TEACHING IDEA by David Seymour and Maria Popova

Vocabulary: My house

Use this activity to practice vocabulary.

Students work in pairs telling each other about the places where they live. Give some examples of questions they can ask, e.g. *Is it an apartment or a house? Do you rent it? What is your favorite room?* Alternatively, students could tell their partner about an interesting place they have lived, e.g. *I used to live on a boat / in a tent* and ask each other questions about it.

TEACHING IDEA by David Seymour and Maria Popova

Vocabulary: Interesting homes

Use this activity to practice vocabulary.

Brainstorm different kinds of accommodations and think of an adjective to describe each one, e.g. palace – luxurious, houseboat – unique. In small groups, students discuss the advantages and disadvantages of living in these places. You can use the suggestions below as prompts if students find it difficult to come up with their own ideas.

basement apartment, high-rise apartment, hotel, camper, cave, tree house

GRAMMAR HUB

2.1 Adverbs of degree

almost	= *nearly*	She **almost** fell from the balcony.
completely	= 100%	This is a **completely** new idea.
extremely	= stronger than *very*	Life here is **extremely** expensive.
very		The city center is **very** lively at night.
so	= *very*	Living here is **so** convenient.
really	= *very*	This building is a **really** smart design.
fairly	= weaker than *very*	The town is **fairly** crowded on weekends.

- We use adverbs of degree to make something stronger or weaker.
- Adverbs of degree usually come **before** the adjective.
- We can also use *very, really, extremely* and *completely* before adjective + noun.

Be careful!

- We don't use *so* or *almost* before adjective + noun.
  It's so noisy. NOT ~~*It's a so noisy area.*~~
- We can also use adverbs of degree before adverbs.
  The pollution problem is improving very slowly.
- We can also use adverbs of degree before verbs.
- When a verb has an auxiliary verb (*have, be, do*), we usually put the adverb between the auxiliary verb and the main verb.

GRAMMAR

A Students complete the sentences with words from the text, before checking their answers in pairs. Give feedback as a class.

B Set a time limit for students to find more adverbs of degree in the text. Give them time to check answers in pairs before giving feedback as a class.

C Students complete the rules in the box using the examples in Exercises A and B to help them. Give feedback as a class.

D Direct students to the **Grammar Hub** (see below). Use the **Grammar Worksheet** on W7 for extra practice.

E Draw students' attention to the pictures of unusual buildings and model the conversation with a strong student. Students work in pairs sharing their ideas using adverbs of degree. Monitor and assist as necessary.

VOCABULARY

A Explain the activity. Read the example with the whole class. Allow students time to complete the exercise individually, before checking their answers with a partner. Give feedback as a class.

B Ask students to think about which of the adjectives from Exercise A they could use to describe their neighborhood. Students write five sentences about their neighborhood. Use the **Vocabulary Worksheet** on W8 for extra practice.

C Model the activity with a stronger student. Students take it in turns to say an adjective for their partner to say the opposite. Encourage stronger students to complete the activity with their books closed. Monitor the activity.

PRONUNCIATION

2.1 **A** Explain the task. Play the audio. Students listen and underline the stressed syllable.

2.1 **B** Play the audio again. Students listen and repeat the words.

C Read the rubric with the whole class. Model the activity. In pairs, students underline the stressed syllables. Check answers with the whole class.

SPEAKING

A Go over the prompts with the whole class and clarify any doubts. Allow students time to prepare their talk and the questions they will ask their partner. Monitor and assist as necessary.

B Model the activity with a stronger student. Then, in pairs, students take turns to talk about their neighborhoods and ask and answer each other's questions. Ask some of the pairs to share their conversations with the whole class. Encourage further questions from the class.

Extra activity
Extend the speaking activity and recycle relevant vocabulary by asking students to decide on the two most important things for deciding on a new neighborhood or place to live, e.g. *peaceful*, *attractive*, etc. Students can decide alone, then compare ideas in pairs, before coming to a consensus as a group. Encourage them to justify their choices.

2.1 Adverbs of degree

A Put the words in order to make sentences.

1 have / they / completely / new / a / designed / building / apartment
They have designed a completely new apartment building.

2 this / extremely / area / expensive / an / is
This is an extremely expensive area.

3 is / park / on / Sundays / crowded / so / the
The park is so crowded on Sundays.

4 cars / move / slowly / city / the / in / very
Cars move very slowly in the city.

5 polluted / is / in / it / places / some / fairly
It is fairly polluted in some places.

6 ready / am / move / to / I / almost
I am almost ready to move.

7 is / really / there / beautiful / park / a / here / near
There is a really beautiful park near here.

B Choose the correct option.

1 I'm **(so)** / ***almost*** happy to be living in London!
2 Cleaning up the city is ***almost*** / **(*extremely*)** expensive.
3 Our new apartment is ***almost*** / **(*really*)** nice. I love it!
4 Architects used a ***so*** / **(*completely*)** new design.
5 In the summer, it gets **(*extremely*)** / ***completely*** hot here.
6 It is **(*almost*)** / ***very*** impossible to get to know everyone in your neighborhood.
7 My last house was ***fairly a*** / **(*fairly*)** big, but I didn't have enough space.

➤ Go back to page 13.

GRAMMAR
Adverbs of degree

A WORK IT OUT Complete the sentences from *The forest in the sky* with the correct adverbs of degree.

1 Sounds ___almost___ impossible!

2 Stefano Boeri has created a ___completely___ new approach to designing buildings.

3 Boeri's team have found a ___very___ green answer to these problems.

B Underline four more adverbs of degree in the article.

fairly, really, extremely, so

C Choose the correct words to complete the rules.

> **Adverbs of degree**
>
> 1 Adverbs of degree are usually used ***before*** / ***after*** the adjective that they modify.
>
> 2 We ***use*** / ***don't use*** adverbs of degree when we want to make something stronger or weaker.
>
> 3 We ***can*** / ***can't*** use adverbs of degree with adverbs and verbs:
>
> - *She is speaking very fast.*
> - *He almost finished the race.*

D Go to the **Grammar Hub** on **page 124**.

E SPEAK Work in pairs. Look at the pictures of unusual buildings and use adverbs of degree to describe them.

A: It's so different from a normal building.

B: It's very strange!

VOCABULARY
Describing places

A Read the sentences and look at the adjectives in **bold**. Then write the opposite adjectives.

1 The air in my city is fairly **clean**. There aren't many factories. ___dirty___

2 My neighbors are very **loud**. They usually play music late at night. ___quiet___

3 It's a very **inconvenient** place to live. Our house is far from the stores and public transportation. ___convenient___

4 The shopping center is very **old-fashioned**. It looks like it's from the 1970s. ___modern___

5 My apartment is in an **ugly** high-rise building. I don't like living there. ___attractive___

6 The main streets are very **dirty**. People regularly drop trash. ___clean___

7 My neighborhood is very **peaceful**. I rarely hear cars or people in the street. ___noisy___

B Use the adjectives in Exercise A to write five sentences about your neighborhood.

C SPEAK Work in pairs. Say an adjective. Your partner says the opposite. Take turns.

PRONUNCIATION
Stress in two-syllable adjectives

2.1 **A** Listen and underline the stressed syllable in each adjective.

1 dirty	3 modern	5 noisy
2 quiet	4 peaceful	

2.1 **B** Listen again and repeat the words.

C Most two-syllable adjectives have the same stress pattern. Read the text below and underline the stressed syllable in all the two-syllable adjectives.

> The Chang (Elephant) Building is in Bangkok, Thailand. Some people think it is modern and interesting; some people think it is strange and funny. Other people think it is ugly and totally awful!

SPEAKING

A Tell your partner about your neighborhood. Use these ideas to help you.

- Location – is it convenient? Close to public transportation?
- Appearance – is the area clean, modern?
- People – who lives there? Families or young professionals?
- Environmentally friendly – are there local parks?

B Work in pairs. Take turns to ask and answer your questions.

Talk about your neighborhood

2.2 The boomerang generation

Talk about your life and routine

V verb + preposition **G** simple present and present progressive **P** consonant pairs at the beginning of words

LISTENING

A Work in pairs. Discuss the questions.

1. Why do people move out of their parents' home?
2. When do people usually leave home in your country?
3. Why do some adults continue to live at home?
4. What problems could this cause?

2.2 **B LISTEN FOR GIST** Listen to the first part of *The boomerang generation* and answer the questions.

1. What does 'boomerang generation' mean? people return to live with parents after college
2. How old is Richard? 25
3. Why is Richard living at home with his parents? he is looking for a job
4. Does he enjoy living at home? no

Glossary

boomerang (n) a curved stick that comes back to you when you throw it
generation (n) a group of people in society who are born and live around the same time
permanent (adj) happening or existing for a long time

2.3 **C** Listen to all of *The boomerang generation* and match two questions with each speaker. Write Richard (R), Gordon (G), Alice (A) or Carla (C).

Who …

1. says their child can live at home for a long time? C
2. seems worried about their child? G
3. isn't working right now? R
4. plans to do something to thank their parents? A
5. wants to make a change to their house? G
6. likes living with their parents? A
7. is happy they are not alone? C
8. isn't happy with the house rules? R

D SPEAK Work in pairs. What are the advantages and disadvantages of living with your parents as an adult?

VOCABULARY

Verb + preposition

2.4 **A** Complete the sentences from the radio show with the correct preposition. Then listen and check your answers.

1. I'm still looking ___for___ a permanent job.
2. We argue ___about___ the rules.
3. He can always rely ___on___ us.
4. I help ___with___ the housework.
5. I can talk ___to___ her.

Verb + preposition

Some verbs can be used with different prepositions to mean different things.

argue + *about* + something

- *We usually argue **about** housework.*

argue + *with* + someone

- *I usually argue **with** my parents.*

It is possible to join the sentences together:

- *I usually argue **with** my parents **about** housework.*

B Complete the email to Stella with the prepositions from Exercise A.

Re: Help?!
Sent: Friday, November 10, 2017, 2:19 pm
To: stella_28@logbox.com
From: d.smith@screen.nett

Hi Stella,

Thanks for calling this morning. Sorry to hear you're having money problems, but we're happy you decided to talk [1] ___to___ us about it. You can always rely [2] ___on___ us. I know you don't like borrowing money, but we'd like to help [3] ___with___ your rent this month. Let's not argue [4] ___about___ it this time. You can pay us back when you have a little more money.

You said you'd like to look [5] ___for___ somewhere cheaper to live. How about coming back to live [6] ___with___ us for a while? It would only be a temporary solution, but we'd like you to think [7] ___about___ it. Give us a call and let's talk [8] ___about___ it.

Lots of love,

Mom and Dad

C SPEAK Work in pairs. What should Stella do? Move home or find somewhere else to live?

A: I think she should definitely …
B: I'm not sure she should …

2.2 The boomerang generation

LEAD-IN

Write *boomerang* vertically down the board. Ask students if they know the meaning of the word. In groups of four, students attempt to come up with the longest word that begins with each letter of the word *boomerang*. Ask groups to read their words. They should cross out repeated words. Give each team a point per accepted word.

LISTENING

A Read the questions with the whole class and clarify any questions students have. Students discuss the questions in pairs. Monitor and assist as necessary. Take feedback from one or two pairs and encourage the other students to respond to one another's ideas. Can they think of a relation between the word *boomerang* and the questions they are discussing?

2.2 **B** Focus students on the glossary. Explain that it contains key words that they might need to understand the audio. Ask students to look at the pictures and elicit the relationship between the people in each photo. Explain the task. Students read the questions. Play the audio. Students discuss their answers in pairs and check with the whole class.

2.3 **C** Go through the task with the whole class. Play the audio. Ask some questions to check understanding (e.g. *Whose parents are happy their child is living at home? Whose parents aren't happy?* etc). Allow students time to answer. Students can check their answers in pairs. Play the audio again for students to check. Check answers with the whole class.

D Students discuss the question in pairs. Encourage them to use information from the *Listening* to support their ideas. Monitor and assist as necessary. Take feedback from one or two pairs and encourage students to respond to one another's ideas.

VOCABULARY

2.4 **A** Focus students on the vocabulary box. Elicit the differences in meaning shown by the examples. Play the audio. Allow time for students to complete the sentences. Play the audio again for students to check their answers. Check answers with the whole class. Elicit other examples from the radio show.

B Students complete the email individually and check their answers in pairs. Number 1 has been done as an example. Use the **Vocabulary Worksheet** on W10 for extra practice.

C Ask what the purpose of the email is (*Stella's parents are suggesting that she should move back home to save money*). Model the conversation with a stronger student. In pairs, students discuss the question using information from the radio show and their own opinions to support their answers. Monitor and assist as necessary. Take feedback from one or two pairs and encourage students to respond to one another's opinions.

AUDIO SCRIPT

2.3

Listening, Exercise C
P = Presenter R = Richard G = Gordon
A = Alice C = Carla

P: More and more of the world's young people are going home to live with their parents after college. Why? And what is it like living at home again as an adult? How do parents feel about the situation?
Ex B Q1 Today, we talk to members of 'The boomerang generation' and their parents about the advantages and disadvantages of living together again. Let's start with Richard …

Ex B Q2 **R:** I'm Richard Woodman, from the US. I'm 25 years old
Ex B Q3 and at the moment, I'm living at home with my mom
Ex C Q3 and dad. I … uh … graduated two years ago, but I'm still looking for a permanent job. I love my parents, but we … um … well, they are difficult to live with.
Ex C Q8 We argue about the rules all the time. I'm sleeping in my old room and living with the people who took
Ex B Q4 me to the park when I was little! I know I'm lucky to be here, but it's … you know … it isn't easy.

G: My name is Gordon Woodman. I'm Richard's dad. Of course, Richard's mom and I are, well, we're happy he is staying with us … most of the time. We're his parents and he can always rely on us, but we uh … we hope he finds the right job and, well, moves out
Ex C Q5 as soon as possible. I want to make his bedroom into my home office. And his music, it's … well you know, thump, thump, thump all day and night. It drives
Ex C Q2 me crazy! Anyway, we think he needs to be more independent. We love him, but he's unhappy, and he isn't learning about adult life living here with us.

A: Hi, I'm Alice Melo from Philadelphia, in the US. I'm 28 years old and I graduated last year. I work as a dentist and, at the moment, I'm living with my parents to save money for my own place. Well, I'm trying to save money anyway, ha ha! I studied in Colorado, but I … uh … couldn't find a job there,
Ex C Q6 so, you know, I came back home. More and more of my friends are moving back home. It's great! Mom cooks and does all my laundry. She won't take any money from me … I tried, but … uh … so I'm not paying any bills. Of course, I help … sometimes … I help with the housework and the yard, I mean, now
Ex C Q4 and again, you know. One day, I will do something special to thank them.

C: I'm Carla Melo, Alice's mom. We're very happy our daughter is home again. She's working hard and she
Ex C Q1 wants to get her own place, but I always tell her she can live here with us forever! She's an adult now, I know, but she's still my baby! This year, my husband is traveling a lot for work, for his job, you know, so
Ex C Q7 I'm very happy Alice is here with me. I don't like being on my own. I can talk to her, and she can save money and enjoy her mom's cooking.

2.2 The boomerang generation

GRAMMAR

A Read through the instructions and do the first sentence as a whole class. This activity could be done in pairs to support slower students and make the activity more communicative. Check answers with the whole class. Elicit how each tense is formed (simple present: base form [+*s* for 3rd person singular] / present progressive: *be* + base form + *-ing*).

B Students work together to complete the rules in the grammar box. Remind them to use the examples from Exercise A to help. Discuss answers with the whole class.

C Direct students to the **Grammar Hub** (see below). Use the **Grammar Worksheet** on W9 for extra practice.

D Model the exercise by completing the first two or three sentences on the board with information about your own country. Then, give students time to complete the sentences themselves, before discussing their ideas in pairs. If you are teaching a multilingual class, students could do this activity in pairs or small groups of different nationalities. Monitor and encourage discussion.

PRONUNCIATION

2.5 **A** Highlight the activity. Explain these consonant pairs are commonly found at the start of words. Play the audio. Students listen and complete the table. Give feedback as a class.

B Students work with a partner to practice saying the words from Exercise A. Encourage students to listen carefully to their partners and correct each other's pronunciation. Monitor students and practice more natural pronunciation when necessary. Students add one more word to each column. Check with the whole class.

SPEAKING

A Focus students on the activity. Students work on writing a question for each prompt individually. Monitor and assist when necessary.

B In pairs, students take turns asking and answering each other's questions from Exercise A. Monitor and assist with pronunciation when necessary. Encourage them to ask follow-up questions to extend their conversation. Take feedback from one or two pairs and encourage students to respond to one another's ideas.

GRAMMAR HUB

2.2 Simple present and present progressive

	Positive	Negative
I/you/we/they	**They love** their house.	**I don't live** in a big city.
he/she/it	**She loves** her family.	**He doesn't cook** every evening.

	Positive	Negative
I	**I'm studying** right now.	**I'm not studying** right now.
he/she/it	**She's living** with her parents.	**She isn't living** with her parents.
you/we/they	**We're moving** to the city.	**We aren't moving** to the city.

Question	Positive short answer	Negative short answer
Does he love cooking?	Yes, **he does**.	No, **he doesn't**.
Are they working?	Yes, **they are**.	No, **they aren't**.

- We use the simple present to talk about routines and things which are always or generally true.
- We use the present progressive to talk about temporary actions happening now or around now.
- We also use the present progressive to talk about trends.

2.2 Simple present and present progressive

A **Correct the mistakes in each sentence. Use contractions where possible.**

1 ~~We be~~ *We're* living in Rome right now.
2 ~~I stay~~ I'm staying at my parents' house this week.
3 ~~She's liking~~ She likes doing the laundry very much.
4 They're usually help~~ing~~ with the housework on Sundays.
5 ~~Paul's doing~~ Paul does the cooking most of the time.
6 We ^are both ~~look~~ looking for a permanent job right now.

B **Complete the sentences with the correct form of the verb in parentheses. Use contractions where possible.**

1 I *'m studying* (*study*) French history this year.
2 My mom still does (*do*) all my laundry.
3 I don't need (*not / need*) you to help me look for a new place.
4 What are you arguing (*you / argue*) about now?
5 They 're / are saving (*save*) money to buy a house.
6 She doesn't always cook (*not / always / cook*) for herself.
7 He 's / is talking (*talk*) to his cousin right now.

➤ Go back to page 15.

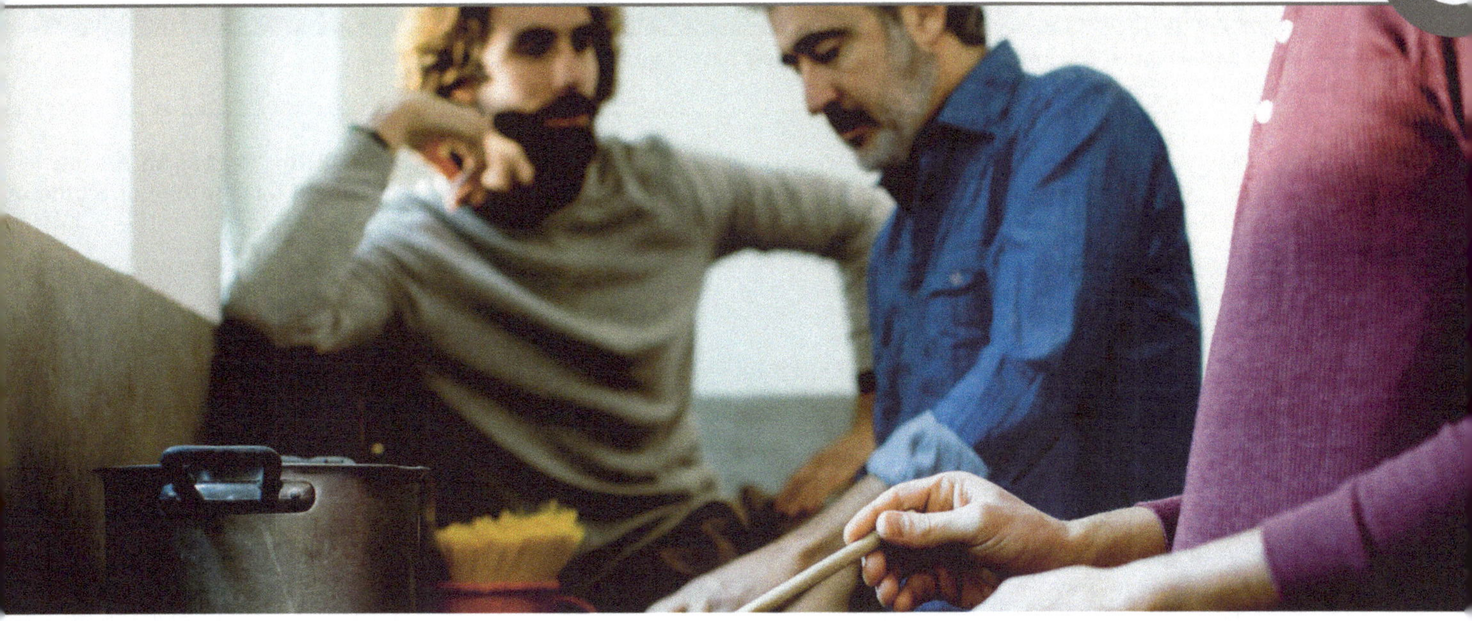

GRAMMAR
Simple present and present progressive

A WORK IT OUT Read the sentences from *The boomerang generation*. Are they simple present (SP) or present progressive (PP)?

1 I love my parents. SP
2 I'm sleeping in my old room. PP
3 Mom cooks and does all my laundry. SP
4 More and more of my friends are moving back home. PP

B Complete the rules with *simple* or *progressive*.

Simple present and present progressive

1 We use the simple present to talk about routines (events that happen every day) and things which are always or generally true.
2 We use the present progressive to describe what is happening now and to talk about trends.
3 We do not usually use the present progressive with state verbs like *be, like, want, understand, believe, know, mean, need, cost*.
4 We usually use the present progressive with time expressions like *now, today, this year*.

C Go to the **Grammar Hub** on **page 124**.

D SPEAK Work in pairs. Complete the sentences with information about your country and discuss with your partner.

1 Recently, more people are living *in apartments in the big cities*.
2 People love ______, but they don't like ______.
3 Everyone's talking about ______ right now.
4 Many young people are studying ______ right now.
5 Some people are happy because ______.

PRONUNCIATION
Consonant pairs at the beginning of words

2.5 **A** Listen to the words and add them to the correct consonant group.

sl	sm	sn	sp	st	sw
sleep	small	snack	speak	start	swim

B SPEAK Work in pairs. Practice saying these words. Can you add one more example to each group?

SPEAKING

A You are going to ask your partner about his/her life and routine. Use the prompts to make simple present or present progressive questions.

1 think about / moving back home again?
Are you thinking about moving back home again?
2 save money / for anything this year?
Are you saving money for anything this year?
3 like / cooking for yourself?
Do you like cooking for yourself?
4 know / your neighbors?
Do you know your neighbors?
5 your own question
______

B Work in pairs. Take turns to ask and answer your questions.

A: Are you thinking of moving back home?
B: I'm not sure. I need to save some money, so maybe!

Talk about your life and routine

2.3 Time flies

Talk about life events

G simple past – regular and irregular verbs P Simple past irregular verbs /ɔː/, /e/ and /eɪ/
V life events S skimming for key words

READING

A Work in pairs. Read the sentence from the article and discuss the questions.

When I was young, … a year was such a long time. Now I'm an adult, time passes so quickly.

1 Do you agree with this sentence? Why/Why not?
2 Can you think of an example when time passed quickly or slowly for you?

B READ FOR MAIN IDEA Read *When did the years get shorter?* quickly and match the headings (a–e) with each theory in the text (1–4). There is one heading you do not need. Use the information in the box to help you.

Skimming for key words

When you read an article for the first time, look for clues to help you understand the main idea of each paragraph.

- Look for key words. These could be numbers or the same words repeated.
- Look for words connected to the main topic.
- Look at the first sentence of each paragraph to help you understand the topic.

a The race against time
b From spring to winter
c New experiences slow down time
d It's all about the numbers
e Counting the days

C READ FOR DETAIL Read again. Are the sentences true (T) or false (F)? Correct the false sentences.

1 Time moved more quickly when the writer was a child. T / F
2 As we grow old, every year becomes a smaller percentage of our life. T / F
3 Many adults feel they have too much free time. T / F
4 Time slows down if we are looking forward to an event. T / F
5 New experiences can help to slow down time. T / F
6 All the theories agree that adults and children experience time differently. T / F

D SPEAK Work in pairs. Which theories in the article best explain why time seems to fly as we get older? Why? Give examples from your own life.

A: I like the one about …
B: I think Theory 3 is best because …

When did the years get shorter?

By Stefan Nyberg January 10, 2019

Glossary
routine (n) your usual way of doing things
stressful (adj) involving or causing a lot of pressure or worry
theory (n) an idea that explains how or why something happens

When I was young, the school summer vacation was six weeks long – it felt like forever. A year was such a long time! Now I'm an adult, time passes so quickly. Why does time seem to fly as we get older? Psychologists have several theories about this. Here are the most popular ones:

Theory 1: ___

The first theory is mathematical. When you were 5 years old, a year was 20 percent of your life, so it seemed like a long time. When you are 50 years old, a year is only 2 percent of your life, so it seems much shorter. Time can feel very different if you are a child or an adult.

Theory 2: ___

As children, we didn't have as much to worry about – we started school and studied, then we came home and played with our friends. Adult life is fast, busy and stressful – it's difficult to do everything we want to do. Days can be tiring. Many of us feel that there isn't enough time in the day. Time seems to pass very quickly because as adults we tend to rush to do something and then move on to the next job with no time to stop and think.

Theory 3: ___

As children we knew exactly how many days it was until our next birthday or holiday. All that counting and waiting made the days seem to pass much more slowly. Some psychologists suggest adults don't notice time passing because they are focused on 'boring adult stuff', like shopping or housework. The days, weeks and months pass quickly. Suddenly, another year is over and a new one is beginning.

Theory 4: ___

The routines of work and family life mean that, for many adults, the days all feel the same. This is different from our early lives, which were full of exciting first-time experiences. Back then, we started school and studied new things. Then we took exams, went on our first dates and learned to drive. When we look back on all these first-time experiences, we feel that the years were much longer because so many new things happened.

All these theories have something in common: there is a clear difference between the way adults and children experience time. Perhaps we need to learn from children and slow down a little more. Stop, look around, notice the blossom on the trees in the spring and the leaves changing color in the fall. The earth will keep spinning, but we are only here for a short time. Let's enjoy it!

LEAD-IN

Write the following sentences with blanks on the board: 1 *I first __________ a long time ago;* 2 *I last __________ three months ago;* 3 *I __________ last week and it was horrible.* Tell students to complete the sentences with true information. Then, nominate students to read aloud only the blanks from their sentences and try to guess as a class which sentence they're completing.

READING

A Ask students to read the lesson title. Ask *Does anyone know what 'time flies' means?* (*time goes by quickly*). Read the sentence from the article with the whole class. Ask a couple of students whether they agree. Focus students on the glossary. Remind them it contains key words they might need for their answers. Students discuss Questions 1–2 in pairs. Monitor and assist with grammar and vocabulary when necessary. Take feedback from one or two pairs and encourage students to respond to one another's ideas.

B Read the skills box as a class, giving further explanation where necessary. Students then read the text to match Headings a–e with the four theories described. Set a time limit to ensure students only have time to skim the paragraphs to do the task. Check answers with the whole class.

C Explain the task to students. Give them time to read the passage again, this time paying attention to detail. They work in pairs to decide whether the sentences are true or false. Help slower students by telling them that they will find the answers in the text in the same order as the sentences.

D Model the activity for the class giving an example about yourself. Give students time to think of an answer. Students work in pairs taking turns to explain to each other the theory they prefer and give their examples. Monitor and assist as required. With a stronger class, you might want to tell students to find an answer they both agree with. Take feedback from one or two pairs and encourage students to respond to one another's opinions.

TEACHING IDEA by David Seymour and Maria Popova

Speaking: Memory

Use this activity to practice conversation.

Ask students to raise their hands if they think they have a good memory. Ask them to take a pen and paper and dictate the following list to the class:

- passwords and pin numbers
- new people's names
- the words to songs
- your phone, keys and wallet
- what you did two weeks ago
- things that happened when you were a child

Ask students to decide whether they are good (✓) or bad (✗) at remembering these things. Ask students to work with a partner to discuss their answers and decide who has a better memory.

TEACHING IDEA by David Seymour and Maria Popova

Grammar: My childhood

Use this activity to practice the past tense.

Arrange students in pairs. Students ask and answer questions about each other's childhood using the prompts below. If students have children, they might want to talk about them instead.

- the day you were born
- the time of day you were born
- the month you were born
- the season you were born
- the year you were born
- the decade you were born

METHODOLOGY HUB by Jim Scrivener

Getting useful feedback – some starting points

- Don't think of feedback as a once-a-term thing or just as a formal requirement from your school. Visualize it as a moment-by-moment need to find out whether you and the class are on track.
- Clearly, you can overdo it – you don't want the class to groan at being asked *How useful was that activity*? again and again – but don't let this worry prevent you from even starting to explore their reactions and responses.
- Whether you go for oral or written feedback, vary it. Don't turn it into a ritual.
- Some common feedback opportunities: feedback at the start of a lesson, at the end of a lesson, at the end of a week, at the start of a new textbook unit, at the end of a unit, before the class does an activity, after an activity, as the core topic of an activity, written at home.
- Ask small questions (e.g. *Which activity today was most difficult for you?*) as well as big ones (e.g. *How useful is the course for you?*). They are easier to answer.
- Ask simple, factual questions (e.g. *How many words today were new for you?*) as well as evaluative questions (e.g. *Which activity did you enjoy most?*).
- Design a simple feedback form. Photocopy and hand it out (or dictate it to students). You could allow them class time to discuss the questions before they write, or ask them to fill it out at home.

2.3 Time flies

GRAMMAR

A Students work in pairs reading *When did the years get shorter?* again and completing each sentence with the missing verbs. They then match each sentence to the words in the box.

B Focus students on the rules in the grammar box. Tell students to choose the correct word to complete the rules, using the sentences in Exercise A to support them. Students check their answers in pairs before checking with the whole class.

C Direct students to the **Grammar Hub** (see below). Use the **Grammar Worksheet** on W11 for extra practice.

PRONUNCIATION

2.6 **A** Play the audio while students write the irregular verbs into the corresponding group.

B Students write questions alone, using the grammar box for help. Then, they work in pairs to ask and answer each other's questions. Monitor and assist where necessary.

VOCABULARY

A Give students time to find the events in the text and match them to Pictures a–d. They then decide what age they were when they experienced these events. Encourage discussion during class feedback.

B Direct students to the **Vocabulary Hub**. Use the **Vocabulary Worksheet** on W12 for extra practice.

C In pairs, students discuss the age at which people generally do each of the bulleted activities and how this compares to their grandparents' generation. Give feedback as a class.

SPEAKING HUB

A Students choose the experiences they want to talk about using the ideas in the box or their own ideas.

B Students answer the questions about the experiences they chose in Exercise A. Monitor and help as required.

C In groups, students take turns telling their experiences and guessing whether they are true or false. Encourage students to ask follow-up questions to extend their conversation.

GRAMMAR HUB

2.3 Simple past – regular and irregular verbs

Subject	Positive	Negative
I/you/he/she/it/we/they	**He talked** to Jim yesterday.	**He didn't talk** to Jim yesterday.

Question	Positive short answer	Negative short answer
Did you talk to Jim yesterday?	Yes, **I did**.	No, **I didn't**.

- We use the simple past to talk about finished actions in the past.
- We usually use the time phrases *yesterday*, *an hour ago*, *on Monday*, *in 2015*, etc. with the simple past.

	Infinitive	Simple past positive
Add *-ed*.	ask	asked
Add *-d* after verbs ending *-e*.	decide	decided
Add *-ed* after verbs ending in a vowel + *-y*.	play	played
Change *-y* after a consonant to *-ied*.	study	studied
For verbs ending in a vowel and a consonant, double the consonant before adding *-ed*.	stop	stopped

2.3 Simple past – regular and irregular verbs

A Put the verbs into the simple past. Use contractions where possible.

1. They (*go*) to Amsterdam yesterday. *went*
2. She (*not / visit*) her parents on the weekend. didn't visit
3. I (*buy*) a new laptop. bought
4. (*you / bring*) your bag with you? Did you bring
5. Dan (*take*) the train to work this morning. took
6. I (*not / leave*) work until 10 last night. didn't leave
7. We (*not / be*) worried when we took our exams. weren't worried

B Complete the conversation with the simple past form of the verbs.

Will: (1) Did you enjoy (*you / enjoy*) your childhood?

Rebecca: Yes, my friends and I (2) went (*go*) to the movie theater a lot, and we played on our bikes. What sort of things (3) did you do (*you / do*)?

Will: I (4) didn't have (*not / have*) a good time. My school (5) was (*be*) terrible. I (6) took (*take*) my exams three times before I passed.

Rebecca: Oh dear! So you didn't have much free time, I imagine.

Will: Exactly!

➤ Go back to page 17.

GRAMMAR

Simple past – regular and irregular verbs

A WORK IT OUT Complete the sentences (1–4) from *When did the years get shorter?* Then match them with the correct simple past forms in the box below.

1 As children we _started_ school and studied. regular
2 We _knew_ exactly how many days it was until our next birthday or holiday. irregular
3 As children, we _didn't_ have as much to worry about. negative
4 When _did_ the years get shorter? question

negative regular question irregular

B Choose the correct options to complete the rules.

Simple past regular and irregular verbs

Simple past positive

1 To talk about *finished* / *unfinished* actions in the past.
2 For most regular verbs in the simple past tense, we add *-ed* / *-ing*.

Simple past negative

3 We make the simple past *negative* / *positive* with subject + *didn't* + base form

Simple past questions

4 We *make* / *don't make* questions with *Did* + subject + base form + ?
5 Question words (*What*, *Where*, *When*, *Why* and *How*) come *before* / *after did*.
6 After *yes/no* questions, we use *did/didn't* in *short* / *long* answers.

C Go to the **Grammar Hub** on **page 124**.

PRONUNCIATION

Simple past irregular verbs /ɔː/, /e/ and /eɪ/

2.6 **A** Complete the table with the words in the box. Listen and check.

~~ate~~ ~~bought~~ fought made paid ~~said~~ sent taught

/ɔː/	*bought*, fought, taught
/e/	*said*, sent
/eɪ/	*ate*, made, paid

B SPEAK Make questions about your childhood using the prompts. Ask and answer them with a partner.

1 Where / meet / your best friend?
Where did you meet your best friend?
2 What / your parents / teach you?
What did your parents teach you?
3 You / a happy teenager?
Were you a happy teenager?
4 Your idea.

VOCABULARY

Life events

A Look at *When did the years get shorter?* again. Find four important life events and match them with the pictures (a–d). How old were you when you did these things?

B Go to **the Vocabulary Hub** on **page 146**.

C SPEAK Work in pairs. At what age do people generally do these things in your country? At what age did your grandparents' generation do these things? Tell your partner.

- learn to swim
- get married
- have a baby
- retire

SPEAKING HUB

A Work in groups. You are going to tell your group about three first-time experiences. Two should be true and one should be false. Use the ideas in the box or your own ideas.

first vacation without your parents
first child first important exams first job
first romantic relationship getting your own place
learning to ride a bike or drive leaving home
starting school or college

B ORGANIZE Answer the questions. Write notes.

- Where and when did you have this first-time experience?
- Who else was part of the experience?
- What happened? What went well? Were there any problems?
- How did you feel? Did you learn anything from the experience?

C DISCUSS Tell the group about your first-time experiences. Take turns. Can you guess which experiences are true and which are false?

Talk about life events

Café Hub

2.4 Noisy neighbors

F – ask for and give advice   P – disagreeing

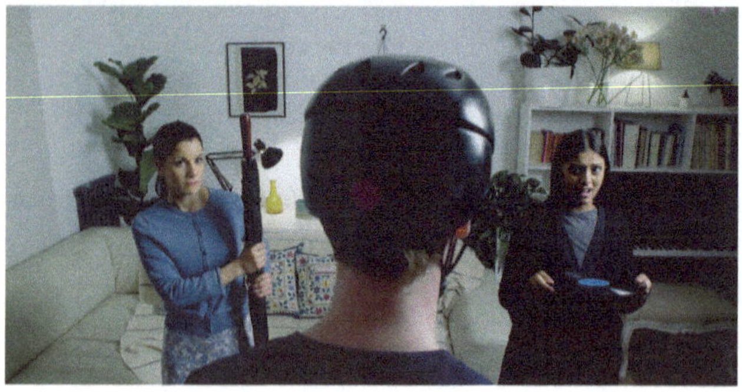

COMPREHENSION

A SPEAK Work in pairs. Describe your neighbors to your partner. What are they like? Use words in the box to help you or your own ideas.

friendly   noisy   old   quiet   unfriendly   young

B Look at the picture. Why do you think Neena, Gaby and Zac are going to see their neighbor like this? Write notes.

Neena's problem	The advice	The decision

C ▶ **00:00–03:40** Watch the first part of the video and check your ideas in Exercise B. What do you think the neighbor is like?

D ▶ **03:40–04:04** Watch the second part of the video. Why does everybody laugh? Relief. They were expecting problems – possibly somebody aggressive. In the end it was a neighbor with hearing loss.

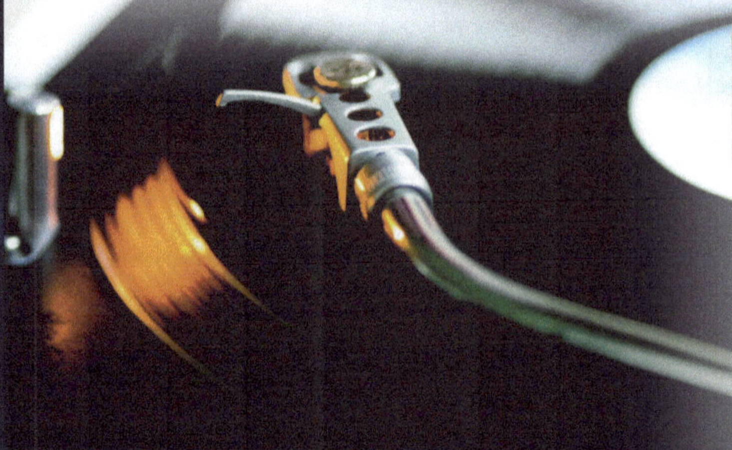

FUNCTIONAL LANGUAGE

Ask for and give advice

A Complete the sentences with the correct verb forms. Then decide who said each sentence, Gaby (G), Neena (N) or Zac (Z).

1. What do you think I should ***do*** / ***to do***? N
2. You could ***ask*** / ***to ask*** them to turn the volume down. G
3. How about ***to use*** / ***using*** some earplugs? G
4. Let me ***help*** / ***to help*** you out here. Earplugs. Z
5. What ***do*** / ***are*** you suggest? N
6. Why don't you ***go*** / ***to go*** upstairs and talk to them? Z
7. I think you should ***go*** / ***to go*** and talk to them. Z
8. And why don't we ***come*** / ***coming*** with you? Z

B ▶ Watch the video again and check your answers to Exercise A. Write the sentences in the correct place.

Ask for advice

What should I do?

1 What do you think I should do?

2 What do you suggest?

Give advice

You should/shouldn't …

3 You could …

4 How about + *-ing*?

5 Let me help you out.

6 Why don't you …

7 I think you should …

8 Why don't we …

Reply

That's a good idea.

Thanks, I'll try them.

I'm not sure it's a good idea.

MILLY

SAM

NEENA

ZAC

GABY

C Complete the job interview advice for Neena with one word in each blank. Which do you think is the best piece of advice?

1 You ___should___ leave plenty of time to get there.
2 I ___think___ you should read about the company before the interview.
3 Here's one idea: you ___could___ practice a few typical interview questions with a friend.
4 Nervous? ___Why___ don't you do some breathing exercises to relax?
5 I think you ___should___ dress for success.
6 You ___shouldn't___ have your phone on during the interview.
7 I ___don't___ think you should ask about salary first.

USEFUL PHRASES

A Match the useful phrases (1–6) with the phrases that come after them in the video (a–f). Then watch the video again and check your answers.

1 Seriously?!
2 What's wrong?
3 Cool!
4 Here you go.
5 What's the problem?
6 You can rely on us.

a No, it's not cool.
b All of us.
c Cool, thanks, Gaby.
d Someone's playing dance music in the flat above my bedroom.
e *(very loud dance music playing)*
f Oh Zac, the people upstairs are playing loud music.

B How do you say these useful phrases in your language?

PRONUNCIATION

Disagreeing

A 00:38–00:49 Watch the scene where Neena disagrees with Gaby again. Read out the conversation at the same time as Gaby and Neena. Copy the word stress and intonation.

Gaby: Really? Cool!
Neena: No, It's not cool. I need to get to sleep.

B **SPEAK** Work in pairs. Make similar conversations. Take turns to comment, disagree and say why. Use the comments in the box or your own ideas.

That's cheap/expensive! That's fair/unfair!
That's funny/serious! That's good/bad!
That's lucky/unlucky!

A: That's cheap!
B: No, it's not cheap. It's really expensive.

SPEAKING

A Work in pairs. Choose one of the problems and write a conversation with one friend giving advice to another one.

1 I usually forget my house keys.
2 My neighbor's dog barks all day.
3 The children in the apartment upstairs are very noisy.
4 My roommate spends too much time in the bathroom.
5 I'm the only person who does the cleaning.
6 My roommate's always hot and I'm always cold.

B Practice your conversation. Take turns giving advice. Then perform it for the rest of the class.

A: I usually forget my house keys.
B: Why don't you leave a key with your neighbor?
A: That's a good idea.

Ask for and give advice

➤ Turn to **page 159** to learn how to write an email of complaint.

2.4 Noisy neighbors

COMPREHENSION

A Model the task for students by describing your own neighbors. Then, give students time to discuss their neighbors in pairs. Monitor and assist as necessary.

B Look at the picture and elicit some ideas about what might be happening. Give students time to complete the exercise alone (or in pairs/groups if they're finding it difficult).

C ▶ 00:00–03:40 Play the first part of the video so students can check their ideas from Exercise B. Give feedback as a class and elicit ideas about the neighbor.

D ▶ 03:40–04:04 Play the second part of the video and ask why everyone laughed. Encourage students to share their ideas.

FUNCTIONAL LANGUAGE

A Students work alone to complete the sentences with the correct form of the verb, before deciding who said them.

B ▶ Play the full video for students to check their answers to Exercise A. Then, ask students to complete the table before giving feedback as a class.

C Students complete the sentences alone. Students share with the class their ideas about which the best advice for Neena is. Encourage them to give reasons and respond to one another's ideas.

USEFUL PHRASES

A ▶ Students do the task individually and check their answers in pairs. Play the video again for students to check their answers.

B Students look at the useful phrases from Exercise A and translate them into their own language. In a multilingual class, you may want to pair students from different countries. Take feedback from different students and encourage them to respond to one another's ideas.

PRONUNCIATION

A ▶ 00:38–00:49 Play the conversation between Neena and Gaby so students can copy the word stress and intonation.

B Model a new conversation with one of the ideas in the box. Then, give students time to practice their own conversations. Monitor and assist as required.

SPEAKING

A Students write a conversation around one of the six problems listed. Monitor and assist as required.

B Allow students time to practice their role plays and ask them to try reading both roles. When the students are confident, encourage the pairs to act out their role plays for the class.

▶ VIDEO SCRIPT

Café Hub 2.4 Noisy neighbors
N = Neena G = Gaby Z = Zac S = Shirley

N: Seriously?
G: Oh, hi, Neena. What's wrong?
N: Someone is playing dance music in the flat above my bedroom.
G: Really? Cool!
N: No! It's not cool, Gaby! I need to get to sleep! I've got another interview tomorrow … What do you think I should do?
G: Hmm. You could ask them to turn the volume down?
N: I guess I could … But who listens to loud dance music on a Sunday night? Maybe they're crazy.
G: You're right, I'm not sure it's a good idea … Hmm … How about using some earplugs?
N: That's a great idea, but I don't have any.
G: I do! Here you go.
N: Thanks, Gaby. I'll try them. Goodnight!
G: Good luck!
N: Aargh!
Z: Enter! Hi, Neena. What's the problem?
N: Oh, Zac, the people upstairs are playing loud music and I need to sleep!
Z: Let me help you out here – earplugs.
N: I tried. They didn't work. I don't know what to do. What do you suggest?
Z: Why don't you go upstairs and talk to them?
N: Really? I'm not sure Zac …
Z: I think you should go and talk to them. And why don't we come with you? You can rely on us. All of us. Let's prepare.
N: Shall I go first?
S: Oh hello! Let me turn the music down. You'll have to speak loudly as I'm quite deaf in this ear! And that ear, too!

TEACHING IDEA by David Seymour and Maria Popova

Grammar: What you should do is …

Put students into groups, and explain they will take turns giving one another advice for different situations using *should* and *shouldn't*, e.g. A – My car won't start. B – You should check the battery. C – You shouldn't have bought that car.

Write the following on the board:

I'm bored. My husband/wife snores. My boss yells at me. The roof is leaking. I'm going skiing. I feel very tired these days. I want to learn to speak Arabic. I'm losing a lot of weight. My neighbors are always arguing. I want to get in shape.

Monitor and give feedback as necessary.

Speaking: Apartment share problems

Put students into pairs and ask them to imagine they are roommates. Students should role-play a discussion and give each other advice about how to change their behavior, e.g. A – You shouldn't leave your bike in the hall, it makes it dirty. B – Why don't you relax more? It's easy to clean up later. Explain that Student A is very neat, likes peace and quiet, studies hard, doesn't go out very much, usually pays the bills on time and does most of the cooking and housework. Student B is very messy, likes loud music/TV, can't be bothered to study, likes parties, is always broke and hates cooking and housework. Model the activity with a stronger student.

Speaking: Bad habits

In two groups, brainstorm a list of adjectives to describe someone who is unbearable to live with. Write a piece of advice next to each one:

e.g. *Lazy – You should clean up the kitchen more often.*

Take turns reading your advice to the other group and see if they can guess the adjectives.

2 Writing — Write an email of complaint

W– linking words

A Read Emma's email about a problem in her neighborhood. What is she complaining about?

To: Mr. Black
Re: Road safety complaint

Dear Mr. Black,

I'm writing to complain about the dangerous roads outside my apartment building.

My main complaint is that the roads are dangerous **because** there are no crosswalks **or** traffic lights outside my apartment building. This is a problem for a number of reasons.

First of all, the traffic is very fast on the main road **and** this makes crossing difficult for older people and mothers with young children. The second problem is that there is a popular children's play area across from the main road, **but** the children have no way to cross the road to use the play area. The last problem is that the grocery store parking lot entrance is on the corner of two busy roads, **so** it makes it more difficult to cross the road.

I would like to offer you two solutions for this problem. First of all, I think you should make a crosswalk on the busy road between the grocery store and the children's play area. I also think you need to make a second crosswalk across the main road from the apartment building to the play area. You could put traffic lights on this intersection to make it safe for children to use.

I hope you will make this dangerous road safer for the older people and children in our neighborhood.

I'm looking forward to hearing from you.

Sincerely yours,
Emma Lopez

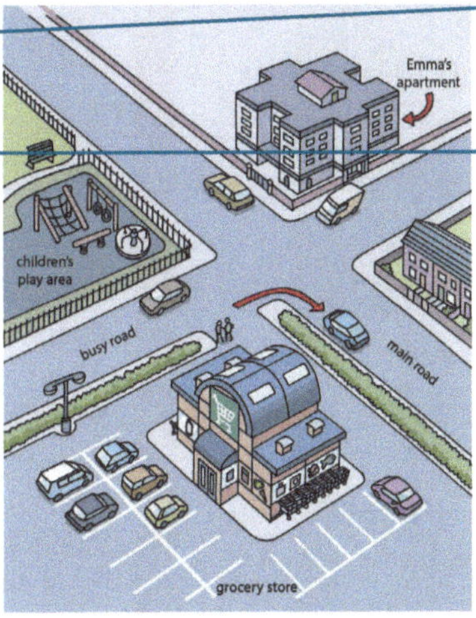

B Read again and answer the questions.

1 How many problems and solutions does Emma mention? *Emma mentions three problems and two solutions.*
2 Do you think Mr. Black will do what Emma wants him to do?
3 What tense does she use to begin and end her email? *Present progressive*

C Look at the words in **bold** in Emma's email. Then complete the rules in the box with *and, but, or, so,* or *because.*

Linking words

We can join sentences and link ideas with *and, but, or, so* and *because*. This helps you to write longer and more interesting sentences.

We use [1] ___and___ to add more information.
We use [2] ___or___ to give contrasting information.
We use [3] ___but___ to give a negative alternative.
We use [4] ___so___ to give a result.
We use [5] ___because___ to explain why.

D Complete the sentences with *and, but, or, so* or *because.*

1 The air is dirty ___because___ there are too many cars.
2 There should be more parks for children ___and___ teenagers.
3 We shouldn't litter ___or___ play loud music.
4 We like the play area, ___but___ it's too small.
5 More children are living here, ___so___ the neighborhood should be safer.

WRITING

A PLAN You are going to write an email of complaint. Think of a problem in your neighborhood and two or more solutions to your problem.

B WRITE Write your email of complaint.

- Use Emma's email and the Writing skills box to help you.
- Check your writing for mistakes with grammar, vocabulary and spelling.

C REVIEW Work in groups. Read your emails and decide which one will be the most successful.

2 WRITING 159

Answer
the roads outside her apartment are dangerous

Refer students to this email as a model for the writing task.

Students can do this in class or for homework.

WRITING

A Students read the email and decide what she is complaining about. Discuss answers with the whole class.

B Read Questions 1–3 as a class. Students read Emma's email again and answer the questions individually. Ask some students to share their answers with the whole class. Encourage students to respond to one another's ideas.

C Focus students' attention on the *Linking words* box. Students complete the rules using the linking words in Emma's email. Check answers with the whole class.

D Ask students to read Sentences 1–5 and complete them with the correct linking word. Remind them to use the information in the Writing skills box to help them. Students check answers with the whole class.

WRITING TASK

A Read the rubric with the whole class. Brainstorm some typical neighborhood problems as a class and write the students' ideas on the board. Students choose one problem and think of two or more solutions for it.

B Focus students on the task. Give them time to write their email and check their writing for mistakes with grammar, vocabulary and spelling.

C In groups students read their emails to one another. Encourage them to listen to one another and then decide as a group which email will be the most successful. Take feedback from each group and encourage students to respond to each other's ideas.

Unit 2 Review

VOCABULARY

A Complete the ad with the correct prepositions.

Samaritans is a UK charity that helps [1] with personal problems. Every six seconds, someone calls looking [2] for support. Callers can talk [3] to volunteers 24 hours a day and can rely [4] on them to listen and help. Many callers don't want to talk [5] about their problems with people they know well or live [6] with. Samaritans volunteers keep all conversations private and are always there to help.

www.samaritans.org

B Complete the profile with the simple past forms of the verbs in the box.

change fall get go to have ~~leave~~

David Attenborough

1926 – born in London

1945 – [1] left school and [2] went to Cambridge University

1946 – met and [3] fell in love with Jane Ebsworth Oriel

1950 – [4] got married to Jane; the couple later [5] had two children, Robert and Susan

1952 – joined the BBC

1965 – became the head of television channel BBC Two

1973 – [6] changed jobs and became the writer and presenter we know and love today

GRAMMAR

A Choose the best adverb of degree to complete the sentences. Use the information in parentheses to help you.

1. The idea of a vertical forest building sounds ***fairly / really*** interesting. (*STRONG*)
2. It's ***almost / totally*** impossible to add trees to every high-rise building. (*WEAK*)
3. The builders worked ***extremely / a little*** quickly. (*STRONG*)
4. The problem with buildings like this is they can be ***very / fairly*** expensive. (*WEAK*)
5. The trees are ***almost / so*** healthy because of rainwater. (*STRONG*)

B Complete the paragraph with the simple past or present progressive form of the verbs in parentheses.

Dreaming of Tokyo

Friends Tatsuo and Daisuki shared a small apartment in Tokyo for three years. Tatsuo [1] speaks (*speak*) French and recently left for a temporary job in Paris. He [2] 's working (*work*) there as a tour guide for the summer. Apartments [3] cost (*cost*) a lot in Tokyo and Daisuki can't afford to stay. Right now, he [4] 's living (*live*) with his parents outside the city. They get along well, but Daisuki [5] doesn't like (*not like*) the two-hour daily train trip into Tokyo.

He is not the only one in this situation. More of his friends [6] are leaving (*leave*) the city these days because it's so expensive. Every morning, the train Daisuki [7] catches (*catch*) is full of young people, making the long trip to work and dreaming of their own place in the city.

C There is one mistake with the simple past in each sentence. Correct the mistake.

1. I ~~falled~~ fell in love when I was 18.
2. I ~~weren't~~ wasn't good at sports when I was a teenager.
3. I didn't ~~thought~~ think money was important when I was a child.
4. When I was young, my parents always ~~knowed~~ knew when I wasn't telling the truth.
5. I ~~leaved~~ left home when I was 19.
6. My father ~~teached~~ taught me how to drive.
7. I ~~wasn't~~ didn't meet my partner at work.

FUNCTIONAL LANGUAGE

A Complete the missing words in the conversation.

Sophie: Peter, I can't stand the course I'm studying in college. [1] What do you think I should do?

Peter: [2] Maybe you should wait and see if things improve.

Sophie: [3] I suppose so, but I'm pretty sure the course is not for me.

Peter: [4] Why don't you talk to your teacher about it?

Sophie: [5] That's a good idea.

Peter: [6] Do you want me to go with you?

Sophie: No, that's OK, but thanks.

Canoeing through the early morning mist near Port Angeles, Washington, US.

Travel (n): the activity of traveling.
Synonyms: backpacking (n), RVing (n), independent travel (n).

Andersen suggests that traveling brings us knowledge and freedom, which makes our lives richer and better.

Hans Christian Andersen (April 2, 1805–August 4, 1875) was a Danish author who is most famous for his fairy tales. He also wrote many plays, travelogues, novels and poems.

OBJECTIVES

- talk about journeys and transportation
- tell a story about a journey
- talk about the kind of vacations you like
- ask for travel information and check understanding
- write an email about a travel experience

Work with a partner. Discuss the questions.

1 What can people learn from traveling?
2 Look at the picture. Do you enjoy doing outdoor activities?
3 Where is the last place you traveled to?

TRAVEL 21

OBJECTIVES

Read the unit objectives to the class.

UNIT OPENER QUESTIONS

Encourage students to look at the quote and take one or two suggestions from the class about what they think it means.

Ask students to look at the picture on the page and encourage them to share their ideas. Ask prompt questions such as 'Where do you think the girl is going? Why?' If students share any good ideas or useful language, write these on the board.

Ask the students to read the questions at the bottom of the page. Answer the question for yourself, explaining what you learned from traveling, e.g. to respect differences, a new language, etc. Students discuss the questions in pairs or in a small group.

Monitor and assist as necessary. When students have finished the activity, ask one or two pairs to share their ideas with the class. Encourage students to listen to one another and respond with their own ideas and opinions.

WORKSHEETS

Lesson 3.1 The four-year journey

Grammar: *all / some / most / no / none* (W13)

Vocabulary: Types of transportation (W14)

Lesson 3.2 Lost at sea

Grammar: Past progressive and simple past (W15)

Vocabulary: Prefixes (W16)

Lesson 3.3 Too good to be true

Grammar: verb + *-ing* and verb + *to* + base form (W17)

Vocabulary: Accommodations and amenities (W18)

3.1 The four-year journey

Talk about journeys and transportation

G – *all / some / most / no / none*   V – types of transportation   P – /p/, /b/, /v/

British man Graham Hughes is the first person to visit all of the countries in the world without flying.

Ex D Q6 Hughes traveled by sea and over land to complete his record-breaking journey.
Ex D Q1 He traveled on a budget of only US $150 a week and paid for everything himself.
Thirty-three-year-old Hughes set off on New Year's Day 2009. His first stop was
Ex D Q2 Argentina, and 1,492 days later, he arrived at his final destination, South Sudan.
Hughes crossed the borders of all of the 193 United Nations countries.
He traveled long distances by boat, and for shorter trips went by train, rode a bus or occasionally took a taxi. None of his trips were by
Ex D Q3 plane. A lot of people helped him on his journey. Some of them gave him directions and food or let him sleep on their couch for
Ex D Q4 free, and others gave him rides.
Of course, not all his experiences were good. He also had some problems. He crossed the Sahara Desert, but had to go back 2,000 miles because he didn't have the correct visa. The most difficult place to get to was the Seychelles. Graham tried
Ex D Q5 three times from three different countries before he finally made it to the islands.

Glossary

budget (n) the amount of money a person has to spend on something
visa (n) an official document that allows you to enter or leave a country for a specific time period

READING

A Work in groups. Think of a country beginning with each letter of the alphabet. You have two minutes.

B SCAN Work in pairs. Read the first line of the article about Graham Hughes. What might the information in the box refer to? Read the article and check your answers.

150 US dollars   193 countries   1,426 days   2,000 miles

C SPEAK Work in pairs. Would you like to do a similar journey to Graham? Why/Why not?

D READ FOR DETAIL Read again. Are the sentences true (T) or false (F)? Correct the false sentences.

1 The United Nations helped Graham pay for his journey. T / (F)
2 His journey finished in Argentina. T / (F)
3 People were kind to Graham during his journey. (T) / F
4 He didn't always pay for accommodations. (T) / F
5 He visited the Seychelles three times. T / (F)
6 He went on his journey because he wanted to help people from all over the world. T / (F)

E SPEAK Work in pairs. Discuss the questions.

1 Would you let a stranger sleep on your couch? Why/Why not?
2 Graham says the world is full of people who want to help each other. Do you agree? Explain your answer.

GRAMMAR

all / some / most / no / none

A WORK IT OUT Look at these sentences from the article about Graham Hughes. Then choose the correct words to complete the rules.

*Hughes crossed the borders of **all of** the 193 United Nations countries.*

***None of** his trips were by plane.*

***Some of** them gave him directions and food …*

*Of course, not **all** his experiences were good.*

*He also had **some** problems.*

all / some / most / no / none

1 We use *all, some, most, no* **before** / **after** nouns.
2 We **can** / **can't** use *all, some, most, none* with *of* + pronoun.
3 We **can** / **can't** use *all, some, most, none* with *of* + *the / this / that / these / those*.
4 We **can** / **can't** use *no* with *of* + pronoun or *the / this / that / these / those*.
5 With *all* we **have to** / **don't have to** use *of* before a pronoun or *the / this / that / these / those*.

B Go to the **Grammar Hub** on **page 126**.

C SPEAK Work in pairs. Make sentences of your own with *all / some / most / no / none*. Talk about:

- my friends
- my travel experiences
- types of transportation
- Graham Hughes or people like him

3.1 The four-year journey

LEAD-IN

Write the following on the board: *I'm going on vacation and I'm taking two suitcases*. Explain that students should repeat the previous sentence and add another object (e.g. *I'm going on vacation and I'm taking two suitcases and an umbrella*). Work around the room. Students should repeat the previous sentence and add an object. If you have a strong group, you may decide to ask students to list items alphabetically (e.g. *I'm going on vacation and I'm taking an animal, a basket, a camera and . . .*).

READING

A Read the task with the whole class. Put students into small groups. Set a timer – if possible use a timer that students can see. When the time has passed, all students should stop working. Ask the different groups to say the words they wrote. Groups should cross out the names of countries in their lists if other groups say them. The group with the most names wins.

B Focus students on the glossary. Remind students that the purpose of scanning a text is to read it quickly to look for specific information. Read the first sentence with the whole class. Focus students on the information in the box. In pairs, students discuss what the information in the box refers to. Take feedback from different pairs. Then, give students two minutes to scan the text and check their answers. How many had the correct answers?

150 US dollars – Graham spent $150 per week.
193 countries – Graham visited 193 countries.
1,426 days – Graham traveled for 1,426 days.
2,000 miles – Graham had to go back 2,000 miles because he didn't have the correct visa.

C In pairs, students discuss the pros and cons of going on a similar journey. Encourage students to give reasons and to use information from the text to support their answers. Monitor and assist students when necessary. Take feedback from one or two pairs and encourage students to respond to one another's ideas.

D Tell students to read the text again. Explain they will have to say whether Sentences 1–6 are True or False and correct the incorrect sentences. Allow time for students to compare their answers in pairs before checking as a whole class.

E Read through the questions as a class. Students discuss the questions in pairs. Monitor and assist as required. Take feedback from one or two pairs and encourage students to respond to each other's ideas.

Extra activity

Encourage students to read again with the following questions:

1 Which of the places Hughes visited would you most/least like to visit? Why?
2 Which types of transportation mentioned do you prefer? Why?

Extend the class discussion with the following questions:

1 What do you think about this kind of travel?
2 Do you prefer an adventure or a normal vacation? Why?
3 Would you give a stranger a lift? Why/Why not?

TEACHING IDEA by David Seymour and Maria Popova

Speaking: Around-the-world trip

Use this activity to provide extra speaking practice.

Put students into pairs and ask them to plan their own around-the-world trip. Give students a budget of 3,000 dollars and explain that this is to cover transportation and accommodations for the whole trip. Encourage students to go online and research actual flights, accommodations and attractions to give their plans detail. Ask students to create a presentation about their travel plans to deliver to the rest of the class.

The presentation should include:

The places they will visit

The places they will stay at

Activities they will do

The budget they will have spent

Writing: Postcards

Use this activity to provide extra writing practice.

Ask students if they have ever sent a postcard and what information they usually write about. Ask students to write a short postcard from a vacation detailing an interesting/exciting/ dangerous experience. Tell students that they can write either about a vacation they have been on or an experience from their imagination. Remind students that postcards are short, so they will not be able to include too many words. To make this activity more realistic, bring blank postcards to class for the students to write on.

METHODOLOGY HUB by Jim Scrivener

Grammar: Substitution tables

Below is a substitution table. By reading from left to right, choosing one word from each section, you can make a large number of grammatically correct sentences (although the meaning may require a little thought). A table such as this could be both a stimulus to practice activities in the classroom and a way of recording the studied grammar in notebooks. After working on new grammar, I usually get learners to help me construct a substitution table on the board, which all the class can then copy into their books. Simple variations on a table can alter the level of challenge involved: for example, removing the horizontal line in the substitution table creates an activity that requires more thought on the student's part. Similarly, blanking out a column or leaving spaces in a column and getting students to invent words to go there adds to the difficulty (and probably the interest).

<table>
<tr><td>Has</td><td>Mary
Juan
he</td><td rowspan="2"></td><td rowspan="2">the</td><td rowspan="2">book
chips
....
....
.............</td><td rowspan="2">?</td></tr>
<tr><td>Have</td><td>you
they
your friends</td></tr>
</table>

Oral practice is frequently based on substitution tables.

3.1 The four-year journey

GRAMMAR

A Students read through the sentences and use them to complete the rules in the grammar box. Allow time for students to check their answers in pairs before checking with the whole class.

B Direct students to the **Grammar Hub** (see below). Use the **Grammar Worksheet** on W13 for extra practice.

C Put students into pairs. Students talk about the prompted subjects making sentences using *all / some / most / no / none.* Monitor and give assistance as necessary. Take feedback from one or two pairs and encourage students to respond to each other's ideas.

VOCABULARY

A Students read the article again and underline five types of transportation (*boat, train, bus, taxi, plane*). They classify them and add them to the table. Then, they do the same for the words in the box. Allow them to check answers with a partner before checking with the whole class.

B Focus students on the *Transportation collocations*. Students work in pairs correcting the mistakes, using the information from the box to support them. Check answers as a class. Use the **Vocabulary Worksheet** on W14 for extra practice.

PRONUNCIATION

3.1 **A** Play the audio so students can listen and repeat. Demonstrate the different mouth shape needed to produce the /v/ sound.

3.2 **B** Play the audio for students to complete the table.

3.2 **C** Play the audio a second time for students to check their answers to Exercise B. Model the pronunciation and ask students to repeat the words.

SPEAKING

A Pre-teach additional vocabulary for travel and transportation to help students with this activity, e.g. *bike, trolley, subway, commute*. Tell students to write notes for each bullet.

B Students work in pairs to write questions. Monitor and give feedback as necessary.

C Students change partners and take turns asking and answering the questions they wrote in Exercise B. Ask students to write notes on the answers their new partners give.

D In their original pairs, students discuss Questions 1–3, comparing the answers of the people they interviewed. Monitor and assist as required. Take feedback from one or two pairs and encourage students to respond to each other's ideas.

GRAMMAR HUB

3.1 *all / some / most / no / none*

- We use *all, some, most* and *no* before nouns.

  *Give him **all** the money.*

  *There are **no** taxis.*

- We can use *all, some, most* and *none* with *of* + pronoun or *the/this/that/these/those*.

  *I've stayed in many hotels and I liked **most of** them.*

  *I like **all of** the Greek islands.*

  ***Some of** her trips were by bus.*

  ***None of** the countries were in Africa.*

- With *all*, we don't have to use *of* before a pronoun + noun or *the/this/that/these/those*.

  *Did you spend **all your** money? OR Did you spend **all of** your money?*

- With *all*, we must use *of* before a pronoun without a noun.

  *Did you spend **all of** it? NOT ~~Did you spend all it~~?*

- We cannot use *no* with *of* + pronoun or *the/this/that/these/those*.

  None of us want to leave. NOT ~~No of us want to leave.~~

3.1 *all / some / most / no / none*

A Put the words in order to make sentences.

1 his / none / journeys / were / by / of / train

None of his journeys were by train.

2 dry / the / of / some / were / seats

Some of the seats were dry.

3 all / the / unhappy / passengers / were

All the passengers were unhappy.

4 trip / us / none / wanted / end / of / to / the

None of us wanted the trip to end.

5 kinds / most / don't / I / like / of / resorts / beach

I don't like most kinds of beach resorts.

6 have / money / no / left / wallets / our / we / in

We have no money left in our wallets.

7 Dilly / problems / airport / some / had / also / the / in

Dilly also had some problems in the airport.

B Choose the correct option.

1 *No* / *None* of the tourists were paying attention.

2 All of *the people* / *people* were yelling.

3 Most *of taxis* / *taxis* in London are black.

4 I met *some of* / *some* nice people on my vacation.

5 How was your vacation? Did you enjoy *all* / *all of* it?

6 *No* / *None* visitors can go in this area.

➤ Go back to page 22.

VOCABULARY
Types of transportation

A Find five types of transportation in the article about Graham Hughes. Write them in the correct place. Then add the words in the box.

car ferry helicopter minibus trolley

Travel by air	Travel over land		Travel by ocean
plane helicopter	train bus taxi	car minibus trolley	boat ferry

Transportation collocations

With all the transportation nouns in Exercise A, we can use the verbs *go* or *travel* + *by*. We don't use *a* / *an* before the noun. We can also use *take* or *get* + *a* / *an*.

- *He traveled long distances by boat, and for shorter trips went by train, rode a bus or occasionally took a taxi.*

When we talk about plane travel, we usually use the verb *fly*.

- *We flew to Portugal last summer.*

B Add (+) or remove (–) one word to make each sentence correct. Use the Transportation collocations box in Exercise A to help you.

1 I go to work by ~~a~~ bus everyday. (–)
2 My brother occasionally gives me a ride on the back of his motorcycle. (+)
3 I took a taxi home last Saturday night. (+)
4 I usually get ~~by~~ a trolley to my English classes. (–)

PRONUNCIATION
/p/, /b/, /v/

3.1 **A** Listen and repeat.

1 /p/ plane 2 /b/ boat 3 /v/ visa

3.2 **B** Listen and write the words in the correct place.

/p/	/b/	/v/
pay park passenger passport	bus bank bike	van visit very

3.3 **C** Listen, check and repeat the words.

SPEAKING

A Interview your classmates about their travel habits. Find out about:

- daily travel to and from college or work
- trips they regularly make on the weekend
- transportation they use to go on vacation

B Work in pairs. Write questions to find out about:

- the different types of transportation people use in each type of travel in Exercise A
- what they like and dislike about each type of transportation they use
- how much they spend on transportation in a normal week

C Interview another student and make a note of their answers to your questions.

D Work with your original partner again and compare the travel and transportation habits of the people you interviewed.

1 Who uses more types of transportation?
2 Who feels most positive about the transportation they use?
3 Who spends the most on transportation in a normal week?

Talk about journeys and transportation

3.2 Lost at sea

Tell a story about a journey

G past progressive and simple past   P *was* and *were* with past progressive   V prefixes

LISTENING

A What famous stories or movies do you know that involve seas, oceans and islands? What happens?

B PREDICT Work in pairs. You are going to listen to a podcast about the Robertson family. Look at the pictures (1–4). What do you think happened?

3.4 **C** Listen and check your answers to Exercise B.

Glossary

brave (adj) a brave decision, action or choice is one that you make even though it involves risk and may cause problems for you

life raft (n) a small rubber boat used for saving people whose boat is sinking

survival expert (n) a person who knows how to stay alive in emergencies if you are far away from help

survive (v) to stay alive, especially in a difficult or dangerous situation, for example injury, illness, war

3.4 **D LISTEN FOR DETAIL** Listen again and put the information in the order that you hear it (1–6).

5 The Robertsons got help.

1 One of the Robertsons' children asked an unusual question.

4 The Robertsons had no more food.

2 The Robertsons left their old life behind.

3 There was a serious accident.

6 The Robertsons made it back to land.

E SPEAK Work in pairs. Discuss the questions.

1 Do you think the Robertsons' decision to sail around the world was a good one? Why/Why not?

2 Why do you think some people do dangerous things?

3 Do you ever do dangerous things, or do you prefer to avoid danger? Give examples.

GRAMMAR

Past progressive and simple past

A WORK IT OUT Read the rules and complete the examples with the words in the box.

bought noticed sold started was passing were living

Past progressive and simple past

We use the past progressive (*was / were* + verb + *-ing*) for actions or situations that were in progress.

- *In 1970, Dougal and Lyn Robertson and their four children* 1 were living *on a farm, in northern England.*

We use the simple past for finished actions or situations, and things that happened one after another.

- *They* 2 sold *their business,* 3 bought *a boat and on January 27th, 1971,* 4 started *their journey across the Atlantic.*

When used together in the same sentence, the past progressive describes a long action and the simple past describes a shorter action.

- *Their boat* 5 was passing *the Galapagos Islands when they* 6 noticed *something large in the water behind them.*

when and *while*

We use **when** or **while** to link past progressive and simple past verbs.

We can use **when** or **while** before the past progressive.

- ***When/While** they were sailing out into the Pacific Ocean, things started to go very wrong.*

We always use **when** before the simple past.

- *They were sailing out into the Pacific Ocean **when** things started to go wrong.*

AMAZING ADVENTURES

1

2

3.2 Lost at sea

LEAD-IN

Tell students that you're a tourist in another country and they can ask you a maximum of 20 yes/no questions to guess where you are. Encourage them to use a range of tenses and count the number of questions they ask. If they can't guess with fewer than 20 questions, they lose the game!

LISTENING

A Elicit some examples (e.g. *Titanic*, *Castaway*, etc) and write them on the board. Then, give students time to discuss the question in pairs before giving feedback as a class.

B Go through the task instructions. Clarify the meaning of the words in the glossary box with examples if necessary. In pairs, students look at Pictures 1–4, and discuss what they think happened to the Robertsons. Take two or three suggestions from pairs before moving on to the next exercise.

3.4 **C** Play the audio for students to check their answers.

3.4 **D** Play the audio. Students put the sentences in the order they're mentioned. Give them time to check answers in pairs, before giving feedback as a class.

E Students work in pairs to discuss Questions 1–3. Monitor and help as required. Take feedback from one or two pairs.

GRAMMAR

A Students complete the examples in the rules box with the verbs in the box. Give them time to check their answers in pairs, before giving feedback as a class.

B Direct students to the **Grammar Hub** (see TB25). Use the **Grammar Worksheet** on W15 for extra practice.

C Read the model with the whole class. Give students time to write notes following Questions 1–4. Monitor and help with grammar and vocabulary as required. Once students have completed their notes, put them into small groups to share their stories. Monitor and encourage students to ask follow-up questions to get more information.

AUDIO SCRIPT

3.4

Listening, Exercise C
C = Chloe M = Matt

C: Welcome to this week's Amazing Adventures podcast. I'm Chloe Cole, and with me is sailor and survival expert Matt Cabral. This week, the amazing story of the Robertson family and how they survived a month lost at sea in the Pacific Ocean.
In 1970, Dougal and Lyn Robertson and their four children were living on a farm in northern England.
Ex D1 One ordinary day, Neil, one of their ten-year-old twins, said he wanted to leave the farm and sail around the world. Most families would probably laugh and say 'don't be silly', but the Robertsons saw the chance for
Ex D2 an adventure. They sold their business, bought a boat and, on January 27th, 1971, started their journey across the Atlantic. Matt, what do you think of their decision?

M: Incredible. I mean, Dougal was an experienced sailor, but it was still a brave decision. Maybe not very sensible, but definitely brave!

C: Ha ha, yes. Well, sensible or not, the Robertsons made it across the Atlantic safely in their 13-meter boat, *The Lucette*. But on June 15th, 1972, while they were sailing out into the Pacific Ocean, things started to go very wrong.
Their boat was passing the Galapagos Islands when they noticed something large in the water behind them. It was a group of killer whales swimming toward the boat. Douglas, the eldest son, has said that when he saw the whales, he thought they were going to kill
Ex D3 and eat the family. Well, the whales hit and sank their boat, but amazingly, the Robertsons all made it onto their small life raft, scared, but alive. I mean, they were very unlucky, weren't they, Matt?

M: Yes, they were. On average, there are only two to three accidents with boats and whales per year. But believe it or not, it wasn't all bad. I mean, first, the whales didn't eat them.

C: Ha! That's true.

M: And the life raft and another very small wooden boat survived the accident. And luckily they were carrying some water, some dry bread, cookies, a bag of onions and some fruit in the life raft.

Ex D4 **C:** Yes, but after six days, all the food was gone, so they collected rainwater to drink, and killed turtles and ate the meat and drank the blood. Then, 17 days after the accident, their life raft failed and they had to move to their wooden boat. It was called *The Ednamair* and was only three meters long. Can you imagine the whole family in that small boat?

M: It sounds like an impossible situation. You have to be strong and stay positive to survive something like this. There was only one dry seat in the boat, so most of the time they were sitting in water. But they didn't give up hope.

Ex D5 + 6 **C:** And finally, 38 days after the accident, a Japanese fishing boat found them and took them to dry land and safety.

M: It's an incredible story of survival.

C: Yes, it is. And now, Douglas Robertson works as an accountant in London, and amazingly, he has said that he actually enjoyed the family's adventure!

3.2 Lost at sea

PRONUNCIATION

3.5 **A** Play the audio. Elicit a few ideas from students before moving on to the next exercise.

3.5 **B** Students choose the correct options to complete the rules. Give feedback as a class, playing the audio again if necessary.

C In pairs, students ask and answer the questions. Monitor and practice the weak forms of *was* and *were* as necessary.

VOCABULARY

A Read the examples and highlight that a prefix is a group of letters that you add to the beginning of a word to change the meaning. Then give students time to complete the rules, before giving feedback as a class.

B If necessary, do the first sentence as an example. Students complete the sentences using the correct prefix, before checking their answers with a partner. Give feedback as a class. Use the **Vocabulary Worksheet** on W16 for extra practice.

C Elicit example sentences using the adjective *unlucky*. Then, students work in pairs to write other sentences using the adjectives in Exercises A and B. Give feedback as a class.

SPEAKING

A Form groups with two pairs (A–B, C–D). Direct students to the **Communication Hub** (see TB121). Read the instructions with the class. Each pair discusses their story.

B Each pair tells their story to the other members of their group.

C Now, ask each group to create a new story that includes all eight images. Monitor and assist students as required. Then, redistribute students to form new groups of four. Make sure that no two members from the old groups are put together. Each student has to tell their story to the new group.

GRAMMAR HUB

3.2 Past progressive and simple past

	Positive	Negative
I/you/he/she/it/we/they	**They traveled** by train all night.	We **didn't go** by ferry.

Question	Positive short answer	Negative short answer
Did they enjoy the vacation?	Yes, **they did**.	No, **they didn't**.

- We use the simple past to talk about finished actions or situations, and things that happened one after another.
- See Grammar Reference 2.3 for more information about the simple past.

	Positive	Negative
I/he/she/it	**He was riding** the bus when his phone rang.	**She wasn't biking** to work when the rain started.
you/we/they	**They were sleeping** when I arrived.	**We weren't driving** when the car crashed.

Question	Positive short answer	Negative short answer
Was it snowing outside?	Yes, **it was**.	No, **it wasn't**.

- We use the past progressive for actions or situations that were unfinished at a past time.
- The past progressive describes a longer action and the simple past describes a shorter action.

  *They **were sailing** (=long action) from Portsmouth to Caen when the storm **hit** (=short action).*
- We use *when/while* before the past progressive to describe an action that was in progress when something else happened.

3.2 Past progressive and simple past

A Correct the mistakes in each sentence.

1. We were living in London when the London Eye was opening. *opened*
2. Jan was having an accident while she was sailing in the Pacific.
3. While they asking for directions, I looked at a guide book.
4. She traveled through China when she first met Clive.
5. The pilot was landing the plane when the crash was happening.
6. When the ferry crossed the ocean, we saw some dolphins.
7. She swam in the lake when something was biting her leg.

B Match to make sentences.

1. We were sailing around the island
2. While I was taking photographs,
3. They were not paying attention
4. Someone stole her bag
5. He met Rob
6. Some birds hit the plane

a. I dropped my phone.
b. while she was lying by the pool.
c. while he was biking across Italy.
d. while it was taking off.
e. when they got on the wrong bus.
f. when I started to feel sick.

➤ Go back to page 25.

B Go to the **Grammar Hub** on **page 126**.

C **SPEAK** Think of an interesting or unusual thing that happened to you on a trip or vacation. Write notes using the questions below. Then work in groups and tell your story.

1 Where and when was the vacation?
2 Who did you go with?
3 What happened that was interesting or unusual?
4 What were you doing when this thing happened?

When I was a teenager, I went camping with my family in Spain. One morning, we were walking to the beach when I found a wallet full of money on the path ...

PRONUNCIATION

was and *were* with past progressive

3.5 **A** Listen and repeat the sentences. What do you notice about *was* and *were*?

1 We were biking to the beach when I fell off my bike.
2 I was swimming in the ocean when I lost my car keys.

B **WORK IT OUT** Choose the correct words to complete the rules.

1 We usually use ***weak*** / ***strong*** pronunciation of *was* and *were* in positive sentences.
2 We do this because we ***stress*** / ***don't stress*** the main verb.

C **SPEAK** Work in pairs. Find out what your partner was doing at these times.

1 7 am this morning
2 last New Year's Eve at midnight
3 10 pm last night

VOCABULARY

Prefixes

A Look at the sentences from *Amazing Adventures*. Choose the correct words to complete the rules.

I mean, they were very ***un****lucky, weren't they, Matt?*

It sounds like an ***im****possible situation.*

1 We use prefixes before ***adjectives*** / ***pronouns*** to change their meanings.
2 Prefixes like *un-*, *im-*, *dis-* and *in-* give the original word a(n) ***opposite*** / ***stronger*** meaning.

B Complete the words with the correct prefix, *un-*, *im-*, *dis-* or *in-*.

1 I don't believe anything he says. I think he's __dis__**honest**.
2 Living on rainwater and turtles sounds very __un__**healthy** to me.
3 I failed the test; a lot of my answers were __in__**correct**.
4 Not many people go to the Galapagos Islands. It's a/an __un__**usual** vacation destination.
5 He doesn't like waiting – he's very __im__**patient**.

C **SPEAK** Work in pairs. Think of other examples of things or people that you can describe with the adjectives with prefixes in Exercises A and B.

SPEAKING

A Work in groups and describe a journey. Students A and B – go to the **Communication Hub** on **page 157**. Students C and D – go to the **Communication Hub** on **page 152**.

B Work in pairs. Take turns telling your story to your group.

C Work in groups. Look at all eight pictures as a group and think of a new story that uses them all. Then tell your story to another group.

3

4

3.3 Too good to be true

Talk about the kind of vacations you like

G verb + *-ing* and *to* + base form | V accommodations and amenities | P /ʃ/, /tʃ/ and /dʒ/ | S identifying tone

READING

A Work in pairs. Discuss the questions.

1. When you are planning a vacation, how do you choose where to stay?
2. Do you find online reviews helpful or not? Why?

B Read two online reviews for a hotel. Which sounds real and which does not? Why?

★★★★★

a I love to travel, but I can't afford to stay in five-star hotels or expensive apartments all the time. If you are on a budget like me, the three-star Hotel Jasmine is a great choice. The service is very good and the rooms are small but clean. The location is a little noisy but central. I hope to return to Hotel Jasmine soon.

★★★★★

b This hotel is EXCELLENT!!! The rooms are BEAUTIFUL and the staff are very kind and WONDERFUL!!! I love shopping and the hotel is in the city center!!! I will definitely go on using this hotel – in fact, I refuse to stay anywhere else!!!!!

C **SCAN** Read *Tips for a happy vacation* quickly. Underline any of the ideas you discussed in Exercise B.

D Choose two words which describe the author's tone. Use the information in the box to help you.

1 serious	3 formal
2 informal	4 funny

Identifying tone

The tone of a text can help you understand the author's opinion on the topic. Notice words and phrases the author uses to communicate this.

- Look at the author's choice of adjectives and adverbs.
- Does the punctuation give you any clues? For example, 'quotation marks', exclamation marks, parentheses or capital letters.
- Is the language formal or informal?

TIPS FOR A HAPPY VACATION

You're **planning** to go on vacation and you've **decided** to try somewhere new. You could **consider** using a travel agent, but it's easy to organize your own vacation online these days. All you **need** to do is visit a travel review site, spend time reading travelers' comments and then choose the accommodations with the best reviews. Simple!

Or is it? How do you know that what you are reading is genuine? Research shows that some hotels and restaurants pay people to write fake reviews. Of course, the websites **manage** to find and delete some of these fake reviews, but they aren't always successful. So, before you **choose** to spend your vacation budget on that 'amazing beach resort' or cruise ship that scored ten out of ten, read our tips and learn how to spot a fake review.

TIP ONE: What you see is not always what you get. If the pictures of the apartment, guest house or campsite **seem** to be too good to be true, they probably are. For example, when you see the photograph below, you **expect** to find a nice quiet beach, but in fact, the beach and all the hotels are right next to a building site!

TIP TWO: Nowhere is perfect – fact! Most genuine reviewers **like** to include a mix of positive and negative comments, so a review that's 100 percent positive or negative is more likely to be fake. If you **want** to know what a hostel or chalet is really like, don't read the very best and very worst reviews. Look at the ones in the middle.

TIP THREE: EXCELLENT!!!!!!! Fake reviewers **like** using capital letters, exclamation marks (!) and lots of extreme adjectives like 'wonderful', 'amazing' and 'excellent'. It can feel like you are being YELLED AT! Genuine reviewers usually **avoid** using so much extreme language. Instead, they usually include helpful details like room size or prices.

Glossary

fake (adj) made to look like something real in order to trick people

genuine (adj) real, rather than pretended or false

3.3 Too good to be true

LEAD-IN

In groups, students ask each other about the places they would like and dislike to go on vacation (e.g. *Would you like to go to Thailand?*). Students should keep asking until they find a place that no one in the group likes. Have a member from each group write that place on the board. See if there is a place where the class wouldn't like to spend a vacation.

READING

A Students discuss the questions in pairs. Share ideas as a whole class, and ask students to justify the answers they give.

B Students read the reviews and answer the question, before checking their ideas with a partner. Give feedback as a class, encouraging students to explain their reasoning.

Possible answers:

A Sounds real – it mentions both good and bad points; the writer hasn't used a lot of strong adjectives like 'fantastic', 'wonderful' or 'beautiful'; it doesn't have unnecessary punctuation or capital letters.

B Doesn't sound real – the writer has used lots of strong adjectives like 'fantastic', 'wonderful' and 'beautiful'; it has lots of unnecessary punctuation and capital letters.

C Read through the glossary as a class, giving further explanation of the words if necessary. Set a time limit of one minute to encourage students to scan the text. Ask them to underline any of the ideas they discussed in Exercise B.

D Read through the information on *Identifying tone* in the box with the class. Students look at the article again and choose two adjectives that describe the author's tone. Check answers with the whole class. Ask students to give reasons for their answers.

E Read the task with the class. Students answer the questions individually and check them in pairs before checking with the whole class.

F Students discuss the questions in groups of three or four. Monitor and assist when necessary. Take feedback from one or two pairs and encourage students to respond to each other's ideas.

Extra activity

For homework, ask students to find examples of good and bad hotel reviews online, ideally one they think is fake and one they think is real. They should underline examples of words and phrases that identify tone. They should also look for features in the article that suggest it is authentic or fake. They can share these in class and compare impressions of the texts with their classmates. Alternatively, you could also have students find a review and then write their own. Groups then have to guess which is the real review.

GRAMMAR HUB

3.3 Verb + *-ing* and *to* + base form

- After some verbs (e.g. *agree*), we use *to* + base form.
- After some verbs (e.g. *enjoy*), we use *-ing*.
- After some verbs (e.g. *hate*), we can use either *to* + base form or *-ing*.

Verb	+ *to* + base form
can't afford	I **can't afford to buy** a new car.
hope	They **hope to meet** again soon.
learn	When did you **learn to drive**?
would like	We **would like to travel** the world.
would prefer	He **would prefer to go** to France.
Other verbs: agree / choose / decide / expect / manage / need / plan / refuse / seem / want	They **decided to go** by plane.

Verb	+ *-ing*
consider	She **considered saying** yes.
enjoy	We **enjoy reading** guide books.
avoid	He **avoided getting** wet on his trip.
spend time	Tina **spent time researching** the Andes.
Other verbs: advise / allow / begin / can't help / continue / finish / keep / mind / regret / stand	I **keep making** mistakes.

Verb	+ *to* + base form or *-ing*
hate	I **hate driving** in bad weather. OR I **hate to drive** in bad weather.
love	We **love visiting** Italy. OR We **love to visit** Italy.
prefer	I **prefer staying** in a hotel. OR I **prefer to stay** in a hotel.
like	They **like going** surfing. OR They **like to go** surfing.
Other verbs: begin / start	It **started to rain**. OR It **started raining**.

3.3 Too good to be true

GRAMMAR

A Students complete the rules with the words/structures in the box. Give feedback as a class, asking students to identify the structures used in each example.

B Students look at the article again, and complete the grammar box with the verbs in bold. Check answers.

C Direct students to the **Grammar Hub** (see TB26 and below). Use the **Grammar Worksheet** on W17 for extra practice.

D Students write their reviews individually and complete the task in pairs. Monitor and help when necessary. Take feedback from one or two pairs and encourage students to respond to each other's ideas.

VOCABULARY

A Focus students on the vocabulary box. Elicit which types of accommodations were mentioned in the article with books closed. With a weaker group, you may want to allow them to work in pairs and/or check back with the article.

B Direct students to the **Vocabulary Hub**. Use the **Vocabulary Worksheet** on W18 for extra practice.

C Model the conversation with a stronger student. Students work in small groups taking turns to describe or draw. Monitor and assist as required.

PRONUNCIATION

3.6 **A** Play the audio. Students listen and identify the differences between the sounds. Play it again for students to listen and repeat.

3.7 **B** Students complete the table with the words in the box. Then play the audio for them to listen, check and repeat.

C Put students into groups of three to discuss the questions. Monitor and assist with new vocabulary and grammar as necessary.

SPEAKING HUB

A Students discuss the questions in groups of three. Encourage them to use the vocabulary from today's lesson to help them. Take feedback from one or two groups and encourage students to respond to each other's ideas.

B Direct Students A, B and C to the **Communication Hub**. Students read the instructions individually. Help with vocabulary if required.

C Read the task with the class. Students take turns describing the accommodations they read about to their group. When the information has been shared, the group decides where to stay and how much spending money they will have left. Take feedback from one or two groups and encourage students to respond to each other's ideas.

TEACHING IDEA by David Seymour and Maria Popova

Speaking: Projects

Visit a cell phone website and look for the best deal for you. Bring the information you get to class and work in small groups to discuss the deals.

Visit the website of a large arts center and find out what's going on, including ticket prices and times of shows. Then decide what kind of show you want to see: music, theater, exhibit, free event. In the next lesson, role-play a telephone call to find out about a show and to book tickets.

TEACHING IDEA by David Seymour and Maria Popova

Speaking: Booking a room

Work in pairs. Student A, you are a guest checking into a hotel. Student B, you are the receptionist. Role-play a conversation using these words. When you have finished, write the conversation down. Compare your conversation with another pair.

> single/double, suite, one night/two nights, suitcases, alarm call/time, champagne, sauna/pool, internet

GRAMMAR HUB

3.3 Verb + *-ing* and *to* + base form

A Choose the correct option.

1 Avoid ***to book*** / ***booking*** a room at this hotel.
2 Consider ***to write*** / ***writing*** your own travel blog.
3 Refuse ***to take*** / ***taking*** no for an answer.
4 Spend time ***to try*** / ***trying*** different foods.
5 Learn ***to enjoy*** / ***enjoying*** life.
6 Don't agree ***to get*** / ***getting*** in the car with a stranger.

B Complete the text messages with the correct forms of the verbs.

Fay: I would like (**1**) ___to stay___ (*stay*) somewhere fun for a weekend trip. Any ideas?

Joy: What about a campsite?

Fay: I can't stand (**2**) ___sleeping___ (*sleep*) outdoors. Maybe a hostel or a guest house?

Joy: I don't mind (**3**) ___going___ (*go*) to either. Which would you prefer?

Fay: I'd prefer (**4**) ___to stay___ (*stay*) at a hostel. Sound OK?

Joy: Yes, I enjoy (**5**) ___meeting___ (*meet*) new people.

Fay: Great! I can't afford (**6**) ___to spend___ (*spend*) much money.

Joy: Then a hostel is a good choice – they usually have low prices.

➤ Go back to page 27.

E READ FOR DETAIL Read again and answer the questions.

1 Why isn't organizing your own vacation online as simple as it seems?
2 Why might someone want to write a fake review?
3 What does the article aim to teach its readers?
4 What are the characteristics of a genuine review?
5 What are the characteristics of a fake review?

F SPEAK Work in groups. Discuss the questions.

1 What other kinds of online reviews do you read or write, for example, movies, books, games, etc.?
2 Do people rely too much on online reviews? Explain.

GRAMMAR

verb + *-ing* and *to* + base form

A WORK IT OUT Look at the underlined verb patterns from the online reviews. Then complete the rules with the words in the box.

either	*to* + base form	verb + *-ing*

1 I love to travel, but I can't afford to stay in five-star hotels or expensive apartments all the time.
2 I hope to return to Hotel Jasmine soon.
3 I love shopping and the hotel is in the city center!!!
4 I will definitely go on using this hotel – in fact, I refuse to stay anywhere else!!!!!

verb + *-ing* and *to* + base form

1 We use *to + base form* after these verbs: *agree, can't afford, hope, learn, refuse, would like, would prefer,* *plan*, *decide*, *need*, *manage*, *choose*, *seem*, *expect*, *want*.
2 We use *verb + -ing* after these verbs: *(don't) mind, enjoy,* *consider*, *avoid*.
3 We can use *either* after these verbs (there is little change in meaning): *hate, love, prefer, (can't) stand,* *like*.

B Look at *Tips for a happy vacation* again. Write the verbs in **bold** in the correct place in Exercise A.

C Go to the **Grammar Hub** on **page 126**.

D SPEAK Work in pairs. Think about the best place you have stayed on vacation. Write a short review. Then swap with a partner and ask questions about your partner's review.

VOCABULARY

Accommodations and amenities

A Look at the words in the box. Which types of accommodations are included in *Tips for a happy vacation?*

apartment	beach resort	campsite	chalet	cruise ship	guest house	hostel	hotel

all of them

B Go to the **Vocabulary Hub** on **page 147**.

C SPEAK Work in groups. Take turns describing or drawing items from the **Vocabulary Hub**. The first person in the group to guess each item gets one point.

A: This keeps your room cool when the weather is hot.
B: Air conditioner!

PRONUNCIATION

/ʃ/, /tʃ/ and /dʒ/

A Listen to the sounds. Are they the same or different? Then listen and repeat. different
3.6

1 /ʃ/ chalet 2 /tʃ/ choose 3 /dʒ/ budget

B Complete the table with the words in the box. Listen, check and repeat.
3.7

~~adjective~~	~~beach~~	genuine	language	manage	picture	~~ship~~	shout	show

/ʃ/	/tʃ/	/dʒ/
ship	*beach*	*adjective*
shout	picture	genuine
show		language
		manage

C SPEAK Work in pairs. Practice saying the words. Listen and check your partner's pronunciation.

SPEAKING HUB

A Work in groups. You are going on vacation together to Barcelona for two nights. Together, you have a budget of 600 dollars for accommodations and spending money. Answer the questions:

1 What kind of accommodations would you like to stay in?
2 Which amenities are most important to your group?

B Read about vacation accommodations in Barcelona. Student A – go to the **Communication Hub** on **page 155** and read about Hotel Rambla Park. Student B – go to the **Communication Hub** on **page 156** and read about Gaudí House Hostel. Student C – go to the **Communication Hub** on **page 157** and read about Olympic Apartments.

C PRESENT Describe the accommodations you read about to your group. Decide where you will stay. How much spending money will you have left?

Talk about the kind of vacations you like

Café Hub

3.4 Overslept

F – ask for travel information and check understanding
P – word stress and intonation

COMPREHENSION

A SPEAK Work in pairs. Are you usually early or late for things? Give examples.

B SPEAK Work in pairs. Number the pictures in order (1–6) to describe a morning when Gaby overslept. What do you think happened?

a 4

b 6

c 1

d 5

e 2

f 3

C Watch the video and compare it with your ideas in Exercise B. What does the ticket officer find? What do you think will happen next?

He picks up a bag Gaby has dropped. The bag has her name and phone number on it.

FUNCTIONAL LANGUAGE

Ask for travel information and check understanding

A Test your memory! Look at the conversation between a customer and a ticket officer. Underline five responses that are different from the video. Try to remember the correct information.

Ask for travel information – trains	
Customer:	1 Could I have a ticket to St. Albans?
Ticket officer:	2 Of course. Would you like a single or a return?
Customer:	3 <u>A single, please.</u> A return/round-trip, please.
Ticket officer:	4 No problem.
Customer:	5 Do I have to change trains? No, most trains are direct.
Ticket officer:	6 <u>Yes, you need to change at Watford.</u>
Customer:	7 What time's the next train?
Ticket officer:	8 The next train's in about <u>ten minutes.</u> three minutes 9 The next train leaves from <u>platform 4B.</u> platform 9
Customer:	10 What time does the train arrive in St. Albans?
Ticket officer:	11 <u>At 9:13.</u> At 9.30.

B Watch the video again and check your answers to Exercise A. Write the correct information.

Glossary

single **(adj) (British)** = one-way **(adj) (American)**
return **(adj) (British)** = round-trip **(adj) (American)**

MILLY SAM NEENA ZAC GABY

USEFUL PHRASES

A Watch the video without sound. Yell *Stop!* when you think the ticket officer is about to use one of the useful phrases. Then listen and check.

1 Here, let me help you. [01:34]
2 Don't worry. [01:38]
3 Follow me. [02:15]
4 Don't forget this. [02:43]
5 You don't want to miss your train. [02:47]
6 Have a good trip. [02:55]

B How do you say these useful phrases in your language?

PRONUNCIATION
Word stress and intonation

3.8 **A** Listen and repeat the conversation. Copy the word stress and intonation.

Ticket officer: The next train's in about three minutes from platform two.
Anna: I'm sorry. Did you say three minutes?
Ticket officer: Yes, three minutes!
Anna: OK, thanks. Oh, and where's platform two?
Ticket officer: Go past the coffee shop, then turn right.
Anna: OK. So I need to go past the coffee shop and then … turn left? Is that right?
Ticket officer: No, you need to turn right after the coffee shop.

B SPEAK Work in pairs. Make a similar conversation.

SPEAKING

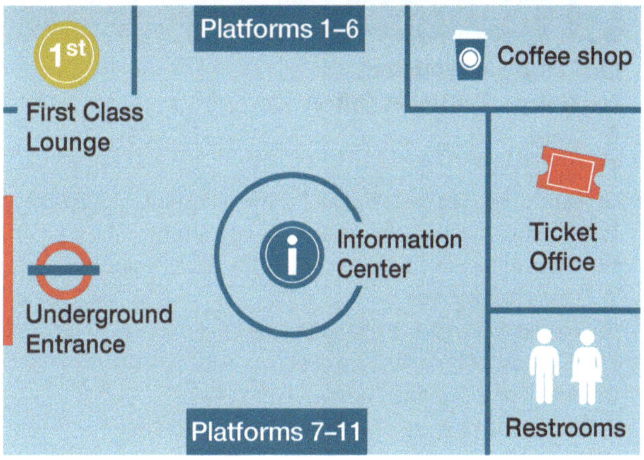

A Work in pairs. Student A is the customer. Student B is the ticket officer. Write a conversation. Use these ideas to help you.

Student A: Ask for information about trains to a place on the departure board.
Student B: Answer Student A's questions.
Student A: Check understanding and then ask for directions to the correct platform.
Student B: Look at the train station plan and give directions.
Student A: Check understanding.

B Practice your conversation. Take turns being the customer and the ticket officer. Then perform it for the rest of the class.

Ask for travel information and check understanding

➤ Turn to **page 160** to learn how to write an email about a travel experience.

3.4 Overslept

COMPREHENSION

A Focus students on the task. Pre-teach *overslept*. Remind students of prefixes. Students discuss in pairs. Make sure they give their partner specific examples. Monitor and assist when necessary. Take feedback from one or two pairs and encourage students to respond to each other's ideas.

B Focus students on the task. Students look at the six images and decide what is happening in each picture. They then number Pictures 1–6 in the order in which they think things happened.

C ▶ Play the video. Students watch and check their answers to Exercise B. Students answer the question. Discuss answers with the whole class.

FUNCTIONAL LANGUAGE

A Students work alone to read the conversation and underline the answers they think are different from the video. They check their answers in pairs. Encourage students to remember the conversation from the video.

B ▶ Play the video again for students to check their answers and rewrite the different sentences.

USEFUL PHRASES

A ▶ Read the task with the class. Play the episode again without the sound. Stop the video when students shout 'Stop!' and ask them to provide the useful phrase that's coming. Then press play to check if they were right.

B As a class, discuss how students would say these phrases in their own language.

PRONUNCIATION

3.8 **A** Play the audio and ask students to read aloud the conversation at the same time. Focus on word stress and intonation.

B Model the conversation with a stronger student. In pairs, students write and perform a similar conversation. Monitor and encourage natural word stress and intonation.

SPEAKING

A Focus students on the station plan and the prompts. Model the conversation with a stronger student. Students work in pairs to write their role play using the prompts. Monitor and give feedback as necessary.

B Give students time to rehearse their role plays. Ask them to practice both roles. When the students are confident, encourage pairs to perform their role plays for the class.

▶ VIDEO SCRIPT

Café Hub 3.4 Overslept

G = Gaby T = Ticket Officer

G: I'm late!
T: Can I help?
G: Oh … Erm, yes please. Could I have a ticket to St Albans?
T: Of course, would you like a single or a return?
G: A return please, I'd like to come back this evening.
T: That's no problem.
G: Thanks. Do I have to change trains?
T: No, most of the trains are direct.
G: Thank you, and what time's the next train?
T: Hmm, the next train leaves in about 3 minutes …
G: I'm sorry, did you say 3 minutes?
T: Yes, 3 minutes! Here's your ticket. The train leaves from platform 9.
G: Oh, and what time does the train arrive in St Albans?
T: About nine-thirty.
G: Argh!
T: Here, let me help you.
G: I'm having a bad day!
T: Don't worry, we all have them.
G: How do you get to platform 9?
T: Go past the coffee shop, then turn right. Then go straight on and it's on the left, you can't miss it.
G: OK, so I need to go past the coffee shop and then … Turn left …? Is that right?
T: Erm, no … You need to turn right after the coffee shop, then … Actually, I'll just show you. 2 minutes! Follow me! Don't forget this!
G: Thank you so much!
T: You don't want to miss your train …
G: No. I should go. It was nice to meet you.
T: You too. Have a good trip!
G: Thanks. Bye!

TEACHING IDEA by David Seymour and Maria Popova

Lead-In Activity: My morning

Draw six pictures about your morning on the board in any order (e.g. *package, alarm clock, bicycle, coffee cup, subway station, police officer*). Make sure you include something unusual. Students work in small groups to decide what happened and in what order. Take feedback from one or two groups. Then ask students to draw six pictures about their own morning. Encourage them to include something unusual. Students mingle around the classroom, showing each other their pictures, for their classmates to guess what happened to them this morning.

TEACHING IDEA by David Seymour and Maria Popova

Extension Activity: I'm sorry I'm late …

Ask students to imagine they have overslept and arrived late for an important appointment. Arrange students in pairs, and ask them to come up with five good excuses for their lateness, e.g. *I'm sorry I'm late. The car broke down and I had to take it to the garage.* Take feedback from the pairs and decide as a class which excuse was the most creative/most believable.

3 Writing

● Write an email about a travel experience

Ⓦ ordering events

A Work in pairs. Discuss the questions.

1 Why do some people feel it is important to have a vacation?
2 What kind of problems do people have on vacation?

B Read Amal's email. Underline any of the problems you thought of in Exercise A.

To: Cleo
Subject: We're back!

Hi Cleo,

How are you? Thanks for feeding the cat. We're home, but there's no electricity, so I'm writing this on my phone. We had a terrible vacation. Scott broke his leg!

First, bad weather delayed our flight. We arrived at the chalet in the middle of the night, so the next morning we were really tired. After breakfast, we went to the ski lifts, but they were closed because it was too windy.

The following day, it wasn't so windy and we had a great time on the slopes in the morning. Then, we stopped for some lunch, but when I wanted to pay I couldn't find my wallet!

Two days later, the real disaster happened. We were skiing down a busy slope when Scott fell over and broke his leg. We had to fly to the local hospital in a helicopter. His leg is in a cast for the next six weeks.

I'll call you tomorrow.

Amal

C Read again and number the events in the order they happened (1–6).

5 Scott had an accident.
6 There was a problem at Amal's home.
1 The flight left the airport late.
2 It wasn't possible to go up the mountain.
4 Amal lost something.
3 The weather was better.

D Find and underline the words that helped you order the events. There are six words or phrases.

E Complete the sentences with the words in the box. Use the information in the box to help you.

Ordering events

When you write about an experience, use sequencing words and phrases like the ones you underlined in Amal's email to help readers follow the order of events.

after first hours morning next then

1 First, we missed the bus, so we had to take a taxi.
2 The following morning, I got the correct visa and crossed the border on foot.
3 The next day, we woke up to the sound of the ocean.
4 We drove for four hours, and then stopped for some lunch.
5 Two hours later, my friend found her cell phone behind the couch.
6 After a quick lunch, we began walking again in the rain.

F Work in pairs. Cover Amal's email and retell the story using sequencing words and the events in Exercise C.

WRITING

A PLAN You are going to write an email to a friend about a good or bad travel experience. Think about the following:

1 Was it a good or bad experience?
2 Where were you and who were you with?
3 What happened?
4 How did the experience end?

B WRITE Write an email to a friend. Use the checklist to help you.

☐ I have written to a friend.
☐ I have started with an informal greeting and finished with an informal sign-off.
☐ I have used sequencing words and phrases to order the events.
☐ I have checked my spelling, vocabulary and grammar.

C REVIEW Work in pairs. Read your partner's email and ask questions about his/her experience.

160 3 WRITING

Possible answers

1 *To take a break from work. To take a break from taking care of a family. To visit and learn about another place. To spend more time as a family or with a partner.*
2 *Bad weather, flight delays.*

Refer students to this card as a model for the writing task.

Encourage students to check each of these objectives off when writing.

WRITING

A Students read and discuss Questions 1 and 2 in pairs. Monitor and assist as required. Elicit different problems from the whole class and write them on the board.

B Students read the email on their own and underline any of the problems that coincide with those they thought of in Exercise A. Elicit their answers and encourage students to respond to each other's ideas.

C Focus students on the activity. Students do the task individually and check their answers in pairs. Check answers with the whole class.

D Read the skills box as a class. Students read the email again in pairs, and underline the six words or phrases that helped them order the events. Ask students to dictate them to you to check, and write them on the board.

E Focus students on the vocabulary box. Students complete the sentences using the words from it. Remind students to use the Writing skills box to help them. Check answers with the whole class.

F Students work in pairs retelling Amal's story from memory to each other. Encourage them to use the sequencing words and the events from Exercise C. Monitor and assist when necessary. Ask one or two pairs to say their retellings to the class to check.

WRITING TASK

A Focus students on the activity. Explain that students should use the prompts to write notes to help them plan their email. With a weak group, you may want to ask two or three students to read their notes to the class.

B Students write their email using their notes. Encourage students to use as many sequencing words as possible and to edit their email using the checklist.

C Students work in pairs reading each other's emails. Encourage them to ask their partner two or three questions to learn more about their experience.

Unit 3 Review

VOCABULARY

A Label the pictures with the correct forms of transportation.

bus ferry helicopter minibus plane trolley

1 ___trolley___

2 ___minibus___

3 ___plane___

4 ___bus___

5 ___helicopter___

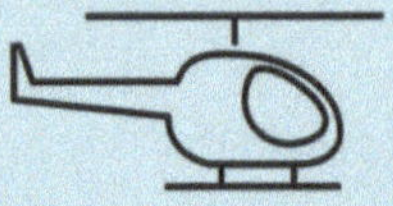

6 ___ferry___

B Write the words in the box in the correct place. Some words can go in more than one place.

accurate happy kind likely organized polite

un-	im-	dis-	in-
happy kind likely organized	polite	organized	accurate

C Complete the definitions with the words in the box.

apartment beach resort campsite chalet cruise ship

1 A ___campsite___ is a place where people on vacation can stay in tents.

2 A ___cruise ship___ is a large, comfortable boat that has similar amenities to a hotel.

3 A ___beach resort___ is a place that many people go to for a vacation by the ocean.

4 A ___chalet___ is a wooden house built in a mountain area where people on vacation can stay.

5 An ___apartment___ is a set of rooms, usually on one floor of a large building, where people on vacation can stay and cook their own meals.

GRAMMAR

A Choose the correct words to complete the sentences.

1 *Most* / ***Most of*** the people I know want to visit other countries.

2 ***Some*** / *Some of* countries are difficult to get into.

3 ***No*** / *None* type of transportation is completely safe.

4 *All the* / ***All*** my money was in my jacket.

B Complete the article with the past progressive or simple past forms of the verbs in parentheses.

Lucky to be alive!

Today, we bring you the story of surfer Mick Fanning.

World champion surfer Mick Fanning is lucky to be alive. In 2015, he [1] ___was surfing___ (*surf*) in a competition in South Africa when a shark [2] ___attacked___ (*attack*) him. Thousands of people [3] ___were watching___ (*watch*) on live television when the attack [4] ___happened___ (*happen*). Mick [5] ___was sitting___ (*sit*) on his surf board when he [6] ___noticed___ (*notice*) the shark next to him. The giant fish tried to pull him under the water, but Mick [7] ___hit___ (*hit*) it on the back, and it [8] ___swam___ (*swim*) away. A rescue boat [9] ___was waiting___ (*wait*) and it brought Mick and another surfer safely back to land.

C Choose the correct form of the verbs to complete the questions. Both forms may be possible.

1 Do you ever refuse ***to leave*** / *leaving* a tip in a restaurant? Why?

2 Do you prefer ***to go*** / ***going*** on vacation in the summer or the winter? Why?

3 What do you hope ***to learn*** / *learning* when you visit a new country?

4 Would you enjoy *to visit* / ***visiting*** a country where no one speaks your language? Why/Why not?

5 Do you like ***to try*** / ***trying*** new foods when you travel? Give an example.

FUNCTIONAL LANGUAGE

A Write the words in the correct order to make questions.

1 have / a / could / I / ticket / to / Central Station / ?
___Could I have a ticket to Central Station?___

2 a / one-way / you / like / would / a / round-trip / or / ?
___Would you like a one-way or a round-trip?___

3 does / train / what / the / arrive / in / time / Amsterdam / ?
___What time does the train arrive in Amsterdam?___

4 next / the / time's / train / what / ?
___What time's the next train?___

5 do / trains / have / I / to / change / ?
___Do I have to change trains?___

6 did / say / platform / sorry, / I'm / 30 / you / ?
___I'm sorry, did you say platform 30?___

7 is that right / at the top of the stairs, / so it's left / ?
___So it's left at the top of the stairs, is that right?___

8 do / get / you / to / platform / 9 / how / excuse me, / ?
___Excuse me, how do you get to platform 9?___

B Work in pairs. Think of different ways to answer the questions in Exercise A.

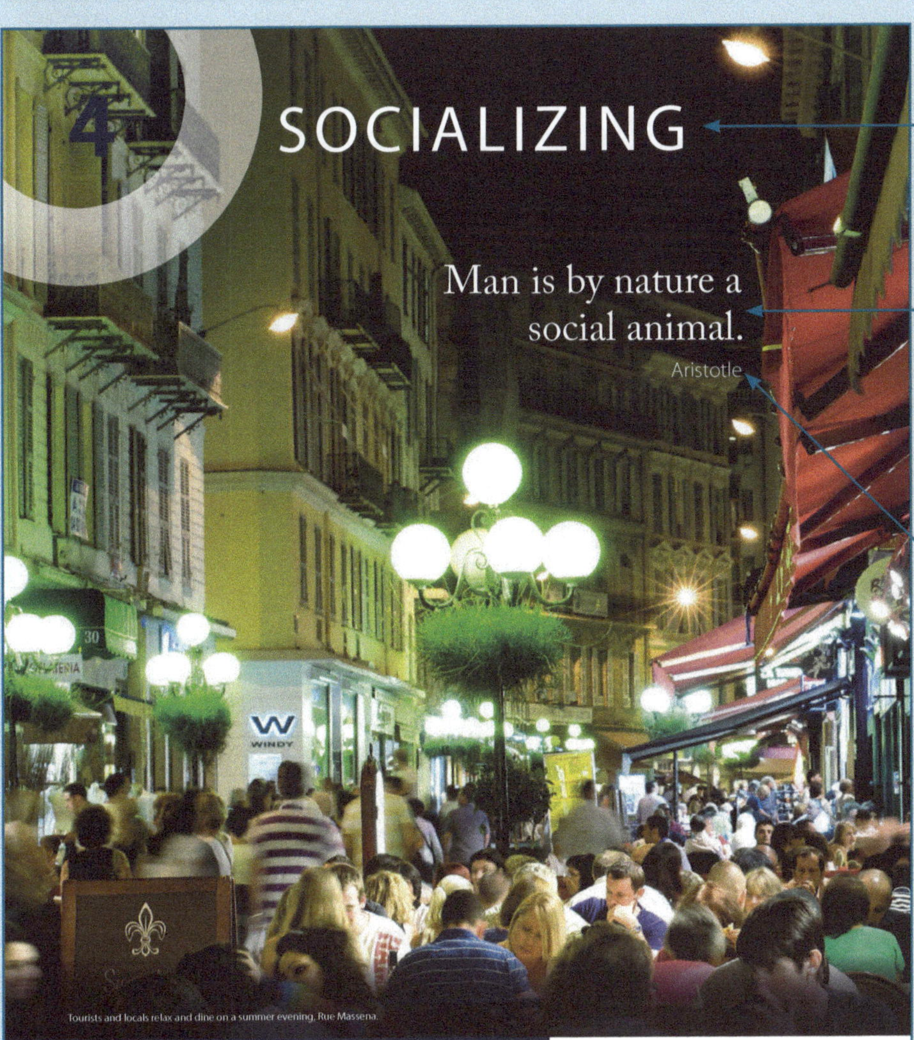

Tourists and locals relax and dine on a summer evening, Rue Massena.

Socializing (n) spending time with other people socially, for example, at a party.

Aristotle is suggesting that human beings cannot survive on their own, but rather are beings that have to live in a community.

Aristotle (384–322 BCE) was an ancient Greek philosopher and scientist. He is considered one of the 'Fathers of Western Philosophy'.

OBJECTIVES

- talk about plans you have made for a weekend with visitors
- present reasons to support or argue against predictions
- ask and answer questions about how you like to spend your free time
- make arrangements to meet up with somebody
- write an invitation and reply

Work with a partner. Discuss the questions.

1 Where do people go out in your country?
2 Look at the picture. Which city do you think it is? Why?
3 What do you enjoy doing with your friends?

SOCIALIZING 31

OBJECTIVES

Read the unit objectives to the class.

UNIT OPENER QUESTIONS

Ask students to read the quote and take one or two suggestions from the class about what they think it means.

Tell students to look at the picture on the page and ask prompt questions such as 'Where are these people? Would you like to be in a place like this? Why? Why not?' If students share any good ideas or useful language, write these on the board.

Call on a student to read aloud the first question. Answer with a list of the places where people in your country may get together in the winter or in the summer. Then ask students to discuss the questions with a partner or in a small group.

Monitor and help with grammar and vocabulary as required. When students have finished the activity, ask one or two pairs or groups to share their ideas with the class. Encourage the students to listen to one another and respond with their own ideas and opinions.

WORKSHEETS

Lesson 4.1 What's the plan?

Grammar: *be going to* + base form and present progressive for the future. Page W19

Vocabulary: Free time. Page W20

Lesson 4.2 The future of free time

Grammar: Making predictions. Page W21

Vocabulary: Suffixes. Page W22

Lesson 4.3 Hygge

Grammar: Subject and object questions. Page W23

Vocabulary: Relaxing. Page W24

4.1 What's the plan?

● Talk about plans you have made for a weekend with visitors

V free time G *be going to* + base form and present progressive for the future P *going to*

VOCABULARY

Free time

A SPEAK Work in pairs. Write down as many free time activities as you can in English. You have two minutes. Then compare your list with another pair.

B Complete the diagrams with the verbs in the box.

go for go to hang out play see or go to

1 go to: the theater / the movies; a museum / a gallery; a market; a friend's place / a party

2 go for: a meal / a drink; sushi/pizza/burgers; a walk / a run / a bike ride; coffee/lunch/dinner

3 see or go to: an exhibit; a concert / a play / a movie; a comedy show

4 play: cards; board games; pool/billiards

5 hang out: in town; at the mall; online; in the park; with friends

C SPEAK Work in pairs. Which of the free time activities in Exercise B are your favorites, and why?

LISTENING

A Work in pairs. What kind of things do you like to do when you visit a city for the first time?

4.1 **B LISTEN FOR GIST** Listen to a conversation between Sylvia and Greg and circle seven free-time activities in Vocabulary Exercise B that they talk about.

Glossary

arrange (v) to make plans for something to happen, for example by agreeing on a time and place

intelligent (adj) good at understanding difficult ideas and subjects

4.1 **C LISTEN FOR DETAIL** Listen again and choose the correct answer a or b.

1 What is the relationship between Sylvia and Greg?
   a brother and sister
   b boyfriend and girlfriend

2 Who is Claire?
   a Greg's friend
   b Greg's girlfriend

3 Sylvia thinks that Greg will like her friend Duncan because they …
   a are both good cooks.
   b both enjoy eating.

4 After dinner, Sylvia and Greg are going to see …
   a a comedy show.
   b a play by Shakespeare.

5 Greg stops Sylvia explaining the plan for the next day because he …
   a doesn't feel very well.
   b wants to order some food.

D SPEAK Work in pairs. When was the last time you visited friends or family for the weekend? Tell your partner.

4.1 What's the plan?

LEAD-IN

Put students into groups to make plans for their dream vacation. They should decide where they want to go, by what means of transportation, where they will stay and what activities they will do. Each group then makes a five-minute presentation.

VOCABULARY

A Read the task with the class. In pairs, students write their lists of free-time activities. When the time is finished, put the pairs in groups of four and ask them to share their ideas with each other. Take feedback from one or two groups and encourage students to add ideas that weren't mentioned.

B Focus students on the diagram and the verbs in the box. If necessary, pre-teach *hang out* as an informal way to say *spend time with*. Students complete the diagrams in pairs. Check answers with the whole class. Use the **Vocabulary Worksheet** on W20 for extra practice.

C In pairs, students discuss free-time activities from Exercise B they enjoy and give reasons. Monitor and assist when necessary. Take feedback from one or two pairs and encourage students to respond to each other's ideas.

LISTENING

A Read the activity with the whole class. Students discuss the question in pairs. Remind them to look at Vocabulary Exercise B for support. Monitor and assist as required. Take feedback from one or two pairs and encourage students to respond to each other's ideas.

4.1 **B** Students read the task and the glossary before listening to the conversation. Play the audio while students focus on Vocabulary Exercise B and work individually circling the free-time activities mentioned. Students compare their answers in pairs. Play the audio again for students to check their answers. Check answers with the whole class.

4.1 **C** Read the activity with the class, focusing on Questions 1–5. Students work individually choosing the correct answer for each question. Allow students to compare their answers. Play the audio again before checking with the whole class.

D In pairs, students tell their partner about the last time they visited friends or family for the weekend. Encourage students to use the vocabulary from this unit and their own ideas. Monitor and assist as required. Take feedback from one or two pairs and encourage students to respond to each other's ideas.

AUDIO SCRIPT

4.1

Listening, Exercise B
S = Sylvia G = Greg

S: Greggy! Ohhhhhh! It's so nice to see you!
G: Hi, Syl. Give me a hug. It's nice to see you, too … Do you have to call me Greggy?
S: Ha ha. Yes, and I'm going to introduce you to all my new friends as 'Greggy'. Was the trip OK?
Ex C Q1 **G:** Sure, sure. Mom gave me a ride to the station. She sends her love. She misses her darling daughter et cetera, et cetera. She's gonna call later.
Ex C Q2 **S:** Oh, good. How's Claire? Are you two OK? Still madly in love?
G: Oh, yeah, you know. Lucky girl.
S: Stop it.
G: She wanted to come this weekend, but tomorrow evening she's having dinner with some old friends. They arranged it a long time ago.
S: Of course. Never mind. Hopefully she'll make it next time. I've got so many plans for us this weekend! It's such a great city. I can't wait to show you around. Are you hungry?
G: Always.
S: Yep, silly question. Let's go for lunch.
G: Wow, this place is cool.
S: Nice, right? I hang out with my friends here a lot. I think I'm going to bring Mom and Dad here, too … if they ever come and visit!
G: Ha! They will. And then they'll never leave!
S: Ha!
G: So, what are all these plans you've got for us then?
S: Well, when we've finished lunch, I'm gonna text Angie and Mark and tell them to come and meet us, and we're going to go for a walk and show you the city center. Then we're meeting Duncan and Alicia at three o'clock, and I think we're going for coffee somewhere, but I'm not sure where.
G: Duncan and Alicia?
S: Oh, they're great. You'll like Duncan. He's a little like you.
G: What, handsome and intelligent?
Ex C Q3 **S:** Uhh … more like he's always thinking about his next meal.
G: I like him already.
S: After that, we're going to the market to look around; it's a beautiful old building, and we're going to do some food shopping because Duncan is making a curry dish for us all tonight. He's a great cook. Alicia says she and Duncan are going to open a restaurant one day. Anyway, …
G: Sounds great.
S: OK, so then tonight, we're going to the theater.
G: The theater?
S: Yes, I have tickets for a Shakespeare play.
G: What?
Ex C Q4 **S:** Ha ha! Only joking. We're seeing a comedy show. One of my friends is filming the show and he got us some free tickets.
G: Phew. That's more like it. What a great day you have planned, Syl! I can't wait.
S: And that's just today. Wait until you hear about tomorrow … In the morning, we're …
G: Uh, Syl, hang on. Did you hear that?
S: What?
G: Listen!
S: What? Is it the music?
Ex C Q5 **G:** No … no … it's … I think … yes, it's the sound of my empty stomach. Are we getting something to eat, or what?
S: Pfffft. You and your stomach. Pass me a menu …

4.1 What's the plan?

GRAMMAR

A Students read the definitions, then categorize the examples. Give feedback as a class.

B Students choose the correct word to complete the rules, before checking in pairs. Give feedback as a class.

C Direct students to the **Grammar Hub** (see below). Use the **Grammar Worksheet** on W19 for extra practice.

PRONUNCIATION

4.2

A Play the audio for students to listen and repeat.

B In pairs, students practice saying the sentences from Grammar Exercise A. Monitor and encourage use of /ˈgʌnə/.

C In pairs, students ask and answer questions. Monitor and encourage use of /ˈgʌnə/.

SPEAKING

A In groups, students decide which type of visitor to plan for.

B Groups write notes on each of the bullets. Monitor and assist as necessary.

C Put students into new groups to present their plans from Exercise B. Monitor and encourage discussion.

GRAMMAR HUB

4.1 *be going to* + base form and present progressive for the future

	Positive	Negative
I	**I'm going to meet** my friends.	**I'm not going to have** a night out.
he/she/it	**He's going to play** billiards.	**She isn't going to relax** at home.
you/we/they	**They're going to spend** the evening at home.	**We aren't going to see** a play on the weekend.

Question	Positive short answer	Negative short answer
Is he going to hang out with us?	Yes, **he is**.	No, **he isn't**.
Are they going to have a party to celebrate?	Yes, **they are**.	No, **they aren't**.

- We use *be going to* to talk about intentions.

	Positive	Negative
I	**I'm meeting** Steff at 6.	**I'm not having** dinner with Steve tonight.
he/she/it	**She's going** to the movies on Saturday.	**She isn't visiting** her grandparents this weekend.
you/we/they	**We're visiting** Tina tomorrow.	**We aren't playing** in the concert next week.

Question	Positive short answer	Negative short answer
Am I meeting you at 8?	Yes, **you are**.	No, **you aren't**.
Are you watching a movie tonight?	Yes, **we are**.	No, **we aren't**.

- We use the present progressive to talk about arrangements in the future.

Be careful!

- We don't use the present progressive for intentions.
  I'm going to open my own restaurant when I'm older. NOT ~~*I'm opening my own restaurant when I'm older.*~~

4.1 *be going to* + base form and present progressive for the future

A Correct the mistakes in each sentence.

1 I'm going to ~~introducing~~ *introduce* you to my friends.
2 She['s] going to the theater with Alice tonight.
3 ~~We meet~~ We're meeting Pamela at 4 pm this afternoon.
4 They [are] going to cook pizza for everyone.
5 She's going [to] buy a cake for his birthday.
6 What time [are] we meeting for lunch?

B Put the words in order to make sentences.

1 to / invite / my colleagues / I'm / to the party / going / all
I'm going to invite all my colleagues to the party.
2 to / I / going / tonight / think / at home / I'm / stay
I think I'm going to stay at home tonight.
3 are / that new sushi place / to / Karl and Inge / going / try
Karl and Inge are going to try that new sushi place.
4 sister / seeing / you / again / when / are / your / ?
When are you seeing your sister again?
5 on Friday night / having / Tom's / a birthday party
Tom's having a birthday party on Friday night.
6 at five o'clock / meeting / we're / in the central square
We're meeting in the central square at five o'clock.

➤ Go back to page 33.

GRAMMAR

be going to + base form and present progressive for the future

A WORK IT OUT **Read the definitions. Then look at the sentences and decide if they are arrangements (A) or intentions (I).**

Arrangements – you have probably booked a ticket or agreed on a time with other people. You usually mention a time, date or place.

Intentions – you have already decided to do something and want to tell someone about it. You don't need to mention a time, date or place.

1 I'm going to introduce you to all my new friends as 'Greggy'. I

2 Tomorrow evening, she's having dinner with some old friends. A

3 I think I'm going to bring Mom and Dad here, too. I

4 We're meeting Duncan and Alicia at three o'clock. A

5 Alicia says she and Duncan are going to open a restaurant one day. I

B **Choose the correct words to complete the rules. Use Exercise A to help you.**

be going to + base form and present progressive for the future

1 We use *be going to* + base form to talk about ***arrangements / intentions***.

2 We use the present progressive (*be* + verb + *-ing*) to talk about ***arrangements / intentions***.

C Go to the **Grammar Hub** on **page 128**.

PRONUNCIATION

going to

4.2 **A** **Listen and repeat the pronunciation of *going to* /ˈgʌnə/ in informal speech.**

1 She's going to call later.

2 I'm going to text Angie and Mark.

B SPEAK **Work in pairs. Look at the sentences that you marked as intentions (I) in Grammar Exercise A. Practice saying the sentences in an informal way. Pronounce *going to* as /ˈgʌnə/.**

C SPEAK **Ask questions about your partner's plans. Talk about your arrangements and intentions.**

A: Are you going to have a party in the next few weeks?

B: Yes, I am! It's my birthday next weekend and I'm having a party.

SPEAKING

A **Work in groups. Plan a weekend. Choose a group of visitors:**

- older family members, for example, an aunt and uncle or grandparents
- younger family members, for example, a brother or sister with their partner and children
- a group of four friends from school or college

B **Make plans for next weekend for you and your visitors in and around a city you know well. Write notes on:**

- meeting
- sightseeing
- entertainment
- food and drink
- evening activities

C **Explain your plan to students from other groups. Which weekend sounds like the most fun?**

My old school friends are coming to visit next weekend. I'm meeting them at the train station. Then we're going to have breakfast in town, probably at Vincent Café. The food there is great and it isn't expensive.

Talk about plans you have made for a weekend with visitors

4.2 The future of free time

Present reasons to support or argue against predictions

G– making predictions   P– *will* and *won't*   V– suffixes

READING

A Work in pairs. Do you agree with the following sentences? Why/Why not?

In the next ten years …

we will do less work and spend more time socializing.

we will do a lot of our socializing in virtual worlds.

we will socialize with artificial intelligence.

B **READ FOR MAIN IDEA** Work in groups. Student A go to **page 156**, Student B go to **page 153** and Student C go to **page 152**. Read your article and discuss the questions below.

1 What does the article say about our social lives?

2 What role will technology play?

3 Which expert or business leader is mentioned, and why?

4 What possible benefits of the development does the article mention?

C **SPEAK** Work in groups. Discuss your article and the following questions.

1 Which predictions do you think will happen?

2 Do you think these will be positive or negative developments for our social lives? Why?

GRAMMAR

Making predictions

A **WORK IT OUT** Look at the sentences from the articles about the future of our social lives. Underline the modal verbs used to make predictions.

1 The good news is some people think it might not be long until every weekend is a long weekend.

2 However, experts agree that the way we use social media will change in the future.

3 Some experts even believe that one day it may be possible for robots to feel love.

B Find and underline four more examples of modal verbs in one of the articles you read in Reading Exercise B. Then work in pairs and compare your answers.

C Complete the rules with *will* or *might/may*.

Making predictions

1 We use ___will___ (*not*) + the base form of a verb when we are certain about our prediction.

2 We use ___might/may___ (*not*) + the base form of a verb when we are less certain about our prediction.

D Look at the sentences from *Robot relationships*. Then choose the correct words to complete the rules.

… humans will probably develop close relationships with robots.

… it definitely won't be long until robots look, sound and move like humans.

1 We use *probably* to make predictions with *will* and *won't* **less** / **more** certain.

2 We use *definitely* to make predictions with *will* and *won't* **less** / **more** certain.

3 We use *probably* and *definitely* **before** / **after** *will*.

4 We use *probably* and *definitely* **before** / **after** *won't*.

4.2 The future of free time

LEAD-IN

Students write anonymous predictions about what their classmates will do or become in the next five years. Collect all the predictions and read each one aloud. The class has to guess who the prediction is about and who wrote it.

READING

A Have a class discussion on whether they agree or not and why.

B Put students into groups of three. Direct students to the **Communication Hub**. Each student reads their corresponding article and answers the questions.

Article A: Work-life balance

1 *Shorter working weeks, longer weekends / more free time / soon every weekend might be a long weekend.*
2 *Better technology will do more of our work for us.*
3 *Carlos Slim – some of his employees work shorter weeks.*
4 *A better work-life balance / offices will use less energy and there will be fewer car trips.*

Article B: Social media

1 *The way we use social media will change in the future.*
2 *Virtual reality will make it possible to meet friends in 3D worlds.*
3 *Mark Zuckerberg – developing VR social media.*
4 *You will be able to meet friends 'inside' pictures and videos and in VR clubs and museums, etc.*

Article C: Robot relationships

1 *Humans will develop close relationships with robots.*
2 *Technology will make robots look, sound and move like humans. Scientists might be able to build robots that really understand human feelings.*
3 *Professor Hiroshi Ishiguro – he is mentioned because he has built a robot called Erica that can show basic feelings on her face.*
4 *Robots could take care of people.*

C Students take turns summarizing their article and discussing the questions as a group.

GRAMMAR

A Highlight the title of the section *(Making predictions)*. Ask students to read the three sentences and underline the modal verbs used to express prediction. Allow students to check their answers with a partner before checking with the whole class.

B Direct students back to the **Communication Hub** articles they read, and ask them to underline four examples of modal verbs. Give feedback as a class.

A: Work-life balance

*... technology **will** do more of ...*
*This **will** allow us to have ...*
*... work-life balance **won't** be the ...*
*Office **will** use less energy ...*
*... there **will** be fewer car trips ...*

B: Social media

*... your friends **will** soon put on ...*
*... it **will** be possible to meet ...*
*... that you **will** be able to ...*
*It **will** also be possible ...*
*... you **might** have to wait ...*

C: Robot relationships ...

*humans **will** probably develop ...*
*... it definitely **won't** be long ...*
*... technology **might** help scientists ...*
*... your robot **might** be able to ...*

C Focus students on the rules in the *Making predictions* box. Students work on their own to complete the rules. Remind them to use the sentences in Exercise A to help them. Check answers as a class.

D Read the sentences with the whole class. Students work on their own, completing Rules 1–4. They compare their answers in pairs before checking with the whole class.

METHODOLOGY HUB by Jim Scrivener

Getting feedback on teaching

Feedback from colleagues

Ask other teachers to come in and observe some of your lessons, and do an exchange observation with them, not to judge each other or score points but to learn from each other. The growth in trust and respect that comes from sharing ideas and skills in this way can really help all involved move forward, as well as having a markedly positive effect on the whole atmosphere of a school.

Even if a colleague cannot come in and observe a lesson, you could still set aside some uninterrupted time (perhaps 15 minutes or so) when they will sit and listen to you talk through your thoughts about the lesson. Your colleague could make a 'contract' with you that he or she will not offer suggestions or advice or help or opinions, but will simply listen and support you. This kind of helping is very simple to describe, but extremely powerful in action. It can be surprisingly beneficial to talk through one's own experience with another person who is really listening.

TEACHING IDEA by David Seymour and Maria Popova

One day

Explain that you are going to dictate one prediction about the future to each person. Invite students to mingle and collect (write down) the other students' opinions on their prediction. (Dictate each sentence quickly, but go through them two or three times so that students get another chance to write down their prediction. After the survey, elicit the results and write them on the board.)

Computers will take over the world.
Time travel will be possible.
We will find life in other solar systems.
Unintelligent clones will do all the hard work.
Disease will be eliminated.
People will live on Mars.
Everyone will live to be 200.
The environment will be destroyed.

4.2 The future of free time

E Direct students to the **Grammar Hub** (see below). Use the **Grammar Worksheet** on W21 for extra practice.

F Read the task with the whole class. Students put the modals in parentheses into the correct place in each sentence. Check answers as a class.

G Students work in pairs to discuss what predictions from Exercise F they disagree with. Encourage students to give reasons for their answers. Monitor and assist when necessary. Take feedback from one or two pairs and encourage students to respond to each other's ideas.

PRONUNCIATION

4.3 **A** Read the task with the class. Model reading aloud the first sentence and checking students understand the task. Elicit that stressed words are the ones that carry information. Play the audio while students underline the stressed words. Stop after each sentence to give students time to do the task. With a weak group, you may have to play the audio more than once. Check answers with the whole class.

4.3 **B** Play the audio again for students to repeat the sentences, paying close attention to stress.

VOCABULARY

A Direct students to the **Vocabulary Hub** (TB121). Use the **Vocabulary Worksheet** on W22 for extra practice.

B Students complete the words using suffixes from the box, then check their answers with a partner. Give feedback as a class.

C In pairs, students discuss Sentences 1, 2 and 5 from Exercise B. Monitor and assist as necessary.

SPEAKING

A Read the three predictions with the whole class. Have a class discussion with students giving their opinions and reasons to support or argue against each of the predictions.

B Arrange students in groups of three. They should discuss each prediction, noting down reasons for or against each of them. To help students focus, give them a target number of ideas to write (e.g. two ideas for and against each sentence). Monitor and help as required.

C In new groups, students take turns to discuss one of the predictions for one to two minutes. Monitor and assist as necessary.

GRAMMAR HUB

4.2 Making predictions

	Positive	Negative
I/you/he/she/it/we/they	**He will go** on a virtual date.	**It won't be** very romantic.
	They may/might fall in love.	**It may/might not be** easy to meet people.

Question	Positive short answer	Negative short answer
Will they go out for dinner?	Yes, **they will**.	No, **they won't**.

- We use *will*, *may* and *might* to make predictions about the future. We use *will* when we are certain. We use *may* or *might* when we are less certain. There is little difference in meaning between *may* and *might*.
- Because *will*, *may* and *might* are modals, they only have one form.

  She might bring her VR headset. NOT ~~*She mights bring her VR headset.*~~
- We use adverbs of probability with *will* to make predictions more or less certain.

  100% *We'll **definitely/certainly** need to bring a warm blanket.*
  75% *She'll **probably** stay at home with her family.*
  50% ***Maybe** they'll go on vacation to Denmark.*
  25% *I **probably** won't cook a meal.*
  0% *You **definitely** won't forget the experience.*

Be careful!

- *Maybe* goes at the beginning of the sentence.

  Maybe you'll play board games. NOT ~~*You'll maybe play board games.*~~

4.2 Making predictions

A Choose the correct option.

1. I *definitely* / *maybe* won't go to the concert because it's raining.
2. *Maybe you will* / *You maybe will* be home early on Friday.
3. They *will* / *might* definitely go sailing tonight.
4. Robots *might* / *definitely* won't understand human feelings in the future. I don't believe that's possible.
5. I *may* / *will* not have enough money for the tickets. Let's see how much they are.
6. We probably *might not* / *won't* have the party next week.
7. I'll definitely *going* / *go* to college when I leave high school.

B Make sentences with *will* or *might*.

1. Robots will definitely do (*definitely / do*) all the work in the future.
2. We might control (*control*) computers with our minds in the future. It's possible.
3. It might not be (*not / be*) a good idea to sell my car. I need to think about it.
4. They probably won't go (*probably / not / go*) to the party.
5. I don't think robots will have (*have*) feelings.
6. It won't cost (*not / cost*) more than 20 dollars. That's for sure.

➤ Go back to page 35.

E Go to the **Grammar Hub** on **page 128**.

F Complete the predictions about artificial intelligence with the words in parentheses.

1 Some people *might not* want three-day weekends every week. (*might not*)
2 It *will* probably be harder to find a job in the future because of technology. (*will*)
3 I don't think we *'ll* have robot friends in my lifetime. (*'ll*)
4 We *might* control computers with our minds in the future. (*might*)
5 VR headsets *will* definitely get much cheaper in the next few years. (*will*)
6 Humans *probably* won't fall in love with robots in the future. (*probably*)
7 I'm sure we *'ll* all have robots in our homes 20 years from now. (*'ll*)
8 We *may* stop working completely one day because of technology. (*may*)

G SPEAK Work in pairs. Are there any predictions in Exercise F that you do not agree with?

I think most people will want three-day weekends every week.

PRONUNCIATION
will and *won't*

4.3 **A Stressed words are the ones that carry the information. Listen and underline the stressed words.**

1 There will be fewer car trips to work in the future.
2 Technology will do more of the work for us.
3 People won't be paid for working fewer days per week.
4 Do you think people will be happier in the future?
5 No, they won't.
6 Yes, they will. They won't have to work so hard.

4.3 **B Listen again and repeat the sentences. Copy the stress.**

VOCABULARY
Suffixes

A Go to the **Vocabulary Hub** on **page 147**.

B Add one of the suffixes in the box to the words in parentheses to make nouns. You may need to change the spelling of some of the words. You will need to use some of the suffixes more than once.

-ion -ity -ment -ness

1 I think there is a ___possibility___ (*possible*) that robots will feel love in the future.
2 I agree with the ___prediction___ (*predict*) that virtual reality will be an important part of social media.
3 There is an ___agreement___ (*agree*) between many experts that technology will help our work–life balance.
4 An important ___development___ (*develop*) is that robots are now beginning to understand our feelings.
5 I don't believe that robots will be able to experience real ___happiness___ (*happy*) or ___sadness___ (*sad*).

C SPEAK Work in pairs. Look at sentences 1, 2 and 5 in Exercise B. Do you agree with these opinions? Why/Why not?

SPEAKING

A Discuss some predictions about the future. Read three predictions for the future and present reasons to support and argue against each.

Fifty years from now …

1 cash in the form of bills and coins will completely disappear.
2 all cars will be self-driving and there will be very few road accidents.
3 all European children will learn Mandarin at school.

B Work in groups. Discuss the predictions and write down reasons to support and argue against each prediction.

C Work in new groups. Take turns speaking for one to two minutes about one of the predictions.

Present reasons to support or argue against predictions

4.3 Hygge

Ask and answer questions about how you like to spend your free time

G subject and object questions **V** relaxing **P** linking a consonant to a vowel **S** summarizing

READING

A Work in pairs. Which of these things have you done recently? What exactly did you do? Tell your partner.

1 spend the evening at a friend's home
2 relax at home on your own
3 invite people over to your home for the evening
4 get together with your extended family
5 have a night out with friends

B SPEAK Look at the pictures. What are the people doing? How do you think they feel? Use the words in the box to help you.

a cozy blanket	a family gathering	a fire	a hot bath
a sleeping pet	candles	warm socks	wool sweaters

C READ FOR MAIN IDEA The pictures all show the Danish idea of *hygge*. What do you think *hygge* means? Read the first paragraph of *Make yourself at home* to check your answer.

Make *yourself* at home

What is *hygge*?

Winters in Denmark are long, dark and cold, but according to the 2016 UN World Happiness Report, Danish people are among the happiest in the world. One reason might be *hygge*, the Danish attitude that focuses on enjoying the simple things in life, such as enjoying a coffee in a relaxed atmosphere with easy-going friends or family.

How do you pronounce *hygge*?

Hygge is easy enough to pronounce – 'hue-gah' – but much more difficult to translate. No single English word describes the idea completely, but being cozy is a big part of it. There may be a connection between the word *hygge* and the English word *hug*, and in Danish *hygge* can be an adjective, verb or noun.

How do I know if it's *hygge*?

Your friends come over on a cold winter evening to sit by the fire, eat homemade food and play board games. That's definitely *hygge*. You have a quiet night in, take a bath, light some candles, then sit down with a good book and a cozy blanket. That's *hygge*, too. You argue about politics, check your phone, play video games and listen to thumping techno music. That's definitely not *hygge*! So how do you know if it's *hygge*? Think warm socks, wool sweaters, sleeping pets and happy family gatherings. Got it now?

Why *hygge*?

Research shows that people who are kind to themselves and take some time out to relax have better mental health and feel happier. *Hygge* encourages us to do this and also to get together with friends and family. Happy groups of people make more caring communities and a happier society. It's no surprise that the Danes are always smiling!

Glossary

cozy (adj) warm and comfortable, and making you feel relaxed
family gathering (phrase) when a family meets and spends time together
translate (v) to change spoken or written words into another language

4.3 Hygge

LEAD-IN

Draw a Tic-Tac-Toe grid on the board (with nine squares), and write nine activities to do in your free time in each space, e.g. *go to the movie theater, hang out at the mall, play video games, chat online, have sushi at a Japanese restaurant, go to a costume party, play cards, go out for a drink and go on a picnic.* Divide the class into two teams. To claim their team's Xs or Os, a team member must attempt to talk about the topic in the chosen square for 30 seconds without pausing, hesitations or repetition.

READING

A Read the activity with the class. Check understanding of *extended family*. In pairs, students look at the list of free-time activities, and discuss which they have done recently, sharing as much information as possible. Monitor and assist as required. Take feedback from one or two pairs and encourage students to respond to each other's ideas.

B Focus students on the task and the phrases in the vocabulary box. Ask students to look at the glossary, as the words there may help them to do the activity. Students look at the four pictures and describe them using the new language.

C Explain that the pictures represent the Danish idea of *hygge*. Ask the class to share their ideas about the meaning of *hygge*, but do not correct or confirm their answers. Students read the first paragraph and check their answers. To discourage students from reading the whole text, set a time limit which ensures they only have time to skim the first paragraph. When students have finished reading, ask them to explain the meaning of *hygge*.

Hygge is the Danish attitude that focuses on enjoying the simple things in life, such as enjoying a coffee in a relaxed atmosphere with easy-going friends or family.

TEACHING IDEA by David Seymour and Maria Popova

Lead-In Activity: Happiness is …

Use this activity as an alternative to introduce the lesson.

Check that students know the meaning of the word *definition*. Arrange students in pairs or small groups and explain that you are going to give them some words to define. Ask students to write the following on a piece of paper (each one will need to be on a separate line):

Love is …, A friend is …, Coffee is …, Winter is …, Time is …, Happiness is …

Give the groups time to talk to each other and come up with an appropriate way to finish each sentence.

Once they have finished, ask the groups to read aloud just their endings and encourage the rest of the class to guess what they are defining.

TEACHING IDEA by David Seymour and Maria Popova

Adjectives

Stand in a circle. Take turns throwing a ball to each other and follow this sequence: (1) say an adjective; (2) say an associated noun; (3) make a sentence with the adjective and noun and so on, e.g.

A (throwing): *Green.*

B (catching): *Tree.*

C (catching): *The trees are very green in the summer.*

D (catching): *Hot …*

(Variation: Students only have to say adjectives, but they must begin with the last letter of the previous adjective, e.g. *green, new, wonderful, lazy …*)

GRAMMAR HUB

4.3 Subject and object questions

- We ask subject questions when we don't know what/who/which/whose something (or someone) is.

  What is hygge?
- We ask object questions when we want to know more information about something (or someone).

  How do you pronounce hygge?
- Subject questions don't include an auxiliary verb. Object questions do.

  Subject question: Whose blanket is this?

  *Object question: Which restaurant **did** you go to?*
- With subject questions, we don't change the word order in the answer.

  Who is your best friend? Friya is my best friend.
- In object questions, the question word is the object of the sentence.

  ***What** do you do to relax? I play **computer games** to relax.*

4.3 Hygge

D Give students time to read the skills box, before completing the summary. During class feedback, elicit where in the text students found their answers.

E Students discuss the questions in pairs. Monitor and assist as necessary.

GRAMMAR

A Give students time to answer the questions alone, before giving feedback as a class.

B Students choose the correct options to complete the rules, before checking their answers with a partner. Give feedback as a class.

C Direct students to the **Grammar Hub** (see TB36 and below). Use the **Grammar Worksheet** on W23 for extra practice.

D Students choose the correct question word to complete the questions, adding an auxiliary verb if necessary. Then, they decide if each is a subject (S) or object (O) question. Give feedback as a class.

E In pairs, students ask and answer the questions from Exercise D. Monitor and assist as necessary.

VOCABULARY

A Put students into pairs and give them a minute to brainstorm a list of ways to relax. Give feedback, adding new or interesting vocabulary to the board.

B Direct students to the **Vocabulary Hub**. Allow time for students to compare answers in pairs before checking with the whole class. Use the **Vocabulary Worksheet** on W24 for extra practice.

PRONUNCIATION

A In pairs, students make a list of vowels and consonants. Give feedback as a class.

4.4 **B** Play the audio. Elicit that the last consonant sound of a word links to the vowel sound at the beginning of the next word.

4.5 **C** Read the task with the class. Students say the phrases aloud and mark the consonant and vowel links by drawing an arrow. Play the audio again for students to check. Check answers with the whole class.

SPEAKING HUB

A Ask students whether they have ever taken a personality quiz online or in a magazine. Discuss with the class what personality tests look like (e.g. *multiple-choice questions with a certain point value, a final explanation of what your answers say about you according to the points obtained*). Explain that students are going to create their own personality quiz. Check that students understand the meaning of *home bird*, also known as a *homebody* (*someone who prefers spending time at home to going out*) and *party animal* (*someone who likes parties, clubs, etc*).

B Students work in pairs writing five questions with two or three possible answers each. They can use the prompts or their own ideas. Monitor and help when necessary.

C Students swap their quiz with another pair and answer their questions. Rearrange the pairs in groups of four. They discuss whether the results are accurate. Take feedback from one or two groups and encourage students to respond to each other's ideas.

Extra activity
Based on their feedback in class, students can write up and refine their quizzes for homework.

GRAMMAR HUB

4.3 Subject and object questions

A Complete the sentences with the question words in the box. Then select the correct question type: subject (S) or object (O).

how what when where who why

1 Who is going on the trip to Denmark? (S) / O
2 When do you leave for Copenhagen? S / (O)
3 What is your favorite board game? (S) / O
4 Where do you want to meet? S / (O)
5 How do you say 'hello' in French? S / (O)
6 Why is our English class canceled? (S) / O

B Put the words in order to make questions. Then match the answers (a–f).

1 you / have / do / when / classes / English
When do you have English classes? f
2 favorite / place / where / your / relaxing / is / for
Where is your favorite place for relaxing? a
3 does / do / she / free / time / what / her / in
What does she do in her free time? e
4 feeling / Sara / is / how / driving test / about / the
How is Sara feeling about the driving test? b
5 they / for / when / leaving / are / Bucharest
When are they leaving for Bucharest? c
6 best / the / is / who / cook / the / in / family
Who is the best cook in the family? d

a the bathtub
b worried
c next weekend
d Fred
e She goes to the gym.
f on Thursdays

➤ Go back to page 37.

D READ FOR DETAIL Read the whole article. Then complete the summary with the words in the box. Use the information in the box to help you.

Summarizing

A summary gives the most important points of a text.

Highlight or underline key points and write notes as you read the text. Try to use your own words rather than copy the writer's.

comfortable explain health important technology

Hygge is a Danish custom for people who want to relax and feel [1] comfortable. It is usually at home and no [2] technology is involved! *Hygge* can be with other people or by yourself – the [3] important thing is to feel happy and cozy. Feeling this way is good for your mental [4] health. This might [5] explain why Danish people were described as some of the happiest people in the world by the 2016 UN World Happiness Report.

E SPEAK Work in pairs. Discuss the questions.

1 When did you last do something '*hygge*'? What was it and who were you with?

2 Is there a word in your language that means *hygge* or something similar?

GRAMMAR
Subject and object questions

A WORK IT OUT Read the rules and look at the questions from *Make yourself at home*. Then look at the examples and answer the questions (1–3).

Subject and object questions

We ask subject questions when we don't know *what/who/which/whose* something or someone is.

We ask object questions when we want to know more information about something or someone.

What is hygge?

How do you pronounce 'hygge'?

1 Which is the subject question? What is hygge?

2 Which is the object question? How do you pronounce 'hygge'?

3 Which question includes an auxiliary verb?
How do you pronounce 'hygge'? (object question)

B Look at the questions and possible answers. Then choose the correct words to complete the rules.

What is hygge? It is an attitude that focuses on enjoying the simple things in life.

How do you pronounce 'hygge'? You pronounce it 'hue-gah'.

1 With subject questions, we *change* / *don't change* the word order in the answer.

2 In *subject* / *object* questions, the question word is the object of the sentence.

C Go to the **Grammar Hub** on **page 128**.

D Choose the best question word and decide if an auxiliary verb is needed to complete the questions. Then choose the correct question type: subject (S) or object (O).

1 *Who* / *Why* is *do* / *–* your best friend? **S** / O

2 *When* / *What do* / *–* you do with your best friend? S / **O**

3 *What* / *Who does smile* / *smiles* more, you or your best friend? **S** / O

4 *What* / *Which do* / *–* you do to relax? S / **O**

E SPEAK Work in pairs. Ask and answer the questions in Exercise D.

VOCABULARY
Relaxing

A Work in pairs. Make a list of different ways of relaxing. You have one minute.

B Go to the **Vocabulary Hub** on **page 148**.

PRONUNCIATION
Linking a consonant to a vowel

A SPEAK Work in pairs. Which letters of the alphabet are vowels and which are consonants? Vowels: a, e, i, o, u
Consonants: b, c, d, f, g, h, j, k, l, m, n, p, q, r, s, t, v, w, x, y, z

4.4 **B** Listen and repeat the phrases. Which words link together?

1 light a candle 'light' and 'a'

2 take a bath 'take' and 'a'

4.5 **C** Say the phrases and draw an arrow where a consonant sound links to a vowel sound. Then listen and check your answers.

1 have some friends over

2 a relaxed atmosphere

3 the simple things in life

4 friends and family

SPEAKING HUB

A Work in pairs. You are going to write a quiz with the title *Are you a home bird or a party animal?*

B PLAN Ask five questions and give two or three possible answers for each. Use the topics below:

- a favorite way of celebrating
- a typical Saturday night
- your ideal vacation
- going to or having parties
- eating out or cooking at home

C Swap quizzes with another pair and answer their questions. Do you agree with the results?

Ask and answer questions about how you like to spend your free time

Café Hub

4.4 Would you?

Ⓕ– make arrangements to meet up with somebody

Ⓟ– saying *yes* or *no*

COMPREHENSION

A SPEAK Work in pairs. Look at the pictures and discuss where the characters are and what you think happens. Then choose the correct words to complete the sentences.

1 Zac and Milly *have* / *haven't* met before.

2 Zac *knows* / *doesn't know* what to say to Milly.

3 Zac *wants* / *doesn't want* to buy a T-shirt.

4 Milly *likes* / *doesn't like* Zac.

5 Zac *likes* / *doesn't like* Milly.

6 Zac and Milly *arrange* / *don't arrange* to go out together.

B ▶ Watch the video and check your answers to Exercise A.

C ▶ **02:58–04:19** Watch part of the video again. When are Milly and Zac free to meet? Put a check mark (✓) or an ✗ in the correct place.

	Milly	Zac
1 tonight	✗	✓
2 on Saturday after 1:30	✓	✗
3 on Sunday at midday	✓	✓

D SPEAK Work in pairs. Why are they not able to meet tonight or on Saturday? Tonight, Milly has to see her sister. On Saturday, Zac is fixing Sam's computer.

Glossary

midday **(n) (British)** = noon **(n) (American)**

FUNCTIONAL LANGUAGE

Make arrangements to meet up with somebody

A Complete the questions with the words in the box. There are three words you do not need.

are can could do how maybe what will ~~would~~ would

Make arrangements (invitations)

1 __Would__ you like to hang out tonight?

2 __Would__ you like to do something, then?

3 We __could__ go for a coffee, or eat something?

4 __Are__ you free on Saturday?

5 __How__ about Sunday instead?

6 __What__ time?

7 __Do__ you want to meet at the park?

Say *yes*

Yeah! Sure. / Sounds great. / Awesome!

I'd love to!

Great. Twelve o'clock it is!

Say *no*

I'm so sorry, I can't.

Oh! Wait a minute. I just remembered …

B ▶ Watch the video again and check your answers to Exercise A.

MILLY SAM NEENA ZAC GABY

USEFUL PHRASES

A Match the useful phrases (1–6) with the phrases which show the correct meaning (a–f).

d **1** Are you looking for anything in particular?
f **2** I'm sorry, I need to get that.
e **3** So, you were saying.
a **4** Well, it was nice to see you again.
c **5** Wait, hold on!
b **6** Sounds great!

a I'm leaving.
b That's a good idea.
c Stay here!
d Do you want to buy something?
e Please continue.
f The phone is ringing.

B How do you say these useful phrases in your language?

PRONUNCIATION
Saying *yes* or *no*

4.6 **A** Listen and write the replies in the correct place.

Saying *yes*	Saying *no*
Sounds great. Awesome. I'd love to. Yeah, sure.	I'm sorry, I'm busy. I can't. Oh, wait a minute, I just remembered …

4.7 **B** Listen and repeat. Can you hear the difference in intonation between saying *yes* and saying *no*? Copy the word stress and intonation.

C **SPEAK** Work in pairs. Practice saying the replies. Listen and check your partner's pronunciation.

SPEAKING

A Work in pairs. Look at some things you could arrange to do. One item in each word set is not correct. Cross it out and replace it with your own idea.

1 go for … a drink / a walk / a drive / a shop
2 go to … the movie theater / swim / a gig / the beach
3 go … shopping / eating / swimming / dancing / biking

B Work in pairs. Practice making arrangements using the ideas in Exercise A. Take turns inviting each other.

Student A: Invite B to do something.
Student B: Say *no*.
Student A: Suggest another time.
Student B: Say *no*.
Student A: Suggest *another* time.
Student B: Say *yes*.

Make arrangements to meet up with somebody

➤ Turn to **page 161** to learn how to write an invitation and reply.

COMPREHENSION

A Read the activity with the class. In pairs, students discuss what they think will happen in the episode. They then complete the sentences with what they think is the correct word. Take feedback from one or two pairs and encourage students to respond to each other's ideas, but do not confirm or correct their answers yet.

B ▶ Play the full video for students to check their predictions. Ask for a show of hands to see how many got the correct answers.

C ▶ 02:58–04:19 Focus students on the task. Play the video. Students watch and decide when Milly and Zac are free to meet. Play the video again so they can check their answers. Check with the class.

D In pairs, students discuss why Milly and Zac can't meet tonight or on Saturday. Monitor and assist when necessary.

FUNCTIONAL LANGUAGE

A Focus students on the boxes *Make arrangements, Say yes* and *Say no*. Read the activity with the class. Give students time to complete the invitations from the video. Remind students there are two words they do not need.

B ▶ Play the video again, for students to check their answers to Exercise A. Check answers.

USEFUL PHRASES

A ▶ Students match the phrases to their meanings. If students need support with this activity, play the video again. Check answers in pairs before doing so with the whole class.

B Students think about how they would say these phrases in their own language. In a multilingual class, you may want to pair students from different countries. Take feedback from different students and encourage them to respond to one another's ideas.

PRONUNCIATION

4.6 **A** Play the audio. Students listen to the replies to the invitations and write them in the correct column, *Saying yes* or *Saying no*. Check answers as a class.

4.6 **B** Play the audio again and ask students to listen for any differences in intonation between saying yes and no. Play the audio again for students to listen and repeat, focusing on their own intonation.

C Students practice saying the replies in pairs. Encourage them to listen to and to correct each other's intonation. Monitor and assist as required.

SPEAKING

A Students work in pairs finding and crossing out the activity that does not match the verb in each set. They then replace it with an activity of their own.

B Pairs read the conversation frame and use it to build a short conversation. Remind students to use the ideas from Exercise A and the phrases from Pronunciation Exercise A to support them. Monitor and assist when necessary.

Extra activity
An alternative approach to the task is to ask students to have 'paper conversations'. Instead of using the frame to prompt spoken conversation, students pass a piece of paper back and forth and write their conversations. This allows you to provide individual or class correction on all conversations before students perform them.

▶ VIDEO SCRIPT

Café Hub 4.4 Would you?
M = Milly Z = Zac M VO = Milly voice-over
Z VO = Zac voice-over

M: Oh! It's you. Hey, Zac?
Z: Hi Milly. Sorry I scared you …
M: No, no. I'm sorry. I didn't hear you come in. I should probably turn the music down.
Z: Really? I like this music.
M: You do?
Z: Yeah, it's awesome.
Z VO: What do I say now?
M VO: What do I do now?
M: Hello Sir! Are you looking for anything in particular?
Z VO: Not really.
Z: Yeah … A T-shirt?
M: A T-shirt? Sure, yeah, we have plenty of T-shirts. There are some over here.
Z VO: Come on! Ask her out!
M VO: I really hope he asks me out!
Z VO: COME ON! DO IT, Zac!
M VO: He's not going to do it.
Z VO: DO IT! DO IT NOW!
M: And I think that's all the T-shirts we have.
Z: Hey, Milly, Would you …
M: I need to get that.
Z: Sure.
M: So, you were saying?
Z: Yes … Would you like to … hang out tonight? I'm going to a concert.
M: Oh … Um … Sorry, Zac, I'm afraid I can't …
Z: OK, I understand. Oh well, it was nice to see you again …
M: Wait! Hold on. I'm seeing my sister tonight but I'm free on the weekend. Would you like to do something then?
Z: Yeah! Awesome! Maybe we could go for a coffee, or eat something? Or go see an exhibition or go to the park? I mean, I, I …
M: I'd love to. Are you free on Saturday?
Z: Yeah. Sounds great!
M: Perfect. I'll probably finish at one thirty.
Z: Sure. Oh! Wait a minute. Ah, I just remembered that I'm fixing the computer at Sam's café on Saturday. How about Sunday instead?
M: Yeah, sure. Sounds great. What time?
Z: Umm, 12 o'clock?
M: OK great. 12 o'clock it is. Do you want to meet at the park?
Z: Sure.
M: OK. See ya on Sunday!
Z: OK, well, bye!
M: Bye!

4 Writing ● Write an invitation and reply

Ⓦ Informal emails

A Read Marta's message and answer the questions.

1 Why is Marta messaging her friends?
To invite them to her place.
2 What kind of evening is she planning on Saturday?
She's planning a hygge evening.
3 What should her guests bring?
Themselves, some warm socks and a wool sweater.

To: elviraandjan, ravi.gupta, stuart.jackson
Subject: Hygge Evening

Hi guys,
[1]How are things? Hope you're OK. [2]Life's good, but as usual, I'm looking forward to the weekend.
Actually, that is why I'm writing. [3]Are you doing anything on Saturday night? I'm planning a *hygge* evening around 7 pm at my place. [4]Can you make it?
I'm going to bake some cookies, light lots of candles and we could play a board game or watch a movie – or both! 😃
Anyway, [5]let me know whether you can come. All you need to bring is yourself, some warm socks and a wool sweater 😉
[6]It would be nice to see you.
Marta

B Look at Marta's message again. Match the underlined phrases (1–6) with the phrases with a similar meaning (a–f).

a Let me know if you're coming. 5
b Would you like to come? 4
c Everything is fine. 2
d Do you have any plans for …? 3
e How's life? 1
f I hope you can make it. 6

C Read two replies to Marta's message. Who is and is not coming to her *hygge* evening?
Elvira and Jan are not coming. Ravi is coming.

Dear Marta,
Nice to hear from you!
Thanks for inviting us on Saturday. We'd love to come, but we're going to Jan's parents' house for dinner, so I'm afraid we can't make it. I'm meeting them for the first time! I'm sure it will be fine, but I am a little nervous. Your *hygge* evening sounds much more relaxing!
Anyway, I'll let you know how it goes. Let's get together soon. I have so much to tell you.
See you soon,
Elvira

Hi Marta,
Long time no see. I hope you're well!
Thanks for the invitation for Saturday. A *hygge* evening sounds like just what I need, and I'd love to come. Who else will be there? Are Elvira and Jan coming?
Are you sure I can't bring any food? I could make some homemade snacks or something.
Let me know. It'll be gr8 to see you.
Love,
Ravi

D Read again and underline the phrases Marta's friends use to:

1 say thank you
2 say yes to the invitation
3 say no to the invitation
4 give a reason for saying no
5 mention the next time they'll meet

E Complete the box with words from the emails in Exercises A and C.

Informal emails

Start informal emails with a friendly greeting.
- *Dear Marta,*
- *Hi/Hello Marta,*
- *Hi* [1] guys (to a group; men, women or mixed)

Mention your last contact with other person.
- *Nice to hear from you.*
- *Long time no* [2] see (when you haven't seen the person for a long time)

Use emoticons and abbreviations, but don't overuse them.
- *It'll be* [3] gr8 *to see you.*

Don't use full forms. Use contractions.
- *I hope ~~you are~~ you're well.*
- *We ~~would~~* [4] 'd *love to come.*

Finish with a friendly goodbye.
- *Bye for now,*
- [5] See you *soon,*
- *Love,*

WRITING

A WRITE Work in pairs. You are organizing a party at your place. Write a message inviting another pair of students. Use Exercise E above to help you. Write 100–150 words.

B WRITE Swap messages with another pair of students and reply to their invitation. Use the Writing skills box to help you. Write 50–100 words. Include the following information:

- say thank you for the invitation
- say yes or no to the invitation (if no, give a reason)
- mention the next time you'll meet

Refer students to this email as a model for the first stage of the writing task.

Refer students to these emails as models for the second stage of the writing task.

WRITING

A Students read Marta's message and answer Questions 1–3. Check answers with the class.

B Students read Marta's message again and match the underlined phrases with the phrases (a–f) that have the same meaning. Check answers.

C Ask students to read the two replies to Marta's message. Elicit the answer from the class.

D Read Questions 1–5 as a class. Students read the two replies again and underline the phrases used for these functions.

E Focus students on the box and complete the expressions with words from the emails in Exercises A and C. Students compare their answers in pairs before checking with the whole class.

WRITING TASK

A In pairs, students decide on another pair to work with. They have to imagine they are organizing a party at home. Each pair writes an invitation to the other pair. Encourage students to use Marta's message to help them. Monitor and assist as required.

B Pairs swap invitations. Each pair writes a reply to the received invitation using the prompts. Remind students to use the phrases in the box. Take feedback from different pairs.

Unit 4 Review

VOCABULARY

A Write the missing words to complete Olivia's email.

To: Natalie
Subject: This weekend

Hi Natalie,

I have a great weekend planned for us. On Friday, I'll meet you at the station – then let's 1 ___go___ for sushi and go 2 ___for___ a drink in town.

On Saturday, we can go for a bike 3 ___ride___. I have two bikes, so let's take them and go 4 ___to___ the market. After we can hang 5 ___out___ in the park and talk or 6 ___play___ cards.

On Saturday evening, we're going 7 ___to___ my friend Alex's place. Then on Sunday, maybe we can 8 ___watch___ a movie before you go.

Can't wait!

Olivia xxx

B Choose the correct words to complete the sentences.

1 This robot can do a lot of different *active* / *activities*.
2 I think we should have a *discussion* / *discuss* about what will happen in the future.
3 What kind of *abilities* / *able* do you think machines will have in 50 years?
4 In my opinion, *happiness* / *happy* is one of the most important things in life.
5 There is the *possible* / *possibility* that people will stop using social media.

GRAMMAR

A Complete the sentences with *be going to* + infinitive or the present progressive form of the verbs in parentheses. Use contractions.

1 I ___'m not going to forget___ (*not forget*) my friend's birthday again this year.
2 We ___'re meeting___ (*meet*) the others tonight on the corner by the coffee shop.
3 Mia ___'s taking___ (*take*) her friend out for dinner tomorrow.
4 I think I ___'m going to lie down___ (*lie down*) for a while before we go out.
5 Go to bed early because we ___'re getting up___ (*get up*) at 6 am to drive to the airport.

B Find and correct the mistake in each sentence.

1 It will be easier to meet people in the future probably because of technology.
It will probably be easier to meet people in the future because of technology.
2 People might going on virtual dates online in the future.
People might go on virtual dates online in the future.
3 A virtual date probably won't very romantic.
A virtual date probably won't be very romantic.
4 We might to use technology to help us choose the perfect partner.
We might use technology to help us choose the perfect partner.
5 The way people meet and fall in love not may change very much.
The way people meet and fall in love may not change very much.

C Complete the questions and answers with the words in the box. You need to use some of the words more than once.

did	do	don't	it's	make
spend	went	what	which	

1 '___Which___ country is *hygge* from, Denmark or Sweden?' '___It's___ from Denmark.'
2 'Who ___do___ you spend time with?' 'I ___spend___ a lot of time with my best friend.'
3 '___What___ is your favorite book?' '___It's___ *The Lord of the Rings*.'
4 'Which board games ___do___ you play?' 'I ___don't___ play board games.'
5 'How ___did___ you celebrate your last birthday?' 'I ___went___ out for dinner.'

FUNCTIONAL LANGUAGE

Look at the beginning and end of the telephone conversation. Put the rest of the conversation in the correct order.

John: Dean, it's your brother. You OK?
Dean: Yep, fine thanks, and you?
5 **John:** That's great. There's just one thing … Jenny and I are going out.
2 **Dean:** Not really. No plans. Why?
9 **John:** Well, yes.
7 **John:** Well, we have an invitation to a new restaurant and …
8 **Dean:** And, you need a babysitter!
1 **John:** I'm great, thanks. Listen, are you doing anything this evening?
3 **John:** Do you want to come over? Jenny has made a curry dish and little Sam says he misses his Uncle Dean.
4 **Dean:** A curry dish and my favorite nephew? I'd love to!
6 **Dean:** What?
Dean: Fine, fine. What time?
John: You are the best. How about seven o'clock?

Electrical lineman Chen Qi cleans snow from a high-voltage transmission tower, Baima Mountain, Wolong County, China.

Work (n) activity that involves physical or mental effort. Synonym: effort (n).

Edison is suggesting that hard work is necessary if you want to achieve anything in life. It improves your chances to succeed, regardless of whether you are talented or not.

Thomas Alva Edison (February 11, 1847–October 18, 1931) was an American inventor and businessperson. He was one of the first inventors to apply the principles of mass production and large-scale teamwork to the process of invention.

OBJECTIVES

- talk about the pros and cons of different jobs and say how they help society
- decide on the rules for a workplace or classroom
- answer questions on topics in which you are an expert
- give information about your work experience in a job interview
- write a cover email

Work with a partner. Discuss the questions.

1 What do you like about your job or the subjects you study?
2 Read the quote. What do you think Edison meant? Do you agree with him?
3 Look at the picture. Would you like to have this man's job? Why/Why not?

WORK 41

OBJECTIVES

Read the unit objectives to the class.

UNIT OPENER QUESTIONS

Encourage students to look at the quote and take one or two suggestions from the class about what they think it means.

Ask students to look at the picture on the page and encourage them to share their ideas. Ask prompt questions such as 'Where's this man working? What's the season? In what way does the photo relate to the quote?' If students share any good ideas or useful language, write these on the board.

Ask students to look at the questions at the bottom of the page. Model one possible answer, explaining why you like your job. Students discuss the questions in pairs or in a small group.

Monitor and assist as necessary. When students have finished the activity, ask one or two pairs to share their ideas with the class. Encourage students to listen to one another and respond with their own ideas and opinions.

WORKSHEETS

Lesson 5.1 Work

Grammar: *can, could, be able to* (W25)

Vocabulary: Work collocations (W26)

Lesson 5.2 Flip-flop entrepreneurs

Grammar: Obligation, necessity and permission: *must, have to* and *can* (W27)

Vocabulary: Adjectives for appearance (W28)

Lesson 5.3 Don't call us

Grammar: Present perfect with *for* and *since* (W29)

Vocabulary: *work* + preposition (W30)

5.1 Work

Talk about the pros and cons of different jobs and say how they help society

G *can, could, be able to* V work collocations P /w/ and /v/

READING

A Match the definitions (1–4) with the words in the box.

pay raise salary self-employed well-paid

1 working for yourself self-employed
2 a fixed amount of money that you earn each month or year from your job salary
3 paid a lot of money well-paid
4 an increase in the amount of money you are paid to do your job pay raise

B SPEAK Work in pairs. What are four things, apart from money, that can make people happy at work?

C SCAN Read *What really makes us happy in our jobs?* quickly. Which of your ideas from Exercise B can you find?

D READ FOR DETAIL Read again. Who says these things make them happy in their job, Helen (H), Lena (L), Bret (B) or Ken (K)?

1 they have flexible vacations and working hours K
2 they learn and use special skills H
3 their employer gives them clear goals L
4 they are independent K
5 they have a relaxed manager B
6 they have time for the family L

E SPEAK Work in pairs. Which of the four jobs in the article would you rather have? Why?

What really makes us ***happy in our jobs?***

In a recent survey about jobs and work, 75 percent of children under ten said 'yes' to the question 'Can money buy happiness?' But is being **well-paid** really so important? Can you still be happy at work if you earn a **low hourly wage**? We asked four working adults what, apart from money, they like about their jobs.

Helen Police Officer

I don't work regular office hours – I do shifts. This means I often work in the evenings and sometimes do the night shift. In my last job I could choose when I wanted to work and I found that I liked working in the evenings. I also like that I am able to use all the different skills I learned when I was training to be a police officer.

Bret Waiter

My job is poorly paid, but I only work weekends, so I can study during the week. I work in a big restaurant. When there are no problems, the boss is usually very easygoing.

Lena Sales Manager

I earn an average salary. However, if I make a lot of sales, I get a bonus and I find that motivating. I also enjoy having clear goals, even when I have to work long hours to achieve them. I recently got a promotion which meant a lot of extra work, but I don't mind. I got a small pay raise and as a manager I was able to take an extra afternoon off each week to spend with my kids.

Ken Architect

The best part of my job is being my own boss. Because I'm self-employed, I can choose when I work and can take long vacations when I want to. The only bad part is I don't get a company car!

Glossary

bonus (n) extra money you are paid in addition to your usual salary, usually because you have done well, for example, *a year-end bonus*

promotion (n) a move to a higher level in your job, usually because you have done well

LEAD-IN

Arrange students in four groups. Prepare four short descriptions: (e.g. *'Max is 28 and has a degree in business but no experience. He is hard working and organized.' 'Susan is 21 and has completed an Administrative Assistant program. She has worked as a receptionist in a big company for a year and has a good command of English. She's a people person and very patient.' 'Alan is 35. He worked in a steel factory for 15 years, but it closed and laid off all workers. He has a license and can drive all kinds of vehicles. He is hard working, able to work well with others and puts pride in his work.' 'Allison is 30 and has a professional certification in catering. She has worked as an assistant cook in a five-star hotel. She is self-motivated and able to work effectively in a busy environment.'*). Have students create a business that they 'run'. They should go over the résumés of the four job candidates and discuss who they would hire for their business and why.

READING

A Focus students on the word box and the activity. Students work alone matching the words in the vocabulary box with the definitions (1–4). Allow them to compare their answers with a partner before checking them with the class.

B In pairs, students discuss the question and list four things, apart from money, that make people happy at work. Encourage students to use their own work experience to help them. Monitor and assist when necessary.

C Students scan the article trying to find any of the ideas on their list. Allow them a limited time to do the task (e.g. one minute) to make sure students don't read the article in detail. Take feedback from the class about which of their ideas were mentioned.

D Students read the article again, in detail. Then, in pairs, they decide which person said which sentence. Remind students that they may not find the exact phrase in the text, they should look for synonyms. With a weaker group, tell them to underline the key words in each.

Helen – likes that she doesn't know what will happen on each shift and can use the different skills she learned during training.
Lena – likes the possibility of getting a bonus, likes clear goals, likes that she can take an extra day off sometimes.
Bret – likes his boss and the hours he works.
Ken – likes that he is his own boss, likes that he can decide when to work and when to take vacations.

E In pairs, students take turns discussing which of the jobs from the article they would rather do. Remind students to give reasons for their answers. Take feedback from one or two pairs and encourage students to respond to each other's ideas.

METHODOLOGY HUB by Jim Scrivener

Dealing with lexis during reading or listening work

While students are mainly working on reading or listening skills, you are less likely to spend time on lexis, as this might clash with the reading, listening or other goals. During such stages, you are likely only to:

- deal with an item when a student specifically asks about it;
- give brief, to-the-point explanations or translations, rather than detailed presentations;
- offer help quietly to the one or two students who ask, rather than to the whole class;
- sometimes refuse help and tell students to do their best without knowing some items.

After the first phase of listening or reading work

Once the learners have become comfortable with the text, you can focus attention on lexical items in the text and how they are used. Here are some things that you could ask:

- Can you guess the meaning of this word from the meaning of the text around it?
- Find some words in the text that mean …
- Find some words in the text connected with the subject of …
- In line X, what does … mean?
- Find words and sort them into three separate groups under these headings: …
- Find words in the text that match this list of synonyms.
- Can you remember any other phrases you know with this word in them?
- What's the opposite of this word?

TEACHING IDEA by David Seymour and Maria Popova

Vocabulary: Work places

Use this activity to practice workplace vocabulary.

Work in pairs. Imagine you have a job in one of these places: a hospital, Disneyland, an airport, an office, a hotel, an EFL school. Your partner will ask you yes/no questions to discover your job, e.g. A – *I work in a hospital.* B – *Do you operate on people?* A – *No. I'm not a surgeon.* B – *Do you clean the floors?* A – *No. I'm not a janitor.*

Vocabulary: What's my job?

Use this activity to practice general work vocabulary.

Work in two teams. Listen to the sentences and yell out the job. The first team to say the job each time wins a point. (Here are four ideas to start with.)

Take two of these three times a day. *(doctor)* The brakes need replacing. *(mechanic)* Are you ready to order? *(waiter)* Now over to Jo in the weather center. *(newscaster)*

Grammar: Something special

- What things can Superman do? Do you know anybody with a lot of abilities? Who is it and what can he/she do?

  In groups of three or four, find out what special abilities you have among you. Here are some topics to think about. Which group has the most special abilities?

cooking, sports, arts and crafts, science, professional skills, music

- In pairs, make a list of special abilities that animals have, e.g. *Bats can find things by echo location.*

  Discuss how your life would change if you could do the same things.

5.1 Work

GRAMMAR

A Students read the example sentences, then complete the grammar box. Give them time to check in pairs, before giving feedback as a class.

B Direct students to the **Grammar Hub** (see below). Use the **Grammar Worksheet** on W25 for extra practice.

C Students discuss the questions in pairs. Monitor and assist as required. Give feedback as a class, encouraging discussion.

VOCABULARY

A Students complete the sentences with the correct form of the verbs in the box. Give them time to check their answers in pairs, before giving feedback as a class. Use the **Vocabulary Worksheet** on W26 for extra practice.

B Students discuss the question in pairs. Monitor and assist as required.

PRONUNCIATION

5.1 **A** Play the audio. Students listen to the difference in pronunciation between /w/ and /v/. Play the audio again and ask students to listen and repeat.

5.2 **B** Students listen and write the words in the correct column.

5.2 **C** Students listen to check their answers. Play the audio again. Students listen and repeat.

D In pairs, students make their list before feedback.

SPEAKING

A Arrange students in three groups (A, B, C) and direct them to the **Communication Hub**. Students read the questions from Exercise A. Model the example and provide an answer to another question if required. Each group reads their list of jobs and discusses each by answering Questions 1–4.

B Rearrange students into new groups of three. Students report back on the jobs they discussed to their new groups, including the category they chose for them in Question 4.

GRAMMAR HUB

5.1 *can, could, be able to*

- We use *can* to talk about general possibility and ability in the present.

  I can choose when I work.
  They can't come to the meeting.
  Can I speak to you for a minute? Yes, you can. / No, you can't.

- We use *could* to talk about general possibility and ability in the past.

  She could work shifts when she was younger.
  They couldn't come to the meeting last Saturday.
  Could you take long vacations in your last job? Yes, I could. / No, I couldn't.

- We use *be able to* to talk about possibility and ability in the present, usually at a particular time or for a particular reason.

  I'm able to work with different people.
  He isn't able to work late tonight.
  Are they able to work nights? Yes, they are. / No, they aren't.

- We use *be able to* directly after another verb because *can* has no *-ing* or *to* + base form.

  I like being able to work nights. NOT *~~I like can work nights.~~*

- We use *was/were able to* to talk about possibility and ability in the past, usually at a particular time or for a particular reason.

  She was able to find a new job.
  They weren't able to get the bus to work.
  Was he able to find the office? Yes, he was. / No, he wasn't.

5.1 *can, could, be able to*

A Complete the sentences with the words in the box.

able can (x2) can't could to were

1 As a manager, you ___can___ have a company car!
2 I ___can't___ do this. Can you help me?
3 She's not ___able___ to work on Saturday.
4 ___Can___ you work the night shift tomorrow?
5 We ___were___ able to get a lot of work done yesterday.
6 At my last job, I ___could___ start late on Fridays.
7 Brenda's self-employed so she's able ___to___ choose when she works.

B Put the words in order to make sentences.

1 hate / not / make / decisions / I / being / to / able
I hate not being able to make decisions.
2 wants / able / she / buy / to / house / be / to / a
She wants to be able to buy a house.
3 last / in / finish / job / my / could / at / four / I
At my last job I could finish at four.
4 wants / able / to / she / take / be / long / vacation / a / to
She wants to be able to take a long vacation.
5 training / he / do / the / can't / because / involves / special / job / it
He can't do the job because it involves special training.
6 they / being / like / from / work / able / home / to
They like being able to work from home.

➤ Go back to page 43.

GRAMMAR

can, could, be able to

A WORK IT OUT Look at the sentences from *What really makes us happy in our jobs?* Then complete the rules with *can*, *could* or *be able to*.

I only work weekends, so I can study during the week.

I am able to use all the different skills I learned when I was training.

In my last job I could choose when I wanted to work.

I was able to take an extra afternoon off each week.

can, could and be able to

1. We use *can* and _be able to_ to talk about possibility and ability in the present.
2. We use _could_ and *was / were able to* to talk about possibility and ability in the past.
3. We usually use _be able to_ or *was / were able to* for possibilities and abilities at a particular time or for a particular reason.
4. We use _be able to_ immediately before the main verb because *can* has no *-ing* form or *to* + base form.

B Go to the **Grammar Hub** on **page 130.**

C SPEAK Work in pairs. Discuss the questions.

1. What are some of your abilities?
2. What were some of your abilities as a child?

VOCABULARY

Work collocations

A Complete the questions with the correct form of the verbs in the box. Sometimes more than one answer is possible. You need to use some verbs more than once.

be earn get take work

1. Do you or anyone you know _work_ shifts? How often do they do a night shift?
2. Do you know anyone who _earns/gets_ a very high salary? What do they do?
3. Do you think people should _get_ an automatic pay raise every year they stay in the same job?
4. Who _works_ the longest hours out of all the people you know? What do they do?
5. When was the last time you _took_ a day off? What did you do?
6. Would you prefer to _get_ a company car or more money?
7. Do people who _are_ unemployed get money from the government in your country?
8. Would you be motivated by a job where you earn an average salary, but have the chance to _get/earn_ a bonus? Why/Why not?

B SPEAK Work in pairs. Would you like to be your own boss? Why/Why not? Tell your partner.

PRONUNCIATION

/w/ and /v/

5.1 **A** Listen to the sounds. Are they the same or different? Listen and repeat. different

1 /w/ work 2 /v/ very

5.2 **B** Listen and write the words in the correct place.

/w/	/v/	
wage	*involve*	achieve
weekend	visa	
with	love	
	have	

5.3 **C** Listen and check your answers. Then listen and repeat.

D SPEAK Work in pairs. Can you think of more words with the sounds /w/ and /v/? Make a list.

SPEAKING

A Work in groups. Go to the **Communication Hub** on **page 157** and look at your group's list of jobs. Discuss the questions for each job.

1. Who do you know that does these jobs? How do they feel about them?
   My brother is a social worker. He works with people that have serious problems, but he still enjoys it.
2. Is each job paid a high, medium or low wage or salary?
3. What are the best and worst parts of each job?
4. Give each job a category which describes how it helps society, for example, *important for entertainment, health, education.*

B Work in new groups. Tell the group about the jobs you discussed and the categories you chose in Exercise A. Discuss which categories of jobs are most valuable to society and why.

Talk about the pros and cons of different jobs and say how they help society

5.2 Flip-flop entrepreneurs

Decide on the rules for a workplace or classroom

G obligation, necessity and permission: *must, have to* and *can* **P** *can / can't* and *must / must not* **V** adjectives for appearance

READING

A SPEAK Work in pairs. How important to you are the things on the list when you are buying new clothes? Decide whether they are very important (1), fairly important (2) or less important (3). Compare your ideas.

The product …

a is available in different colors and designs. ___

b is fashionable. ___

c is popular with celebrities. ___

The company …

a pays its staff fair wages. ___

b gives money to charity. ___

c does charity work. ___

B SCAN Read *How do you build a children's home out of flip-flops?* Which things in Exercise A are mentioned?

is fashionable, is popular with celebrities, gives money to charity, does charity work

C READ FOR DETAIL Read again and answer the questions.

1 What was unusual about Rob and Paul's education? Their parents took them out of school and away to India to travel and do charity work.

2 How did the brothers become orphans? Their parents died in the Asian tsunami.

3 Why did the brothers start Gandys? In memory of their parents and to help other orphans

4 Which six adjectives are used to describe the company's flip-flops? attractive, casual, comfortable, stylish, fashionable, colorful

5 What was unusual about the brothers' visit to Buckingham Palace? They wore flip-flops.

D SPEAK Work in groups. Discuss the questions.

1 Who do the biggest charities help in your country? What do they do to help?

2 Do you give money to charity? Why/Why not?

How do you build a children's home out of flip-flops?

British brothers Rob and Paul Forkan have experienced tragedy and success in their short and unusual lives. When they were still children, their parents took them out of school in the UK and moved the family to India to travel and do charity work. The experience taught them about life in other places and made them confident and independent.

Tragedy struck in 2004 when the Asian tsunami hit the coast of Sri Lanka, where the Forkans were staying. The giant wave killed their parents, but Rob (17), Paul (15) and their younger brother and sister survived. The children, now orphans, managed to hitchhike across Sri Lanka to the airport. From there, they flew back to Britain, where friends and family were waiting.

Six years later and now adults, the brothers decided to do something in memory of their parents. Their idea was simple. Make and sell attractive casual footwear and use the profits to help other orphans. Their company *Gandys* and their charity *Orphans for Orphans* were born.

After a lot of hard work and with the support of celebrity customers such as Richard Branson and Jamie Oliver, the comfortable rubber flip-flops became a hit. Customers love *Gandys*' stylish and fashionable designs and that the brothers give ten percent of the profits to their charity. In 2014, three years after *Gandys* began, *Orphans for Orphans* opened its first children's home in Sri Lanka.

Gandys' head office now employs a large team and is possibly the only office in London where you can wear flip-flops to work! Rob and Paul's charity work has even gotten them an invitation to meet British princes William and Harry. Normally of course, you must wear dress clothes at Buckingham Palace, but the brothers ignored the dress code and looked cool in their colorful flip-flops!

Rob and Paul's story shows that positive can follow negative and that you don't have to wear a business suit to be successful in business!

Glossary

hitchhike (v) to have people give you a ride in their car, usually by standing on the side of the road and holding out your thumb or a sign

in memory of someone (phrase) in honor of someone who has died, so that people will remember them

tragedy (n) a very sad event that causes people to suffer or die

5.2 Flip-flop entrepreneurs

LEAD-IN

Explain that you are going to discuss the rules for class discussion. Give some examples like *you must not interrupt others* or *you have to listen to the speaker.* Ask students to brainstorm the rules in groups. Collect them and compile them, eliminating redundancies. Write them up on the board and tell students that these will be the rules for the term.

READING

A Read the activity as a class. You may need to pre-teach *charity* and *fair wages*, and discuss the difference between *giving to charity* and *working with a charity* (*simply giving versus being involved in organizing projects*). Students give a score to the factors that influence their buying decisions on their own. Then, they discuss their scores in pairs. Take feedback from one or two pairs and encourage students to respond to each other's ideas.

B Focus students on the activity and the glossary. Remind them they will find in it words that may help them understand the text. If necessary, check that students know the meaning of *entrepreneur*. Students scan the article to find the ideas mentioned in Exercise A. Set a time limit which only allows time to scan, not read, the article. Take feedback from the class about which ideas were mentioned.

C Students read the article again and answer Questions 1–5. Take feedback from the class and encourage students to respond to each other's ideas.

D In groups, students think of one or two big charities in their country and discuss who they help and how. Take feedback from one or two groups and encourage students to respond to each other's ideas.

TEACHING IDEA by David Seymour and Maria Popova

Extension activity: Definitions

Arrange the class into four groups and give each group one of the following words from the reading passage:

a fair wage.

dress code.

orphan.

tsunami.

Students should work together to write three definitions for their word, one correct and two incorrect. The groups should then read aloud their word and three definitions to the class, while the other groups decide which is the correct definition.

TEACHING IDEA by David Seymour and Maria Popova

Extension activity: Rules for success

Arrange students in pairs. Ask each pair to choose one of the following topics and write six rules for success:

- How to be a good boss.
- How to do well at college.
- How to get a promotion.
- How to sell something to someone.
- How to work on a team.

Students should try to use all of the modal verbs from this lesson.

GRAMMAR HUB

5.2 Obligation, necessity and permission: *must*, *have to* and *can*

	Positive	Negative
I/you/he/she/it/we/they	**You can wear** casual clothes in the office. **You must get** to work before 9 am.	**You can't wear** jewelry. **You must not be** late.
I/you/we/they	**You have to get** to work before 9 am.	**They don't have to use** English at work.
he/she/it	**He has to get** to work before 9 am.	**She doesn't have to work** on Sundays.

Question	Positive short answer	Negative short answer
Can she wear earrings?	Yes, **she can**.	No, **she can't**.
Do we have to wear a tie?	Yes, **you do**.	No, **you don't**.
Does he have to have special training?	Yes, **he does**.	No, **he doesn't**.

- We use *can* for something that is allowed.
- We use *can't* for something that is not allowed.
- We use *must* and *have to* for something that is necessary or a rule.

Be careful!

- *Must not* has a different meaning to *don't have to*.

  must not = not allowed

  *You **must not** wear sportswear in the office.*

  must not = modal of deduction (in American English but NOT in British English)

  *They **must not** be at home. The car is gone.*

  don't have to = not necessary (but possible)

  *You **don't have to** wear dress clothes to work, but you can if you want.*
- In questions, we usually use *have to* and not *must*.

  Do you have to wear boots? NOT ~~*Must you wear boots?*~~

GRAMMAR

A Ask students to reread the last two paragraphs of *How do you build a children's home out of flip-flops?* and complete Sentences 1–3.

B Focus students on the grammar box. They work on their own matching the modal verbs with their definitions. Allow time for students to compare their answers with a partner before checking with the whole class.

C Students read through the grammar box and choose the correct word to complete the rule.

D Direct students to the **Grammar Hub** (see TB44 and below). Use the **Grammar Worksheet** on W27 for extra practice.

PRONUNCIATION

5.4 **A** Play the audio. Students listen to the difference in pronunciation between *can* and *can't* and *must* and *must not*.

5.5 **B** Ask students to read the pairs of sentences. Play the audio. Students apply check marks to the sentence that they hear. Play the audio again for them to check their answers in pairs before checking with the whole class.

VOCABULARY

A Put students in pairs. Give them a minute to make a list of adjectives that describe what people look like. When the time is finished, ask the pair with the longest list to read aloud their ideas. The rest of the class shares any ideas that weren't mentioned.

B Students work alone matching the adjectives to their definitions. They compare their answers with a partner. Check answers with the whole class. Use the **Vocabulary Worksheet** on W28 for extra practice of *Adjectives for appearance*.

C Students complete the sentences, before discussing their ideas with a partner. Monitor and assist as necessary.

SPEAKING

A Students discuss the questions in groups. Monitor and assist as required.

B In groups, students write ten rules for either the perfect workplace or classroom (ideally on a large piece of paper). Monitor and encourage students to use the modal verbs from the grammar section.

C Hang each set of rules on the wall and ask groups to take turns presenting their ideas. Encourage students to explain their answers and allow time for questions at the end of each presentation.

GRAMMAR HUB

5.2 Obligation, necessity and permission: *must*, *have to* and *can*

A Choose the correct option.

1 You *can't* / *can* do this job unless you have training. (can't)
2 You *must not* / *don't have to* do this work today. Next week's fine. (don't have to)
3 We *can* / *must* wear casual clothes on a Monday. It's our choice. (can)
4 You *can* / *have to* believe in your idea for it to be a success. (have to)
5 Simon *must not* / *doesn't have to* be rude to the manager. He'll lose his job! (must not)
6 I *can* / *don't have to* take the bus. It's easy to walk there. (don't have to)
7 Everyone *can* / *must* start work at 9. It's a rule. (must)

B Complete the text messages with the words in the box.

can can't don't have to has to have to

Hannah: (**1**) ___Can___ you meet me and Lily for coffee after work – at five thirty?

Fatima: No, I (**2**) ___can't___ . We (**3**) ___have to___ work late today, remember?

Hannah: Oh, yeah. Well, I (**4**) ___don't have to___ work late because I did all my work this morning. Have you asked Lily?

Fatima: She (**5**) ___has to___ stay too. She told me this morning.

Hannah: OK. Another time then.

➤ Go back to page 45.

GRAMMAR

Obligation, necessity and permission: *must*, *have to* and *can*

A WORK IT OUT Look at the last two paragraphs of *How do you build a children's home out of flip-flops?* and complete the sentences.

1 You ___can___ wear flip-flops to work.

2 You ___don't have to___ wear a business suit to be successful in business.

3 You ___must___ wear dress clothes at Buckingham Palace.

B Match the modal verbs (1–4) with the meanings (a–d).

Obligation, necessity and permission: *must*, *have to* and *can*

1 *don't have to*
2 *must / have to*
3 *can*
4 *can't / must not*

a This is necessary or is a rule.
b This is not necessary but allowed.
c This is allowed but not necessary.
d This is not allowed.

C Choose the correct word to complete the rule.

Obligation, necessity and permission: *must*, *have to* and *can*

Modal verbs, such as *have to*, *can* and *must* are followed by the ***base form*** / ***simple present*** form of a verb.

D Go to the **Grammar Hub** on **page 130**.

PRONUNCIATION

can / *can't* and *must* / *must not*

5.4 **A** Listen to the pairs of sentences. Can you hear the differences?

1 a You can wear casual clothes.
  b You can't wear casual clothes.
2 a Staff must not wear sportswear.
  b Staff must wear sportswear.

5.5 **B** Listen and check (✓) the sentence you hear.

1 a You must wear large earrings. ☐
  b You must not wear large earrings. ☑
2 a You can wear a baseball cap. ☑
  b You can't wear a baseball cap. ☐
3 a You must leave your coat downstairs. ☑
  b You must not leave your coat downstairs. ☐
4 a You can hang your coat on your chair. ☐
  b You can't hang your coat on your chair. ☑

VOCABULARY

Adjectives for appearance

A SPEAK Work in pairs. Make a list of adjectives to describe appearance. You have one minute.

cool, casual …

B Match the adjectives (1–7) with the definitions (a–g).

1 attractive
2 casual
3 colorful
4 cool
5 fashionable
6 well-dressed
7 stylish

a show good judgement about how to dress well
b relaxed and comfortable
c pleasant to look at
d impressive and modern
e clean and neat
f popular at a particular time
g has bright or many different colors

C Choose the words that you agree with most. Then work in pairs and explain why.

1 I ***do*** / ***don't*** think it's important to wear dress clothes to work.
2 I think that flip-flops are ***too casual*** / ***perfect*** for wearing around town.
3 I prefer clothes with ***colorful*** / ***cool and simple*** designs.
4 I think it ***is*** / ***isn't*** important to wear fashionable clothes.
5 You ***can*** / ***can't*** be stylish without wearing expensive clothes.
6 People ***spend too much*** / ***don't spend enough*** time and money trying to look attractive.

SPEAKING

A Work in groups. Think about the place where you work or study. Answer the questions.

1 What are the most important rules?
2 What annoying or unnecessary rules are there?
3 What rules would you add to make it a better place to work or study?

B Work in groups. Write ten rules for the perfect workplace or classroom. Think about what is/isn't allowed and what is/isn't necessary. Use these ideas:

Workplace: rules for workers, managers and directors; working hours; pay; dress code, etc.

Classroom: rules for students and teachers; during classes; homework; tests and exams, etc.

C Look at the rules written by other groups. Which are the most useful? Why? Are there any you do not agree with? Why?

Decide on the rules for a workplace or classroom

5.3 Don't call us

Answer questions on topics in which you are an expert

G present perfect with *for* and *since* | P *has, have, for, since* | V *work* + preposition | S listening for inference

LISTENING

A Work in groups. Complete the tips for job interviews with *do* or *don't*.

1 __Don't__ eat smelly food or smoke before the interview.

2 __Do__ arrive ten minutes before your appointment.

3 __Do__ listen carefully to introductions and try to remember names.

4 __Don't__ answer your phone or check messages during the interview.

5 __Don't__ be negative about yourself or your last job.

6 __Do__ ask one or two questions at the end.

5.6 **B LISTEN FOR GIST** Barry has a job interview with Gemma. Listen and choose the summary (1–3) that best describes the interview.

1 The interview goes well. Gemma and Barry have a good conversation. Barry will probably get the job.

2 The interview goes fairly well. Barry has a lot of experience working on a team. Barry might get the job.

3 The interview does not go well. Barry lies. Gemma is annoyed. Barry will definitely not get the job.

Glossary

call center (n) a place where a large number of people are employed to deal with customers by telephone, either in order to sell something or to answer questions

résumé (n) a document giving details of your certifications and the jobs you have had in the past that you send to someone when you are applying for a job

teamwork (n) work that you do together with other people

telemarketing (n) the activity or job of using the telephone to sell goods or services

5.6 **C** Test your memory! Check (✓) the things Barry has done and put an ✗ on the things he has not. Listen and check.

1 worked in a call center ✓

2 worked on a team ✗

3 worked for a telemarketing company ✓

4 been skydiving ✗

5 read French poetry ✗

5.7 **D** Listen to three extracts from the interview. Then answer the questions about each extract. Use the information in the box to help you.

Listening for inference

When you listen to a foreign language, use vocabulary and context clues and your wider knowledge to figure out the meaning of what you hear.

Think about the speaker's tone and attitude, as well as what they don't say.

Extract one

1 Does Barry check whether he needs to tell the truth? *(yes) / no*

2 Does he give a real example? *yes / (no)*

3 Do you think he has ever worked as part of a team? *yes / (no)*

Extract two

4 Is Barry interested in skydiving? *(yes) / no*

5 Does he think it's exciting? *(yes) / no*

6 Do you think he has ever actually done it? *yes / (no)*

Extract three

7 Does Barry remember what he wrote on his résumé? *yes / (no)*

8 Does he tell the truth about what he wrote on his résumé? *yes / (no)*

9 Do you think he enjoys French poetry? *yes / (no)*

E SPEAK Work in groups. Have you ever had an interview for a job, course or scholarship? Tell your group about it.

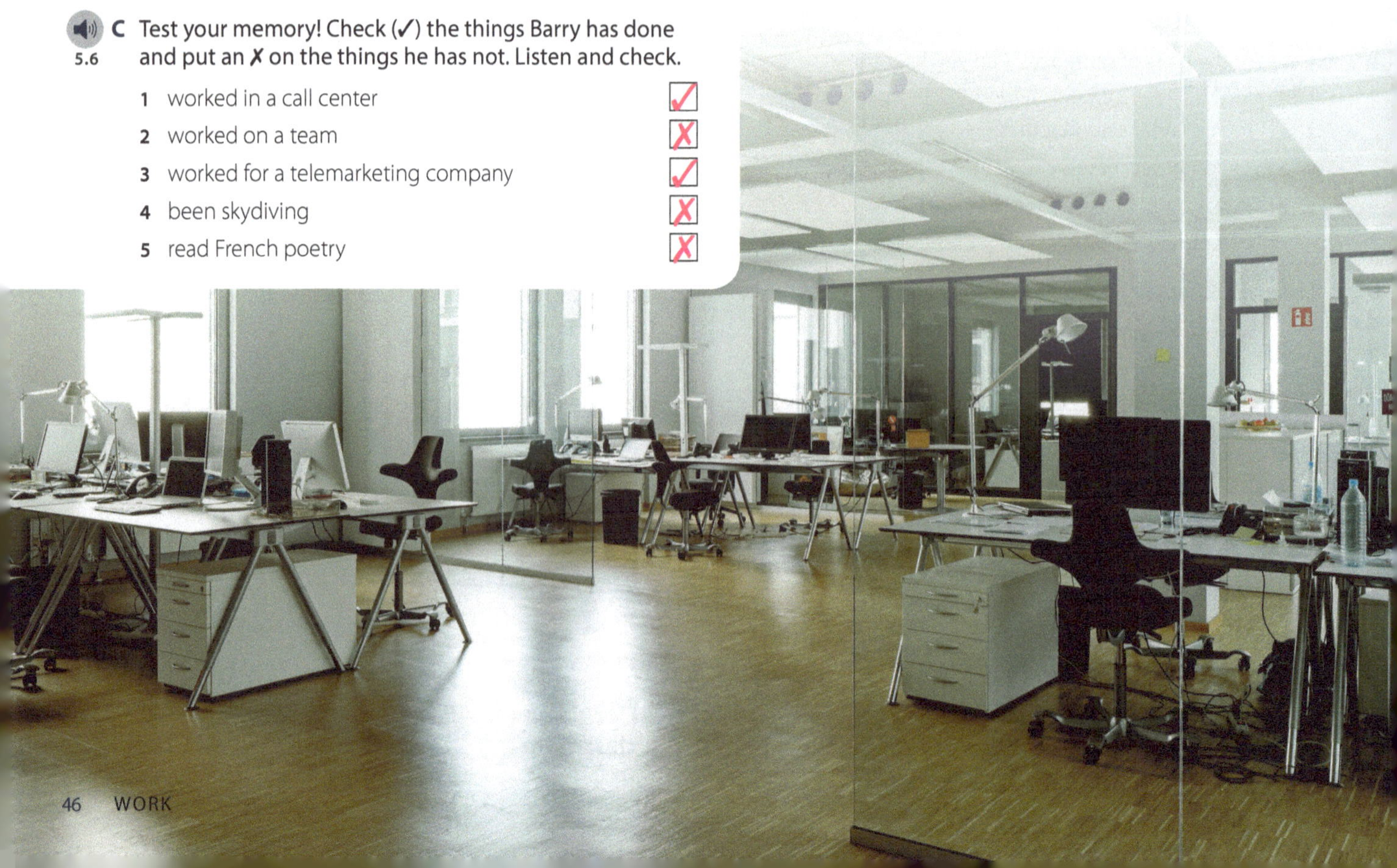

5.3 Don't call us

LEAD-IN

Tell students: *Imagine you can change three things about either your school or workplace. What would you change and why?* Then, give students time to write down their ideas. Monitor and assist as required. Next, put students into groups to discuss their ideas. Monitor and encourage discussion. Finally, ask groups to report back and encourage further discussion as appropriate.

LISTENING

A In small groups, students read and complete the tips with *do* or *don't*. Take feedback from one or two groups and encourage students to respond to each other's ideas.

5.6 **B** Focus students on the glossary. Remind them it may help them to understand the audio. Play the audio. Students choose the sentence that best summarizes the interview. With a weaker group, you may have to play the audio again for students to check their answers.

5.6 **C** Students read through Sentences 1–5 and put a check (√) or an ✗ according to whether they think that Barry has or hasn't done those things. Play the audio again for students to check their answers.

5.7 **D** Read the skills box as a class. Highlight that speakers don't always say what they mean. Instead, we have to guess meaning from context. Play the audio. Students complete the extracts, then answer the questions. Give them time to discuss their ideas in pairs, before giving feedback as a class. This is a difficult exercise, so don't be afraid to play the audio multiple times.

E In groups, students tell each other about the last interview they had. Monitor and assist as required. Take feedback from each group about one of the interview stories they heard.

AUDIO SCRIPT

5.6

Listening, Exercise B
G = Gemma B = Barry

G: Good morning. You must be Barry. I'm Gemma.
B: Oh mmmm hmmfff … sorry. I'm just finishing my sandwich!
G: That's OK … Egg sandwich, is it?
B: Uh … Yes, egg. Sorry. My favorite. Nice to meet you, Emma.
G: It's Gemma.
B: Excuse me?
G: It's Gemma, not Emma.
B: Sorry! What a terrible start.
G: Please don't worry, Barry. Gemma. Lockwood. Base One IT Services. I work in Human Resources. Sorry we're a little delayed today. Have you been here long?
B: Actually, I've been here since 9 am.
G: You've been here for … three hours?
B: Yes, well, I didn't want to be late. That's why I was hungry.
G: OK … well … uh … good! Come in and have a seat.
B: Thanks.
G: So, Barry, we are looking for people to work at our head office on the customer service team. First, could you tell me a little about yourself?
B: Ha ha. OK. Well, I'm Barry. I'm uh … 23 years old. Single, male, blond hair. Rather nervous in interviews … ha. I uh … I'm one meter tall, I have a cat named Yoda and I love … uh … egg sandwiches, ha ha, and … um … computers and … wait, did I just say one meter tall? Ha ha sorry. Uh … I'm one meter 70 centimeters tall, and I …
G: Uh … Barry, maybe we could focus on your work
Ex C Q3 experience. You work for a telemarketing company at the moment, is that right? How long have you worked there?
B: Uh, well, I left my old job in June … and now it's …
Ex C Q1 well, I … I've worked at the call center for six weeks. Have you read my résumé? I did send one. I mean, I wrote everything there, so …
G: Uh … yes, but … tell me more. For example, why do you want to change jobs and work for Base One?
B: Oh, well, that's easy; I hate my job at the call center! I sit on the phone all day long asking people questions and nobody wants to talk to me. People get really angry and sometimes, well, they hang up the phone.
G: I … see. Uh … So, what do you know about Base One?
B: About what? OH! Yes … well … I'm … I think it's … could you repeat the question, please?
G: Uh … well … OK. What do you know about Base One IT Services?
B: Um, well Base One is a … great IT company, with … great services … and the office here is … um … really cool. And, you seem very nice, and I …
G: Barry, ahem! Teamwork is very important for us here at Base One. Can you tell me about a time
Ex C Q2; when you worked as part of a team?
B: Um, you mean a real example?
Ex D Q1, Q3 **G:** Uh, yes.
B: Let me think … uhh, I … um, actually … uhh …
G: Um … OK. It says on your résumé that you enjoy skydiving. Wow! How long have you been interested in that?
B: Oh, well. I've liked skydiving since I was a teenager.
Ex C Q4; It just looks so exciting! I've always wanted to try it.
G: So you haven't actually tried skydiving?
Ex D Q2; **B:** Well, I really want to.
Ex D Q4–Q6 **G:** And French poetry?
B: What?
Ex C Q5; **G:** Your résumé says you enjoy French poetry.
B: Does it? Oh yes! That's right. Of course, French
Ex D Q7–Q9 poetry – love it.
G: Uh, Barry, I, uh, I think we've finished for today.
B: Oh, great – that was quick.
G: Yes, uh … do you uh … do you have any questions?
B: Um … No! No, I don't!
Ex B **G:** OK, so thanks again and … please don't call us … we … uh, we'll contact you. Thank you, Barry.
B: No, thank YOU, Gemma.

5.3 Don't call us

GRAMMAR

A Students use the examples to help them answer the questions. Give feedback as a class, clarifying with further examples where necessary.

B Students choose the correct options to complete the rules. Give them time to check their answers in pairs, before giving feedback as a class.

C Students complete the second rules box with the words in bold. Give feedback as a class.

D Students read the sentence and choose the correct tense to complete the rules for *since*. Give feedback as a class.

E Direct students to the **Grammar Hub** (see below). Use the **Grammar Worksheet** on W29 for extra practice.

PRONUNCIATION

5.8 **A** Play the audio for students to listen and repeat.

VOCABULARY

A Direct students to the **Vocabulary Hub**. Use the **Vocabulary Worksheet** on W30 for extra practice.

B Students mingle and interview each other about jobs. Encourage them to write notes. Model the activity for the class. Elicit what subjects might be interesting to ask about and write them on the board (e.g. *job title, degree, duties, location of office*, etc).

C In pairs, students discuss what they found out in Exercise B. Monitor and assist as necessary.

SPEAKING HUB

A Read the task with the class. Students look at the prompts and decide what they want to talk about. Encourage weaker students to write down what they want to say.

B Ask students to think of questions they could ask each other about their topics.

C In groups, students interview each other about their chosen subjects. Monitor and encourage students to ask follow-up questions. Give feedback as a class, encouraging students to highlight the most interesting things they learned.

GRAMMAR HUB

5.3 Present perfect with *for* and *since*

	Positive	Negative
I/you/we/they	**I've worked** here for 12 years.	**They haven't called** since last week.
he/she/it	**She's worked** in telemarketing since 2017.	**She hasn't checked** her messages for two days.

Question	Positive short answer	Negative short answer
Have you worked in a restaurant before?	Yes, **I have**.	No, **I haven't**.
Has he finished the project?	Yes, **he has**.	No, **he hasn't**.

- We use the present perfect to talk about actions and situations that started in the past but are unfinished and so continue until the present time.

  *I have **worked** here **for** three weeks. (= and I am still working here now)*

- We use *for* to show the amount of time, and *since* to show when the action or situation started.

  *She has been at this company **since** January.*
  *She has been at this company **for** six months.*

- We use *How long* plus the present perfect to ask about the length of time until the present.

  How long has Maria worked there?

- We also use the present perfect to talk about things that happened in the past at an unspecified time and our experiences up to now.

  I've done a lot of different jobs.

Be careful!

- The verb *go* has two past participles: *been* and *gone*.
- We use *been* when someone has gone somewhere and come back.

  Bill has been to a lot of job interviews.
- We use *gone* when someone has gone somewhere and not come back yet.

  Jeff has gone for an interview and he'll be back later.

5.3 Present perfect with *for* and *since*

A Choose the correct option.

1. I have wanted to work there (for) / *since* a long time.
2. I have worked here *for* / (since) 2014.
3. We haven't had a day off (for) / *since* a long time.
4. They've worked in recruitment (for) / *since* the last 10 years.
5. She hasn't spoken to the manager (for) / *since* months.
6. Giles hasn't worked *for* / (since) he lost his job in accounts.
7. Things have changed *for* / (since) we did our research.

B Make sentences with the present perfect.

1. she / do / a lot of charity work
   She's done a lot of charity work.
2. they / be / in your office / for an hour
   They've been in your office for an hour.
3. you / change / your appointment / three times
   You've changed your appointment three times.
4. we / not have / a pay raise / for a while
   We haven't had a pay raise for a while.
5. How long / she / be / the owner of the company / ?
   How long has she been the owner of the company?

➤ Go back to page 47.

GRAMMAR

Present perfect with *for* and *since*

A WORK IT OUT Look at the sentences from Barry's interview and answer the questions.

I left my old job in June.

1 Does Barry still do his old job? no
2 Is the action *leave* finished or unfinished? finished
3 What tense is the verb *leave* in? simple past

I've worked at the call center for six weeks.

4 Does Barry still work at the call center? yes
5 Is the action *work* finished or unfinished? unfinished
6 What tense is the verb *work* in? present perfect

B Choose the correct words to complete the rules.

Present perfect and simple past

1 We use the ***present perfect / simple past*** to talk about actions or situations that started and finished in the past.
2 We use the ***present perfect / simple past*** to talk about actions or situations that started in the past, but are unfinished and so continue until the present.

C Look at the words in **bold** in the sentences from Barry's interview. Complete the rules with *how long*, *for* or *since*.

How long *have you worked there?*

Actually, I've been here ***since*** *9 am.*

You've been here ***for*** *three hours?*

Present perfect with *how long*, *for* and *since*

1 We use How long + present perfect to ask about the duration of an action.
2 We use since to talk about the point in time when something started, e.g. *yesterday, I was young*.
3 We use for + present perfect to talk about a length of time until the present time, e.g. *three hours, two weeks*.

D Look at the sentence from Barry's interview and choose the correct words to complete the rule.

I've liked skydiving since I was a teenager.

since

After *since* we usually use a verb in ***present perfect / simple past***.

E Go to the **Grammar Hub** on **page 130**.

PRONUNCIATION

has, have, for, since

5.8 Listen and repeat.

1 How long has he lived there?
2 How long have you worked there?
3 He's lived there for three years.
4 I've worked there since last summer.

VOCABULARY

work + preposition

A Go to the **Vocabulary Hub** on **page 148**.

B SPEAK Work as a class. Talk to as many different people as possible in five minutes about their job or the job of someone they know. Write notes for each person you talk to.

Cassie: She works in IT for a software company. She's a computer programmer. She works in their office in the center of the city.

C SPEAK Work in pairs. Compare your notes. Which jobs were the most unusual or interesting?

SPEAKING HUB

A You are going to talk about a topic in which you are an expert. Consider the following areas:

- your profession and/or studies
- a skill you've learned, e.g. cooking, skiing, car mechanics, piano

B PLAN Think of some questions you could ask your classmates about their topics.

How long ...?
What can/can't you do?

C DISCUSS Work in a group. Interview each student in your group about their expertise. What were the most interesting things you learned about your classmates?

Answer questions on topics in which you are an expert

Café Hub

5.4 The cat

F– give information about your work experience in a job interview
P– singular and plural forms

COMPREHENSION

A ▶ **SPEAK** Work in pairs. Look at the pictures above from Neena's job interview. What do you think goes wrong in the interview? Watch the video and check.

B ▶ 03:09–05:00 Watch the last part of the interview again. Answer the questions.

1 Whose cat was it? The interviewer's cat
2 What was the cat's name? Mittens
3 What is Neena doing on Monday? Starting a new job

C ▶ 00:27–03:06 Complete the job interview form for Neena. Then watch part of the video again and check your answers.

JOBS, JOBS, JOBS AND JOBS

Job interview

Name: Neena Patel
Current job: Working for a [1] ___law___ firm. Responsible for international [2] ___accounts___.
Time in current job: [3] ___four___ years.
Reasons for changing job: Is looking for a [4] ___new___ challenge.
Strengths: Is good at working [5] ___under___ pressure. Can [6] ___manage___ her time. Is very organized. Is good at [7] ___project___ management. Works well on a [8] ___team___.
Weaknesses: Is a perfectionist – enjoys getting everything [9] ___right___.
A good candidate for the job: [10] Yes / No

MILLY

SAM

NEENA

ZAC

GABY

FUNCTIONAL LANGUAGE

Give information about your work experience in a job interview

A Cross out the word that is NOT possible to complete the sentences.

1 Currently, I'm working for *a law firm* / *Citibank* / ~~*architect*~~.
2 I have to manage *a team* / *five sales representatives* / ~~*a company car*~~.
3 I've worked there for ~~*last year*~~ / *a long time* / *four years*.
4 People say I'm good at *working under pressure* / ~~*manage my time*~~ / *my job*.
5 I've learned how to *manage my time* / ~~*working on a team*~~ / *deal with clients*.
6 I work well *on a team* / *under pressure* / ~~*my job*~~.

B Look at Exercise A. Think of another word for each sentence to replace the one you crossed out.

USEFUL PHRASES

A ▶ Complete the conversations with the useful phrases in the box. Then watch the video again and check your answers.

Go on.	How did it go?	It was going so well …
Just go!	Let me think.	Please take a seat.
Tell me about yourself.	That's a good question.	

Gaby: 1 How did it go?
Neena: Oh, Gaby, it was awful.
Gaby: What happened?
Neena: 2 It was going so well …
Interviewer: Good afternoon, Neena. 3 Please take a seat. So Neena, 4 Tell me about yourself. What have you learned from your current job?
Neena: 5 That's a good question.
Interviewer: And any weak points?
Neena: 6 Let me think. Well, I have one question.
Interviewer: 7 Go on.
Neena: So, will you call me?
Interviewer: 8 Just go!

B How do you say these useful phrases in your language?

PRONUNCIATION

Singular and plural forms

5.9 **A** Listen and repeat the singular and plural forms of the nouns in the box. Which noun has an extra syllable in the plural form? challenge(s)

account(s)	challenge(s)	job(s)	perfectionist(s)
pressure(s)	project(s)	question(s)	strength(s)

B SPEAK Work in pairs. Practice saying the words in Exercise A. Listen and check your partner's pronunciation.

SPEAKING

A Think about the things you are good at. Write down three strengths and one weakness. Then work in pairs and compare your ideas.

B Work in pairs. Write down three important skills for each of the jobs in the box.

accountant	soccer team manager
teacher	website manager

C Role-play a job interview. Use the job interview form in Comprehension Exercise C to help you. Include at least two useful phrases. Take turns.

Student A: Choose a job from Exercise B and interview Student B for the job.
Student B: Answer Student A's questions.
Student A: Decide if Student B is suitable for the job.

Give information about your work experience in a job interview

➤ Turn to **page 162** to learn how to write a cover email.

5.4 The cat

COMPREHENSION

A ▶ In pairs, students predict what goes wrong in the interview. Play the video for students to check their ideas.

B ▶ 03:09–05:00 Play the last part of the video again. Students answer the questions, before checking in pairs. Give feedback as a class.

C ▶ 00:27–03:06 Students complete the interview, then watch part of the video again to check their answers. Give feedback as a class.

FUNCTIONAL LANGUAGE

A Students cross out the incorrect option in each sentence. Give them time to check their answers with a partner, before giving feedback as a class.

B Students replace the crossed out phrases in Exercise A with suitable alternatives. Check answers as a class.

USEFUL PHRASES

A ▶ Students complete the conversations with the phrases in the box. Play the video again for students to check their answers.

B As a class, discuss how students would say the phrases in Exercise A in their own language.

PRONUNCIATION

5.9 **A** Play the audio. Students listen and repeat the nouns in the box and answer the question.

B Students practice saying the words in pairs. Monitor and continue practicing correct pronunciation as required.

SPEAKING

A Students write down three of their strengths and one weakness, before discussing their answers in pairs. Monitor and assist as required.

B In the same pairs, students write three vital skills required for each job. With a weak group, write one skill for each job on the board (e.g. *Accountant – good with numbers, Soccer team manager – experienced in playing soccer, Teacher – patience, Website manager – knowledge of programing languages*).

C Students role-play the job interviews in pairs. Remind students that the questions must be based on the skills they listed for each job (e.g. Soccer team manager – *Can you tell me a little bit about your experience as a soccer player?*). The answers are based on the notes they made about their strengths and weaknesses. Student A will then decide whether Student B is suitable for the job. Students take turns being the interviewer and interviewee.

▶ VIDEO SCRIPT

Café Hub 6.4 The cat
G = Gaby N = Neena I = Interviewer J = Jenny

G: How did it go?
N: Oh Gaby, it was awful!
G: What happened?
N: It was going so well …
I: Come in.
N: Hello, I'm Neena Patel.
I: Good afternoon Neena, please take a seat.
N: Thank you.
I: My name is Matthew Williams and I've been head of staff here at Jobs, Jobs, Jobs and Jobs since 2012. This is Jenny Bridges – she's an account manager.
N: Good afternoon.
J: Hello.
I: So Neena, tell me about yourself.
N: Well, currently I'm working for a Law Firm called Jones and Jones. I'm responsible for International accounts and I have to manage a team. I've worked there for 4 years, but I'm looking for a new challenge. I like working hard and people say I'm good at working under pressure.
I: Well, we like hard workers here! Tell me – what have you learnt from your current job?
N: Let me think … I've learnt how to manage my time. We are a small team, so I have to be very organised.
I: Good. Good. Do you have any special strengths?
N: I think I'm good at project management. I enjoy organising difficult projects.
I: And any weak points?
N: That's a good question … Maybe, I'm a perfectionist? I enjoy getting everything right. Every time.
I: We like perfectionists here at Jobs, Jobs, Jobs and Jobs. Well thank you very much Neena. Finally, do you have any questions for us?
N: Well, I have one question.
I: Go on.
N: Does the job involve much teamwork? I work well in a team.
I: Yes. You must be able to work well in a team. We like everyone to work closely together. Communication is very important here. Thank you for coming Neena, I'm sure we'll be in touch soon.
N: Thanks. Thank you. That's a beautiful cat.
I: Yes … Yes she is … I mean … She was … So very beautiful …
J: It's OK Matthew, it's OK …
N: What … Erm, what was her name?
I: Mittens … She was called Mittens.
J: I think you should leave now Miss Patel.
N: So … Will you call me …?
J: Just go!
G: … Just go? She said: 'Just. Go.'?
N: Yes.
G: That's not good.
N: No. It's not good. Maybe it's them? It's them! Hello … It is … OK … Yes. Thank you. Goodbye.
G: Well? What did they say?
N: I got the job. I start on Monday.

Unit 5 Writing

5 Writing

Write a cover email

W beginning and ending emails and letters

English-speaking vacation nannies and mannies (job s632)

Vacation Hands agency is looking for English-speaking nannies and mannies (male nannies) to travel with families on their summer and winter vacations. You will take care of the children during the day and babysit in the evenings. Experience is an advantage. Good pay, plus all travel, accommodations and food included. Reply with a résumé and a copy of your passport to Olga Zatorska at ol.zator@vacationhands.nett

A Work in pairs. Read the advertisement. Would you or anyone you know be interested in this job? Why/Why not?

B Read Maurice's cover email. Do you think Maurice will be offered an interview? Why?

To: Ms. Zatorska
Subject: Vacation manny job

1 Dear Ms. Zatorska, [Dear Sir/Madam]
2 I am writing to apply for [I would like to apply for] the job of vacation manny with the Vacation Hands agency. 3 I attached [Please find attached] a copy of my résumé.
4 Right now, I am studying at the University of Edinburgh and am available to work from July 1st to September 30th.
5 I speak fluent [I am fluent in] English and Spanish and enjoy working with children. Last summer, I was an activities supervisor at a summer camp for 6–12-year-olds. My energy and creativity made me popular with the children. I believe this experience [the knowledge and skills I developed there] will be very useful. 6 A job with [Working for] the Vacation Hands agency would be an exciting opportunity to learn new skills and work in an international environment.
7 I look forward to hearing from you. [I hope to hear from you soon.]
8 Sincerely yours, [Yours truly,]
Maurice Garcia

C Read again. Put the different parts of a cover email in the correct order (1–7).

6 why you want this job
4 what you are doing now and when you are available
7 polite ending
2 reason for writing
1 a formal greeting
5 details about your experience and character
3 attachments, for example, your résumé

D Look at the box. Which beginnings and endings are formal (F)? Which are informal (I)?

Beginning and ending emails and letters

Beginning			Ending		
1	Hello,	I	7	See you soon,	I
2	Dear Sir/Madam,	F	8	Bye for now,	I
3	Dear all,	I	9	Lots of love,	I
4	Hi everyone,	I	10	Sincerely yours,	F
5	Dear Mr. Cox,	F	11	Yours truly,	F
6	Dear Diane,	I/F	12	Kind regards,	F
			13	Best wishes,	I

E Replace the underlined phrases in the email with similar phrases in the box.

Dear Sir/Madam, I am fluent in
I hope to hear from you soon.
I would like to apply for Please find attached
the knowledge and skills I developed there
Working for Yours truly,

F Work in pairs. What kind of skills, experience and personality would be helpful for this summer job?

Waiters and waitresses wanted (job h384)
Are you looking for part-time work? We need friendly, hard-working people to join our evening table service team at Blue Moon Asian Food Center. Experience is an advantage, but we will give full training. Attractive wages and free meals. Write with a résumé to noi.warumdee@mail.nett.

WRITING

A PLAN You are going to write a cover email to apply for the job in Writing Exercise F. Take notes for a cover email. Use Exercise C to help you.

B WRITE Write your cover email. Use the strategies in the box and Maurice's email to help you.

162 5 WRITING

Refer students to this email as a model for the first stage of the writing task.

Remind students to use appropriate openings and endings for their email, and to maintain a formal tone.

WRITING

A In pairs, students read the job advertisement for English-speaking nannies and mannies. Students discuss whether they, or anyone they know, would be interested in the job and why. Take feedback from one or two pairs and encourage students to respond to each other's ideas.

B Students read Maurice's cover email on their own. Elicit ideas as to whether Maurice will be offered an interview. Encourage students to share their reasons, using information from the email to support them.

C Students reread Maurice's email and put it in the correct order in pairs. Check answers with the class.

D Focus students on the writing box. Students work on their own deciding whether the beginnings and endings are formal (F) or informal (I). They compare their answers in pairs.

E Read the phrases in the box with the class. In pairs, students find the underlined phrases in Maurice's email and replace them with similar phrases from the vocabulary box. Check answers with the class.

WRITING TASK

A Read the task with the class. Ask students to write notes for their email using Exercise C and the words and phrases on the board to help them.

B Students write their cover emails. Encourage students to use Maurice's email and the information from the box to support them. Monitor and assist when necessary.

Unit 5 Review

VOCABULARY

A Match beginnings of the sentences (1–5) with the ends of the sentences (a–e).

1 What advantages are there to a job where you work
2 How important do you think it is to earn
3 What are the disadvantages of being
4 When did you last take
5 Do you think people should get

a a day off from work or school and what did you do?
b shifts, so sometimes you start at night or early in the morning?
c a pay raise every year or only when they have done well at work?
d your own boss?
e a high salary in your job?

B Write the missing words to complete the sentences.

1 My brother is very c_o_o_l_; he always looks good.
2 She's not allowed to wear c_a_s_u_a_l_ clothes to work.
3 I love those high-heeled shoes – they have a very s_t_y_l_i_s_h_ design.
4 I don't like that T-shirt. I don't think those colors look a_t_t_r_a_c_t_i_v_e_.
5 In our country, you must wear d_r_e_s_s_ clothes to a wedding.

C Choose the correct prepositions. In three examples, both are possible.

1 They work *at* / *for* the IT department.
2 He works *in* / *at* marketing.
3 She works *at* / *for* Bluemoon Software Services.
4 She works *at* / *for* an advertising firm.
5 I work *at* / *in* a library.
6 We work *in* / *for* a telemarketing company.

GRAMMAR

A Choose the best words to complete the sentences.

1 When I was young, I *can* / *could* stay up late, but these days I get tired early.
2 I really enjoy *being able to* / *can* work for myself.
3 Johann *able to* / *can* speak four languages.
4 I *was able to* / *could* speak to my boss last Friday about getting a pay raise.
5 I'd like *can* / *to be able to* speak perfect English one day.

B Match the rules (1–8) with the meanings (a–d).

Memo: Information for palace staff

1 _c_ You can park your car in the staff parking lot.
2 _d_ You must not bring your own cell phone inside the palace.
3 _d_ You can't take any pictures while at work.
4 _a_ You have to be nicely dressed at all times.*
5 _a_ You must call the Queen 'Your Majesty'.
6 _d_ You must not mention anything you see or hear at work to anyone.
7 _c_ You can smoke in the staff smoking area.
8 _b_ *If the Royal family are away, you don't have to wear the full uniform.

a This is necessary or is a rule.
b This is not necessary but allowed.
c This is allowed but not necessary.
d This is not allowed.

C Complete the conversations with the simple past or present perfect form of the verbs in parentheses.

Erin: How long [1] _have you worked_ (*you / work*) here?
Paulie: Oh, not long. [2] _I started_ (*I / start*) work last December. But, you see that lady there? Well, [3] _she's been_ (*she / be*) here for 20 years. [4] _She became_ (*she / become*) a cook when she was only 17.

Karl: I thought you worked for a newspaper? When [5] _did you change_ (*you / change*) jobs?
Crystal: Years ago! [6] _I haven't worked_ (*I / not work*) in journalism since about 2004.

Pippa: [7] _I wanted_ (*I / want*) to be a doctor when I was a child, but now I'm a vet.
Gianni: A vet? That's so cool. [8] _I've loved_ (*I / love*) animals since I was little.

FUNCTIONAL LANGUAGE

A Complete the phrases to use in job interviews with the words in the box.

enjoy learned problem question responsible team

1 I've _learned_ how to motivate other people.
2 Well, I have one _question_ I'd like to ask.
3 I'm _responsible_ for customer service.
4 I _enjoy_ working in a busy office.
5 I work well on a _team_.
6 Well, I have a _problem_ with the weekend hours.

6 Health

HEALTH

Health is not valued until sickness comes.

Thomas Fuller

Yoga enthusiasts take part in the annual Times Square event celebrating the Summer Solstice, the longest day of the year, New York.

OBJECTIVES

- give a presentation on health dos and don'ts
- plan an exercise event for your local community
- encourage people to make a lifestyle change
- talk about your symptoms at a pharmacy
- write a product review

Work with a partner. Discuss the questions.

1 What do you do to stay healthy?
2 Read the quote. Do you agree with it?
3 Would you like to take part in an event like the one in the picture? Why/Why not?

HEALTH 51

Health (n) the condition of your body, especially whether or not you are ill.
Synonyms: condition, fitness.

Fuller is suggesting that while we are healthy, we don't give health any importance. We only realize how important health is when we are ill.

Thomas Fuller (1608–August 16, 1661) was an English historian. He is famous for his writings, particularly his *Worthies of England*, published after his death. He was a prolific author, and one of the first English writers who was able to live by his pen.

OBJECTIVES

Read the unit objectives to the class.

UNIT OPENER QUESTIONS

Encourage students to look at the quote and take one or two suggestions from the class about what they think it means.

Ask students to look at the picture on the page and encourage them to share their ideas. Ask prompt questions such as 'Where are these people? Do you think what they are doing is healthy? In what way does the photo relate to the quote?' If students share any good ideas or useful language, write these on the board.

Ask students to look at questions at the bottom of the page. Model possible answers, like whether you do any physical activity or what you think about what the people on the photo are doing. Students discuss the questions in pairs or in a small group.

Monitor and assist as necessary. When students have finished the activity, ask one or two pairs to share their ideas with the class. Encourage students to listen to one another and respond with their own ideas and opinions.

WORKSHEETS

Lesson 6.1 Health myths

Grammar: Quantifiers *too* and *enough* (W31)

Vocabulary: Minor illnesses (W32)

Lesson 6.2 Keep fit

Grammar: *-ing* forms (W33)

Vocabulary: Exercise (W34)

Lesson 6.3 We may never 'meat' again

Grammar: Present perfect with *just, already* and *yet* (W35)

Vocabulary: Food groups (W36)

6.1 Health myths

Give a presentation on health dos and don'ts

G quantifiers *too* and *enough* **V** minor illnesses **P** /ʌ/, /ɔː/, /uː/, /eɪ/ and /ɜː/

LISTENING

A Match the definitions (1–7) with the words in the box.

a balanced diet antibiotics confused expert liquid myth reality

1 something that people wrongly believe to be true myth
2 someone who has a particular skill or who knows a lot about a particular subject expert
3 a fact, event or situation as it really exists reality
4 a range of food that a person eats to provide all the good things their body needs a balanced diet
5 drugs that cure illnesses and infections caused by bacteria antibiotics
6 unable to understand something or think clearly about it confused
7 a substance (such as water) that can flow, has no fixed shape and is not a solid or a gas liquid

B SPEAK Work in pairs. Check (✓) the sentences about health you have heard before. Which ones do you think are true and which ones are myths? Give reasons.

1 Everyone should drink eight glasses of water per day. ☐
2 Eating fatty food makes you fat. ☐
3 Eggs are bad for your heart. ☐
4 Cold weather causes colds. ☐
5 Take antibiotics when you have a cold. ☐

6.1 **C LISTEN FOR GIST** Look at the glossary. Then listen to the introduction of *Live with Pippa* and answer the questions.

Glossary

calorie (n) unit for measuring how much energy you get from food
carbohydrate (n) a substance found in foods such as sugar, bread and potatoes. Carbohydrates supply your body with heat and energy.
fatty (adj) containing a lot of fat
virus (n) a thing that can enter your body and make you sick

1 How many experts does Pippa speak to? four experts
2 Choose the best summary of Pippa's message in the introduction to the show.
 a It is better to ask a medical professional than look online for information about health.
 b It is difficult to know which online information about health is true.
 c Bad online advice about health is making healthy people sick.

6.1 **D LISTEN FOR DETAIL** Listen again and choose a, b or c.

1 Doctor Singh says that …
 a most headaches are due to a lack of water.
 b we get some of the water we need from our food.
 c more than eight glasses of water per day is dangerous.
2 Michael says that …
 a everyone needs some fat in their diets.
 b most people get fat because they eat too much sugar.
 c we shouldn't eat fatty food.
3 Dr. Tremblay says you are more likely to catch a cold or flu …
 a if you spend time outside in cold weather.
 b if you don't get enough vitamins in your diet.
 c if you spend time indoors with a lot of people.
4 Lia says that …
 a advice on eating eggs changes regularly.
 b advice on eating eggs is not the same as it was in the past.
 c advice on eating eggs is the same as it has always been.

GRAMMAR

Quantifiers *too* and *enough*

A WORK IT OUT Complete the sentences from the radio show (1–5) using the audio script on **page 173**. Then match the sentences with the rules (a–c).

1 You drink too __much__ coffee. rule _a_
2 You don't sleep __enough__. rule _c_
3 It's because you go to bed __too__ early. rule _a_
4 Make sure you are getting __enough__ vitamins. rule _b_
5 Too __many__ eggs are bad for your heart. rule _a_

Quantifiers *too* and *enough*

a We use *too* + adjective or adverb, *too much* and *too many* to mean more than the right amount.
b We use *enough* to mean the right amount.
c We use *not enough* to mean less than the right amount.

6.1 Health myths

LEAD-IN

Put students in groups and give them three minutes to come up with answers.

1 *Write four kinds of vegetable that are yellow.*

2 *Which activity burns more calories: watching TV or ironing?*

3 *Write two types of food that belong to the carbohydrates category.*

The winner is the group with more correct answers.

LISTENING

A Students match the words in the box with the definitions using the images on the page.

B In pairs, students read through Sentences 1–5 and check (✓) those they have heard or been told before. Students discuss which sentences they think are true and which are myths, giving reasons to support their answers.

6.1 **C** Play the audio introduction. Students answer the questions alone and compare their answers in pairs. Play the audio again for students to check their answers.

6.1 **D** Play the full interview. Students listen and select the correct answer (a, b or c). Play the audio again for students to check.

GRAMMAR

A Students complete Sentences 1–5 using the **Audio script** (see below). With a weaker group, you may want students to work in pairs with one student looking at the Audio script and the other looking at the questions. With a stronger class, students can complete the sentences from memory, using the Audio script to confirm their answers. Once the sentences have been completed, focus student on the grammar box. Students decide which rule is exemplified by each sentence.

AUDIO SCRIPT

6.1

Listening, Exercise C
P = Pippa DS = Doctor Singh M = Michael
DT = Doctor Tremblay L = Lia

P: G'day, Australia! Pippa Chan on chatfmmelbourne.nett. Today, we are talking about health myths. Half an hour on the internet leaves most people pretty confused about what's good for their health and what isn't. You know, one article says 'you drink too much coffee, but you don't drink enough water', then the next says coffee is good for you, but too much water is dangerous! Confusing? Very!
I mean, let's say you are one of the many people who goes through life feeling tired a lot of the time. If you look online, you'll find one expert that says 'you don't sleep enough' and another that says 'you sleep too much'. Ha! And if you can't sleep? Oh, it's because you go to bed too early. No, no, no, it's because you don't go to bed early enough! And of course EVERYthing makes you fat.
So how do we know what to believe? Well, we've been down to Melbourne City Hospital to ask some medical professionals about the reality behind some common health myths. Let's hear from the experts …

DS: Hi. I'm Dr Singh and I work at Melbourne City Hospital. My myth concerns how much water we need to drink. Most people have probably heard that not drinking enough water can cause headaches. And they are right – that isn't a myth. But many of us have probably also heard that we need to drink eight glasses of water per day to stay healthy – well, that isn't exactly true. The eight glasses, or around two liters, includes all liquids: tea, coffee, juice, et cetera – plus the water you get from food, which is around one-fifth of your daily total. So how much water should we drink? Well, my advice is drink when you are thirsty and you'll be OK. (Ex D Q1)

M: Hi, my name is Michael. I'm a nurse here in Melbourne. Many people believe that eating fatty food makes them fat, but in fact, that isn't the whole truth. Eating more calories than you need makes you fat. Yes, it's true that fat has lots of calories, but so do carbohydrates and sugars. It isn't actually too much fat that makes you fat, it's too many calories. Some fat is necessary, so you can still enjoy your burger as part of a balanced diet. And to burn those extra calories? Get up off that couch and get moving! (Ex D Q2)

DT: Hi, I'm Dr Tremblay from Canada. The Australian winter is here and so are colds and flu. You remember Grandma's advice … 'Hat! Scarf! Keep warm, or you'll catch a cold.' Well, Australia isn't as cold as Canada, but it is sensible to make sure you're warm enough. However, the truth is that cold weather doesn't cause colds and flu. They are caused by viruses. You are more likely to catch a cold inside, where there are lots of people. And remember, if you have a cold and are suffering with a headache, a cough or a sore throat, get plenty of rest, drink warm drinks – unless you have a temperature – and make sure you are getting enough vitamins. Don't take antibiotics! They don't kill viruses and they won't help a cold. (Ex D Q3)

L: Hi, I'm Lia. I'm a medical student from London and I want to talk about eggs! Some people believe that you shouldn't eat more than one or two eggs a week. This is probably because of old advice. In the past, the warning was always 'too many eggs are bad for your heart', but we now know that an egg or two per day doesn't increase the risk of heart disease in healthy people. Egg-cellent news for egg lovers – Egg-xactly what they wanted to hear! Ha ha – sorry! (Ex D Q4)

P: Wow! Thank you to all our egg-sperts. Interesting stuff! We'll be back with music from Enrique Egg-lesias after the break.

6.1 Health myths

B Students complete the rules, before checking their answers with a partner. Give feedback as a class.

C Direct students to the **Grammar Hub** (see below). Use the **Grammar Worksheet** on W31 for extra practice.

D Model a sentence for the class. With a weaker group, you may want to elicit some possible activities to complete the sentences. Students complete the sentences for themselves. Take feedback from one or two stronger students and encourage others to read their ideas.

E In pairs, students compare and discuss their sentences for Exercise D. Monitor and assist where necessary.

VOCABULARY

A Direct students to the **Audio script** (see TB52). They should reread Dr. Tremblay's Audio script and underline the six health problems he talks about.

B Focus students on the word box and Pictures 1–10. Students work alone labeling each picture with the words from the box. Students compare their answers in pairs before checking them with the class. Use the **Vocabulary Worksheet** on W32 for extra practice.

PRONUNCIATION

6.2 **A** Play the audio and ask students to listen to the five vowel sounds and repeat.

6.3 **B** Play the audio. Students match the words with the sounds and then underline the letters that represent each sound.

C Students work in pairs discussing what people do when they have one of the health problems from Vocabulary Exercise B. They can use either the prompts or their own ideas. Monitor and assist when necessary. Take feedback from one or two pairs and encourage students to respond to each other's ideas.

SPEAKING

A In pairs, students prepare a presentation called *The dos and don'ts of staying active and healthy*. Depending on the resources you have available, you may wish to ask students to create slides or posters to support their presentation.

B Pairs write a list of dos and don'ts for each of the five topic areas. If you have limited time, you may want to ask each pair to focus on one or two topics, rather than all six. With a weaker class, suggest for the pairs to write just a do and a don't for each topic. Monitor and assist as required.

C Ask the pairs to deliver their presentation to the rest of the class. Explain that students should listen carefully and try to identify if there is any bad advice. Once the presentations are finished, take feedback from the class on which pieces of bad advice they heard.

GRAMMAR HUB

6.1 Quantifiers *too* and *enough*

- We use *too* + adjective or adverb, *too much* and *too many* to mean more than the right amount.

  *I am **too tired**.*

  *You drink **too much** cola and you eat **too many** candies.*

Be careful!

- We use *too many* with countable nouns.

  *They buy **too many** snacks.*
- We use *too much* with uncountable nouns.

  *We eat **too much** sugar.*
- We use *enough* + noun to mean the right amount.

  *We have **enough** drinks for everyone.*
- We use *not enough* + noun to mean less than the right amount.

  *She **doesn't** have **enough** time to cook.*

Be careful!

- When we use *too* and *enough* with adjectives or adverbs, we put *too* **before** the adjective or adverb and *enough* **after** the adjective or adverb.

  *I feel **too sick** to have dinner.*

  *I don't feel **well enough** to have dinner.*

  *You exercise **too hard**.*

  *You don't exercise **hard enough**.*

6.1 Quantifiers *too* and *enough*

A Choose the correct option.

1 Don't eat too *much* / *many* eggs.
2 I am *enough* / *too* tired to jog.
3 Make sure you are getting *enough* / *too much* sleep.
4 You don't drink *enough* / *too much* water.
5 I have eaten too *many* / *much* candy.
6 The gym closes *too* / *enough* early.
7 We don't have *enough* / *too much* food in the fridge.

B Match to make sentences.

1 We have too __e__
2 You don't do __a__
3 We don't have __d__
4 There are too many __c__
5 She has too much __f__
6 He's too __b__

a enough exercise.
b sick for soccer practice.
c people in this yoga class.
d enough milk.
e many cups on the table.
f energy to sit still.

➤ Go back to page 53.

B Look at the sentences from the radio show in Exercise A and complete the rules.

too much and too many

1 We use ***too much*** / ***too many*** with countable nouns.
2 We use ***too much*** / ***too many*** with uncountable nouns.

C Go to the **Grammar Hub** on **page 132**.

D PRACTICE Complete the sentences so they are true for you.

1 I spend too much time ________________ and not enough time ________________.
2 I eat too much/many ________________ and not enough ________________.
3 I don't ________________ enough and I ________________ too much/often.
4 I find ________________ too difficult.
5 I have enough ________________, but not enough ________________.

E SPEAK Work in pairs. Discuss your answers to Exercise D.

VOCABULARY
Minor illnesses

A Read Dr. Tremblay's audio script on **page 173** and underline six health problems he talks about.
cold, flu, a headache, a cough, a sore throat, a temperature

B Label the pictures (1–10) with the health problems in the box.

a broken bone ~~a cold~~ a cough
a headache a temperature a sore throat
flu stomachache sunburn toothache

PRONUNCIATION
/ʌ/, /ɔː/, /uː/, /eɪ/ and /ɜː/

6.2 **A** Listen and repeat.

1 /ʌ/ but
2 /ɔː/ caught
3 /uː/ do
4 /eɪ/ pay
5 /ɜː/ fur

6.3 **B** Each word contains one of the sounds in Exercise A. Listen and match the words with the sounds. Then underline the letter(s) that make the sounds.

1 burn — e
2 ache — d
3 stomach — a
4 flu — c
5 sore — b

a /ʌ/
b /ɔː/
c /uː/
d /eɪ/
e /ɜː/

C SPEAK Work in pairs. What do people usually do for each of the problems in Vocabulary Exercise B? Use ideas below to help you and your own ideas.

- go to bed
- take medicine
- go to the doctor
- take painkillers
- put on lotion
- stay home from work

SPEAKING

A Work in pairs. Plan and give a short presentation called *The dos and don'ts of staying active and healthy*.

B Write a list of dos and don'ts for each of the topics:

- food and drink
- sleep
- exercise
- stress
- avoiding and recovering from illness

C Present your advice to the class. Ask them to guess which piece of advice is a myth or bad advice.

1

a cold

2

a cough

3

a headache

4

flu

5

toothache

6

sunburn

7
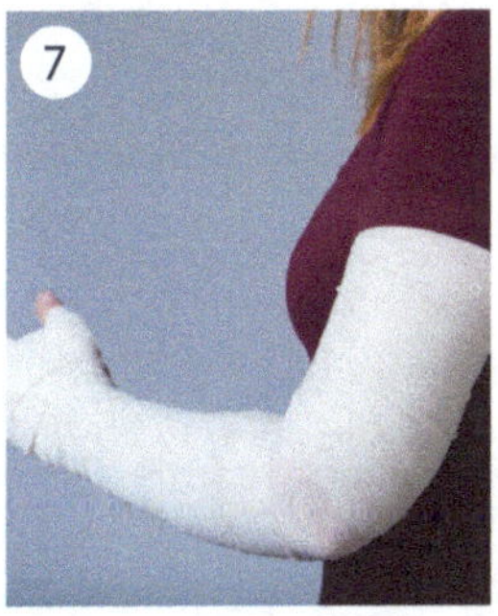
a broken bone

8

a temperature

9
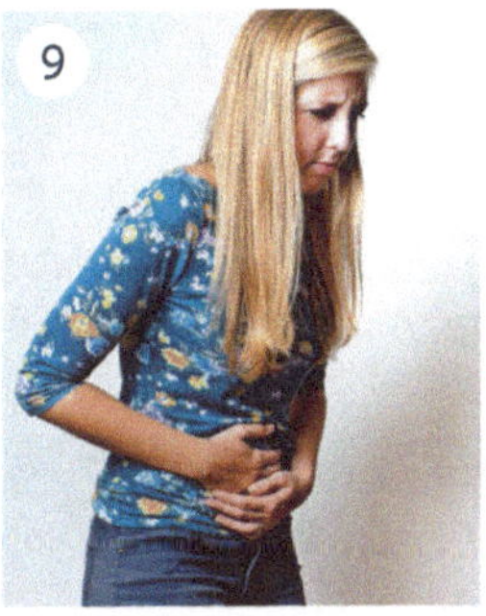
stomachache

10
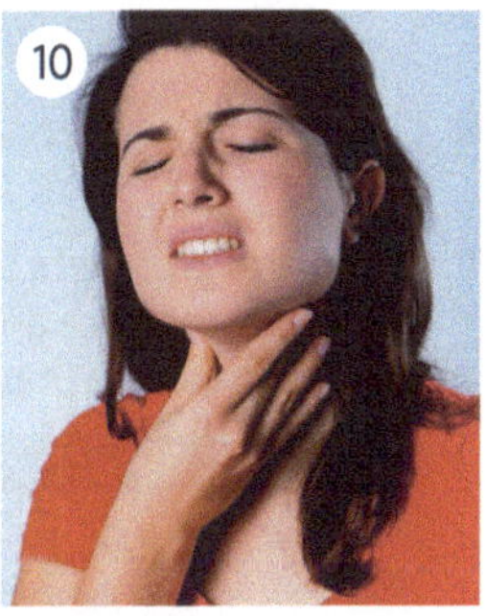
a sore throat

Give a presentation on health dos and don'ts

6.2 Keep fit

Plan an exercise event for your local community

V exercise P /ŋ/, /n/ and /m/ G -*ing* forms

VOCABULARY

Exercise

A Work in pairs. Make a list of different ways of exercising. You have one minute.

Walking, swimming ...

B Go to the **Vocabulary Hub** on **page 148**.

C **SPEAK** Look at the **Vocabulary Hub** Exercise B on **page 149**. Go around the class and ask the questions. If someone answers *yes*, write their name and ask a follow-up question.

A: Do you hate working out at the gym?
B: Yes, I do.
A: Why?
B: I like to exercise outdoors and I don't like to exercise with so many other people watching me. I find most gyms too busy.

PRONUNCIATION

/ŋ/, /n/ and /m/

6.4 **A** Listen to these sounds. Do they sound the same or different? different

1 /ŋ/ biking 2 /n/ run 3 /m/ team

6.4 **B** Listen again and repeat the sounds.

6.5 **C** Listen and complete the table with the words you hear. Do the words have an /ŋ/, /n/ or /m/ sound? Some words have more than one of the sounds.

/ŋ/	/n/	/m/
walking	burn marathon	swim stomach remember marathon

READING

A Check (✓) the sentences you agree with. Then work in pairs and explain your choices.

Running is great exercise and great fun. ☐
I'd like to run a marathon one day. ☐
I prefer team sports, like racquetball or field hockey. ☐
Jogging is exercise, not fun. ☐
Running is boring. ☐
The only time I run is to catch the bus. ☐

B **SCAN** Read texts 1–3. What is the purpose of each?

Text 3 : to inform Text 2 : to persuade
Text 1 : to entertain

1

Funny fitness

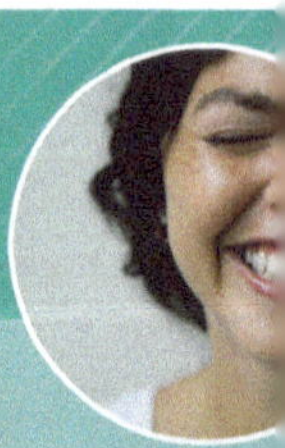

Did you know that laughing for 15 minutes can burn up to 40 calories? We hope these jokes and quotes will keep you smiling as you walk to the store, jog around the park or run your next marathon.

Q What is a runner's favorite school subject?
A Jog-raphy

'If you are in a bad mood, go for a walk. If you are still in a bad mood, go for another walk.'
Hippocrates

Patient: Doctor, can you give me something to stop sleepwalking?
Doctor: I'm afraid I can't, sir. You need the exercise!

6.2 Keep fit

LEAD-IN

Explain to students that you are going to discuss what they do to keep fit, or stay in shape. Hold a board pen in one hand and explain that students can only speak when they are holding it. Model the game by saying: *In order to keep fit, I run for half an hour every morning. What do you do?* Pass the pen to a stronger student for them to say what they do to keep fit or stay in shape or why they don't do anything. They then ask the question and pass the marker to the next speaker, and so on. Look for any opportunities to highlight/teach emergent language.

VOCABULARY

A Ask students to look at the picture and say what sport it is (*speed skating*). Students work in pairs writing their lists. When time is up, ask the pair with the longest list to share their words with the class. The other pairs have to share any words that were not mentioned.

B Direct students to the **Vocabulary Hub** (TB121). Use the **Vocabulary Worksheet** on W34 for extra practice.

C Read the activity with the class. Model the activity with a stronger student. Direct students to the **Vocabulary Hub** Exercise B (TB121). Then, give students five minutes to mingle, ask the questions to their classmates, write down the name of the student who answered yes and ask a follow-up question. Monitor and assist when necessary.

PRONUNCIATION

6.4 **A** Play the audio. Ask students whether the consonants sound the same or different.

6.4 **B** Play the audio again. Students listen and repeat.

6.5 **C** Play the audio. Students listen to a list of words that contain the sounds /ŋ/, /n/ and /m/. Students repeat and identify the sounds they hear and then write them in the corresponding column. Check answers with the whole class. With a stronger class, you may ask them to make a list of other words they know containing one or more of the three sounds.

READING

A On the basis of the *Lead-in* activity, ask those students who run, one or two follow-up questions (e.g. how often? where? longest distance?). Ask students to look at the six sentences about running and check (✓) any that they agree with. Arrange students in pairs. They discuss their answers giving reasons for their choices. Take feedback from one or two pairs and encourage students to respond to each other's ideas.

B Explain that authors have a purpose when they write. When reading, students should think what the purpose of a text is: to inform? to entertain? to persuade? Elicit the meanings of *to inform, to persuade* and *to entertain*. Ask students to scan the three texts and decide their purpose. Set a time limit to do the task, e.g. two minutes, to prevent students from reading the full texts in detail.

METHODOLOGY HUB by Jim Scrivener

Knowing a lexical item

Seeing real examples of language being used is usually more important than hearing 'cold' definitions. How can we do this? Here are some ideas.

Record lexical items in useful ways

Encourage learners to keep word pages that let them collect collocations, pronunciation, idioms, etc. Help learners by giving out blank formats (e.g. word lists, collocation grids, etc) and teaching them how to use them.

Revisit lexical item pages

Encourage students to revisit their word collections and keep amending and adding new examples, collocations, etc. Keep referring back to and making use of these pages in class, for homework, etc.

Collect lexical items

When students read a text or listen to a recording, encourage them to notice interesting items and 'collect' them on their word pages.

Sort and classify items

Get students to read specific texts to collect and classify items together on single word pages (e.g. from a cooking article: 'things found in the kitchen'; from a vacation story: 'travel words'; from a love letter: 'happy words'; from a job advertisement: 'adjectives describing people'; etc).

When an error comes up, review a range of collocations

In class, a student says *I made the exam last week*. Rather than just swiftly giving the correct verb, have students take a look at a number of useful 'exam' collocations and chunks: *took the exam, failed the exam, passed the exam, exam questions, exam results*, etc.

C Students read the texts again and decide which, if any, contains the information in Sentences 1–6. Give them time to check their answers in pairs, before giving feedback as a class.

D Students discuss the questions in pairs. Monitor and assist as required.

GRAMMAR

A Students use the example sentences to help them complete the rules. Give feedback as a class, clarifying the use of each *-ing* form as necessary.

B Direct students to the **Grammar Hub** (see below). Use the **Grammar Worksheet** on W33 for extra practice.

C Arrange students in pairs and ask them to discuss Questions 1 and 2. Monitor and assist when necessary. Take feedback from one or two pairs and encourage students to respond to each other's ideas.

SPEAKING

A Read the task with the class. Focus students on the prompts and elicit some ideas for each category (e.g. Will the event be directed toward children, students, pregnant women? Will they use posters, advertisements, or flyers to promote it? With a stronger class, you could add a further discussion category such as where the event will be held or how much it will cost). Students work in groups planning their event. Monitor and help when necessary.

B Ask the groups to present their ideas to the class. Once each group has presented their ideas, ask the class to decide which event they think will have the most impact.

TEACHING IDEA by David Seymour and Maria Popova

Use this activity to practice using gerunds.

My opinion

Work in three teams. I'll give each team three adjectives. Use these adjectives with a gerund to write sentences, e.g. stupid.
– *Drunk-driving is stupid.*

1 tiring, boring, stressful 2 dangerous, exciting, unhealthy
3 illegal, healthy, relaxing

Read aloud your adjectives. The rest of the class will guess what gerund you have written. In pairs, write down four opinions using a gerund, e.g. *Working more than 40 hours a week should be illegal.* Choose one of the opinions each and do a survey of the class to find out how many students agree.

GRAMMAR HUB

6.2 *-ing* forms

- We use the present participle *-ing* form to talk about things that are happening now or around now and that are not finished. This is the present progressive.
  *You're **doing** really well at yoga.*
- We use the *-ing* form as an adjective to describe a noun.
  *He has developed a **growing** interest in Nordic walking.*
- We use the *-ing* form as a gerund to make a noun.
  *They like **working out** at the gym twice a week.*

6.2 *-ing* forms

A Correct the mistakes in each sentence.

1. We both enjoy ~~go~~ going for walks.
2. ~~To jog~~ Jogging is my favorite form of exercise.
3. I'm ~~watch~~ watching a good TV show about superfoods.
4. She doesn't like ~~swim~~ swimming in the ocean.
5. Recently, there has been an ~~increase~~ increasing number of accidents in the home.
6. My nextdoor neighbor isn't ~~to do~~ doing very well right now.
7. A ~~rise~~ rising number of people can't afford to buy medicine.

B Put the words in order to make sentences. Then choose gerund (*G*), adjective (*A*) or present participle (*PP*) for the words in **bold**.

1. doesn't / **being** / her / on / like / she / own — (G) / A / PP
   She doesn't like being on her own.
2. love / doctor / **visiting** / we / family / our — (G) / A / PP
   We love visiting our family doctor.
3. now / **growing** / in / there / is / interest / a / pilates — G / (A) / PP
   There is now a growing interest in pilates.
4. **studying** / food / we're / health / in / class / groups — G / A / (PP)
   We're studying food groups in health class.
5. my / **cooking** / free time / activity / favorite / is — (G) / A / PP
   My favorite free-time activity is cooking.
6. now / people / vitamins / of / taking / **increasing** / are / numbers — G / (A) / PP
   People are taking vitamins in increasing numbers.

➤ Go back to page 55.

2

Parkrun

Are you looking for an easy way to stay in shape and lose weight? Would you like to run 5 km in a family-friendly atmosphere? Would you like to compare your results with other runners from all over the world? If so, then check out *Parkrun*.

Parkrun organizes free weekly timed runs in parks all over the world. The 5 km runs take place on weekend mornings and are open to everyone. After each race, runners receive detailed results via email.

Parkrun is an international community of over one million runners in 17 countries and there is always space for more! So come and join the *Parkrun* family and get fit for free!

Glossary

atmosphere (n) the mood or feeling in a place

3

MARATHON MAN

What do you think it takes to become a running master? Fauja Singh, from east London, finished a 10 km race in Hong Kong in one hour and 32 minutes – and he did it at the age of 101.

In 2011, Singh became the oldest person to run a marathon. At 100 years of age, he completed the Toronto Marathon in just over eight hours.

As a young man, Mr. Singh was a farmer in Punjab, India. Then in the 1960s, he went to live in Britain and only began running when he was 89 years old.

Mr. Singh plans to run again for charity, but the Hong Kong 10 km was his final competitive race. 'I will remember this day. I will miss it,' Mr. Singh said after the event.

C READ FOR DETAIL Read again and answer the questions. Write *Funny fitness* (FF), *Parkrun* (PR), *Marathon man* (MM) or none of the texts (N).

Which text …

1 tells the story of an individual? MM
2 offers readers the chance to read more online? PR
3 tries to sell readers something? N
4 reports the results of a research project? N
5 tries to make readers laugh? FF
6 describes the purpose of a particular organization? PR

D SPEAK **Work in pairs. Discuss the questions.**

1 Why is running such a popular form of exercise?
2 Would you like to do a parkrun? Why/Why not?

GRAMMAR

-ing forms

A **Look at the examples of different *-ing* forms used in the texts. Then complete the rules with the words in the box.**

1 Did you know that **laughing** for 15 minutes can burn up to 40 calories? (gerund)
2 Are you **looking** for an easy way to stay in shape and lose weight? (present participle)
3 What do you think it takes to become a **running** master? (adjective)

adjectives gerunds present participle

-ing forms

1 We use the *present participle* -*ing* form with the verb *to be* to talk about things that are happening now or around now, and are not finished.
2 We use -*ing* form as *adjectives* to describe nouns.
3 We use -*ing* form as *gerunds* to make nouns.

B Go to the **Grammar Hub** on **page 132**.

C SPEAK **Work in pairs. Discuss the questions.**

1 What is your favorite form of exercise?
2 Do you like working out? Why/Why not?

SPEAKING

A **Work in groups. Plan an event to encourage local people to start doing more exercise. Think about:**

- who your event is for
- how it will help people get in shape or start exercising
- what people need to bring to the event
- how you will promote the event

B **Describe your event to the rest of the class. Which event is the most popular. Why?**

Plan an exercise event for your local community

6.3 We may never 'meat' again

Encourage people to make a lifestyle change

G present perfect with *just, already* and *yet* **V** food groups **P** /s/ and /ʃ/ **S** scanning for key words

READING

A Match the words in the box to pictures (1–6).

avocado broccoli fur grain kale wheat

B **READ FOR GIST** Read *A fresh start*. Which three reasons for going vegetarian or vegan are given in the article?

1 wheat 2 avocado 3 grain 4 broccoli 5 fur 6 kale

A fresh start

Large numbers of people are saying 'never again!' to meat and becoming vegetarian or vegan. For some it's about health, for others it's about concern for the environment. Whatever the reason, many people are changing the way they eat forever.

Ex C Q1 Research by the Vegan Society states that in 2016 there were around 542,000 vegans in the UK alone. Veganism is also on the Ex C Q2 rise thanks to celebrity supporters including Ellie Goulding, Liam Hemsworth and Venus and Serena Williams.

There are various reasons why people decide to go vegetarian Ex B or vegan. Some do it for their health. Vegans get all the vitamins, minerals and other things they need for a balanced diet from grains, Ex C Q3 fruits, seeds, nuts and vegetables such as kale, broccoli, beans and avocados. A vegetarian diet can help people lose weight because it is low in fat. High-fat diets are linked to serious health problems including diabetes, heart disease and cancer.

Ex B Some people give up meat because they are worried about the environment. A 2006 FAO (The Food and Agriculture Organization of the United Nations) study reported that 18 percent of greenhouse gases come from farm animals such as cows, sheep and chickens. That's more than all of the world's cars, trains and planes put together. Ex C Q4 We use over 36 percent of the world's grain to feed farm animals, yet a quarter of the people in the world do not have enough food. If we made food for people from the grain instead, there would be enough for everyone. Ex C Q5

Other people go meat-free because they feel it is wrong to kill animals. Ex B Animals feel pain and fear. Many farmed animals are kept in poor conditions with little space and no time outdoors. In the UK, around 990 million farmed animals are killed for food each year.

With so many grocery stores and restaurants now offering vegetarian and vegan goods, it's easier than ever to give up or reduce the amount of meat we eat. Ex C Q6 Why not try a few meat-free days a week – you could help reduce world hunger and even help with climate change!

Are you vegan or vegetarian?

We want your comments!

Nora_27: **I've just changed to a vegetarian diet after years of eating meat.** It's only been a week, but I feel much healthier and I highly recommend it!

M-M-Maxine: I feel bad about killing animals, but I really enjoy meat. **I've already eaten two sausages and a chicken sandwich today, and it's only lunchtime!** I don't think I'd last very long without meat.

Cool_keith2: **I've been vegetarian for a while, but I haven't managed to go vegan yet.** It seems like a lot of work to plan and prepare the food. Any advice?

Kellykale: Great article. Vegan food is great! **Have you tried kale chips yet?** They are really tasty and great as a healthy snack.

Glossary

billion (number) the number 1,000,000,000

greenhouse gas (n) a gas that stops heat from escaping the atmosphere and causes the greenhouse effect, the gas that makes global warming worse

mineral (n) a natural substance in some foods that you need for good health, for example, iron and calcium

vitamin (n) natural substances found in food that are necessary to keep your body healthy

6.3 We may never 'meat' again

LEAD-IN

Draw a table with the following headings on the board: *Your own country / US / Other countries*. Tell students they have one minute to write as many national or typical dishes as they can under each heading. Then have a class discussion by asking the following questions:

1. *Have you ever tried any of these dishes? Which ones? Did you like them?*
2. *Which is the strangest food you've ever eaten? What did it taste like?*
3. *Do you like trying new foods?*
4. *Do you prefer your own country's food or other kinds of food? Why?*
5. *If you were living in another country, which food would you miss most from this country?*

READING

A Students look at the six images on the page and match them with the words from the vocabulary box. Check answers as a class. Follow up by asking which of these items the class has bought recently.

B Focus students on the glossary. You may profit from pre-teaching *meat-eater, vegan* and *vegetarian*. You may also want to pre-teach *veggie* as a shortened, informal form of vegetable. Model and practice pronunciation. Tell students they have one minute to read the article and find three reasons for choosing a vegan or vegetarian diet.

METHODOLOGY HUB by Jim Scrivener

Guided Discovery

When explaining new grammar to students, two minutes of focused explanation can be really helpful; 20 minutes of the same is likely to get students confused, bored and embarrassed. An alternative to giving explanations would be to create activities that allow learners to generate their own discoveries and explanations. Tasks at just the right level will draw attention to interesting language issues. Teacher questions will 'nudge' the learners toward key points.

Guided discovery: typical comments, instructions and questions

The following list shows various ideas and examples of guided discovery questions from different lessons.

Questions about form

What word goes in this space? How many words are there in the sentence? How do you spell that? Is that a verb?

Questions about function

Do they know each other? Where do you think they are speaking? Is this formal or informal? How does he feel?

Reflecting on use

Write down some of the sentences you heard. Why did you use that tense? Where was the problem? Which of those two sentences is correct?

Hypothesizing rules – Is this possible?

What will the ending be in this example? Why is that incorrect? Can you think of another word that could go here?

Contexts and situations

This is Paul. Where does he work? Tell me what he does every day. Jo has a full schedule. What's she doing tonight? Look at this picture. What's going to happen? If I throw this pen at the picture on the wall, what'll happen?

GRAMMAR HUB

6.3 Present perfect with *just, already* and *yet*

	Positive	Negative
I/you/we/they	I**'ve** just **seen** the doctor.	**I haven't seen** the doctor yet.
he/she/it	**She's left** the hospital already.	**He hasn't gone** to the gym yet.

Question	Positive short answer	Negative short answer
Have you taken your painkillers yet?	Yes, **I have**.	No, **I haven't**.
Has the nurse just **given** you some medicine?	Yes, **he has**.	No, **he hasn't**.

- We use the present perfect with *just* in positive statements to say that something happened very recently.

  *I have **just** passed my fitness test.*
- We use the present perfect with *already* in positive statements to say that something happened before now, or earlier than expected.

  *We have been to the grocery store twice today **already**.*
- We use the present perfect with *yet* in negative statements to say that something hasn't happened, but it still might.

  *You haven't finished your vegetables **yet**.*
- We use the present perfect with *yet* in questions to ask if something has happened.

  *Have you cleared the dinner table **yet**?*

Be careful!

- *Just* goes before the past participle.

  *I've **just** eaten some fruit.* NOT ~~*I've eaten some fruit just.*~~
- *Yet* goes at the end of the sentence.

  *Have you gone vegetarian **yet**?* NOT ~~*Have you yet gone vegetarian?*~~
- In American English, *already* usually goes at the end of the sentence. In British English, *already* goes before the past participle.

  *I've stopped eating meat **already**.* OR *I've **already** stopped eating meat.*
- See Grammar Reference 5.3 for more information about the present perfect.

6.3 We may never 'meat' again

C Focus students on the activity and on the skills box. Give them one minute to scan the article to decide whether Sentences 1–6 are true or false. Check answers as a class.

D Students work in pairs to discuss the arguments for and against farming and killing animals for food. Monitor and assist when necessary. Take feedback from one or two pairs and encourage students to respond to each other's ideas.

GRAMMAR

A Focus students on the activity. Students work in pairs looking at the sentences in bold again and completing the sentences in the grammar box with *just, already* and *yet*. Check answers with the whole class.

B Students read through Rules 1–3 as a class. They work on their own to choose the correct word. Allow them to check in pairs before checking the answers with the whole class.

C Direct students to the **Grammar Hub** (see TB56 and below). Use the **Grammar Worksheet** on W35 for extra practice.

D In pairs, students discuss the questions using sentences with the present perfect and *just, already* and *yet*. Monitor and assist as required. Take feedback from one or two pairs and encourage students to respond to each other's ideas.

VOCABULARY

A Give students one minute to make a list of different food items in pairs. When time is up, ask the pair with the longest list to share their words with the class. The other pairs share any words that were not mentioned.

B Direct students to the **Vocabulary Hub** for further practice of vocabulary on food groups and to complete the exercises. Use the **Vocabulary Worksheet** on W36 for extra practice.

C Model the activity for the class by either reading the example or by giving a personal example. In pairs, students discuss the questions. Remind students to use *just, already* and *yet* in their answers. Monitor and assist when necessary. Take feedback from one or two pairs and encourage students to respond to each other's ideas.

PRONUNCIATION

A Students work in pairs writing the words from the vocabulary box into the correct columns in the table (/s/, /ʃ/ or /s/ and /ʃ/). Check answers with the whole class.

6.6 **B** Play the audio. Students check their answers to Exercise A. Play the audio again and ask students to listen and repeat.

C Students take turns practicing saying the words in pairs. Encourage them to listen to and to correct each other's pronunciation. Monitor and assist as required.

SPEAKING HUB

A Arrange students in small groups of three or four. Focus them on the task. Groups discuss and choose which subject to write their leaflet, or flyer, about.

B Students read the prompts and work together to plan their leaflets. Monitor and assist when necessary.

C Collect the leaflets from each group and place them around the classroom. Ask students to move around the room and look at the leaflets from each group. Students decide which leaflet would be the most effective and give reasons for their answers.

Extra activity

If it is not possible for students to complete the leaflets in class, this could be set as a group homework task. Students can work on the leaflets based on the feedback they received in class. Each member of the group could be assigned a different task, e.g. image research, health benefits, etc. Students would then be allowed to further research their topics online.

GRAMMAR HUB

6.3 Present perfect with *just*, *already* and *yet*

A Write *just*, *already* or *yet*.

1. Have you had anything to eat ___yet___?
2. He hasn't asked her to work out with him ___yet___.
3. I've run two marathons this year ___already___.
4. She's ___just___ finished her workout – she's showering now.
5. It's only 11 a.m., but Jack's eaten his lunch ___already___.
6. **A:** Who was on the phone?
   B: Frida. She's ___just___ returned home from the hospital.

B Make sentences with the present perfect and *just*, *already* and *yet*.

1. you / see / your exam results / ?
   Have you seen your exam results yet?
2. they / lose / 5 pounds / from their diet
   They have already lost 5 pounds from their diet.
3. I / have / a phone call / from the nurse
   I have just had a phone call from the nurse.
4. we / not use / our new oven
   We haven't used our new oven yet.
5. she / take / her medicine / today
   She has already taken her medicine today.
6. you / buy / the food / for tonight / ?
   Have you bought the food for tonight yet?
7. I / see / Pamela / in the grocery store
   I've just seen Pamela in the grocery store.

➤ Go back to page 57.

C SCAN Read again. Are the sentences true (T) or false (F)? Use the information in the box to help you.

> **Scanning for key words**
>
> When you are reading to find specific information, such as names, dates and statistics, move your eyes quickly over the text and look for titles, numbers, symbols and names. Read around these items to find the information you are looking for. This is called scanning.
>
> Scanning helps save time in exams and is useful for previewing texts to decide whether to read them in more detail.

1. There are about half a million vegetarians in the UK. There are around half a million vegans in the UK. T / (F)
2. A fair number of famous people are vegans. (T) / F
3. Vegans need to take extra vitamins to stay healthy. T / (F) Vegans get all the vitamins they need from grains, fruits, seeds, nuts and vegetables.
4. Vehicles produce less air pollution than farming animals for meat. (T) / F
5. If we produced less meat, there would be more food for those people who do not have enough. (T) / F
6. It is difficult to buy vegan products. Many Supermarkets and restaurants now offer vegetarian and vegan products. T / (F)

D SPEAK Work in pairs. What are the arguments for and against farming and killing animals for food?

GRAMMAR

Present perfect with *just*, *already* and *yet*

A WORK IT OUT Look at the sentences in **bold** in the comments section of *A fresh start*. Then complete the rules with *just*, *already* or *yet*.

> **Present perfect with *just*, *already* and *yet***
>
> 1 We use the present perfect with *just* in positive statements to say something happened very recently.
>
> 2 We use the present perfect with *already* in positive statements to say that something happened before now or earlier than expected.
>
> 3 We use the present perfect with *yet*:
> - in negative statements to say that something hasn't happened, but it still might.
> - in questions to ask if something has happened.

B Look again and choose the correct words to complete the rules.

> 1 *Just* comes ***before*** / ***after*** the past participle in a sentence.
>
> 2 *Already* usually comes ***before*** / ***after*** the past participle in a sentence.
>
> 3 *Yet* comes at the ***beginning*** / ***end*** of a sentence or question.

C Go to the **Grammar Hub** on **page 132**.

D SPEAK. Work in pairs. Have you done any exercise today? Make true sentences with present perfect and *just*, *already* or *yet*.

VOCABULARY

Food groups

A Work in pairs. Make a list of different food items. You have one minute.

B Go to the **Vocabulary Hub** on **page 149**.

C SPEAK Work in pairs. Have you eaten any healthy food today? Who has been kinder to their body?

I had two oranges with my breakfast, and I've just eaten an apple and two kiwis, so I've had five pieces of fruit today already.

PRONUNCIATION

/s/ and /ʃ/

A SPEAK Work in pairs. Write the words in the box in the correct place. Use the examples to help you.

> chefs fish fresh lettuce ~~lobster~~ rice sandwich sauce spinach sushi ~~sugar~~

/s/	/ʃ/	/s/ and /ʃ/
lobster sauce lettuce spinach rice sandwich	*sugar* fresh fish	chefs sushi

6.6 **B** Listen and check. Then listen again and repeat the words.

C SPEAK Work in pairs. Student A – point to a word in Exercise B. Student B – say the word. Take turns.

SPEAKING HUB

A Work in groups. You are going to design a leaflet to help other students make a lifestyle change. Choose one of the following:

- eat less meat
- stop drinking bottled water
- use more fresh ingredients when cooking
- eat less sugar

B PLAN What information will you include on the leaflet? Think about the areas below and then design your leaflet.

- health benefits
- environmental benefits
- how your school or college will help
- how you or someone you know changed their lifestyle in this way and how they benefited

C REFLECT Read the other groups' leaflets. Which do you think would be most successful and why?

Encourage people to make a lifestyle change

Café Hub

6.4 Painful experience

F – talk about your symptoms at a pharmacy

P – vowel sounds

COMPREHENSION

A ▶ **00:00–02:13** Watch the first part of the video without sound and answer the questions.

1 How does the pharmacist feel? terrible

2 How does Gaby feel? terrible

3 Check (✓) the parts of their bodies that hurt.

arm ☐	back ☐	ears ☑	eyes ☑	foot ☐
hand ☐	head ☑	leg ☐	nose ☑	throat ☑

B ▶ **00:00–02:13** Watch the first part of the video again with sound and check your answers to Exercise A.

C SPEAK Work in pairs. What advice would you give Gaby? What advice would you give the pharmacist?

D ▶ **02:26–04:54** Watch the second part of the video and check your answers to Exercise C.

FUNCTIONAL LANGUAGE

Talk about your symptoms at a pharmacy

A Write the headings in the box in the correct place (a–c).

Explain symptoms | Ask about health | Give advice

Useful language

a Ask about health

Are you OK?

Are you [1] sure you're OK ?

What's painful?

What are your symptoms?

Do you have anything for a sore throat / a [2] headache ?

Do you have sore eyes / [3] a temperature ?

Are you allergic to anything?

b Explain symptoms

It's very painful.

My nose / [4] back hurts.

I'm not feeling very well.

I have a terrible cold.

You don't have a cold, you have hay fever / [5] flu .

c Give advice

I suggest these tablets / [6] this medicine .

Take one every eight hours.

You could try drinking a hot lemon and honey.

I think you should rest / [7] relax .

MILLY

SAM

NEENA

ZAC

GABY

B Write the words and phrases in the box in the correct place in Exercise A.

back flu a temperature headache relax sure you're OK this medicine

USEFUL PHRASES

A Match the useful phrases (1–6) with similar phrases which show the meaning (a–f).

1 I know how you feel.
2 We are both not very well today.
3 It's common at this time of year.
4 I'll be fine.
5 Is one enough?
6 That usually makes me feel better.

a A lot of people get this in the summer.
b Don't I need more?
c I have the same symptoms as you.
d It's my favorite cure.
e You and I are sick today.
f Don't worry about me.

B How do you say these useful phrases in your language?

PRONUNCIATION

Vowel sounds

A Match the words which have the same vowel sound.

1 cough
2 hurt
3 pain
4 sore
5 throat

a allergic
b door
c nose
d same
e wrong

6.7 **B** Listen and check. Then listen again and repeat the words.

C **SPEAK** Work in pairs. Practice saying the words. Listen and check your partner's pronunciation.

SPEAKING

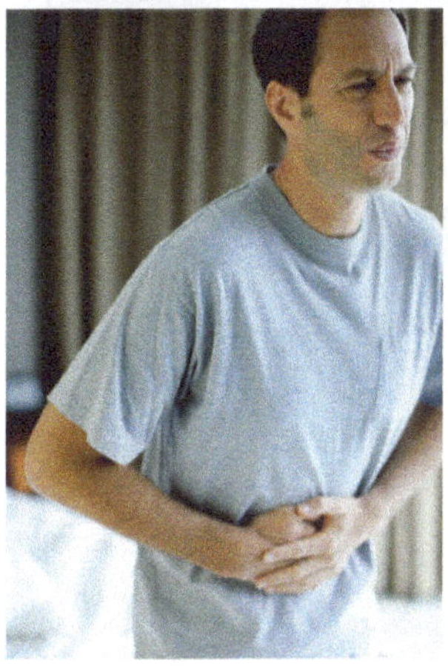

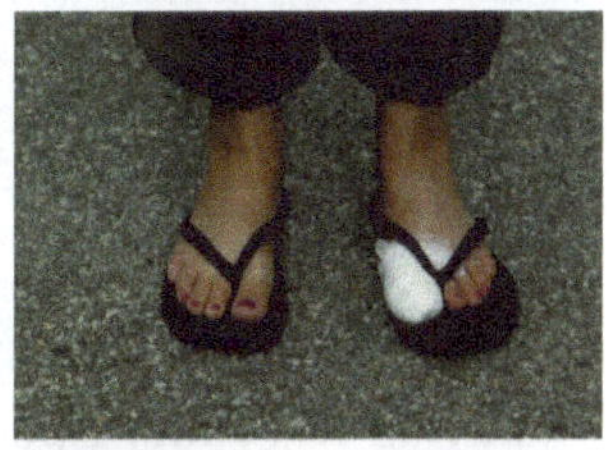

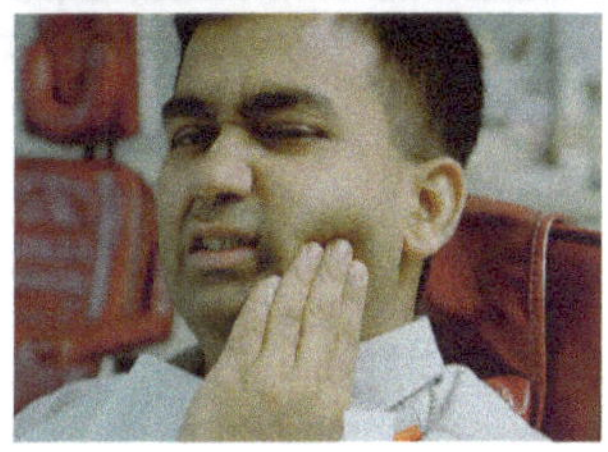

Work in pairs. Role-play a conversation about health. Take turns being Student A and Student B.

Student A: Choose an ailment from the pictures and explain the symptoms.

You must use the following words: *feeling, have, hurt(s), painful.*

Student B: Ask questions and give advice.

You must use the following words: *allergic, take, temperature, try.*

Talk about your symptoms at a pharmacy

➤ Turn to **page 163** to learn how to write a product review.

6.4 Painful experience

COMPREHENSION

A ▶ 00:00–02:13 Elicit from the images where Gaby is (*the pharmacy*) and what will happen in the episode. Pre-teach *symptoms*. Play the first part of the video without sound and ask students to answer Questions 1–3. Ask for one or two answers, but do not confirm or correct them.

B ▶ 00:00–02:13 Play the video again with sound for students to check their answers to Exercise A.

C In pairs, students discuss what advice they would give Gaby and the pharmacist. Monitor and assist students when necessary. Give feedback as a class and encourage discussion.

D ▶ 02:26–04:54 Play the second part of the video. Students compare their advice from Exercise C to the advice in the video.

FUNCTIONAL LANGUAGE

A Focus students on the *Useful language* box. Students complete the table with the correct headings. Give feedback as a class.

B Students complete the phrases with the words in the box. Give them time to check their answers in pairs, before giving feedback as a class.

USEFUL PHRASES

A Students match sentence to the phrases with the same meaning. Check answers as a class.

B As a class, discuss how students would say these phrases in their own language. Encourage discussion.

PRONUNCIATION

A Students match the words that contain the same vowel sounds. Don't take feedback at this stage.

6.7 **B** Play the audio for students to check their answers to Exercise A. Play it again for students to listen and repeat.

C In pairs, students practice saying the words from Exercise A. Monitor and continue practicing correct pronunciation as needed.

SPEAKING

A Elicit the problems the pictures show. In pairs, students read the conversation frame and take turns role-playing their conversation. Monitor and assist as required. Ask some pairs to perform their role plays for the class.

VIDEO SCRIPT

Café Hub 1.4 Painful experience
G = Gaby P = Pharmacist

G: Hello? Is anyone here?
P: Hello. How can I help?
G: Are you okay?
P: It's very painful!
G: What's painful?
P: Everything. My head, my throat, my eyes … My nose hurts … My ears hurt … Everything … hurts!
G: Oh, I am sorry.
P: Argh! Too much noise! My head! It really hurts! Anyway, I'm sorry. What can I do for you?
G: I'm not feeling very well.
P: What are your symptoms?
G: I have a terrible cold and ah… Ah… Ah… Choo!
P: I know how you feel.
G: Well, we are both not very well today. Do you have anything for a sore throat?
P: Do you have sore eyes?
G: Yes. Very sore!
P: And do you have a temperature?
G: No. Not really.
P: No … You don't have a cold. You have hay fever!
G: Hay fever. Really?
P: Yes, it's common at this time of year. I suggest these tablets.
G: Are you sure you are okay?
P: Yes. Yes. I'll be fine. Are you allergic to anything?
G: No.
P: Good. Here you are.
G: Great, thanks. How many do I have to take?
P: Take one every eight hours.
G: Is one enough?
P: Yes, they're very strong.
G: You could try drinking a hot lemon and honey? That usually makes me feel better. And I think you should rest …
P: Thank you, I'll try that.
G: Good. Also, do you have any tissues?
P: Yes, they're over there.

TEACHING IDEA by David Seymour and Maria Popova

Lead-In Activity: Healthcare

Arrange students in groups and give each group one of the discussion topics below and a piece of poster paper. Explain to students that they have five minutes to discuss the ways in which healthcare has changed over the years and write notes about this on their poster. After five minutes, ask the groups to move around the room to the next poster. Students should read the information from the first group and try to add two new ideas. Repeat the process until all the groups have discussed each of the topics. When students have returned to their original questions, take feedback from each group.

Old and modern medicine: How have medical techniques improved?

Nutrition: How has what we eat changed?

Institutions: How have hospitals and surgeries changed?

Extension Activity: What's wrong?

Write out some symptoms of minor illnesses (I feel tired all the time, I can't get to sleep, I have a sore throat, I have a bad cough, I have a high temperature, My chest hurts, etc) on sticky notes. Make sure you have one per student. Put the sticky notes on the backs of each student, ensuring that they do not see what is written. Explain that they will walk around the class, look at the sticky notes of their classmates and offer them some advice. Students should listen to the advice they receive and try to guess what their problem is.

6 Writing ● Write a product review

Ⓦ ordering information

A Read the product reviews from an online shopping website and match each review (1–3) with a picture (a–c).

Answers
1 a; 2 c; 3 b

1 Really useful ★★★★★
I bought this cool little device to help me get in shape, and **I'm very** [1] *happy* **with it**. It's comfortable and **I like the color.** It tells me how many steps I've taken, and how many calories I've burned each day. It also gives me information about how I slept. **It's very** [2] *useful* and I find it motivates me to do more exercise than before. **It's made of** rubber, so it's waterproof and also very light. **It was definitely** [3] *worth* **the money** and it arrived the day after I ordered it. [4] *Highly* **recommended** for anyone who is interested in health and fitness.

2 Ouch! ★★★
I bought this a few weeks ago to help me exercise. **It was a** [5] *reasonable* **price** and it seems to be **well made. It was easy to put together** and **came with** a book full of different exercises to try. **The only** [6] *problem* **is** it is really difficult to use! My stomach muscles aren't very strong and I find most of the exercises in the book impossible. I'm sure with enough practice it will get easier, but for now I have to say I don't look forward to using it. [7] *Recommended* **for** those who don't mind the pain!

3 Save your money ★
My girlfriend bought me these as a birthday present, but **I was very** [8] *disappointed* **with them.** Yes, **they look nice** and are comfortable to wear, but there's one big problem. **They are really** [9] *poor* **quality.** I wore them in the gym once, and after about half an hour, I noticed there was a hole in the side. Obviously these were very **badly** [10] *made*. I sent them back to the website and got a new pair, but after a few more trips to the gym … it happened again! **I don't recommend these** at all. They were **a real** [11] *waste* **of money.**

B Read again. Complete the phrases in **bold** with the words in the box.

disappointed highly made happy poor problem reasonable recommended useful waste worth

C Read again. Which phrases in **bold** describe positive things about the products, which describe negative and which are neutral?

I'm very happy with it. = positive
I was very disappointed with them. = negative
It's made of … = neutral

D Read the information in the box. Then read the reviews again and number the parts of a review in the correct order (1–4).

Ordering information
Think carefully about the order in which you present information in reviews and other types of factual writing. Organize your ideas into clear and logical paragraphs to make your writing easy for readers to follow.

negative points *3*
recommendation (or not) *4*
positive points *2*
why you bought the product *1*

E Work in pairs. Describe one product you have bought recently that you recommend and one that you do not.

WRITING

A PLAN Imagine you have bought one of the products below. Take notes on the following questions.

a pair of running sneakers

a fitness game for a game console

a winter sports jacket

a mountain bike

1 What positive points does the product have?
2 What negative points does the product have?

B WRITE Write a 100-word review of the product for a shopping website. Explain why you bought it and what positive and negative points it has. Then make a recommendation.

C REVIEW Work in groups. Read you classmates' reviews. Which are the best and worst products?

6 WRITING 163

Refer students to the three reviews as models for the first stage of the writing task.

Students can do this in class or for homework.

WRITING

A Students work on their own, reading the three product reviews and matching them to the pictures. Allow students to compare their answers in pairs before checking with the class.

B In pairs, students read the reviews again and complete the expressions in bold with the words from the vocabulary box. Check answers with the whole class.

C In pairs, students decide whether the phrases from the reviews are positive, negative or neutral. Take feedback from one or two pairs and encourage them to respond to one another's ideas.

Possible answers:

Positive: I like the color; It's very useful; It was definitely worth the money; Highly recommended; It was a reasonable price; It is well made; It was easy to put together; Recommended for…; They look nice.

Neutral: It came with …

Negative: The only problem is …; I was very disappointed with them; They're really poor quality; These were badly made; I don't recommend these; a real waste of money

D Read the box on *Ordering information* as a class. Ask students to read the reviews again and number the parts of a review in the correct order. Allow students to compare their answers with a partner before checking with the whole class.

E Students work in pairs taking turns describing a product they have bought recently that they recommend and one that they don't. Ask students to use as many of the words and phrases from the reviews as possible. Monitor and assist when necessary.

WRITING TASK

A Ask students to look at the four pictures and the list in Exercise B, and choose one to write a review about. Focus students on Questions 1 and 2. Ask them to write notes.

B Students write a 100-word review for the chosen product. Remind students to use the language from this lesson. Monitor and help as required.

C Arrange students in groups of four. They should read each other's reviews and decide which the best and worst products are.

Unit 6 Review

VOCABULARY

A Complete the crossword.

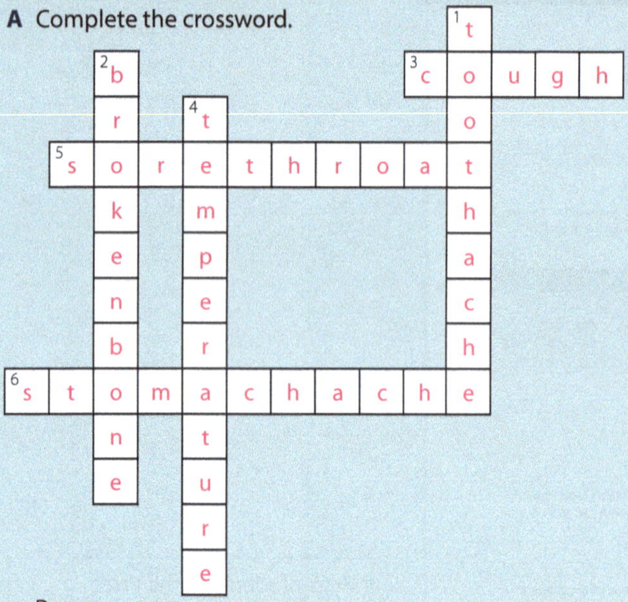

Down

1 See the dentist with this problem.

2 Leg, arm, finger? Go to the hospital. (two words)

4 You are warmer than you should be.

Across

3 Cover your mouth with your hand when you do this.

5 Try not to talk. Drink hot drinks. Suck a candy. (two words)

6 Did you eat too much?

B What are the missing words? Choose a, b or c to complete the survey.

WELCOME TO *SUNNY'S GYM*

Check (✓) your fitness goals.

1 c weight ☐

2 get or a in shape ☐

Do you …

3 b at a gym? ☐

4 c jogging? ☐

5 b a team sport? ☐

6 c yoga? ☐

	a	b	c
1	get	put	lose
2	stay	work	go
3	work it	work out	work on
4	run	do	go
5	go	play	join
6	play	go	do

C Choose the correct words to complete the sentences.

1 Pasta is made from *nuts* / *wheat*.

2 You can eat the shell of *shrimp* / *lobster*, but a lot of people choose not to.

3 Pizza is made with bread, cheese and *avocado* / *tomato* sauce.

4 British-style fish and chips usually includes *tuna* / *cod*.

5 One of the main salad ingredients is *rice* / *lettuce*.

GRAMMAR

A Complete the sentences with *too many*, *too much* and *not enough*.

1 We can't make a cake today. There are not enough eggs in the fridge.

2 There are too many flavors of ice cream – I can't decide!

3 There are not enough chairs here. I'll get two more from the kitchen.

4 We shouldn't eat too much sugar in our diets. It's unhealthy.

5 I've eaten too much pie. I don't feel well.

B Write the word in parentheses in the correct place. Then circle the correct *-ing* form. Choose gerund (G), adjective (A) or present participle (PP).

1 She left the gym because of the rising prices. (*rising*) *G* / *(A)* / *PP*

2 Lucien is becoming very fit these days. (*becoming*) *G* / *A* / *(PP)*

3 He isn't doing any exercise right now. (*doing*) *G* / *A* / *(PP)*

4 My brother loves running marathons. (*running*) *(G)* / *A* / *PP*

5 I want to try practicing yoga by myself. (*practicing*) *(G)* / *A* / *PP*

C Complete the comments from a health website with *just*, *already* or *yet*.

HART_27: I became vegetarian about two weeks ago. I feel lighter and I have clearer skin [1] already. I've [2] just weighed myself but I haven't lost any weight [3] yet.

KENNYKEN: This morning, I finally decided to go vegan. I've [4] just come back from the store with vegan ingredients and a cookbook. Actually, I have one vegan cookbook [5] already, but I haven't made anything from it [6] yet.

FUNCTIONAL LANGUAGE

A Complete the words in the conversation at a pharmacy.

Pharmacist: Good morning. [1]How can I help?

Customer: Oh, good morning. [2]I feel terrible.

Pharmacist: [3]What are your symptoms?

Customer: [4]I have a sore throat and a cough. [5]It really hurts.

Pharmacist: Oh, dear. Anything else?

Customer: Well, I think [6]I have a temperature, too, because I feel hot all the time.

A little boy tries to solve the Sunday crossword puzzle, Lancashire, United Kingdom.

Mind (n) the part of you that thinks, knows, remembers and feels things.
Synonyms: intelligence, intuition, intellect (n).

Ford is suggesting that physical age is not important, but your attitude toward life is. Keeping an open mind, following your dreams, learning something new is what keeps you young.

Henry Ford (July 30,1863– April 7, 1947) was an American businessperson, who founded the Ford Motor Company.

OBJECTIVES

- discuss what makes you happy
- write an online comment about the effects of the internet
- talk about intelligence and achievements
- describe an object and say what you use it for
- write a survey report

Work with a partner. Discuss the questions.

1 How can people 'stay young'?
2 Look at the picture. Who is helping whom?
3 What do you do to keep your mind healthy?

MIND 61

OBJECTIVES

Read the unit objectives to the class.

UNIT OPENER QUESTIONS

Encourage students to look at the quote and take one or two suggestions from the class about what they think it means. If they are at a loss, read to them the complete quote.

Ask students to look at the picture on the page and encourage them to share their ideas. Ask prompt questions such as 'What's the relationship between the people in the photo? What are the people doing? In what way does the photo relate to the quote?' If students share any good ideas or useful language, write these on the board.

Ask students to look at questions at the bottom of the page. Model one possible answer, explaining different ways people have kept their minds young, e.g. learning a new language or a new skill and working with young people. Students discuss the questions in pairs or in a small group.

Monitor and assist as necessary. When students have finished the activity, ask one or two pairs to share their ideas with the class. Encourage students to listen to one another and respond with their own ideas and opinions.

WORKSHEETS

Lesson 7.1 Smile

Grammar: Articles (W37)

Vocabulary: Feelings (W38)

Lesson 7.2 The internet and the brain

Grammar: *used to* (W39)

Vocabulary: Shortened words (W40)

Lesson 7.3 Intelligence

Grammar: No article (*school, the school*) (W41)

Vocabulary: Phrasal verbs (W42)

7.1 Smile

Discuss what makes you happy

G – articles P – /ə/ (schwa) in *a* / *an* V – feelings

Mona Lisa

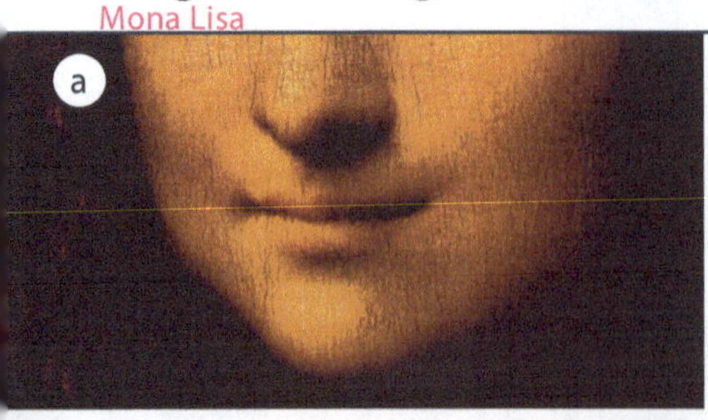

a

Marilyn Monroe

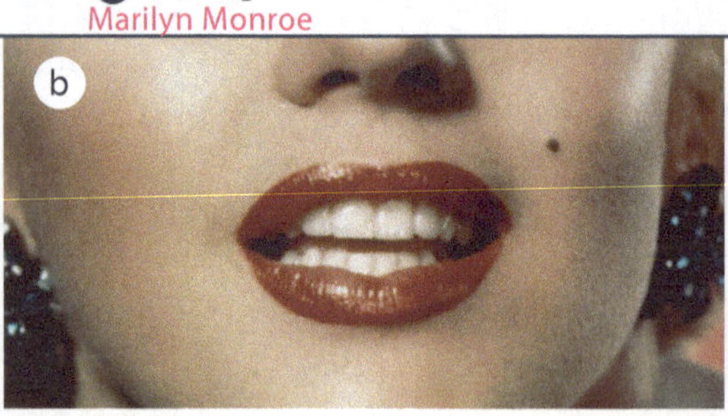

b

Drama Mask

c

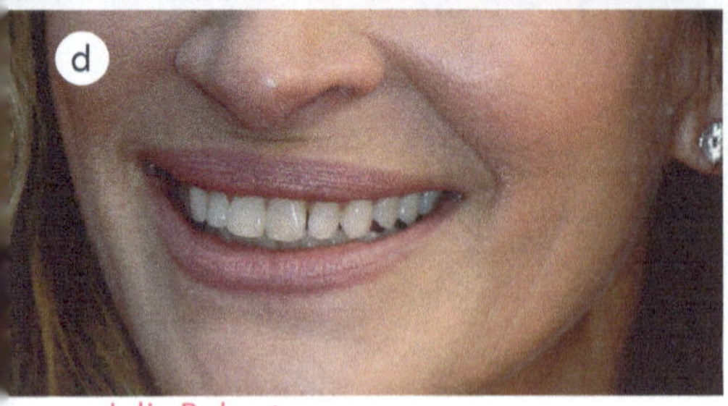

d

Julia Roberts

e

Smiley

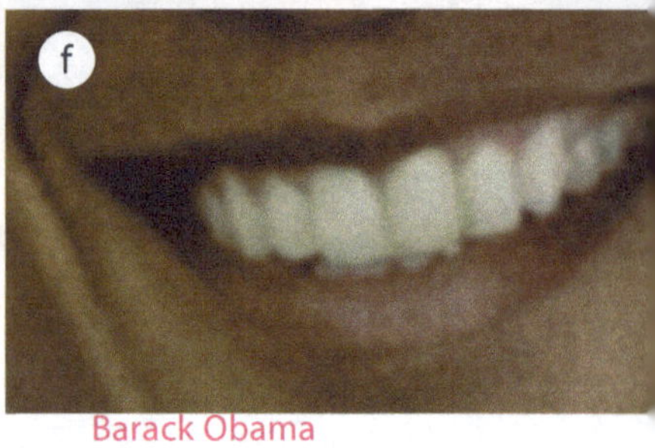

f

Barack Obama

READING

A Work in groups. Discuss the questions.

1 Do you recognize these famous smiles? What do you know about them?
2 'Laugh and the world laughs with you.' What does this saying mean? Do you agree with its message? Do you have a similar saying in your language?
3 How many times a day do you think a person laughs on average?
4 How is laughing good for our health?
5 How do smiling and laughing help social relationships?

B READ FOR GIST Read *A smile a day …* quickly and check your answers to questions 3, 4 and 5.

C READ FOR DETAIL Are the following statements true (T) or false (F)? Correct the false sentences.

1 Happy people are likely to live to an older age. T / F
2 Laughing can have a similar effect to working out in the gym. T / F
3 Laughing slows our heartbeat and blood flow. T / F
4 Laughing can prevent small health problems. T / F
5 The production of chemicals in our brain causes laughter. T / F
6 Smiling and laughter began in humans to show there was danger. T / F

D SPEAK Work in pairs. Discuss the questions.

1 How many times do you think you laugh each day? When did you last laugh? What did you laugh at?
2 What everyday things make you feel good and put you in a positive mood? (For example, good food, music, new clothes)

A *smile* a day …

We all know that a cheerful state of mind makes us happy but it could also help us to live longer. Ex C Q1

Laughing out loud, something we do on average 17 times a day, is particularly good for you. Laughter is a short sound which is repeated, on average, five times a second. It is widely believed that laughing 100 times is equal to ten minutes' light exercise in the gym. Ex C Q2 In addition, a 2005 study by the University of Maryland School of Medicine showed that laughter lowers blood pressure and there is a healthy increase in heart rate and blood flow. Ex C Q3 This can lead to a healthier heart and also make you less likely to catch colds and other minor illnesses. Ex C Q4 The research also suggests that people who are happy are likely to live longer. Laughing also produces chemicals in the brain that make us feel pleased and puts us in a positive mood. Ex C Q5 Smiling and laughing are also important for social relationships. Experts believe that smiling and laughing in humans began as a way to show relief when danger had passed. Ex C Q6 It helped the mind and body to feel relaxed and therefore showed trust between people. This stopped people from feeling scared of each other and helped people to connect. So the next time you want to connect with someone, why not start with a smile? It will help them to feel at ease and you might even make a new friend!

Glossary

minor (adj) not very important in comparison with things of the same type
relief (n) a relaxed, happy feeling that you get because a bad situation has ended
state of mind (phrase) the way that you are thinking and feeling at the present time
trust (n) a feeling of confidence in someone that shows you believe they are honest, fair and reliable

LEAD-IN

Draw seven columns on the board. Write a day of the week as a heading for each. Students write an adjective to show how they felt on each day for the past week (e.g. *happy, sad, bored*, etc). Fill in the chart for yourself and model the activity with a stronger student: e.g. 'Why were you sad last Friday?' 'Because my best friend moved to a different city.' Give students time to write. In pairs, students exchange their charts and take turns asking and answering each other's questions.

READING

A Arrange students in small groups to discuss Questions 1–5. To make this activity more heads-up, write the questions on the board and display the images. Take feedback from one or two groups and encourage students to respond to each other's ideas. Do not confirm or correct the answers to Questions 3, 4 or 5 at this time.

Possible answers:

3 *17*
4 *It lowers blood pressure, and there is a healthy increase in heart rate and blood flow. It can create a positive mood and lower stress.*
5 *It helps people to connect. It says 'I like you and I want to be your friend'.*

B On their own, students read the article quickly to check their answers to Questions 3, 4 and 5 from Exercise A. Set a time limit to prevent students from reading the text in detail.

C Focus students on the glossary. Remind them they will find words here that may help them understand the reading. Tell students to read the article again in more detail. Students decide whether the sentences are true or false and correct the false sentences. Allow students to check their answers with a partner before checking with the whole class.

D In pairs, students discuss Questions 1 and 2. Monitor and assist when necessary. Take feedback from one or two pairs and encourage students to respond to each other's ideas.

Extra activity

You can use this speaking activity to extend or replace the discussion questions in Exercise D. Put students into two groups. Group A should brainstorm as many things that make people laugh, smile or feel good as they can think of. Group B should brainstorm as many things that make people cry or feel bad as they can think of. Give students a time limit of two to three minutes. Ask students to find a partner from the other group. Together they should come up with a list of the top five things that make people feel good and the top five that make them feel bad. In class feedback, make sure to encourage students to explain and justify their choices. As a class discussion you can compare the lists and try to decide on the top five together.

METHODOLOGY HUB by Jim Scrivener

Error Correction

Five teacher decisions have to be made when working with oral errors in class:

1 What kind of error has been made (grammatical? pronunciation? etc).
2 Whether to deal with it (is it useful to correct it?).
3 When to deal with it (now? end of activity? later?).
4 Who will correct (teacher? student self-correction? other students?).
5 Which technique to use to indicate that an error has occurred or to enable correction.

Look back at Decision 2 in the list above. What are your criteria for whether or not to give on-the-spot immediate correction?

An important consideration here is the goal of the activity. Is it to improve learners' accurate use of English? If this is the case, then correction may be helpful. However, if the activity is meant to encourage fluency, interruptions and corrections might get in the way of the work.

There are other factors to take into account when deciding if a correction should be made: Will it help or hinder learning? Am I correcting something they don't know? (If so, there doesn't seem much point.) How will the student take the correction? What is my intention in correcting?

Decision 3 is about when to correct. The options include immediately, after a few minutes, at the end of the activity, later in the lesson, at the end of the lesson, in the next lesson, later in the course and never. The distinction between accuracy and fluency goals is important here. If the objective is accuracy, then immediate correction is likely to be useful; if the goal is fluency, then lengthy, immediate correction that distracts from the flow of speaking is less appropriate. We either need to correct briefly and unobtrusively as we go or save any correction for after the activity has finished or later.

Main objective of speaking activity	When to correct
accuracy	focused immediate correction *or* later *or* not at all
fluency	later *or* brief, unobtrusive, immediate correction (scaffolding) *or* not at all

One strategy used by many teachers during fluency activities is to listen in discreetly and collect a list of overheard errors. Later on, you can use this list to provide sentences to discuss, to set an exercise, to plan the next lesson, etc.

7.1 Smile

GRAMMAR

A Focus students on the sentences. Using them as support, students complete the rules for the use of the article in the grammar box. Check answers with the class.

B Direct students to the **Grammar Hub** (see below). Use the **Grammar Worksheet** on W37 for extra practice.

C Students read Sentences 1–3 and find and correct the mistakes. Students compare their answers with a partner before checking with the whole class.

D Monitor and assist as required. Encourage students to respond to each other's ideas.

PRONUNCIATION

7.1 **A** Play the audio. Ask students whether the articles are stressed or unstressed. Explain that *schwa* is a name given to the most common sound in English – the sound of an unstressed vowel. Play the audio again. Students listen and repeat.

B Students work in pairs (A and B). Direct students to the **Communication Hub** (TB121).

VOCABULARY

A In pairs, students choose the correct options in Questions 1–3. Check answers with the whole class.

B Direct students to the **Vocabulary Hub** (TB121) for further practice of *Feelings* and complete the exercises. Use the **Vocabulary Worksheet** on W38 for extra practice.

C Monitor and assist when necessary. Take feedback from one or two pairs and encourage students to respond to each other's ideas.

SPEAKING

A Explain *survey* (a set of questions you ask a large number of people). Students write down three everyday things that make them happy. If students struggle for ideas, suggest some (e.g. *a warm drink, running, taking a bath*, etc). In pairs, students tell each other about these things. If necessary, model the activity with a stronger student.

B Ask students to mingle and ask their classmates the three everyday things that make them happy. Encourage students to talk to as many of their classmates as possible and write down their answers. Set a time limit or a target number of people to talk to. Monitor and assist as required.

C Students compare their findings. Provide feedback as a class.

GRAMMAR HUB

7.1 Articles

- We use *a/an* to refer to something indefinite when it is one example of many. We usually use it when we refer to something for the first time.

  *Petros told me **a** funny joke.*

- We use *the* to refer to something definite, which we know. This is usually because it has already been mentioned.

  *Petros told me a funny joke. **The** joke was about ...*

- We use *the* when there is only one of something.

  *Do you usually use **the** internet?*

- We use – (no article) to refer to a plural or uncountable noun or something in a general sense.

  *I love finding **bargains** when I go shopping.*

Be careful!

- We don't use *the* before meals, days, streets, and singular place names.

  I eat dinner at 6 every evening. NOT ~~*I eat the dinner at 6 every evening.*~~

- We use *the* before the names of oceans and rivers and countries whose names are plural.

  ***the** Atlantic Ocean / **the** Nile River / **the** United States / **the** Philippines*

- We use *an* before a vowel sound. We use *a* before a consonant sound, even if the word begins with *a, e, i, o* or *u*.

  an article, an old friend
  a university, a European citizen

7.1 Articles

A Choose the correct option.

1 **The** / A / – way you feel about life can affect your health.
2 I heard a great saying. **The** / A / – saying goes: 'Smile and the world smiles with you'.
3 George wasn't in *the* / **a** / – very good mood this morning.
4 What did you have for *the* / *a* / **–** lunch today?
5 **The** / A / – research they did into the effects of laughter was very interesting.
6 Sarah put *the* / **an** / – angry face at the end of her text message.
7 We usually have a lot of *the* / *a* / **–** fun at parties.

B Complete the text messages with *the*, *a*, *an* or –.

Emma: Do you want to see (**1**) __a__ movie on the weekend?

Ian: Great! (**2**) __The__ movie theater on Orwell Street has four screens. I'll see what's playing.

Emma: Maybe try to find (**3**) __a__ comedy because (**4**) __–__ horror movies and thrillers make me too scared!

Ian: Sure! I need (**5**) __a__ good laugh! I'll find out and let you know.

Emma: OK. 😀

➤ Go back to page 63.

GRAMMAR

Articles

A WORK IT OUT Look at the sentences from *A smile a day ...* Then complete the rules with *a/an*, *the* or – (no article).

__The research__ also suggests that people who are happy are likely to live longer.

Laughter is __a short sound__ which is repeated, on average, five times a second.

Smiling and laughing are also important for __social relationships__.

Articles

1. We use ___*a/an*___ to refer to something indefinite when it is one of many. We usually use it when we refer to something for the first time.
2. We use ___*the*___ to refer to something definite and which we know. This is usually because it has already been mentioned.
3. We use ___*– (no article)*___ to refer to a plural or uncountable noun or something in a general sense.

B Go to the **Grammar Hub** on **page 134**.

C PRACTICE There are two mistakes in each question. Correct the mistakes.

1. The smiley face is a famous image all over ^the world. Why do you think ~~an~~ the image is so successful and popular?
2. Do you own or have you ever owned anything with ^a smiley face on it, such as ~~the~~ a T-shirt? Where else do we see it?
3. Do you use ~~an~~ emojis or icons in your online messaging? Do you have a favorite emoji? Are there ~~the~~ emojis for your country or culture?

D SPEAK Work in pairs. Ask and answer the questions in Exercise C.

PRONUNCIATION

/ə/ (schwa) in *a* / *an*

7.1 **A** Listen and repeat. What do you notice about the pronunciation of *a* and *an*? They are pronounced using the weak sound /ə/ (schwa). *a/an* is connected to the end of the word before it.

1. Have **a** nice day.
2. We had **a** great time.
3. She's **an** old friend.
4. A smile **a** day keeps the doctor away.

B SPEAK Work in pairs. Student A – go to the **Communication Hub** on **page 156.** Student B – go to the **Communication Hub** on **page 153.**

VOCABULARY

Feelings

A WORK IT OUT Look at the sentences from *A smile a day ...* Then choose the correct words to complete the sentences (1–3).

We all know that a __cheerful__ state of mind makes us happy ...

It helped the mind and body to feel __relaxed__ and therefore showed trust between people.

This stopped people from feeling __scared__ of each other and helped people to connect.

1. The words in bold are ***adjectives*** / ***nouns***.
2. They describe *opinions* / *feelings and states of mind*.
3. Words like these *are always positive* / *are always negative* / *can be positive or negative*.

B Go to the **Vocabulary Hub** on **page 149.**

C SPEAK Work in pairs. When was the last time you felt anxious, confused, pleased, relaxed? Tell your partner.

SPEAKING

A Work in pairs. Do a class survey about what everyday things make people happy. Think of three everyday things that make you happy. Write them down and tell your partner about them.

A: *I feel happy when I have a cup of tea in the morning. How about you?*
B: *Me, too, but I prefer coffee. And going for a walk on a sunny day with a clear blue sky makes me feel good.*
A: *I agree. A nice day makes everyone feel good!*

B Go around the class and ask your classmates what three everyday things make them happy. Write down their answers.

A: *Getting into bed after a long day.*
B: *When I find a bargain in the stores.*
C: *Relaxing with a good book.*

C Work in pairs. Compare your findings. What were the most common answers? What were the most interesting or unusual answers? Work with other pairs and share your answers.

Discuss what makes you happy

7.2 The internet and the brain

Write an online comment about the effects of the internet

G – *used to* P – *used to* V – shortened words

READING

A Work in pairs. Discuss the questions.

1. Look at the picture on the opposite page. What are the people doing?
2. How much time do you spend online? Which devices do you use?
3. What do you like or dislike about the internet?

B Match definitions (1–4) with the words in the box.

addicted attention span distracted memory

1. the length of time that you can pay attention to one thing without becoming bored or thinking about something else ___attention span___
2. the ability to remember things ___memory___
3. not able to concentrate on something ___distracted___
4. enjoying a particular activity very much and spending as much time as you can doing it ___addicted___

C READ FOR MAIN IDEA Work in pairs. Look at the title of the show and think of three ways the internet could be killing or damaging our brains. Then read the blog and check your answers.

D READ FOR DETAIL Read the comments. Match the comments with the person.

Who …

1. doesn't think the internet is a negative thing?
   Tom6 / JennyH / Sue123
2. is losing the ability to concentrate on something for long periods?
   Tom6 / JennyH / Sue123
3. thinks the internet has many negative effects on people?
   Tom6 / JennyH / Sue123
4. can't remember some things as well as in the past?
   Tom6 / JennyH / Sue123
5. thinks it's normal to change the way we use our memory?
   Tom6 / JennyH / Sue123

E SPEAK Work in pairs. What does 'use it or lose it' mean? What other skills could 'use it or lose it' apply to?

Glossary

adapt (v) to change your ideas or behavior so that you can deal with a new situation

approval (n) a positive opinion that you have towards someone or something that you think is good or suitable

impress (v) if someone or something impresses you, you admire them

Did you see …?

The TV blog for the TV lover *by Anna Frese*

Show: *Is the internet killing our brains?*

Did anyone see that TV show last night, *Is the internet killing our brains?* It was really interesting! First, it looked at the human memory in the 21st century and at how the internet is destroying our memory. This is because today most information is instantly available online and we don't need to remember things. And it said that over time, this could have a negative effect on the brain's memory system – a case of use it or lose it. The show then focused on how the human attention span is decreasing. It said that the brain is naturally easily distracted, and on the internet there is a lot of opportunity for this distraction. Evidence suggests that this is negatively affecting our attention spans and our ability to concentrate.

Finally, the show examined how the 'likes' and other positive comments and approval we receive on social media can be addictive. As a result, people are constantly trying to impress, and social network addiction is becoming a serious issue.

What do you think? Add your comments below:

Tom6 I don't agree with all the points. But, as soon as I start using the net, I find myself looking at site after site. It's very addictive. I can spend hours online and I suddenly realize it's dark outside!
Ex D Q2 I didn't use to be like that. I really do think my attention span is decreasing because of the net. However, they used to say the same thing about the radio and TV when they became popular.

JennyH The Greek philosopher Socrates said that writing would destroy memory because we would not have to remember things. However, Einstein believed that remembering facts was not a good use of our brains or our time. He said we had books to do that for us.
Ex D Q5 What's different about the internet? Humans will adapt to it
Ex D Q1 as they have in the past. I don't see a problem.

Sue123 I disagree with JennyH. I read somewhere that more than 70 percent of people
Ex D Q4 don't know important phone numbers. I used to know all my friends' numbers. Now, I don't know any.
Ex D Q3 We rely on our devices and the internet too much. So I do think it's killing our brains, and in a lot of ways, not just our memories.

7.2 The internet and the brain

LEAD-IN

Write *internet* on the board and have students brainstorm what they know about it. Alternatively, with a stronger group, you may divide the board into two columns headed 'Pros' and 'Cons' for students to come up with the pros and cons of the internet. Write students' ideas on the board.

READING

A Students discuss Questions 1–3 in pairs. To make this activity more heads-up, write the questions on the board. Take feedback from one or two pairs and encourage students to respond to each other's ideas.

B Focus students on the vocabulary box. Students read through the definitions and match them to the correct words from the vocabulary box. Allow students to compare their answers with a partner before checking them with the whole class.

C Focus students on the glossary and on the title and first line of the blog post. Elicit from the class the topic of the show (the internet is damaging our brains). Arrange students in pairs to think of three ways in which the internet could be damaging our brains. To encourage discussion, this part of the exercise could be done with closed books. Once the pairs have come up with three possible answers, ask students to read the blog post quickly to check them against the text.

A possible negative effect on our memory because we do not need to remember things.
Possibly affecting our attention spans because we are easily distracted.
Social network addiction is becoming a serious problem because people are constantly trying to impress and get approval.

D Ask students to read the comments again and decide who said each point. Students work alone but check answers with a partner. Review answers with the whole class.

E In pairs, students discuss the meaning of 'use it or lose it' and the skills that it could apply to. Take feedback from one or two pairs and encourage students to respond to each other's ideas.

If you don't use an ability or skill, you will lose that ability or skill. This could apply to abilities and skills such as using your memory, playing a musical instrument or something physical such as fitness, stamina or strength.

Extra activity

Extend the discussion and allow the students to revisit the text by asking:

1 Which of the three problems in the article do you think is most serious? Which is least serious? Why?
2 Which of the three comments do you most agree with? Why?

For writing practice, students could write a short comment in response to the article. However, make sure that students react to the article rather than respond to the comments. They will have an opportunity to write responses to the comments in the Speaking section.

TEACHING IDEA by David Seymour and Maria Popova

Speaking: Changes

Arrange students in three groups and ask them to list the ways life used to be different, e.g. 1,000 years ago most people used to go everywhere on foot.

Ask Group A to talk about life 100 years ago, Group B to talk about life 1,000 years ago and Group C to talk about life 10,000 years ago. Write the following prompts on the board to help them:

transportation, politics, food, work, health, education

Ask the groups to pass their list to the next group. Challenge the groups to add three things to the new list. Take feedback from the class.

TEACHING IDEA by David Seymour and Maria Popova

Speaking: Question focus

Arrange students in small groups. Explain that they will ask each other questions about how they've changed in the last five years, e.g.

A – Did you use to have a different hairstyle five years ago?

B – Oh, yes. I used to dye my hair all the time, too. Once I even dyed it green!

Write the following prompts on the board:

physical appearance (clothes, hair, build), habits (food, smoking, alcohol, going out), personality (problems, hopes, fears), people (friends, family, heroes and heroines)

7.2 The internet and the brain

GRAMMAR

A Students complete the sentences with the missing words. With a stronger group, ask students to complete them from memory. Read the grammar box as a class.

B Direct students to the **Grammar Hub** (see below). Use the **Grammar Worksheet** on W39 for extra practice.

C Focus students on the task and read the examples. Students write five true sentences. Monitor and assist as required. Take feedback from several students to check.

D Take feedback from one or two pairs and encourage the students to respond to each other's ideas.

PRONUNCIATION

7.2 **A** Play the audio. Students should notice that *d* and *t* combine to make one /t/ sound. Play the audio again for students to listen and repeat.

7.3 **B** Students practice saying the sentences in pairs. Play the audio for students to check their pronunciation.

VOCABULARY

A Students read the sentence to find the shortened words. Elicit the full word.

B Direct students to the **Vocabulary Hub** (TB121). Use the **Vocabulary Worksheet** on W40 for extra practice.

C Monitor and assist when necessary. Take feedback from one or two pairs and encourage students to respond to each other's ideas.

SPEAKING

A Encourage students to choose one or two points from the article or comments that they want to respond to.

B Students write down their ideas. Remind them that they should include a sentence with *used to* or *didn't use to*.

C Remind students to check their writing for grammar and spelling mistakes.

D In pairs, students decide whether they agree or disagree with each other and add a further point to their partner's comment.

E Encourage students to read and respond to each other's ideas. With less confident classes, ask students to discuss in pairs or small groups before taking feedback from the class.

GRAMMAR HUB

7.2 *used to*

	Positive	Negative
I/you/he/she/it/we/they	**I used to be** able to speak French.	**They didn't use to have** the internet in the 80s.

Question	Positive short answer	Negative short answer
Did you use to work hard at school?	Yes, **I did**.	No, **I didn't**.

- We use *used to* to talk about past situations that do not exist now. These include past habits and past states.

  Past habit: *We **used to watch** more TV before we had the internet.*

  Past state: *He **used to be** very anxious but he's more relaxed these days.*

Be careful!

- We use *use to* with the auxiliary verb *did*.

  I didn't use to chat online for hours. NOT ~~*I didn't used to chat online for hours.*~~

  Did you use to be addicted to video games? NOT ~~*Did you used to be addicted to video games?*~~

- In the negative, we can also say *never used to*.

  *I **didn't use to** chat online for hours.* OR *I **never used to** chat online for hours.*

7.2 *used to*

A Correct the mistakes in each sentence.

1. I used ~~working~~ *to work* in a restaurant.
2. Did you ~~used~~ use to live here?
3. They didn't ~~used~~ use to be friends.
4. She ~~use~~ used to study all the time.
5. We used ^to live in Germany.
6. He used ~~surfing~~ to surf the internet for hours every day.
7. You used to be~~ing~~ good at remembering names.

B Make sentences with *used to*.

1. your school / give you / all your books / ?
   Did your school use to give you all your books?
2. in the past, / people / not have / things like the internet
   In the past, people didn't use to have things like the internet.
3. in the 1990s, / cell phones / be / much bigger
   In the 1990s, cell phones used to be much bigger.
4. in the early days, / the internet / be / very unreliable
   In the early days, the internet used to be very unreliable.
5. you / find / it hard / to study at school / ?
   Did you use to find it hard to study at school?

➤ Go back to page 65.

GRAMMAR
used to

A WORK IT OUT Look at the sentences from *Did you see ...?* Find the missing words and complete the sentences. Then choose the correct words to complete the rule.

1 I can spend hours online, and I suddenly realize it's dark outside! I didn't use to be like that.
2 However, they used to say the same thing about the radio and TV when they became popular.
3 I used to know all my friends' numbers. Now, I don't know any.

used to

We use *used to* to talk about past situations that ***do not exist now*** / ***continue now***. The negative form is *didn't use to*.

- I used to work in a phone store.
- She used to have long hair.
- I didn't use to like chatting online.

B Go to the **Grammar Hub** on **page 134**.

C PRACTICE Write five sentences that are true for you with *used to* or *didn't use to*. Use the verbs in the box or your own ideas.

be be able to buy drive eat go have like listen to live play read smoke watch

I used to read comic books a lot when I was younger.
I didn't use to enjoy learning English.

D SPEAK Work in pairs. Discuss your answers to Exercise C.

PRONUNCIATION
used to

A 7.2 Listen and repeat. What do you notice about the pronunciation of *used to*? *Used to* is pronounced as /ju:s tə/.

1 used to We don't usually pronounce the final sound in *used* and *to* has the weak form /ə/ (schwa).
2 I used to play video games.
3 Phones used to be much bigger.

B 7.3 **SPEAK** Work in pairs. Practice saying the sentences. Then listen and check your pronunciation.

1 We used to speak on the phone a lot more.
2 Computers used to be much bigger.
3 I didn't use to go online much.

VOCABULARY
Shortened words

A Look at the words in **bold** in the sentence from *Did you see ...?* They are shortened words. What are the words short for? net = internet site = website

But, as soon as I start using the ***net****, I find myself looking at* ***site*** *after* ***site****.*

B Go to the **Vocabulary Hub** on **pages 149** and **150**.

C SPEAK Work in pairs. Discuss the questions.

1 Why do you think we shorten some words? To express ourselves quickly
2 Is it better to use shortened words in an informal or a formal situation? Informal
3 Can you think of any other shortened words in English?

SPEAKING

A Read *Did you see ...?* again. Comment on the blog or one of the comments.

B Write notes. Include at least one example of *used to* or *didn't use to*.

C Write about 50 words. Read your comment carefully and check for spelling and grammar.

D DISCUSS Work in pairs. Swap your comments and say whether you agree or disagree with your partner then add a further point.

E Display the comments for your classmates to read. Which ideas and opinions are the most common?

Write an online comment about the effects of the internet

7.3 Intelligence

● Talk about intelligence and achievements

V phrasal verbs G no article (*school, the school*) P practicing *the*: /ðiː/ or /ðə/ S listening for the order of events

Wolfgang Amadeus Mozart

Pablo Picasso

Venus Williams

William James Sidis

Garry Kasparov

LISTENING

A SPEAK Work in pairs. Look at the pictures. What do you know about these people? What do they all have in common?

B Match the words (1–2) with the correct definitions (a–b).

1 intelligence b

2 knowledge a

a all the facts that someone knows about a particular subject

b the ability to understand and think about things

7.4 **C LISTEN FOR KEY WORDS** Listen to the podcast about William James Sidis. Check (✓) what the presenter talks about.

1 Sidis's IQ ✓

2 where he was born ✓

3 his grandparents ☐

4 his language skills ✓

5 his college studies ✓

6 his jobs ✓

7 his friends ☐

8 how he died ☐

Glossary

child prodigy (n) a child who is extremely skillful at something that usually only adults can do

in/out of the public eye (phrase) well known or not well known to people in general

IQ = intelligence quotient (n) a number that represents a person's intelligence, based on the results of a particular type of test

turning point (n) a time when an important change takes place in a situation

7.4 **D** Number the events (a–h) in William James Sidis's life in the order they happened (1–8). Use the information in the box to help you. Then listen again and check.

Listening for the order of events

Listen for words and phrases to help you follow the order of events in a story.

- Words and phrases that tell us when something happened:

  when he was nine by four years old at 11
  at age 16 in 1898

- Words and phrases that tell us that something happened before, at the same time or after something else:

  before before that earlier previously
  while during at the same time
  after after this soon after then next

- Words and phrases that tell us that one thing was a consequence of another:

  as a result therefore

a He received a prison sentence. 7

b He became interested in politics. 6

c He taught math at Rice University. 4

d He studied math at Harvard University. 3

e He went to Harvard University to study law. 5

f He gave a lecture in math at Harvard University. 2

g He traveled around the US doing different jobs. 8

h He learned seven languages and also invented one. 1

E SPEAK Work in pairs. Discuss the questions.

1 What were the key events and turning points in William James Sidis's life?

2 Sidis didn't go to school, his mother taught him at home. What are the advantages and disadvantages of this?

7.3 Intelligence

LEAD-IN

Write the following questions on the board:

Do you prefer …

1 to hear directions or see directions?

2 reading or doing hands-on activities?

3 to study alone or with other people?

4 to use words or to use logic and reasoning systems?

Explain that each student's answers will define their learning style, i.e. the way in which they learn. Give students two minutes to answer the questions. Students read their answers. Explain what styles correspond to each question: 1 (*aural vs. visual*), 2 (*visual vs. physical*), 3 (*solitary vs. social*), 4 (*verbal vs. logical*). Ask for a show of hands to see how many students belong to each group.

LISTENING

A Display the images and read the activity with the class. Students discuss the questions in pairs. Monitor and assist when necessary. Take feedback from one or two pairs and encourage students to respond to each other's ideas.

Background notes:

Mozart was an Austrian composer who started writing music from the age of five.

Picasso is considered one of the most influential artists of the 20th century and demonstrated extraordinary talent from a young age.

Kasparov is a chess grandmaster who became the youngest ever world champion at the age of 22.

William James Sidis was an American child prodigy who was exceptionally good at mathematics and languages. He was accepted into Harvard University at the age of 11 and by the time he was an adult could speak over 40 languages.

Venus Williams is an American tennis player and is seen as one of the all-time greats. She was first spotted by a tennis coach at the age of seven, and made her professional debut at the age of 14.

B Elicit students' opinions about the difference between *intelligence* and *knowledge*. Ask them to match the words with the correct definitions. Check answers with the class.

C (7.4) Focus students on the glossary. Remind them that the words will help them understand the podcast. Play the audio. Students listen, read the list of topics and check (√) those the presenter talks about. Play the audio again for students to check their answers. With a weaker group, you may have to play the audio more than twice.

D (7.4) Focus students on the listening box. Tell students to look at Sentences a–h and underline any key words that will help them find the answers. Students work alone reading the sentences and putting them in order using the information from the listening box. Play the audio. Encourage students to listen for the key words in the recording. Students check their answers.

E Students discuss Questions 1 and 2 in pairs. Monitor and assist when necessary. Take feedback from one or two pairs and encourage students to respond to each other's ideas.

AUDIO SCRIPT

7.4

Listening, Exercise C
S = Shauna

S: Welcome to Great Minds. I'm Shauna Andrews, and today we're talking about William James Sidis. You have possibly never heard of him. But he is perhaps one of the most intelligent people who ever lived.

Ex C Q1 He had an IQ of between 250 and 300.

Ex C Q2 He was born in the United States in 1898, and grew up in New York. His parents, who were originally from Ukraine, were doctors and were both highly intelligent. They wanted to give their son the best possible chance in life. So, his mother gave up her job and taught him at home. He didn't go to school. And they brought him up to have a 'love of knowledge'.

As a result, Sidis was reading and writing at 18 months, and enjoyed reading the *New York Times* newspaper. He wrote several books and newspaper articles before he was four and, by the time he was

Ex C Q4 / Ex D h eight, he spoke seven languages. He also made up his own language, which he called 'Vendergood'.

Ex C Q5 / Ex D d / Ex D f At 11, he went to college to study math – to Harvard University, actually. And in fact, he had previously given a math lecture there when he was nine. Sidis became front page news and news reporters followed him everywhere at the college. He became known as a child prodigy all over the country. Sidis graduated from Harvard University with a degree

Ex C Q6 / Ex D c in mathematics at age 16. He then joined Rice University as a teacher of math. However, he found teaching difficult, especially because of his age. After only eight months, he left Rice University and went

Ex C Q5; Ex D e back to Harvard, this time to study law.

Ex D b While studying law, he became more and more interested in the political and social issues of the day. And as a result, he dropped out of the university before he finished his degree. This was a big turning point in his life. Soon after, in 1918, he was arrested while

Ex D a he was taking part in an anti-war demonstration. He received an 18-month prison sentence. However, he didn't go to prison and instead he spent a year in a hospital. It was actually the hospital where his parents worked.

After this, Sidis tried to stay out of the public eye.

Ex C Q6 / Ex D g He moved from city to city around America and he had a number of simple low-paid jobs. He became more and more lonely and finally, he had a falling-out with his parents and lost contact with them. The newspapers printed stories about how the child prodigy had failed as an adult.

After his death in 1944, many people questioned his high IQ and many of his other childhood achievements. Despite this, Sidis has been the subject of a number of books and academic studies and he is still one of the world's greatest child prodigies.

7.3 Intelligence

VOCABULARY

A Elicit that *phrasal verbs* consist of a verb + an adverb or a preposition that changes the meaning of the verb. Students read the sentences and match the phrasal verbs in bold with their definitions.

B Students use the phrasal verbs from Exercise A to complete Questions 1–6. Students check their answers with a partner before checking with the whole class. Use the **Vocabulary Worksheet** on W42 for extra practice.

C Students take turns asking and answering the questions in Exercise B in pairs. Monitor and assist as required. Take feedback from one or two pairs and encourage students to respond to each other's ideas.

GRAMMAR

A Focus students on the grammar box. Using the sentences to support them, students choose the correct words to complete the grammar rules. Check answers with the class.

B Direct students to the **Grammar Hub** (see below). Use the **Grammar Worksheet** on W41 for extra practice.

C Students work on their own completing the texts by choosing the correct words. Check answers with the whole class.

D Arrange students in pairs. They close their books and take turns telling their partner one of the stories from Exercise C. Encourage students to listen to and correct each other when necessary. Monitor and assist when necessary.

PRONUNCIATION

A Focus students on the way 'the' is pronounced in English. In pairs, students practice saying Sentences 1–3 with their partner.

7.5 **B** Play the audio and ask students to focus on the pronunciation of 'the' in the two sentences. Check whether students noticed any differences in pronunciation and why they think they occur. Elicit that we pronounce **/ðiː/** when 'the' occurs before a vowel sound, including **/juː/** in the 'United States', and **/ðə/** when 'the' occurs before a consonant.

SPEAKING HUB

A Split the class in half (As and Bs). Direct students to the **Communication Hub**.

B Students read the file and write notes on the five areas listed.

C Set students who have read the same text in groups of four or five. Each group should plan their presentation and decide who will present each topic. Encourage students to use the sequencing words and phrases from the listening box in their presentations. Allow the groups time to practice their presentations. Monitor and assist as required.

D Each group gives their presentations to the class. Encourage students to listen and give each other feedback.

Extra activity

For homework, students can be asked to research another child prodigy they find interesting. They should be prepared to answer some questions about the person and justify their choice in class.

GRAMMAR HUB

7.3 No article (*school, the school*)

- When we are referring to a place in terms of the **activity** associated with a place, we use **no** article.

  He studied Math in college. NOT *~~He studied Math in the college.~~*

  My grandfather never went to high school. NOT *~~My grandfather never went to the high school.~~*

- When we are referring to the **physical place**, we use an article.

  The college I go to is called Cambridge University. NOT *~~college I go to is called Cambridge University.~~* *This is a good school.* NOT *~~This is good school.~~*

7.3 No article (*school, the school*)

A Complete the sentences with the words in the box. Use the definite article *the* if necessary.

college ~~college~~ prison school school

1 I started studying math in *college* but I soon dropped out.

2 They brought the child up badly and he ended up in prison for robbery.

3 The school next to my house is called Gregory's. It's for talented children.

4 It's easy to make friends at school. I had lots as a kid.

5 Anna also went to the college where I studied Law.

B Complete the text with *the* or – (no article).

(1) *The* college I work at is called St. Anne's. I'm a professor there. When I was a kid, I used to hate (2) – school. (3) The school I went to was very bad and it didn't have good amenities. I loved it when I went to (4) – college, though, because (5) the college I studied at was very modern, and it's also where I met my best friend, Jillian.

➤ Go back to page 67.

VOCABULARY

Phrasal verbs

A Look at the phrasal verbs in **bold** from the podcast about William James Sidis. Match the phrasal verbs (1–6) with the correct meanings (a–f).

b 1 He was born in 1898 and **grew up** in New York.
f 2 They **brought** him **up** to have 'a love of knowledge'.
c 3 His mother **gave up** her job and taught him at home.
a 4 He also **made up** his own language.
d 5 He **dropped out** of the university before he finished his degree.
e 6 He had a **falling out** with his parents and lost contact with them.

a invented
b spent his childhood
c stopped doing something
d left something before finishing it
e stopped being friendly because he had had a disagreement with them
f took care of him until he became an adult

B PRACTICE Complete the sentences with the correct form of a phrasal verb from Exercise A. Use each phrasal verb once.

1 Where did you ___grow up___? What is the neighborhood like? Do you still live there?
2 Who ___brought___ you ___up___? Do you have a big family or a small family?
3 Name something you have ___given up___. When and why did you stop doing it?
4 When you were a child, did you play traditional games or did you ___make up___ your own games?
5 Do you know anyone who ___dropped out___ of school or college? Why didn't they finish?
6 Have you ever had a ___falling out___ with someone? Did you become friends again?

C SPEAK Ask and answer the questions in Exercise B.

GRAMMAR

No article (*school*, *the school*)

A WORK IT OUT Look at the sentences from the podcast. Then choose the correct words to complete the rules.

No article (*school*, *the school*)

Sometimes we use an article (*a*, *the*) with the words *school*, *college*, and *prison*. But sometimes we use no article.

- *He didn't go to school.*
- *News reporters followed him everywhere at the college.*
- *At 11, he went to college to study math.*
- *He didn't go to prison and instead he spent a year in a hospital.*

1 When we are referring to the *activity* associated with the place (studying / being a student, being a prisoner) we use *an article* / *no article*.
2 When we are referring to the *physical* place, we use *an article* / *no article*.

B Go to the **Grammar Hub** on **page 134**.

C PRACTICE Choose the correct words to complete the texts.

Most people go to [1]*the college* / *college* at age 18 or 19. However, in 1981, at the age of just 12, Ruth Lawrence became the University of Oxford's youngest ever student. She didn't go to [2]*the school* / *school* and her father gave up his job to teach her at home. He also accompanied her everywhere at [3]*the college* / *a college*.

Nelson Mandela was president of South Africa from 1994 to 1999. Before that, he spent 27 years in [4]*the prison* / *prison* for crimes against the government. Eighteen years of this was in [5]*the prison* / *prison* on Robben Island, which is seven kilometers out in the ocean from Cape Town.

D SPEAK Work in pairs. Close your books. Tell your partner a story from Exercise C.

PRONUNCIATION

Practicing *the*: /ðiː/ or /ðə/

A SPEAK Work in pairs. Practice saying the sentences.

1 Have you ever been to the East Coast of the United States?
2 No, but I've been to the West Coast.

7.5 **B** Listen and compare your pronunciation. What do you notice about the pronunciation of *the* in each sentence? Why is there a difference?

SPEAKING HUB

A You are going to give a short presentation about a child prodigy. Student A – go to the **Communication Hub** on **page 152**. Student B – go to the **Communication Hub** on **page 157**.

B PLAN Read the biography and write notes about:

- the person's early life and education
- his/her talents and abilities
- any key moments or turning points in his/her life
- achievements he/she is famous for
- what he/she did later in life

C ORGANIZE Work in groups. Decide who is going to present which topics and practice your presentation. Use words and phrases from the Listening box to help you.

D PRESENT Give your presentation to your classmates.

Talk about intelligence and achievements

Café Hub

7.4 Neena's dinner

F– describe an object and say what you use it for   P– objects

COMPREHENSION

A SPEAK Work in pairs. Look at the picture. Who do you think says the following, Zac (Z), Gaby (G) or Neena (N)? What do you think happens and who cooks Neena's dinner?

1. Gaby, what's wrong? Z
2. And we promised to cook dinner for her tonight. G
3. And it's 6:30! G
4. Who's going to cook? Z
5. I can make pizza! G
6. I can't think of the word in English. G
7. A knife? Z
8. You used to work at Pizza Roma? G
9. Yeah, but I ate too much pizza. Z
10. It looks like Pizza Roma! N

B ▶ Watch the video and check your answers to Exercise A. What is *rallador* in English? a grater

FUNCTIONAL LANGUAGE

Describe an object and say what you use it for

A Complete the phrases with the verbs in the box. You need to use two verbs twice.

forgotten   know   made   think   use

Find out the English word for something

Problem

I've [1] forgotten the name of it.

I can't [2] think of the word in English.

It's *rallador* in Spanish.

Oh, what's it [3] made of?

Description

You [4] use it to …

It's a thing you [5] use to …

It's [6] made of metal.

Check understanding

Do you [7] know what I mean?

B ▶ 01:09–02:43 Watch part of the video again and check your answers to Exercise A.

USEFUL PHRASES

A ▶ Match the useful phrases (1–5) with the phrase that comes before or after it (a–e). Then watch the video again and check your answers.

c 1 Let me think …
e 2 Who's going to cook?
d 3 You can be my assistant chef.
a 4 You know! 'Un rallador'.
b 5 Neena says she'll be home soon.

a I'm sorry, I don't understand Spanish.
b Oh, no! We have no time!
c Who's going to cook?
d Cool, good plan.
e Me, for sure.

B How do you say these useful phrases in your language?

MILLY

SAM

NEENA

ZAC

GABY

PRONUNCIATION
Objects

7.6 **A** Match the pictures (a–c) with the conversations (1–3). Then listen and repeat the conversations.

a

b
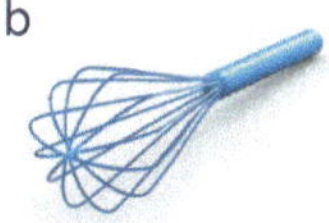
c

b **1** **A:** What's it made of?
B: It's made of metal. You use it to beat eggs.

a **2** **A:** What's it made of?
B: It's made of wood. You use it to roll pastry.

c **3** **A:** What's it made of?
B: It's made of plastic. You use it to wash the dirty dishes.

B SPEAK Work in pairs. Choose another object and write a conversation. Practice saying your conversation.

SPEAKING

1

2

3

4
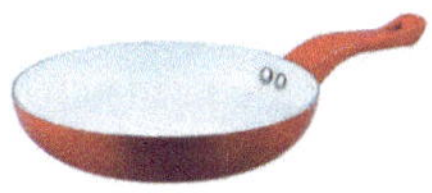
5

6

7

8

Work in pairs. Take turns being Student A and B.

Student A: Look at the pictures and choose an object. Tell your partner:

- the word in your language
- what it's made of
- what you use it for

Student B: Listen and guess the object your partner describes. Tell him/her the number of the object and the name in English.

Describe an object and say what you use it for

➤ Turn to **page 164** to learn how to write a survey report.

7.4 Neena's dinner

COMPREHENSION

A If possible, enlarge the image from the video. Elicit the names of the characters. Students read the quotes and decide which character said which lines. Ask them what they think will happen in the episode and who will cook Neena's dinner. Monitor and assist when necessary. Take feedback from one or two pairs, but do not confirm or correct their answers.

B ▶ Play the video. Students check their answers to Exercise A. With a weaker group, you may want to play the video again. Ask students what the English for *rallador* is.

FUNCTIONAL LANGUAGE

A Focus students on the functional language box and the vocabulary box. Students read and complete the phrases with the words in the vocabulary box. Elicit answers from the class but do not confirm or correct them.

B ▶ 01:09–02:43 Play part of the video. Students check their answers to Exercise A.

USEFUL PHRASES

A ▶ Read through the task with the class. Students match the phrases (1–5) to those that came before or after them. Play the video again for students to check their answers.

B Students think about how they would say these phrases in their own language. In a multilingual class, you may want to pair students from different countries. Invite students to share their phrases with the class.

PRONUNCIATION

7.6 **A** Students look at the pictures. Elicit the names of the objects (*rolling pin, beater and plastic basin*). In pairs, students read the conversations and match them with the pictures. Play the audio for students to check their answers. Play it again for students to listen and repeat. Have students practice pronunciation and word stress.

B Students work in pairs using the conversations in Exercise A as a model to write about another object. They then take turns saying both sides of the conversations. Monitor and assist as required.

SPEAKING

A Focus students on the pictures and elicit the names of the objects (*strainer, potato peeler, blender, frying pan, cutting board, bowl, jug* or *pitcher, teapot*). In pairs, students take turns choosing an object, saying the word in their own language, explaining what it is made of and what it is used for. Their partners listen, guess the object and say the name of the object in English. Monitor and assist when necessary.

▶ VIDEO SCRIPT

Café Hub 7.4 Neena's dinner
Z = Zac G = Gaby N = Neena

Z: Gaby? What's wrong?
G: Today is Neena's first day in her new job!
Z: Yep.
G: And we promised to cook dinner for her tonight!
Z: Yep.
G: And she gets home at about 7 o'clock.
Z: Yep.
G: And it's six thirty!
Z: Yep. Oh! Let me think … OK! Who's going to cook?
G: Me! For sure. I can make pizza. She loves pizza! You can be my assistant chef!
Z: Cool. Good plan. Let's do it!
G: You don't need those! So the first thing I need is … oh … I've forgotten the name of it. Umm, I can't think of the word in English. It's rallador in Spanish. You use it to 'mm mm' cheese. Oh, what's it called? You know! Un Rallador!!
Z: Sorry, I don't understand Spanish!
G: It's a thing you use to make cheese smaller. Do you know what I mean?
Z: Make cheese smaller? Hmm… What's it made of?
G: What?
Z: I mean. Is it made of plastic or metal or something else?
G: Yes. Yes! It's made of metal. Yes.
Z: A knife?
G: No! Not a knife! That's it!!! What's it called?
Z: It's called a grater.
G: A grater? Really? A grater. Great!
Z: Uh oh!
G: What?
Z: Neena says she'll be home soon and she's really excited about dinner!
G: Oh no! We have no time!
Z: OK! I have a plan. There's a pizza place called Pizza Roma just round the corner. I used to work there.
G: Really? You used to work at Pizza Roma!
Z: Yeah, but I ate too much pizza … OK! I'll order the pizzas now.
G: Good plan! Go! Go!
N: It looks like Pizza Roma. It smells like Pizza Roma. It tastes like Pizza Roma …
Z and G: It's Pizza Roma.

TEACHING IDEA by David Seymour and Maria Popova

Speaking: Shopping list

Arrange the class in small groups. Write the occasions or situations from the list below on strips of paper and hand one to each group. Explain to students that they need to prepare a meal for this occasion. Students should agree on a shopping list of all the things they need for this meal. When they have finished, ask students to look at the other groups' lists and try to guess the occasion or situation they are preparing for.

> A Sunday meal. A picnic in the park. A romantic dinner for two. A breakfast buffet. A healthy meal for a fitness fanatic. A child's birthday party.

Functional language: Things

Explain to students that you are going to describe some objects hidden in a bag. Collect objects from the students and include a few of your own. Put your hand in the bag and feel an object. Describe it to the class, but don't tell them what it is, e.g. It feels soft and furry. It's made of wool. They will try to guess. After a few guesses, invite the student to remove the object and show it to the class. Arrange students in pairs and ask them to repeat the activity by asking yes/no questions about these aspects:

size, material, color, when you use it, where you use it, what you use it for

7 Writing

Write a survey report

W – using survey report language

A Look at the chart. What does it show? Do any of the findings surprise you? The percentage of 24–34-year-olds in English-speaking countries with a college degree in 2015.

Percentage of population aged 25–34 with a college degree in English-speaking countries in 2015

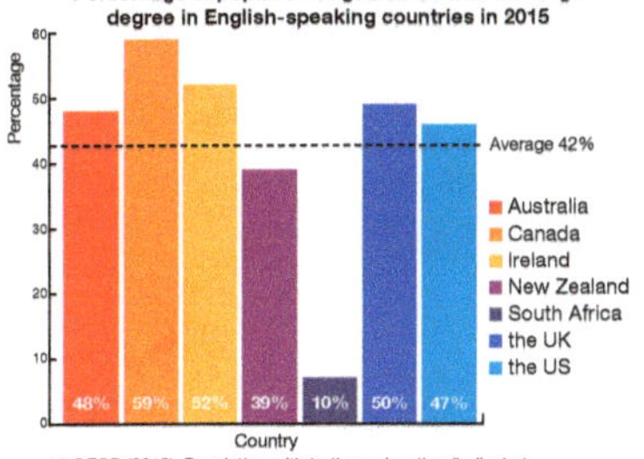

(c) OECD (2018), Population with tertiary education (indicator).

B Complete the survey report with the correct country.

The survey compares the percentage of people aged 25 to 34 with a college degree in English-speaking countries. According to the survey, an average of 42 percent of the population of these countries are graduates. [1] Canada has the highest percentage of graduates at 59 percent. In contrast, [2] South Africa has the lowest with just ten percent of the population having a college degree. The number of graduates in [3] Ireland is just over 50 percent, while in [4] Australia the figure is just under 50 percent. Similarly, the figure for [5] the US is 47 percent, while in [6] New Zealand, 39 percent of people aged 25 to 34 are graduates.

C Look at the survey report again and complete the words and phrases in the box.

Using survey report language

We can say what the survey is about with:
- *The survey shows …*
- *The survey* [1] compares *…*
- *According* [2] to *the survey, …*

We can express differences with:
- *By/In comparison, …*
- *By/In* [3] contrast *, …*

We can express similarities with:
- [4] Similarly *, …*
- *Both …*

We can give data and statistics by using:
- *… has the highest percentage of graduates at 59 percent.*
- *… an average of 42 percent of the population …*
- *… has the lowest with just 7 percent …*
- *… the figure for the US is 47 percent …*

Note the different uses of prepositions (*at, of*).

D Complete the sentences with the best words or phrases. Use the strategies in the box to help you.

1 As of 2015 the birth rate in the US is just under two children per family. By/In comparison, in Europe it is around 1.5.

2 According to the survey, 41 percent of both men and women play sports to keep fit. Thirty percent say they play sports for social reasons.[1]

3 The survey compares IQs of brothers and sisters. It shows that the oldest generally has the highest IQ.

WRITING

A PREPARE You are going to write a survey report about World Happiness. Read about the report. What areas of life do you think the survey asks questions about?

The World Happiness report is an annual survey. It collects data from over 150 countries to find out which country has the happiest population. The survey asks people to decide how happy they are with different areas of their life.

B PLAN Look at the survey results.
- Decide which of the data you will include.
- Decide how you can compare and contrast the data.
- Use the report in Writing Exercise B to help you.
- Use the information in the *World Happiness* report.
- Use phrases from the Writing skills box.

C WRITE Write about 100–120 words. Check your writing for grammar, vocabulary and spelling.

World Happiness report

Top four countries	score (out of 10)
Norway	7.54
Denmark	7.52
Iceland	7.50
Switzerland	7.50
Bottom four countries	**score**
Syria	3.46
Tanzania	3.35
Burundi	2.91
Central African Republic	2.69

Helliwell, J., Layard, R., & Sachs, J. (2017). World Happiness Report 2017, New York: Sustainable Development Solutions Network.

D DISCUSS Work in groups. Why do you think the countries in the survey are the happiest in the world?

1 Special Eurobarometer 412 "Sport and physical activity". © European Union, 1995-2017

164 7 WRITING

Refer students to this survey report as a model for the writing task.

Students can do this in class or for homework.

You could mention that this is mostly used in formal writing.

WRITING

A Use the Digital Students' Book to display the bar chart. Elicit from students what it shows. Ask whether they find the information surprising.

B Students read and complete the survey report using the information from the bar chart. Allow students to compare their answers in pairs before checking with the whole class.

C Focus students on the *Using survey report language* box. In pairs, students complete the information in the box with words and phrases from the survey report in Exercise B.

D Focus student on the task. Students complete the sentences using the information from the box. Allow them to compare their answers in pairs before checking with the whole class.

WRITING TASK

A Read the task with the class. Elicit students' ideas on the areas of life the survey is about.

B Focus students on the steps to write their survey report. Remind students that they will only write between 100 and 120 words, so they should choose the most interesting information. Encourage them to use the writing skills box and the example report to help them.

C Students write their report. Encourage them to check their work for any grammar, vocabulary or spelling mistakes they have made. Monitor and assist when necessary.

D Students work in groups discussing why they think the countries in the survey are the happiest and least happy in the world. Monitor and assist when necessary. Elicit ideas from each of the groups and encourage students to respond to their classmates' ideas.

VOCABULARY

A Choose the best adjective to complete the sentences. Use the information in parentheses to help you.

1 I feel really ***anxious*** / ***cheerful*** now that the holidays have started. (*positive*)
2 Lola is a little ***nervous*** / ***glad*** about the interview tomorrow. (*negative*)
3 I always feel ***scared*** / ***happy*** when I get a lot of 'likes' for my posts on Twitter. (*positive*)
4 I'm really ***nervous*** / ***glad*** that you liked the cake I made. (*positive*)
5 Casper didn't go to the top of the building because he was too ***relaxed*** / ***scared***. (*negative*)

B Look at the shortened words. Write the missing letters to complete the full words.

1 cell _ _ _ _ _
2 info _ _ _ _ _ _ _
3 lab _ _ _ _ _ _ _
4 _ _ _ plane
5 _ _ _ _ _ net
6 mic _ _ _ _ _ _ _
7 _ _ _ _ case
8 _ _ _ site

C The phrasal verbs are in the wrong places in the texts. Write them in the correct place. Change the tense if necessary.

I [1]**brought up** in Sheffield. It was just me and my mom, so she [2]**made** me **up** on her own. We had a good relationship, although we argued sometimes and had a [3]**gave up** from time to time. Because I was an only child, I played on my own a lot of the time. This was OK because I had a good imagination and I used to [4]**grew up** my own games. To be honest, I had a really good childhood.

I didn't enjoy college. I found it really difficult. Studying took up all of my time and I had to [5]**drop out** a lot of my hobbies and other activities. I just went to lectures in the day and then studied all evening. So, I decided to [6]**falling out** and get a job instead. It was the best decision I ever made.

GRAMMAR

A Choose the correct article or no article to complete the text.

Humans are not [1]*the* / – only animals that laugh. Other animals such as [2]*the* / – gorillas, chimpanzees and orangutans also laugh. [3]*A* / *The* main reason for laughter in [4]*the* / – animals is when they are playing. [5]*A* / *The* laughter indicates that it is [6]*a* / *the* game and that no one is going to get hurt. [7]*A* / – Laughter has also been observed in [8]*the* / – rats.

B Think about everyday life forty years ago. For each pair of words or phrases, write what we *used to* and *didn't use to* do. Use the verbs in the box.

chat ~~use~~ use watch write and send

1 online maps and GPS / paper maps
We didn't use to use online maps and GPS. We used to use paper maps.
2 on social media / on the phone
3 videos / movies online
4 emails / letters

C Complete the questions about school and college with *a*/*an*, *the* or – (no article).

SCHOOL AND COLLEGE QUESTIONNAIRE

1 Where did you go to ___ school as a child? Was ___ school close to where you lived?
2 Did you enjoy ___ school? What were your favorite subjects at ___ school?
3 Did you, do you or will you go to ___ college? If so, is ___ college well known for anything?
4 Is there ___ college in the town or city where you grew up? Do most cities in your country have ___ college?

FUNCTIONAL LANGUAGE

Write the missing letters to complete the words. Then match the conversations (1–3) with the pictures (a–c).

a 
b 
c 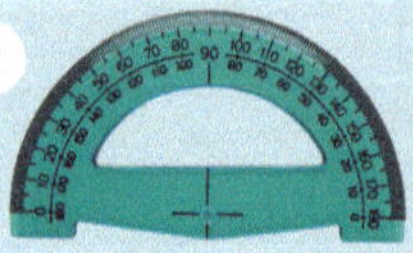

1 **A:** What's a protractor?
B: It's a thing you u _ _ to measure and draw angles. It's shaped like half a circle and usually m _ _ _ of plastic.
2 **A:** I can't t _ _ _ _ of the English word for *agrafeuse*. Do you know?
B: Yes, it's stapler, I think.
3 **A:** What's this for?
B: You u _ _ it to draw circles. It's c _ _ _ _ _ a compass.

ART

Art is not what you see, but what you make others see.
Edgar Degas

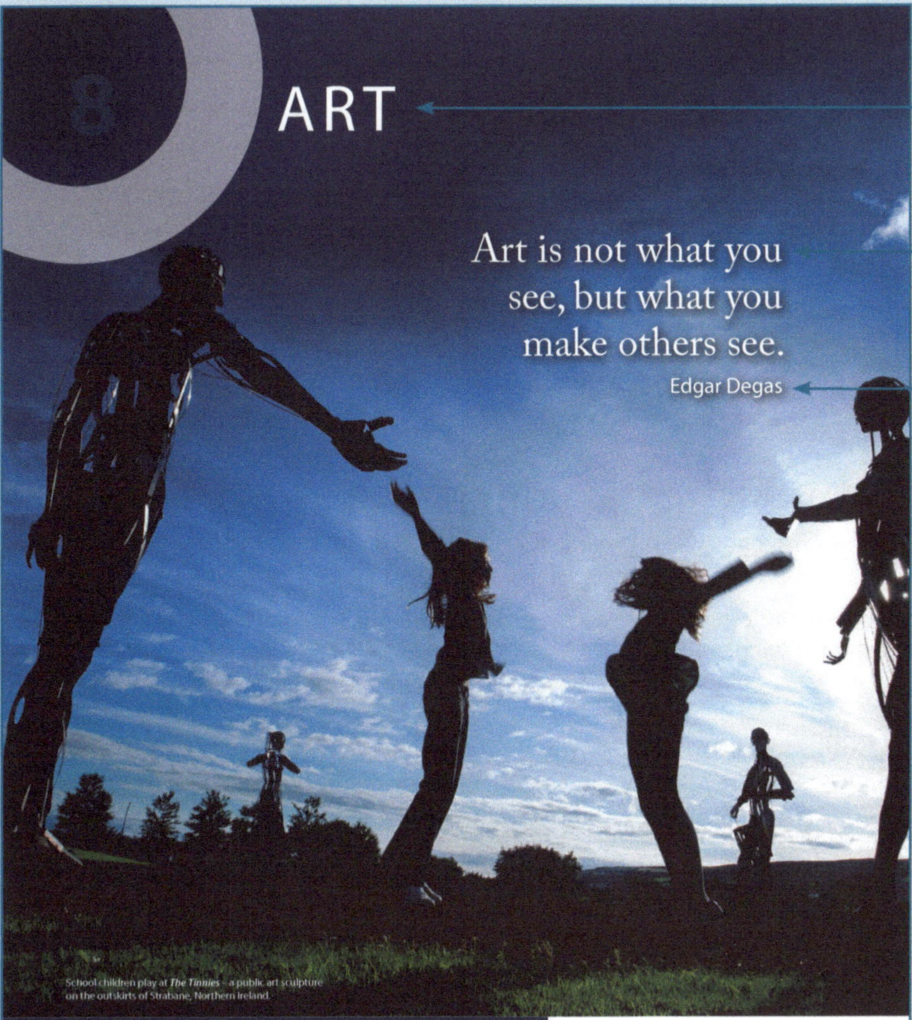

School children play at *The Tinnies* – a public art sculpture on the outskirts of Strabane, Northern Ireland.

Art (n) the activity of painting, drawing or creating sculptures. Synonyms: art form, arts and crafts, the arts.

Degas is suggesting that the artistic process is not simply about an artist describing their own reality but about their capacity to open other people's eyes to new realities.

Edgar Degas (July 19, 1834–September 27, 1917) was a highly celebrated 19th-century French painter and sculptor. His work influenced several major modern artists, including Pablo Picasso.

OBJECTIVES

- talk about taste in music and your favorite songs
- talk about art and artists
- describe movies and books
- show interest in a topic
- write a review

Work with a partner. Discuss the questions.

1 What different types of art can you name?
2 Look at the picture. Would you like to visit this place?
3 Do you think museums and art galleries should be free? Why/Why not?

ART 71

OBJECTIVES

Read the unit objectives to the class.

UNIT OPENER QUESTIONS

Encourage students to look at the quote and take one or two suggestions from the class about what they think it means.

Ask students to look at the questions at the bottom of the page. Model possible answers. You may provide different types of art forms or what you think about art galleries. Students discuss the questions in pairs or in a small group.

Monitor and assist as necessary. When students have finished the activity, ask one or two pairs to share their ideas with the class. Encourage students to listen to one another and respond with their own ideas and opinions.

WORKSHEETS

Lesson 8.1 Musical taste

Grammar: Reflexive pronouns (W42)

Vocabulary: Music (W43)

Lesson 8.2 Unusual art

Grammar: Infinitive of purpose (W44)

Vocabulary: Types of art (W45)

Lesson 8.3 Telling stories

Grammar: First conditional (W46)

Vocabulary: Movie and book genres (W47)

8.1 Musical taste

Talk about taste in music and your favorite songs

G reflexive pronouns **V** music **P** consonant clusters in words

LISTENING

8.1 **A** Listen to the music extracts (1–7) and match them with the different types of music (a–g).

a rap	5		**e** blues	4	
b jazz	6		**f** reggae	7	
c rock	3		**g** classical	2	
d disco	1				

B SPEAK Work in pairs. Discuss the questions.

1. Can you think of any other types of music?
2. What types of music do you like? What don't you like? Why?
3. Who are your favorite bands or musicians?
4. Why do we like certain types of music? Think of three reasons.

8.2 **C LISTEN FOR MAIN IDEA** Listen to the podcast *Music matters* with Professor Suzy Harrison. What are the three things which explain our taste in music?

Glossary

comforting (adj) making you feel less sad, worried or disappointed
energize (v) to make someone feel excited and enthusiastic
influence (v) to affect the way someone thinks or behaves, also *be influenced by*

8.2 **D LISTEN FOR DETAIL** Choose the correct answer a, b or c, to complete the sentences. Then listen again and check your answers.

1. When we are older, the music from our childhood makes us feel …
   - **a** old.
   - **b** sad.
   - **c** happy. (circled)
2. Our first big music influence is generally …
   - **a** our younger brothers and sisters.
   - **b** our older brothers and sisters. (circled)
   - **c** our school friends.
3. Music brings people together because we can share …
   - **a** music files and records.
   - **b** our opinions of the music.
   - **c** the mood it creates. (circled)
4. We sometimes choose a particular type of music …
   - **a** to create the right conditions for an activity. (circled)
   - **b** to give us a break from an activity.
   - **c** to help us forget about an activity.
5. Compared with the past, people today generally like …
   - **a** fewer kinds of music.
   - **b** more kinds of music. (circled)
   - **c** the same variety of music.

E SPEAK Work in groups. Discuss the questions.

1. Who has influenced your taste in music, your parents, brothers and sisters, friends or someone or something else?
2. Do you generally like the same kinds of music as your friends? Do you think music is an important part of your friendships?
3. Do you tend to play different kinds of music at different times and when you are in different moods? Give some examples.

GRAMMAR

Reflexive pronouns

8.3 **A** Complete the sentences from the podcast *Music matters* with the pronouns in the box. You need to use one of the pronouns more than once. Then listen and check.

ourselves (x2) themselves yourself

1. **We** don't choose this music ___ourselves___, of course.
2. So, when **we** start to discover music by ___ourselves___, it is influenced by what we listened to when we were growing up.
3. In contrast, for **other people**, musical taste is a way to make ___themselves___ different from other people.
4. And when **you're** preparing for a night out, **you** might want to energize ___yourself___ and play something loud and full of energy.

8.1 Musical taste

LEAD-IN

Write on the board: *Find someone who … listens to rap music, can play a musical instrument, has changed their taste in music in the last five years, has met a famous singer, likes the same music as you.*

Give students five minutes to mingle. Then, take feedback from one or two students and encourage the rest of the class to respond to and complete their information.

LISTENING

8.1 **A** Read the task with the class. Play the audio. Students listen to the extracts and match them to the types of music. Play the audio again for students to check their answers. Compare answers with the whole class.

B In pairs, students read and discuss the questions, giving as much detail as possible. If students are struggling for ideas about different types of music, prompt discussion by writing some suggestions on the board (*hip-hop, soul, folk, country, heavy metal, etc*). Monitor and assist when necessary. Take feedback from one or two pairs and encourage students to respond to each other's ideas.

8.2 **C** Read the task and the glossary with the class. Remind students the words in the glossary may help them understand the interview. Arrange students in pairs. Play the audio. Students listen and discuss the question. Take feedback from one or two pairs and encourage students to respond to each other's ideas.

8.2 **D** Play the audio again for students to choose the correct answers. Allow them to compare their answers with a partner before checking with the whole class.

E Students discuss the questions in groups, giving as much detail as possible. Monitor and assist when necessary.

Extra activity

For homework, students can be asked to research popular types of music and popular musicians in different countries. Ask students to write notes on any particularly interesting musicians. Ask students to prepare to give a five minute presentation about one of the musicians or genres of music that they found out about in their next class.

AUDIO SCRIPT

8.2

Listening, Exercise C
L = Lizzie S = Suzy

L: Welcome to *Music matters* with me, Lizzie Reid. Our taste in music says a lot about who we are. But why do we have different tastes in music? To answer this question, we are joined by Professor Suzy Harrison, an expert in the psychology of music. Welcome, Suzy.

S: Hello, thank you.

L: So, why do some people, say, prefer rock music or blues or jazz, while other people prefer pop or rap music?

S: Well, there are three main points which might
Ex C explain our taste in music. The first is the music we grew up with. We don't choose this music ourselves, of course. But as a child, the music that we
Ex D Q1 hear at home is familiar and comforting. Later in life, these same sounds bring back these feelings and this gives us pleasure. So, when we start to discover music by ourselves, it is influenced by what we listened to when we were growing up.

L: So, you're saying our first musical influence is our parents and our brothers and sisters?

Ex D Q2 **S:** Yes, that's right – particularly, our older brothers and
Ex C sisters. Secondly, music brings people together. It
Ex D Q3 creates an atmosphere and mood that people can share. So the second point is that we listen to certain types of music to help us form or join social groups. We want to be with people similar to ourselves. In contrast, for other people, musical taste is a way to make themselves different from other people. It's a way to be an individual. If you listen to music that others don't like, people will see you differently.

L: Yes, and I suppose it's true that we are generally attracted to people with similar music tastes to our own.

Ex C **S:** Yes, that's generally the case. And the third point is about how we feel when we listen to the music.
Ex D Q4 Music can help to create a mood! For example, when you want to study, you might listen to something in the background, something without words – classical music, for example. And when you're preparing for a night out, you might want to energize yourself and play something loud and full of energy – maybe some rock or pop or reggae music. At other times, you might play the same sad song over and over again. Because of the internet, finding music is very quick and easy for our different moods. Interestingly, studies have shown that because of this easy access to different kinds
Ex D Q5 of music, people today like a much wider range of music styles compared to previous generations.

L: I see. So, our individual taste in music is a combination of three things: the music we grew up with, the need to fit in with other people and finally, to match our different moods?

S: Yes, that's right. Of course, one thing may be stronger than the others. But, yes, over time it is most likely a combination of these things which influence our music choices.

L: Very interesting, Professor Harrison. Thank you for speaking to us today.

S: You're welcome.

TEACHING IDEA

by David Seymour and Maria Popova

Vocabulary: Music

Read aloud the following questions and ask students to write their answers on a piece of paper. When you have finished, arrange students in small groups and tell them to ask each other the same questions using their answers as prompts.

Name four instruments in an orchestra.

Write two adjectives to describe music.

What was the first record you bought?

What subjects are most lyrics about?

What was the last song you heard?

What do you know about the Beatles?

Describe an instrument from your country.

What's your first memory of music?

Describe a concert you have been to.

What's a didgeridoo?

8.1 Musical taste

GRAMMAR

8.3 **A** Students read and complete the sentences. With a stronger class, students may complete the sentences from memory. With a weaker class, you may have to play the audio once before students complete the sentences.

B In pairs, students match the rules to the example sentences in Exercise A. Check answers as a whole class.

C Direct students to the **Grammar Hub** (see below). Use the **Grammar Worksheet** on W42 for extra practice.

D Encourage students to use reflexive pronouns in their answers. Monitor and assist as required.

VOCABULARY

A Direct students to the **Vocabulary Hub** (TB121). Use the **Vocabulary Worksheet** on W43 for extra practice.

B Allow students to work with a partner. Check answers as a class.

C Write on the board *'Hello' by Adele is a great song. I love the lyrics.* Students work in pairs. Using the sentences on the board as an example, they choose a minimum of four sentences from Exercise B and then rewrite them.

PRONUNCIATION

8.4 **A** Explain that *consonant clusters* are two or more consonants with no vowels between them. Play the audio to check answers.

8.4 **B** Play the audio for students to listen and repeat.

SPEAKING

A Discuss as a class whether there is a similar radio show in their country.

B Students work on their own choosing three songs.

C Read the task with the class. Give students time to write notes about their chosen songs, using the prompts in Exercise C.

D Take feedback from one or two pairs and encourage students to respond to each other's ideas.

GRAMMAR HUB

8.1 Reflexive pronouns

Subject pronoun	Reflexive pronoun	
I	myself	I see **myself** performing in this band for two more years.
you (singular)	yourself	You know **yourself** better than anyone else does.
him	himself	He works for **himself** as a photographer.
her	herself	She's the only actress I know who likes watching **herself** on TV.
it	itself	This problem won't fix **itself**. We need to do something.
we	ourselves	We are going to treat **ourselves** to front row seats at the theater.
you (plural)	yourselves	I hope you all enjoyed **yourselves** at the show.
they	themselves	They bought **themselves** an expensive sculpture.

- We use a reflexive pronoun as the object of a verb when the subject and the object are the same person or thing.
  *I taught **myself** how to play the guitar.*
- We can use a reflexive pronoun after the object of a verb. This is to emphasise the person or thing that does the action.
  *She chose the costumes for the play **herself**.*
- We use *by* + reflexive pronoun to say we do something alone or with no help.
  *He worked out what had happened **by himself**.*
- For emphasis, we can also use *all by* + reflexive pronoun.
  *I can't believe you did it **all by** yourself!*
- We use *each other* when two or more people or things perform the same action to the other person/people.
  *Eric and Patricia sang **each other** a song.* NOT ~~*Eric and Patricia sang **themselves** a song.*~~

Be careful!

- We don't use reflexive pronouns after prepositions of place. We use object pronouns.
  *I took my camera with **me**.* NOT ~~*I took my camera with myself.*~~

8.1 Reflexive pronouns

A Correct the mistakes in each sentence.

1. I bought ~~me~~ *myself* a membership to a book club.
2. We didn't give ~~ourself~~ ourselves enough time to set up the exhibit.
3. Paul, be careful! Please don't hurt ~~himself~~ yourself climbing over those seats.
4. He wrote the songs for his album all by ~~itself~~. himself
5. You look tired, Eleni. You should look after ~~yourselves~~ yourself and get more sleep.
6. I wish our friends Pete and Lynne could be ~~ourselves~~ themselves around strangers.
7. The show I organized ran ~~myself~~ itself – it didn't take a lot of work.

B Write the missing reflexive pronoun.

1. We bought *ourselves* a new piano.
2. Jane, please don't compare yourself to other people.
3. Rachel hurt herself singing on stage.
4. The problem with my music player fixed itself.
5. They bought themselves tickets to see Adele in concert.
6. He asked himself if he was happy as a writer.
7. We must learn to love ourselves before we can love others.

➤ Go back to page 73.

B WORK IT OUT Match the sentences in Exercise A (1–4) with the rules (a–c).

Reflexive pronouns

There are several ways we can use reflexive pronouns. The most usual are:

a We use a reflexive pronoun as the object of a verb. This is when the subject and the object are the same person or thing. 3, 4

b We also use a reflexive pronoun after the object of a verb. This is to emphasize the person or thing that does the action. 1

c We use *by* + reflexive pronoun to say we do something alone or with no help. 2

C Go to the **Grammar Hub** on **page 136.**

D SPEAK Work in pairs. Have you ever …

1 taught yourself to do something (for example, play a musical instrument, play a sport, learn a skill)?
2 designed and/or built something yourself?
3 bought yourself something special?

VOCABULARY

Music

A Go to the **Vocabulary Hub** on **page 150.**

B Replace the words in **bold** with words in the box with the same or similar meaning.

album band members catchy cover songs gig live lyrics on tour

1 It's a great song. I love the **words.** lyrics
2 It's the best **concert** I've been to. gig
3 They play their own songs and **songs by other bands.** cover songs
4 This song is **very easy to remember.** catchy
5 They are **doing a series of concerts** soon. on tour
6 Their first **collection of songs** is their best. album
7 I would love to see them **performing a concert.** live
8 They have some great **people in the group,** who are excellent musicians. band members

C SPEAK Work in pairs. Replace the pronouns in Exercise B to make true sentences. Tell your partner.

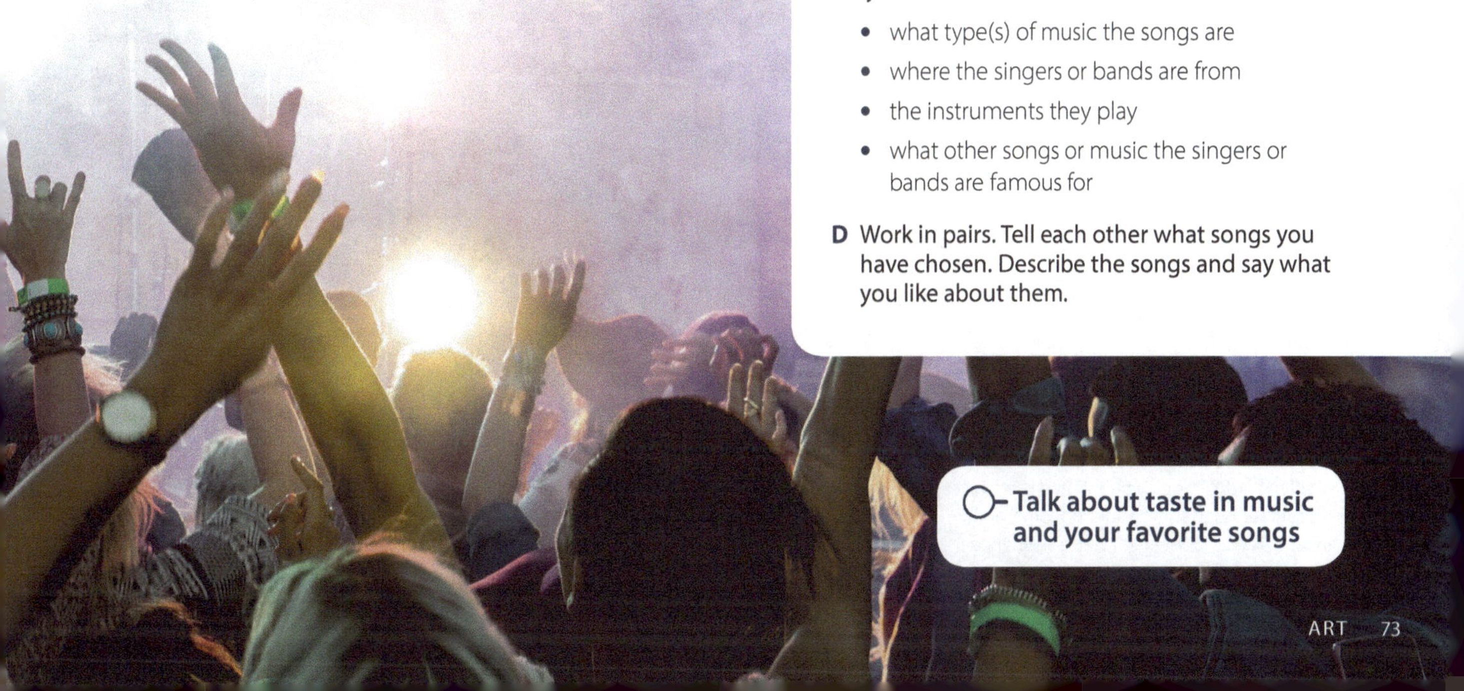

PRONUNCIATION

Consonant clusters in words

8.4 **A** Underline the consonant clusters in each word. Then listen carefully. Are all the letters in the consonant clusters pronounced?
No, the 'ck' together make one /k/ sound.

1 background
2 electric yes
3 individual yes
4 influenced yes
5 keyboards yes
6 ourselves yes

8.4 **B** Listen again and repeat the words.

SPEAKING

A Read the text about a radio show. Do you have a similar show in your country?

DESERT ISLAND DISCS

Desert Island Discs is a BBC Radio 4 show in the UK. It was first broadcast in 1942 and since then 3000 episodes have been recorded. Each week, a guest is asked to choose eight songs or other pieces of music they would take if they had to go on a desert island. The guest explains the reasons for their choices.

B Choose three songs or pieces of music to take to a desert island. Which is your number one song?

C Think about how to describe the songs and what you like about them, for example, the lyrics. Write notes about:

- what type(s) of music the songs are
- where the singers or bands are from
- the instruments they play
- what other songs or music the singers or bands are famous for

D Work in pairs. Tell each other what songs you have chosen. Describe the songs and say what you like about them.

Talk about taste in music and your favorite songs

8.2 Unusual art

Talk about art and artists

V types of art P /ɪ/ and /iː/ G infinitive of purpose

VOCABULARY

Types of art

A SPEAK Work in pairs. How many artists can you name? What do you know about them or their paintings? Who are the most famous artists from your country?

B Go to the **Vocabulary Hub** on **page 150**.

PRONUNCIATION

/ɪ/ and /iː/

8.5 Listen to the sounds /ɪ/ and /iː/. Then listen and underline the word you hear.

	/ɪ/	/iː/		/ɪ/	/iː/
1	slip	<u>sleep</u>	4	sit	<u>seat</u>
2	<u>ship</u>	sheep	5	<u>pitch</u>	peach
3	<u>live</u>	leave	6	bit	<u>beat</u>

READING

A Work in pairs. Look at the works of art (a–d). What material do you think the artist uses in each one? Tell your partner.

a, packing tape; b, dirt; c, matches; d, toilet paper rolls and paper

B SCAN Read *Unusual art* quickly and check your answers to Exercise A. Then match the works of art (a–d) with the correct paragraphs (2–5). a 3; b 5; c 4; d 2

C READ FOR DETAIL Read again. Are the following sentences true (T) or false (F)?

1 Anastassia Elias cuts up toilet paper rolls to produce her works of art. She cuts up paper and places it inside toilet paper rolls. T / **F**

2 Max Zorn uses different colored tape to produce light and dark. He uses thin layers of brown packing tape to produce light and dark. T / **F**

3 Stanislav Aristov uses more than one picture to create his art. **T** / F

4 Scott Wade mostly creates images of cars and things connected with the automotive industry. He creates images of different subjects. T / **F**

D SPEAK Work in pairs. Which of the works of art do you like best? Why?

UNUSUAL ART

1 Art and artists come in many forms. In this post, we look at four artists who use unusual materials to produce their art.

2 French artist Anastassia Elias uses toilet paper rolls and paper to create everyday scenes of life. She cuts out the image from paper and places it inside the roll. She then illuminates the images from the back, which creates a silhouette. (Ex C Q1)

3 Max Zorn uses brown packing tape to create his works of art. He sticks the tape on glass sheets and illuminates them from the back. He creates dark and light by using thick or thin layers of tape. Originally, he used street lights in Amsterdam in the Netherlands, which is where he is from. (Ex C Q2)

4 Russian artist Stanislav Aristov uses burned matchsticks to create his art. First, he photographs a match after it has finished burning. He then photographs a separate burning flame. Aristov then combines these two images to produce the final picture using picture software. He produces images from nature, such as flowers and animals, as well as everyday objects. (Ex C Q3)

5 Scott Wade creates works of art on the dirty windows of cars. He usually uses artificial dirt to make the car dirty. Wade creates his own images and also recreates famous paintings, such as landscapes and still life. He also produces portraits of famous people. Wade has displayed his work at car shows and other automotive events around the world. He believes that 'dirt is beautiful.' (Ex C Q4)

Glossary

artificial (adj) made by people and used instead of something natural
illuminate (v) to shine a light on something
layer (n) an amount or sheet of a substance that covers a surface
silhouette (n) the dark shape of something

a

b

c

d

8.2 Unusual art

LEAD-IN

Take a reproduction of a well-known picture or a photo of a sculpture to class. Cover the reproduction leaving just a small part for students to see and, gradually, reveal some other parts of the picture. Students work in groups to decide what type of art it is, who painted or sculpted it, what materials were used, where you can see the original, etc. Discuss answers with the whole class.

VOCABULARY

A Arrange students in pairs. Tell them they have one minute to think of a list of artists from their countries and the world. Take feedback from one or two pairs and encourage students to share names to complete the list.

B Direct students to the **Vocabulary Hub** (TB121). Use the **Vocabulary Worksheet** on W45 for extra practice.

PRONUNCIATION

8.5 **A** Model and focus students on the pronunciation difference between /ɪ/ and /iː/. Play the audio. Students underline the word they hear. Play the audio again for students to listen and repeat.

READING

A Enlarge the images next to the reading passage. Read the task and the glossary with the class. Students discuss the question in pairs. Take feedback from one or two pairs and encourage students to respond to each other's ideas but do not confirm or correct their answers at this time.

B Give students a limited time to read the article, check their answers to Exercise A and match the works of art with the paragraph that talks about them. Make sure they have enough time to do the task but not enough to read the article in detail.

C Students read the article again and decide if the sentences are true or false. Check answers as a class.

D Students work in pairs discussing which of the works of art they like best and why. Monitor and assist when necessary. Take feedback from one or two pairs and encourage students to respond to each other's ideas.

TEACHING IDEA by David Seymour and Maria Popova

Speaking: Desert Island Discs

Ask students what they know about the radio show *Desert Island Discs*. Explain that the guests on the show are allowed to choose one book and one luxury item to take with them to a desert island, as well as eight pieces of music. Arrange students in groups of four and ask them to share their ideas about what books and luxury items they would take with them and why.

METHODOLOGY HUB by Jim Scrivener

Fillers

Most teachers find they need a small collection of fillers, i.e. things to do when they've run out of other materials, perhaps because the main activity went much faster than expected and there is still seven-minutes remaining at the end of the lesson before the bell rings. Fillers are also useful at the start of a lesson as a warm-up (particularly when you are waiting for some latecomers) or mid-lesson as a way of changing the pace or of breaking up similar activities. Some common fillers:

Revision dictation

Divide the class into teams. Choose between five and fifteen sentences (or words) from the lesson. Dictate the words, challenging the teams to write down the sentences / words with correct spelling. Allow them time for arguing and agreeing. At the end, go through the whole list. Give points for completely correct answers.

***Yes* and *no* questions**

Quick story puzzles usually go over well. Describe a slightly cryptic basic situation or problem; the learners have to ask questions, discuss and find a solution that explains the story. You can only answer *yes* or *no* to any questions asked.

For example:

'A stranger crawled all over my living room today'. (*'I'd dropped a contact lens; the TV repair man helped me find it.'*)

'A man is pushing a car on a road. When he gets to the hotel, he will lose all his money. What's happening?' (*It's a game of Monopoly.*)

The hotel receptionist game

Prepare a list of likely (and unlikely) sentences that a guest would say to a hotel receptionist (e.g. 'What time is breakfast?' 'Where's the restaurant?' 'My TV has exploded!' 'I've lost my wallet'). Hand one of these sentences to a student who must mime it well enough for the class to guess the original sentence. It could be a team game with points; it could use other situations or locations such as airport, theater, family at dinner, etc.

TEACHING IDEA by David Seymour and Maria Popova

Vocabulary: High culture

Ask students what cultural activities they take part in. Arrange students in pairs and ask them to tell each other about what they do and the places they go, e.g. movie theaters, the theater, galleries, museums, etc. Ask students to specify movies, plays and exhibits. Students should then mingle with the rest of the class and find out everyone's favorite painting, building and piece of music. Ask students to write down the name of anyone who shares their opinion. Did anyone find someone with the same three favorites?

8.2 Unusual art

GRAMMAR

A Focus students on the sentences. Students complete the sentences with two words from the article. Students compare their answers with a partner before checking with the whole class.

B Students read the grammar box. In pairs, they complete the rule using the sentences in Exercise A to help them. They then underline further examples of *infinitive of purpose* from the text.

In this post, we look at five artists who use unusual materials to produce their art.
French artist Anastassia Elias uses toilet paper rolls and paper to create everyday scenes of life.
Russian artist Stanislav Aristov uses burned matchsticks to create his art.
Aristov then combines these two images to produce the final artwork using picture software.

C Direct students to the **Grammar Hub** (see below). Use the **Grammar Worksheet** on W44 for extra practice.

D Focus students on the sentence starters and ask them to write complete sentences expressing purpose or reason. Arrange students in pairs. They take turns discussing their sentences with their partner. Encourage students to share as much information as they can. Take feedback from one or two pairs and encourage students to respond to each other's ideas.

Possible answers:
1 *I go to museums and galleries to learn about art and artists.*
2 *We take pictures to remember special moments.*
3 *People go on vacation to relax.*

SPEAKING

A Focus students on the pictures. Elicit from the class what they know about the art, the artists and which they like best. Encourage students to use facts and reasons to support their answers.

B Explain that students are going to give a two-minute presentation about art. Focus students on the activity. Students choose either one of the four works of art or an artist. Alternatively, they may want to choose their favorite work of art or artist. Students work on their own using the question prompts to guide their notes. If students have chosen a female artist, they should change the questions accordingly, e.g. *What is* ***her*** *name? Where is* ***she*** *from?*
Allow time for students to do the research about their chosen topic either in the classroom – on their cell phones – or on the school computers. Monitor and help with grammar and vocabulary when necessary.

C Arrange students in groups of four or five. They take turns giving their presentation to their group. Monitor students as they give their presentations. Take feedback from each of the groups on which artists and art works were mentioned.

GRAMMAR HUB

8.2 Infinitive of purpose

- We can use *to* + base form when we express the purpose or reason for doing something.

*I went to the art store **to get** some paint.*
*We went to the ticket office early **to avoid** the lines.*

Be careful!

*Trine went to the concert **to see** her favorite band perform.* NOT ~~*Trine went to the concert seeing her favorite band perform.*~~

8.2 Infinitive of purpose

A Make sentences with *to* + base form.

1 I / play / the violin / relax
I play the violin to relax.

2 she / attend / drawing classes / spend / time / with other artists
She attended drawing classes to spend time with other artists.

3 we / go / to the movie theater / early / get / good seats
We go to the movie theater early to get good seats.

4 some people / visit / Paris / just / see / the Louvre
Some people visit Paris just to see the Louvre.

5 they / sell / their art / on the street / last weekend / make / money
They were selling their art on the street last weekend to make money.

6 she / go / to voice lessons / every evening / improve / her singing
She is going to voice lessons every evening to improve her singing.

7 we / travel / to Florence / next year / do / some photography
We are traveling to Florence next year to do some photography.

➤ Go back to page 75.

TEACHING IDEA by David Seymour and Maria Popova

Grammar: Purpose

Write on the board: *theater, bus station, DIY shop, movie theater, café, bakery, pharmacy, travel agency, post office*

Arrange students in pairs. Students choose five places from the list that they have been to in the last few days. Then they swap lists with their partner and take turns asking and answering the question *Why did you go?* Model the activity with two stronger students:

Student A – Why did you go to the bank?

Student B – I went there to take out money.

1 Little Dancer by Edgar Degas

2 The Scream by Edvard Munch

3 Self-Portrait by Vincent Van Gogh

4 Girl with Balloon by Banksy

GRAMMAR

Infinitive of purpose

A Complete the sentences from *Unusual art*. Write two words in each blank.

1 Max Zorn uses brown packing tape ___to create___ his works of art.

2 Aristov then combines these two images ___to produce___ the final picture.

3 He usually uses artificial dirt ___to make___ the car dirty.

B WORK IT OUT Look at the sentences in Exercise A and complete the rule. Then find and underline three more examples in the article.

Infinitive of purpose

We use ___to___ + ___infinitive___ to express the purpose or reason for doing something.

C Go to the **Grammar Hub** on **page 136**.

D SPEAK Complete the sentences with your own ideas to express purpose or reason. Then work in pairs and compare your ideas.

1 I go to museums and galleries …

2 We take pictures …

3 People go on vacation …

SPEAKING

A Look at the pictures above. What do you know about the works of art and the artists (1–4)? Which do you like the best? Why? What other famous works of art do you know?

B Choose one of the works of art or the artist who produced it (1–4) or use your own ideas. Write notes about:

Work of art

- What is the title?
- Who painted or made it? When?
- Is it in a museum or gallery? Where?
- What does it show?
- What materials are used?
- How does it make you feel?
- Have you seen the original?
- Any other information?

Artist

- What is his name?
- Where is he from?
- When was he alive?
- What is his style?
- What are his famous works of art?
- Do you have a favorite picture by him?
- Do you like this artist? Why/Why not?
- Any other information?

C Work in groups. Give your presentation to the group.

Talk about art and artists

8.3 Telling stories

Describe movies and books

V movie and book genres; adjectives for describing movies and books **P** word stress in longer words
G first conditional **S** identifying contrasts

VOCABULARY

Movie and book genres

A Match the pictures (1–6) with the genres in the box. Then work in pairs to think of movies and books which match the other genres in the box.

> action adventure animated autobiography biography biopic comedy costume drama fairy tale fantasy historical horror musical romantic comedy (rom-com) science fiction (sci-fi) thriller western

1 sci-fi

2 horror

3 autobiography
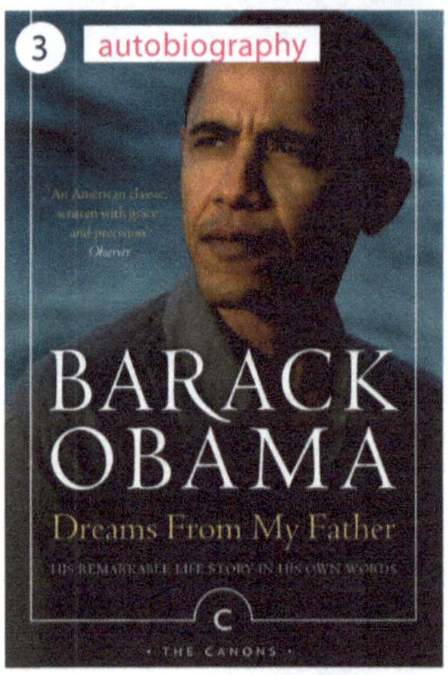

4 comedy

5 costume drama

6 animated

PRONUNCIATION

Word stress in longer words

A Write the movie and book genres in the box in the correct place.

> adventure animated biography comedy fantasy historical musical romantic comedy science fiction

1 •●•	2 ●•••	3 •●••
adventure	animated	historical biography
4 ●••	**5 •●•●••**	**6 ●•●•**
fantasy comedy musical	romantic comedy	science fiction

8.6 **B** Work in pairs. Compare your answers. Then listen and check.

C **SPEAK** Work in pairs. What genres of movies and books do you enjoy?

LISTENING

A Match the definitions (1–5) with the words in the box.

> engaging gripping memorable sense visualize

1 easy to remember because of being special in some way memorable
2 attracting and keeping someone's attention engaging
3 to form a picture of something in your mind visualize
4 one of the natural abilities most people have to see, hear, smell, taste and feel things sense
5 very exciting and interesting gripping

B **PREDICT** Do you think the following statements refer to movies (M) or books (B)?

1 They allow us to imagine and see things in our own way. B
2 We get to know the characters more. B
3 They connect with our different senses at the same time. M
4 It is an experience we usually share with friends. M

8.7 **C** **LISTEN FOR GIST** Listen to a podcast comparing movies and books and check your answers to Exercise B.

Glossary

book club (n) a group of people who meet regularly to discuss books
chapter (n) one of the sections into which a book is divided; a chapter usually has a number or a title
character (n) a person in a book or movie
dialogue (n) the words that characters speak in a book or movie

8.3 Telling stories

LEAD-IN

Arrange students in groups of four. With books closed, they have to think of a movie and write a short summary. Give students five minutes to do the task. Then, each group reads their summary aloud, without saying the title, for the rest of the class to guess the movie.

VOCABULARY

A Ask students what kinds of movies and books they enjoy. Read through the genres in the vocabulary box and clarify meanings. Take feedback from one or two pairs and encourage students to respond to each other's ideas.

PRONUNCIATION

A Model the first word. Explain that the larger dot represents the stressed syllable. With a weaker group, you may want to do one or two more words with the whole class.

8.6 **B** Play the audio for students to check their answers.

C Monitor students, paying close attention to their pronunciation.

LISTENING

A Students work alone matching the words to the definitions. With a weaker group you may want to allow students to compare their answers in pairs before checking them as a class.

B Take feedback from one or two students and encourage the class to respond to each other's ideas but do not confirm or correct their ideas at this time.

8.7 **C** Ask students to look at the glossary, and check understanding. Play the audio for students to check their answers to Exercise B.

8.7 **D** Focus students on the information in the box. Remind students of the listening passage in Exercise C and ask them to match Sentences 1–5 with their contrasting ideas a–e. Then, play the audio again for students to check their answers.

8.8 **E** Read the activity with the class. Play the audio. In pairs, students listen and make a list of the linking words and phrases.

1 *Books allow the reader to use their imagination. With movies, on the other hand, we see what the director and the actors want us to see.*
2 *With books, the story generally moves more slowly. With a movie, though, the whole story needs to start and finish in 90 minutes.*
3 *We generally watch a movie with other people … But reading a book is more individual and personal.*
4 *Reading is a less sociable activity. Although book clubs are very popular these days.*
5 *People usually say they are disappointed by the movie. However, in many cases people actually prefer the movie.*

Extra activity

You can use this speaking activity to consolidate work on presenting contrasting ideas. Put students into small groups and give them a topic to discuss, e.g. hobbies, education or entertainment. Each student should give an opinion on a topic and the other students should then disagree with this. Tell students to use the linking words and phrases from the language box in Exercise D to help them to present their ideas.

AUDIO SCRIPT

8.7

Listening, Exercise C

A: … Well, I'd say the main difference between movies and books is how they tell the story and how we connect with it.

Ex D Q1 **B:** Yes, I agree. Books allow the reader to use their imagination. We can visualise the story and the people and the places in our own way. With movies, on the other hand, we see what the director and the actors want us to see. There's much less possibility for us to use our own imagination.

A: I agree. And another important difference is that
Ex D Q2 with books, the story generally moves more slowly and goes into more detail. With a movie, though, the whole story needs to start and finish in 90 minutes. So, in a book, we have more time to get to know the characters and to understand them. I think this makes the experience more personal and engaging.

B: Well, yes, I see what you mean – a book can be more engaging, but at the same time, a movie can be much more exciting and gripping than a book. It can use sounds and images and dialogue all at the same time. We use our different senses. And for many people, this is more entertaining than reading a book. Music can also make the movie more interesting and memorable.

A: That's true. I think another important difference is that with a book, the chapters provide natural breaks in the story. This gives us time to think about what we have read. A movie doesn't give us this opportunity.

B: Yeah, and also, of course, watching a movie is usually a social experience. We generally watch a movie with
Ex D Q3 other people and then talk about it and share our opinions. But reading a book is more individual and personal. I think that's a really important difference.

A: Yes, I agree that reading is a less sociable activity.
Ex D Q4 Although, book clubs are very popular these days. I guess that's a similar social experience.

B: And one more thing is that people usually say that the book is better than the movie. Compared to the book, people usually say they are disappointed by the movie – especially if they have read the book first.
Ex D Q5 However, I think in many cases people actually prefer the movie.

A: Interesting. That's something that we can …

8.3 Telling stories

VOCABULARY

A Students work on their own before checking answers in pairs.

8.9 **B** Students work in pairs. Play the audio to check answers.

GRAMMAR

A Students work alone. Check answers as a class.

B Direct students to the **Grammar Hub** (see below). Use the **Grammar Worksheet** on W46 for extra practice.

SPEAKING HUB

A Play the audio. Students circle the subjects Salli talks about.

8.10 **B** Students work on their own. Monitor and assist when necessary.

C Encourage students to use the adjectives for describing movies or books from this lesson. Use the **Vocabulary Worksheet** on W47 for extra practice.

D When everyone has spoken, ask each group to summarize the recommendations and share them with the class.

GRAMMAR HUB

8.3

First conditional

Condition *If* + simple present,	Result *will/won't*
If **you go** to the festival,	**you'll have** a great time.
If **it doesn't rain**,	**we'll go** to the street fair.
If **it's** busy,	**we won't go** to the theater.
If **you don't ask** for help,	**you won't get** any.

Result *will/won't*	Condition *if* + simple present
You'll meet the artist	if **you visit** the gallery tonight.
She won't go to the concert	if **it's** expensive.

Question	Positive short answer	Negative short answer
If Star Wars **is** playing at the movie theater, **will you go**?	Yes, **I will**.	No, **I won't**.
Will you go if Star Wars **is** playing at the movie theater?		

- We use the first conditional to talk about possible situations in the future.
- The *if*-clause describes the action or condition.

  *If **he sells all his art**, he'll get a bigger studio.*

  The result clause says what will happen.

  *If he sells all his art, **he'll get a bigger studio**.*
- We can use other modal verbs (e.g. *can, could, might, should*) instead of *will*.

  *If you sing really well, you **can** become famous.*
  *If it's open, we **might** go to the museum.*
  *If you win an award, we **should** celebrate.*
- We can use *should* to ask questions and make suggestions.

  ***Should** we work on our paintings if you're not too tired?*

Be careful!

- We use a comma (,) when the *if*-clause comes first.

  If you go, I'll come too. NOT ~~*If you go I'll come too.*~~
  I'll buy your ticket if you get the popcorn. NOT ~~*I'll buy your ticket, if you get the popcorn.*~~

8.3 First conditional

A Check (✓) the sentences that are correct. Correct the mistakes in the others.

1 She will give you an autograph if you ~~will~~ ask her.
2 If I have time, I will paint your portrait tomorrow. ✓
3 He ~~stars~~ will star in the movie if they pay him well.
4 I 'll go with you to the movie theater if we can watch a comedy.
5 The audience will love us, if we play our best songs. ✗
6 If we all join the book club, it will be a lot of fun. ✓

B Complete the sentences with the correct form of the verbs in the box.

ask buy ~~call~~ go have like

1 I *'ll call* Claire if you call Simon.
2 If you get the movie tickets, I 'll buy the snacks.
3 If it rains tomorrow, we won't have a concert in the park.
4 I 'll go to the audition if you come with me.
5 You'll love *Wicked* if you like musicals.
6 If she asks for my help, I'll give it to her.

C Complete the conversation with the correct form of the verbs in parentheses.

Wes: (1) What about next week's gallery opening? If you *organize* (*organize*) the food, I *'ll take care of* (*take care of*) the drinks.

Trisha: (2) OK. What about setting up the artwork? If I do (*do*) that, will you send (*you / send*) out the invitations?

Wes: (3) Sure. Should I invite students from the university? If they come (*come*), we won't have (*not have*) enough food and drinks.

Trisha: (4) I know … It's a problem. If we invite (*invite*) all of them, the gallery will get (*get*) too full!

Wes: (5) If everyone shows (*show*) up, there probably won't be (*probably / not be*) enough space.

Trisha: (6) If that happens (*happen*), people might damage (*might damage*) the art.

Wes: You're right. Let's not invite them, then.

➤ Go back to page 77.

8.7 **D** Match the sentences (1–5) with their contrasting ideas (a–e). Then listen again and check your answers. Use the information in the box to help you.

Identifying contrasts

Listen for linking words and phrases that express a contrast between two ideas:

but, though, however, although	*(but) at the same time*
on the other hand	*compared to*

Listen for phrases that introduce a further contrast:

another (important) difference is	*and one more thing*

1 Books allow the reader to use their imagination.
2 With books, the story generally moves more slowly.
3 We generally watch a movie with other people.
4 Reading is a less sociable activity.
5 People usually say they are disappointed by the movie.

a Book clubs are very popular these days.
b In many cases people actually prefer the movie.
c Reading a book is more individual and personal.
d With a movie the whole story needs to start and finish in 90 minutes.
e With movies we see what the director and the actors want us to see.

8.8 **E** **LISTEN FOR KEY WORDS** Listen to the extracts. Which linking words or phrases express the contrasting ideas in Exercise D? Make a list.

VOCABULARY
Adjectives for describing movies and books

A Look at the sentences from the podcast. Complete the adjectives with the missing vowels (*a*, *e*, *i*, *o*, *u*).

1 I think this makes the experience more personal and _ng_g_ng.
2 A movie can be much more _xc_t_ng and gr_pp_ng than a book.
3 Music can also make the movie more _nt_r_st_ng and m_m_r_bl_.
4 Compared to the book, people usually say they are d_s_pp_ _nt_d by the movie.

8.9 **B** Read the information in the box and choose the correct option in the sentences below. Listen and check.

Adjectives for describing movies and books

We use adjectives ending in *-ing* to talk about what caused the feeling.

- *The movie was disappointing.*

We use adjectives ending in *-ed* to talk about how we feel.

- *I was disappointed.*

1 It was totally *engaged* / *engaging* and the acting was *amazed* / *amazing*.
2 I was, well, a little *bored* / *boring* by the end. It isn't very memorable I'm afraid.
3 You won't be *disappointed* / *disappointing*. The singing was incredible.
4 It's really *gripped* / *gripping*. And it's very *moved* / *moving* and sad, too.

GRAMMAR
First conditional

A **WORK IT OUT** Look at the first conditional sentences below. Then choose the correct words to complete the rules.

*If you **want** a great night out, you **should see** this movie.*

*If you **remind** me, I'**ll lend** it to you.*

*If you **like** musicals, you'**ll love** it.*

First conditional

1 We use the first conditional to talk about *impossible* / *possible* situations in the future.
2 Conditional sentences usually have two clauses: the *if*-clause and the main clause. To make a first conditional sentence, we use:
   - *If* + *present tense* / *will* and *present tense* / *will* + base form.
3 We *can* / *can't* use other modal verbs (for example, *can, could, might, should*) instead of *will* in the main clause.

B Go to the **Grammar Hub** on **page 136**.

SPEAKING HUB

8.10 **A** Listen to Salli recommending a movie. What does she talk about?

1 the movie type or genre
2 the main story
3 the actors, the director, the writer
4 what she likes about it
5 how it made her feel

B **PLAN** You are going to recommend a movie or book. Decide which movie or book you are going to talk about and write notes about the topics in Exercise A.

C **ORGANIZE** Use adjectives for describing movies or books and at least one first conditional sentence (*If you like …, you'll love …*).

D **DISCUSS** Work in groups. Recommend the movie or book you chose to your group.

Describe movies and books

8.4 First date

F– show interest in a topic   P– intonation

COMPREHENSION

A ▶ **SPEAK** Work in pairs. Which topics do you think Milly and Zac will talk about on their first date? Then watch the video and check your answers.

children (culture) (family) (food) (home) marriage money (music) the weather work

B ▶ Are the sentences true (T) or false (F)? Correct the false sentences. Then watch the video again and check your answers.

1 Zac arrives first at the park. (T) / F
2 Milly knows the band Zac is listening to. (T) / F
3 Zac and Milly have tickets to the same show. (T) / F
4 It's Milly's birthday today. T / (F) Milly's birthday is next week.
5 Zac loves English food. T / (F) Zac isn't crazy about English food.
6 Milly likes English culture. (T) / F
7 Zac thinks Milly is shy. T / (F) Milly thinks Zac is shy.
8 Milly wants to go home. T / (F) Milly wants to keep walking.

FUNCTIONAL LANGUAGE

Show interest in a topic

A Complete the replies (1–11) with the words in the box.

are believe did do for kidding neither no really so too

Comment	Reply
	Show surprise
[music playing]	[1] No way! Is this Gold Sounds?
It's their new record.	[2] For real?
I have tickets to their show.	You're [3] kidding ! I don't [4] believe it!
I'm going with my sister.	[5] Are you?
She got the tickets for my birthday.	She [6] did ?
It's today.	[7] Really ? It's your birthday today?
I like that about you.	You [8] do ?
	Show you understand
I miss my family.	[9] So do I.
I'm not crazy about English food.	[10] Neither am I.
I feel like I can be myself here.	Me, [11] too .

B ▶ Watch the video again and check your answers.

MILLY

SAM

NEENA

ZAC

GABY

Glossary

Really? **(interjection) (British)** = For real? **(phrase) (American)**
You're joking! **(phrase) (British)** = You're kidding! **(phrase) (American)**

PRONUNCIATION

Intonation

8.11 **A** Listen to the replies from Functional language Exercise A. Write them in the correct place. Then listen again and check your answers.

Rising intonation	Falling intonation
For real? Are you? She did? Really? You do?	*No way!* Me, too. You're kidding! I don't believe it! So do I. Neither am I.

8.11 **B** Listen again and repeat the replies. Copy the intonation.

SPEAKING

A Write a short sentence about the following topics:

1 something surprising
I have tickets for Rihanna!
2 something shocking
______
3 something that isn't true
______
4 something about the past
______
5 something about the future
______
6 something you like
______
7 something you don't like
______

B Work in pairs. Take turns. Student A – read out your sentences. Student B – show interest and reply.

Show interest in a topic

➤ Turn to page 165 to learn how to write a review.

8.4 First date

COMPREHENSION

A ▶ Students look at the still images and decide what is happening (*Milly and Zac are going on a date*). Focus students on the vocabulary box. In pairs, students discuss what they think Milly and Zac will talk about on their date. Take feedback from one or two students, but do not correct or confirm their answers. Play the video for students to check their answers.

B ▶ Students decide whether the sentences are true or false. Take feedback from the class but do not correct or confirm their answers at this time. Play the video again for students to check their answers

FUNCTIONAL LANGUAGE

A Focus students on ways to show interest in a topic. Students read the expressions in the box and complete the blanks with the words from the vocabulary box. Take feedback from the class but do not correct or confirm their answers at this time.

B ▶ Play the video again for students to check their answers. Focus students' attention on the differences between American and British English. Explain that both forms are correct and they can use either in their speaking.

PRONUNCIATION

8.11 **A** Focus students on intonation. Elicit that intonation is the rise and fall of your voice when you speak. Model and practice some examples of rising and falling intonation. Play the audio. Students write the replies in the correct column. Play the audio again for students to check their answers.

8.11 **B** Play the audio again for students to listen and repeat. Monitor students, paying close attention to word stress and intonation.

SPEAKING

A Focus students on the activity and the prompts. Model one or two sentences for the class. Students write their sentences. Monitor and assist when necessary.

B In pairs, students take turns responding to each other's sentences using the *Functional Language* from this lesson. To make this activity more challenging, encourage stronger students to keep their books closed and try to remember the responses from the lesson. Take feedback from one or two pairs about any interesting things they have learned and encourage students to respond to each other's ideas.

▶ VIDEO SCRIPT

Café Hub 8.4 First date
Z = Zac M = Milly

Z: Hey!
M: Hey Zac. No way! Is this Gold Sounds?
Z: Wow! You know Gold Sounds?
M: What?
Z: Yeah! It's their new record.
M: For real? They're awesome, I really love them! I have tickets to their show at the Seachange Arms next weekend.
Z: On the Friday or Saturday?
M: Saturday I think.
Z: You're kidding! So do I.
M: I don't believe it! I'm going with my sister.
Z: Are you? That's cool.
M: Yeah, she's totally cool. She got the tickets for my birthday.
Z: She did? When's your birthday?
M: Well … It's today!
Z: Really? It's your birthday today? Oh … I didn't know …
M: I'm just kidding. It's next week! Sorry. So, where are we going?
Z: Have you ever been to Breeze Park?
M: Breeze Park? Nope, I don't think so.
Z: Really? I think you'll like it! If we go this way we'll be there in 10 minutes.
M: Great! Let's go!
Z: Do you ever miss home?
M: Yeah, sometimes. You?
Z: Yeah, I miss my family.
M: Yeah. So do I …
Z: I miss the food too. I'm not crazy about English food.
M: Neither am I. I love the culture and British humour though … I feel like I can be myself here.
Z: Yeah. Me too. Hey, I'm sorry it took me so long to ask you out.
M: Yeah I noticed that.
Z: I'm kind of shy.
M: Yeah, I noticed that too. But I like that about you.
Z: You do?
M: Yeah … How high can you swing?
Z: Higher than you!
M: No chance!
Z: So where to now?
M: I don't mind. Let's just … Keep walking …

TEACHING IDEA by David Seymour and Maria Popova

Functional language: Love

Ask the students if they believe in love at first sight. Ask whether anyone knows the story of Romeo and Juliet. Elicit the story from those who know it, one sentence at a time. Those who don't know it ask a question about each line, e.g. 'They met at a party'. 'Whose party was it?' Arrange students in small groups and ask them to discuss the way relationships begin in different cultures. What are the most important foundations of a successful relationship? When they have finished discussing, ask students to compare their ideas with another group.

Speaking: First dates

Elicit from the class the topics that Milly and Zac talked about on their first date. Ask students whether there are any topics that you shouldn't discuss on a first date and elicit two or three ideas. Ask students to work with their partner and come up with two lists of conversation topics: a green list of topics that are suitable for a first date, and a red list of topics that are inappropriate. When students are finished, ask them to compare their ideas with another group.

8 Writing — Write a review

W – describing and recommending

A Read the movie review. Is it positive or negative? Positive
Underline the words and phrases that tell you this.

Ex A

La La Land is set in modern-day Los Angeles. It stars Emma Stone and Ryan Gosling. It tells the story of a romance between Mia (played by Emma Stone) and Seb (played by Ryan Gosling). She is an actress and he is a jazz pianist. The movie is a musical, but it is also a classic love story with some wonderful music and singing and some old-fashioned dancing. At the same time, it is exciting, beautiful and heart-breaking. I found myself completely engaged with the story and with the lives of Mia and Seb. The acting was excellent. Emma Stone and Ryan Gosling were perfect as Mia and Seb. If you like musicals, you'll love this movie.

Share Like Comment

Ex C

Comments:

Stacey99: I agree. Great movie. I wasn't expecting that ending, but it's definitely worth seeing.

BillyTom: I liked the ending. I didn't imagine the story would finish that way. It was a nice twist!

DashaV: This movie is a work of art, full of color and life. A modern-day classic.

Rob78: Not my favorite movie. But to be fair, I don't like musicals!

> Refer students to this review as a model for the writing task.

B Number the topics in the order they are written about in the review.

The movie
2 the plot or story
1 where the movie is set (location)
4 writer's opinion of the movie
5 writer's opinion of the actors
6 writer's recommendation
3 movie genre

> You can elicit some of these at the beginning of the class or as a reminder before writing by asking *What does the reader of a review want to know?*

C Read the comments again. Does each person like or dislike the movie? Underline the words and phrases in the comments that tell you this. Stacey99, BillyTom and DashaV like the movie. Rob78 doesn't like the movie.

D Cover Exercises A, B and C. Complete the missing words in the phrases from the review and comments.

Describing and recommending

1 *La La Land* is s e t in …
2 It s t a r s Emma Stone and Ryan Gosling.
3 It tells the s t o r y of …
4 The m o v i e is a musical.
5 The a c t i n g was …
6 It's (definitely) w o r t h seeing.

E Write the missing words to complete the review.

The movie is s e t in Los Angeles in 1961. It t e l l s the true s t o r y of the author PL Travers and moviemaker Walt Disney. Disney wants to make a movie using one of Traver's books. It s t a r s Tom Hanks. The a c t i n g is excellent. This movie is definitely w o r t h seeing.

WRITING

A PREPARE You are going to write review of a movie that you have seen.

B PLAN Take notes for each topic in Writing Exercise B.

C WRITE Use the review in Exercise A and the strategies in the Writing skills box to help you write your review. Write about 100 words.

> Students can do this in class or for homework.

D REVIEW Work in pairs. Can you find someone in the class who has seen the same movie? Read your partner's review and write a comment. Then work with another pair and add comments to their reviews.

8 WRITING 165

WRITING

A Students read the review of *La La Land* and decide whether it is positive or negative. Ask students to underline the words and phrases that helped them to decide.

B Focus students on the topics. Students look again at the review and number the topics (1–6) in the order they appear in the review.

C Students read the comments below the review and decide whether the people liked or disliked the movie. Ask students to underline the words and phrases that helped them decide.

D Ask students to cover Exercises A, B and C with a piece of paper. Students complete the phrases in the box with words from the review and comments. Each space represents one letter of the missing word.

E Students complete the movie review on their own and compare their answers in pairs.

WRITING TASK

A Explain that students will now write their own movie review. Ask them to think of a movie they have seen recently or that they know well.

B Ask students to look again at the topics in Exercise B and write notes for each topic about the movie they have chosen. Monitor and assist when necessary.

C Students write their reviews. Encourage them to write approximately 100 words. Remind them to use the example review and the information in the box to help them.

D Check what movies have been reviewed. In pairs, students see whether other students have reviewed the same movies. Then, they take turns reading their partner's review and write a brief comment on it. Arrange groups of four by putting together two pairs. Students read and respond to each other's reviews.

Unit 8 Review

VOCABULARY

A Rearrange the letters of the words in **bold**. The first and last letters are in the correct place.

1 Do you listen to whole **ablmus** [albums] or do you usually listen to individual songs?

2 Do you pay much attention to the **lriyes** [lyrics] of a song or do you mostly listen to the music?

3 Do you have a favorite **sigenr** [singer] or musician (**giuristat** [guitarist], **dmruemr** [drummer])?

4 Do you go to many **ggis** [gigs]? What was the last band you saw **lvie** [live]? Was there a good **lhgit sohw** [light show]? Where were you in the **aduenice** [audience] – near the **satge** [stage] or far away from it?

B Complete the quiz questions with the words in the box. There is one word you do not need. Then take the quiz.

abstract exhibit gallery landscape portrait sculpture still life

ART QUIZ
How much do you know?

1 Which is the world's most visited art _gallery_**?**
- a The British Museum, London
- b The Metropolitan Museum of Art, New York
- c The Louvre, Paris (circled)

2 It toured the world in the 1970s and is the most visited _exhibit_ **of all time. What was it?**
- a *The Treasures of Tutankhamun* (circled)
- b The *Art of the Aztecs*
- c *The Visions of Van Gogh*

3 *David* by Michelangelo is perhaps the most famous _sculpture_ **in the world. How tall is it?**
- a 5.17 meters (circled)
- b 7.15 meters
- c 1.75 meters

4 *Sunflowers* is one of the world's most famous collections of _still life_ **paintings. Who painted them?**
- a Leonardo da Vinci
- b Vincent van Gogh (circled)
- c Pablo Picasso

5 *Girl with a Pearl Earring* by Johannes Vermeer is a famous _portrait_ **painting. When did Vermeer paint it?**
- a 1465 (circled)
- b 1665
- c 1865

6 Pablo Picasso was most famous for his _abstract_ **art. Where was Picasso born?**
- a France
- b Italy (circled)
- c Spain

C Match the movie and book genres (1–5) with the descriptions (a–e). Then choose the correct adjectives. Which of the descriptions are positive (P) and which are negative (N)?

1 comedy — b
2 thriller — e
3 biography — d
4 fantasy — c
5 horror — a

a It isn't scary at all and I was pretty <u>*bored*</u> / *boring* for most of it. N

b It's really funny. Go see it, you won't be <u>*disappointed*</u> / *disappointing*. P

c It has a lot of strange creatures in it. The visuals are *amazed* / <u>*amazing*</u>. P

d The story of his life was very *engaged* / <u>*engaging*</u> and very *moved* / <u>*moving*</u>. P

e It's very *excited* / <u>*exciting*</u> and *gripped* / <u>*gripping*</u>. I couldn't stop reading it. P

GRAMMAR

A Complete the conversations with the correct reflexive pronouns.

1 **A:** Great gig! Who's the last song by?
B: We wrote it _ourselves_.

2 **A:** I like Jenny's website. Who designed it for her?
B: I think she designed it _herself_.

3 **A:** Did you have guitar lessons or teach _yourself_?
B: I taught _myself_.

B Complete the sentences with the best verb to express purpose. Use *to* + infinitive.

1 We're going to the museum _to see / to visit_ the Picasso exhibit.
2 I mostly use my laptop _to watch_ movies.
3 I started a hobby _to meet / to get to know_ new people.
4 Can I use your phone _to call_ my friend?

C Complete 1–3 with the correct form of the verbs in parentheses.

1 If you _see_ (*see*) Janice this evening, _will you say_ (*you / say*) hello from me?

2 **A:** If we _miss_ (*miss*) the bus, we _'ll get_ (*get*) a taxi.
B: OK, or if it _stops_ (*stop*) raining, we _can walk / 'll walk / could walk_ (*walk*). It isn't far to the movie theater.

3 If you _like_ (*like*) reggae, you _'ll love_ (*love*) this band. I _'ll get_ (*get*) you a ticket if you _like_ (*like*).

FUNCTIONAL LANGUAGE

A Complete the conversations with the words in the box.

believe did do real so too

1 **A:** Alice got a place in the art course.
B: She _did_? That's great news.

2 **A:** Jimmy's band has a record contract.
B: For _real_?

3 **A:** Did you know that the movie won three Oscars?
B: Really? I don't _believe_ it! It was terrible.

4 **A:** I'm going see Jake's new band tonight.
B: Yeah. Me, _too_.

5 **A:** I want to go to the Damien Hirst exhibit.
B: You _do_? I didn't think you liked his stuff.

6 **A:** I love musicals.
B: _So_ do I!

The money piles up in a museum's voluntary donation box, Milan, Italy.

Money (n) what you earn, save, invest and use to pay for things.
Synonyms: bill, bread, cash (n).

Emerson is suggesting that sometimes we sacrifice too many important things like time with our families or friends, health and happiness to obtain money.

Ralph Waldo Emerson (May 25, 1803–April 27, 1882) was an American essayist, lecturer, philosopher and poet. He was a champion of individualism and freedom from the pressures of society. His work has greatly influenced the thinkers, writers and poets that followed him.

OBJECTIVES

- talk about attitudes toward money and about spending money
- talk about philanthropy and charities
- discuss your skills and how they could help others
- go shopping for clothes and ask for a refund
- write a 'for sale' advertisement

Work with a partner. Discuss the questions.

1 Is money important?
2 Read the quote. What do you think Emerson meant? Do you agree?
3 Do you spend money every day? What do you buy?

MONEY 81

OBJECTIVES

Read the unit objectives to the class.

UNIT OPENER QUESTIONS

Encourage students to look at the quote and take one or two suggestions from the class about what they think it means.

Ask students to look at the picture on the page and encourage them to share their ideas. Ask prompt questions such as 'Do you recognize the currency? How important is money to you? What are you ready to sacrifice for money?' If students share any good ideas or useful language, write these on the board.

Students look at the questions at the bottom of the page. Model one possible answer, explaining what money means to you. Students discuss the questions in pairs or in a small group.

Monitor and assist as necessary. When students have finished the activity, ask one or two pairs to share their ideas with the class. Encourage students to listen to one another and respond with their own ideas and opinions.

WORKSHEETS

Lesson 9.1 Spending money

Grammar: Second conditional (W48)

Vocabulary: Prepositions in money phrases (W48)

Lesson 9.2 Getting and giving

Grammar: Essential adjective clauses (W49)

Vocabulary: Verbs connected with money (W50)

Lesson 9.3 Who needs money?

Grammar: Gerunds (W51)

Vocabulary: *make* and *do* expressions (W52)

9.1 Spending money

Talk about attitudes toward money and about spending money

P /ɑː/, /ʌ/ and /æ/ **G** second conditional **V** prepositions in money phrases

READING

A Match the words (1–4) with the definitions (a–d).

1 obsessed a something that you own
2 gain b to get something
3 inspire c to give someone the enthusiasm to do something
4 possession d considering something so important that you are always thinking about it

B READ FOR MAIN IDEA Read *How to buy happiness*. Write the paragraph headings in the correct place. There is one heading you do not need.

a Try something new
b Discover yourself
c Take your time
d Open your mind

C READ FOR DETAIL Read again and answer the questions.

1 Which makes us feel better for longer, possessions or experiences?
2 In what three ways does Julie benefit from traveling?
3 What does Carmen learn from meeting people?
4 According to Carmen, how can traveling improve our character?
5 What does Hugo think can make us lazy?
6 Why does Hugo think experiences inspire us to do more?

D SPEAK Work in pairs. Discuss the questions.

1 Do you agree with the article? Why/Why not?
2 Have you spent money on experiences such as travel? What did you do? Were the experiences positive or negative? Why?

HOW TO BUY HAPPINESS

We live in a society that is obsessed with spending money – a society that is obsessed with materialism. When we buy things, it gives us happiness. But this feeling usually lasts only for a short time. Experiences, on the other hand, stay with us for a long time after they have finished. Therefore, if we spent more of our money on experiences, we would gain something that can last a lifetime. Here are three more reasons we should spend more time and money on experiences and three people who agree with this advice. Ex C Q1

1 b Discover yourself

Julie from the UK believes travel is an important experience. She says, 'Traveling helps us to discover our interests. I'm always saving up so I can go away at least once or twice a year. It helps me to discover what I like and what I don't like. It helps me to understand who I am. I think we wouldn't find out these things if we didn't spend money on experiences.' Ex C Q2

2 d Open your mind

Carmen from Italy also believes that travel is important. She says, 'I spend a lot of my money on traveling. It helps us to see different points of view. As you travel, you meet new people with different ideas and opinions to your own. This teaches us some important life lessons and helps us to understand the world.' Carmen also believes that traveling helps you to become more independent and more confident. Ex C Q3 Ex C Q4

Glossary

materialism (n) the belief that money and possessions are the most important aspects of human existence

3 a Try something new

According to Hugo from Brazil, our experiences can inspire us. He says, 'It's always good to do something that is new. If we didn't do anything different, we might become lazy. We don't have to climb Mount Everest, but we can do things like learn to play a musical instrument, start a new sport or simply do something new for the first time. This will make us feel good and give us a sense of achievement. This will then inspire us to try more things in life. So, my attitude toward money is to spend it on experiences as much as possible!' Ex C Q5 Ex C Q6

So, before you buy your next possession, ask yourself 'Is there an experience I can spend my money on instead?' This could be a night out with friends, a concert or a sporting event, or maybe a weekend away or a vacation. Whatever we choose, it will make us rich with memories and life lessons.

9.1 Spending money

LEAD-IN

Arrange students in pairs. Ask them to imagine that they have a business together, e.g. a bar, a clothing store, a restaurant, a newsstand, a bakery, a bookstore, etc. Tell them to make a list of at least five items that they sell and decide how much each item costs. Form new pairs. Students take turns asking and answering what they sell and how much the items cost.

READING

A In pairs, students match the words with their definitions. Check answers with the whole class.

B Read aloud the title of the article *How to buy happiness.* Call on a stronger student to read the glossary aloud. In what way is 'materialism' linked to the title of the article? Elicit some ideas from the class. Tell students to read the article and decide which heading matches each paragraph. Explain that they should look for synonyms in the article to help them decide which headings to use.

C Ask students to work alone to do the task. Allow students to compare and discuss their answers with a partner before checking them with the whole class.

D In pairs students discuss the questions using specific examples from the article and their own ideas. Monitor and assist when necessary. Take feedback from one or two pairs and encourage students to respond to each other's ideas.

Extra activity

You can use this activity to extend Reading Exercise D. Put students into pairs. Ask them to look back at the *How to buy happiness* article, and then summarize the opinions of the three people in the article. Students should discuss which type of experiences they would be prepared to spend their money on, and say why.

PRONUNCIATION

A Focus students on the three vowel sounds /ɑː/, /ʌ/ and /æ/. Write three examples not in the box on the board and model the sounds, e.g. B<u>ar</u>t, c<u>u</u>t, b<u>a</u>t. Students do the activity in pairs. Take feedback from one or two pairs but do not correct or confirm their answers at this time.

9.1 **B** Play the audio for students to check their answers. Ask for a show of hands to see how many students got the correct answers. Comment on the mistakes.

C In pairs, students practice saying sentences 1–3, focusing on the pronunciation of /ʌ/, /æ/ and /ɑː/. Encourage students to listen to their partners and correct them when necessary.

GRAMMAR

A Students should look back at the article to find the missing words. With a stronger class, you may want students to work in pairs, completing the sentences from memory. Using the completed sentences, students choose the tense to complete the rules for the second conditional.

B Direct students to the **Grammar Hub** (see TB83 and below). Use the **Grammar Worksheet** on W48 for extra practice.

GRAMMAR HUB

9.1 Second conditional

Condition *If* + simple past,	Result *would/wouldn't*
If **you spent** less money,	**you would be** happier.
If **I didn't work** all the time,	**I'd make** more friends.
If **it were** expensive,	**I wouldn't buy** it.
If **they didn't travel** a lot,	**they wouldn't gain** new experiences.

Result *would/wouldn't*	Condition *if* + simple past
You'd discover your interests	if **you traveled** more.
She wouldn't do it	if **she didn't want** to.

Question	Positive short answer	Negative short answer
If **you had** a lot of money, **would you give** it to charity? **Would you give** money to charity if **you had** a lot?	Yes, **I would**.	No, **I wouldn't**.

- We use the second conditional to talk about hypothetical situations in the present or future. The *if*-clauses can be an unlikely or impossible situation.
  Unlikely: *<u>If I won the London marathon,</u> I **would be** so happy!*
  Impossible: *<u>If I were you,</u> I **wouldn't lend** him the money.*
- We only use a comma (,) when the *if*-clause comes first.
- We can use other modal verbs (e.g. *could*, *might*) as an alternative to *would* in the main clause.
  *If she tried something new, it **could open** her mind.*
  *If you had more free time, you **might feel** happier.*
- When the *if*-clause is clear or is implied, we usually only state the result clause.
  What would you do if you won a million dollars?
  I'd leave my job! And I might buy a new house.

Be careful!

- With *I*, *he*, *she* and *it*, we usually use *were* in the *if*-clause, not *was*.
  If I were rich, I would give money to my favorite charity.
- We only use *would* in the result clause.
  If we had children, we'd buy a bigger house. NOT ~~*If we would have a family, we'd buy a bigger house.*~~

9.1 Spending money

VOCABULARY

A Students read sentences 1–3 and complete them with the correct preposition. Direct students back to the article to check their answers. Check answers with the whole class.

B Students complete the sentences with the prepositions in the box. They compare their answers in pairs before checking with the class. Use the **Vocabulary Worksheet** on W48 for extra practice.

C Model the activity with a stronger student, or ask two students to read the example. Students rewrite the sentences on their own and compare their new sentences in pairs. Encourage students to ask each other one or two follow-up questions.

SPEAKING

A Arrange students in groups of three or four and give each group a label A or B. Direct both groups to the **Communication Hub** (TB121).

B Set up pairs with an A and a B student. Students take turns asking and answering their questions and write down the answers.

C Students return to their original groups and compare the answers they received. They work together comparing the answers and deciding which were the most common or unusual. Take feedback from each group and encourage students to respond to each other's ideas.

TEACHING IDEA by David Seymour and Maria Popova

Speaking: Money talks

Arrange students in groups of three (if possible, group students from different countries). Write the following questions on the board for the groups to discuss:

- What is the currency in your country?
- What is the exchange rate with the Euro / the US dollar?
- What's the rate of income tax and VAT in your country?
- How would society work without money?
- Do you think poor countries should be required to pay their debts to the rich countries?
- What are the advantages and disadvantages of credit cards?

Monitor and help students where necessary. When the students have finished discussing the questions, call on each group to share some of their answers with the rest of the class.

TEACHING IDEA by David Seymour and Maria Popova

Speaking: Bills

In pairs, make a list of all the regular bills you can think of, e.g. electricity, gas, water, insurance, etc. Discuss which you think you could reduce, and how.

In your country, what does an electricity company do when someone doesn't pay their bill? Imagine you haven't paid your bill for six months. Role-play this conversation with your partner.

METHODOLOGY HUB by Jim Scrivener

Dictation

Traditional dictation – where you read a text aloud and the learners must write it down accurately – is usually fairly unpopular with learners. It can feel like an unfair test. Could we make it more enjoyable and useful? Maybe the key question is: Who does what? Usually the teacher makes all the decisions about a dictation. How about turning the tables? Let the learners choose the text. Or let them decide how many times it should be read. Or who should read it. In fact, could the learners choose everything and then dictate to the teacher? Here are a few ideas:

Key words dictation

Find an interesting short story and underline 15–20 of the most important words in it (e.g. key nouns and verbs). Dictate these words to the class, but don't tell them the original story. They now must make a new story that uses those words, in exactly the original order and the original form you dictated. At the end, the class can swap stories, reading or telling them. You could also tell them the original if you wanted.

The 'bad cold' dictation

Explain that you have a bad cold today (sneeze or cough a little to prove it!). Tell the class that you're going to do a normal dictation, but if you have to sneeze or cough (and they can't hear a word), they should write any good word that fits the space. For example, you might dictate *Last Thursday, Maria decided to have some [cough] for breakfast.* The learners could write the sentence with a word like *eggs* or *cornflakes* instead of the cough.

GRAMMAR HUB

9.1 Second conditional

A Correct the mistakes in each sentence. Make second conditionals.

1. If I could travel, I *would* discover more about myself.
2. If people ~~aren't~~ weren't obsessed with money, the world would be a better place.
3. If I had the choice, I ~~will~~ would buy experiences, not possessions.
4. Carol would travel more if she ~~have not~~ didn't have children.
5. You would inspire other people if you ~~would do~~ did something amazing.
6. ~~Did~~ Would you throw away ~~your all~~ all your possessions if I asked you?
7. If I could take two months off work, ~~I traveled~~ I'd travel around India.

B Complete the conversation with the correct form of the verbs in parentheses.

Molly: I just played the lotto. It's $10 million tonight. Imagine what (1) *would happen* (*happen*) if I (2) won (*win*)!

Nelly: Well, you (3) would be (*be*) rich – that's for sure! What (4) would you do (*you / do*) with the money?

Molly: If I (5) had (*have*) $10 million, I (6) would give (*give*) most of it to my family, or to charity, you know?

Nelly: Really? I (7) wouldn't do (*not / do*) that. I'd buy a big house, and some expensive artwork.

➤ Go back to page 83.

PRONUNCIATION
/ɑː/, /ʌ/ and /æ/

A Look at the underlined letters in each word. What sound do they make? Write the words in the correct place.

after discover happiness last money much ~~past~~ travel up

/ɑː/	/ʌ/	/æ/
past after last	discover up money much	happiness travel

9.1 **B** Listen and check. Then listen again and repeat the words.

C SPEAK Work in pairs. Practice saying the sentences. Listen to your partner and check their pronunciation.

1 Happiness usually lasts only for a short time.
2 Traveling helps us to discover our interests.
3 Is there an experience I can spend my money on instead?

GRAMMAR
Second conditional

A WORK IT OUT Look at the second conditional sentences from *How to buy happiness*. Write the missing words. Then choose the correct words to complete the rules.

1 If we __spent__ more of our money on experiences, we __would gain__ something that can last a lifetime.
2 We __wouldn't find out__ these things if we __didn't spend__ money on experiences.
3 If we __didn't do__ anything different, we __might become__ lazy.

Second conditional

1 We use the second conditional to talk about *real* / *unreal or impossible* situations in the present or future.
2 Conditional sentences usually have two clauses: the *if*-clause and the main clause. To make a second conditional sentence, we use:
- *If* + *simple past* / *would* and *simple past* / *would* + *base form*.

3 We *can* / *can't* use other modal verbs (for example, *can*, *could*, *might*, *should*) instead of *would* in the main clause.

B Go to the **Grammar Hub on page 138.**

VOCABULARY
Prepositions in money phrases

A Complete the sentences with the correct prepositions. Then read *How to buy happiness* again and check your answers.

1 I'm always saving __up__ so I can go away at least once or twice a year.
2 I spend a lot of my money __on__ traveling.
3 My attitude __toward__ money is to spend it on experiences as much as possible.

B Complete the sentences with the prepositions in the box.

by for from in out out of to

1 I usually take money __out of__ the ATM once or twice a week. I take __out__ 20 or 30 dollars each time.
2 For things under, say, five dollars, I generally pay __in__ cash. I usually pay __for__ things over five dollars __by__ card.
3 I occasionally borrow money __from__ my friends and I also sometimes lend it __to__ them. But it's never usually more than 10 or 20 dollars.

C SPEAK Work in pairs. Change the sentences in Exercises A and B so they are true for you. Ask your partner questions to find out more information.

A: I'm always saving up so I can go to concerts and music festivals.
B: My attitude toward money is spend a little and save a little.

SPEAKING

A Work in groups. Think about different situations and make choices. Group A – go to the **Communication Hub** on **page 157**. Group B – go to the **Communication Hub** on **page 153**.

B Work in pairs. Ask your partner your new questions and make a note of their answers.

C Work in groups. Compare your findings. How similar or different are they? What are the most common or unusual answers?

Talk about attitudes toward money and about spending money

9.2 Getting and giving

Talk about philanthropy and charities

V – verbs connected with money P – /s/ and /z/ G – essential adjective clauses

VOCABULARY

Verbs connected with money

A Complete the facts below with the correct form of the verbs in the box.

donate	~~earn~~	give away	lose
make	owe	raise	support

MONEY facts

1. In 1979, baseball player Nolan Ryan became the first professional athlete to ___earn___ $1 million a year.
2. Microsoft's Bill Gates, businessman Warren Buffet and Facebook's Mark Zuckerberg have all said they will ___give away___ 95 percent of their money to charity. A number of other philanthropists have also made the same promise.
3. Spanish actress Penélope Cruz ___supports___ many charities (organizations that give money and help to people who need it). In fact, she gave all of her salary from her first Hollywood movie to charity.
4. On September 16, 1992, Hungarian-born businessman George Soros ___made___ $1 billion. This is the biggest single-day profit in history.
5. Eike Batista was once Brazil's richest person with $30 billion. However, unfortunately he ___lost___ it all. In fact, in 2014, he ___owed___ $30 billion to the banks.
6. The London Marathon ___raises___ more money for charity than any other sports event. In 2016, this was almost £60 million.
7. Philanthropy is about giving money to people who need it. Philanthropists across the world ___donate___ around $500 billion a year to charity and other organizations. The main givers include the United States, China, United Kingdom, Russia, Australia and Switzerland.

B Complete the questions with the correct verbs. Use the *Money facts* to help you.

1. Have you ever d___onated___ money to a charity? If so, what does the charity r___aise___ money for?
2. If you could give a lot of money to charity, which charities or organizations would you s___upport___? Why?
3. Do you agree that all people who e___arn___ a lot of money or who have m___ade___ a lot of money should g___ive___ some of it a___way___ to charities? Why/Why not?

C **SPEAK** Ask and answer the questions in Exercise B.

PRONUNCIATION

/s/ and /z/

A **SPEAK** Work in pairs. Look at the words in the box. Do the letters in **bold** make a /s/ or a /z/ sound? Underline the /s/ sounds and circle the /z/ sounds.

across	also	baseball	Facebook	givers	promise
raises	salary	same	supports	Switzerland	visit

B Listen and check. Then listen again and repeat the words.

9.2

LISTENING

A Work in pairs. Discuss the questions.

1. What you know about the people in the pictures? What do you think they have in common?
2. Which other philanthropists do you know?

Andrew Carnegie

John D. Rockefeller

Bill Gates, Melinda Gates, Warren Buffet

Oprah Winfrey

9.2 Getting and giving

LEAD-IN

Draw a Tic-Tac-Toe grid (nine squares) on the board and write in each square the verbs from the vocabulary box: *donate, earn, give away, lose, make, owe, raise, support* and *receive*. Divide the class into two teams. One team chooses a verb and provides a sentence with it. If the sentence is correct, they win that square and mark it with an O or X symbol. When a team gets three Os or Xs in a row horizontally, vertically or diagonally, they win the round.

VOCABULARY

A Students complete the article using the correct forms of the verbs. Check answers with the class.

B Students complete the questions. They check their answers in pairs before checking with the class. Use the **Vocabulary Worksheet** on W50 for extra practice.

C In pairs or small groups, students take turns asking and answering the questions from Exercise B. Take feedback from one or two pairs/groups and encourage students to respond to each other's ideas.

PRONUNCIATION

A Write *sit, box, cats* and *zip, buzz, boys* on the board. Model the pronunciation of the sounds /s/ and /z/. In pairs, students underline the words with /s/ sounds and circle the words with /z/ sounds. Take feedback from one or two pairs but do not correct or confirm their answers.

9.2 **B** Play the audio for students to check their answers to Exercise A. Play the audio again. Students listen and repeat, paying close attention to their pronunciation of /s/ and /z/ sounds.

LISTENING

A Arrange students in groups. Make sure there is at least one student with a smartphone in each group. Give students time to look up who the people in the pictures are. With the information they found, students discuss the answers to the questions. Elicit the meaning of philanthropists (people who believe in helping people, especially by giving money to those who need it). Take feedback from one or two pairs and encourage students to respond to each other's ideas.

AUDIO SCRIPT

9.3

Listening, Exercise B

Today's lecture is about philanthropy. Philanthropy, as you know, is the act of giving away a large amount of money which is used to benefit society.

There are many famous and not so famous people who have given away large amounts of money. Two of the 20th century's most famous philanthropists are John D. Rockefeller and Andrew Carnegie. Rockefeller of course made his money from oil and Carnegie from the steel industry. Rockefeller gave away about $540 million before his death in 1937, and Carnegie gave away about $350 million. This was about 90 percent of his wealth.

And today there are many celebrities who have given money to charity. For example, the TV personality Oprah Winfrey has so far given away around half a billion dollars.

But perhaps today's most well-known philanthropists are Bill Gates and his wife Melinda, and Warren Buffett. Their main aim is to improve global health and to end poverty. And between them, they have already given away tens of billions of dollars. In 2010, they also created the Giving Pledge. The Giving Pledge asks …

9.4

Listening, Exercise D

But perhaps today's most well-known philanthropists are Bill Gates and his wife Melinda and Warren Buffett. Their main aim is to improve global health and to end poverty. And between them, they have already given away tens of billions of dollars. In 2010, they also created the Giving Pledge. The Giving Pledge asks
Ex D the world's richest people to give away at least half of their wealth in their lifetime. In its first ten years,
Ex E many people agreed to this, including Facebook's Mark Zuckerberg, Virgin boss Richard Branson and Ann Gloag, who started the international transportation group Stagecoach.

However, not everyone agrees that the Giving Pledge is a good thing, and some people have decided not to join. So, let's now look at five modern-day philanthropists that you may or may not have heard of.

First, Carlos Slim. Slim is a Mexican businessman and is one of the world's richest men. He made his money in telecommunications and is worth around $80 billion. He
Ex E has so far given away about $8 billion. However, he has not joined the Giving Pledge because he disagrees with
Ex F Q5 the approach of Bill Gates and Warren Buffet. Instead, he believes that education and jobs are the best way to end poverty.

Next, we have Sara Blakely, an American businesswoman. She recently became the world's youngest self-made
Ex E female billionaire, and she was also the first woman to join the Giving Pledge. Her philanthropy focuses mainly on women's and girls' education and career possibilities.
Ex F Q4 She believes that if there are more women in powerful positions, this will make the world a better place.

Li Ka-shing is a Hong Kong businessman and has promised to give away one third of his $30 billion
Ex F Q6 fortune. His aim is to promote education and health, but
Ex E mainly in China. He has not joined the Giving Pledge. This is because he wishes to keep control of how and when he gives his money away.

Billionaire Meg Whitman was the president of eBay
Ex F Q3 for ten years. She has said that she would refuse if she
Ex E was invited to join the Giving Pledge. Instead, she has her own charity that focuses on the environment and education.

And finally, Azim Premji. Premji is one of India's richest
Ex E people. He has joined the Giving Pledge and has already
Ex F Q2 given away one quarter of his wealth. Premji's aim is to improve Indian school education and he has also set up a university which promotes educational thinking.

So, what do you think? Is the Giving Pledge a good thing? And what about philanthropy in general? What are the pros and the cons of this …

9.3 **B** Focus students on the task and the chart. Read the example. Play the first part of the audio and give students time to complete the information.

9.3 **C** Read the example in the last column with the class. Play the audio again. Students complete the last column of the table.

9.4 **D** Focus students on the activity. Play Part 2 of the audio. Students listen and choose the best explanation of the Giving Pledge. Check answers with the whole class.

9.4 **E** Students read the activity and the options. Play the audio. Students apply a check mark or an X in the boxes next to the names of the philanthropists accordingly. Students compare their answers in pairs before checking with the whole class.

9.4 **F** Focus students on the task. Play the audio again for students to complete the sentences. Take feedback from some students and encourage students to respond to their ideas.

GRAMMAR

A Write the first sentence on the board. Explain that the underlined words constitute *an essential adjective clause*. Elicit that *who* refers back to *celebrities*, and that the underlined words give information about them. In pairs, students underline the essential adjective clause in each sentence. Take feedback. Ask students to complete the rules in the grammar box with *who, which* or *that*. Check answers with the class.

B Direct students to the **Grammar Hub** (see below). Use the **Grammar Worksheet** on W49 for extra practice.

C Arrange students in pairs (A and B). Direct students to the **Communication Hub**. Students complete their definitions and take turns guessing their partner's word.

D Students complete the sentences on their own. Take whole-class feedback.

SPEAKING

A Students discuss the questions in groups. Encourage students to respond to each other's ideas.

GRAMMAR HUB

9.2 Essential adjective clauses

	Relative pronoun	
Person	who	The friend **who** lent me the money is named Jack.
	that	The person **that** gave away the money is a billionaire.
Thing	which	The salary **which** I earn is too small.
	that	The donation **that** he made is very large.
Possession	whose	The man **whose** wallet I found thanked me.
Place	where	The company **where** I work supports many charities.
Time	when	The year **when** Rockefeller died was 1937.

- We use an essential adjective clause to give information about and identify a noun (person or thing).
- We can use *who* or *that* for people, and *which* or *that* for things.
  The person **who** lent me the money is named Jack. OR The person **that** lent me the money is named Jack.
  The donation **that** he made is very large. OR The donation **which** he made is very large.
- We can leave out the relative pronoun when it is followed by a subject and verb, rather than just a verb.
  Relative pronoun + subject and verb: The charity **that** she supports helps animals. OR The charity she supports helps animals.
  Relative pronoun + verb: The person **that lent** me the money is named Jack. NOT ~~The person lent me the money is named Jack.~~

9.2 Essential adjective clauses

A Choose the correct option.

1 I know many people *which* / *who* would love to travel.
2 The student *who* / *whose* father is a well-known philanthropist has plenty of money.
3 The charity *who* / *that* I usually donate to is *Help the Children*.
4 This is the city *where* / *which* I went to college.
5 Wealthy people *that* / *which* join the Giving Pledge can inspire others.
6 That was the time *when* / *where* Rockefeller gave away most of his fortune.
7 He started his own charity *which* / *whose* helps protect the environment.

B Match to make sentences.

1 My cell phone is the possession b
2 The London Marathon is an event d
3 Andrew Carnegie was another person who a
4 The money e
5 She's the woman g
6 South America is where c
7 She gained a lot of experience f

a gave away most of his wealth.
b that I could never give away!
c she traveled as a student.
d that raises millions of dollars for charity.
e that he left will be given to charity.
f when she was traveling in India.
g who set up the charity.

➤ Go back to page 85.

9.3 **B LISTEN FOR KEY WORDS** Listen to Part 1 of a lecture about philanthropists. Complete the first column with the people in the pictures on page 84.

Names of philanthropists	Numbers	What the numbers mean
John D. Rockefeller	$540m, 1937	John D. Rockefeller gave away about $540 million. He died in 1937.
Andrew Carnegie	$350m, 90 percent	He gave away $350m – 90% of his wealth.
Oprah Winfrey	half a billion dollars	Money she has given away so far.
Bill and Melinda Gates and Warren Buffet	tens of billions of dollars, 2010	Money given away. *Giving Pledge* set up in 2010.

9.3 **C LISTEN FOR KEY INFORMATION** Listen again. What do the numbers mean? Write your answers in the third column in Exercise B.

9.4 **D LISTEN FOR GIST** Listen to Part 2 of the lecture. Which is the best explanation of the Giving Pledge? Choose a, b or c.

The Giving Pledge asks people to give at least 50 percent of their wealth to charity …

a when they die.

b before they die. (circled)

c in the next ten years.

9.4 **E LISTEN FOR MAIN IDEA** Listen again. Check (✓) the names of the philanthropists who have joined the Giving Pledge. Put an ✗ in the box for the ones who have not.

1 Mark Zuckerberg ✓
2 Richard Branson ✓
3 Ann Gloag ✓
4 Carlos Slim ✗
5 Sara Blakely ✓
6 Li Ka-shing ✗
7 Meg Whitman ✗
8 Azim Premji ✓

9.4 **F LISTEN FOR DETAIL** Listen again. Write the names of the philanthropists.

1 ___Azim Premji___ has set up a university.

2 ___Azim Premji___ has given away one quarter of his or her wealth.

3 ___Meg Whitman___ would refuse to join the Giving Pledge if he or she was invited.

4 ___Sara Blakely___ believes that there should be more women in powerful positions.

5 ___Carlos Slim___ believes the best way to end poverty is through education and jobs.

6 ___Li Ka-shing___ is mostly concerned with education and health in his or her own country.

GRAMMAR

Essential adjective clauses

A WORK IT OUT Underline the adjective clauses in the sentences from the lecture. Then complete the rules with *who*, *which* or *that*.

1 And today, there are many celebrities who have given money to charity.

2 Let's now look at five modern-day philanthropists that you may or may not have heard of.

3 Instead she has her own charity that focuses on the environment and education.

4 He has also set up a university which promotes educational thinking.

Essential adjective clauses

1 An essential adjective clause gives information about and identifies a noun (a person or thing). It comes after the noun and starts with a relative pronoun.

We use [a] ___who___ when the noun is a person.

We use [b] ___which___ when the noun is a thing.

We can use [c] ___that___ for a person or a thing.

2 We can leave out the relative pronoun when the word following the noun is a subject (*I, you, people, the charity*).

- *Let's now look at five modern-day philanthropists ~~that~~ you may or may not have heard of.*

B Go to the **Grammar Hub** on **page 138**.

C You are going to write some definitions. Student A – go to **page 152**. Student B – go to **page 154**.

D SPEAK Complete the sentences with the correct relative pronouns and your own ideas. Leave out the relative pronoun if possible. Then, work in groups and share your ideas.

1 A famous person _____ I admire is …
A famous person I admire is Michelle Obama.

2 A charity ___which___ does a lot of good is … Oxfam.

3 Someone ___who___ has influenced me a lot is … my English teacher.

4 A global issue ___(which)___ I think is important is … poverty.

5 A person ___who___ has positively influenced society is … Tim Berners-Lee.

SPEAKING

A Work in groups and discuss the questions.

1 Which charities do you know?

2 What do you know about them?

3 Why do people give to charity?

4 Do you think it is better to give time or money? Why?

Talk about philanthropy and charities

9.3 Who needs money?

● Discuss your skills and how they could help others

G gerunds V *make* and *do* expressions P /ʒ/ and /dʒ/ S using context to guess unknown words

READING

A Did you exchange anything with other people when you were younger, for example, toys, books or soccer cards? What about later in life?

B **PREDICT** Look at the title of the article and at the glossary. What do you think the article is about? The article is about how it is becoming more common for people to trade goods or services instead of paying money for them.

C **SCAN** Read *Bartering is back* and complete the notes.

1. Kyle McDonald started a website, and after one year exchanged a ___red paperclip___ for a ___house___.
2. Websites such as Craigslist.org: People can exchange ___items or services___ with each other.
3. Antonio Puri exchanged a ___($1200) painting___ for ___dental treatment___.
4. Time banks: For every ___hour___ you work, you earn (a certain amount of) time credits.
5. Basic rule: Ask a ___realistic price___ for what you are offering. Need to agree what is ___a fair exchange___.

BARTERING IS **BACK**

Back in 2005, Canadian Kyle MacDonald was making a living delivering pizzas, but he dreamed of owning his own house. So, one day he set up a website and offered a red paper clip in exchange for 'something bigger and better'. One year later,
Ex C **and after 14 exchanges, he had swapped the paper clip for**
Q1 **a house! First, he swapped the paper clip for a pen. After that, the trades included a snowmobile, a van, an afternoon with rock star Alice Cooper and a role in a Hollywood movie. Finally, he swapped the movie role for a house.**

But trading or bartering one item for another is nothing new. It was how people 'shopped' before the invention of money. And today, bartering is back. The number of people who use
Ex C websites such as Craigslist.org, where you can exchange one
Q2 item or service for another, is increasing. Some websites, such as babysitterexchange.com, provide just one service, while other sites cover a range of items and services. People have exchanged yoga lessons and language lessons for decorating, offered dog-walking and rides to the airport in exchange for theater and concert tickets, and some people will offer to do your shopping, cleaning or ironing in exchange for items they need. People also offer to trade professional services such as legal advice and accountancy. Antonio Puri, an artist based in Philadelphia in the US, was in his dentist's chair when he noticed there were no paintings on the walls. He told his dentist 'You need art. How about doing a trade?' Puri made him an offer and
Ex C swapped a $1200 painting for his dental treatment.
Q3

Time banks are another recent development. You register at your local *Time Bank*'s website and list the
Ex C services you have to offer or like doing. For each hour
Q4 of work you provide to another member, you earn a certain number of 'time credits'. You can then spend your 'time credits' on another service on the site that someone else enjoys doing.

Ex C Doing your research and suggesting realistic prices
Q5 are the basic rules with both barter sites and time banks. It's important not to try to make a profit. At the same time, if someone does you a favor, don't give them something below its value. If you do this, the system will break down and stop working. If you are bartering, it is important to agree with the other person what is a fair exchange. So, for example, you might agree that a driving lesson is equal to two haircuts or that fixing someone's washing machine is equal to a half-hour guitar lesson.

So, next time you need something, don't reach for your wallet or bankcard. Who needs money when you can trade?

Glossary

barter (v) to exchange goods or services for other goods or services instead of using money

9.3 Who needs money?

LEAD-IN

Write on the board *If I had a lot of money, I would ...* In pairs, students create their own lists of what they would do if they were rich. Change pairs. Students take turns interviewing each other. Take feedback from one or two pairs and encourage students to respond to each other's ideas.

READING

A Ask students to look at the picture and elicit what is happening (*the boys are exchanging or swapping cards*). Check student understanding of exchange/swap (*to give each other something*). Ask students the questions in Exercise A as a class discussion. Encourage students to listen and respond to each other's ideas. Ask follow-up questions to prompt discussion.

B Ask students to look at the title of the reading passage *Bartering is back* and the glossary. Encourage students to share their ideas on what the passage is about.

C Remind students that scanning means looking for specific information in a text. Focus students on the sentences and encourage them to underline the key words that will help them find the missing information. Ask students to scan the article and find the missing words. To prevent students from reading the whole article in detail, set a time limit that ensures they only have time to scan for the answers. Ask some students to read the finalized answers and encourage the class to respond to their ideas.

D Focus students on the words in the box. Ask for a show of hands and a short discussion to see how many students know their meanings. Read the information in the box with the class and clarify its meaning and give examples if necessary. Students work in pairs to find the words in the text and try to guess their meanings. Ask different pairs to read their answers and say what cues they used to guess the meanings.

making a living = earning (enough) money to live
set up = started something
swapped = gave something to someone in exchange for something else
dental = relating to teeth
treatment = the process of providing medical care
favor = something you do for someone in order to help them
break down = stop working

E Students read the paragraph and match the words in bold to the definitions. Check answers with the class.

F Students discuss the questions in small groups. Monitor and assist when necessary. Take feedback from one or two groups and encourage students to respond to each other's ideas.

TEACHING IDEA by David Seymour and Maria Popova

Speaking: Sayings

Write the sayings below on the board. Ask students to work in small groups and discuss what these sayings mean. Then ask students to decide whether they agree or disagree with the sayings and tell the group a saying about money from their countries.

You can't buy love.

Property is theft.

Money talks.

Time is money.

Money makes the world go around.

A fool and his money are soon parted.

Money is the root of all evil.

TEACHING IDEA by David Seymour and Maria Popova

Speaking: Speaking personally

Ask students to work in pairs. They should take turns finishing the prompts below truthfully. They should then share the most interesting thing they learned about their partner with the class, e.g. *Pavel's thinking of going to China next year.*

I'm good at ...

I'm looking forward to ...

I'm thinking of ...

I get very excited about ...

I often dream about ...

Sometimes I get fed up with ...

I'm interested in ...

I sometimes regret not ...

METHODOLOGY HUB by Jim Scrivener

Skimming and scanning

Many activities designed to increase reading speeds are variations on the following two ideas:

- Skimming: Read quickly to get the gist of a passage (e.g. to discover key topics, main ideas, overall theme, basic structure, etc.). A typical skimming task would be a general question from the teacher, such as *Is this passage about Jill's memories of the summer or the winter?* or *Is this story set in a school or a restaurant?* The learners would attempt to find the answer quickly, without reading every word of the passage, by 'speed-reading' through some portions of the text.
- Scanning: Move eyes quickly over the text to locate a specific piece of information (e.g. a name, address, fact, price, number, date, etc) without reading the whole text or unpacking any subtleties of meaning. A common scanning activity is searching for information in a brochure or directory, and a typical scanning task would be *What time does the train to Boston leave?* or *What does Cathy take with her to the meeting?*

Skimming and scanning are both 'top-down' skills. Although scanning is involved with finding individual points from the text without reading carefully through every word of the text, the way that a reader finds that information involves some degree of processing of the overall shape and structure of the text, moving his/her eyes quickly over the whole page, searching for key words or clues from the textual layout and the content that will enable him/her to focus in on smaller sections of text that he/she is likely to get answers from.

9.3 Who needs money?

GRAMMAR

A Students look at the *-ing* forms in bold in the article. Elicit they are all gerunds. Students complete the information about gerunds in the grammar box.

B Direct students to the **Grammar Hub** (see below). Use the **Grammar Worksheet** on W51 for extra practice.

C Focus students on the questions. Students discuss them in pairs. Monitor and pay close attention to their use of gerunds. Take feedback from one or two pairs and encourage students to respond to each other's ideas.

VOCABULARY

A Ask students to work on their own, completing the sentences with *make* or *do*. Students check their answers in the article. With a weaker group, allow them to find the sentences before filling in the blanks.

B Direct students to the **Vocabulary Hub** (TB121). Use the **Vocabulary Worksheet** on W52 for extra practice.

PRONUNCIATION

9.5 **A** Play the audio, pausing after each word for students to answer.

9.5 **B** Play the audio again for students to listen and repeat. Pay close attention to their pronunciation of /ʒ/ and /dʒ/.

SPEAKING HUB

A Read through the instructions as a class. You may wish to model an example.

B Students must talk to at least five classmates to find out and write down the skills and services they are offering and how much they are charging.

C When students have finished mingling, ask them to choose three skills and services that they would like to try.

D Explain to the class that they have to barter their chosen services or skills. Remind students that in order to make a trade they might need to offer more time or added services. Monitor and assist when necessary.

GRAMMAR HUB

9.3 Gerunds

- Gerunds are a type of noun.

  Noun: *He likes **clothes**.*

  Gerund: *He likes **shopping**.*

  Noun: ***Money** doesn't bring happiness.*

  Gerund: ***Owning** things doesn't bring happiness.*

- We use gerunds after prepositions.

  *I dream **about setting up** my own business.*

  *He's good **at trading** things online.*

- We can use gerunds directly after some verbs. See Grammar Reference 3.3 for more information.

  *They **like** making a profit.*

  *We **love** doing online research.*

- We can use gerunds as either subjects or objects.

  *Subject: **Cleaning** the house is boring.*

  *Object: She hates **cleaning** the house.*

- Gerunds can act like verbs and take an object.

  *She hates doing **the ironing**.*

Be careful!

- If the verb ends in *-e*, remove the final *-e* before adding *-ing*.

  make → making *give → giving*

  *He enjoys **making** money.* *She likes **giving** money to charity.*

9.3 Gerunds

A Complete the sentences with the gerund form of the verbs in the box.

do give have make ~~save~~ set up spend

1 He isn't very good at *saving* money.
2 She usually dreams of having a family of her own.
3 Gareth is looking forward to setting up his own business.
4 Andrew Carnegie was famous for giving away almost all his money.
5 Doing research is one of the most enjoyable things about my course.
6 We really need to stop spending so much money on entertainment.
7 We hope that our business will start making a profit.

B Complete the sentences with the gerund form of the verb in parentheses. Then choose subject gerund (*S*) or object gerund (*O*).

1 They aren't good at *making* (*make*) a living. S / (O)
2 Dreaming (*dream*) of new places to visit is my favorite way to pass the time. (S) / O
3 Spending (*spend*) money on designer clothing is a total waste. (S) / O
4 The most important thing to practice and be good at is being (*be*) yourself. S / (O)
5 Saving money may involve doing (*do*) without certain luxuries. S / (O)
6 Being (*be*) a successful trader is harder than it sounds. (S) / O
7 You cannot enjoy life unless you spend it living (*live*) for today. S / (O)

➤ Go back to page 87.

D Do you know the meaning of the words and phrases in the box? Find them in the text and use the information in the box to work out or check their meaning.

break down dental favor making a living set up swapped treatment

Using context to guess unknown words

If there is a word or phrase in a text that you don't know or understand, try to guess the meaning from context. Read the sentence before and the sentence after to help you.

Think about the wider context, for example, the topic and message of the paragraph.

Identify the word's grammatical form and function to help give it meaning.

If you can't work out the meaning, keep reading. You may read something later which helps you to understand the word.

E Guess the meaning of the words in **bold** (1–3). Then match them with their definitions (a–c).

Bartering is about communities. It connects people. It [1]**fosters** human contact. For something [2]**tangible**, like a couch or a bike, it is easy to decide a price. But to work out a price for a service is more [3]**tricky**.

3 **a** difficult to do
1 **b** helps something to develop over a period of time
2 **c** something that you can touch

F **SPEAK** Work in groups. Do you think bartering items and services is a good idea? What are the pros and the cons?

GRAMMAR
Gerunds

A Look at the gerunds in **bold** in the phrases from *Bartering is back*. Then choose the correct words to complete the rules.

... but he dreamed of ***owning*** *his own house.*

... that someone else enjoys ***doing****.*

Doing *your research and suggesting realistic prices are the basic rules ...*

... the system will break down and stop ***working****.*

Gerunds

1 Gerunds are types of *nouns* / *verbs*.
2 We use gerunds *after* / *before* prepositions.
3 We can use gerunds directly after *some* / *all* verbs.
4 We can use gerunds as *subjects only* / *objects only* / *subjects or objects*.

B Go to the **Grammar Hub** on **page 138**.

C **SPEAK** Work in pairs. Discuss the questions.

- What are you looking forward to doing this weekend?
- What do you like/dislike spending your money on?
- Are you good at saving money? Why/Why not?

VOCABULARY
make and *do* expressions

A Complete the sentences from *Bartering is back* with the correct form of *make* or *do*. Then check your answers in the article.

1 Back in 2005, Canadian Kyle MacDonald was ___making___ **a living** delivering pizzas.
2 Some people will offer to ___do___ your **shopping, cleaning** or **ironing** in exchange for items they need.
3 Puri ___made___ him **an offer** and swapped a $1200 painting for his dental treatment.
4 ___Doing___ your **research** and suggesting realistic prices are the basic rules with both barter sites and time banks.
5 It's important not to try to ___make___ **a profit**. At the same time, if someone ___does___ you **a favor**, don't give them something below its value.

B Go to the **Vocabulary Hub** on **page 151**.

PRONUNCIATION
/ʒ/ and /dʒ/

9.5 **A** Listen to the sounds /ʒ/ and /dʒ/. They are very similar. Then listen and say whether you hear the sound /ʒ/ or /dʒ/ in each word.

1 exchange /dʒ/ 3 decision /ʒ/ 5 suggest /dʒ/
2 language /dʒ/ 4 Asia /ʒ/

9.6 **B** Listen, check and repeat the words.

SPEAKING HUB

A You are going to swap skills and services with your classmates. Follow the instructions.

- Think about two or three skills and services that you can offer (music, language or driving lessons; help with cleaning, gardening; accounting advice).
- Decide on the price of your service. For example, a one-hour driving lesson = $30, or an hour's ironing = $10.

B **SPEAK** Walk around the class and find out what skills and services your classmates are offering and how much they cost.

C **PLAN** When you have spoken to at least five people, decide which three skills and services you would like.

D **DISCUSS** Try to exchange skills or services with your classmates. For example, you could offer a one-hour driving lesson in exchange for three hours of ironing.

Discuss your skills and how they could help others

Café Hub

9.4 Difficult customer

F – go shopping for clothes and ask for a refund
P – adding emphasis

COMPREHENSION

A SPEAK Work in pairs. Think of a time when you bought something in a clothing store (or any store) and then returned it. Discuss the questions.

1 What was the item?
2 What was the problem?
3 What happened in the end?

B ▶ Watch the video and answer the questions in Exercise A.

C How would you describe Milly? How would you describe the customer? Choose adjectives from the box or use your own ideas.

anxious dishonest friendly kind relaxed scared shy

Milly – relaxed/kind
Customer – dishonest/anxious

FUNCTIONAL LANGUAGE

Go shopping for clothes and ask for a refund

A Work in pairs. Change the highlighted words for more polite words in the box.

Can you enter Here's your refund I'd like a refund I'd like to I'll take it I'm looking for kind of thing would you like

Sales clerk	Customer
Can I help you?	I want [1] ___I'm looking for___ a gift for my nephew. He's 15.
What exactly [2] ___kind of thing___ are you looking for?	A blue sweater.
	How much is this sweater?
$15	Great. I want it [3] ___I'll take it___.
How do you want [4] ___would you like___ to pay, cash or card?	Card, please.
Put in [5] ___Can you enter___ your pin?	
Would you like me to gift wrap it for you?	Yes, please.
OK.	
Two weeks later	
	I want to [6] ___I'd like to___ return this, please. It doesn't fit my nephew. It's the wrong size.
	I want my money back [7] ___I'd like a refund___, please.
Do you have your receipt?	It's in here somewhere.
Don't worry about it. Take your money. [8] ___Here's your refund.___	

B ▶ Watch the video again and check your answers to Exercise A.

MILLY SAM NEENA ZAC GABY

USEFUL PHRASES

A Complete the useful phrases. Who says them, Milly (M) or the customer (C)?

about be must only over right

1 You're a yoga teacher, *right*? (M) / C
2 The sweaters are *over* there. (M) / C
3 It says 'hand wash *only*' on the label. (M) / C
4 I have to *be* quick. M / (C)
5 It *must* be here! M / (C)
6 Don't worry *about* it. (M) / C

B How do you say these useful phrases in your language?

PRONUNCIATION
Adding emphasis

9.7 **A** To emphasize a point, you can change the stressed word. Listen and underline the stressed word in each sentence.

1 a He is so special to me.
  b He is so special to me.
2 a My niece is really tall.
  b My niece is really tall.
3 a These shoes are very comfortable.
  b These shoes are very comfortable.
4 a You've been extremely helpful.
  b You've been extremely helpful.

9.7 **B** Listen again and repeat the sentences.

C **SPEAK** Work in pairs. Student A – say a sentence from Exercise A. Student B – point to the sentence. Take turns.

SPEAKING

A Work in pairs. Role-play buying a gift for your mother, father or best friend. Take turns being the customer and the sales clerk. Use the Functional language box to help you.

- Customer: Tell the sales clerk you want to buy a gift. Choose one of the items in the pictures. Ask for the price and for gift-wrapping.
- Sales clerk: Answer the customer's questions and sell the item.

B Role-play returning the gift you bought in Exercise A.

Customer: Tell the sales clerk you want to return something. Choose one of the following problems:

- it is the wrong size
- it is damaged
- the person you bought it for doesn't like it

Sales clerk: Listen to the customer and give them a refund.

Go shopping for clothes and ask for a refund

➤ Turn to **page 166** to learn how to write a 'for sale' advertisement.

9.4 Difficult customer

COMPREHENSION

A Ask students to look at the images and elicit their ideas about what is happening. Students discuss the questions in pairs. Take feedback from some pairs and encourage students to respond to their ideas.

B ▶ Play the video. Students watch and answer the questions from Exercise A.

1 *A blue sweater*
2 *It was too small.*
3 *Milly asked if the sweater had been in the washing machine. The woman said no. Then the woman got upset and Milly gave her the money back.*

C Ask students to look at the personality adjectives in the box and decide which they would use to describe Milly and the customer. Encourage students to share their own ideas as well as the words in the box.

FUNCTIONAL LANGUAGE

A Focus students on the polite phrases in the box and in the activity. In pairs, students replace the highlighted words with the more polite phrases. Take feedback from one or two pairs but do not correct or confirm their answers at this time.

B ▶ Play the video again for students to check their answers to Exercise A. Ask for a show of hands to see how many pairs got correct answers.

USEFUL PHRASES

A Focus students on the words in the box. They complete the sentences on their own. Allow them to compare answers in pairs and to decide whether they were said by Milly (M) or the customer (C).

B Ask students to think about how they would say these useful phrases in their own language. In a multilingual class, this can be done as a pair work activity with a student from another country.

PRONUNCIATION

9.7 **A** Explain that in English you can modify the emphasis in a sentence by changing word stress. Model the first sentence and elicit which the important words in *a* and *b* are. Focus students on sentences 2–4. Play the audio for students to do the activity. Allow them to compare their answers in pairs.

9.7 **B** Play the audio again for students to listen and repeat, paying close attention to word stress.

C Focus students on the activity. In pairs, students take turns saying the sentences from Exercise A for their partners to point to the sentence they hear. Monitor and assist when necessary.

SPEAKING

A Focus students on the task. In pairs, they take turns role-playing a conversation between a customer and a sales clerk. Encourage students to use the useful phrases and functional language from this lesson. Monitor and assist when necessary. Take feedback from one or two pairs to check with the whole class.

B Students take turns role-playing a new conversation, when the customer returns the item they bought. Monitor and assist as required.

Extra activity
An alternative approach is to make one or both of the role plays a 'paper conversation'. Instead of speaking the conversations, the students write them in real-time on a shared piece of paper that is passed between them. This allows you to monitor, correct and give feedback in more detail. The students can then perform the role plays aloud.

▶ VIDEO SCRIPT

Café Hub 9.4 Difficult customer
C = Customer M = Milly

C: No. No. No.
M: Oh, hi – you're uh, a yoga teacher, right. I've been to your class.
C: Yes I am! Nice to see you again.
M: Welcome to my store, can I help you?
C: Yes please. I'm looking for a gift for my nephew. He's 15.
M: What kind of thing are you looking for?
C: A blue sweater.
M: The sweaters are over there.
C: Thank you!
How much is this sweater?
M: £15
C: Great. I'll take it. I think my nephew will love it.
M: Yeah, it's a cool sweater. How would you like to pay, cash or card?
C: Card, please.
M: No problem, here you go.
Can you enter your pin please … would you like me to gift wrap it for you?
C: Yes please.
C: I'd like to return this please.
M: Um … OK …
C: It doesn't fit my nephew. It's the wrong size.
M: Did someone put it in the washing machine? It says hand wash only on the label …
C: No.
M: Are you … sure? It looks much smaller now …
C: Look … I didn't realize it was too small … I just wanted to get something that Jimmy would love. He is so special to me!
Hi Lucy. What do you mean you're late? No! I can't teach your yoga class! You're fired … again! Argh! I'm sorry I have to be quick. Yoga class to teach! I'd like a refund please.
M: OK … have you got the receipt?
C: Yes. It's in here somewhere. It must be here … I'm sure it's here … Where is it?
M: Hey, hey, hey, listen … Look, don't worry about it. Here's your refund.
C: Thank you, thank you so much.

9 Writing — Write a 'for sale' advertisement

W — describing a product

A Read the advice for writing a 'for sale' advertisement. Complete the advice with the words in the box.

accessories buyer condition details specifications

The key to a great ad

Attention: The title of the advertisement needs to get the [1] buyer 's attention. Keep it short and simple. Start with the best or key feature of your item. This could be the price, its [2] condition or simply that it is a very popular item. If it has a fixed price, use words like 'only' and 'bargain'.

Description: Your advertisement needs a detailed description of the item. If needed, include the [3] specifications such as size, height and width. Include any [4] accessories that it comes with, such as a battery charger. Include pictures to show what condition the item is in.

Action: Encourage the buyer to take action. For example, invite them to contact you with questions or for more [5] details . Say how you will post the item and offer free postage if possible.

B Look at the advertisements. Do they follow the advice? Find and underline examples of:

- best or key features
- how good the price is
- specification (size or dimensions)
- accessories
- condition
- contacting the seller

digital camera – only $150

The camera is almost new and hardly used. It comes in the original box and with a case, strap and spare battery. See picture. Please contact me if you have any questions.

Pen and ink drawing – auction

This is an original and signed pen and ink drawing by British illustrator William Miller. It shows a mountain scene in Scotland. The dimensions are 35 cm x 18 cm. The work is in good condition with a few minor marks. Please contact me for further information.

Men's sneakers (size 40) – $40

I am selling a pair of sneakers. They are size 40 and are yellow with gray stripes. They are in excellent condition with just a few light marks. I am selling them for the bargain price of $40. Free delivery. If you have any questions, just ask.

C Complete the box with words from the advertisements.

Describing a product

Introducing the item
- *This is …*
- *I am* [1] selling *…*

Describing its condition, specification and accessories
- *In excellent/good* [2] condition *, almost* [3] new *, hardly* [4] used
- *It comes in the original* [5] box
- *… with (just) a few (light/minor)* [6] marks
- *It comes with …*
- *The dimensions are …*

Contacting the seller
- *Please contact me if you have any (further)* [7] questions *.*
- *Please contact me for further* [8] information */details.*
- *If you have any questions, just* [9] ask *.*

D Correct the mistakes and rewrite the sentences from online 'for sale' advertisements.

1 The phone comes in the origin box.
The phone comes in the original box.

2 I sell a Sony Bravia 65XE9005 TV.
I am selling a Sony Bravia 65XE9005 TV.

3 The camera is near new and is excellent condition.
The camera is nearly new and is in excellent condition.

4 The item in good condition with a few lightly marks.
The item is in good condition with a few light marks.

5 Please contact for further informations and details.
Please contact me for further information and details.

WRITING

A PLAN You are going to write a 'for sale' advertisement. Choose one of the items in the pictures or choose an item of your own. Invent some details about the condition of the item.

B WRITE Write your advertisement. Use the Writing skills box, the ads and the advice to help you. Write 50–75 words.

C DISCUSS Work in groups. Show your advertisement to your group. Is anyone interested in buying your item?

166 9 WRITING

Answers

best or key features: *This is an original and signed pen and ink drawing …*

how good the price is: *only $150 / I am selling them for the bargain price of $40.*

size or dimensions: *The dimensions are 35 cm x 18 cm. / They are size 40.*

accessories: *It comes in the original box and with a case, strap and spare battery.*

condition: *almost new and hardly used / in good condition with a few minor marks / in excellent condition with just a few light marks*

contacting the seller: *Please contact me if you have any questions. / Please contact me for further information. / If you have any questions, just ask.*

Students should write their 'for sale' ad on a separate piece of paper.

Refer students to these ads as a model for the writing task.

WRITING

A Focus students on the vocabulary box and the article. Students complete the blanks with the words from the box. Check answers with the class.

B Students read the ads and decide whether they follow the advice from Exercise A. They underline any words or phrases that match the bullet points. Students check in pairs before whole-class feedback.

C Focus students on the box and the task. Students complete the phrases in the box with words from the ads in Exercise B.

D Students correct the mistakes of the sentences using the ads. Allow them to compare their answers in pairs before checking with the class.

WRITING TASK

A Students choose one of the items to write a 'for sale' advertisement. They should write notes about the condition of their chosen item. Ask students if they remember the advice from the article. Ask them also to think about what their reader will want and expect to know about their product.

B Students write an ad of between 50 and 75 words. They should use the phrases from the box to support them.

C Arrange students in groups of four. Ask them to share their ads with their group and find out whether anyone in the group wants to buy their item. You can also include a stage of peer correction here. Students exchange and correct each other's ads. If you feel this might be too sensitive, you can also take a few representative errors from students' work and write them on the board. Students then correct the errors.

Unit 9 Review

VOCABULARY

A Complete the questions with the prepositions in the box.

by for from in ~~on~~ out of to up

1 What do you **spend** most money ___on___?
2 Do you ever **lend** money ___to___ your friends? Or **borrow** it ___from___ them?
3 How often do you **take money** ___out of___ the ATM?
4 Do you **pay** ___for___ things mostly ___by___ **card**, cash or do you use your phone?
5 What kind of things do you pay for ___in___ **cash**?
6 What kind of things do you **save** ___up___ for?

B Complete the sentences with the correct form of *make* or *do*. Then finish the sentences so they are true for you.

1 I need to ___make___ **a decision** about *what to do on the weekend.*
2 I usually ___make___ **mistakes** when ...
3 I ___made___ **a mess** when I was ...
4 I usually ___do___ **my homework** ...
5 I'd love to be able to ___make___ **a living** as a ...
6 I ___did___ my friend **a favor** when ...

GRAMMAR

A What would you do in these situations? Write sentences using the second conditional.

If I were you ...

Get answers to your dilemmas.

1 The other day, I found a $100 bill in the street. What would you do? Would you keep it or take it to the police?

If I found a $100 bill in the street, I'd take it to the police.

2 I bought a phone from an online company, but they sent me two by mistake. What would you do? Would you tell them or keep both phones?

I'd tell them. / I'd keep both phones.

3 I am the best at math in my class. Some of my classmates want to give me money to copy my homework. What would you do? Would you accept the money or tell the teacher?

I'd accept the money. / I'd tell the teacher.

4 I saw someone who looked homeless steal some food from the local store that I shop at regularly. Would you offer to pay for the food for them or tell the store manager?

I'd pay for the food. / I'd tell the store manager.

B Complete the news report with the adjective clauses in the box.

that Matt has hidden that is useful who finds one who has received a favor who needs food you don't know you spend it on

Man hiding money in Cardiff

A man from Cardiff in South Wales has hidden twenty £10 notes around the city (£10 is roughly $15). Anyone [1]___who finds one___ has to use the £10 to do something good for someone else. And this has to be someone [2]___you don't know___. The man behind the idea, Matt Callanan, says that you could give it to a person [3]___who needs food___ or, if it's raining when you find the note, you could buy something [4]___that is useful___, like an umbrella, and give it to someone! Callanan believes that a person [5]___who has received a favor___ will then do something good for someone else, and so on. So, if you find £10 [6]___that Matt has hidden___, you could be helping more than just the person [7]___you spend it on___.

FUNCTIONAL LANGUAGE

Put the words in the correct order to complete the conversations.

Sales clerk: [1]I / help / you / can / ? *Can I help you?*
Customer: [2]for / I'm looking / for / a gift / my mother I'm looking for a gift for my mother. It's her birthday.
Sales clerk: [3]thing / kind / what / of / are you looking for / ? What kind of thing are you looking for?
Customer: Well, maybe a scarf or some gloves ... I like these gloves. [4]much / they / are / how / ? How much are they?
Sales clerk: Let me see. They're $20.
Customer: Great. [5]them / I'll / take I'll take them.
Sales clerk: [6]for / would you like me to / gift-wrap / you / them / ? Would you like me to gift-wrap them for you?
Customer: Yes, please.
Sales clerk: [7]like / you / how / would / pay, / to / cash or card / ? How would you like to pay, cash or card?
Customer: Card, please.
Sales clerk: Thanks a lot!

Engineers of the future – two young Serbians work together to repair a robot.

Science (n) the study and knowledge of the physical world and its behavior that is based on experiments and facts that can be proved and is organized into a system.

Technology (n) advanced scientific knowledge used for practical purposes, especially in industry.

Marie Curie is suggesting that we can enrich our lives by finding out about the ideas that interest us, rather than by gossiping.

Marie Curie (November 7, 1867–July 4, 1934) was a Polish and naturalized French physicist and chemist who conducted pioneering research on radioactivity. She was the first woman to win a Nobel Prize.

OBJECTIVES

- describe and compare personal possessions
- describe types of technology
- discuss the requirements for a job
- make and receive formal and informal phone calls
- write a recommendation

Work with a partner. Discuss the questions.

1 Look at the picture. What were you curious about when you were a child?
2 What was your dream job when you were younger? Is it different now or the same?
3 What would you like to learn more about?

SCIENCE AND TECHNOLOGY 91

OBJECTIVES

Read the unit objectives to the class.

UNIT OPENER QUESTIONS

Encourage students to look at the quote and take one or two suggestions from the class about what they think it means.

Ask students to look at the picture on the page and encourage them to share their ideas. Ask prompt questions such as 'What do you know about Marie Curie? Why do you think the photo is about two girls doing science? What are you curious about?' If students share any good ideas or useful language, write these on the board.

Ask students to look at the questions at the bottom of the page. Model possible answers. You may answer the question about what you were curious about when you were a child and expand to what you are curious about now. Students discuss the questions in pairs or in a small group.

Monitor and assist as necessary. When students have finished the activity, ask one or two pairs to share their ideas with the class. Encourage students to listen to one another and respond with their own ideas and opinions.

WORKSHEETS

Lesson 10.1 Devices

Grammar: Comparatives and superlatives (W53)

Vocabulary: Electronic devices (W54)

Lesson 10.2 It's only good when it works

Grammar: More comparative structures (W55)

Vocabulary: Using devices and the internet (W56)

Lesson 10.3 The best view in the universe

Grammar: *need to* (W57)

Vocabulary: Collocations: science and research (W58)

10.1 Devices

Describe and compare personal possessions

V – electronic devices   G – comparatives and superlatives   P – /ɪst/ and superlative adjectives

VOCABULARY
Electronic devices

A SPEAK Work in pairs. Make a list of words to name or describe electronic devices. You have one minute.

A: Can you think of anything?
B: OK, a tablet and a cell phone.

B Go to the **Vocabulary Hub** on **page 151**.

LISTENING

10.1 **A LISTEN FOR MAIN IDEA** Listen to four people talking about devices. What question are they answering?

a Which device do you use every day?
b What is the most useful device you own?
c What device do you most regret buying?

Glossary

package (n) an object or set of objects wrapped in a box or in paper and sent or given to someone
regret (v) to feel sorry or sad about something that has happened or about something you have said or done
reliable (adj) a reliable vehicle, piece of equipment or system always works well

10.1 **B LISTEN FOR DETAIL** Listen again and match the speakers (1–4) to the devices (a–h) they are describing. There are four devices you do not need.

a	drone	4	e	power bank	___
b	e-reader	1	f	tablet	3
c	fitness tracker	___	g	USB drive	___
d	GPS	2	h	laptop	___

C SPEAK Work in groups. Discuss the questions.

1 Which of the devices in the list in Exercise B do you own or would you like to own?
2 Which do you think is most useful and why?

GRAMMAR
Comparatives and superlatives

A Underline the comparative and superlative adjectives and adverbs in the sentences from the radio show.

1 My bag is a lot lighter than it used to be.
2 It's the best gadget I've ever bought.
3 I bought the cheapest one.
4 You can check words so much more quickly than in a paper dictionary.
5 This is definitely the most useful piece of technology I own.
6 It was more expensive than an old-fashioned paper map.
7 We spend a lot of time arguing about which turns the most quickly.

10.1 Devices

LEAD-IN

Think of an electronic device, e.g. a GPS, a drone, a USB drive, etc. Tell students they have to guess what it is through yes-no questions. Tell students that they can ask a maximum of twenty questions, so they need to think logically about the best questions to ask. Remind them that you can only respond to their questions with 'yes' or 'no' answers.

VOCABULARY

A Ask the class to look at the picture and name any devices that they can see (*cell phone, e-reader/tablet*). Model the activity with a stronger student or ask two stronger students to read the example. Students work in pairs listing as many words as they can to name or describe electronic devices. When the time is up, ask the pair with the most words to share their list with the class. Ask the other students to share any words on their lists that have not been mentioned. Write any new or useful vocabulary on the board.

B Direct students to the **Vocabulary Hub** (TB121). Use the **Vocabulary Worksheet** on W54 for extra practice.

LISTENING

10.1 **A** Focus students on the glossary and the activity. Play the audio. Students listen and decide which of the questions (a–c) the four people are answering. Allow students to compare their answers in pairs before checking with the whole class.

10.1 **B** Play the audio again. Students listen and decide which device each person is talking about. Remind students that there are only four speakers, so there are four devices they do not need. Check answers with the class.

C Focus students on the activity. Students discuss the questions in groups of three or four. Monitor and assist when necessary. Take feedback from one or two groups and encourage students to respond to each other's ideas.

GRAMMAR

A Read the rubric with the class. Elicit examples of comparative and superlative adjectives and adverbs. Students do the activity in pairs. Check answers as a class.

B Remind students that to count syllables in English, we pay attention to how the words are pronounced and not to how they are written, e.g. polite /pə'lait/ has two syllables, as does likely /'laikli/. Students complete the table using the underlined word. Allow them to compare their answers in pairs before checking with the whole class.

C Focus students on the activity. Model the first sentence for the class. Students read the sentences and answer the questions.

D Direct students to the **Grammar Hub** (see TB93). Use the **Grammar Worksheet** on W53 for extra practice.

AUDIO SCRIPT

10.1

Listening, Exercise A

1 I travel and fly a lot for work, and this device means my bag is a lot lighter than it used to be. I can honestly say it's the best gadget I've ever bought.
Ex B b Before I got it, I always used to carry three or four heavy novels with me, but now I can fit hundreds into my coat pocket. I got the cheapest one, but the battery lasts for a long time and it has a dictionary. You can check words so much more quickly than in a paper dictionary. You just touch the word you don't know and it shows you the meaning.

Ex A **2** This is definitely the most useful piece of technology I own. I don't enjoy driving in new cities or foreign
Ex B d countries, but I can find my way so much more easily than in the past thanks to this smart device. Obviously, it was more expensive than an old-fashioned paper map, but I don't regret buying it. My wife and I don't argue about which way to go anymore! It's very reliable – it never makes mistakes and even tells you when there is traffic or a speed camera.

3 This has to be the greatest invention of the 21st century! I take it everywhere with me and it is just the right size to fit in my bag. They are getting cheaper and cheaper – mine cost less than a lot of phones do
Ex B f these days. I don't have many apps on it, and most of the time, I just use it to go online or watch videos – the screen is so much bigger than on my phone. The best thing about it is that it starts so quickly. It's much faster and more convenient than my old laptop. The worst thing about it is that I now spend even more time online!

4 Every Saturday morning, I go to the city park and meet other … uh … fans. We spend a lot of time talking about our favourite 'toys', as my girlfriend calls them, and arguing about which is the best, or which turns the most quickly, or a thousand other things!
Ex B a And of course we fly and race them. Mine is a little heavier than some of them because it has a camera, but I can take pictures and videos from the air. And of course, they are not just for fun – they have many possible uses. You know, delivering packages, helping the police, taking pictures for scientific research and so on.

10.1 Devices

PRONUNCIATION

10.2 **A** Model and practice the sound with the class.

10.3 **B** Play the audio twice. Have students practice for accuracy.

SPEAKING

A Students work in groups of three or four. Encourage them to use the question prompts as a guide.

B Ask two stronger students to read the example for the class. With a weaker group, you may have to model another example.

C Encourage students to use superlatives and the modeled conversation frame. Take feedback from each group and encourage students to respond to each other's ideas.

GRAMMAR HUB

10.1 Comparatives and superlatives

	Comparative	Superlative
One syllable adjective	adj + *-er* (+ *than*) slow → slow**er**	*the* + adj + *-est* cheap → **the** cheap**est**
Short adjectives ending in *-e*	adj + *-r* (+ *than*) late → late**r**	*the* + adj + *-st* late → **the** late**st**
Short adjectives ending in one vowel + one consonant	double the consonant + *-er* (+ *than*) big → big**ger**	*the* + double the consonant + *-est* big → **the** big**gest**
Adjectives ending in *-y*	adj without *-y* + *-ier* (+ *than*) easy → easi**er**	*the* + adj without *-y* + *-iest* heavy → **the** heav**iest**
Longer adjectives (two + syllables)	*more* + adj (+ *than*) expensive → **more** expensive	the most + adj useful → **the most** useful
Irregular adjectives	good → **better**	good → **the best**
Regular adverbs	*more* + adv (+ *than*) quickly → **more** quickly	the most + adv efficiently→ **the most** efficiently
Irregular adverbs	badly → worse far → farther/further fast → faster hard → harder well → better	badly → the worst far → the farthest/furthest fast → the fastest hard → the hardest well → the best

- We use comparatives to say how two or more things are different.
- We use superlatives to say that something is top or bottom of a group.
- To make a negative comparative, we use *less* instead of *more*.

  *My e-reader was **less** expensive than yours.*
- To make a negative superlative, we use *the least* instead of *the most*.

  *This phone works **the least** efficiently of them all.*
- We use the pattern *get/become* + comparative adjective + *and* + the same comparative adjective to talk about change over time.

  *Computers are **getting smaller and smaller**.*
- For longer adjectives, we use *get/become* + *more and more* + comparative adjective.

  *Computer games are **becoming more and more realistic**.*

Be careful!

- We only use *than* when it is followed by the thing we are comparing.

  This phone is better than this phone.
  NOT ~~This phone is good but this one is better than.~~
- We don't put *the* before a superlative when we use a possessive adjective.

  What was your biggest mistake when buying gadgets? NOT ~~What was your the biggest mistake when buying gadgets?~~

10.1 Comparatives and superlatives

A Correct the mistakes in each sentence.

1. Exercising is a lot more ~~interested~~ *interesting* with a fitness tracker.
2. This is the ~~better~~ best device I've ever owned.
3. You bought the ~~more~~ most expensive phone in the store.
4. This laptop is ~~worst~~ worse than my old one.
5. Your tablet is ~~more light~~ lighter than mine.
6. This tablet starts ~~the~~ more quickly than my other devices.
7. Technology is getting more ~~the~~ and more advanced.

B Complete the sentences with the correct form of the adjectives and adverbs in parentheses.

1. This new cell phone is *lighter* (*light*) than my old one.
2. My computer is the most expensive (*expensive*) thing I own.
3. An e-reader is better (*good*) for reading books than a laptop.
4. Computers are getting cheaper and cheaper (*cheap*) every year.
5. You can check spelling more quickly (*quick*) online than you can by using a dictionary.
6. Although my phone was the heaviest (*heavy*) one in the store, I bought it for all its features.

➤ Go back to page 93.

B WORK IT OUT Write the words you underlined in Exercise A in the correct place.

Comparatives and superlatives				
	Comparative	Example	Superlative	Example
one syllable adj	adjective + *-er* (+ *than*)	cheaper [1] lighter	*the* + adjective + *-est*	the [4] cheapest the lightest
adj with two + syllables	*more* + adjective (+ *than*)	more useful [2] more expensive	*the most* + adjective	the [5] most useful the most expensive
adj with two + syllables ending in *-y*	we cut the *-y* and add *-ier*	heavier easier	we cut the *-y* and add *- iest*	the heaviest the easiest
irregular adj	adjective (+ *than*)	better worse	*the* + adjective	the [6] best the worst
regular adv	*more* + adverb	more slowly [3] more quickly	*the most* + adverb	the most slowly [7] most quickly

C Look at the sentences and answer the questions.

1. 'My bag is a lot lighter than it used to be.'
   Which two words make the comparative adjective *lighter* stronger? a lot
2. 'You can check words so much more quickly.'
   Which two words make the comparative adverb *quickly* stronger? so much
3. 'Mine is a little heavier than some of the others because it has a camera.'
   Which two words make the comparative adjective *heavy* weaker? a little

D Go to the **Grammar Hub** on **page 140**.

PRONUNCIATION

/ɪst/ and superlative adjectives

A Listen and repeat. 10.2

/ɪst/ heaviest, strongest, fastest

B Listen and underline the sound /ɪst/ in the sentences. Then listen and repeat. 10.3

1. The cheapest devices aren't the best.
2. The lightest laptop is better than the rest.
3. It's the fastest phone in our product test.

SPEAKING

A Work in groups. Show and describe your cell phone to the rest of the group. Use the questions to help you.

- When did you buy your phone? How old is it? How much was it? (If you don't mind saying!)
- How is it different from any other phones you have owned?
- What do you like about it?
- What don't you like about it?

B Use comparatives to compare your phones.

A: Jenny's phone is a little heavier than Marvin's.
B: Carly's phone was a lot more expensive than Mohammed's.

C Talk to the other groups in the class. Use superlatives to tell them about your group's phones.

A: Lucia's phone is the newest.
B: Fa's phone is the most interesting.

Describe and compare personal possessions

10.2 It's only good when it works

Describe types of technology

V using devices and the internet G more comparative structures P /əz/ in comparative structures

READING

A Complete the definitions (1–6) with the words in the box.

advertise (v) annoying (adj) mix (n) rely on (phr verb) security (n) symbol (n)

1 ___annoying___ = making you feel slightly angry

2 ___rely on___ = to trust someone or something to do a job or task for you

3 ___mix___ = a combination of different types of people who form a group, for example: *There was a good* ___mix___ *of people at the party.*

4 ___advertise___ = to try to persuade people to buy a product or service by announcing it on television, on the internet, or in newspapers

5 ___symbol___ = a picture or shape used to represent something: &*+@

6 ___security___ = safety from attack, harm or damage

B Read the posts on the online forum *Is it just me?* Do you agree or disagree with the users' opinions?

	Agree	Disagree	Not sure
User 1			
User 2			
User 3			
User 4			

C Read again. Match the sentences to the users.

Which user …

1 says that other people might not have the same problem as they do? ___User 2___

2 regularly forgets important personal information? ___User 4___

3 feels that technology is often unreliable? ___User 1___

4 thinks that people waste money on technology? ___User 3___

5 feels that it is important to protect your money online? ___User 4___

6 gets annoyed when trying to communicate online? ___User 1___

7 finds it hard to concentrate when using the internet? ___User 2___

D SPEAK Work in groups. What would you post on the site? Are the other students in your group annoyed by the same thing?

Is it just me? Tell the internet what annoys you and find out who agrees and who doesn't!

Glossary

benefit (n) an advantage you get from a situation

distracted (adj) not able to concentrate on something

waste time (phrase) to spend time doing things that aren't important

You say: People say technology and the internet have made life better. Sure, there are benefits, but there are also lots of annoying things. Does anyone agree?

The internet says:

(User 1) Dancingmaggie

I agree! The worst thing is how often things go wrong. Many times, when I try to make a video call, for example, the screen freezes. Video calls seem to fail as often as they work! Other things, too – you connect a drive and your computer crashes. You install a new app and everything stops working. Technology is only good when it works.

(User 3) Aoneandatwo

The internet is amazing, and technology, too, in general. My problem is with the technology companies. They are always advertising new devices, so many people feel they have to own the latest model. If you ask me, the old models are usually just as good as the new ones, but, you know, 'your device is not as new as my device, so you're just not cool'. It annoys me that people stop using perfectly good phones and laptops. Ex C Q4

(User 2) RossM8

We rely on the internet, but we also waste time because of it. I'm usually searching for something online, but then I notice something interesting, click on a link and ten minutes later I'm reading about a cat that looks like Beyoncé or a man that married himself! Sometimes I forget what I was searching for in the first place. Some people are probably not as easily distracted as me.

(User 4) ABC123

I know online security is important, especially when it comes to your bank details, but trying to remember passwords is not as easy as it sounds. Ex C Q5 They usually have to be a mix of symbols, numbers and letters, and of course, you shouldn't write them down or use the same password on different websites. My memory is not reliable and I forget passwords as often as I remember them. Ex C Q2 I have blocked my accounts so many times!

10.2 It's only good when it works

LEAD-IN

Start the class off with a sentence, e.g. *I lost my tablet on the subway, but fortunately* .... Point to a student to finish the sentence. Then say ...*but unfortunately*... and point to another student to finish that sentence.

Go on pointing to students around the classroom saying *Fortunately* or *Unfortunately* alternatively.

READING

A Ask students to read the title of the unit and guess what it might be about (*the benefits and disadvantages of technology*). Focus students on the words in the vocabulary box. Students work in pairs matching them to their definitions. With a weaker group, you may have to model one item for the class. Take feedback from one or two pairs and encourage students to respond to each other's ideas.

B Focus students on the title and *You say* section. Elicit that the opinion that has been shared is that technology can sometimes be annoying. Read the task with the class. Remind students to read the glossary to help them with unknown words. Students complete the chart on their own. Check answers with the whole class.

C Students read the article again in more detail and decide who says each sentence. Encourage students to underline any key words in the sentences that will help them find the relevant information in the text. Allow students to compare their answers with a partner before checking answers with the class.

D Arrange students in small groups. Students take turns telling each other what annoys them about the internet. They have to find out whether the other people in their group agree or disagree. Monitor and assist as required. Take feedback from each group and encourage students to respond to each other's ideas.

TEACHING IDEA by David Seymour and Maria Popova

Speaking : Discoveries and inventions

Ask students *What technological developments and scientific discoveries have there been in the last 200 years?* Arrange students in small groups and ask them to brainstorm discoveries/ inventions and the advances that have resulted from them.

The groups should agree on a list of the top five most significant discoveries and inventions.

If students need help coming up with ideas, write the following suggestions on the board:

electricity, the light bulb, vaccinations, nuclear fission, the silicon chip, the internal combustion engine, algorithms

TEACHING IDEA by David Seymour and Maria Popova

Grammar *As ... as*

Write on the board:

food, clothes, transportation, entertainment, housing, cars

Ask students to take turns asking you questions about the prices of these items in a country you know well (the US, the UK, Australia, etc).

After each answer, ask students to write a sentence comparing the price in the foreign country with that in their own country, e.g. *Transportation is almost twice as expensive in the US.*

Ask students to compare their sentences with a partner. In pairs, students should then write some more comparisons, e.g. 'It's not nearly as rainy in the United States as it is in my country'.

METHODOLOGY HUB by Jim Scrivener

Practicing

Practicing provides intensive oral repetition of selected sentences, giving the learners a chance to practice 'getting their mouths around' the language without worrying too much about meaning. The basic technique involves simple repetition:

Teacher: *He's going to open the door.*

Students: *He's going to open the door.*

Practicing is important for 'getting your tongue around it' problems. They can also help with other things, for example, on issues to do with selecting the right form quickly (again, something that improves with familiarity).

Variations on practice techniques

- Repeat the grammar item on its own.
- Repeat the intonation pattern as hummed music, no words.
- Repeat by 'backchaining', i.e. build up sentences little by little starting at the end.

TEACHING IDEA by David Seymour and Maria Popova

Speaking: Telephone

Elicit from the class some problems that they might call their friends, family or roommates about. Write their ideas on the board. If students have difficulty coming up with ideas, write a few prompts on the board (late for dinner, can't find something, etc). Arrange students in a semi-circle and whisper one of the problems to the student on the left. Each student should listen to the problem, and then whisper it to the person next to them. When the message reaches the end of the semi-circle, ask the final student to say what the message was. The first student should now choose another problem and repeat the activity.

10.2 It's only good when it works

VOCABULARY

A Write on the board *to make a video call* and *to click on a link*. Elicit that what these phrases have in common is that they are always used together. That's why they are called *collocations*. Ask students if they can think of other examples. Focus students on the task. In pairs, students read the article again and complete the collocations. Check answers with the class. Use the **Vocabulary Worksheet** on W56 for extra practice.

B Students work in small groups discussing Questions 1 and 2. Encourage students to share as much information as they can to maintain the conversation. Monitor and assist when necessary. Take feedback from one or two groups and encourage students to respond to each other's ideas.

GRAMMAR

A Focus students on the sentences. What do they have in common with the comparative sentences from the previous lesson? Elicit that these sentences are also comparatives, but they establish whether things are the same or different. Focus students on the grammar box and ask them to choose the correct words to complete the rules. Allow them to compare their answers in pairs before checking with the whole class.

B Ask students to read through sentences and match them with their definitions. Remind students to use the information in the grammar box to support them. Check answers with the class.

C Direct students to the **Grammar Hub** (see below). Use the **Grammar Worksheet** on W55 for extra practice.

PRONUNCIATION

10.4 **A** Focus students on the pronunciation of *as* in comparative structures. Remind them of the schwa /ə/ from Unit 7 and of the effects of stress for emphasis they learned in Unit 9. Elicit that /ə/ is the sound of unstressed vowels in English and that stress can sometimes change the quality of a vowel. Play the audio. Ask students if they notice any difference in the pronunciation of *as* between the two speakers.

'As' is usually unstressed and pronounced **/əz/**. *Here, the second speaker uses* **/æz/** *(strong pronunciation) to emphasize their argument.*

10.4 **B** Play the audio again and ask students to listen and repeat the conversation. Focus on their pronunciation of **/æz/**and **/əz/**. Pause the recording after each speaker to allow students enough time to repeat the sentence.

C In pairs, students make similar conversations using conversation prompts 1–3. Monitor and assist when necessary. Take feedback from one or two pairs and encourage students to pay attention to each other's pronunciation.

SPEAKING

A Arrange students in pairs (A and B). Ask them to turn to the **Communication Hub** (TB121). Students follow the instructions and complete the activity. Take feedback from some pairs to check.

> **Extra activity**
> If you have time, divide the class into two groups to debate the use of technology in the classroom. One group should be in favor of, and the other against, using technology.

GRAMMAR HUB

10.2 More comparative structures

- We use *as* + adjective/adverb + *as* to say that two things are the same in some way.
  *Your phone is **as good as** mine.*
  *My drone flies **as quickly as** yours.*
- For emphasis, we use *just as … as*.
  *You are **just as** good **as** I am at this video game.*
- We use *not as* + adjective/adverb + *as* to say that two things are different in some way.
  *Your computer **isn't as fast as** mine.*
  *I **don't** use technology **as regularly as** you do.*

10.2 More comparative structures

A Choose the correct option.

1. When my computer crashes, I get *just* / *as* annoyed as everyone else does.
2. My tablet is *as not* / *not as* useful as I thought it would be.
3. Is your drone *as much fun* / *fun as much* as you expected it to be?
4. Getting more computer memory is *just as simple as* / *simple as just* connecting a USB.
5. Video calls are as cheap *than* / *as* normal calls on a computer.
6. This GPS is not *as reliable as* / *reliable as* it should be.
7. Your internet connection is just *as fast as* / *fast as* mine.

B Make sentences. Use contractions where possible.

1. tablets … = useful … laptops
   Tablets are just as useful as laptops.
2. tablets … > useful … laptops
   Laptops aren't as useful as tablets.
3. TV advertising … > effective … advertising on the radio
   Radio advertising isn't as effective as TV advertising.
4. the GPS on my phone … = good … the GPS in the car
   The GPS on my phone is as good as the GPS in the car.
5. 4G … > fast … 3G internet
   3G internet isn't as fast as 4G.
6. new models … > reliable … old models
   Old models aren't as reliable as new models.

➤ Go back to page 95.

VOCABULARY
Using devices and the internet

A **Read** ***Is it just me?*** **again. Complete the collocations with verbs from the posts.**

1 ___make___ **a video call** – use the internet to talk to and see someone else

2 ___block___ **your account** – if a bank or a social media provider does this, they stop your account from working because you have done something wrong

3 ___remember___ **your password** – keep in your mind the secret word you chose to keep your email, bank or social media account safe

4 ___connect___ **a drive** – add a small device with extra memory to your computer

5 ___click___ **on a link** – press the button on your mouse to connect quickly to a website

6 **your computer** ___crashes___ – your computer stops working; often you see a blue screen and a warning

7 **the screen** ___freezes___ – there's a problem that means the screen on your device won't change

8 ___install___ **an app** – add a new application to your phone or tablet

B **SPEAK** **Work in groups. Discuss the questions.**

1 What was the last really good app you installed on a device? Why do you like it?

2 How do you remember passwords? Have you ever blocked an account by entering the wrong password?

GRAMMAR
More comparative structures

A **WORK IT OUT** **Look at the sentences from** ***Is it just me?*** **and choose the correct words to complete the rules.**

If you ask me, the old models are usually ***just as good as*** *the new ones.*

Video calls seem to fail ***as often as*** *they work!*

Some people are probably ***not as easily distracted as*** *me.*

Comparative structures

1 To say that two things or people are ***the same*** / ***different*** in some way, we use (*just*) *as* + adjective/adverb + *as*.

2 To say that two things or people are ***the same*** / ***different*** in some way, we use *not as* + adjective/adverb + *as*.

B **Match the sentences (1–4) with the correct meanings (a–d).**

1 I don't get as annoyed with technology as my boyfriend does. — b
2 I get just as annoyed with technology as my boyfriend does. — a
3 I don't forget my passwords as often as my girlfriend does. — c
4 I forget my passwords just as often as my girlfriend does. — d

a We get equally annoyed with technology.
b He gets more annoyed with technology than me.
c She forgets her passwords more often than me.
d There is no difference in how often we forget our passwords.

C Go to the **Grammar Hub** on **page 140**.

PRONUNCIATION
/əz/ in comparative structures

10.4 **A** **Listen to the sentences. How does each speaker pronounce** ***as*****?**

1 I don't think online banking is as secure as personal banking. /əz/

2 Sending an email is not as thoughtful as making a phone call. /æz/

10.4 **B** **Listen again and repeat the conversation.**

C **SPEAK** **Work in pairs. Make similar conversations about these topics. Use** ***as … as*** **in its weak form.**

1 going to the movie theater vs. watching movies online

2 paying in cash vs. paying by credit or debit card

3 shopping online vs. shopping in town

SPEAKING

Work in pairs. You are going to talk about different types of technology. Student A – go to the Communication Hub on page 154. Student B – go to the Communication Hub on page 155.

Describe types of technology

10.3 The best view in the universe

● Discuss the requirements for a job

G *need to* V collocations: science and research P /ʊ/ and /uː/ S facts and opinions

READING

A Work in pairs. Describe the picture. Try to use all the words in the box.

astronaut Earth International Space Station (ISS) space spacesuit spacewalk view

B SPEAK Work in groups. Discuss the questions.

1. What do you know about the history of human space travel?
2. What do you think would be the best and worst parts about visiting the ISS?

C READ FOR GIST Read the glossary and quickly read the article. Then choose the best subtitle.

1. A bridge to Mars
2. The laboratory in the stars
3. Just another day in space

INTERNATIONAL SPACE STATION

There are more than seven billion human beings living on Earth, and then there are a very special group of people who live somewhere completely different. Four hundred kilometers above us and circling the planet at 7.7 km per second, there are between six and ten astronauts who call the International Space Station (ISS) home.

Since the first crew members arrived in November 2000, records confirm that over 200 people from 18 countries have visited the ISS. (Ex D Q1) Many only need to stay for a short time, but others need to spend several months there. So, what is the average zero-gravity day like on the ISS?

Living in space may seem exciting, but in fact, the daily routine is fairly repetitive. (Ex D Q2) The crew needs to follow a detailed schedule. Days begin each morning at 6 am when, instead of an alarm clock, a different song chosen by the crew's families back on Earth is played to wake them up. As on Earth, the first stop is the bathroom. Keeping clean is difficult because without gravity everything floats, including water. Residents of the ISS report that washing your hair is particularly difficult in space. (Ex D Q3)

After a challenging start comes breakfast. Almost all the food on the ISS is either dried or canned. Most people would agree that the daily menu is not one of the highlights of life in space. (Ex D Q4) Next, it's time to exercise. Research has shown that muscles and bones quickly become weak in space, so astronauts need to work out for at least two hours each day, using special zero-gravity gym equipment. (Ex D Q5)

The ISS is a large floating laboratory and astronauts spend much of the day doing research. Crew members work with scientists on Earth to do experiments and collect data, usually about the effects of space travel on the mind and body. It is thought that one day humans will travel to Mars, so astronauts test new technologies and look for solutions to the challenges of spending large amounts of time in space. (Ex D Q6)

ISS crews have made many important discoveries. For example, they have proved that it is possible to grow a range of different vegetables to provide food in space. (Ex D Q7) They have also found new ways to develop drugs to help treat diseases. (Ex D Q8)

Crews also need to repair equipment and solve any problems with the station itself. Sometimes this means going outside. Because of the obvious risks, the astronauts spend weeks making preparations. Incredibly, it takes four hours just to put on a spacesuit before going out for a 'spacewalk'.

When they don't need to do any other tasks, the astronauts usually use their free time to contact relatives, read or watch movies. However, there is no doubt that the most popular activity is simply looking out of the window at what is probably the best view in the universe. (Ex D Q9) (Ex D Q10)

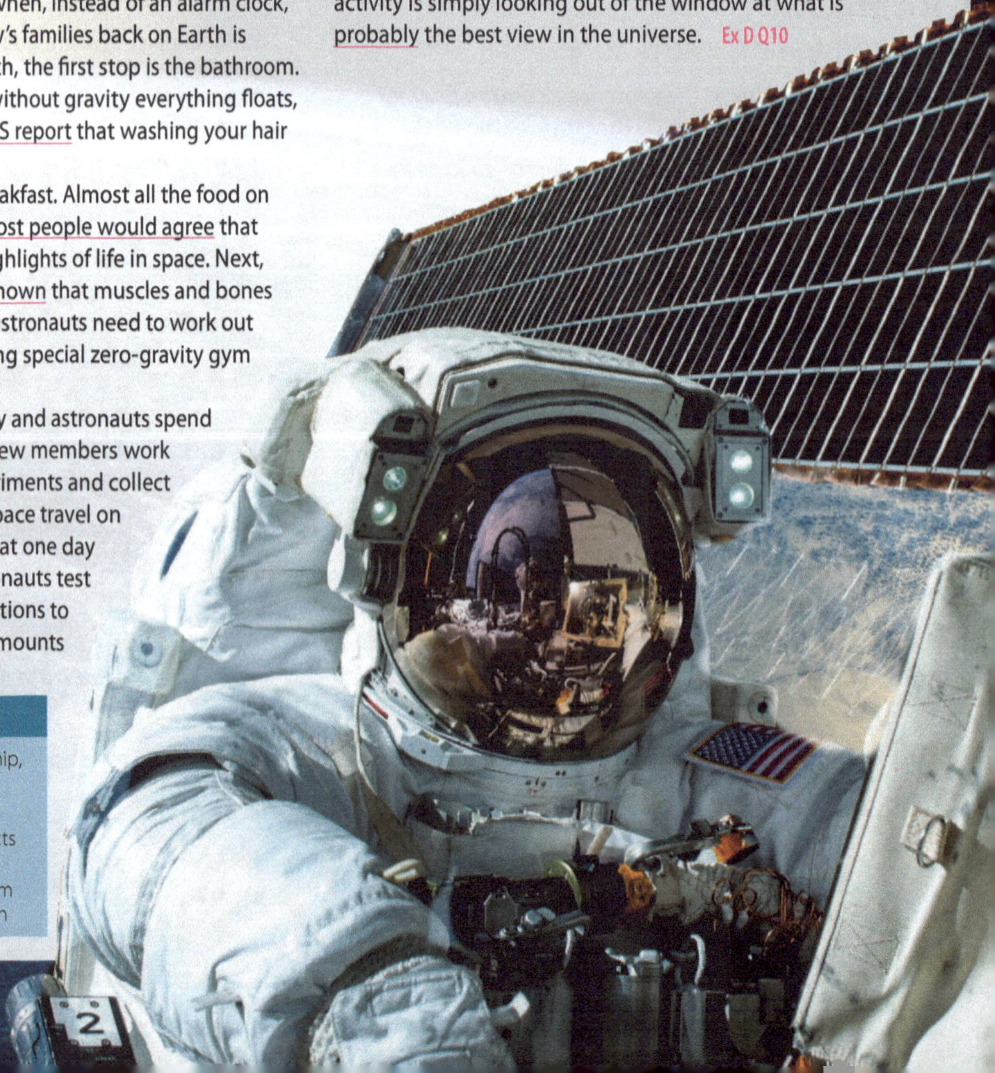

Glossary

crew (n) the people who work on a ship, aircraft, or space station
float (v) to move slowly through air
gravity (n) the force that makes objects fall to the ground
laboratory (n) a building or large room where people do scientific research

10.3 The best view in the universe

LEAD-IN

Students make an outline of their own résumés. List possible jobs students might apply for. Discuss what information goes into a résumé, e.g. educational background, work experience, etc. If students have no job record, discuss possible alternatives to employment, e.g. volunteer work, special courses or workshops, apprenticeships, etc. Remind students that they should order their characteristics in such a way as to convince a potential employer that they are suitable for the job. Give students five minutes to write their outlines. Take feedback from three or four students. Would the rest of the class give them the job they are applying for? Why? Why not?

READING

A Focus students on the vocabulary box. In pairs, students describe what they can see in the picture. Encourage them to use all the words in the box. Monitor and assist when necessary. Write any useful vocabulary on the board. Take feedback from one or two pairs and encourage students to respond to each other's ideas.

B Read the questions with the class. Arrange students in small groups to discuss the questions. Monitor and assist when necessary. Take feedback from each group and encourage students to respond to each other's ideas.

C Focus students on the glossary and the activity. Students work on their own choosing the best subtitle. Encourage students to read the first line of each paragraph to understand the topics. To prevent students from reading the article in too much detail, set a time limit that ensures they just have time to read the article for general meaning.

D Focus students on the box as a class. Give one or two examples of facts and opinions and elicit others from students. Students reread the article and decide if Sentences 1–10 are facts or opinions.

E In small groups, students discuss Questions 1 and 2 in their groups, using information from the article to support their ideas. Monitor and assist as required. Take feedback from one or two groups and encourage students to respond to each other's ideas.

TEACHING IDEA by David Seymour and Maria Popova

Speaking: Now hiring

Arrange students in small groups and ask them to write a job advertisement for a position on the International Space Station. Elicit ideas from the class on what information needs to be included (duties, personality characteristics, certifications, etc). Tell students that they can use the information from the two **Communication Hub** activities in this lesson to help them. When students have completed their job advertisements, combine groups and ask them to compare what they wrote.

Vocabulary: Astronaut's diary

Use this activity to practice vocabulary:

Ask students whether any of them keep a diary and elicit their ideas on the kinds of information that they include. Ask students to imagine that they are an astronaut on the International Space Station. Ask students to write a diary entry for a day aboard the ISS. Encourage students to use the language from the lesson in their diary entries.

METHODOLOGY HUB by Jim Scrivener

Research better, search better

If students are going to research online, make sure that they have some training in basic skills – especially in effective ways of searching. Most people just type a word into a search engine and wait for the results – but it's possible to refine your search criteria a lot more than this, for example, by saying what you want to include and exclude.

A few key tips that work on many search engines:

- Use two or three words rather than one. You can pin down what you need more precisely by searching a range of relevant terms rather than just one. For example, if you are looking for a picture of an apple, a search on 'apple' will return a lot about computers. But looking for 'apple fruit' removes most of these and gives you relevant results.
- Use quotation marks to search for a whole phrase, e.g. 'Learning teaching' (otherwise you will turn up thousands of results which contain those words somewhere, but not necessarily together).
- Use the minus sign to exclude words you don't want, e.g. 'Tom Jones –singer' will bring up more results on the Fielding novel than just entering Tom Jones.
- Use wild cards to stand for whole words you don't know, e.g. 'conference on * language teaching' will bring up results about conferences on many different languages and specializations.

10.3 The best view in the universe

GRAMMAR

A Focus students on the sentences and the rules in the grammar box. Students work on their own using the information from the sentences to choose the correct words to complete the rules. Allow them to compare their answers in pairs before checking with the whole class.

B Direct students to the **Grammar Hub** (see below). Use the **Grammar Worksheet** on W57 for extra practice.

VOCABULARY

A Remind students of what collocations are and elicit some examples. Focus them on the activity. Students read the ISS schedule memo in pairs and choose the correct words to complete the collocations. Remind students to use the article to help them. Use the **Vocabulary Worksheet** on W58 for extra practice.

B Direct students to the **Communication Hub** (TB121). Students complete the survey on their own and then compare their answers with a partner. Monitor and assist when necessary. Ask a couple of pairs to report the results of their survey to the class and encourage students to react to their results.

PRONUNCIATION

10.5 **A** Focus students on the pronunciation of /ʊ/ and /uː/. Write on the board: *book, stood* and *room, move* and model the pronunciation. Play the audio. Students listen to the word pairs and identify the differences in pronunciation of the underlined vowels.

10.5 **B** Play the audio again. In pairs, students listen and repeat the words, focusing on their pronunciation of /ʊ/ and /uː/. Encourage them to listen to and correct each other's pronunciation.

10.6 **C** Focus students on the words in the box. In pairs, students decide whether they contain the /ʊ/ or /uː/ sounds, and write them in the correct column. Elicit the answers from one or two pairs but do not correct or confirm them. Play the audio for students to check their answers.

10.6 **D** Play the audio again for students to listen and repeat the words, focusing on their pronunciation of /ʊ/ and /uː/. Encourage them to listen to and correct each other's pronunciation.

SPEAKING HUB

A Arrange students in small groups and direct them to the **Communication Hub** (TB121). Students read the information and discuss the questions. Monitor and assist when necessary.

GRAMMAR HUB

10.3 *need to*

	Positive	Negative
I/you/we/they	**You need to prove** what you're saying.	**We don't need to do** any more research.
he/she/it	**He needs to make** preparations.	**She doesn't need to wear** a spacesuit.

Question	Positive short answer	Negative short answer
Do you need to prepare for the test?	Yes, **I do**.	No, **I don't**.
Does she need to report her findings?	Yes, **she does**.	No, **she doesn't**.

- We use *need to* like *have to* to say that something is or isn't necessary.

  *Astronauts **need to** be fit. OR Astronauts **have to** be fit.*

  *Astronauts **don't need** to be young. OR Astronauts **don't have to** be young.*

- The verb *need* is followed by *to* + infinitive.

  *Astronauts need **to be** fit. NOT ~~Astronauts need being fit.~~*

10.3 *need to*

A Make questions with *need to*. Then write short answers.

1 you / need / find / a solution ✓
Do you need to find a solution? Yes, I/we do.

2 astronauts / need / wear / spacesuits all the time ✗
Do astronauts need to wear spacesuits all the time? No, they don't.

3 she / need / follow / a schedule ✗
Does she need to follow a schedule? No, she doesn't.

4 the food / need / be / canned ✓
Does the food need to be canned? Yes, it does.

5 astronauts / need / be / fit ✓
Do astronauts need to be fit? Yes, they do.

6 I / need / repair / this computer ✗
Do I need to repair this computer? No, I don't.

B Make sentences with *need to*.

1 You / not / use a telescope to see the ISS
You don't need to use a telescope to see the ISS.

2 the scientists / do / more research on the subject
The scientists need to do more research on the subject.

3 people / think / about the future
People need to think about the future.

4 you / find / a solution
You need to find a solution.

5 he / confirm / what he believes
He needs to confirm what he believes.

6 they / not / install / an app
They do not / don't need to install an app.

➤ Go back to page 97.

D READ FOR DETAIL Read again. Are the sentences fact (F) or opinion (O)? Use the information in the box to help you decide.

Facts and opinions

With so much written information online these days, it is important to question what you read. To do this, you need to recognize the difference between facts and opinions. Facts are clearly true and usually presented with support. Opinions are things that people believe, but may not be true.

Language regularly used to present facts

report, confirm, show, prove, find

There is no doubt that …

Language often used to present opinions

seem, think, believe, feel, hope

Most people would agree that …

1 There have been more than 200 visitors to the ISS. F / O
2 Life in space is exciting. F / O
3 It is hard to wash your hair when there is no gravity. F / O
4 The food on the ISS is not particularly enjoyable. F / O
5 The human body quickly loses strength in space. F / O
6 People will travel to Mars in the future. F / O
7 Plants can grow successfully in space. F / O
8 Research on the ISS is helping people with serious illnesses. F / O
9 The astronauts' favorite free time activity is looking down at Earth. F / O
10 There is no better view than the one from the ISS. F / O

E SPEAK Work in groups. Discuss the questions.

1 Would you visit the ISS if you had the chance? Why/Why not?
2 What would you miss most from Earth if you lived on the ISS for several months?

GRAMMAR

need to

A Look at the sentences from *International Space Station*. Choose the correct words to complete the rules.

The crew needs to follow a detailed schedule.

Crews also need to repair equipment and solve any problems with the station itself.

When they don't need to do any other tasks, the astronauts usually use their free time to contact relatives, read or watch movies.

need to

1 We use *need* to say something is ***possible*** / ***necessary***.
2 When *need* is followed by a verb, we use ***-ing*** / ***to*** + ***base form***.
3 We ***add*** / ***don't add*** -*s* to *need* when the subject is *he*, *she* or *it*.
4 We use the auxiliary ***do*** / ***have*** with negative and question forms of *need*.

B Go to the **Grammar Hub** on **page 140**.

VOCABULARY

Collocations: science and research

A Choose the correct verbs to complete the collocations in **bold** in the ISS schedule memo. Use *International Space Station* to help you.

ISS schedule memo 1174639 – Schedule number 4077

Good evening from Earth and the Control Center.
As always, please [1]***do*** / ***follow*** tomorrow's **schedule** carefully.
9:00 am – IMPORTANT [2]***repair*** / ***solve*** broken gym **equipment**. This must be fixed today. Exercise program must return to normal.
10:00 am – Live link with University of Beijing – Give a presentation to students on Chinese astronauts who have [3]***made*** / ***found*** important **discoveries** on the ISS.
11:00 am – Continue [4]***testing*** / ***making*** **new technologies** for long-distance communication.
1:00 pm – Meeting to [5]***look for*** / ***collect*** **solutions** to the recent computer problems.
2:00 pm – Continue [6]***making*** / ***doing*** **research** into growing fruit in space. [7]***Do*** / ***Test*** **experiments**, numbers 146 to 149 and [8]***collect*** / ***follow*** more **data** on water levels.
5:00 pm – [9]***Make*** / ***Do*** more **preparations** for the next spacewalk. Try to [10]***test*** / ***solve*** the **problems** with spacesuit number 4.

B SPEAK Work in pairs. Go to the **Communication Hub** on **page 155** and complete the survey. Then compare your results. Which of you would be best at working in space?

PRONUNCIATION

/ʊ/ and /uː/

The vowel sounds are different in each pair. *Foot* and *woman* have the short /ʊ/ sound. *Food* and *routine* have the long /uː/ sound.

10.5 **A** Listen to the word pairs. How is the pronunciation of the vowel sounds different?

1 foot food 2 woman routine

10.5 **B** Listen again and repeat the words.

10.6 **C** Write the words in the correct place in the table. Listen and check.

~~crew~~ group look move room would

/ʊ/	/uː/	
look	crew	move
would	group	room

10.6 **D** Listen again and repeat the words.

SPEAKING HUB

PREPARE You are going to talk about working in space. Go to the **Communication Hub** on **page 156** and follow the instructions.

Discuss the requirements for a job

Café Hub

10.4 Locked out

Ⓕ– make and receive formal and informal phone calls
Ⓟ– word stress and intonation

COMPREHENSION

A ▶ **Cover the video screen. Listen to the video and put the events (a–j) in the correct order (1–10).**

- **a** The front door closes and locks shut. 2
- **b** Gaby phones Neena's work. 7
- **c** The signal is bad. 4
- **d** Gaby is put on hold. 8
- **e** Gaby phones Zac's mobile. 3
- **f** Gaby leaves a voice message for Neena. 9
- **g** It starts raining. 10
- **h** Neena's phone is switched off. 6
- **i** Gaby phones Neena's mobile. 5
- **j** Gaby opens the front door to take the rubbish out. 1

Glossary

phones **(v) (British)** = calls **(v) (American)**
mobile **(n) (British)** = cell phone **(n) (American)**
rubbish **(n) (British)** = trash **(n) (American)**

B ▶ **SPEAK** Work in pairs. Predict the answers to the questions. Then watch the video and check your answers.

1. Where is Gaby? Outside the flat/apartment.
2. How does Gaby get locked out? She is taking the rubbish/trash out and the door slams shut.
3. Where is Zac? Outside, walking down a street.
4. Where is Neena? We don't know.
5. What is the music we hear three times? Holding music.
6. How does the video end? Gaby finds the keys in her dressing gown/bathrobe.

MILLY

SAM

NEENA

ZAC

GABY

FUNCTIONAL LANGUAGE

Make and receive formal and informal phone calls

A Write the words in the correct order to make useful phrases. Then write each phrase in the correct place.

1 up / breaking / You're / .
You're breaking up.

2 you / hear / can't / I / .
I can't hear you.

3 me / Can / you / hear / ?
Can you hear me?

4 cut / out / You / again / .
You cut out again.

5 that / What / was / ?
What was that?

6 very / The / isn't / signal / good / .
The signal isn't very good.

Describe a phone problem	Ask for clarification
You're breaking up. I can't hear you. You cut out again. The signal isn't very good.	Can you hear me? What was that?

B Complete the receptionist's replies with two of the words in the box.

just over soon through

Receptionist: Good morning. You're [1] through to Jobs, Jobs, Jobs and Jobs. How can I help?

Gaby: Hello, is it possible to speak to Neena Patel?

Receptionist: Yes, of course. I'll [2] just try to put you [3] through. I'm afraid the line is busy. Would you like to hold?

Gaby: Yes, please.

[MUSIC ON HOLD]

Receptionist: Thank you for calling. [4] Just putting you [5] through.

C **SPEAK** Work in pairs. Practice the conversation in Exercise B with your own ideas.

PRONUNCIATION

Word stress and intonation

10.7 **A** Listen and repeat Amelia's voicemail greeting. Copy the word stress and intonation.

Amelia: Hi, this is A<u>me</u>lia <u>Jones</u>. I <u>can't</u> take your <u>call</u> at the <u>mo</u>ment. Please leave a <u>mes</u>sage after the <u>beep</u>.

B **SPEAK** Work in pairs. You are going to record your own voicemail greeting in English.

- Practice your voicemail greeting.
- Record your voicemail greeting on your phone.
- Call your partner and listen to his/her greeting.
- Leave a message for your partner.

SPEAKING

Work in groups. Choose a problem from the box or use your own ideas. Then role-play calling two friends to ask for help. Use the Functional Language box to help you.

You've locked yourself out. You've lost your car keys. You've lost your house keys. You've missed the last bus home. You've forgotten your passport.

Student A: Call a friend (Student B). The signal is bad.

Student B: Answer Student A. The signal is bad.

Student A: Call another friend at Jones & Jones. You can't get through. You speak to Student C (the receptionist).

Student C: You are the receptionist at Jones & Jones. Answer Student A. The line is busy.

Student A: Answer Student C (the receptionist).

Make and receive formal and informal phone calls

➤ Turn to **page 167** to learn how to write a recommendation.

10.4 Locked out

COMPREHENSION

A ▶ Students look at the images and guess what is happening *(Gaby has been locked out of the house)*. Ask students whether they have ever been locked out of their home and what they did. Elicit some ideas from the class.

Focus students on the events in the episode. Cover the video screen and play the video in full. Students complete the activity on their own. Allow them to compare their answers in pairs before checking with the class.

B ▶ In pairs, students predict the answers to Questions 1–6, using the images from the video and their answers to Exercise A. Play the video again, this time with the visuals, for students to check their answers. Take feedback from one or two pairs and encourage students to respond to their ideas.

FUNCTIONAL LANGUAGE

A Ask students how often they use the phone in English and how they feel about it. Focus on the useful language section. Students write the words in the correct order to make sentences on their own. Then, they write them in the corresponding column in the table below. Allow students to compare their sentences in pairs before checking with the class.

B Focus students on the task. They complete the conversation between Gaby and the receptionist with the words in the box. Students complete the blanks on their own, then they check the answers as a class.

C Students work in pairs practicing the conversation from Exercise B with their partner. Encourage students to replace the words *Good morning, Jobs, Jobs, Jobs and Jobs, Neena Patel* and *[MUSIC ON HOLD]* with their own ideas. Monitor and assist as required. Encourage students to switch roles and repeat the conversation. If you are working with a confident class, encourage them to cover the conversation and try to say the conversation from memory.

PRONUNCIATION

A (10.7) Elicit the meaning of voicemail *(an inbox for voice messages, sometimes called an answering machine in American English)*. Explain that both forms are correct and they can use either in their speaking. Focus students on the stressed words. Play the audio. Students listen and repeat, imitating word stress and intonation. Pause the audio at the end of each sentence for students to repeat.

B Check that all students have access to a phone for recording their voicemail greeting. If a student doesn't have access, ask other students to help with the use of their phones, or use yours. Students work individually writing and practicing their voicemail greeting in a natural way, paying close attention to their stress and intonation. Monitor and assist as required. Once students are confident with their greetings, ask them to record them. In pairs, students call each other's phone and listen to their voicemail greeting. They then leave a message on their partner's phone. If students are not allowed to use cell phones in class, this part of the activity can be done for homework.

SPEAKING

A Focus students on the task. In groups of three, students choose a problem from the box. Then, they write the role play, following the conversation prompts. Allow students some time to write and rehearse their role plays. Encourage the groups to perform their role plays for the rest of the class.

Extra activity

As a class, elicit from students some problems they have when communicating over the telephone. Students could work in groups to brainstorm ways to improve their communication skills while using the phone. You could prompt them with a few ideas , e.g. speak slowly, ask the speaker to spell complicated words, take time to plan what you want to say before calling, etc. For homework, ask students to write a list of ten tips for improving telephone communication skills. Compare their ideas with the other students in the next class.

▶ VIDEO SCRIPT

Café Hub 10.4 Locked out
Z = Zac G = Gaby R = Receptionist
N (*P*) = Neena (*Pre-recorded*)

Z: See you later.
G: Bye! Noooo! Quick, phone Zac.
Z: Hello?
G: Hi, it's me. Sorry, you're breaking up – I can't hear you…
Z: How's this?
G: That's better. Can you hear me? Oh, you've gone again… That's worse now. What did you say?
Z: What was that? Listen, the signal isn't very good. I'll call you back later.
G: What? Could you speak up? Zac? Zac? Great, he's gone… OK, I'll try Neena.
N (*P*): The telephone you are calling is switched off, please try again later.
G: Great. She's at work.
R: Good morning, you're through to Jobs, Jobs, Jobs and Jobs, helping you to find the perfect job. How can I help?
G: Hello, is it possible to speak to Neena Patel?
R: Yes of course, I'll just try to put you through. …Good morning, you're through to Jobs, Jobs, Jobs and Jobs, helping you to find the perfect job. How can I help?
G: Err. I just spoke to you and I've been on hold…
R: Sorry about that. How can I help?
G: Could I speak to Neena Patel please – it's very important.
R: I'll just try to put you through. Hello?
G: Hi.
R: I'm afraid the line's busy, would you like to hold?
G: Ah… Yes please.
R: Thank you for calling, just putting you through…
N (*P*): Hi this is Neena Patel, I can't take your call at the moment. Please leave a message after the beep.
G: Neena, it's Gaby, please phone me as soon as you get this – I've lost my key! And it's raining…

10 Writing

Write a recommendation

W– making recommendations

A Work in groups. Answer the questions.

1 How many school subjects can you think of in one minute?

2 Which were your favorite and least favorite subjects at school, and why?

3 Were/Are you more interested in science, art, language or humanities (history, geography, etc)?

B Work in pairs. Read Bee's question on an online message board. What recommendation would you make for Bee and why?

Woohaa Answers

Bee, Thailand: Should I buy a laptop or a tablet?
I'm not sure whether to buy a laptop or a tablet. I need a computer for work, but also for entertainment at home and while I'm traveling. What do you think?

C Now read Dylan's answer and underline any ideas you or your partner said in Exercise B. What other advantages and disadvantages of laptops and tablets does Dylan mention?

Best answer
Dylan, US
This is not an easy decision, Bee. If you choose the wrong computer, you might regret it. Before you decide, think about size and weight, performance and price.
Most laptops are bigger and heavier than the average tablet. This is partly because they have a normal keyboard. Size and weight may be a problem if you travel a lot or need to carry your computer to work each day.
When it comes to performance, laptops are usually faster and have a bigger memory than tablets. They are also better for people who need to have several apps or programs open at the same time. On the other hand, the battery in a tablet computer will probably last longer between charges than the one in a laptop.
Of course, your budget is also important. Generally speaking, laptops are more expensive than tablets. If you travel regularly and want to spend less money, I'd recommend a tablet. If you want better performance and a normal keyboard, I'd suggest buying a laptop.
I think you should do some more research online. You could also talk to someone in a computer store and ask for their opinion. Good luck!

Ex D

D Read the information in the box. Then find and underline four examples of the structures in the box in Dylan's answer.

Making recommendations

You can tell people what you think they should do using the following language:
- *I think you should* + base form
- *You could* + base form
- *I'd suggest* + noun **or** verb + *-ing* **or** *you* + base form
- *I'd recommend* + noun **or** verb-*ing* **or** *you* + base form

E There is one mistake in each recommendation. Correct the mistakes.

1 I think you should getting a new phone rather than a used one.
I think you should get a new phone rather than a used one.

2 I'd recommend you checking a used phone carefully before you buy it.
I'd recommend checking a used phone carefully before you buy it.

3 You could reading more about different brands online.
You could read more about different brands online.

4 I'd suggest to buy a used phone because you'll get better performance for your money.
I'd suggest buying a used phone because you'll get better performance for your money.

F Work in pairs. Imagine a friend has asked you the following questions. What would you recommend and why? Compare your ideas.

1 Should I travel for six months or get a job right away when I finish college?

2 What brand of computer do you think I should buy?

3 Should I study science or language?

WRITING

A WRITE Read Corey's question on the *Woohaa Answers* website. Write a reply of at least 100 words comparing the two options and making recommendations.

Woohaa Answers

Corey, Germany: Should I buy a new or used phone?
Should I buy a new cell phone or a used one? I don't have a lot of money to spend on it, but I'd like the best one I can afford. What do you think?

B REVIEW Work in groups. Read your group's recommendations. In what ways are they similar or different to yours?

10 WRITING 167

Answers

Laptops. Advantages: faster, bigger memory, good if you want several apps or programs open at the same time. Disadvantages: big and heavy, more expensive

Tablets. Advantages: battery lasts longer between charges, good for travel. Disadvantages: small memory

Refer students to this recommendation as a model for the writing task.

Students can do this in class or for homework.

WRITING

A Focus students on the questions. In groups, students discuss Questions 1–3. Monitor and assist when necessary.

B Students work in pairs reading Bee's question. Elicit ideas from each pair on what recommendations they would make for Bee and why. Write any useful words or phrases on the board.

C Students read Dylan's response and underline any ideas that they mentioned in Exercise B. Take feedback from the class and elicit any other advantages and disadvantages of laptops and tablets that Dylan mentions.

D Students should read the information in the box before completing the task.

E Read the instructions with the class. Remind them to use the information in the box and Dylan's answer to help them. Allow students to check their answers in pairs before checking with the whole class.

F Arrange students in pairs. First, they come up with answers to the questions alone. Then students compare their recommendations with their partner. Monitor and assist as required.

WRITING TASK

A Students write a response of 100 words talking about the pros and cons of the two options. Remind students to use the useful language from the lesson in their answers.

B Ask students to discuss the similarities and differences they can find. Take feedback from each group. You can also include a stage of peer correction here. Students exchange and correct each other's replies. If you feel this might be too sensitive you can also take a few representative errors from students' work and write them on the board. Students then correct the errors.

Unit 10 Review

VOCABULARY

A Choose the correct words to complete the sentences.

1. My new ***drone*** / *fitness tracker* has arrived. Should we go to the park and fly it?
2. I'm so bad at directions – this *USB drive* / ***GPS*** is really useful!
3. I think a ***fitness tracker*** / *tablet* would make me exercise more.
4. I always take my ***e-reader*** / *power bank* on vacation with me. I love books.
5. My son wants a *drone* / ***tablet*** so he can watch his favorite TV shows.
6. A *GPS* / ***USB drive*** is very useful when I go on business trips. I can take my work everywhere!
7. I don't know what I would do without my ***power bank*** / *e-reader* – my phone battery is always running out.

B Complete the information with the verbs in the box. You need to use one of the verbs twice.

collect do look make test

Higgerfield University
SCIENCE DEPARTMENT

Why study science at Higgerfield?

We asked three first-year students why they chose science subjects.

Sergei: I want to [1] ___collect___ data and [2] ___look___ for solutions to the problem of climate change.

Masha: I want to [3] ___do___ research on space travel and [4] ___test___ new technologies to help get us to other planets.

Melissa: I want to [5] ___make___ discoveries and [6] ___do___ experiments that will help save people's lives.

To find out more about studying Science at Higgerfield, join us at one of our open houses.

GRAMMAR

A Complete the article with comparative and superlative forms of the missing adjectives and adverbs.

Hi-fi & Wi-fi Magazine **Awards**

Cell phones

1st Chitchat 8
2nd Speakup 4 3rd Talkabout 2

Overall

The Talkabout 2 is a good phone, but the Speakup 4 is [1] ___better___. And this year, the Chitchat 8 is [2] ___the best___.

Is it reliable?

The Talkabout 2 is fairly reliable, but the Speakup 4 is [3] ___more reliable___. Again, the Chitchat 8 is [4] ___the most reliable___.

Is it easy to use?

The Talkabout 2 is fairly easy to use, but the Speakup 4 is definitely [5] ___easier___ to use. However, the Chitchat 8 is [6] ___the easiest___ to use.

Does it charge quickly?

The Talkabout 2 charges quickly, but the Speakup 4 charges [7] ___more quickly___. Again, the Chitchat 8 wins this year because it charges [8] ___the most quickly___.

B Add *as … as* to complete each sentence.

1. I get just (as) annoyed with pop-up ads (as) anybody else.
2. That messaging service is not (as) private (as) this one.
3. My wife doesn't forget passwords (as) easily (as) I do.
4. My dad's phone is just (as) old-fashioned (as) my mom's.
5. I don't learn how to use new devices (as) quickly (as) I used to when I was young.
6. This game is just (as) good (as) the other soccer games on the market.

FUNCTIONAL LANGUAGE

Complete the words in the phone conversation. The first letter of each word has been given to help you.

Derek: Hello, this is Derek Lebarge. [1]Sorry, I can't t**ake** your call at the m**oment**. [2]Please leave a m**essage** after the b**eep**.

Murray: Derek? Derek? It's Murray. [3]Sorry, the s**ignal** isn't very g**ood**. [4]What was t**hat**? [5]You're b**reaking** up. Hello?

An urban fox begins his nightly hunt for food, Twickenham, United Kingdom.

Natural world (n) nature as it exists without the effects produced or caused by people.

Muir is suggesting that nature is as important as food to human beings. Being in nature has the power to make us feel better and give us both physical and mental strength.

John Muir (1838–1914) was an influential Scottish-American author and naturalist. He played an important role in protecting wilderness areas in the United States and founded the Sierra Club, an American conservation organization. He is sometimes called the 'Father of the National Parks'. The quote was originally published in Muir's book *The Yosemite* (1912).

OBJECTIVES

- talk about natural wonders
- read and talk about wildlife photography
- talk about the causes and effects of plastic pollution
- tell a story
- write an email giving suggestions and advice

Work with a partner. Discuss the questions.

1 Do you find the city or the country more relaxing? Why?
2 Read the quote. Do you agree with Muir?
3 Look at the picture. What wildlife is there in your city?

NATURAL WORLD 101

OBJECTIVES

Read the unit objectives to the class.

UNIT OPENER QUESTIONS

Encourage students to look at the quote and take one or two suggestions from the class about what they think it means.

Ask students to look at the picture on the page and encourage them to share their ideas. Ask prompt questions such as 'Where do you think this photo was taken? How important is nature and being outside for you? Do you think it is worthwhile to prevent the building of an airport or of a road to save a rare animal species?' If students share any good ideas or useful language, write these on the board.

Students look at the questions at the bottom of the page. Model one possible answer, explaining why the countryside or the city is more relaxing for you. Students discuss the questions in pairs. Monitor and assist as necessary. When students have finished the activity, ask one or two pairs to share their ideas with the class. Encourage students to listen to one another and respond with their own ideas and opinions.

WORKSHEETS

Lesson 11.1 Natural wonders

Grammar: The passive voice (simple present and simple past) (W59)

Vocabulary: Natural features (W60)

Lesson 11.2 Animal images

Grammar: Adjective + infinitive (W61)

Vocabulary: Animals (W62)

Lesson 11.3 Throw-away world

Grammar: *even* (W63)

Vocabulary: *somewhere, nowhere, everywhere, anywhere* (W64)

11.1 Natural wonders

● Talk about natural wonders

V natural features **P** /e/ and /iː/ **G** the passive voice (simple present and simple past)

VOCABULARY
Natural features

A Label the pictures (1–7) with the words in the box.

canyon harbor lights mountain reef volcano waterfall

B Go to the **Vocabulary Hub** on **page 151**.

C **SPEAK** Work in pairs. Name other examples of the natural features in Exercise A and in the Vocabulary Hub.

A: Well, there's Mount Fuji and The Great Barrier Reef. But I can't think of a famous canyon.
B: What about The Grand Canyon in Arizona?

PRONUNCIATION
/e/ and /iː/

11.1 **A** Listen to the vowel sounds /e/ and /iː/. What is the vowel sound in each word in the box? Write the words in the correct place.

be get leave met reef rest see ten

/e/	/iː/
get met rest ten	be leave reef see

11.2 **B** Listen and check your answers. Then listen again and repeat the words.

LISTENING

A The places in the pictures above have recently been named as the *Seven Natural Wonders of the World*. Match the names (a–g) with the pictures (1–7). What do you know about them?

a Mount Everest 4
b Great Barrier Reef 6
c Grand Canyon 2
d Northern lights (aurora borealis) 1
e Rio de Janeiro harbor 7
f Victoria Falls 3
g Paricutin volcano 5

11.3 **B** **LISTEN FOR KEY WORDS** Listen to a radio travel show about the *Seven Natural Wonders of the World*. In which order did the travel writer visit the places?

1 *the Great Barrier Reef*
2 Grand Canyon
3 Mount Everest
4 Victoria Falls
5 Paricutin volcano
6 Rio de Janeiro harbor
7 northern lights

Glossary

coral (n) a very small ocean creature that lives in large groups that look like plants, in places where the water is warm
crater (n) the round hole at the top of a volcano
form (v) to make something exist
promote (v) to support something
unique (adj) not the same as anything else

11.1 Natural wonders

LEAD-IN

In pairs, students discuss the most beautiful natural wonders in their country. If you are working in a class with only one nationality, ask them to work together and make a list of the top five most beautiful places in their country. Write the names of the places on the board.

VOCABULARY

A Allow students to work with a partner.

B Students turn to the **Vocabulary Hub** (TB121) for further practice. Use the **Vocabulary Worksheet** on W60 for extra practice.

C If students are at a loss, remind them of the words on the board and suggest others like the Etna, Niagara Falls, etc.

PRONUNCIATION

11.1 **A** Write *best* and *beast* on the board and model the two vowel sounds. Play the audio. **NB** The international phonetic alphabet has been used in this course. However, /iː/ is represented as /i/ in the American English phonetic alphabet.

11.2 **B** Play the audio for students to listen and check their answers to Exercise A. Then play the audio again for students to listen and repeat.

LISTENING

A Ask students to match the places with their pictures. Elicit what they know about them. Can they say in which country they are?

11.3 **B** Play the audio. With a weaker group, you may have to play it twice.

11.3 **C** Focus students on the questions. Ask them to underline any key words that will help them find the answer in the audio. Play the audio for students to answer the questions. Play it again for them to check their answers.

D Students work in pairs to answer the question. Monitor and assist when necessary. Take feedback from one or two pairs and encourage students to respond to each other's ideas.

Extra activity

Put students into pairs to describe a place that they love to visit. Students should say where the place is and what it is about that place which makes it so special. Draw upon pairs to talk about what their partner told them in whole-class feedback.

AUDIO SCRIPT

11.3

Listening, Exercise B

P = Presenter M = Mike

P: Welcome to this week's edition of the *Travel Show*. Today, we are joined by travel writer Mike Harold. A year ago, Mike decided to visit the Seven Natural Wonders of the World. Last week, he finally achieved his goal. Mike, tell us a little bit about the seven natural wonders.

M: Well, the Seven Natural Wonders of the World was the idea of the Seven Natural Wonders organization. Ex C Q1 The organization was created to promote and to protect the natural wonders of the world. Not just these seven, but many others as well.

P: So, how did they choose the seven places?

Ex C Q2 **M:** The decision was based on three main things. The places were chosen according to how unique the place is, how important it is and, finally, its pure natural beauty.

P: And why did you decide to visit them?

Ex C Q3 **M:** Well, I've always loved traveling and I like a challenge! As a travel writer, I thought this was an interesting thing to do professionally.

P: OK, so, what are the seven natural wonders?

M: First, I visited the Great Barrier Reef. The reef is 2600 km long and is located off the northeastern coast of Australia. It's made of over 400 different Ex C Q4d kinds of coral and is the largest and most colorful coral reef in the world. It really was amazing. After that, I went to the Grand Canyon, in the US. It was chosen as a natural wonder because of its enormous size and incredible scenery. The canyon was created by the Colorado River, which you can see at the very Ex C Q4f bottom. It's the most popular of the seven natural wonders and is visited by over five million people a year. The next place was the most difficult to get to, as it's located in the Himalayan mountain range.

P: Ohh, this has to be Mount Everest!

Ex C Q4e **M:** Yes, the highest place on Earth. I didn't go to the top, but I went to the base camp, which is at about 5000 meters. The views were unbelievable.

P: I can imagine. And where did you go next?

M: My fourth natural wonder was Victoria Falls. This, of course, is the famous waterfall on the Zambezi River Ex C Q4c in southern Africa. It is actually on the border of two countries, Zambia and Zimbabwe. The waterfall is almost two kilometers wide and over 100 meters high. It really was an incredible sight. For numbers five and six, I travelled to Central and South America. The first is perhaps the least well known. It's the Paricutin volcano in Mexico.

P: Yes, I must admit, I've never heard of this.

Ex C Q4b **M:** Well, it was only formed in 1943, so it's quite new! It was also the first time modern science saw the creation of a volcano – and that's why it's a natural wonder. I was able to climb the volcano and walk around the crater and look inside. I then went to South America to see a more familiar 'wonder' – the bay and natural harbor of Rio de Janeiro in Brazil. The bay includes several islands and is surrounded by beautiful beaches and spectacular mountains with some great views.

P: And I understand for the final natural wonder, you had some good luck.

M: Yes, I did. The final natural wonder I saw was the northern lights, or aurora borealis. I went to Iceland Ex C Q4a to see them. You can only see them at certain times of the year. And yes, I was very lucky. It really was amazing. And the perfect way to finish my challenge.

P: That sounds amazing! Thanks for sharing your journey with us.

GRAMMAR

A Students complete the rules using the words in the box. Allow students to compare their answers in pairs before checking with the whole class.

B Direct students to the **Grammar Hub** (see below). Use the **Grammar Worksheet** on W59 for extra practice.

C Students work in pairs and discuss what they know about these places.

2 The White Cliffs of Dover are made of chalk and similar minerals.
3 The Himalayas were formed 40–50 million years ago.
4 The Niagara Falls are visited by around 30 million people a year.
5 Uluru in Australia is also known as Ayers Rock.
6 The Galapagos Islands were discovered by the Bishop of Panama in 1535.

SPEAKING

A 11.4 Play the audio. Students listen to the presentation and answer the questions.

The Gullfoss Waterfall is located in a canyon on the Hvita River in South-Western Iceland. It was formed at the end of the Ice Age about 15,000 years ago. The waterfall is unusual as it has two large steps, rather than one single drop. It is surrounded by open land and fields, and it is reached by road and then a short walk. It is visited every year by thousands of people who are attracted by the spectacular views and by the incredible power of the water as it passes through the waterfall.

B Students work in pairs preparing a presentation about a natural wonder in their country or continent. Monitor and assist when necessary.

C Ask the different pairs to give their presentations to the class.

GRAMMAR HUB

11.1 The passive voice (simple present and simple past)

	Positive	Negative
I	**I am told** the desert is beautiful.	**I'm not expected** to be an expert on the environment.
he/she/it	It **is visited** by lots of people.	**It is not understood** by many people. **It isn't understood** by many people.
you/we/they	**You are advised** to stay away from the volcano.	**They aren't studied** by scientists.

Question	Positive short answer	Negative short answer
Am I allowed to take photographs?	Yes, **you are**.	No, **you aren't**.
Are we permitted to get close to the waterfall?	Yes, **we/you are**.	No, **we/you aren't**.

	Positive	Negative
I/he/she/it	**I was told** to read the article.	**She wasn't asked** to help.
you/we/they	They **were invited** to the island.	The clothes **weren't needed** on the journey.

Question	Positive short answer	Negative short answer
Was she joined by her friends?	Yes, **she was**.	No, **she wasn't**.
Were they told what to do?	Yes, **they were**.	No, **they weren't**.

- We use the passive voice when we don't say who or what causes the action (usually because the person or thing is not known, not important or obvious).

  *The new road to the site **was opened** last year.*

- We also use the passive voice with *by* when we know who does/did an action and we want to emphasize it.

  *This report was produced **by** scientists from Cambridge University.*

- We can sometimes say the same thing in the active or passive voice. The choice usually depends on the topic we are talking about.

  Active: *Many tourists **visit** the site.* (The topic is tourists.)
  Passive: *The site **is visited** by many tourists.* (The topic is the site.)

Be careful!

- We don't use *by* + the agent unless it is important, useful information.

  The research is paid for by the World Wildlife Fund. NOT ~~*The research is paid for by someone.*~~

11.3 **C LISTEN FOR DETAIL** Listen to the radio show again and answer the questions.

1 What is the goal of the Seven Natural Wonders organization? To promote and protect the natural wonders of the world.
2 What three main factors were used to choose the Seven Natural Wonders? How unique the place is, how important it is, and its pure natural beauty.
3 Why did Mike decide to visit the Seven Natural Wonders? He loves traveling and likes a challenge.
4 Which of the seven natural wonders …
   a is visible only at certain times of the year? northern lights
   b was formed the most recently? Paricutin volcano
   c is located in two countries? Victoria Falls
   d is famous for its different colors? Great Barrier Reef
   e is the highest? Mount Everest
   f is the most visited? The Grand Canyon

D SPEAK Work in pairs. Which of the Seven Natural Wonders you would most like to visit and why?

GRAMMAR

The passive voice (simple present and simple past)

A WORK IT OUT Look at the sentences from the radio show about the seven natural wonders. Then complete the rules using the words in the box.

1 The decision **was based** on three main things.
2 The places **were chosen** according to how unique the place is …
3 It'**s made** of over 400 different kinds of coral.
4 It **was** only **formed** in 1943.
5 The canyon **was created** by the Colorado River.
6 It'**s visited** by about four-and-a-half million people a year.

be | *by* | do not say | past participle

The passive voice (simple present and simple past)

1 We make the passive voice with the auxiliary verb ___be___ + the ___past participle___ of the main verb.
2 We most commonly use the passive voice when we ___do not say___ who or what performs or causes the action. This is usually because the person or thing is not known, not important or obvious.
3 We sometimes use the passive voice with an agent (the person or thing that performs or causes the action). We use ___by___ to introduce the agent.

B Go to the **Grammar Hub** on **page 142**.

C SPEAK Work in pairs. Test your general knowledge! Make sentences about these natural wonders using a word from each column. Discuss what you know about each place.

Jeju Island is located off the coast of South Korea.

1 Jeju Island	form	around 30 million people a year
2 The White Cliffs of Dover	locate	40–50 million years ago
3 The Himalayas	visit	as Ayers Rock
4 The Niagara Falls	make	off the coast of South Korea
5 Uluru in Australia	discover	of chalk and similar minerals
6 The Galapagos Islands	also/know	the Bishop of Panama in 1535

SPEAKING

11.4 **A** Listen to a presentation about the Gullfoss Waterfall in Iceland and answer the questions.

- Where is it located? In a canyon on the Hvita River in southwestern Iceland.
- When was it formed or created? At the end of the Ice Age, 15,000 years ago.
- What is it surrounded by? By open land and fields.
- How is it reached? By road and a short walk.
- Who and how many people visit it? Thousands of people each year.
- Why are people attracted to it? The spectacular views and the incredible power of the water.

B Work in pairs. Choose a natural wonder in your country or continent to give a presentation about. Use the questions in Exercise A to help you.

C Give your presentation to the class.

Talk about natural wonders

11.2 Animal images

Read and talk about wildlife photography

V animals **G** adjective + infinitive **P** *to* /tə/

VOCABULARY
Animals

A SPEAK Work in pairs. Make a list of animals. You have one minute.

B Go to the **Vocabulary Hub** on **page 151**.

C SPEAK Work in pairs. Write down your three favorite animals. Tell your partner what you wrote. Explain your choices.

D SPEAK Work in pairs. Go to the **Communication Hub** on **page 157** to see what your answers to Exercise C mean. Do you agree or disagree?

My first animal is a dolphin. I think I'm like a dolphin because it's smart, moves quickly, is very sociable and always in groups.

READING

A Match the words and phrases (1–5) with the definitions (a–e).

d **1** habitat
c **2** wildlife
e **3** make eye contact
b **4** facial expression
a **5** life cycle

a the series of changes that happen to an animal or plant during its life
b the look on someone's face that shows what their thoughts or feelings are
c animals, birds and plants that live in natural conditions
d the type of place that a particular animal usually lives in or a particular plant usually grows in
e situation in which two people look at each other's eyes

Behind the lens:
Anthony Remy, wildlife photographer

You may not know Anthony Remy's name but you will almost certainly have seen one of his photos. He spoke to us about his 30-year career close-up with wildlife.

Where did your interest in wildlife photography come from?
I grew up in Canada with nature right on my doorstep. I just had to step outside and I could see all manner of mammals, reptiles, birds and amphibians. One day my older cousin, Julian, took me to see a
Ex B Q1 grizzly fishing with her cub … from a safe distance, of course. Julian passed me his camera so that I could zoom in. It was great to watch
Ex C Q1 them so closely, I never wanted to forget it. I pressed the shutter and that's when I decided what I wanted to do for the rest of my life.

Is it easy to find work? I imagine it's fairly difficult.
It is at first when no one knows your name and you don't have any contacts at magazines. Over time your reputation grows. You ask local stores to put up framed photos or sell some of your cards … you know, anything to make a living!

I guess you're asked this a lot but what's your favorite animal?
Well … I love dogs … I have four at home. In terms of
Ex B Q2 photography though orangutans without a doubt.
Ex C Q2 Their name literally means 'person of the forest' in Malay and you can see why. It's not just their body language and facial expressions that are so like ours, but also their social interactions. Over my career I've also taken a lot of photos
Ex B Q2 of spiders, which you may not
Ex C Q3 understand! But most people come to realize, like me, that up close they are unexpectedly fascinating.

And which animal don't you enjoy taking photos of?
Well some animals are so 'seen' there are hundreds of Ex C Q4
Ex B photographs of them … you know, elephants, eagles, tigers.
Q3 It isn't easy to take something amazing that everyone would be interested in. Certain types of monkeys are challenging Ex B Q3
too as they don't want to make eye contact with people. Ex C Q5
Then there are lemurs which will look you in the eye, in Ex B Q3
fact they'll climb all over you, but they live deep in the Madagascan rainforest. Habitats like that are hard to get to, especially carrying camera equipment.

So any top tips for future wildlife photographers out there?
Don't rush out and spend a fortune on a new camera. It Ex C Q6
really isn't the most important thing. An interest in animals is obvious but essential. Unless you are incredibly lucky, be prepared for uncomfortable hours or even weeks waiting for the perfect shot. Researching habitats and life cycles can
Ex B certainly help this. If you watch an animal for long enough,
Q4 you can predict its behavior. For example, I always know when a grizzly will swipe for the salmon and so I am there ready to capture the moment.

Glossary
body language (n) the movements or positions of your body that show others what you are thinking or feeling
close-up (n) a picture of someone or something taken from a position very near them
make a living (phrase) to earn money from a job

11.2 Animal images

LEAD-IN

With books closed, arrange students in pairs and ask them to take turns describing an animal to their partner. Their partner should guess what animal they are describing.

VOCABULARY

A Arrange students in pairs. Tell them they have one minute to list all the animals they know. When the time is up, ask the pair with the longest list to share it with the rest of the class. Ask the other pairs to add any other animals which weren't mentioned.

B Direct students to the **Vocabulary Hub** (TB121). Use the **Vocabulary Worksheet** on W62 for extra practice.

C Students write down their three favorite animals. Arrange students in pairs. They tell their partner what animals they chose and why. Monitor and assist when necessary.

D Direct the pairs to the **Communication Hub** (TB121). Students discuss the information with their partner and decide whether they agree with what is written. Encourage them to model their exchanges on the example. Take feedback from one or two pairs and encourage students to respond to each other's ideas.

READING

A In pairs, students match the words and phrases with their definitions. Share answers as a class.

GRAMMAR HUB

11.1 The passive voice (simple present and simple past)

A Correct the mistakes in each sentence.

1 The volcano ^is located in the middle of a jungle.
2 The cliffs were ~~form~~ formed 200 million years ago.
3 The museum ^was opened by the President last night.
4 The mountain is ~~make~~ made of a strong type of rock.
5 The city ~~doesn't~~ isn't known for its art.
6 The new park wasn't ~~open~~ opened by anyone famous.
7 She ^was attracted to Africa because of the wildlife.

B Complete the text messages with the correct passive form of the verbs in parentheses.

Gloria: How was your trip to Uluru?

Toby: Great! I learned a lot. I (**1**) __was helped__ (*help*) by all the tourist information there.

Gloria: Like what?

Toby: Well, it (**2**) __is made__ (*make*) of sandstone and it's nearly 350m high.

Gloria: Cool. What else did you learn?

Toby: It (**3**) __was created__ (*create*) over 600 million years ago.

Gloria: Wow, that's really old!

Toby: I know! Also, it (**4**) __is owned__ (*own*) by the native Australian people.

Gloria: I thought the government owned it.

Toby: It's (**5**) __not owned__ (*not own*) by them. They just manage it.

➤ Go back to page 103.

TEACHING IDEA by David Seymour and Maria Popova

Speaking: Animal characteristics

In pairs, match each animal with the adjective which is traditionally used to describe them. (Re-order the adjectives when you write them up on the board; they appear here in the correct order.)

- owl, fox, mouse, monkey, lion, wise, clever, small, cheeky, proud
- dog, bat, ox, donkey, dinosaur, loyal, blind, strong, stubborn, extinct
- pig, cat, fish, greedy, independent, slippery

Think of animals that these adjectives could describe:

lazy, thoughtful, selfish, kind, sensible, sensitive, cold, cheerful, impatient, hard-working, easy-going, stylish, reserved, antisocial, moody

Think of another adjective to describe each animal and explain why you chose it.

TEACHING IDEA by David Seymour and Maria Popova

Vocabulary: Animal extremes

Write the following superlatives on the board:

the biggest, the most beautiful, the most dangerous, the fastest, the slowest, the most unusual, the cuddliest, the ugliest, the smelliest, the friendliest

Arrange students in pairs and ask them to agree on an animal to fit each of the descriptions. When students have finished, ask them to compare their ideas with another pair and see how many answers they agree on.

TEACHING IDEA by David Seymour and Maria Popova

Speaking: My hobby

Write on the board:

a) What is your hobby? b) What inspired you to start this hobby? c) How have you improved or changed the way you do your hobby since you started?

In small groups, students tell their group about one of their hobbies. Allow students time to prepare their ideas before speaking.

Following their discussion, ask students to create a poster that will encourage other students to take up their hobby.

11.2 Animal images

B Focus students on the questions and the glossary. Tell them to underline the key words that will help them find the answers. Students scan the article and answer the questions on their own. Set a time limit which ensures students only have time to scan for the answers. Check answers with the class.

C Ask students to read the article again, in more detail, to answer Questions 1–6. Allow students to check their answers in pairs before checking with the whole class.

D Arrange students in pairs. Ask them to discuss the skills, qualities and characteristics needed to be a wildlife photographer. Monitor and assist when necessary. Take feedback from one or two pairs and encourage students to respond to each other's ideas.

GRAMMAR

A Focus students on the task and the grammar box. With a stronger group, ask students to complete the sentences from memory, and then to check them against the text in pairs. With a weaker group, arrange students in pairs and allow them to go back to the text to find and complete the sentences. When students have completed the sentences, ask them to complete the rule in the grammar box. Check with the whole class.

B Direct students to the **Grammar Hub** (see below). Use the **Grammar Worksheet** on W61 for extra practice.

C Direct students to the **Communication Hub**. Students work in pairs talking about hobbies and using adjective + infinitive. Monitor and assist when necessary.

PRONUNCIATION

11.5 **A** Focus students on the pronunciation of *to*. Remind them of the schwa and when it is used in English. Play the audio.

11.5 **B** Play the audio again. Students listen and repeat, paying close attention to their pronunciation of *to*.

SPEAKING

A Students read the tips for taking photographs of animals on their own. In pairs, they decide whether they agree and add a tip of their own. Take feedback from one or two pairs and encourage students to react to their ideas.

B Ask students to look at the pictures and answer the questions. Remind them to use the tips from Exercise A to help them make their choices. Students rank the pictures in order of their preferences. Encourage them to write notes about their reasons for ranking the pictures in that order.

C Arrange students in groups of four or five. Students compare their ideas from Exercise B. Monitor and assist as required. Students vote on the best photographs as a group. Take feedback from each group and encourage students to respond to each other's ideas.

GRAMMAR HUB

11.2 Adjective + infinitive

- When we want to use an adjective to describe an action, we can use adjective + infinitive.

  *It's **interesting to study** the life cycle of a mammal.*
  *It was **nice to watch** animals in their natural habitat.*

- When we want to say that an adjective doesn't describe an action, we use the negative form of the verb.

  *It **wasn't** easy to make a living as a scientist.*

- When we want to say that an adjective describes the opposite of an action, we use *not* + infinitive.

  *It's important **not to do** any damage to the environment.*

11.2 Adjective + infinitive

A Put the words in order to make sentences.

1 easy / understand / a person's / it's / to / body language
It's easy to understand a person's body language.

2 necessary / be / it's / quiet / to / near / wild animals
It's necessary to be quiet near wild animals.

3 fascinating / take / was / photos of insects / to / it
It was fascinating to take photos of insects.

4 good / live / green / a / it's / to / lifestyle
It's good to live a green lifestyle.

5 to / is / educational / it / wildlife shows / watch / ?
Is it educational to watch wildlife shows?

B Choose the correct option.

1 It's ***good not*** / ***not good*** to feed the animals in the zoo.
2 It's ***important not*** / ***not important*** to make wild animals angry or upset.
3 It's ***not easy*** / ***easy not*** to take the perfect photo.
4 It's ***necessary not*** / ***not necessary*** to be an expert to enjoy studying animals.
5 It's ***not essential*** / ***essential not*** to go near crocodiles.
6 It's ***not safe*** / ***safe not*** to go traveling in the wild on your own.
7 It's ***essential not*** / ***not essential*** to have top quality equipment in order to take great photos.

➤ Go back to page 105.

B SCAN Read *Behind the lens* and answer the questions.

Which animal(s) …

1 did Anthony Remy first take pictures of? grizzly bears

2 is/are his favorite to photograph? orangutans, spiders

3 is/are difficult to get a good picture of? elephants, eagles, tigers, monkeys, lemurs

4 does he think has/have predictable behavior? grizzly bears

C READ FOR DETAIL Choose the correct answers, a, b or c.

1 Anthony Remy started taking pictures of bears …
   a to show his cousin what he had seen.
   b to help him remember them (circled)
   c to capture the beauty of where he is from.

2 He thinks orangutans are …
   a shy.
   b dangerous.
   c similar to humans (circled)

3 He thinks his pictures of spiders usually …
   a surprise people. (circled)
   b frighten people.
   c disappoint people.

4 He thinks some animals, such as elephants …
   a are not interesting to photograph.
   b don't do anything surprising.
   c have been photographed too much. (circled)

5 He says monkeys …
   a don't like to look at humans. (circled)
   b try to hide from humans.
   c behave like humans.

6 In Anthony's opinion, it is <u>not</u> necessary …
   a to know about the animals you are photographing.
   b to spend time watching and have a lot of patience.
   c to have a lot of expensive camera equipment. (circled)

D SPEAK Work in pairs. Discuss the skills and characteristics you need to be a wildlife photographer.

GRAMMAR

Adjective + infinitive

A WORK IT OUT Look at the sentences from *Behind the lens*. Add the missing adjective + infinitive. Then complete the rule.

1 It was ____great to watch____ them so closely …

2 It isn't ____easy to take____ something amazing that everyone would be interested in.

3 Habitats like that are ____hard to get____ to, especially carrying camera equipment.

Adjective + infinitive

When a verb comes after an adjective, we use the ____infinitive____ form of the verb.

B Go to the **Grammar Hub** on **page 142**.

C SPEAK Go to the **Communication Hub** on **page 153** and follow the instructions.

PRONUNCIATION

to /tə/

A Listen to the weak pronunciation of *to* /tə/ in the sentences. 11.5

1 It's easy to take a good picture.

2 It's important to be patient.

3 Are you ready to leave?

B Listen again and repeat the sentences. 11.5

SPEAKING

A Read the tips about what makes a good animal picture. Do you agree? Add a tip of your own.

- ✓ It's important to show the animal in its natural habitat.
- ✓ It's important to be able to see the animal's face and eyes. It gives an idea of how the animal is feeling or what it's thinking.
- ✓ It's good to photograph the animal doing something. It's even better to catch it doing something unusual or maybe something funny.
- ✓ A good animal picture shows detail and color that you don't normally see.
- ✓ A good picture is one where you see something new. You learn something about the animal.

B Look at the pictures (a–f) above and answer the questions.

- Which of the features in the tips above does each picture have?
- Choose the best animal picture in your opinion.
- Put the others in order of second favorite, third favorite.

C Work in groups. Compare your ideas. In your group, decide on the best animal picture.

Read and talk about wildlife photography

11.3 Throw-away world

Talk about the causes and effects of plastic pollution

P /l/ pronounced and silent **G** *even* **V** *somewhere, nowhere, everywhere, anywhere*
S looking for ways of expressing cause and effect

READING

A Work in pairs. Discuss the questions.

1 Do you recycle? What kind of things do you recycle? Is it easy to recycle things where you live? What happens to things you throw away that are not recycled?

2 Look at the picture. What can you see on the beach? How do you think it got there?

B READ FOR GIST Read *The nightmare of Plastic Island* and decide which is the best summary.

a Plastic is usually blown into the ocean and is carried around the world by ocean currents. The pictures of Henderson Island show how we should clean the beaches before the plastic enters the ocean.

b Plastic is carried to certain parts of the world by ocean currents, but it does not reach other parts of the world. The pictures of Henderson Island suggest that the situation is worse than it actually is.

c Plastic is carried around the world by ocean currents and reaches the most remote beaches and other places. The pictures of Henderson Island show how serious the problem is.

C READ FOR DETAIL Answer the questions. Use the information in the box to help you. Then read again and check your answers.

Looking for ways of expressing cause and effect

Look for verbs, linking words and nouns that express cause and effect:

- **verbs:** *This **means** there are … This has **led** to …*
- **linking words:** *This is **because** … **Because of** this, … **If** we do this, …*
- **nouns:** *And as a **result**, …*

1 Why is there plastic everywhere?

2 Why was plastic successful when it first appeared?

3 Scientists believe that there are five trillion pieces of plastic in the oceans. What is this number based on?

4 Some marine animals eat plastic. How can this affect humans?

5 Experts believe plastic pollution in the oceans is a serious problem. How have some governments responded to this?

6 What can individuals do to help reduce the amount of plastic pollution?

The nightmare of PLASTIC ISLAND

Plastic is everywhere. It is at the bottom of the oceans, on tropical beaches and at the top of Mount Everest. It is even on the surface of Mars. This is because each year, over 300 million metric tons of plastic is produced, used and then most of it is thrown away. Ex C Q1

Plastic was invented over 100 years ago. When it first appeared, it was an instant success. It was cheap, convenient, had many uses and was long-lasting. And that is the problem. Plastic will not go away. It may break into smaller and smaller pieces, but every piece of plastic ever made still exists somewhere in the world. Ex C Q2

Up to 12 million metric tons of plastic enters the world's oceans every year. This means there are around five trillion pieces of plastic currently in our oceans. Once there, it can be carried by the currents for many years and travel thousands of kilometers. Some of it is eaten by marine wildlife and enters the food chain. As a result, thousands of pieces of marine plastic are consumed by humans each year when they eat fish and other seafood. However, most of the plastic in the seas and oceans eventually washes up on beaches. Nowhere on Earth has as much plastic as the beaches of Henderson Island in the South Pacific. The remote island is the most polluted anywhere in the world, and 99.8 percent of this pollution is plastic. The island's beaches contain around 38 million pieces of plastic; most of this is from everyday consumer goods. (Ex C Q3, Ex C Q4)

Henderson Island is a UNESCO World Heritage site and it is an important habitat for wildlife. Jennifer Lavers, of the University of Tasmania, says that the situation on Henderson Island shows that 'nowhere is safe from plastic pollution'. She even believes that marine plastic pollution is 'as important as climate change'. Other experts describe the situation as 'a major ecological disaster' and 'an environmental emergency'.

Because of this, there is a global effort to reduce the amount of plastic pollution. For example, Indonesia has promised to spend up to $1 billion on reducing plastic and other waste products which pollute its waters. This has led to other governments making similar pledges. Ex C Q5

However, the best way to prevent trash from washing up on beaches would be for us as individuals to use less plastic, especially things that we don't even need. These are single-use and 'disposable' items, such as cutlery and even toothbrushes. We should also buy products with less packaging and recycle more. If we do this, we will reduce the amount of plastic that ends up in our oceans and on our beaches. We will also be less likely to find plastic returning to us on our dinner plates. Ex C Q6

Glossary

consumer goods (n) things you buy for personal or home use, such as food and clothing
current (n) a strong movement of water in one direction
marine (adj) living or happening in the ocean
remote (adj) far away from other cities, towns or people

11.3 Throw-away world

LEAD-IN

With books closed, students work in small groups to discuss and come up with the three biggest problems that our planet is facing. Take feedback from each group and encourage students to respond to each other's ideas.

READING

A Arrange students in pairs. Ask them to discuss Questions 1 and 2 with their partner. Monitor and assist when necessary. Take feedback from one or two pairs and encourage students to respond to each other's ideas.

B Remind students that when we read for gist we read quickly to try to get a general idea of the text. Students read the article quickly on their own. Focus students on the summaries. Tell them to underline the key words to help them decide which is the best summary for the article.

C Focus students on the box and the questions. Students read the article again and underline the verbs, linking words and nouns that will help them find the answers. Check answers with the class.

TEACHING IDEA by David Seymour and Maria Popova

Speaking: Green manifesto

Ask students to think again about the main threats facing our environment. How can they be avoided? Arrange students in pairs and ask them to discuss the questions below, comparing their experience of different countries.

What are the most well-known ecological threats?

Are people environmentally conscious?

Is there a Green Party?

How is trash dealt with?

What recycling facilities are there?

In groups, ask students to write a Green Party manifesto, giving proposals for an environmentally friendly lifestyle.

TEACHING IDEA by David Seymour and Maria Popova

Speaking: Public consultation meeting

Explain the following to students:

A paper factory is planned for your town, which is very beautiful but high in unemployment. There are concerns from the local community about pollution and the destruction of an ancient forest nearby.

In groups of eight, students are going to role-play a public consultation meeting to listen to local views. Allocate the roles below. If the class does not divide into groups of eight, drop one or two of the roles.

In favor of the factory: the mayor, a representative of the paper company, the building contractor, an unemployed person.

Against the factory: a member of the Green Party, an environmental scientist, a local craftsman, a local hotel owner.

Before the meeting, arrange all the students with the same role together and ask them to discuss their arguments, considering pollution, visual impact, tourism, jobs and effects on other businesses. Role-play the meeting.

METHODOLOGY HUB by Jim Scrivener

Deciding on your role while students do an activity

Let's distinguish two steps.

Step 1: The first 30 seconds: are they doing the task?

Immediately after you have given the instructions for a task and students start doing it, there is often an immediate need to check to make sure that students are doing the activity that you asked them to do and have understood the basic mechanics of the activity.

You could do this by quietly and relatively inconspicuously wandering around the room, listening briefly to parts of the discussion from many groups and assuring yourself that students are doing what they are supposed to. We could call this 'monitoring to check the mechanics'.

Step 2: The task itself

In many activities, the prime goal is for learners to get a chance to work on their own, speaking fluently and trying out things without too much interference and correction. If they are doing the task correctly, then possibly they don't need you once the task is under way. Your presence might actually be an interference. If you are around and very visible, they might look to you for language items and help whenever they hit a problem, whereas it might be more useful for them to struggle a little and learn to make use of their own resources. So once an activity is safely under way, your options often boil down to the following choices: monitor discreetly or vanish.

METHODOLOGY HUB by Jim Scrivener

Fluency, accuracy and communication

Imagine a switch inside your head – it swings between two settings: 'working mainly on accuracy' and 'working mainly on fluency'.

It's probably a huge simplification, but I suspect that something like this is at work in my head through most of my language teaching, changing its setting from activity to activity, stage to stage – and, in some teaching, changing moment by moment in response to things happening in class. And I think initially getting that switch installed and working may be a key skill for anyone learning to be a language teacher.

Certainly there are activities in which you are arguably working on both accuracy and fluency in relatively equal measure, but many everyday language teaching lesson stages are focused on one more than the other, and at any one moment, in any one activity, it is likely you will be focusing on accuracy rather than fluency, or fluency rather than accuracy. The danger of correcting students in the middle of a mainly fluency-based task is that you interrupt their flow and take the focus off their message. Students often find it hard to continue after a correction, while others in class may become more reluctant to speak for fear of similar interruptions.

11.3 Throw-away world

PRONUNCIATION

11.6 **A** Focus students on the /l/ sound. Write on the board *plastic, should,* and *pollution* and model the pronunciation. Play the audio. Students listen to the words and decide whether the /l/ sound is pronounced in each word. Take feedback from students but do not confirm or correct their answers at this time.

11.7 **B** Arrange students in pairs and ask them to put the words from Exercise A into the correct columns. Play the audio again for students to check their answers.

C Keep students in their pairs and ask them to discuss why the letter *l* is pronounced in some words but not in others. Take feedback from one or two pairs and encourage students to respond to each other's ideas.

The letter 'l' is usually not pronounced when it follows the vowels 'a', 'o' or 'u'.

GRAMMAR

A Focus students on the sentences and the information about *even* in the grammar box. Pairs work together to complete the rules. Check answers with the class.

B Direct students to the **Grammar Hub** (see below). Use the **Grammar Worksheet** on W63 for extra practice.

C Model the activity. Say *I was hiking with some friends in the Pyrenees when we decided to start counting plastic bottles left by other climbers. We counted 110 plastic bottles along the most frequented paths. Hikers hadn't even bothered to carry their bottles back to throw them into the trash cans along the paths*. Brainstorm possible situations. In groups of three or four, students tell each other three things that they think are surprising. Encourage students to use *even* and *don't even* in their answers. Monitor and assist when necessary. Take feedback from each group and encourage students to respond to each other's ideas.

VOCABULARY

A Write the suffix *-where* on the board and elicit words that can take this suffix (*some, every, no, any*). Elicit the meaning of the new words. Students complete Sentences 1–5. Ask students to scan the article and check their answers. Ask for a show of hands to see how many had correct answers.

B Students complete Sentences 1–4 with *somewhere, nowhere, everywhere* and *anywhere*. Allow students to compare their answers in pairs before checking as a class.

C Ask students to rewrite the sentences from Exercise B using their own ideas. In pairs, students discuss their sentences and ask each other follow-up questions to learn more about their partner's ideas. Monitor and assist as required. Take feedback from one or two pairs and encourage students to respond to each other's ideas.

SPEAKING HUB

A Focus students on the *Plastic Challenge*. They read the paragraph and discuss how realistic the challenge may be. Ask students to provide pros and cons of the challenge.

B Ask students to read Questions 1 and 2 and write notes on their answers. Monitor and assist when necessary.

C Arrange students in groups of four or five. Students discuss their lists and ideas about the *Plastic Challenge* as a group. They then decide on a plan for doing the *Plastic Challenge*. Explain that they must all agree to do the same things. Monitor and assist when necessary. Take feedback from each group and encourage students to respond to each other's ideas.

GRAMMAR HUB

11.3 *even*

- We use *even* as an adverb to suggest that something is surprising.

  Recycling is not difficult – there is ***even*** *a recycling bin at the office.*

  You don't ***even*** *have to leave your room to find things made of plastic.*

  She doesn't ***even*** *know where the Pacific Ocean is!*

- We use *even* before main verbs and after auxiliary verbs and modals.

  We ***even found*** *plastic waste on Mount Everest.*

  NOT ~~We found even plastic waste on Mount Everest.~~

  Plastic ***can even*** *be found on Mars NOT ~~Plastic even can be found on Mars.~~*

- We can also use *even* before nouns.

  Even *experts make mistakes sometimes.*

11.3 *even*

A Choose the correct place to put *even*, A or B.

1. Most (A) people haven't (B) thought about it before.
2. (A) some experts are surprised (B) that the problem is so serious.
3. A lot of people (A) don't (B) realize that plastic lasts so long.
4. There (A) is (B) a place to recycle glass on my street.
5. You (A) can't (B) walk 100 meters without seeing some plastic that has been thrown away.

B Put *even* in the correct place in each sentence.

1. A lot of people don't ^even notice the pollution.
2. ^Even the base camp for Mount Aconcagua is very high.
3. There are many solutions – we can ^even stop using plastic.
4. There are a lot of organizations in my town – there's ^even a bird-watchers' club.
5. I love all animals, and I ^even like spiders.
6. I know some adults who don't ^even know the difference between a lion and a tiger.

➤ Go back to page 107.

PRONUNCIATION
/l/ pronounced and silent

11.6 **A** Listen to the words. Is the letter *l* pronounced in each word? No.

1 plastic yes 3 smaller yes 5 calm no 7 should no
2 travel yes 4 would no 6 climate yes 8 folk no

11.7 **B** Work in pairs. Write the words in the correct place. Listen and check.

l is pronounced	*l* is not pronounced
plastic	would
travel	calm
smaller	should
climate	folk

C SPEAK Work in pairs. Why is the letter *l* pronounced in some words and not in others?

GRAMMAR
even

A WORK IT OUT Look at the phrases from *The nightmare of Plastic Island*. Then choose the correct words to complete the rules.

It is even on the surface of Mars.

She even believes that marine plastic pollution is 'as important as climate change.'

… especially things that we don't even need.

These are single-use and 'disposable' items, such as cutlery and even toothbrushes.

even

1 We use *even* to suggest that something is ***surprising*** / ***obvious***.
2 We use *even* ***before*** / ***after*** verbs, but ***before*** / ***after*** auxiliary verbs (*be, have, can, don't*).
3 We ***can*** / ***cannot*** use *even* before nouns.

B Go to the **Grammar Hub** on **page 142**.

C SPEAK Work in groups. Tell your group three things that you think are surprising. You can talk about natural wonders, animals or pollution. Use *even* and *don't even*.

VOCABULARY
somewhere, nowhere, everywhere, anywhere

A Complete the sentences from *The nightmare of Plastic Island* with *somewhere, nowhere, everywhere* or *anywhere*. Then read again and check your answers.

1 Plastic is everywhere.
2 Every piece of plastic ever made still exists somewhere in the world.
3 Nowhere on Earth has as much plastic as the beaches of Henderson Island.
4 The remote island is the most polluted anywhere in the world.
5 Jennifer Lavers says that 'nowhere is safe from plastic pollution'.

B Complete the sentences with *somewhere, nowhere, everywhere* or *anywhere*.

1 I'd like to live by the ocean – ideally, somewhere near a big sandy beach and without too many people.
2 There is nowhere like India. It's unique. There's a lot of pollution and poverty, but it's an amazing place. Everywhere you go, you see something incredible.
3 If I could visit anywhere in the world, I'd go to California. I've always wanted to go there. If not California, I'd like to go somewhere similar with big cities, lots of beaches and warm weather.
4 I was very impressed by Singapore. Everywhere was so clean. There was no trash anywhere.

C SPEAK Rewrite the sentences in Exercise B using your own ideas. Then work in pairs and share your ideas. Ask questions to find out more information.

I'd like to live in a town – ideally, somewhere with a few stores and surrounded by nice countryside.

SPEAKING HUB

A You are going to do the Plastic Challenge. Read about the Plastic Challenge, which is organized by the Marine Conservation Society.

The Plastic Challenge asks people to stop using plastic items for as long as they can. This could be for a day, a week or a month. Our message is 'reduce, reuse, recycle'. We're challenging people to give up their single-use plastics, such as prepackaged sandwiches, prepackaged meals, bottled drinks and so on. Do the Plastic Challenge and you'll never look at your grocery shopping in the same way again!

B PLAN Spend a few minutes thinking about the following.

1 Make a list of all the plastic you have used …
  a today.
  b in the last week.
  c How much of this was single-use items?
2 Imagine you are going to do the Plastic Challenge.
  a Which items would be easier to stop using and which would be more difficult?
  b What changes would you need to make in your daily life to do the challenge?
  c How long do you think you could do the challenge for?

C DISCUSS Work in groups.

1 Compare and discuss your lists and your ideas about the Plastic Challenge.
2 Decide on a plan for doing the Plastic Challenge. You must agree to do the same things.

Talk about the causes and effects of plastic pollution

Café Hub

11.4 Power cut

F – tell a story   P – showing interest

COMPREHENSION

A ▶ **00:00–03:33 Watch the first part of the video and answer the questions.**

1 What is a 'power cut'? What is the American English word for this? When all the lights go out and there is no power. The American English word for *power cut* is *power outage* or *power out*.

2 What kind of story does Sam tell Neena and Gaby? A story about a time he was scared when the power went out.

3 How do Neena and Gaby feel as Sam tells the story? More and more frightened.

4 How do you think Sam's story ends?

B ▶ **03:33–04:29 Watch the second part of the video. Compare the end of Sam's story with your ideas in Exercise A. Is it a good story?**

C ▶ **Work in pairs. Put the events of Sam's story in the correct order (1–10). Then watch the video again and check your answers.**

a After that, I tried to switch the lights on, but there was no power. 7

b I wasn't alone. 10

c It was stormy. Very stormy. 2

d I arrived back at my uncle's house, got out of the car and walked up to the front door. 3

e So anyway, I went inside and called out to see if my uncle was home. 'Uncle Mike' I shouted – there was no answer. 5

f It all started on a stormy night when I was in Cornwall staying with my uncle. 1

g I walked into the kitchen and sat down in the dark. My uncle was missing – I was scared. 8

h I pushed the door and the wind blew it open. 4

i In the end, I sat there alone in the dark. 9

j Then the front door slammed shut behind me. 6

D Match Sam's sentences (1–5) with the replies (a–e).

1 This reminds me of a very scary experience I once had. — d

2 It all started on a stormy night when I was in Cornwall staying with my uncle. — a

3 Can I continue my story now? — e

4 I was scared. — b

5 My phone was dead. — c

a Where is Cornwall?

b You poor thing!

c How awful!

d So, tell us. What happened?

e Sure. Go on.

MILLY

SAM

NEENA

ZAC

GABY

FUNCTIONAL LANGUAGE

Tell a story

A Look at the underlined words in Comprehension Exercises C and D. Complete the box with one of the words.

Tell a story and listen to a story
Give background information
It was [1] stormy */windy/raining.*   *The sun was shining and it was hot.*
Use linking phrases
Beginning: *At first … / To start with … / It all* [2] started …
Middle: *Then … / After* [3] that … / *So* [4] anyway, …
End: *In the* [5] end, …
Say how you felt
I was excited/surprised/worried/relieved/frightened/ [6] scared.
Keep the story going
Go on. / So, [7] tell us. *(Then) What happened?*
Respond to dramatic events
You [8] poor */lucky thing.*   *How* [9] awful */frightening/funny.*   *That's terrible/awful/funny.*

B SPEAK Work in pairs. You are going to practice responding to events.

1 Look at the responses in the box. Choose three responses you want your partner to give. Circle them.

> How awful/frightening/funny. That's terrible/awful/funny. You poor/lucky thing.

2 Write down three things you could tell your partner to get him/her to give those responses.

3 Tell your partner your ideas. How does he/she respond?

Student A wants Student B to say 'You lucky thing'.

A: I found $5 in the street this morning.
B: You lucky thing!

Glossary

power cut **(n) (British)** = power outage **(n) (American)**
torch **(n) (British)** = flashlight **(n) (American)**

PRONUNCIATION

Showing interest

11.8 **A** Listen and write how the responses sound in the correct place.

Very interested	Not very interested
That's awful. That's terrible. You poor thing.	You lucky thing. How frightening. How interesting.

11.8 **B** Listen again and repeat the responses.

C SPEAK Work in pairs. Practice saying the responses. Listen to your partner and say whether he/she sounds very interested or not very interested.

SPEAKING

A Work in pairs. You are going to tell your partner a story. Choose one of the topics or use your own ideas. Include background information, linking phrases and say how you felt.

A time when … you got lost / you lost your keys / you met an old friend / you won a prize / something happened on vacation.

B Tell each other your stories and react and respond appropriately.

A: I lost some car keys once.
B: That's awful!
A: I was on vacation with the family in Menorca …
B: Where is Menorca?

Tell a story

➤ Turn to **page 168** to learn how to write an email giving suggestions and advice.

COMPREHENSION

A ▶ 00:00–03:33 Students look at the images and guess what is happening (*there has been a power cut*, or *power outage*). Play the first part of the video for students to answer the questions. Play the section again. Students check their answers before checking with the class. Elicit answers to Question 4, but do not correct or confirm their ideas.

B ▶ 03:33–04:29 Play the second part of the video. Elicit similarities and differences. Ask the class whether Sam's story was good.

C ▶ Students put the events of Sam's story in order in pairs. Play the complete video for students to check their answers.

D Allow students to compare their answers in pairs before checking with the whole class.

FUNCTIONAL LANGUAGE

A Students look back at Comprehension Exercises C and D and complete the phrases in the box with the underlined words.

B Focus students' attention on the activity and the differences between American and British English. Explain that both forms are correct and they can use either when speaking.

PRONUNCIATION

11.8 **A** Play the audio. Students write the responses in the correct columns. Check answers with the class.

11.8 **B** Play the audio again for students to listen and repeat.

C Students practice saying the responses in pairs.

SPEAKING

A Give students time to work on their story.

B Model the example with a stronger student. Students work in pairs telling each other their stories and responding appropriately. Take feedback from one or two pairs and encourage students to respond to each other's intonation.

▶ VIDEO SCRIPT

Café Hub 11.4 Power cut

G = Gabby S = Sam N = Neena Z = Zac

G: Did I win? I'm pretty sure I won.
S: The whole street is dark. No lights. I think it's a power cut!
N: Maybe it's the storm?
S: Brrr… This reminds me of a very scary experience I once had.
N: So tell us… What happened?
S: It all started on a stormy night when I was in Cornwall staying with my uncle.
G: Where is Cornwall?
S: Cornwall's in the South-West of England. It's known for its storms. Can I continue my story now?
G: Sure, go on.
S: So as I was saying, it was stormy. Very stormy. I arrived back at my uncle's house, got out of the car and walked up to the front door. It was so windy…
G: Then what happened?
S: Well, the house was covered in leaves and branches. I pushed the door and the wind blew it open.
G: Woah! What was that?
N: I think it was my bedroom door, it does that sometimes…
S: So anyway, I went inside and I called out to see if my uncle was home. 'UNCLE MIKE', I shouted. There was no answer. Then the door slammed shut behind me. After that, I tried to switch the lights on, but there was no power.
N: Where was your uncle?
S: Good question… It was very dark as I slowly walked down the hallway. It was so windy outside that the whole house was shaking. There was a loud crack of thunder.
G: So go on?
S: I walked into the kitchen and sat down in the dark. My uncle was missing. I was scared.
G: You poor thing!
N: Yeah that's terrible!
G: Why didn't you use a torch?
S: I didn't have one, and my phone was dead.
G: How awful!
N: So what happened?
S: Well… In the end, I sat there, and I waited. Alone in the dark. Except… I wasn't alone…
Z: Whoa! Take it easy – it's me!
S: Are you okay Neena?
N: Yes. Of course. I'm fine. I'm absolutely fine.
G: Sam! Finish the story! Who was there?
S: Oh, just my uncle, he was upstairs, trying to fix the power…
N: What? Is that it? Is that the story?
S: Er, yeah that's it. OK! Who wants to play another game?
Z: I'm in!
N: Why not…
G: Perfect. I can win again! Did I win? I'm pretty sure I won.

TEACHING IDEA by David Seymour and Maria Popova

Speaking: Storyboard

Explain that you will tell a story without speaking: you will only draw on the board and mime, and students will have to guess each line of the story. When they get a correct sentence, you'll nod and they will write it down.

It was a beautiful morning. The sun was shining and the birds were singing. I got up early, had breakfast and took the dog for a walk along the beach. After an hour or so, it got cloudy and the wind started blowing. I turned for home but got caught in a heavy downpour. Then the thunder and lightning started. The ocean waves got higher and higher…

Arrange students in small groups and ask them to continue the story, e.g. *The storm got a lot worse.*

Speaking: Story words

In small groups, students select 20 recently learned items of vocabulary and write them on a large piece of paper. Ask groups to swap their lists. Each group puts the list of words that they received in the middle and group members take turns using the words in a story, adding one line each. Encourage students to use the useful phrases from this lesson.

11 Writing

Write an email giving suggestions and advice

W– making suggestions and giving advice

A Look at the places in the pictures. Where do you think they are? Read the emails quickly and match them with the pictures. Were your ideas correct?

1 b. Halong Bay, Vietnam

2 c. Lindisfarne, Northumberland, the UK

3 a. Joshua Tree National Park, California

a
To: Sam
Subject: RE: Any advice?

You really must visit the Joshua Tree National Park when you're in California. It isn't far from Los Angeles and it's really easy to get to by car. It's named after the famous Joshua trees that are found there. It's an amazing desert landscape with huge rocks and boulders everywhere. If I were you, I'd spend at least two days there. You can camp there, but it's a good idea to book in advance.

b
To: Carlos
Subject: RE: Vietnam tips

In Vietnam, Halong Bay is a must. There are thousands of different-sized islands and rock formations coming out of the ocean. It really is an incredible place. According to legend, the bay was formed when an angry dragon destroyed a mountain with its tail. It isn't too far from Hanoi. I'd recommend taking an organized tour from there.

c
To: Teresa
Subject: RE: Where to go

If you're in northern England, you really should visit the island of Lindisfarne. It's about a mile from the mainland and you can drive across to it when the tide is out. But when the tide comes in, it becomes a true island. It's a magical place with some beautiful beaches. I suggest you head to the north part of the island to get away from the crowds of people. Make sure you check the times of the tides so you know when it's safe to cross.

B Read again and complete the table.

	a	b	c
Name of place			
Location			
Key features			
How to travel there			

C Complete the box with words from the emails.

Making suggestions and giving advice

When/If you're in …
I suggest you …
I'd [1] recommend + verb + -ing …
You (really) [2] should / ought to / must …
If I [3] were *you, I* [4] 'd …
… is a must.
Make [5] sure *you …*
It's a good [6] idea *to …*

D Write the words in the correct order to make sentences.

1 It's / to / a / book the train in advance / idea / good
2 I / in April or May / suggest / go / you
3 I'd / at least two or three days / staying / recommend
4 If / in Krakow, / you're / the Wieliczka Salt Mine / visit / really / you / should
5 When / in Oxford, / you're / make / you / sure / the Natural History Museum / visit
6 If / I'd / you, / were / I / for a few days / rent a car

WRITING

A PLAN Imagine a friend is visiting your country or a country you know. You are going to write a short email (50–100 words) to make some suggestions and to give some advice about a place to visit.

B WRITE Use the Writing skills box and include information about:

- where it is
- how to get there
- the main features of the place

C REVIEW Work in groups. Read each other's emails. Which place would you most like to visit?

168 11 WRITING

Refer students to these emails as models for the writing task.

Answers

1 *It's a good idea to book the train in advance.*
2 *I suggest you go in April or May.*
3 *I'd recommend staying at least two or three days.*
4 *If you're in Krakow, you really should visit the Wieliczka Salt Mine.*
5 *When you're in Oxford, make sure you visit the Natural History Museum.*
6 *If I were you, I'd rent a car for a few days.*

Students can do this in class or for homework.

Answers for B

a: Joshua Tree National Park; California; Joshua trees, desert, landscape, rocks and boulders; by car (from Los Angeles)

b: Halong Bay; Vietnam; different-sized islands and rock formations; by organized tour (from Hanoi)

c: Lindisfarne; north of England; beautiful beaches; by car (when the tide is out)

WRITING

A Point out images 1–3 and elicit ideas from the class on where these places are. Students scan the emails, match them to the pictures and check their answers.

B Students read the emails again and complete the table.

C Focus students on the box. They complete the phrases with words from the emails. With a weaker group, you may want students to do this activity in pairs. Check answers with the class.

D Students rewrite the sentences on their own and compare their answers with a partner. Check answers with the whole class.

WRITING TASK

A Focus students on the activity. Give them time to choose the place they are going to give advice about and write notes.

B Students write their emails. Encourage them to use the writing prompts and useful language box to help them. Monitor and assist when necessary.

C Arrange students in small groups to share their emails. Ask the groups to choose the place they would most like to visit. Take feedback from each group and encourage students to respond to each other's ideas. You can also include a stage of peer correction here. Students exchange and correct each other's emails. If you feel this might be too sensitive you can also take a few representative errors from students' work and board them. Students then correct the errors.

Extra activity
For homework, ask students to research a place they would like to visit. They should imagine that they work for a travel agency and write a short promotional leaflet to encourage people to visit the place they have researched. Students could swap leaflets with their classmates in the next lesson and give feedback on each other's writing.

Unit 11 Review

VOCABULARY

A Complete the sentences using a word from box a and box b.

a Amazon Atlas Death Grand Lascaux Panama ~~Sahara~~ San Francisco

b Bay Canal Canyon Caves ~~Desert~~ Mountains Rainforest Valley

1 The *Sahara Desert* is 9.3 million square kilometers, which is almost the same size as China.
2 The Atlas Mountains stretch for 2,500 km in Morocco, Algeria and Tunisia.
3 The Golden Gate Bridge is 2,737 meters long and crosses the San Francisco Bay.
4 The Grand Canyon is 446 km in length and 29 km across at its widest point.
5 The Amazon Rainforest is 9.3 million square kilometers and is located in nine countries in South America.
6 In 1913, a temperature of 56.7°C was recorded in Death Valley in eastern California.
7 The Panama Canal connects the Atlantic Ocean with the Pacific Ocean.
8 The walls of the Lascaux Caves in southwestern France are decorated with 17,000-year-old paintings of animals, such as cows, horses and deer.

B Find 17 animals and write them in the correct place.

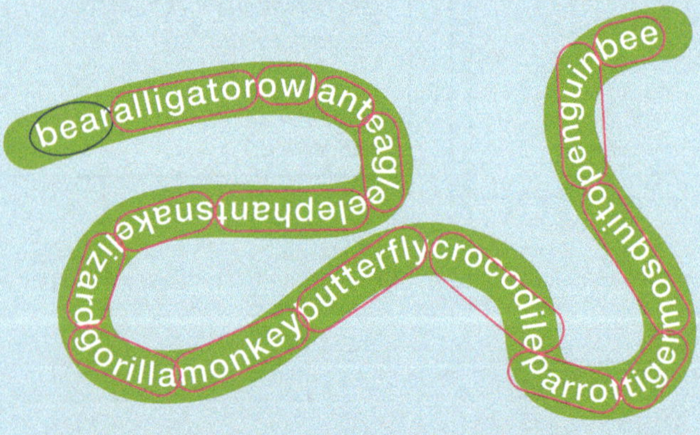

Mammals	Birds	Reptiles	Insects	Fish
bear elephant, gorilla, ~~monkey~~, tiger	owl, eagle, parrot, penguin	alligator, snake, lizard, crocodile	ant, butterfly, mosquito, bee	

C Choose the correct words to complete the sentences.

1 Plastic is ***anywhere*** / ***everywhere***. It has more forms and uses than any other material on the planet.
2 About 30 percent of all the plastic ever made is still in use ***anywhere*** / ***somewhere*** in the world today.
3 Recycling rates of plastic are not the same ***somewhere*** / ***everywhere*** in the world. For example, in Europe about 30 percent is recycled, in China around 25 percent and in the US the figure is just 10 percent.
4 There is almost ***anywhere*** / ***nowhere*** on Earth that does not have plastic pollution.

GRAMMAR

A Complete the text with the correct passive form of the verbs in parentheses. Add *by* where it is needed.

Ayers Rock [1] is located (*locate*) in the Uluru-Kata Tjuta National Park in central Australia. It [2] is also known (*also / know*) as Uluru, which is its original Aboriginal name. The rock [3] was formed (*form*) over 600 million years ago and it [4] was originally located (*originally / locate*) under the ocean. The summit is generally flat but, there are valleys and caves that [5] were created by (*create*) the wind and rain over millions of years.

B Complete the conversations with the words in the box.

easy/use lucky/see necessary/have safe/drink unusual/see

1 **A:** Is your camera easy to use?
B: Yes, it's very easy. Anyone can use it.
2 **A:** It isn't safe to drink the water here.
B: OK, I'll get some bottled water.
3 **A:** It isn't necessary to have expensive equipment to take good pictures.
B: I agree. A creative eye is all you need.
4 **A:** It's unusual to see the northern lights at this time of year.
B: Yes, we were very lucky to see them.

C Rewrite the sentences with the correct form of *even / don't even*.

1 I use plastic bags. (*not even*)
I don't even use plastic bags.
2 Ella does a lot of recycling; she recycles clothes. (*even*)
Ella does a lot of recycling; she even recycles clothes.
3 I never buy plastic. I let my children play with plastic toys. (*not even*)
I never buy plastic. I don't even let my children play with plastic toys.

FUNCTIONAL LANGUAGE

Add the missing words to complete the conversation.

A: It all [1]**s**tarted when we decided to walk along the Samaria Gorge in Crete.
B: [2]**G**o on.
A: Well, Sandy, my friend, didn't want to do it. It's a fairly long and steep walk to get down in the gorge. But she finally agreed to it.
B: So, what [3]**h**appened?
A: After about two hours, Sandy fell over and hurt her leg.
B: Oh, no! [4]**H**ow awful! [5]**P**oor thing!
A: So, [6]**a**nyway, she took some painkillers and decided to go back to the hotel.
B: [7]**T**hen what happened?
A: Well her leg was broken …
B: [8]**T**hat's terrible.
A: Yes, but in the [9]**e**nd, everything was OK.

12 MEDIA

I do not take a single newspaper, nor read one a month, and I feel happier for it.

Thomas Jefferson

A printer works through the night to get out the news on time.

Media (n, pl) radio, television, newspapers, the internet and magazines, considered as a group: can be followed by a singular or plural verb. Synonyms: the media, medium, mass media, multimedia.

Jefferson is suggesting that reading the news and keeping updated is not always a good thing. Paying too close attention to the news can make you feel unhappy.

Thomas Jefferson (1743–1826) was one of the Founding Fathers of the United States of America. He was the main author of the *Declaration of Independence* and served as the third president of the United States from 1801 to 1809. After retiring from public office, Jefferson founded the University of Virginia.

OBJECTIVES

- talk about the pros and cons of online news
- talk and debate about different TV viewing habits
- talk about advertising and what makes a good advertisement
- give and respond to opinions
- write a story

Work with a partner. Discuss the questions.

1 How often do you read the news?
2 Look at the picture. Do you think newspapers will exist in the future?
3 Do you think 24-hour news on TV and the internet is a positive thing? Why/Why not?

MEDIA 111

OBJECTIVES

Read the unit objectives to the class.

UNIT OPENER QUESTIONS

Encourage students to look at the quote and take one or two suggestions from the class about what they think it means.

Ask students to look at the picture on the page and encourage them to share their ideas. Ask prompt questions such as 'What is this a photo of? Do you read any newspapers? What do you prefer, reading the news or watching it on TV? Do you have an application in your phone to keep updated as to the most important current news?' If students share any good ideas or useful language, write these on the board.

Ask students to look at questions at the bottom of the page. Model possible answers. You may answer the question saying how often you read a newspaper and/or watch the news on TV or follow them on your smartphone. Students discuss the questions in pairs or in a small group.

Monitor and assist as necessary. When students have finished the activity, ask one or two pairs to share their ideas with the class. Encourage students to listen to one another and respond with their own ideas and opinions.

WORKSHEETS

Lesson 12.1 The news

Grammar: Reported speech (W65)

Vocabulary: News expressions (W66)

Lesson 12.2 On the box

Grammar: Past perfect (W67)

Vocabulary: Television (W68)

Lesson 12.3 Advertising

Grammar: *should* (W69)

Vocabulary: Advertising (W70)

12.1 The news

Talk about the pros and cons of online news

V news expressions G reported speech P /ɒ /, /ɔː/ and /oʊ/

VOCABULARY

News expressions

A Replace the words in **bold** with the words and phrases with the same meaning in the box.

breaking news follow ~~get~~ journalist news headlines report share

1. How do you generally ~~watch / listen to~~ ___get___ the news? TV? Radio? Online?
2. How closely do you **pay attention to** ___follow___ the news?
3. What are the current **biggest news stories** ___news headlines___?
4. How do you usually find out about **the very latest news** ___breaking news___?
5. How often do you **repost** ___share___ news stories on social media?
6. What characteristics and qualities do you need to be a **person who writes about the news** ___journalist___?
7. Do different news organizations **communicate** ___report___ the news in different ways? How?

B Work in pairs. Ask and answer the questions in Exercise A.

READING

A READ FOR GIST Read the article and choose the best subtitle. Give reasons. The article is about how to identify fake news.

a here and now b good or bad?
c past and present (d truth or lies?)

B READ FOR DETAIL Read again and answer the questions.

1. Today, what are the main ways we get our news?
2. Do people trust newspapers, radio and TV news more or less than online news sites?
3. Why is there less control over the quality of journalism today than in the past?
4. What is fake news and what is the main reason for it?
5. Why is it usually difficult to know if something is fake news or not?
6. What can help us to decide if a news story is fake or not?

C SPEAK Work in pairs. Discuss the questions.

1. What are the pros and cons of online news?
2. Do you think fake news is a problem? Why/Why not?

The news: ____________

Not long ago, television, radio and newspapers were the main ways of receiving the latest news. But the way we get our news today is very different. Most of us have mobile devices and the internet is available almost everywhere. As a result, online news sites and social media give us quick and easy access to what is going on in the world. Headlines change constantly, we get breaking news as it happens and we can follow the latest developments minute by minute. (Ex B Q1)

(Ex B Q2) Most people still believe traditional media more than news found online – stating that online articles tend to have a very one-sided view. When questioned further one person said they thought the news was usually unreliable or that they did not trust it. In contrast, those who get their news from the TV, radio or paper said that 'fake' or biased news was not really a concern. This lack of trust in online news is mostly because (Ex B Q3) it is so easy for anyone to set up a website and report the news. This means there is less control over online journalism, and separating fact from fiction is becoming more difficult.

(Ex B Q4) 'Fake news' has become a familiar term. It describes invented news stories that are designed to seem real. Fake stories are usually used for political reasons or to support some other way of thinking. There were a number of famous fake news stories, for example, during the 2016 United States presidential election. Some fake (Ex B Q5) news websites are designed to look like genuine news sites and have similar web addresses, for example ABCnews.nett. Also, the fake news stories are usually mixed in with real stories, which makes it difficult to notice them.

So, how do we know if a story is fake or not? First, check the source of the story. (Ex B Q6) If the story comes from an unfamiliar organization, check the 'about' section to learn more. Look closely at the website address. When you are reading, notice how much information there is to support the story. Genuine stories will have a lot of supporting facts. Also, look carefully at the pictures – false news stories usually contain fake images. Finally, check to see if other reliable organizations are reporting the story. If not, it may mean that the story is false. Also most important of all, use your own common sense and think critically about the stories being reported – don't believe everything you read!

Glossary

balanced (adj) considering all arguments and opinions fairly and equally
fake (adj) made to look like something real in order to trick people
genuine (adj) real rather than false
source (n) someone who provides information for a journalist

12.1 The news

VOCABULARY

A Students do the activity on their own before comparing answers with a partner. Use the **Vocabulary Worksheet** on W66 for extra practice.

B Arrange students in pairs. Monitor and assist when necessary. Take feedback from one or two pairs and encourage students to respond to each other's ideas.

READING

A Give the class one minute to read the article.

B Allow students to compare their answers in pairs before checking with the whole class.

C Monitor and assist when necessary. Take feedback from one or two pairs and encourage students to respond to each other's ideas.

GRAMMAR HUB

12.1 Reported speech

Direct speech	Reported speech
simple present '**We like** Channel 4 News best.' '**Do you like** Channel 4 News best?'	simple past Most people said (that) **they liked** Channel 4 News best. She asked them if **they liked** Channel 4 News best.
present progressive '**We are watching** the news.'	past progressive They said (that) **they were watching** the news.
will '**I will** watch TV later.'	*would* She said (that) **she would** watch TV later.
may '**Elle may** buy the box set.'	*might* He said (that) **Elle might** buy the box set.
can '**We can** record the episode.'	*could* They said (that) **they could** record the episode.

- We use reported speech to report what people say or report their thoughts or ideas.
- We use a reporting verb in the simple past.

  *He **said** … They **told** me … She **asked** him if …*
- We usually go back one tense from the tense the speaker used, but we usually don't go back one tense with the simple past.

  *'I'm **watching** TV.' → He said he **was watching** TV.*

  *'We usually **went** to the movie theater.' → He said they usually **went** to the movie theater.*
- We also need to change some pronouns (*I* to *he/she*, *my* to *his/her*, *your* to *my*, etc).

  *'I like **your** radio show,' said Lola. →*

  *Lola told me that **she** liked **my** radio show.*
- We sometimes also need to change other words.

Direct speech	Reported speech
now 'We're going to watch the news **now**.'	*then / right now* They said they were going to watch the news **then / right now**.
tonight 'I will be on social media **tonight**.'	*that night* He said he would be on social media **that night**.
tomorrow 'We'll set the budget **tomorrow**.'	*the next day / the following day* She said they would set the budget **the next day**.
today 'That new show is on TV **today**.'	*that day* He said that new show was on TV **that day**.
here 'There are some reporters **here**.'	*there* She said there were some reporters **there**.

12.1 Reported speech

A Report the statements.

1 Paul and James: 'We're going shopping tonight.'
They said *(that) they were going shopping that night.*

2 Tina: 'I'll post it online later.'
She said (that) she would post it online later.

3 Roy: 'I can't help with the budget.'
He said (that) he couldn't help with the budget.

4 James: 'Don't watch the show without me!'
He told me not to watch the show without him.

5 Helen: 'Can I borrow your box set?'
She asked me if she could borrow my box set.

6 Alan: 'Are they going to show the ad tonight?'
He asked me if they were going to show the ad that night.

7 Nora: 'You may need to speak to a journalist today.'
She told me that I might need to speak to a journalist that day.

B Complete the text messages with the correct form of the verbs in parentheses.

Pat: Fred said you (**1**) *went* (*go*) to the movie theater with him the other night.

Nuala: Yeah. He told me he (**2**) wanted (*want*) to watch a new sci-fi movie, but I asked him if we (**3**) could (*can*) see a comedy instead. I said I (**4**) didn't feel (*not feel*) like seeing a serious movie.

Pat: He said you (**5**) had seen (*see*) *Ride Away* in the end. Was it good?

Nuala: That's right. We (**6**) were going to (*be going to*) choose *Hideout*, but it was on too late. *Ride Away* was the best option.

➤ Go back to page 113.

12.1 The news

GRAMMAR

A Say, *I watch the news every day.* Write it on the board. Then say, *My sister told me that she watched the news every day.* Write the second sentence on the board. Elicit the meanings of *direct speech (exact words as said by a speaker)* and *reported speech (reported by someone else)*. Focus students on the verbs in the two sentences. In what way are they different? Ask students to look at the example sentences. Discuss the sentences as a class, using the prompt questions to guide you.

The sentences are reporting speech and ideas.
The tense used is simple past because when we report someone's ideas or their actual words, we usually 'go back one tense'.

B Focus students on the rules in the grammar box. Students work on their own completing Examples 1–4 using the correct tenses. Allow students to compare their answers with a partner before checking with the whole class.

C Direct students to the **Grammar Hub** (see TB112). Use the **Grammar Worksheet** on W65 for extra practice.

D Students complete the question prompts with their own endings. Arrange students in pairs. They take turns asking and answering each other's questions. Then, rearrange the pairs so that students have a new partner. Students report what their first partner told them to their new partner.

PRONUNCIATION

A 12.1 Focus students on the pronunciation of /ɒ/, /ɔː/ and /oʊ/. Write on the board *pot, bought,* and *boat*. Model the pronunciation of the three vowels. Play the audio and ask students to listen carefully.

B 12.1 Play the audio again. Students listen and repeat.

C 12.2 Focus students on the activity and the vocabulary box. Students work in pairs writing the words in the correct column. Play the audio for students to check their answers. Check answers with the whole class.

SPEAKING

A Read the activity with the class. Arrange students in groups of four. Ask them to read the questions and come up with four similar ones to conduct their survey. Monitor and assist as required.

B Each student in the group interviews one or two of their classmates and writes down the answers they receive.

C Students return to their original groups and discuss what they have learned about their classmates. Give students time to prepare a report on their findings.

D Ask the groups to present their findings to the class using the example as a model. Encourage students to listen carefully to the reports and respond to each other's ideas.

TEACHING IDEA by David Seymour and Maria Popova

Vocabulary: Newspaper survey

Arrange students in small groups and ask them to write a list of ten questions about the newspaper reading habits of the rest of the class, e.g. *Do you read a newspaper every day? Which part do you read first?*

Rearrange students so that they are working with a partner from another group. Tell students to ask each other their questions then report back to their group about their findings.

TEACHING IDEA by David Seymour and Maria Popova

Vocabulary: The news

Tell students that their homework for the evening is to watch the news in English, either on TV or through a trusted online source. Students should write notes about the stories, sports news and weather forecast. Ask students to turn their notes into headlines before the next lesson. In the following lesson, arrange students in groups of four and ask them to compare their headlines and decide how similar or different they are. The group decides on the most effective or attention catching headlines.

Vocabulary: Class paper

In small groups, ask students to brainstorm the sections of a newspaper (local news, international news, horoscopes, help wanted, fashion, TV and radio, sports, etc). Ask each group member to choose one topic and write a short article for a class newspaper.

GRAMMAR

Reported speech

A WORK IT OUT Look at the sentences from *The news.* Do they show direct speech or are they reporting speech and ideas? What tense are the verbs in **bold**? Why is this?

*When questioned further one person said they **thought** the news **was** usually unreliable or that they **did not trust** it.*

*In contrast, those who get their news from the TV, radio or paper **said** that 'fake' or biased news **was** not really a concern.*

B Read the rules and complete the example sentences (1–4) with the correct form of the verbs.

> **Reported speech**
>
> When we report what people say or report their thoughts or ideas, we use a reporting verb (*said, told, asked*) and we usually change the tense of the verb(s) in the sentence (simple present → simple past, present progressive → past progressive, *will* → *would*).
>
> - *65 percent of people said they had a preferred news website.*
> - *The survey asked how often people checked the news.*
> - *Most people said they would think more carefully about the news stories.*
>
> We also do this when we report someone's words directly. We also change the pronoun (*I* → *he/she, you* → *me*)
>
> - *'Do you like your job?' → She asked me if I* [1] ___liked___ *my job.*
> - *'I'm doing some work.' → He said he* [2] ___was doing___ *some work.*
> - *'I don't think there's a lot of fake news.' → She said she* [3] ___didn't think___ *there* [4] ___was___ *a lot of fake news.*
> - *'I'll get back to you later.' → He said he* [5] ___'d get___ *back to me later.*

C Go to the **Grammar Hub** on **page 144**.

D SPEAK Complete the questions with your own ideas. Then work in pairs and ask and answer each other's questions. Then work with another person and tell them what your partner's answers were.

1 What's your favorite …?

2 How often do you …?

3 Do you think you'll …?

Sara said her favorite TV show was Game of Thrones.

PRONUNCIATION

/ɒ/, /ɔː/ and /oʊ/

A 12.1 Listen to the sounds /ɒ/, /ɔː/ and /əʊ/. They are easily confused.

1 /ɒ/ hot   2 /ɔː/ report   3 /oʊ/ hope

B 12.1 Listen again and repeat.

C 12.2 **SPEAK** Write the words in the correct place in the column. Be careful! One word contains two of the sounds. Listen and check.

box caught episode follow honest more online short show

/ɒ/	/ɔː/	/oʊ/
follow online box honest	more short caught	follow episode show

SPEAKING

A Work in groups. You are going to conduct a short survey about people's attitudes to the news. Write at least four survey questions to ask your classmates.

Where do you get most of your news?
Do you always use the same news source?
Do you think that news on the internet is generally reliable?

B Each of you interview one or two classmates and write down their answers.

C Work in groups. Discuss your findings and prepare a report of your results.

D Present your results to the class.

First, we asked where people got their news. Four people said they got it mostly from the internet, including social media. And two said they got it mostly from TV.

Talk about the pros and cons of online news

12.2 On the box

Talk and debate about different TV viewing habits

V– television   G– past perfect   P– word stress in past perfect sentences

VOCABULARY
Television

A SPEAK Work in groups. Check you understand the words in **bold**. Discuss the questions.

1. Which TV **channels** do you watch the most often? What kind of **shows** do you generally watch?
2. Do you own any box sets? Do you watch on-demand TV or online streaming services?
3. Are there any **series** that you always try to watch on TV or online? How long is each **episode**? How many **seasons** of this show are there? Have there been any exciting **season finales**?

HOW BINGE-WATCHING HAS CHANGED TV FOREVER

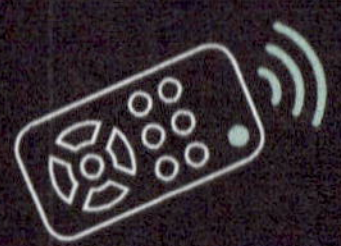

Once upon a time
Not long ago, once a week, people regularly discussed what had happened in the previous night's episode of a certain television show. They knew that they had to wait seven long days to find out what happened next. If it was a season finale, the wait was even longer. Those days are gone.

What changed?
It all started with the DVD box set. And now, thanks to on-demand TV and internet streaming services such as Netflix (which actually
Ex B started as a mail-order DVD rental service) and Amazon Prime, the
Q1 way we watch television has changed forever. At the heart of this is binge-watching.

The 'now' generation
Thirty to sixty minutes of our favorite series is no longer enough. Instead, people spend hours and even whole weekends watching
Ex B episode after episode. As a result, audiences are now watching more
Q2 TV than ever, and around 75 percent admit to binge-watching. It is now the 'new normal'.

Ex B People want new content and they want it now. They don't want to
Q3 wait to find out what happens next. Because of this, TV companies now release a complete series at one time, rather than releasing the shows episode by episode as they have done in the past.

Some of the most popular shows of all time became so successful
Ex B because they could be binge-watched. As a result, a whole industry has
Q4 built up around binge-watching and TV has been changed forever.

A new kind of show
Ex B Today, shows are made differently. Now, there is no need for a whole story
Q5 to be contained in one episode. There is also less need for the traditional end-of-episode 'cliffhanger'. This is changing the familiar format of TV series, and show-makers now can be much more creative. For example, shows usually include actual real-world events that are happening at the same time.

TV is the new movie theater
Budgets for this new generation of TV shows are high and the shows have
Ex B huge international audiences. Consequently, a lot of Hollywood stars are
Q6 moving away from making traditional theater movies and appearing more on TV. At the same time, binge-watching is replacing going to the movie theater as a social occasion, with friends getting together for an evening of television. You don't actually need to be in the same physical place. Thanks to social media sites such as Twitter and Facebook, even watching alone can be a social event.

Is binge-watching here to stay?
In today's online world, people are becoming more demanding and more impatient. They want and expect everything to be immediately available. TV companies will therefore need to make more and more shows that meet this demand. As other media companies are starting to make their own TV shows, too, binge-watching will continue to be big business.

Glossary
binge-watching (n) the activity of watching TV for an extended period of time, for example, several episodes of a series

budget (n) the amount of money a person or organization has to spend on something

cliffhanger (n) an exciting end to a television show that makes you want to watch the next part

format (n) the arrangement, design or organization of something

release (v) to make a movie, TV show, etc. available for people to see or buy

12.2 On the box

LEAD-IN

Arrange students in pairs and tell them they have one minute to list any English language TV shows they watch. When time is up, ask the pair with the longest list to share their ideas with the class. Ask the other pairs to share any of their shows that were not mentioned. Write some of them on the board.

VOCABULARY

A Read through Questions 1–3 as a class and check students' understanding of the questions and the words in bold. Arrange students in small groups and ask them to discuss the questions. Monitor and assist when necessary. Take feedback from each group and encourage students to respond to each other's ideas. Use the **Vocabulary Worksheet** on W68 for extra practice.

READING

A Focus students on the title of the article and the glossary. Elicit students' ideas and write them on the board. Students read the article and check their answers.

B Students read the article again and decide whether the sentences are true (T) or false (F). Check answers with the whole class.

C Arrange students in pairs and direct them to the **Communication Hub** (TB121). Students complete the quiz on their own before comparing their results. Take feedback from some pairs and encourage students to share and respond to their results.

TEACHING IDEA by David Seymour and Maria Popova

Vocabulary: TV survey

Prepare one question about television for each member of the class; you can see some ideas below. Give each student a different question and ask them to mingle with all the other members of the class, asking their question and writing notes on the answers they receive. Ask students to prepare a short report about their survey. Students should then take turns sharing their report with the rest of the class.

Is there more than one TV in your home?

Would you like to live without a TV?

How many hours a week do you watch TV?

Do you watch soap operas?

How often do you watch English language shows?

Do you watch sports?

What is your favorite TV show?

Do you watch nature shows?

Is there too much violence on TV?

TEACHING IDEA by David Seymour and Maria Popova

Speaking: TV guide

Bring in a TV guide for the evening of the lesson or find one online. Arrange students in small groups and give each group a copy of the TV guide. Tell students that they are going to try and agree on an evening's viewing. Explain that they can only watch one TV show and that they can't record anything. Monitor students as they discuss their viewing schedule.

TEACHING IDEA by Jim Scrivener

Grammar: Past perfect

Hero and villain

Invent an adventure story involving a continuing pursuit or chase between a hero and a villain; the story should include a lot of situations in which the hero repeatedly gets to places just after the villain has done something. Draw pictures to elicit the story, scene by scene (*By the time Karina reached the docks, Harry had already left on the cargo ship*).

Changing the 'story starting point'

Prepare a short story in the simple past and display it for students. Ask them to choose a different story starting point and rewrite/retell the story from this new perspective.

Why?

Write up a 'mystery' sentence on the board (*He bought five cans of pink paint*). Students speculate about what had happened earlier that led to this (*He had promised to decorate a toy castle in a children's playground. His wife had just given birth to a baby girl*). Other example mystery sentences include *He laughed very loudly on the bus. She shouted at the computer. They jumped into the river.*

Backwards story

Prepare a short story about Jen's day yesterday relating a chronological sequence of events up to a certain time (5 pm), using simple past verbs (*She drove into town. She chose some new socks at Primark® and then had some coffee at Mr. Bean*). In class, tell the story and ask students to note all the verbs or hand out a list at the end. Write up 'Before 5 o'clock . . .' and encourage students to retell the story from this new starting point, using past perfect verbs (. . . *she had driven into town, chosen some new socks at Primark®*).

12.2 On the box

GRAMMAR

A Focus students on the sentence and the two verbs in bold. Elicit which action came first. Elicit other examples from the class.

B Focus students on the grammar box. Students complete the rules on their own. Allow them to compare their answers in pairs before checking with the class.

C Direct students to the **Grammar Hub** (see below). Use the **Grammar Worksheet** on W67 for extra practice.

PRONUNCIATION

12.3 **A** Remind students what they learned about the schwa and about the way stress affects sentences. Play the audio. Students underline the stressed words and say what happens to the words that are not stressed.

12.3 **B** Play the audio again for students to listen and repeat, paying close attention to stress.

C In pairs, students underline the stressed words and practice saying the sentences. Encourage students to listen to and correct each other's pronunciation.

D Students write an ending for each sentence. They share their sentences in small groups. Each group decides who has the most interesting or unusual ending for each sentence. Take feedback from each group and encourage students to respond to each other's ideas.

SPEAKING

A Divide the class in two groups (A and B). Ask students to turn to the **Communication Hub** (TB121).

B Focus students on the box. Explain that these expressions will help them organize their arguments. Remind groups to anticipate the arguments the other group might prepare against them.

C Hold the debate. Explain that the idea is to persuade the other group to agree with your arguments. Set a time limit for each group to share their arguments and make sure that students listen to and don't interrupt each other. When the students have finished the debate, let the class decide which team won.

GRAMMAR HUB

12.2 Past perfect

	Positive	Negative
I/you/he/she/it/we/they	**I'd heard** the story before you read it.	**She hadn't seen** the ad before yesterday.

Question	Positive short answer	Negative short answer
Had you visited the news website before?	Yes, **I had**.	No, **I hadn't**.

- When we are talking about two events in the past, we use the past perfect to show that one event happened before the other.

past ⟶ present

↑ I saw you on the news. ↑ You told me about it.

*I **had seen** you on the news before you told me about it.*

- We usually use *just* and *already* with the past perfect.

*The movie had **just** started when we arrived at the movie theater.*

*Had they seen the show **already**?*

Be careful!

- If we use the simple past with *when*, the meaning is different to when we use the past perfect.

*I **checked the news** when I left. (= I checked the news **after** I left.)*

*I **had checked the news** when I left. (= I checked the news **before** I left.)*

12.2 Past perfect

A Correct the mistakes in each sentence.

1 Someone had ~~drop~~ *dropped* a newspaper on the ground.

2 I was late, but the movie ~~wasn't starting~~ hadn't started, so it was OK.

3 The show ~~have~~ had just begun when we arrived.

4 They had ~~saw~~ seen the movie twice already.

5 The journalist ~~has~~ had already left when she got to the meeting.

6 Had you ~~just~~ already seen the show before last night?

7 **A:** Had she posted it before?
B: Yes, she ~~did~~. had

B Complete each sentence with the correct form of the verb in parentheses.

1 The movie *had already begun* (*already begin*) when I arrived.

2 I didn't watch the movie because I had already seen (*already see*) it.

3 They didn't want to watch the news because they had already read (*already read*) the newspaper.

4 We had just started (*just start*) the trip home when the accident happened.

5 I found (*find*) the DVD that my girlfriend had dropped behind the couch.

➤ Go back to page 115.

READING

A Look at the title of the article and the glossary. How do you think binge-watching has changed TV? Read the article and check your answer.

B READ FOR DETAIL Read *How binge-watching has changed TV forever*. Are the sentences true (T) or false (F)? Correct the false sentences.

1 Netflix was originally a DVD manufacturer. T / (F)
It was originally a mail-order DVD rental service.
2 We are now watching less TV than in the past. T / (F)
We are now watching more TV than in the past.
3 People binge-watch because they want to find out what happens next. (T) / F
4 Many shows have become successful because people could binge-watch them. (T) / F
5 Today, TV shows need to have a complete story in one episode. Now there is no need for one story to be contained within one episode. T / (F)
6 More and more famous movie actors are starring in TV shows. (T) / F

C SPEAK Work in pairs. Are you a binge-watcher? Are you addicted to TV? Go to the **Communication Hub** on **page 154** and take the quiz! Compare your answers.

GRAMMAR

Past perfect

A WORK IT OUT Look at the verbs in **bold** in this sentence from *How binge-watching has changed TV forever*. Which action was first, 1 or 2? 2

Not long ago, once a week, people regularly [1]***discussed*** *what* [2]***had happened*** *in the previous night's episode of a certain television show.*

B Choose the correct words to complete the rules.

Past perfect

1 We make the past perfect with ***had*** / ***have*** + past participle.
2 When we are talking about two events in the past, we use the past perfect to show that one event happened ***after*** / ***before*** the other.
- *I found a ticket that someone had dropped.*
- *I'd seen a couple of episodes before the one last night.*
- *I was late, but the movie hadn't started.*

3 We usually use the past perfect with *already* and *just*.
- *The bus had already left when we got to the station.*
- *The meeting had just finished when we arrived.*
- *Had you already seen the movie?*

C Go to the **Grammar Hub** on **page 144**.

PRONUNCIATION

Word stress in past perfect sentences

12.3 **A** Listen and underline the stressed words. What happens to words that are not stressed? weak, reduced or contracted forms are used

1 I was late, but the movie hadn't started.
2 I found a ticket that someone had dropped.

12.3 **B** Listen and repeat.

C SPEAK Work in pairs. Underline the stressed words in the sentences. Practice saying them.

1 I'd seen a couple of episodes before the one last night.
2 The meeting had just finished when we arrived.
3 Had you already seen the movie?

D SPEAK Complete the sentences using the past perfect. Then work in groups and compare your sentences. Who has the most interesting or unusual idea for each sentence?

1 We arrived late because … we'd got stuck in traffic.
2 We didn't watch any more TV because … we'd watched enough already.
3 We talked for a long time because … we hadn't seen each other for months.

SPEAKING

A Work in groups. You are going to hold a debate about which is better, box sets and on-demand viewing or more traditional weekly TV shows.

- Decide who will be in Group A and Group B.
- Group A are going to argue that box sets and on-demand viewing is better, and Group B are going to argue that more traditional weekly TV shows are better.
- Group A – go to the **Communication Hub** on **page 153**. Group B – go to the **Communication Hub** on **page 154**.

B Using the ideas in the **Communication Hub** and your own ideas, plan what you are going to say and prepare your argument. Also, think about what the other group's arguments might be and prepare to argue against this.

C Hold the debate. Can you convince the other group to agree with you or to agree with some of your points?

Debating language

Building an argument
- *First, …*
- *Also, …*
- *Furthermore, …*
- *On top of that, …*

Agreeing and disagreeing
- *I (don't) agree.*
- *Yes, but …*
- *I see what you mean, but …*
- *You have a point, but …*

Talk and debate about different TV viewing habits

12.3 Advertising

● Talk about advertising and what makes a good advertisement

G *should* **V** advertising **P** /æ/ and /e/ **S** identifying opinion and attitudes of speakers

LISTENING

A SPEAK Work in pairs. What do you think makes a successful advertisement?

B Look at the pictures of two different advertising campaigns. What is the product? How do you think each campaign works?

sneakers and a vacuum cleaner

12.4 **C LISTEN FOR MAIN IDEA** Listen to two people discussing the advertising campaigns and check your answers to Exercise B.

Glossary

ad (n) an advertisement on television or radio, on the internet, in a newspaper or magazine, etc

billboard (n) a large board for advertisements in an outside public place

suck (v) to pull air or liquid somewhere

Campaign 1

Campaign 2

12.3 Advertising

LEAD-IN

With books closed, elicit the meaning of the unit word *advertisement* from the class (*a short arrangement of video, words, or words and images that is intended to persuade people to buy something*). Arrange students in small groups and ask them to share an advertisement, or ad, that has caught their eye recently. Tell students to say what product the ad is for, and what made it memorable.

LISTENING

A Arrange students in pairs and ask them to discuss what makes a successful advertisement. Monitor and assist when necessary. Take feedback from one or two pairs and encourage students to respond to each other's ideas.

B Use the Digital Students' Book to display the two advertising campaigns on the board. Ask students to look at the two campaigns and elicit their ideas about what the products they might be for and how the campaigns work. Write the students' ideas on the board, but do not correct or confirm their answers at this time.

12.4 **C** Focus students on the activity and the glossary as a class. Play the audio and ask students to check their answers to Exercise B.

Campaign 1 is for Reebok sneakers. People have to run past the billboard and if they run fast enough they win a pair of sneakers. Campaign 2 is for a Miele vacuum cleaner. A video was taken of cars driving into a tunnel and then a billboard was added to make it look like the cars were being sucked into the vacuum cleaner.

12.4 **D** Focus students on the information in the box. Model and ask for examples of the different expressions. Play the audio. Students work on their own matching Sentences 1–6 with the person who shared the opinion. Check answers as a class.

E Arrange students in pairs to discuss the two advertising campaigns with their partner. Students decide which of the ads is the most creative, smart or original. Ask them to give evidence to support their ideas. Monitor and assist when necessary. Take feedback from one or two pairs and encourage the students to respond to each other's ideas.

AUDIOSCRIPT

12.4

Listening, Exercise C
K = Kerry A = Alex

K: Hi, Alex, over here!
A: Hey, Kerry, long time no see! Isn't this amazing?!
K: What's going on? It's so busy!
A: YES! She did it.
K: Did what? What is this?
A: Well, it's an ad campaign for sneakers. If you run past the ad, past the billboard, … if you run fast enough, you win a pair of sneakers. It's smart, isn't it? (Ex D Q1)
K: Oh, yeah. That's really cool. And yes, a really smart idea. What brand is it for? I can't see a logo or anything.
A: It's for Reebok, I think. Yes, look, there's the Reebok logo.
K: And what's 'fast enough'? Does it say how fast you have to run?
A: I'm not sure, but everyone seems to be going pretty quickly. Look, watch this guy … Go! Go! … Oh, no. He didn't do it.
K: You should try it, Alex. Go on. Win yourself some new sneakers. You're a fast runner, aren't you? (Ex D Q2)
A: Actually, I'm not so sure I am, to be honest. I think I'll just watch.
K: We were talking about advertising in a class at the university last week. Have you seen that one for vacuum cleaners? That's another smart one.
A: I'm not sure. What is it?
K: Well, they made a video of cars going through a tunnel. They then added a billboard to the background which showed a huge vacuum cleaner so that it looked like the cars were sucked into the vacuum cleaner.
A: Oh, I think I have seen that, actually.
K: And when they put the video online, people didn't know if it was real or just a video. It created a lot of interest and discussion. It was a very successful ad.
A: Oh, I see. I thought it was a real billboard. (Ex D Q3)
K: No, it's just a video. They did it because they didn't have enough money for an actual billboard campaign.
A: Oh, that's really smart. Really original. And simple.
K: Yes, that's what we were talking about in the class last week – what makes a good ad. And it's exactly that in my opinion – something simple and original. (Ex D Q4)
A: Yeah, and something with a clear message, something you can connect with. And a catchy slogan you can easily remember, you know, like McDonald's 'I'm loving it'. (Ex D Q5)
K: Yeah, but I think the most important thing is that it catches your eye and gets your attention in the first place. Like this Reebok one. (Ex D Q6)
A: Yeah, I agree. You know what, I think I might try it. Should I?
K: Yes, go for it. You can do it. Alex, Alex, Alex …

TEACHING IDEA by David Seymour and Maria Popova

Speaking: Mini-presentations

Arrange students in groups of four or five. Tell them that they each have one minute to talk about a topic you will give them. Write the following rules on the board:

1 *You must not hesitate, repeat words or deviate from the topic.*
2 *If you do, another student can challenge you and end your turn.*
3 *Students that are still talking at the end of a minute get a point.*

Check that students understand the rules. Then write *an ad I hate* on the board. Monitor students as they speak.

TEACHING IDEA by David Seymour and Maria Popova

Speaking: Advertising

Tell students that before the next lesson you want them to look in the press and find two advertisements: one they like and one they don't. Ask students to prepare a short report about the two advertisements. In the next lesson, arrange students in small groups and ask them to explain the ads they chose and why they like or dislike them. As a group, students should choose their favorite and least favorite ads and report back to the class.

12.3 Advertising

GRAMMAR

A Say *It's hot in here. Should I open the window?* Write *Should I open the window?* on the board. Provide other situations, e.g. *Imagine I'm carrying a lot of books / I want to watch a live concert of a music group, etc.* What can students offer/suggest to do to help you? Elicit that we use *Should I* to offer help or make suggestions. In pairs, students choose the correct options to complete the rules for *should*.

B Direct students to the **Grammar Hub** (see below). Use the **Grammar Worksheet** on W69 for extra practice.

C Students work on their own writing two questions with *should*, using the information from the **Grammar Hub** to support them. They take turns asking and answering each other's questions. Monitor and assist as required. Ask one or two pairs to share their questions and answers with the class.

VOCABULARY

A Students complete the advice about advertisements with the words in the box. Allow students to compare their answers in pairs before checking with the whole class.

B In pairs, students discuss Questions 1 and 2. Monitor and assist when necessary. Take feedback from one or two pairs and encourage students to respond to each other's ideas.

PRONUNCIATION

12.5 **A** Focus students on the /æ/ and /e/ sounds. Write on the board *bat* and *bet*. Model the sounds. Play the audio.

12.6 **B** Ask students to listen and check their answers to Exercise A.

12.6 **C** Play the audio again. Students listen and repeat. In pairs, students take turns pronouncing the sounds paying close attention to the pronunciation of /ae/ and /e/. Encourage students to listen to and correct each other's pronunciation.

SPEAKING HUB

A Focus students on the task. Arrange students in groups of four and ask them to turn to the **Communication Hub** (TB121) to choose a product to plan an advertising campaign for.

B Students discuss in their groups the type of campaign they want to run, e.g. online, billboard, magazine, live campaign or a mixture of these. Encourage students to look at the prompts and reread the article *What makes a good advertisement?* Monitor and assist as required.

C The groups take turns presenting their advertising campaign to the class. Encourage students to listen to each other's presentations and write notes about the good/problematic points in their campaigns using the information from the lesson to help them.

D When all the groups have finished their presentations, take a class vote to decide which advertising campaign was the best. Encourage students to use their notes from Exercise C to help them with their decision.

GRAMMAR HUB

12.3 *should*

Subject	Question
I/we	**Should I buy** tickets for the movie?

- We use *should* to make offers and suggestions.
  offer: *Should I turn the TV on?*
  suggestion: *Should we go to the movie theater tonight?*
- We also use *should* to ask for suggestions.
  *Which episode **should we watch** this evening?*

Be careful!

- We only use *should* with *I* and *we*.
  *Which episode **should we watch** this evening?* NOT ~~*Which episode should you watch this evening?*~~

- We use *will* to ask questions about the future.
  ***Will you binge-watch** the show this weekend?*

12.3 *should*

A Choose the correct option.

1 *Should* / *Will* we see what's on TV?
2 *Should* / *Will* I invite Amy over to watch the show?
3 *Should* / *Will* they release the show on DVD soon?
4 *Should* / *Will* we binge-watch the show this weekend?
5 *Should* / *Will* this catch people's attention?
6 What movie *should* / *will* we see at the movie theater?
7 What *should* / *will* you say to the journalist?

B Write questions using *should* or *will*.

1 we / share / our photos online tonight
Should we share our photos online tonight?
2 they / release / the new movie / this weekend
Will they release the new movie this weekend?
3 I / pay / for the movie tickets
Should I pay for the movie tickets?
4 she / finish / her journalism course this year
Will she finish her journalism course this year?
5 we / watch / something exciting this weekend
Should we watch something exciting this weekend?

➤ Go back to page 117.

12.4 **D** Listen again. Match the sentences to *Alex*, *Kerry* or *both*. Use the information in the box to help you.

Identifying opinion and attitudes of speakers

Listen for expressions that people use to express their opinions and attitude and to agree or disagree.

Expressing opinion or attitude

I (don't) think …

In my opinion, …

… to be honest.

To agree

I agree.

Yes, … / Yes, and … / And yes, … / Yes, but …

To disagree

I don't agree. / I disagree.

Actually, …

I'm not (so) sure …

Which person (Alex, Kelly or both) think(s) …

1 the Reebok ad campaign is smart? both
2 Alex is a fast runner? Kerry
3 the vacuum ad was a real billboard? Alex
4 the best ads are simple and original? both
5 an advertisement needs a clear message that you can connect with? Alex
6 the most important thing about an advertisement is that you notice it? Kerry

E SPEAK Work in pairs. Discuss your opinion of the two ads. Which do you think is the more creative, smart or original ad? Why?

GRAMMAR
should

A Look at the sentences from the conversation between Alex and Kerry. Choose the correct words to complete the rules.

You know what, I think I might try it. ***Should*** *I?*

should

1 We usually use *should* to **ask permission** / **make suggestions or offers**.
2 *Should* has **a different meaning from** / **the same meaning as will**.
3 We use *should* with **I and we** / **me and us**.

B Go to the **Grammar Hub** on **page 144**.

C SPEAK Work in pairs. Make two questions with *should*. Ask and answer the questions with your partner.

VOCABULARY
Advertising

A Complete the advice about advertisements with the words in the box.

attention brand connect eye logo message slogan

What makes a good advertisement?

A good advertisement must catch your [1] eye. It needs to be original and needs to grab your [2] attention. It needs to make you stop and look at it. The image should also be something the viewer can [3] connect with on a personal level. A good ad also needs to have a clear and simple [4] message and also have a catchy [5] slogan, such as Nike's 'Just do it' or Microsoft's 'Where do you want to go today?' It should also have the company name or [6] logo on the ad somewhere. But above all, the advertisement needs to tell you that the product or [7] brand is the best there is and it needs to make you go and buy it.

B SPEAK Work in pairs. Discuss the questions.

1 How many famous logos and slogans can you think of?
2 What famous ads or advertising campaigns do you know? Do you have any favorites?

PRONUNCIATION
/æ/ and /e/

12.5 **A** Listen to the sounds /æ/ and /e/. Then underline the letters that represent /æ/ and circle the letters that represent /e/.

best brand can connect grab message

12.6 **B** Listen and check.

12.6 **C** Listen again and repeat the words.

SPEAKING HUB

A Work in groups. You are going to plan an advertising campaign for an everyday item. Go to **page 155** and choose the product for your campaign.

B PLAN Decide if your campaign will be an online, billboard, magazine or 'live' (like the Reebok) campaign. You may want to have a mix of these.

- Think about what makes a good advertising campaign. Consider all the points in the article *What makes a good advertisement?*
- Plan your campaign in detail. Think of a name, logo and slogan.

C PRESENT Present your advertising campaign to the class.

D REFLECT Take a class vote for the best advertising campaign.

Talk about advertising and what makes a good advertisement

Café Hub

12.4 Watch this

F– give and respond to opinions P– agreeing and disagreeing

COMPREHENSION

A SPEAK Work in pairs. Make a list of ten different types of shows you can watch on TV. Then discuss how often you watch them.

I never watch … I usually watch …

A: I watch dramas and movies, but I never watch documentaries. How about you?

B: I like documentaries, but most of the time I watch series.

B ▶ **00:00–01:04** Watch the first part of the video. What do Zac, Neena and Gaby want to watch? Zac - action movie Neena - wildlife show Gaby - football match/soccer game

C SPEAK Work in pairs. The roommates argue about the pros and cons of football. Predict some of the arguments.

In favor of football	Against football
	Players are paid far too much money

D ▶ **01:04–04:15** Watch the second part of the video. Do the roommates use any of your arguments in Exercise C? What do they watch in the end? They watch the movie.

Glossary

football **(n) (British)** = soccer **(n) (American)**

MILLY

SAM

NEENA

ZAC

GABY

FUNCTIONAL LANGUAGE
Give and respond to opinions

A Write the phrases in the correct place.

I don't have a strong opinion. I'm not so sure about that. It seems to me that … That's a good idea.

Give an opinion
Personally, I think …
1 It seems to me that …
In my view, …
Look, all I'm saying is (that) …
Agree
I completely agree!
Exactly!
Yeah, that's true.
That's fair enough.
2 That's a good idea.
Neutral
3 I don't have a strong opinion.
I don't mind.
Disagree
I totally disagree, I think …
Oh please! I mean, what about …
I'm sorry, Gaby, but I think …
4 I'm not so sure about that.
I see what you mean, but …
I see what you're saying about … but …

B Highlight the phrases that show *strong* agreement or disagreement.

PRONUNCIATION
Agreeing and disagreeing

12.7 **A** Listen to and read a conversation about agreeing and disagreeing. Then work in groups and practice the conversation copying the word stress and intonation.

Tim: Personally, I think soccer's pretty boring.

Sarah: It seems to me that soccer these days is just all about the money.

Tim: In my view, it's just some guys running around a field kicking a ball.

Beth: I completely agree.

Sarah: Exactly.

Andy: I totally disagree.

Sarah: Oh, please!

B **SPEAK** Work in pairs. Practice agreeing or disagreeing with each other. Talk about other professional sports, for example basketball, golf, rugby, tennis or your own ideas.

A: Personally, I think tennis players earn far too much money.

B: I see what you mean, but it's a very popular sport.

SPEAKING

A Complete the sentences with your own opinions.

1 I think __________ is the greatest band of all time.

2 In my view, __________ food is the best food in the world.

3 I think the safest way to travel is __________.

4 It seems to me that most celebrities are __________.

5 Personally, I think money makes people __________.

B Work in pairs. Student A – read one of your sentences in Exercise A. Student B – agree or disagree. Take turns.

Give and respond to opinions

➤ Turn to **page 169** to learn how to write a story.

12.4 Watch this

LEAD-IN

With books closed, write the words *agree* and *disagree* on the board. Split the class in half. Ask students in one group to come up with as many ways as they can think of to say they agree with someone, and the others to come up with ways of saying they disagree.

COMPREHENSION

A In pairs, students come up with a list of ten different types of TV shows. Ask students to compare their answers with their partner using the conversation frame. Monitor and assist as required. Take feedback from one or two pairs and encourage students to respond to each other's ideas.

B ▶ 00:00–01:04 Play the first part of the video and ask students what the three roommates want to watch on TV.

C Set a target number of arguments for students to come up with e.g. three pros and three cons. Elicit ideas from several pairs.

D ▶ 01:04–04:15 Play the second part of the video. Students apply a check mark to any of their arguments from Exercise C that the roommates use. Check answers as a class.

FUNCTIONAL LANGUAGE

A Focus students on some phrases for giving and responding to opinions. Students read through the phrases in the box and complete the table with them. Check answers as a class.

B Explain that some of these phrases show strong agreement or disagreement. In pairs, students decide which phrases show strong agreement or disagreement. Support weaker students by letting them know that there are four strong phrases to find.

PRONUNCIATION

12.7 A Read the task with the class. Play the audio. Students read and listen to the conversation. Focus them on the underlined words – they are stressed – and on intonation. Students practice the conversation in groups of four. Monitor and assist when necessary. Ask the groups to read their conversations to the class.

B Model the conversation with a stronger student. In pairs, students choose one subject to discuss and practice agreeing or disagreeing with each other. Encourage them to use the expressions from the box. Monitor and assist as required. Take feedback from one or two pairs and encourage students to respond to each other's ideas.

SPEAKING

A Students read and complete the sentences with their own opinions. Monitor and assist when necessary.

B In pairs, students take turns reading their sentences and agree or disagree with their partner. Take feedback from one or two pairs and encourage students to respond to each other's ideas.

▶ VIDEO SCRIPT

Café Hub 12.4 Watch this
Z = Zac N = Neena TV v = TV voiceover G = Gaby S = Sam

Z: I love this movie! Hey, I was watching that!
N: Come on, you've already seen it loads of times. Look – it's a nature program – this is much more interesting.
TV v: … The hunt is over and the lions begin to eat the baby elephant …
N: Ugh!
Z: That is not cool.
G: Football time! Look it's just started.
Z: Soccer? Really? Personally I think it's pretty boring.
N: I'm sorry Gaby, but I think football is the worst thing ever.
G: I totally disagree! I think it's the best thing ever!
N: Oh please! I mean … What about the players? They get paid far too much money and often behave very badly!
G: OK … I see what you mean, but they are under a lot of pressure to play well and millions and millions of people watch them. I wouldn't like to have that job, even for the money.
S: Pizza time!
Z: Sam! That's my guy!
S: Move up a bit. So what's going on?
Z: Neena and Gaby are having an argument about soccer. Neena said she thought it was the worst thing ever and Gaby said she thought players were under a lot of pressure or something like that.
N: Look, I'm just saying it seems to me that these days football is all about the money.
S: Yeah, that's true, I completely agree.
G: I'm not so sure about that. I mean, OK, I see what you're saying about the money, but football brings people together in a way that nothing else does. And it makes me think of my dad – he doesn't really say very much, but if you talk to him about football, he becomes excited and passionate. I love talking to him about football.
S: That's fair enough. What do you think Zac?
Z: I don't have a strong opinion. In my view, it's just some guys running around a field and kicking a ball.
N: Exactly!
G: I totally disagree. It's amazing. I love it.
Z: Can we put the movie back on?
G: But I want to watch the football!
S: Listen guys, we don't need to argue! Why don't we have a vote?
N: That's good idea.
Z: Sure.
G: Hmm … OK …
S: Hands up who wants to watch the movie? Hands up who wants to watch the football?
G: Sam!
S: Hey, I don't mind, I'm happy to watch either!
Z: Two votes to one. Movie wins.

12 Writing — Write a story

W– writing a story

A Work in pairs. Read the news story then close your books and retell the story to your partner. What do you think of Brett Sanders's actions?

Texan driver paid speeding ticket with over 22,000 pennies.

Brett Sanders was driving at 39 mph in a 30 mph zone when he was stopped by police and was given a $212 fine.

Sanders said the fine was too much and that he wanted to make some kind of complaint. So, he ordered over $212 in pennies from the bank and put them into two large buckets. He then went to the payment office and poured the 22,000 coins onto the counter. When he had finished this, he immediately walked out of the building. A friend filmed him while he was doing this. He told reporters that after he had done it, he 'felt great'.

According to the payment office, Sanders had actually overpaid by $7.81. They called him to offer a refund, but Sanders was happy to let them keep the change.

Many people have said Sanders's actions were wrong. At the same time, other people think it was a good way to make a point. What do you think?

B Look at the box. Find and underline more examples of the three tenses in the news story.

Writing a story

Tenses

When we tell a story, we usually use three main tenses.

We use the simple past for the main events in the story.

- *So, he ordered over $212 in pennies from the bank and put them into two large buckets.*

We use the past progressive for background activities or situations that were in progress when the main events happened.

- *Brett Sanders was driving at 39 mph in a 30 mph zone when he was stopped by police and was given a $212 fine.*

We use the past perfect for events that happened before one of the main events or that happened before the time of the story.

- *When he had finished this, he immediately walked out of the building.*

Sequence words

We use sequence words to connect the events and make the sequence clear.

- *Brett Sanders was driving at 39 mph in a 30 mph zone when he was stopped by police …*
- *So, he ordered over $212 in pennies from the bank …*
- *He then went to the payment office and poured the 22,000 coins onto the counter. When he had finished this, he immediately walked out of the building.*
- *A friend filmed him while he was doing this. He told reporters that after he had done it, he 'felt great'.*

C Choose the correct words to complete the news story.

A surfer [1]***was rescued / had been rescued*** yesterday [2]***while / after*** he [3]***was spending / had spent*** 32 hours at sea. It [4]***got / was getting*** dark [5]***when / then*** the helicopter rescue team [6]***spotted / were spotting*** him 13 miles off the coast of Scotland. He [7]***was / had been*** exhausted and thirsty, but he survived as he [8]***wore / was wearing*** a wetsuit and [9]***was / had been*** still on his surfboard.

WRITING

A PREPARE Look at the pictures and imagine what the story is. You are going to write a short story using all the pictures. Use this as you first sentence:

A man was arrested yesterday for driving a children's electric car.

B PLAN Takes notes and think about the tenses and the sequence words you need to use.

C WRITE Write the story (130–150 words). Check what you have written and make any necessary changes.

D REVIEW Work in groups. Read some of your classmates' stories. How similar are your stories?

12 WRITING 169

You could hold a larger class discussion about this and ask students if they have ever heard any similar stories.

Answers

Simple past: *was stopped; was given; said; wanted; ordered; put; went; poured; walked; filmed; told; felt; called; was/were*

Past progressive: *was driving; was doing*

Past perfect: *had finished; had done; had (actually) overpaid; have said*

Students can do this in class or for homework.

WRITING

A Students read the story on their own. Ask them to close their books and arrange them in pairs. Students take turns retelling the story to their partner and give their opinions. Elicit what students think of Brett Sander's actions from the class.

B Elicit from students examples of the uses of the simple past, the past progressive and past perfect. With a weaker group, you may have to allow them to go back to the Units in which they were discussed. Focus students on the information in the box. In pairs, students reread the story looking for examples of the three tenses.

C Students read the news story and choose the correct form of the verb. Allow them to compare their answers in pairs before checking with the whole class.

WRITING TASK

A Focus students on the six pictures and read the task with the class. Explain that each picture is a sequence in the story and that students have to start the story with the sentence given.

B Ask students to write notes about each picture and decide what tenses and sequence words they will need in each sequence. Monitor and assist as required.

C Students now write a story of between 130 and 150 words. Remind them to check their writing for any grammar, vocabulary or spelling mistakes.

D Arrange students in groups and ask them to share their stories. Elicit ideas from each group about the similarities and differences between their stories. Have each group vote on the best / most interesting / funniest story. Each group presents their choices to the class.

Unit 12 Review

VOCABULARY

A Complete the sentences with the words in the box.

breaking follow headlines report share

1 I generally follow the news pretty closely and check it every hour or so.
2 I always check the news headlines as soon as I get up in the morning.
3 I have an alert on my phone that gives me any breaking news.
4 I sometimes share news stories on social media.
5 I think different news channels report the news in different ways.

B Complete the crossword.

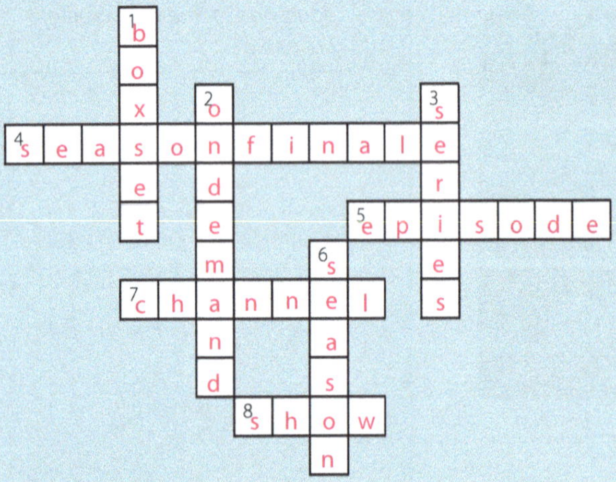

Across
4 The last episode of a season (6, 5)
5 One show in a TV series (7)
7 For example, BBC, HBO, Cartoon Network, MTV, al Jazeera (7)
8 A program that is broadcast on television or radio (4)

Down
1 A collection of DVDs or Blu-rays of the same series (3, 3)
2 You can watch at any time (2, 6)
3 A set of shows that have the same main characters or the same topic (6)
6 A set of shows as part of a series, traditionally broadcast a year before the next one (6)

C Complete the sentences with the words in the box.

attention brands connect eye logos message slogan

1 In recent years, the world's most powerful brands have included Lego, Google and Visa.
2 A recent survey has shown that the world's most recognizable logos that don't contain the company name are Nike, Apple and McDonald's.
3 A good slogan gives a clear message that people can connect with. One of the most successful is McDonald's 'I'm lovin' it'.
4 A good advertisement needs to catch your attention and grab your eye.

GRAMMAR

A Dasha was interviewed about her attitude to online news. Read the questions and her answers. Complete what Dasha says when she reports the questions and her answers.

Q Do you have a favorite news website?
1 She asked me if *I had a favorite news website.*
A There are two or three I usually look at.
2 I said there were two or three I usually look at.
Q What kind of news stories are you interested in?
3 She asked me what kind of news stories I was interested in.
A I don't have a preference.
4 I said I didn't have a preference.
Q Are you following a news story right now?
5 She asked me if I was following a news story at the moment.
A I'm following the election.
6 I told her I was following the election.

B Complete the fact file with the verbs in parentheses. Use simple past or past perfect.

THE INVENTION OF THE TELEVISION

Before it [1] became (*become*) a reality, television [2] had been (*be*) a dream of inventors for over 100 years. And by the time it was finally invented there [3] had been (*be*) many different ideas for television. Despite the many scientists and inventors who [4] had each played (*each / play*) an important part in the development of the television, it was the British inventor John Logie Baird who on January 26, 1926 [5] gave (*give*) the world's first demonstration of true television.

C Choose the correct words to complete the questions.

1 *Should* / *Will* I give you some help? (Should)
2 Who do you think *should* / *will* be interested in this? (will)
3 *Should* / *Will* we meet at six? (Should)
4 *Should* / *Will* everyone understand this ad's message? (Will)
5 Who *should* / *will* I invite to the meeting? (should)

FUNCTIONAL LANGUAGE

Complete the conversation with the words in the box.

disagree see seems strong true view

A: It [1] seems to me that things are getting more and more expensive all the time.
B: Yeah, that's [2] true. Each time I go to the grocery store, things have gone up in price.
A: In my [3] view, soccer players' pay is disgusting!
B: I [4] see what you're saying, but they do give pleasure to millions of people.
A: I'm sorry, but I totally [5] disagree. What do you think, Chris?
C: I don't have a [6] strong opinion either way, to be honest. I'm not at all interested in soccer.

Vocabulary and Communication Hub

Contents

1.1 People

A SPEAK Work in pairs. Look at the pictures. Describe the people and their relationships. Use the words in the box to help you.

children colleagues couple friends grandparents parents relatives strangers students teacher

B Choose the correct words to complete the sentences.

1 Sally and Nicole are good *friends* / *strangers* and they go to the same college.
2 Jamal is a photography *colleague* / *teacher*. He knows a lot about cameras.
3 Every weekend, I go to stay at my *grandparents'* / *couple's* house.
4 I never know what to say to *strangers* / *parents* when I meet them for the first time.
5 Janelle and Carla are *colleagues* / *students*, and they work together in the office very well.
6 All of my *relatives* / *teachers* live in the same town – we're a very close family.

➤ Go back to page 3.

1.2 Types of people

A Match the descriptions (1–10) with the types of people in bold in *Three of the best*.

1 a person who likes animals animal lover
2 a woman who has three children mother of three
3 a person who is very interested in food foodie
4 a person who enjoys seeing other places traveler
5 a person who watches or takes part in sports sports fan
6 a person who plays computer games gamer
7 a person who enjoys spending time with others people person
8 a person who loves reading book lover
9 a person who writes online regularly blogger
10 a person who listens to music regularly music fan

B Complete the sentences with the words in the box.

coffee dog father positive soccer

1 I'm a dog owner. I take it for a walk twice a day.
2 I'm a big coffee drinker. Cappuccino is my favorite, but I also like espresso.
3 I'm a father of two. My wife and I have two daughters.
4 I'm a positive person. I try not to worry or complain.
5 I'm a soccer fan. My favorite team is Manchester United.

➤ Go back to page 4.

2.3 Life events

Match the life events (1–10) with the pictures (a–j).

1 have a baby / children c
2 go to college f
3 get a job i
4 get married b
5 leave home h
6 fall in love e
7 get your own place j
8 retire a
9 learn to swim g
10 leave school d

➤ Go back to page 17.

3.3 Accommodations and amenities

A Label the pictures with the words in the box. Which types of accommodations have you stayed in?

apartment beach resort campsite chalet cruise ship five-star hotel guest house hostel

B SPEAK Work in pairs. What do the words in **bold** mean? Explain them. Then decide who would say each sentence. Write guest (*G*) or receptionist (*R*).

R **1** The **front desk** is open 24 hours. Just dial nine on the phone in your room.

R **2** We don't have any **double** or **twin rooms** for tonight, I'm afraid, but there are two **single rooms** available.

G **3** I understand the **dorms** in the hostel are non-smoking, but can I smoke on the **balcony**?

R **4** All our rooms have **safes** for your valuables, quiet **air conditioners** and beautiful **ocean views**.

G **5** Hello, is that **room service**? I'd like to order some food, please. It's room 442.

R **6** If you'd like to exercise or have a massage, our **gym**, pool and **spa** are on the fourth floor.

G **7** We're **checking out** tomorrow and we'd like to book an **airport transfer** for 10 am, please.

R **8** You have booked a **self-service apartment**, but there is a restaurant by the pool if you'd like to eat there.

➤ Go back to page 27.

4.2 Suffixes

A Complete the diagrams with the verbs in the box. Check your answers in the *Macmillan English Dictionary*.

agree ~~develop~~ ~~discuss~~ improve invent predict

-ION: *discuss*, invent, predict

-MENT: *develop*, agree, improve

B Complete the diagrams with the adjectives in the box. You need to change the spelling in some of the words when you add a suffix. Which ones? Check your answers in the *Macmillan English Dictionary*.

~~able~~ active ~~happy~~ kind possible sad

-NESS: *happi*, kind, sad

-ITY: *abil*, possibil, activ

➤ Go back to page 35.

4.3 Relaxing

A Complete the blanks in blue in the survey with the words in the box. Read *Make yourself at home* on page 36 again to help you.

a good book | board games | by the fire | friends or family | get together | homemade food | hot bath | quiet night | relaxed atmosphere | simple things | some candles | some time out

How *hygge* is your lifestyle?

1 It's a rainy Sunday afternoon. Do you prefer to …

a go to a shopping center and spend some money?
b order delivery food and switch on the game console?
c sit down with [1] __a good book__ and read all afternoon under a cozy blanket?

2 How would you rather celebrate your birthday?

a Go out with friends and stay out until late.
b Meet friends in the [2] __relaxed atmosphere__ of a café or restaurant and have a nice meal.
c Have [3] __friends or family__ over to eat [4] __homemade food__ and play [5] __board games__.

3 What makes you happiest?

a Money, shopping, vacations, etc.
b A chance to [6] __get together__ with family and friends.
c The [7] __simple things__ in life, like a [8] __quiet night__ in or a long walk in the country.

4 It's Friday night and your workweek is over. Would you rather …

a go out with your colleagues?
b go home, watch TV and have an early night?
c go home, have a nice, [9] __hot bath__ and then sit [10] __by the fire__ and dry off?

5 How do you create the perfect atmosphere at home?

a Turn on the lights, turn up the music and dance around the living room.
b Close the curtains, turn on the TV and lie on the couch.
c Light [11] __some candles__, play some soft music and take [12] __some time out__ to relax.

Finished? Work out your score: a = 0, b = 1, c = 2

B SPEAK Work in pairs. Ask and answer the questions in Exercise A. Make a note of your partner's answers. Go to the **Communication Hub** on **page 155** and check your scores. Who has more *hygge* in their lives?

➤ Go back to page 37.

5.3 *work* + preposition

A Complete the diagram with the words in the box.

a design firm | a hospital | accounts | Volkswagen

work

+ *at/for* + a named company, for example, [1] __Volkswagen__

+ *for* + type of company, for example, [2] __a design firm__

+ *in* + area of business or department, for example, [3] __accounts__

+ *at/in* + place, for example, [4] __a hospital__

B Write the correct prepositions to complete the sentences.

1 He works __at/for__ Base One IT Services.
2 We work __for__ a law firm.
3 They work __at/in__ a restaurant.
4 She works __for__ a telemarketing company.
5 He works __in__ the IT department.
6 They work __in__ Human Resources.

➤ Go back to page 47.

6.2 Exercise

A Label the pictures of sports and activities with the words in the box.

biking | field hockey | jogging | marathon running | Nordic walking | racquetball | working out at the gym | yoga

1 __jogging__

2 __racquetball__

3 __yoga__

4 __field hockey__

5 __biking__

6 __Nordic walking__

7 __marathon running__

8 __working out at the gym__

B **Complete the instructions with the correct form of the verbs in the box. You will need to use some of the verbs more than once.**

burn do go lose play run stay ~~work out~~

Find someone who …

1 hates working out at the gym.
2 can give a tip on how to lose weight in a healthy way.
3 goes jogging or running regularly.
4 knows someone who has run/done a marathon, a half-marathon or a 10 km race.
5 knows how to play racquetball.
6 keeps in shape by walking or biking to school or work.
7 knows how many calories an average person burns in a day.
8 does yoga or goes to an exercise class.
9 has a parent or grandparent who goes Nordic walking.
10 regularly played a team sport such as field hockey or soccer when they were in school.

➤ Go back to page 54.

6.3 Food groups

A **Write the food words in the box in the correct place.**

avocado banana cod lettuce lobster oats rice shrimp tomato tuna wheat

Fruits and vegetables	Grains	Seafood
avocado lettuce banana tomato	oats wheat rice	shrimp cod lobster tuna

B **Complete the lists with words from Exercise A.**

1 Foods that are mostly used in salads: cucumber, lettuce, tomato. (possibly avocado, tuna)
2 Foods that are used in breakfast cereals: nuts, oats, wheat, banana.
3 Examples of shellfish: crab, lobster, shrimp.

C **Complete the sentences with words from Exercise A.**

1 I think I'll have a tuna sandwich.
2 The wheat is ground into flour, and this is the main ingredient of bread.
3 A prawn looks just like a shrimp, but is smaller.
4 Sushi is made with raw fish, rice and sometimes shrimp and avocado.
5 I prefer white fish, like haddock and cod.

➤ Go back to page 57.

7.1 Feelings

A **Match the adjectives (1–6) with their meanings (a–f).**

1 pleased
2 cheerful
3 confused
4 anxious
5 relaxed
6 scared

a frightened or worried
b calm and not worried
c worried because you think something bad might happen
d happy and satisfied
e behaving in a happy, friendly way
f unable to understand something or think clearly about it

B **Which words in Exercise A have similar meanings to these words? Are the words positive or negative?**

glad: pleased, cheerful – positive
nervous: anxious, scared – negative

C **Complete the sentences with adjectives from Exercise A. More than one answer may be possible.**

1 I'm feeling anxious because I have an exam tomorrow. (scared is too strong for this situation)
2 Olaf's finished all of his work, so he's in a cheerful mood. (relaxed could also be possible, we rarely use pleased with mood)
3 That was a hard day, but now it's over I can feel relaxed. (pleased and cheerful also possible)
4 I'm not going anywhere near that spider – I'm too scared. (anxious may be possible, but scared is the most natural choice)
5 I don't understand these questions – they just make me feel confused.
6 Jordi's really pleased now that he has passed his driving test. (cheerful is also possible)

➤ Go back to page 63.

7.2 Shortened words

A **Work in pairs. How do you shorten these words? Circle the parts of the words that can be shortened.**

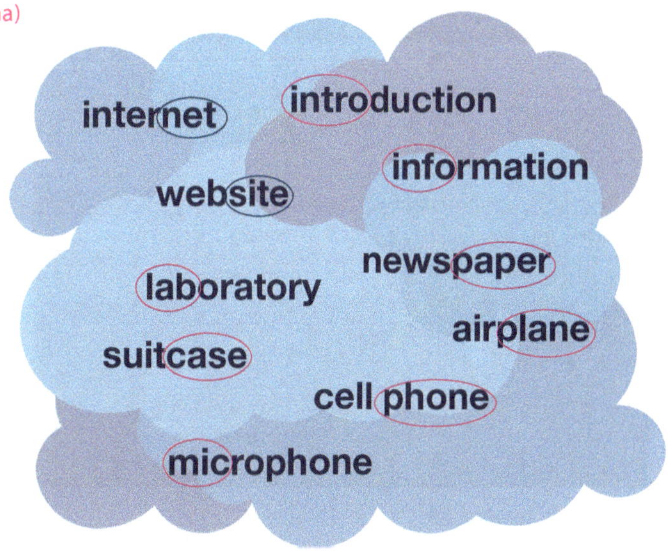

Vocabulary Hub

B Complete the sentences with shortened words from Exercise A.

1 We need more ___info___ before we can make a final decision.

2 The singer dropped the ___mic___ halfway through the song.

3 So many of the ___sites___ on the ___net___ are basically just full of pictures of people's cats.

4 I asked the staff to let me take my ___case___ on to the ___plane___ as carry-on luggage.

5 Read the ___intro___ to this article in the ___paper___ and see if you can understand it.

6 My parents are going to buy me a new ___phone___ when I start working in the ___lab___ at college.

➤ Go back to page 65.

8.1 Music

Label the pictures (1–2) with the words in the box. You will need to use some words more than once.

audience drummer drums guitar guitarist keyboard player keyboards light show microphone singer stage

1 guitar guitarist keyboards keyboard player microphone drums drummer singer

2 audience stage light show guitar guitarist microphone drums drummer

➤ Go back to page 73.

8.2 Types of art

Look at the pictures (1–8). Label them with the words in the box.

abstract art exhibit gallery landscape photograph portrait sculpture still life

The Hay Wain by John Constable

1 ___landscape___

Sunflowers by Vincent van Gogh

2 ___still life___

Mona Lisa by Leonardo da Vinci

3 ___portrait___

Guitar on chair by Juan Gris

4 ___abstract art___

David by Michelangelo

5 ___sculpture___

Lunch atop a Skyscraper by Charles C. Ebbets

6 ___photograph___

A collection of landscapes

7 ___exhibit___

The Louvre, Paris

8 ___gallery___

➤ Go back to page 74.

9.3 *make* and *do* expressions

Match the expressions (1–6) with the pictures (a–f).

1 make a mess f	4 make a decision b
2 make a mistake a	5 do your homework d
3 do some damage c	6 make a complaint e

➤ Go back to page 87.

10.1 Electronic devices

A Label the pictures of electronic devices (1–6) with the words in the box.

drone e-reader fitness tracker power bank tablet USB drive

1 fitness tracker

2 tablet

3 power bank

4 drone

5 e-reader

6 USB drive

B Complete the sentences with the devices in Exercise A. There is one word you do not need.

1 A power bank is great when you are not at home and your phone battery runs out.

2 He always uses his USB drive to transfer large files.

3 I wear my fitness tracker 24 hours a day. I love it because it tells me how many steps I take.

4 Tina got a drone for her birthday, but she was flying it in the backyard and it got stuck up in a tree!

5 My husband won't buy an e-reader because he says he loves the feel and smell of paper books.

➤ Go back to page 92.

11.1 Natural features

Label the pictures (1–8) with the words in the box.

bay canal cave cliff desert ocean rainforest valley

1 desert
2 valley
3 bay
4 cliff
5 cave
6 canal
7 ocean
8 rainforest

➤ Go back to page 102.

11.2 Animals

Write the animal words in the box in the correct place.

alligator ant ~~bear~~ bee butterfly crocodile duck eagle elephant fly frog gorilla lion lizard monkey mosquito moth owl panda parrot penguin shark snake tiger toad tuna

Mammals	Birds	Insects
bear, elephant, gorilla, lion, monkey, panda, tiger	duck, eagle, owl, parrot, penguin	ant, bee, butterfly, fly, mosquito, moth
Reptiles	**Amphibians**	**Fish**
alligator, crocodile, lizard, snake	frog, toad	shark, tuna

➤ Go back to page 104.

7.3 Student A

MICHAEL KEARNEY: the world's youngest college graduate

1984: born and grew up in Honolulu, Hawaii

4 months: spoke his first words

6 months: told his doctor, 'I have a left ear infection'

10 months: learned to read

School: didn't go to school; his parents taught him at home; went to high school for one year; graduated and received his high school diploma when he was six

College: went to college to study anthropology; graduated from the college at age ten; *The Guinness Book of Records* lists him as the world's youngest college graduate; appeared on TV chat shows; received a master's degree in biochemistry when he was 14, a master's degree in computer science when he was 18 and a doctorate in chemistry at age 22

Career: started teaching at a college at age seventeen

Other information

2006 and 2008: competed in several TV quiz shows and won over $1,000,000

➤ Go back to page 67.

9.2 Student A

A Write a definition for each word. Start your sentences with '*This is* ...' and use an adjective clause.

1 a philanthropist

This is someone who gives money to help people.

2 a course book

This is something which/that you use in class to help you learn English.

3 a vegetarian

This is someone who doesn't eat meat.

4 a hashtag

This is a symbol which/that you use when you are tweeting.

5 a cell phone

This is something which/that enables you to communicate with other people at all times.

6 money

This is something which/that we need to buy things with.

B Read your definitions to Student B. Can he/she guess what you are describing?

➤ Go back to page 85.

4.2 Student C

ROBOT RELATIONSHIPS

Meet Pepper, the world's friendliest robot. Pepper's Japanese makers say the cute little robot can understand 70–80 percent of conversations with a human. They even say Pepper can understand when someone is happy or sad. And this is just the beginning. Experts predict that in the future, humans will probably develop close relationships with robots.

Right now, most of the robots in Japan look like Pepper, but it definitely won't be long until robots look, sound and move like humans. Erica, a robot developed by Professor Hiroshi Ishiguro of Osaka University, can show basic feelings on her face and gives us a better idea of what is already possible.

Experts such as Ishiguro think that developments in technology might help scientists to make machines that really understand human feelings. This means your robot might be able to figure out if you are happy or sad and use this information to talk and behave like a friend. That could make it possible for robots to take care of people. Some experts even believe that one day it may be possible for robots to feel love.

Glossary

expert (n) someone who knows a lot about a particular subject

➤ Go back to page 34.

3.2 Students C and D

Work in pairs. Look at the pictures to tell a story. Think about:

1 What happened during the journey?

2 What decisions did people make?

3 How did the people feel at the end of the journey?

➤ Go back to page 25.

11.2 Students A and B

Work in pairs. Choose one of the hobbies or activities and give suggestions and advice to improve. Use the phrases in the box.

It's better (not) It's easy It's essential It's good
It's important It's (not) necessary It's useful It's sensible

learn a musical instrument
play a sport
learn a language
keep fit and healthy
live a 'green' lifestyle
keep an animal as a pet
have a job interview
host a party

➤ Go back to page 105.

7.1 Student B

A Listen to Student A and write down the sentences he/she says.

B Read these sentences to Student A, who will write them down. Be careful to pronounce *a* and *an* using the weak sound /ə/ (schwa). Check Student A's sentences are correct.

1. It's **a** great idea.
2. We had **a** fun day.
3. It was **an** amazing time.
4. It was **a** total surprise.
5. He told **a** funny story.

C Tell your partner about events or situations that the sentences in Exercise B describe.

➤ Go back to page 63.

9.1 Group B

A SPEAK Look at questions 1–3 in Exercise B. What would you do in each situation? Why?

B Think of two more questions. Write them down. Use the second conditional.

1. If you had to choose between a luxury break for two in your country's capital and the very latest smart television with theater sound, which would you choose?
2. If you had to choose between a well-paid job in a city you don't like and a slightly lower-paid job in a city you like, what would you do?
3. If you won $500, what would you spend it on? What about if you won $5000 or $50,000?
4. ______________________________
5. ______________________________

➤ Go back to page 83.

4.2 Student B

Social media

Social media is everywhere and is a normal part of many people's lives. However, experts agree that the way we use social media will change in the future.

Ten years ago, people used social media to share messages. Then everyone got cameras on their phones and began sharing pictures and video. But if Mark Zuckerberg of Facebook is right, you and your friends will soon put on your VR (Virtual Reality) headsets and meet in amazing 3D virtual worlds. Zuckerberg and Facebook are spending a lot of money on developing VR social media.

With VR social media, it will be possible to meet your friends 'inside' pictures and videos. This means, for example, that you will be able to spend time together at the top of mountains or the bottom of oceans! It will also be possible to hang out in virtual versions of real clubs or museums, or just about anywhere in the world (or the universe) you can imagine.

There is still a lot of work to do on the technology, so you might have to wait a while before you can share your selfies from the far side of the moon! However, experts agree that VR is the future of social media.

Glossary

expert (n) someone who knows a lot about a particular subject
virtual (adj) almost the same as the real thing

➤ Go back to page 34.

12.2 Group A

Box sets and on-demand viewing are better.

Here are some ideas for your argument. Add some ideas of your own.

- You can watch episodes when you want to and when is convenient for you.
- You will never miss an episode.
- It is easier to find a time to watch an episode or several episodes with other people, which can …

  be a fun social event.

  bring people closer together because of shared interest.

  help people to get to know each other.

➤ Go back to page 115.

12.2 Group B

Traditional weekly TV shows are better.

Here are some ideas for your argument. Add some ideas of your own.

- You look forward to the show more.
- You don't become too obsessed with the show.
- There is no danger of binge-watching, which can …
  - be bad for your health or eyesight.
  - make your brain too active and cause sleeplessness.
  - waste time.

➤ Go back to page 115.

10.2 Student A

A Look at the pictures. Think about how you will answer the questions. Write notes.

1 Can you describe the two pictures on page 155?
2 Which of these two ways of managing your money do you prefer and why?
3 What computer skills and knowledge about the internet does someone need to manage an online bank account?

B **DISCUSS** Your partner will ask you the questions in Exercise A.

C **CHANGE** Now ask your partner the following questions.

1 Can you describe the two pictures on page 155?
2 Which of these ways of communicating with other people do you prefer and why?
3 What computer skills and knowledge about the internet does someone need to make video calls?

D Can you think of one more question to ask?

➤ Go back to page 95.

9.2 Student B

A Write a definition for each word. Start your sentences with '*This is …*' and use an adjective clause.

1 a businessman or businesswoman
This is someone who works in business, especially in a top position.
2 a magazine This is something which/that we read, usually for entertainment.
3 a professor This is someone who teaches at a university.
4 an emoji This is a symbol which/that you use when you are sending online messages.
5 the internet This is something which/that connects people all over the world.
6 food This is something which/that we need to eat to stay alive.

B Read your definitions to Student A. Can he or she guess what you are describing?

➤ Go back to page 85.

12.2 Students A and B

Are you a binge-watcher? Are you addicted to TV?
Take the quiz! Check (✓) the sentences that are true for you. Then read what it means below.

You know you're a binge-watcher and addicted to TV if …

- you have ever said or thought 'Just one more episode'. ☐
- you dream, or daydream, about the show you're currently watching. ☐
- you feel that you know the show's characters as well as your actual friends. ☐
- when the series ends, you feel depressed (for around ten seconds until you start the next one). ☐
- you've stayed up all night, or at least until 3 am, watching episodes of a show. ☐
- the show is your favorite topic of conversation. ☐
- you want other people to watch the show and love it as much as you do. ☐
- watching the show, or even thinking about watching the show, is the best part of your day. ☐

What it means:

1–3 checks: You enjoy watching TV shows. You are not addicted to TV, yet, but you are perhaps an occasional binge-watcher.
4–6 checks: You are addicted to TV and probably a frequent binge-watcher. Be careful this doesn't take over your life.
7–8 checks: You need to get a life!

➤ Go back to page 115.

3.3 Student A

The central three-star Hotel Rambla Park is 50 m from Barcelona's famous Las Ramblas walking street and close to some of its best stores, markets and restaurants. This attractive hotel has a good restaurant with room service and a small pool. All rooms are non-smoking and have air conditioners, free wi-fi and a TV. One-way airport transfers are available for 15 dollars per person. The front desk is open 24 hours.

Room type: Double or twin room (extra bed available) – 40 dollars per person, per night including breakfast.
Single room: 60 dollars per night including breakfast.

Share Like Comment

➤ Go back to page 27.

10.2 Student B

A Look at the pictures. Think about how you will answer the questions. Write notes.

1. Can you describe the two pictures?
2. Which of these ways of communicating with other people do you prefer and why?
3. What computer skills and knowledge about the internet does someone need to make video calls?

B **DISCUSS** Your partner will ask you the questions in Exercise A.

C **CHANGE** Now ask your partner the questions below.

1. Can you describe the two pictures on page 154?
2. Which of these two ways of managing your money do you prefer and why?
3. What computer skills and knowledge about the internet does someone need to manage an online bank account?

D Can you think of one more question to ask?

➤ Go back to page 95.

12.3 Groups

Choose one of the products for your advertising campaign.

a

b

c

➤ Go back to page 117.

4.3 *Hygge* scores

What does your score mean?

7–10 points: Your lifestyle is already very *hygge*. Have you thought about moving to Denmark?!

4–6 points: Your lifestyle is fairly *hygge*, but you could still learn a thing or two from the Danes.

0–3 points: Your lifestyle is not *hygge* at all. Be kind to yourself and let some more *hygge* into your life!

➤ Go back to page 148.

10.3 Students A and B

Do you have what it takes to work in space? Complete our survey to find out.

Check (✓) the things you do or would like to do in your job.

- Follow a detailed schedule ○
- Do research and collect data ○
- Do experiments and make discoveries ○
- Test or work with new technologies ○
- Solve problems ○
- Repair equipment ○
- Work away from home ○
- Study the mind or body ○
- Do dangerous work ○
- Work alone ○
- Work in a team ○

Results

1–4 checks: Space is probably not your place.
5–8 checks: You could try a job in the sky.
9+ checks: You'd be great for work on Mars or in the stars.

➤ Go back to page 97.

3.3 Student B

Gaudí House Hostel is a half-hour walk or ten-minute bus trip from the center of Barcelona and is perfect for travelers on a budget. The eight-person dorms (choose between male only, female only or mixed) are comfortable, the bathrooms are clean and the kitchen area has everything you need to cook for yourself. Guests can leave their valuables in the safe at the front desk. Wi-fi is available in the front desk area. (Note: air conditioning is not available in dorm rooms.)

Room type: Dorm bed 25 dollars per person, per night. (Add breakfast for only 5 dollars per person, per day!)

Share Like Comment

➤ Go back to page 27.

10.3 Groups

SPEAK Work in groups. Read the fact file and discuss the questions.

Mission to Mars

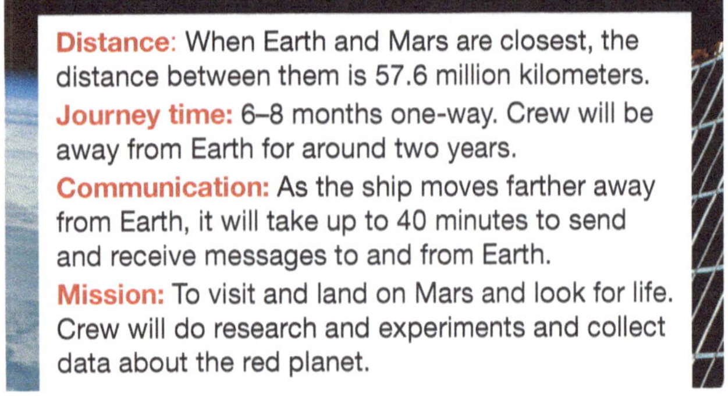

Distance: When Earth and Mars are closest, the distance between them is 57.6 million kilometers.
Journey time: 6–8 months one-way. Crew will be away from Earth for around two years.
Communication: As the ship moves farther away from Earth, it will take up to 40 minutes to send and receive messages to and from Earth.
Mission: To visit and land on Mars and look for life. Crew will do research and experiments and collect data about the red planet.

1 What will be the biggest challenges for the crew on the mission to Mars?
2 What are the five most important skills and personal qualities crew members will need?
3 What kind of problems might they have to solve on the journey?
4 What will an average day be like on the space ship?

➤ Go back to page 97.

7.1 Student A

A Read the sentences to Student B who will write them down. Be careful to pronounce *a* and *an* using the weak sound /ə/ (schwa). Check Student B's sentences are correct.

1 It was **a** great party.
2 It's **a** really funny movie.
3 It was **an** amazing view.
4 We had **a** lot of fun.
5 It put **a** smile on my face.

B Listen to Student B and write down the sentences he/she says.

C Tell your partner about events or situations that the sentences in Exercise B describe.

A: My sister's 18th birthday was a great party. It was an amazing time and we had a lot of fun. We …
B: It was an amazing view from the top of the Eiffel Tower. I went there last year with …

➤ Go back to page 63.

4.2 Student A

Work–life balance

Everybody loves long weekends, so why do they happen so rarely? When we have three full days off work, there is more time to relax and spend time with friends and family. The good news is that some people think it might not be long until *every* weekend is a long weekend.

Experts and business leaders predict that better technology will do more of our work for us. This will allow us to have shorter workweeks in the future. In fact, it is already beginning to happen. Carlos Slim, the famous Mexican telecoms billionaire, has introduced a shorter week for some of his older, more experienced employees. In Japan, companies such as car maker Toyota have found that working shorter hours leads to happier employees, and higher profits.

A better work–life balance won't be the only good thing about shorter workweeks. Offices will use less energy for lighting, computers and air conditioning. Also, there will be fewer car trips to work, which is better for the environment.

Glossary

expert (n) someone who knows a lot about a particular subject
profit (n) money you make by selling something or from your business

➤ Go back to page 34.

9.1 Group A

A SPEAK Look at questions 1–3 in Exercise B. What would you do in each situation? Why?

B Think of two more questions. Write them down. Use the second conditional.

1 If you had to choose between having a new cell phone and seeing your favorite band, which would you choose?

2 If you had to choose between a meal for two and an item of clothing, which would you choose?

3 If you could have a weekend break anywhere in the world, where would you go?

4 ______________________________

5 ______________________________

➤ Go back to page 83.

3.3 Student C

The Olympic Apartments are close to Barcelona's beaches and have beautiful ocean views. The famous Las Ramblas walking street is a 20-minute walk away. The two- and three-bedroom with room service apartments are simple and clean. Guests can pay to use the gym and spa on the first floor. Stores, public transportation and restaurants are all very close. All apartments have a balcony and air conditioners. Wi-fi is available for an extra 5 dollars per day.

Room type: Two-bedroom with room service apartment – 100 dollars per night for up to four people.

➤ Go back to page 27.

5.1 Groups

Group A jobs: banker, nanny, professional soccer player, politician

Group B jobs: doctor, pilot, social worker, actor

Group C jobs: lawyer, nurse, soldier, teacher

➤ Go back to page 43.

11.2 Students A and B

According to psychologists, the first animal you chose is how you like to see yourself. The second animal is how other people see you. And your third choice is what you are really like.

➤ Go back to page 104.

7.3 Student B

Judit Polgár:
chess Grandmaster

1976: born in Hungary

Education: did not go to school; her parents brought her and her two sisters up as part of an 'educational experiment'; chess was the subject her parents chose

6 years: started playing in international tournaments

9 years: won her first international tournament

15 years: became the youngest person ever to become a chess Grandmaster

Career: was the world's number one female chess player for 20 years; has beaten 11 current or former male world champions

Other information

2012: started the Judit Polgár Chess Foundation; the aim is to introduce children around the world to chess

2014: retired from competitive chess; became head coach of the Hungarian National Men's Chess Team

➤ Go back to page 67.

3.2 Students A and B

Work in pairs. Look at the pictures and tell a story. Think about:

- what happened during the journey.
- what decisions the people made.
- how the people felt at the end of the journey.

➤ Go back to page 25.

1.1 Grammar

Question forms

A Complete the questions. Use the answers to help you.

1 What ____________?
My name is Elisa.

2 Where ____________?
I live just outside Milan.

3 Do ____________?
I have a younger brother.

4 Where ____________?
I went to college in Brighton.

5 What ____________?
I studied architecture and design.

6 Have ____________?
No, I've never been to America, but I would like to go.

B Now ask the questions from Exercise A to three classmates. Write their answers in the table below.

Name	Question 1	Question 2	Question 3	Question 4	Question 5	Question 6

1.1 Vocabulary

People

A Complete the web below with the names of the people in your network and their relationship to you. Include your family, friends, colleagues and classmates.

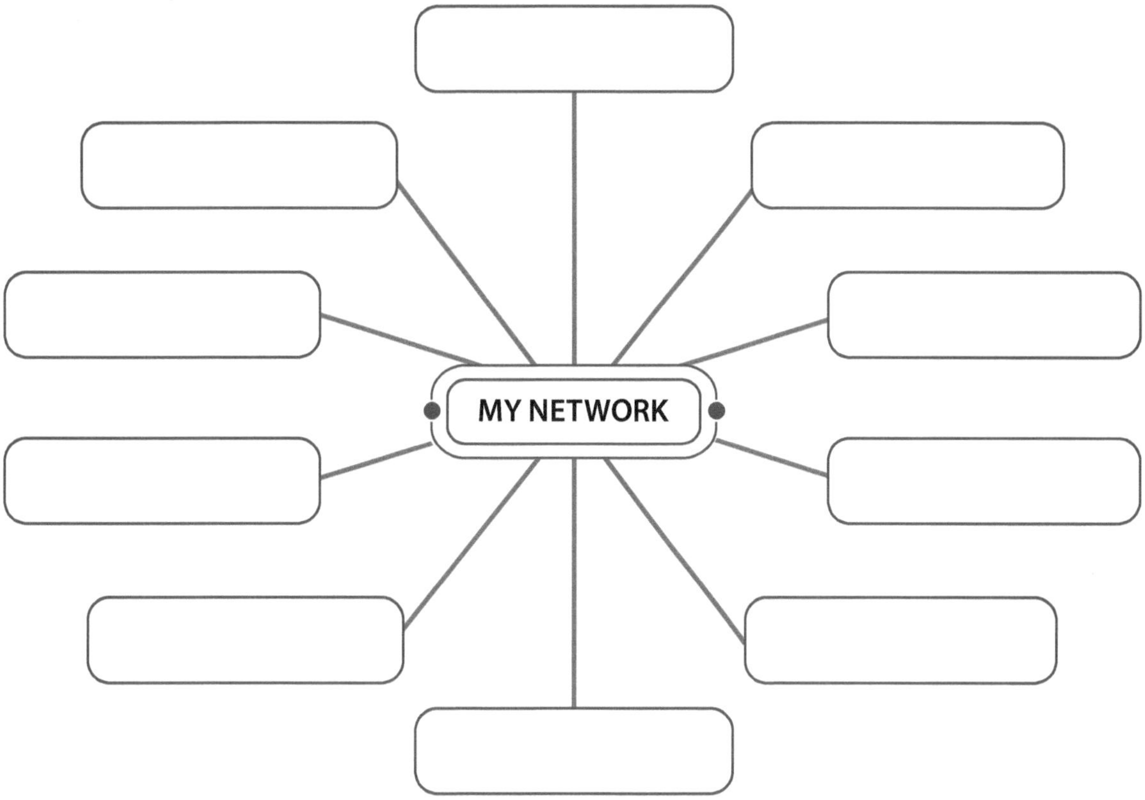

B Work with a partner. Ask and answer questions about each other's networks.

A: Is Yulia your sister?

B: No, she's my colleague.

Frequency words and phrases

A Circle the adverbs of frequency and frequency phrases in the text.

A week in the life . . .

Hello. My name is Jonathan and I'm 28 years old. I have always liked gaming, so I am lucky because I design computer games for a living. I ride my bike to my office three times a week, but on the other two days I work from home.

In my free time I enjoy playing sports. I hardly ever go to the gym, but I usually go swimming on Saturdays, and I play basketball once a week.

I also really like movies and go to the movie theater every so often. I normally watch action movies, but now and then I watch a horror movie, as long as it isn't too scary!

B How often do you do the activities in the table? Write your answers in the first column. Use the language you circled in Exercise A.

Activity	You	Your Partner
go to the grocery store		
eat fish		
play soccer		
cook		
go to the theater		
read books		
write emails		
watch videos online		

C Now ask your partner the questions and fill in their answers in the second column.

A: *How often do you go to the grocery store?*

B: *Hardly ever. I do my food shopping online.*

Types of people

A Complete the types of people in the table below.

	Name	Information
1 is an a_______ l____.		
2 is a f______.		
3 is a m_____ f__.		
4 is a c__ o_____.		
5 is a m_______ or f_______.		
6 is a s_______ f__.		
7 is a c_______ d_______.		

B Ask your classmates. Find someone for each of the boxes. Ask a follow-up question to get more information about them.

Indefinite pronouns

A Look at the sentences below and decide if they are correct or incorrect. Change the incorrect sentences.

1 We never go nowhere on the weekends.

____

2 Did you do anything interesting this summer?

____

3 There is anything wrong with the TV. It isn't working.

____

4 I can't wait to visit New York next year. I've never been anywhere in America.

____

5 Can somebody help me carry this box please?

____

6 Have you seen my glasses? I can't find them everywhere.

____

B Work with a partner. Write six more sentences with indefinite pronouns.

1 ______________________________

2 ______________________________

3 ______________________________

4 ______________________________

5 ______________________________

6 ______________________________

Personality adjectives, adjective + preposition

A Read the sentences and correct the mistakes.

1 I've never been good in talking to people.

____

2 I'm very serious for the environment. I always recycle.

____

3 I was disappointing with the results of my last English test.

____

4 I am a confidence person. I can talk to anyone.

____

5 I study English at home. I think I am hard-worker.

____

6 I am very sensitive. I think about things carefully.

____

7 I am really interesting in history.

____

8 I'm a very creating person. I like to paint and draw.

____

B Work in groups. Discuss the sentences in Exercise A. Which sentences are true for you? What are the similarities and differences in your group?

2.1 Grammar

Adverbs of degree

A Unscramble Questions (1–8).

1 felt / was / When / last time / you / tired / the / extremely / ? ______

2 English / for / Can / think / way / completely / you / of / new / practicing / a / ? ______

3 you / almost / Have / a / flight / missed / ever / ? ______

4 What / happy / makes / extremely / you / ? ______

5 do / Who / really / you / admire / ? ______

6 is / traffic / bad / in / Why / so / cities / the / ? ______

7 angry / you / What / very / makes / ? ______

8 visit / Which / really / to / country / you / do / want / ? ______

B Work in groups. Ask and answer the questions in Exercise A. Write the most interesting answers in the spaces below.

1 ______

2 ______

3 ______

4 ______

5 ______

6 ______

7 ______

8 ______

2.1 Vocabulary

Describing places

A Complete the crossword with opposite adjectives.

Across

3 loud

5 peaceful

7 convenient

8 polluted

Down

1 ugly

2 clean

4 old-fashioned

6 dull

B Work with a partner. Try to think of a place you know for each of the adjectives.

Simple present and present progressive

A Read the paragraph and put the verbs in parentheses in the simple present or present progressive.

My name is Jennifer and I [1]____________ (*have*) a confession: I am 34 years old and, currently, I [2]____________ (*live*) with my parents. Sometimes it [3]____________ (*feel*) like I am 17 years old again. They always [4]____________ (*want*) to know where I am and when I [5]____________ (*come*) home for dinner. Of course, there are some benefits too. I [6]____________ (*not pay*) rent right now, although I [7]____________ (*help*) out with bills and food shopping. But I [8]____________ (*think*) my parents are great roommates. They [9]____________ (*take care*) of me when I [10]____________ (*feel*) unwell and they never [11]____________ (*borrow*) my clothes without asking. Actually, I [12]____________ (*think*) of staying for another year.

B Work with a partner. Write a conversation between Jennifer and her parents. Try to use the simple present and present progressive. The first line is written for you.

Jennifer: I am thinking of staying for another year, is that ok with you?

____

____

____

____

____

C Act out your conversation in your class, then watch your classmates act out their conversations. Were they similar or different to yours? Why?

Verb + preposition

A Complete the questions with the correct prepositions.

1 Which websites do you use when you are looking ____________ a job?
2 Who do you talk ____________ about your problems?
3 What piece of technology do you rely ____________ ?
4 What do you think ____________ education in your country?
5 What do you and your friends argue ____________?
6 What do you and your friends talk ____________?
7 What is difficult about living ____________ roommates?
8 Who helps ____________ the housework in your family?

B Work in pairs to ask and answer the questions in Exercise A. Write down your partner's answers.

1 ______________________________
2 ______________________________
3 ______________________________
4 ______________________________
5 ______________________________
6 ______________________________
7 ______________________________
8 ______________________________

Simple past – regular and irregular verbs

A Put the verbs in the vocabulary box in the past tense, then add them to the correct box.

go eat live try stop study play make
talk want say fly leave buy need

Regular Verbs	Irregular Verbs

B Work with a partner. Choose five verbs and write five sentences in the past tense. Compare your sentences with your partner and ask them questions to get more information.

1 ______________________________.

2 ______________________________.

3 ______________________________.

4 ______________________________.

5 ______________________________.

Life events

A Work in pairs. What life events do you think the pictures show?

B Circle the life events in the word spiral below.

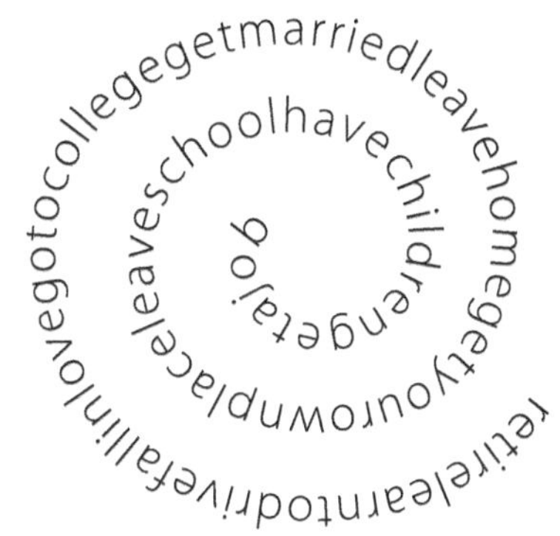

C Work with a partner. Put the life events in the order you think they usually happen.

1 ____________

2 ____________

3 ____________

4 ____________

5 ____________

6 ____________

7 ____________

8 ____________

9 ____________

10 ____________

all / some / most / no / none

A **Rewrite the sentences, using the word in parentheses.**

1 I don't speak to anyone from school anymore. (*none*)

I speak to none of the people from school anymore.

2 Everyone in this class is trying to improve their English. (*all*)

____

3 I'd like to go to the movie theater tonight, but I don't have any money. (*no*)

____

4 62.9% of the people in the world own a cell phone. (*most*)

____

5 Not all people like eating fish. (*some*)

____

6 I asked, but nobody would help me. (*none*)

____

B Work with a partner. Think of four questions to ask your classmates about their studying habits. Ask your questions to the class, then write sentences about your findings using *all*, *some*, *most*, *no* and *none*.

1 ______________________________

2 ______________________________

3 ______________________________

4 ______________________________

Types of transportation

A Read the transportation facts and complete the sentences with the correct verbs.

FUN FACTS – TRAVEL AND TRANSPORTATION

1 In 2016, 75 million people **f**__ __ __ into or out of Heathrow Airport in London.

2 7.5 million people took a **t**__ __ __ __ each day in Mumbai.

3 With 8,600 buses in London, it's always easy to **g**__ __ a bus.

4 In 2015, a driver **g**__ __ __ __ a ride to a Belarusian traveller from Tajikistan to Ukraine – that's over 12,000 km.

5 The first person to **t**__ __ __ __ __ __ __ by helicopter was Igor Sikorsky on September 14, 1939.

B Work in pairs. When was the last time you used the forms of transportation mentioned in Exercise A? Where did you travel to?

Past progressive and simple past

A Read the story and underline the simple past and circle the past progressive.

One night, Carlos was driving home from his mother's house. It was a clear night and the moon was shining brightly. Suddenly, he saw an old man step out in front of his car. Carlos tried to stop the car in time, but he was too late.

He jumped out of the car and ran to check if the old man was OK, but there was no one there. While he was looking under his car, he heard the sound of a woman crying. Carlos felt scared, but he couldn't see anyone around and the car looked fine. No damage at all. He decided to call the police as soon as he got home.

When Carlos arrived home, his phone was already ringing, so he answered it. It was his mother who wanted to know if he was home safely. Carlos told his mother what happened, but she didn't seem surprised.

'Oh son', she said, 'You are not the first person to tell this story. Fifty years ago, an old man was walking along that road with his daughter when he was hit by a car. He died. You must have seen his ghost'.

B Work in groups. Write a story using simple past and past progressive. When you have written one line, pass your story to the next person in the group who will write the next line, and so on.

It was a cold, rainy evening . . .

3.2 Vocabulary

Prefixes

A Put the words in the box with the correct prefix. Use the Macmillan online dictionary to help you with your answers.

complete afraid like experienced possible organized kind trust patient accurate true mature similar paid perfect visible

Un ____________________
____
____
____

Im ____________________
____
____
____

Dis ____________________
____
____
____

In ____________________
____
____
____

B Work in pairs. Complete the questions below, then ask and answer them with your partner.

1 What foods do you dis__ __ __ __?

2 Would you like to be in__ __ __ __ __ __ __ for a day?

3 Why do people do un__ __ __ __ work?

4 When did you last behave in an im__ __ __ __ __ __ way?

5 What is something you think is im__ __ __ __ __ __ __ __?

6 Who is someone you dis__ __ __ __ __?

verb + *-ing* and *to* + base form

A Match the sentence beginnings (1–8) with their endings (a–h).

1 Instead of traveling to another country on vacation, many people choose

2 I love Italy! I can't help

3 I expect that all airlines will begin

4 We usually stay in hotels, but this year I have agreed

5 I refuse

6 If you want to see Japan, I advise

7 There are so many places I want

8 Next year, we are planning

a letting people use their cell phones on planes.

b visiting in the spring. It's beautiful then.

c to explore their own countries.

d to go camping!

e to see in the world.

f visiting every year.

g to use trains, they are too expensive.

h to visit Machu Picchu.

B Work in groups. Try to add more verbs to the table below.

Verb + *-ing*	*to* + base form
Avoid	Learn

Accommodations and amenities

A Complete the table with the words in the box.

double room guest house chalet balcony hostel safe air conditioning beach resort ocean view reception campsite apartment

Accommodations	Amenities

B Work in pairs. Discuss the questions.

1 Which types of accommodations from Exercise A have you stayed in? Which do you prefer?

2 What amenities are important to you when you choose a hotel?

be going to + base form and present progressive for the future

A Read the sentences below and write five more sentences using *be going to* or present progressive for the future.

Find someone who ...	Name	Further detail
1 is going on vacation this summer.		
2 is having a dentist appointment soon.		
3 is planning to buy a house in the future.		
4 is going to do their homework tonight.		
5 is going to watch a movie this weekend.		
6 ______		
7 ______		
8 ______		
9 ______		
10 ______		

B Now talk to your classmates. Try to find a different person for whom each sentence is true and write their name next to it. Ask more questions to get further details.

Are you going on vacation this summer?

Yes I am.

Where are you going? Who are you going with?

I'm going to Ibiza with my friends.

4.1 Vocabulary

Free time

A Complete the sentences with the correct form of the verbs. Each verb can be used more than once.

meet for go to hang out play see go to

1 Mehmet and his wife ________ the theater at least once a month.
2 On Saturday, I ________ a movie at the movie theater.
3 Have you ________ with your friends recently?
4 ________ board games is becoming much more popular again.
5 When I was a child, I loved to ________ at the park.
6 Each weekend, Melissa and Leyla ________ coffee at the local café.
7 I spent all weekend ________ video games.
8 The last time I ________ an exhibit was when I visited the modern art museum.

B Put the activities from Exercise A in order of how much you like them (1 = I love it, 8 = I dislike it). Compare your list with a partner.

1 ________
2 ________
3 ________
4 ________
5 ________
6 ________
7 ________
8 ________

Making predictions

A Unscramble the sentences below to make predictions about the future.

1 cars / will / people / definitely / self-driving / have

____

2 world / might / be / there / a / government

____

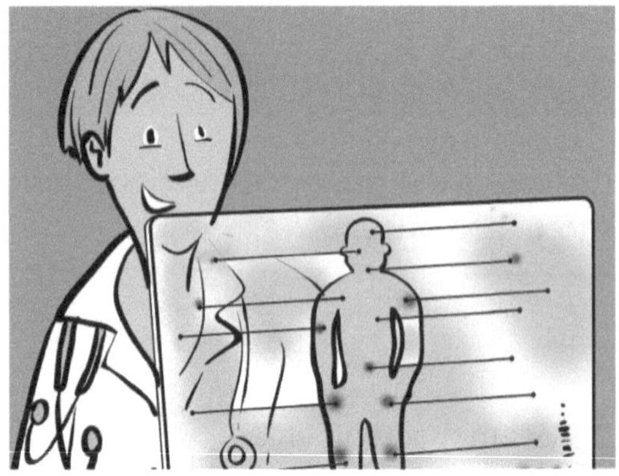

3 probably / learn / will / people / need / Chinese / to

____

4 certainly / Earth / be / there / will / more / on / people

____

5 maybe / something / replaced / computers / will / with / be / else

____

6 water / the / could / world / run out / of

____

7 vacations / visit / space / people / will / on / their

____

8 extinct / languages / may / some / become

____

B Work in pairs. Which of the predictions do you agree with? Why? Make four more predictions of your own.

1 ____

2 ____

3 ____

4 ____

American Language Hub Level 2 Teacher's Book.

Suffixes

A Choose the correct ending (*-ion, -ity, -ment, -ness*) for the words in parentheses, then add them to the sentences below.

1 When people have different opinions, it can be hard to reach an ____________ (*agree*).

2 Spending time with friends can help you overcome feelings of ____________ (*sad*).

3 Making ____________ (*predict*) about the future is difficult. Things change very quickly.

4 We had a ____________ (*discuss*) in the class. All the students participated.

5 Smartphones are an ____________ (*invent*) that has changed the way we live.

6 There is a ____________ (*possible*) that the world will be a different place in a few years.

7 Vacations are the best thing for rest and ____________ (*relax*).

8 This year I have seen a real ____________ (*improve*) in my English.

B Work in groups. How many other words can you find that take the suffixes *-ion, -ity, -ment* and *-ness.* Make a list in the table below.

-ion	*-ity*	*-ment*	*-ness*

Subject and object questions

A Read the paragraph below, then write six questions about the text. You should write three subject questions and three object questions.

Mindfulness

It is easy to rush through life without stopping to notice anything. But paying more attention to the world around you can improve your mental wellbeing. Some people call this awareness 'mindfulness'. Mindfulness can help us enjoy life more and understand ourselves better.

Mindfulness involves sitting silently and paying attention to thoughts, sounds, the sensations of breathing or parts of the body, and bringing your attention back whenever your mind loses focus. You can take steps to develop it in your own life. Here are three ideas to help you be more mindful:

1 Try something new.

Trying new things, such as sitting in a different seat in meetings or going somewhere new for lunch, can help you notice the world in a new way.

2 Keep it regular.

It can be helpful to pick a regular time, for example, the morning trip to work, when you decide to focus on the sensations created by the world around you.

3 Free yourself from the past and future.

You can practice mindfulness anywhere, but it can be especially helpful if you realize that, for several minutes, you are 'trapped' in reliving past problems or worrying about things that might happen in the future.

1 __________

2 __________

3 __________

4 __________

5 __________

6 __________

B Test your memory. Without reading the text again, work with a partner to ask and answer your questions from Exercise A.

4.3 Vocabulary

Relaxing

A Complete the sentences.

1 My friends and I really like playing **b**__ __ __ __ **g**__ __ __ __. Our favorite is Scrabble.

2 In the winter, I really enjoy sitting **b**__ **t**__ __ **f**__ __ __ and watching TV.

3 I usually spend my free time relaxing with **f**__ __ __ __ __ __ or **f**__ __ __ __ __.

4 When my sister feels stressed, she always takes a **h**__ __ **b**__ __ __.

5 There is nothing like cooking **h**__ __ __ __ __ __ __ **f**__ __ __ to make you feel happy.

6 I try to have a **q**__ __ __ __ **n**__ __ __ __ in every Sunday evening. I watch my favorite TV shows in my pajamas.

7 I like to light some **c**__ __ __ __ __ __ to create a **r**__ __ __ __ __ __ **a**__ __ __ __ __ __ __ __ __.

B Work in groups. Which of the sentences do you agree with? What else do you do to relax?

5.1 Grammar

can, could, be able to

A Work in pairs. Discuss the changes that the pictures above show.

B Look at the topics below. For each topic, think about how your abilities have changed. Use *can, could, be/was able to*. Write sentences on these topics in each column.

Learning English   Using technology   Your job   Your favorite hobby

Five Years Ago	Today
1 ______	1 ______
2 ______	2 ______
3 ______	3 ______
4 ______	4 ______

C Now talk to your classmates. Try to find people who have similar answers to yours. How do your experiences compare?

5.1 Vocabulary

Work collocations

A Match the work collocations to the verbs below.

long vacations   shifts   a day off   a high salary   long hours
a company car   unemployed   a bonus   your own boss

EARN ____________ **GET** ____________ **TAKE** ____________

BE ____________ ____________ ____________

____

WORK ____________

____

B Work in groups. Make up six questions using the collocations from Exercise A and discuss them in your group.

1 ____________________________________?

2 ____________________________________?

3 ____________________________________?

4 ____________________________________?

5 ____________________________________?

6 ____________________________________?

Obligation, necessity and permission: *must, have to* and *can*

A Work in pairs. Look at the pictures. What rules do they show?

B Look at these laws from around the world. Complete them with the verbs in the box.

can	have to	must not	must not	must not
must not	must	don't have to	had to	

1 In Denmark there are rules for naming your child. If you want to name your baby something unusual, you ______________ ask permission from the government.

2 When you ride a bike in Mexico, you ______________ take your feet off the pedals. It is a safety rule.

3 Feeding the birds in St. Mark's Square in Venice is not allowed. You ______________ pay a fine of up to $700.

4 In Ontario, Canada, there is a law to prevent loud noises. You ______________ shout, sing or whistle at any time.

5 In 2001, a governor in Cambodia announced that stores ______________ stop selling water guns.

6 In Singapore, you ______________ chew gum, but you ______________ use it for medical reasons.

7 In Western Australia, you ______________ own more than 50 kg of potatoes at one time.

8 In Samoa, it is illegal to forget your wife's birthday, but you ______________ buy her a present.

C Work in groups. Look at the laws from around the world. Do you think they are real? Do you know any other unusual laws?

Adjectives for appearance

A Use the adjectives for appearance below to write sentences about your classmates. Do not use their names.

colorful casual attractive well-dressed fashionable stylish cool

1 ______________________________

2 ______________________________

3 ______________________________

4 ______________________________

5 ______________________________

6 ______________________________

B Work with a partner. Read your sentences to each other. Can you guess who they are describing?

He is very fashionable. He always wears designer labels.

I think you are talking about Ahmet! Am I right?

5.3 Grammar

Present perfect with *for* and *since*

A Look at the pictures below. For each picture write a sentence using the present perfect with *for* or *since*.

B Talk to your classmates. Find someone who agrees with the sentences below. Write their name next to the sentence and ask them one question to learn more about the answer.

Find someone who …

a has spent more than three hours cleaning this week.

b has done the same hobby since they were a child.

c has been married for at least one year.

d has studied another language.

e has been driving since they were a teenager.

f has been delayed at an airport.

work + preposition

Student A

Complete the paragraph below with the correct prepositions (*in*, *at*, *for*). You will need to use the prepositions more than once.

My name is Helena, and I work [1] ______________ a hospital. I'm not a doctor or a nurse though. I work [2] ______________ the IT department. I design their databases. Right now, I am looking for a new job. I'd like to work [3] ______________ an internet firm because I am very interested in programing. My dream job is to work [4] ______________ Google, or somewhere in Silicon Valley.

Now work with a partner. Tell them about Helena.

Student B

Complete the paragraph below with the correct prepositions (*in*, *at*, *for*). You will need to use the prepositions more than once.

I'm Justin, and I think I am really lucky because I love my job. I work with children [1] ______________ an after-school club called Active Kids. We work [2] ______________ a sports center and we do a lot of sports activities with the children. Working [3] ______________ Active Kids is great! Sometimes we work [4] ______________ schools to help children learn how to keep fit and stay healthy, which I really enjoy because it keeps me fit and healthy too!

Now work with a partner. Tell them about Justin.

Quantifiers *too* and *enough*

A Find and correct six mistakes in the sentences with *too* and *enough*.

1 I am too sick to go to work.

____

2 There are too much people in my town. It is overcrowded.

____

3 If you study enough hard, you will pass your exam.

____

4 We don't have eggs enough to make a cake.

____

5 You spend time too much playing computer games.

____

6 I am too much tired to go to the party tonight.

____

7 We didn't have enough money to visit the museum.

____

8 I am not enough rich to buy a Ferrari.

____

B Write three more sentences with *too* and *enough*. You should write two correct sentences and one incorrect sentence. Test your partner.

1 ______________________________

2 ______________________________

3 ______________________________

Minor illnesses

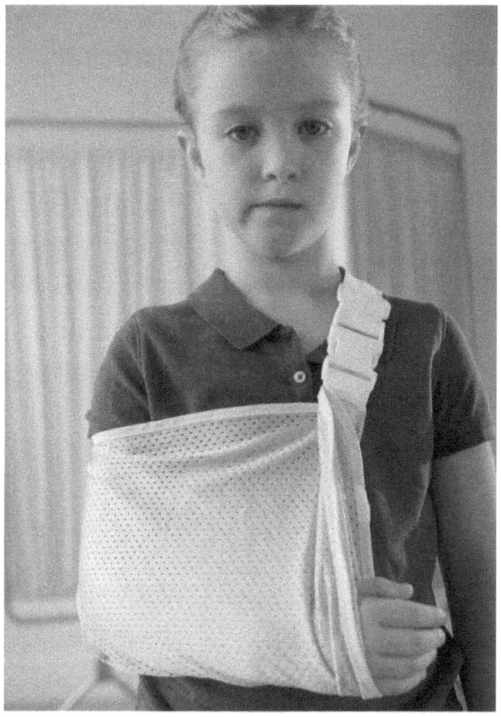

A **Complete the questions with the minor illnesses in the box below.**

broken bone   flu   headache   sore throat   sunburn   toothache

1 Have you ever had a ________________?

I fractured my arm last summer.

2 What do you do when you get a ________________?

I always drink water first. If it doesn't go away, I take some aspirin.

3 What is the best remedy for a ________________?

You should probably see a dentist!

4 When was the last time you had the ________________?

Last winter, I was in bed for a week and I had a high fever.

5 Do you know any natural remedies for ________________?

My friend says you should put yogurt on your skin to cool it down.

6 What do you do when you get a ________________?

I drink a hot honey and lemon drink. It takes away the pain.

B **Work with a partner. Ask and answer the questions from Exercise A. Write down your partner's answers.**

-ing forms

A Read the paragraphs below. For each of the *-ing* forms in **bold** choose and circle whether (G) gerund, (A) adjective or (PP) present participle.

1 Jenny, 22

Playing (G/A/PP) tennis is my favorite way to keep fit. I am a member of my local club and I play three nights a week. You use a lot of energy because you are **running** (G/A/PP) around the court all the time. It is a **challenging** (G/A/PP) game, but I really enjoy it.

2 Paul, 30

Last year, I joined a water sports club. Since then, I have tried lots of different water sports, but my number one is **surfing** (G/A/PP). It's such an **exciting** (G/A/PP) sport! I was quite bad at first and fell off a lot. Now I am much stronger and I can stay on the board easily. Next weekend, I am **entering** (G/A/PP) my first competition.

3 Marina, 42

I go to Zumba twice a week. It is the most **entertaining** (G/A/PP) way to stay in shape that I have ever tried. Actually, it is more like a party than an exercise class. **Learning** (G/A/PP) the moves can be difficult sometimes but there are so many benefits. I have made some good friends, I am in better shape than before and I am **becoming** (G/A/PP) a better dancer.

B Work in groups. Prepare to talk about your favorite way to keep fit, or stay in shape. Write about the sport or activity, how often you do it and why you like it. Now talk to your group.

Exercise

A Decide if the sports and activities in the vocabulary box are usually done inside or outside. Place the words in the Venn diagram below. Some sports might be both – put these in the middle section.

climbing   bike riding   soccer   ice hockey   Pilates   running   skiing   racquetball   volleyball   yoga

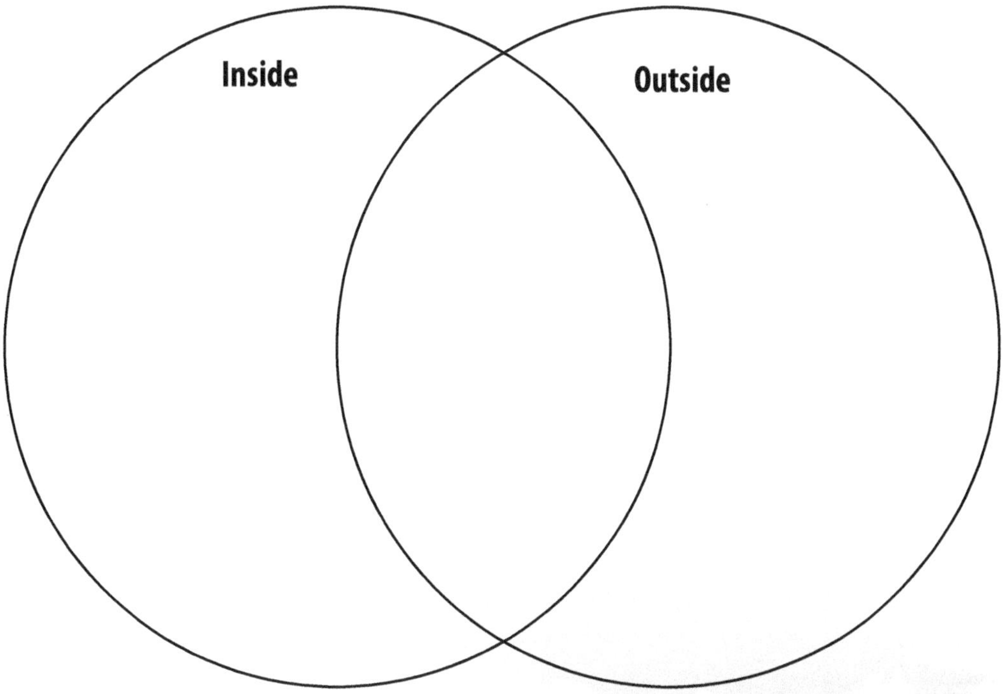

B Work with a partner. Answer the questions below.

1. Can you add two more sports and activities to the diagram in Exercise A?
2. Which of these sports or activities have you tried?
3. How often do you exercise?
4. What is your favorite way to keep fit or stay in shape?
5. Which new sports or activities would you like to try?

Present perfect with *just*, *already* and *yet*

A Match the question to the answer. Fill in the blanks with *just, already* and *yet*.

1 Do you want to go *and see the new Marvel movie tonight*?

2 Are you excited about *the play this weekend*?

3 Have you finished *your English homework* __________?

4 How was your trip to *France*?

5 Hello, is Katie there please?

6 Are you hungry?

a No, not at all. I've __________ eaten.

b I can't wait! I love Hamlet, I've __________ seen it twice.

c Sorry, I've __________ seen it. I went last week with my brother.

d She has __________ left. I saw her walking out about three minutes ago.

e We haven't been to France __________. We arrive in Paris next week.

f No, I am planning on doing it tonight.

B Change the words in *italics* in 1–4 above to make new questions, then write two questions of your own. With a partner, ask and answer your new questions. Try to use *just*, *already* and *yet*.

1 Do you want to go __________________________?

2 Are you excited about __________________________?

3 Have you finished __________________________?

4 How was your trip to __________________________?

5 __________________________?

6 __________________________?

Food groups

A Find the ten words from the box in the word search above.

tomato   avocado   oats   banana   tuna   wheat   shrimp   lobster   rice   cod

B Complete the table below with the ten words. Choose which food group each word belongs to.

Fruits and veggies	Grains	Seafood

Articles

A Complete the passage with *a*, *an*, *the* or – (no article).

Happiness 101

Would you like to take [1] ______ course that teaches you to be happy? At [2] ______ Yale University you can! Twice a week, nearly 1,200 students participate in [3] ______ university's most popular class ever, 'Psychology and the Good Life'. It is [4] ______ largest class size in [5] ______ history of Yale. But why is it so popular?

Laurie Santos, [6] ______ professor who teaches [7] ______ class, says that students are more depressed than ever before. In social science, many new theories on achieving happiness are being developed and [8] ______ students want to learn about them. Homework for [9] ______ class includes being grateful, performing acts of kindness and developing social connections.

Sound interesting? Well, you don't have to be [10] ______ Yale student to take part. [11] ______ course is now being offered for free, through [12] ______ online course.

B **Work in groups. Read the paragraph again and then discuss the questions.**

1 Would you join a class like this one?

2 Do you think you can learn to be happy?

3 Do the colleges or universities in your country offer any unusual courses?

4 Imagine you were starting a new university course. What subject would you offer?

Feelings

Student A

Complete your part of the crossword. Then test your partner.

Across

4 Flying makes me _____________. I get worried in the turbulence.

6 I always get _____________ before tests.

7 I was really _____________ by the homework. I didn't understand it.

8 I am _____________ we didn't miss our train.

Student B

Complete your part of the crossword. Then test your partner.

Down

1 _____________ to meet you. My name's Owen.

2 She is such a _____________ person, always smiling.

3 I feel _____________ when I can sit with my book on my couch.

5 I am _____________ of spiders. When I see one I scream.

used to

A Look at the picture of Dubai. What do you think is different about Dubai now and the way it was fifty years ago? Write six sentences with *used to* and *didn't use to.*

1 ______________________________

2 ______________________________

3 ______________________________

4 ______________________________

5 ______________________________

6 ______________________________

B Work with a partner. Think about the changes in your home town or city and write notes for the prompts below. Tell your partner how your city has changed. Use *used to* and *didn't use to.*

- Houses
- Stores
- Entertainment
- Scenery
- Restaurants

Shortened words

A **Underline the words which can be shortened in each sentence. Rewrite the sentences, using the shortened form. There may be more than one in each sentence.**

1 Can you give me some information about the meeting next week?

____

2 I never buy newspapers any more. I read the news on the internet.

____

3 I get scared every time I get on an airplane.

____

4 Sally usually changes her cell phone every year.

____

5 The airline website said that the weight limit for suitcases is 20 kg.

____

6 The science club is meeting in the laboratory this evening. Are you going?

____

7 I really didn't like that book. I couldn't even understand the introduction.

____

8 I was giving a presentation last week and the microphone stopped working.

____

B **Work with a partner. Test each other. Student A says the shortened word. Student B should say the full word. Take turns.**

No article (*school, the school*)

A Fill in the blanks with *a*, *an*, *the* or – (no article).

Sebastian: Hey Mina, how are you doing?

Mina: OK I guess, [1]____________ college is hard to get used to!

Sebastian: Tell me about it! I have three essays due this week.

Mina: The work is OK; it's just very different from [2]____________ high school.

Sebastian: What do you mean?

Mina: There are so many students here, and [3]____________ campus is huge.

Sebastian: Yes, it is [4]____________ busy and big college. What was your [5]____________ high school like?

Mina: I went to [6]____________ small school. There were only 50 students and we all knew each other.

Sebastian: Wow! That is small.

Mina: Yeah. [7]____________ school was in my village so all the students lived nearby.

B Work with a partner. Check your answers to Exercise A then practice saying the conversation.

7.3 Vocabulary

Phrasal verbs

A Complete the quotations with the correct form of the phrasal verbs in the box.

bring up	drop out	fall out	give up	grow up	make up

1 'I ____________ with six brothers. That's how I learned to dance – waiting for the bathroom.' Bob Hope, entertainer

2 'My mom ____________ me ____________ to believe that my talent is a gift.' Christina Aguilera, pop singer

3 'I didn't have anyone to play with, so I ____________ my own world.' Maya Lin, artist

4 'I never ____________. Doesn't matter what the score is'. Caroline Wozniacki, tennis player

5 'I never liked being told what to do. It's one of the reasons I ____________ of school.' Dave Grohl, rock musician

6 'London is like a girlfriend I loved, then really ____________ with.' Lapo Elkann, businessman

B Work in groups. Discuss the quotes in Exercise A. What do they mean? Which one is your favorite? Why?

8.1 Grammar

Reflexive pronouns

A Complete the sentences with the words in the box. Think of an answer for each clue.

themselves	itself	all by	himself	each other	yourself	herself	yourselves

1 The place you and your closest friend met ____________.

2 Somewhere you would like to visit ____________ yourself.

3 Someone who learned a skill all by ____________.

4 Something that can switch ____________ off.

5 Something that you bought for ____________.

6 Someone who lives by himself or ____________.

7 A man you know who cooks for ____________.

8 A time when you and your friends enjoyed ____________.

8.1 Vocabulary

Music

Student A

Complete the sentences below with the words in the box. Then test your partner.

keyboard   lyrics   catchy   on tour   album   band members

1 An ______________ is a collection of songs.

2 A ______________ is an electronic piano.

3 ______________ are the words to a song.

4 When a band goes ______________ ______________, they play concerts in many towns and cities.

5 The people in a group are called the ______________ ______________.

6 A ______________ song is one that is popular and easy to remember.

Student B

Complete the sentences below with the words in the box. Then test your partner.

light show   gig   stage   audience   cover song   guitar

1 A ______________ ______________ is a song that was originally performed by another band or singer.

2 ______________ is another word for a concert.

3 The people who watch a concert are called the ______________.

4 A ______________ is the raised area at the front of a theater, arena or concert hall.

5 A ______________ is an instrument with six strings.

6 A ______________ ______________ is a colorful display.

8.2 Grammar

Infinitive of purpose

A **Write answers to the questions below using infinitives of purpose.**

1 Why are you learning English?

2 Why did you want to visit the last place you went to on vacation?

3 Why do people go to college?

4 Why do you go to see a comedy movie?

5 Where did you go last weekend? Why did you go there?

6 Why do people save money?

B **Now ask the questions to three of your classmates. Write their names and answers in the table below.**

	Name:	Name:	Name:
1			
2			
3			
4			
5			
6			

Types of art

A Find eight art words in the word search below.

F	L	J	I	D	N	B	T	O	N	R	K
G	I	O	A	X	L	K	K	J	N	D	E
M	L	K	J	G	X	D	T	A	W	P	X
E	F	I	L	L	L	I	T	S	H	P	H
M	Y	L	Z	K	A	H	O	O	T	B	I
A	B	S	T	R	A	C	T	A	R	T	B
N	K	W	T	Z	F	O	B	R	J	X	I
Z	L	R	T	X	G	S	A	X	Z	Z	T
U	O	A	S	R	Z	W	A	G	T	O	I
P	E	P	A	C	S	D	N	A	L	H	R
R	B	P	G	A	L	L	E	R	Y	C	N
M	H	S	C	U	L	P	T	U	R	E	B

B Work in groups. Complete the spaces with the eight words below. Write examples of the types of art next to each word.

______________ ______________

______________ ______________

______________ ______________

______________ ______________

8.3 Grammar

First conditional

A Match the beginning of the first conditional sentences (1–8) with their endings (a–h).

1 We might go to the movie theater on Sunday
2 If you enjoy rock music,
3 If I work hard enough,
4 You can improve your English
5 If it doesn't snow,
6 If you pass your exams,
7 If they have time,
8 We should leave now

a you should come to the Foo Fighters concert with me.
b I will get a promotion.
c they will close the ski slopes.
d if we want to miss the traffic.
e if you practice enough.
f they will come and visit us.
g we should celebrate.
h if the movie hasn't sold out.

B Write three sentences beginning with *I like* … Use the ideas in the box or your own ideas. Then work in pairs. Tell your partner your sentences. Your partner will make recommendations.

genres of movies or books | types of food | types of music | types of TV shows

I like rock and blues music.

If you like rock and blues, you'll love a band called Blackberry Smoke.

I like Thai food.

If you like Thai food, you might like that new Vietnamese restaurant next to the school.

I like ______________________________

I like ______________________________

I like ______________________________

Movie and book genres

A Find and circle 16 movie and book genres in the word spiral below.

biographyrom-comactionfantasyadventurehistoricalsci-ficomedyfairytaleanimatedhorrormusicalthrillerwesterncostumedramaautobiography

B Work with a partner. Put the letters in bold in the correct order to make words. Then ask and answer the questions.

1 What do you prefer **amenatid** movies or **friay tlaes**?

____

2 Would you rather read a famous person's **abhorogapituy** or watch a **bpiioc** about their life?

____

3 Do you have a favorite **roo-cmm**?

____

4 Do you enjoy **hroorr** movies and **tlrhriles**?

____

5 Who is the best **aitocn** star?

____

6 What was the last **hirisaotcl** movie or **csmtoue dmara** that you watched?

____

9.1 Grammar

Second conditional

A Complete the second conditional questions below using the verbs in parentheses.

1 What ____________ you ____________ (*do*) if you ____________ (*win*) the lottery?

2 Where ____________ you ____________ (*go*) if you ____________ (*can visit*) anywhere in the world?

3 If you ____________ (*have*) to move to a new house, what ____________ you ____________ (*miss*) about your current home?

4 If you ____________ (*can have*) dinner with anyone, who ____________ you ____________ (*choose*)?

5 If you ____________ (*be*) famous, what ____________ you ____________ (*be*) famous for?

6 What ____________ you ____________ (*do*) if you ____________ (*can speak*) English perfectly?

7 If you ____________ (*be*) a superhero, what ____________ your superpower ____________ (*be*)?

8 If you ____________ (*can travel*) through time, which year ____________ you ____________ (*visit*)?

B Work in groups. Discuss the questions from Exercise A. Who has the most interesting answers?

9.1 Vocabulary

Prepositions in money phrases

A Match the beginnings of the sentences (1–8) with the endings (a–h).

1 This year, I am saving
2 I spend most of my money
3 These days I rarely take money
4 Some stores only let you pay
5 Last week, I had to pay
6 Debit cards have made paying
7 When I was a teenager I borrowed
8 My attitude

a in cash.
b by card much quicker.
c up for a vacation to South America.
d out of the ATM.
e for my brother's movie ticket. He forgot his wallet.
f toward money is to save 10% of my salary each month.
g on going out to eat.
h a lot of money from my parents.

B Work in pairs. Check (✔) the sentences you agree with, then discuss them with your partner.

Essential adjective clauses

Student A

Look up the words in bold in the dictionary. Write one correct and two false definitions for each word, using essential adjective clauses.

1 An **otter** is

a ______

b ______

c ______

2 An **element** is

a ______

b ______

c ______

3 A **courier** is

a ______

b ______

c ______

Now work in pairs and test your partner.

Student B

Look up the words in bold in the dictionary. Write one correct and two false definitions for each word, using essential adjective clauses.

1 A **fishmonger** is

a ______

b ______

c ______

2 An **income** is

a ______

b ______

c ______

3 A **hammer** is

a ______

b ______

c ______

Now work in pairs and test your partner.

Verbs connected with money

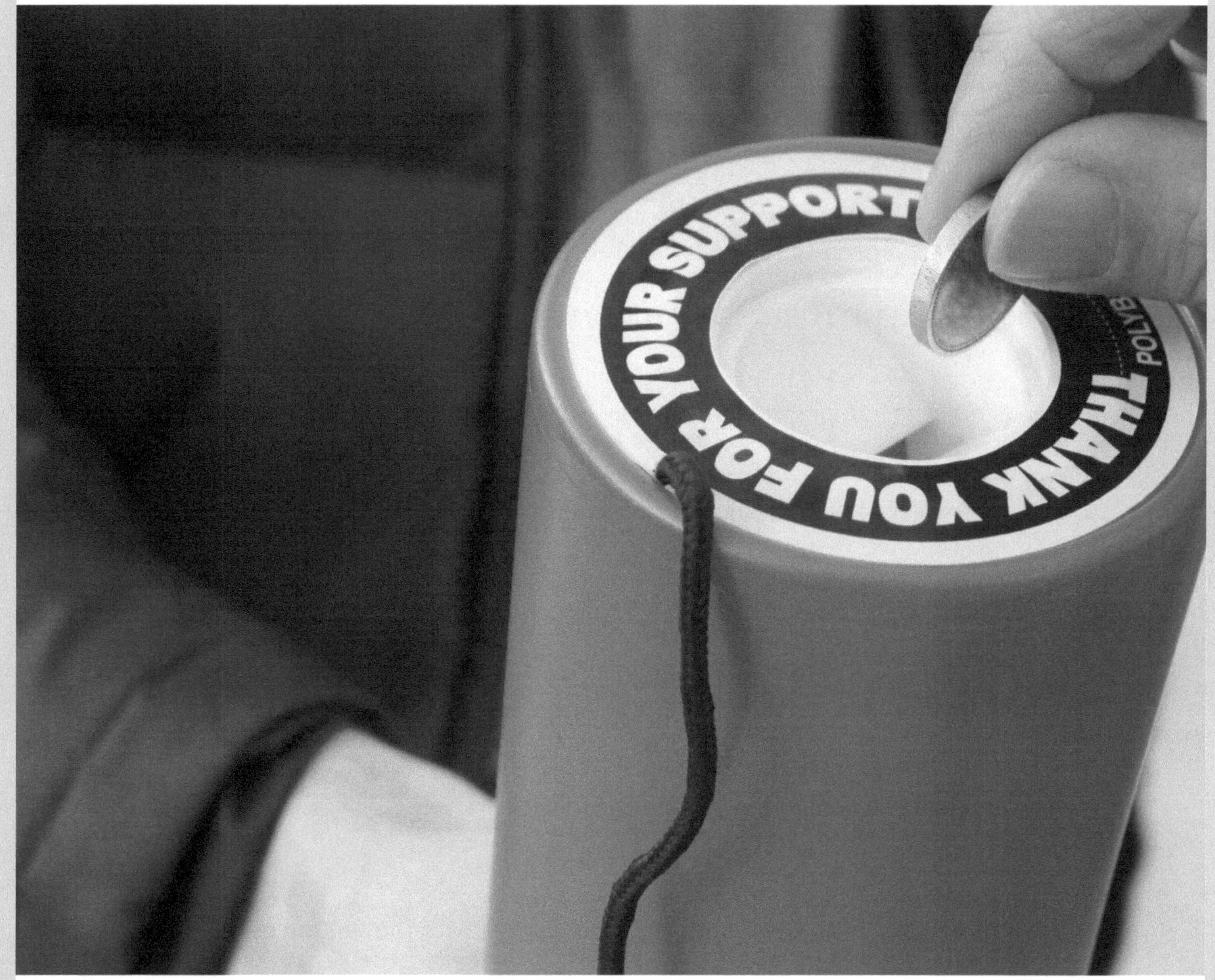

A Choose the correct words to complete the sentences below.

1 The Giving Pledge asks people to ***give away*** / ***lose*** at least half of their money.

2 In the US, about 60 percent of people ***support*** / ***donate*** to charity each year. Seventy-five percent of all donations ***support*** / ***raise*** medical research, animal welfare and children or young people.

3 In 2002, internet and media company AOL Time Warner ***lost*** / ***gave away*** $99 billion. This remains the biggest annual loss in history.

4 In the UK, baking and selling cakes for charity ***raises*** / ***earns*** over £150 million each year.

5 Teachers in Luxemburg ***raise*** / ***earn*** around 30 percent more than any other teachers in the world.

6 Many famous inventors didn't ***raise*** / ***make*** any money from their inventions. These include Tim Berners-Lee (World Wide Web), Douglas Engelbart (computer mouse) and Laszlo Biro (ballpoint pen).

B Work in groups. Check your answers to Exercise A, then discuss the sentences. Which is the most surprising fact?

Gerunds

A **Put the gerunds in parentheses in the correct place to complete the sentences.**

1 I really like new things for my house. (*buying*)

____

2 I always look forward to my bank account on payday. (*checking*)

____

3 Money is something I find difficult to do. (*saving*)

____

4 Is an alternative to money (*bartering*, *using*)

____

5 I always enjoy time with my friends. (*spending*)

____

6 He's famous for so much of his money to charity. (*donating*)

____

7 She enjoys shopping for new clothes. (*going*)

____

8 New restaurants is something I like to do. (*visiting*)

____

B **Discuss Sentences (1–8) with a partner. Do you agree with the sentences?**

make and *do* expressions

A Complete the questions with the correct form of *make* or *do*.

1 Do you always ______________ your homework?

2 What kind of mistakes do you ______________ when speaking English?

3 How would you like to ______________ a living?

4 Have you ever ______________ an offer for something on eBay or a similar website?

5 When did you last ______________ a complaint?

6 When did you last ______________ someone a favor?

7 Have you ______________ any research this week?

8 Have you ______________ any important decisions this week?

B Work in groups. Check your answers to Exercise A, then ask and answer the questions.

Comparatives and superlatives

A Write the missing words to complete the review. Sometimes more than one word is possible.

T9plus – the details

T-net has taken a great tablet (the 8) and made it so [1]__________ better. A lot faster [2]__________ last year's model, the T9plus is also a [3]__________ smaller and a [4]__________ lighter. T-fone has improved the screen; it isn't perfect, but you can see it a little [5]__________ clearly in bright sunlight. The battery now charges [6]__________ more quickly, too. Amazingly, T-net's tablets just keep getting [7]__________ – this is the third year that the price has gone down. It might not be the [8]__________ tablet available, but certainly in the top five! Highly recommended.

B Work in pairs. Write six questions about technology use to ask your classmates. You can use the ideas in the box or your own ideas. Compare your findings and present them to the class.

internet use | new technology | types of technology

1 ______________________________

2 ______________________________

3 ______________________________

4 ______________________________

5 ______________________________

6 ______________________________

10.1 Vocabulary

Electronic devices

Find the twelve words related to using electronic devices in the word search puzzle.

app call computer connect drive install internet link password tablet usb video

d	n	y	j	n	p	p	c	g	p	j	l	r	y	z
e	r	p	h	w	b	o	p	t	s	u	l	z	k	a
t	d	i	h	f	m	m	c	z	k	e	a	c	n	u
t	e	h	v	p	w	e	f	c	r	n	t	a	i	c
h	c	n	u	e	n	i	y	p	o	v	s	x	l	d
a	p	t	r	n	t	p	b	r	e	i	n	x	h	g
m	e	n	o	e	o	n	a	h	i	a	i	v	f	r
r	k	c	f	k	t	a	b	l	e	t	a	i	w	v
x	r	m	g	f	p	n	s	x	j	s	r	d	g	x
z	p	m	m	n	g	b	i	k	y	v	d	e	v	z
d	h	o	m	s	o	b	c	l	p	r	o	o	n	b
s	o	m	q	s	m	a	h	r	r	t	c	o	a	v
b	u	x	x	u	l	n	j	a	y	m	d	t	x	k
k	s	h	q	l	o	g	e	a	p	s	p	p	a	c
n	m	u	c	y	d	n	d	r	o	w	s	s	a	p

More comparative structures

A Look at the sentences below. Rewrite the sentences using *(not) as … as*.

1 Math is harder than English.

____

2 Children and adults are both creative. There is no difference between them.

____

3 It is safer to travel with friends than alone.

____

4 Experience is more useful than education.

____

5 Men and women are equally good at cooking.

____

6 Traveling by plane and by car are both safe.

____

B Work in groups. Do you agree? Rewrite the sentences and make them true for you. Discuss your reasons with your group.

1 ______________________________
2 ______________________________
3 ______________________________
4 ______________________________
5 ______________________________
6 ______________________________

Using devices and the internet

A Complete the sentences with the collocations in the box.

the screen freezes	make a video call	block your account
install an app	remember your password	connect a USB drive
click on a link	your computer crashes	

1 To ____________ ____________ ____________ ____________ to a friend, you both need an app like Skype or FaceTime on your devices.

2 If ____________ ____________ ____________ I think the easiest way to fix it is to turn it off, then turn it back on again.

3 There is only one place to ____________ ____________ ____________ ____________ on my computer. It's on the side, next to the power cable.

4 Don't ____________ ____________ ____________ ____________ in an email unless you know and trust the person or company who sent it.

5 If you can't ____________ ____________ ____________, click here and we'll send a new one to your email account.

6 If you type the wrong details three times, the system will ____________ ____________ ____________ and you will need to call your bank.

7 Before you ____________ ____________ ____________ or game on your phone, check that it was made by a reliable company.

8 When ____________ ____________ ____________ on my phone, I just take the battery out and then put it back in. That usually fixes it.

B Write four questions using the collocations from Exercise A. Ask and answer your questions with a partner.

1 ____?

2 ____?

3 ____?

4 ____?

need to

A Correct the mistakes in the sentences below.

1 I not need to do anything tomorrow.

____

2 My brother need buy a new book on space travel.

____

3 What do astronauts need do to prepare for a spacewalk?

____

4 You need connect the USB drive?

____

5 She not need to install an app.

____

6 Someone needs telling me what to do.

____

B Work in pairs. Make questions from the prompts. Ask and answer the questions.

1 Where / you / need / go / after the class?

2 What / you / need / do / this weekend?

3 You / need / ask / teacher / any questions?

4 When / need / get / a haircut?

5 What / need / do / improve your English?

Collocations: science and research

A The words in bold are in the wrong sentences. Swap the words to make the sentences correct.

1 It can be difficult to collect **experiments** from wild animals because they move around so much.

____

2 NASA is making **data** to send people to Mars.

____

3 Are you any good at solving **discoveries**?

____

4 I was never very good at doing **problems**. I always got bored.

____

5 These days most companies avoid doing **solutions** on animals because it is cruel.

____

6 It is important to test new **preparations** well before selling it to the public.

____

7 Inventors are always looking for **research** to our problems.

____

8 New **technology** are being made every day.

____

B Work with a partner. Say a verb and ask your partner to complete the collocation. Take turns.

The passive voice (simple present and simple past)

A Read about Chichen Itza, one of the man-made wonders of the world. Complete the passage with the verms in parentheses using the active or passive voice.

Chichen Itza

Chichen Itza [1] ________ (*locate*) in Yucatan, Mexico. It [2] ________ (*be*) home to the Mayan people who [3] ________ (*live*) around AD 600–900. The site [4] ________ (*cover*) an area of at least 5 km^2 and [5] ________ (*make*) of hundreds of paved roads. You [6] ________ (*can see*) many stone buildings. Some of the buildings [7] ________ (*restore*). These stone buildings [8] ________ (*look*) very different from each other. They [9] ________ (*built*) in different styles. This [10] ________ (*show*) that the population [11] ________ (*be*) very diverse. The site [12] ________ (*protect*) by the National Institute of History and Anthropology.

B Work in groups. What are the seven wonders of the man-made world? Choose one and research it. Make a poster about the site. Include the information below.

1 Where is it located?

2 When was it built?

3 What is it surrounded by?

4 Who is it visited by?

5 Is it protected?

11.1 Vocabulary

Natural features

Student A

Work with a partner to complete the crossword.

Across

5 an area of woodland in tropical regions where the weather is very wet

6 a large hole in the side of a cliff or under the ground

7 a mountain that forces hot gas, ash, rocks and lava into the air through a hole in the top

9 an artificial river

10 an area of coast where the land curves inward

11 a long line of rock or coral in the ocean

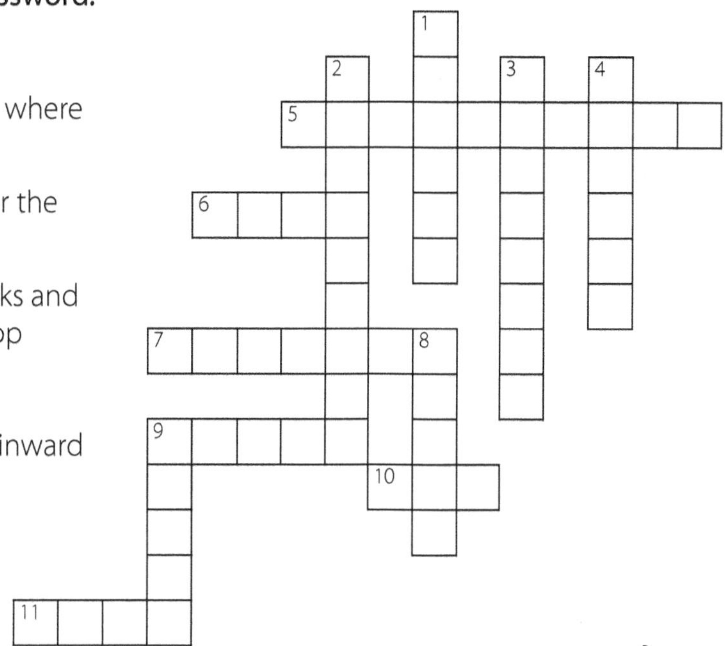

Student B

Work with a partner to complete the crossword.

Down

1 a long deep valley made of rocks

2 a place where water flows over the edge of a cliff or rock

3 a very big hill that is much higher than the land around it

4 an area of land where the weather is very dry

8 a large area of salt water

9 the steep side of an area of high land

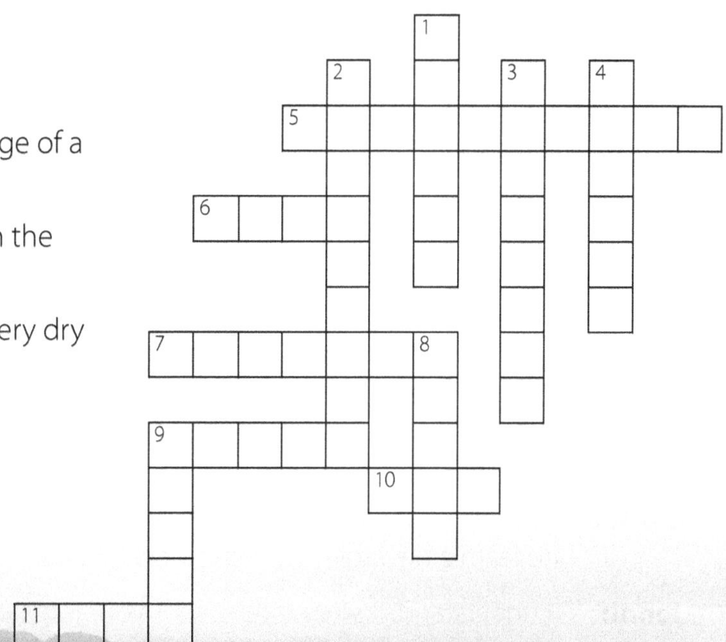

American Language Hub Level 2 Teacher's Book.
Published by Macmillan Education Limited.

Adjective + infinitive

A Complete the conversation with the adjectives and verbs from the box.

great/see   not fun/ wait   impossible/find   hard/know   important/be   not easy/change

Martha: Hey Jenni, over here!

Jenni: Hi Martha, sorry I'm late! It was [1]__________ a parking space.

Martha: Don't worry about it. It's [2]__________ you!

Jenni: Yes, you too! It has been too long. How are you?

Martha: I'm OK thanks. I am thinking about applying for a new job, but it's [3]__________ what to do.

Jenni: Can I help?

Martha: Maybe!

Jenni: Well, I think it is most [4]__________ happy. Are you happy where you are?

Martha: Most of the time. I really like the work but the commute is a nightmare. It's [5]__________ in traffic for two hours every morning.

Jenni: What about the other job?

Martha: The office is much closer to my home. The salary is better but I'd have to learn a new role and make new friends.

Jenni: I understand. It's [6]__________ your job.

B Work with a partner. What should Martha do? Write an ending for the conversation, then practice saying it with your partner.

Martha: ______________________________

Jenni: ______________________________

Martha: ______________________________

Jenni: ______________________________

11.2 Vocabulary

Animals

A **Complete the idioms with words from the box below.**

horse mice dogs fly bird chickens worm cat fish lion

1 The early ______________ catches the ______________.

2 Don't look a gift ______________ in the mouth.

3 Don't count your ______________ before they are hatched.

4 Let sleeping ______________ lie.

5 When the ______________ is away, the ______________ will play.

6 Like a ______________ out of water.

7 He wouldn't hurt a ______________.

8 The ______________'s share.

B **Work in groups. Discuss the questions.**

1 Do you know the meanings of the idioms in Exercise A?

2 Do you have the same or similar idioms in your language?

3 Do you know any other animal idioms in English?

even

A Read the comments below about recycling. Add *(not) even* to each comment.

1 Hannah (19)

I have always recycled. I recycle clothes.

2 Juan (54)

We have recycling bins at work, but nobody uses them. I do think people realize they are there.

3 Filipe (32)

I really care about the environment. I recycle things like bottle tops and drinking straws.

4 Zarah (32)

I went on vacation recently and the most remote beaches were polluted.

5 Katy (41) and Joe (41)

In our house, we recycle everything: food waste, plastic, glass, paper and toilet paper.

6 Irina (38)

It makes me happy to see people are taking recycling seriously. These days restaurants are banning plastic.

B Work with a partner. Interview three people about their recycling habits. Work together and come up with five questions to ask. Report back to the class using *even* and *not even*.

1 ____________________

2 ____________________

3 ____________________

4 ____________________

5 ____________________

11.3 Vocabulary

Somewhere, nowhere, everywhere, anywhere

A Look at the sentences. Correct the mistakes.

1 Traffic cameras are anywhere these days.

____

2 I looked all over, but I couldn't find my phone nowhere.

____

3 I'm not sure where Jeff is. He must be anywhere in the building.

____

4 There is anywhere on earth I like more than my hometown.

____

5 I put my keys anywhere and now I can't find them.

____

6 Somewhere in the world is higher than La Rinconada, Peru. It is the highest town in the world.

____

B Work in pairs. Complete the sentences with your own ideas.

1 __________ is everywhere these days.

2 There isn't anywhere as __________ as __________.

3 There is nowhere on earth more __________ than __________.

4 I'd like to live somewhere __________.

12.1 Grammar

Reported speech

A **Add the missing word in parentheses in the correct place in the sentences below.**

1 Marcus said he was reading the news. (*that*)

2 I said I check the arrival time before I went to the station. (*would*)

3 They told they didn't need the documents. (*us*)

4 She asked me I wanted to see a movie. (*if*)

5 Lydia said they watching TV. (*were*)

6 They asked where I lived. (*me*)

7 We told we might be late. (*them*)

8 Kevin us that the news was fake. (*told*)

B **Work in pairs. Talk to your partner about one of the topics below. Write notes on what they tell you. Change partners. Tell your new partner what you learned. Use reported speech.**

- Movies and TV
- Music
- News
- Sports

12.1 Vocabulary

News expressions

A Find six news expressions in the word spiral. Match them to the definitions below.

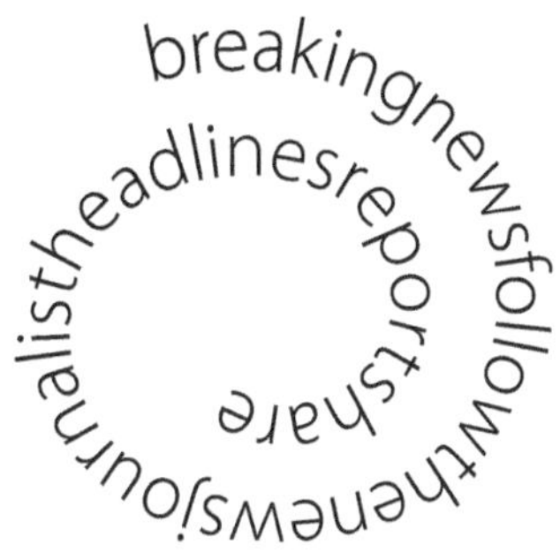

1 __________: To post a link to a story on social media.

2 __________ __________: A story that the media have just learned about.

3 __________: A person who works in news media.

4 __________: The most important news stories.

5 __________: To tell the stories in the news.

6 __________ __________ __________: To keep up to date with what is happening in the world.

B Work in pairs. Discuss the questions below.

1 Who are the most respected journalists in your country?

2 Do you get notifications on your phone when news stories break?

3 What was the last news story you shared?

4 Do you think it is unhealthy to follow the news too closely?

Past perfect

A Read the story below. Put the verbs in the correct tenses (past perfect or simple past).

Last night, my friend and I [1] ______________ (*decide*) to go to the movie theater. We [2] ______________ (*check*) what movies were playing and [3] ______________ (*choose*) a romantic comedy – we both really enjoy them. She [4] ______________ (*tell*) me that she would pick me up, so I [5] ______________ (*wait*) on the street but I [6] ______________ (*can see*) her car. I [7] ______________ (*wait*) for about ten minutes when she finally [8] ______________ (*arrive*). We quickly [9] ______________ (*drive*) to the movie theater. The trailers [10] ______________ (*already start*) when we [11] ______________ (*get*) there, but luckily, we [12] ______________ (*buy*) our tickets online so we [13] ______________ (*go*) straight in.

B Work in groups. Write about something interesting that has happened to you this year. Use the past perfect and simple past. Tell your story to the group. Who has the most interesting story?

____

____

____

____

____

____

____

____

Television

A Read the comments about television. Put the letters in bold in the correct order to make words.

Giulia, 23

1 To be honest, I don't really watch television anymore. I mainly use **olnnie srnmtieag** services.

Rita, 37

2 When I was younger, we only had four **cleanhns**. These days we have hundreds, but they play the same **wohss** all the time.

Dean, 28

3 My favorite TV show is Criminal Minds. They always have gripping **seosan fanlies** that make you excited about the next **saeosn**.

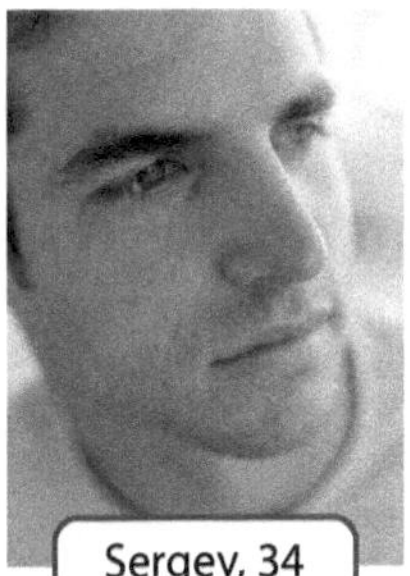

Sergey, 34

4 The first **oxb est** I ever saw was '24'. I was completely hooked from the beginning.

Danilo, 36

5 A **sriees** that I love is Grand Designs. Each **eposdie** follows a different family who is building their dream house.

B Work in groups. Which of the comments above do you agree with? Have you heard of these TV shows?

should

A Look at the questions with *should*. Decide if the question is an offer (O) or suggestion (S). Circle the correct answer.

1 Should I answer the phone? O / S

2 Should we go on vacation this year? O / S

3 Should we go shopping this weekend? O / S

4 Should we help you wash the dishes? O / S

5 Should we check what's on at the theater? O / S

6 Which show should I choose? O / S

7 When should we go out for coffee? O / S

8 Should I carry that for you? O / S

B Work in pairs. Think of three problems you are having right now. Ask your partner for suggestions. Write three questions with should I …?

Problem: ____________________

Question: ____________________

Problem: ____________________

Question: ____________________

Problem: ____________________

Question: ____________________

Advertising

A Fill in the blanks in the sentences.

1. What are your favorite **b** __________? What products or services do they create?
2. What was the last advertising campaign that really **g** ____________ **y** ______ **a** ______________?
3. What makes a product **c** ________ **y** ______ **e** ____?
4. Can you remember any company **s** ____________? What are they?
5. Which company **l** ________ do you think are the most recognizable?
6. Do you think it is important for an ad to have a **m** ____________?

B Work in groups. Discuss the questions from Exercise A.

Answer key

1.1 Grammar

A

1 is your name?
2 do you live?
3 you have any brothers or sisters?
4 did you go to college?
5 did you study?
6 you ever been to the US?

1.2 Grammar

A

always; three times a week; hardly ever; usually; once a week; every so often; normally; now and then

1.2 Vocabulary

A

1 animal lover **2** foodie **3** muisic fan
4 cat owner **5** mother or father
6 soccer fan **7** coffee drinker

1.3 Grammar

A

1 ~~nowhere~~ anywhere **2** correct
3 ~~anything~~ something **4** correct
5 correct **6** ~~everywhere~~ anywhere

1.3 Vocabulary

A

1 ~~in~~ at **2** ~~for~~ about **3** ~~disappointing~~ disappointed **4** ~~confidence~~ confident
5 ~~hard-worker~~ hard-working
6 ~~sensitive~~ sensible **7** ~~interesting~~ interested **8** ~~creating~~ creative

2.1 Grammar

A

1 When was the last time you felt extremely tired?
2 Can you think of a completely new way for practicing English?
3 Have you ever almost missed a flight?
4 What makes you extremely happy?
5 Who do you really admire?
6 Why is the traffic in cities so bad?
7 What makes you very angry?
8 Which country do you really want to visit?

2.1 Vocabulary

A

Across: 3 quiet; **5** noisy; **7** inconvenient; **8** clean
Down: 2 dirty; **4** modern; **6** lively

2.2 Grammar

A

1 have **2** am living **3** feels **4** want
5 am coming **6** 'm not paying **7** help
8 think **9** take care **10** feel
11 borrow **12** am thinking

2.2 Vocabulary

A

1 for **2** to **3** on **4** of/about
5 about **6** about **7** with **8** with

2.3 Grammar

A

Regular Verbs: lived, tried, stopped, studied, played, talked, wanted, needed
Irregular Verbs: went, ate, made, said, flew, left, bought

2.3 Vocabulary

B

retire, learn to drive, fall in love, go to college, get married, leave home, get your own place, leave school, have children, get a job

3.1 Grammar

A

2 All the students in this class are trying to improve their English.
3 I'd like to go to the movie theater tonight, but I have no money.
4 Most of the people in the world own a cell phone.
5 Some people like eating fish.
6 I asked, but none of the people would help me.

3.1 Vocabulary

A

1 flew **2** taxi **3** get **4** gave **5** travel

3.2 Grammar

A

Simple past: was(x3), saw, tried, was, jumped, ran, was, heard, felt, couldn't see, looked, decided, arrived, answered, was, wanted, was, told, didn't seem, said, was hit, died
Past progressive: was driving, was shining, was looking, was already ringing, was walking

3.2 Vocabulary

A

Un: afraid, kind, paid, true (*also, like*)
Im: possible, patient, mature, perfect
Dis: like, organized, trust, similar
In: complete, experienced, accurate, visible

B

1 dislike **2** invisible **3** unpaid
4 immature **5** impossible **6** distrust

3.3 Grammar

A

1 c **2** f **3** a **4** d **5** g **6** b
7 e **8** h

3.3 Vocabulary

A

Accommodations: guest house, chalet, hostel, beach resort, campsite, apartment
Amenities: double room, balcony, safe, air conditioning, ocean view, reception

4.1 Vocabulary

A

1 go to **2** saw **3** hung out **4** Playing
5 hang out / play **6** meet for **7** playing
8 went to / saw

4.2 Grammar

A

1 People will definitely have self-driving cars.
2 There might be a world government.
3 People will probably need to learn Chinese.
4 There will certainly be more people on Earth.
5 Maybe computers will be replaced with something else. / Computers will maybe be replaced with something else.
6 The world could run out of water.
7 People will visit space on their vacations.
8 Some languages may become extinct.

4.2 Vocabulary

A

1 agreement **2** sadness **3** predictions
4 discussion **5** invention **6** possibility
7 relaxation **8** improvement

4.3 Vocabulary

A

1 board games **2** by the fire
3 friends, family **4** hot bath
5 homemade food **6** quiet night
7 candles, relaxed atmosphere

5.1 Vocabulary

A

Earn: a high salary **Get:** a company car; a bonus **Take:** long vacations; a day off
Be: unemployed; your own boss
Work: shifts; long hours

5.2 Grammar

B

1 must / have to **2** must not **3** have to
4 must not **5** had to **6** must not, can
7 must not **8** don't have to

5.3 Vocabulary

Student A
1 at / in 2 in 3 for 4 for

Student B
1 at 2 in 3 for 4 in

6.1 Grammar

A
1 correct 2 There are too many people in my town. It is overcrowded. 3 If you study hard enough, you will pass your exam. 4 We don't have enough eggs to make a cake. 5 You spend too much time playing computer games. 6 I am much too tired to go to the party tonight. 7 correct 8 I am not rich enough to buy a Ferrari.

6.1 Vocabulary

A
1 broken bone 2 headache 3 toothache 4 flu 5 sunburn 6 sore throat

6.2 Grammar

A
1 G, PP, A 2 G, A, PP 3 A, G, PP

6.2 Vocabulary

A
Inside: racquetball, yoga, Pilates, ice hockey
Outside: bike riding, skiing, soccer,
Both: running, climbing, volleyball

6.3 Grammar

A
1 c – already 2 b – already 3 f – yet 4 e – yet 5 d – just 6 a – just

6.3 Vocabulary

Fruits and veggies: avocado, tomato, banana
Grains: rice, wheat, oats
Seafood: lobster, shrimp, tuna, cod

7.1 Grammar

A
1 a 2 – 3 the 4 the 5 the 6 the 7 the 8 – 9 the 10 a 11 The 12 an

7.1 Vocabulary

Student A
4 nervous 6 anxious 7 confused 8 glad

Student B
1 Pleased 2 cheerful 3 relaxed 5 scared

7.2 Vocabulary

A
1 information – info
2 newspapers – papers / internet – net
3 airplane – plane
4 cell phone – phone
5 website – site / suitcases – cases
6 Laboratory – lab
7 introduction – intro
8 microphone – mic

7.3 Grammar

A
1 – 2 – 3 the 4 a 5 – 6 a 7 the

7.3 Vocabulary

A
1 grew up 2 brought, up 3 made up 4 give up 5 dropped out 6 fell out

8.1 Grammar

A
1 each other 2 all by 3 themselves 4 itself 5 yourself 6 herself 7 himself 8 yourselves

8.1 Vocabulary

Student A
1 album 2 keyboard 3 Lyrics 4 on tour 5 band members 6 catchy

Student B
1 cover song 2 Gig 3 audience 4 stage 5 guitar 6 light show

8.2 Vocabulary

A
abstract; art; sculpture; photograph; gallery; landscape; exhibit; portrait

8.3 Grammar

A
1 h 2 a 3 b 4 e 5 c 6 g 7 f 8 d

8.3 Vocabulary

A
biography; rom-com; action; fantasy; adventure; historical; sci-fi; comedy; fairy tale; animated; horror; musical; thriller; western; costume drama; autobiography

B
1 animated, fairy tales 2 autobiography, biography 3 rom-com 4 horror, thrillers 5 action 6 historical, costume drama

9.1 Grammar

A
1 would, do, won
2 would, go, could visit
3 had, would, miss 4 could have, would, choose? 5 were, would, be 6 would, do, could speak 7 were, would, be
8 could travel, would, visit?

9.1 Vocabulary

A
1 c 2 g 3 d 4 a 5 e 6 b 7 h 8 f

9.2 Vocabulary

A
1 give away 2 donate, support 3 lost 4 raises 5 earn 6 make

9.3 Grammar

A
1 I really like buying things for my house.
2 I always look forward to checking my bank account on payday. 3 Saving money is something I find difficult to do.
4 Bartering is an alternative to using money. 5 I always enjoy spending time with my friends. 6 He's famous for donating so much of his money to charity.
7 She enjoys going shopping for new clothes. 8 Visiting new restaurants is something I like to do.

9.3 Vocabulary

A
1 do 2 make 3 make 4 made 5 make 6 do 7 done 8 made

10.1 Grammar

A
1 much 2 than 3 little / lot 4 little / lot 5 more 6 much / a lot 7 cheaper 8 the best

10.1 Vocabulary

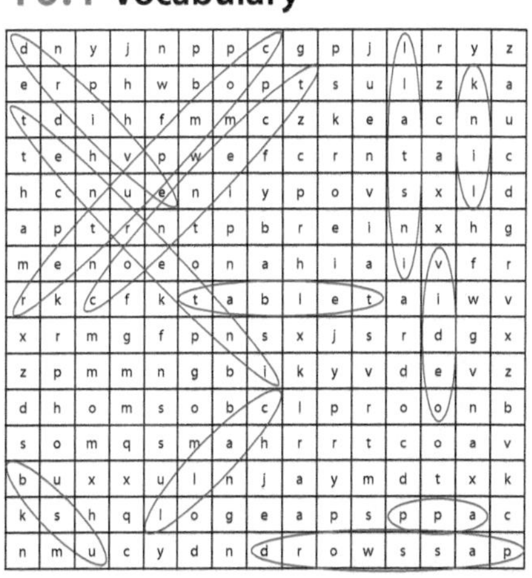

10.2 Grammar

A

1 English is not as hard as math.
2 Children are as creative as adults.
3 Traveling alone is not as safe as traveling with friends.
4 Education is not as useful as experience.
5 Men and women are as good at cooking as each other.
6 Traveling by plane is as safe as traveling by car.

10.2 Vocabulary

A

1 make a video call **2** your computer crashes **3** connect a USB drive **4** click on a link **5** remember your password **6** block your account **7** install an app **8** the screen freezes

10.3 Grammar

A

1 I don't need to do anything tomorrow.
2 My brother needs to buy a new book on space travel.
3 What do astronauts need to do to prepare for a spacewalk?
4 Do you need to connect the USB drive?
5 She doesn't need to install an app.
6 Someone needs to tell me what to do.

B

1 Where do you need to go after the class?
2 What do you need to do this weekend?
3 Do you need to ask the teacher any questions?
4 When do you need to get a haircut?
5 What do you need to do to improve your English?

10.3 Vocabulary

A

1 data **2** preparations **3** problems **4** research **5** experiments **6** technology **7** solutions **8** discoveries

11.1 Grammar

A

1 is located
2 was
3 lived
4 covers
5 is made
6 can see
7 were restored / have been restored
8 look
9 were built
10 shows
11 was
12 is protected

11.1 Vocabulary

Student A

5 rainforest **6** cave **7** volcano **9** canal **10** bay **11** reef

Student B

1 canyon **2** waterfall **3** mountain **4** desert **8** ocean **9** cliff

11.2 Grammar

A

1 impossible to find
2 great to see
3 hard to know
4 important to be
5 not fun to wait
6 not easy to change

11.2 Vocabulary

A

1 bird, worm **2** horse **3** chickens **4** dogs **5** cat, mice **6** fish **7** fly **8** lion

11.3 Grammar

A

1 I have always recycled. I even recycle clothes.
2 We have recycling bins at work, but nobody uses them. I don't think people even realize they are there.
3 I really care about the environment. I even recycle things like bottle tops and drinking straws.
4 I went on vacation recently and even the most remote beaches were polluted.
5 In our house, we recycle everything: food waste, plastic, glass, paper and even toilet paper.
6 It makes me happy to see people are taking recycling seriously. These days even restaurants are banning plastic.

11.3 Vocabulary

A

1 ~~anywhere~~ everywhere **2** ~~nowhere~~ anywhere. **3** ~~anywhere~~ somewhere **4** ~~anywhere~~ nowhere **5** ~~anywhere~~ somewhere **6** ~~Somewhere~~ Nowhere

12.1 Grammar

A

1 Marcus said that he was reading the news.
2 I said I would check the arrival time before I went to the station.
3 They told us they didn't need the documents.
4 She asked me if I wanted to see a movie.
5 Lydia said they were watching TV.
6 They asked me where I lived.
7 We told them we might be late.
8 Kevin told us that the news was fake.

12.1 Vocabulary

A

1 share **2** breaking news **3** journalist **4** headlines **5** report **6** follow the news

12.2 Grammar

A

1 decided
2 checked
3 chose
4 told
5 waited
6 couldn't see
7 had waited
8 arrived
9 drove **1**
0 had already started
11 got
12 had bought
13 went

12.2 Vocabulary

A

1 online streaming
2 channels, shows
3 season finales, season
4 box set
5 series, episode

12.3 Grammar

A

1 O
2 S
3 S
4 O
5 S
6 S
7 S
8 O

12.3 Vocabulary

A

1 brands **2** grabbed your attention **3** catch your eye **4** slogans **5** logos **6** message